THE GARDENER'S BUG BOOK

PESTS

The rose-bug on the rose
Is evil—so are those
Who see the rose-bug
Not the rose.

ELLA M. BOULT

The Gardener's Bug Book

FOURTH EDITION
Completely Rewritten and Reset

By Cynthia Westcott

*With Full-Color Illustrations of 102 Pests
by Eva Melady*

DOUBLEDAY & COMPANY, INC.
GARDEN CITY, NEW YORK
1973

ISBN: 0-385-01525-9
Copyright © 1946, 1956, 1964, 1973 by Cynthia Westcott
Library of Congress Catalog Card Number 72–89822
All Rights Reserved
Printed in the United States of America

PREFACE TO THE FOURTH EDITION

The preparation of this fourth edition of *The Gardener's Bug Book* has been more a process of deletion than addition. First, of course, we have had to eliminate DDT and some other controversial chemicals and to treat other pesticides with some caution. There are now restrictions on the use of chemicals by home gardeners but these are by no means uniform across the country. They vary from town to town, from state to state, and year to year. In 1971, chlordane could not be legally purchased by laymen in New York State; it was restricted to professionals with a permit. In 1972 New York gardeners were allowed to buy chlordane for certain specific purposes.

The most time-honored and reliable nonchemical method of pest control has been sanitation. But now, with the emphasis on air pollution, I must delete my recommendations to clean up and *burn* your infested material. How you can dispose of it safely, I don't really know. Perhaps some can be spaded under and some can go out with the garbage for landfill operations but undoubtedly our pest problems will increase with restrictions on immediate destruction by fire.

We are constantly told now what *not* to do with leftover chemicals but there is little positive information on safe disposal. If you still have banned chemicals on hand some authorities say that the best thing to do is to use them up; others suggest burying them deeply; others say to wrap the container in newspaper and put it out with the garbage; and still others advise locking it up until someone figures out how to get rid of it without harm to the environment. I wish I had the answers for you, but I don't.

In the beginning this *Bug Book* included some garden pests, such as mice, moles, rabbits, and dogs, that were not remotely related to insects. These have been eliminated in favor of more space for "bugs." In this edition we are deleting the section on Nematodes. Although they are animals they are not related to insects and they cause plant

disease, not injury. They more properly belong in the field of Plant Pathology, rather than Entomology, although Nematology is rapidly becoming a highly specialized science on its own. Nematodes are microscopic organisms, like bacteria and fungi, and are included in my companion volume, *Plant Disease Handbook*. The third edition was published in 1971 and was an American Garden Guild selection in 1972.

Finally, to accord with the latest list approved by the Entomological Society of America, I have deleted all the hyphens from the common names of insects. In some cases this means two separate words; in other cases the two halves are run together.

On the plus side, this edition includes a few new insects and some that were omitted earlier, although most insects with common names were treated in the third edition. There are a few more host plants and the latest changes in scientific names (or as many as I could discover) have been incorporated. The pesticides have been updated to include those marketed in 1972 for either the home gardener or the professional growers. Some alternative methods of control are given and there is emphasis on beneficial insects as well as pest species.

As I have stated in an earlier preface, descriptions and life histories of insects are reasonably stable; control measures are subject to constant revision. Please supplement this book with current information from your state extension service.

CYNTHIA WESTCOTT

Springvale
Croton-on-Hudson, New York
June 1972

PREFACE TO THE THIRD EDITION

During the many years that I have doctored gardens and studied their pests a major source of help has been *Insects of Western North America* by Professor E. O. Essig. This was published in 1926, but not until I started to write the preface to the present edition of *The Gardener's Bug Book* did I stop to read the title page of Dr. Essig's exhaustive manual. Belatedly I learn that the book was introduced as a "Manual and Textbook for Students in Colleges and Universities and a Handbook for County, State and Federal Entomologists and Agriculturists as well as for Foresters, Farmers, Gardeners, Travelers, and Lovers of Nature."

Now I hopefully address my own book to exactly the same audience as envisioned by Dr. Essig, nearly forty years ago. It is for the student, of course—for anyone working in entomology, plant pathology or horticulture, including floriculture, pomology, vegetable culture, and landscape design.

Primarily, however, this book is oriented toward the serious gardener and those who serve him, from the farmer who grows his food to the County Agricultural Agent who advises him on growing his own food. It is for the forester who provides wood for his shelter and woods for his recreation; for the nurseryman who produces the trees and shrubs for home planting, and for the tree expert who keeps them healthy. It is for the florist who provides the material for home arrangements and for the flower lover who wants to grow her own decorative material.

This book is for the manufacturing chemist and for the dealer who sells chemicals in small packages and must aid the home gardener in using them wisely. And because it includes friendly insects as well as pests and discusses alternative control methods, this book is even for the organic gardener who shuns all chemicals and for the wildlife enthusiast who is worried about them.

Because previous editions have been increasingly used by professional entomologists, this revision is a bit more scientific, giving the authors of scientific names and some other items of interest to taxonomists. Such details need not worry the gardener.

Because so many people have said, "I can't find my bug in your book," this revision includes many more insects—nearly 1,900, as against 1,100 in the second edition. Of course this by no means exhausts the possibilities; there are still many, many more injurious insects in the United States than can be mentioned here, but I hope there is a reasonable representation of the more important pests that occur in various sections of the country.

Because the field of nematology has expanded so rapidly since 1956, much more attention has been paid to nematodes. In the previous edition, for instance, there were no nematodes in the check list of pests of Lawn Grasses. In this edition twenty types of nematodes that may injure turf are included.

Because the *Bug Book* has been used in warm climates and because travelers are interested in exotic plants, the Host Plants have been expanded from 450 to 700. Many of the additions are subtropical, but some are cover crops that the gardener or nurseryman might use. We still do not include grains and other plants that would have no place in a home garden.

There has been no attempt to increase the number of illustrations, the space being used for information. Eva Melady's exquisite color paintings have been retained, as have many of the line drawings. Nor has there been any attempt at changing the general format, for gardeners continue to find it easy to use for finger-tip reference. Although the additions have made this third edition a more ponderous tome, it should not be more difficult. However, if this increased array of pests and hosts seems too formidable, and perhaps too extensive, try instead *Are You Your Garden's Worst Pest?* (Doubleday, 1961), which deals only with the more common problems of the more important ornamental plants. The book, unfortunately, is out-of-print but perhaps your library will have a copy.

CYNTHIA WESTCOTT

Springvale
Croton-on-Hudson, New York
November 1963

PREFACE TO THE SECOND EDITION

When *The Gardener's Bug Book* was published, in 1946, we were on the threshold of an exciting new era of chemical control of plant pests. Since then, synthetic chemicals have come on the market so rapidly it has been difficult to keep them sorted out, to know which one is best for a particular pest. I have been repeatedly asked, in person, by telephone, and by letter, "When are you going to revise the *Bug Book* and put in the modern chemicals?"

It is gratifying to know that the book has proved useful to others as well as myself. Seed dealers tell me they keep it beside the telephone to answer inquiries. Some universities and some tree companies use it for their students. Garden writers, nurserymen, and professional gardeners refer to it, while plain dirt gardeners from every state in the union, as well as a few from abroad, have written that they find it understandable and helpful, though usually this politeness is preliminary to asking for information on some pest *not* included.

So here is the new *Gardener's Bug Book*, rewritten to include a few pests omitted from the first edition, a few pests that have become problems since 1946, many new chemicals, and numerous name changes. One or two new hosts have been added and the listing of pests under hosts has been simplified.

The general format has been retained because the book has proved in practice to be the easy, finger-tip reference we hoped for. At least the layman so considers it. Some scientists have found it difficult to find their way around insects grouped by common names rather than taxonomic relationships, but for them there is always the Index, with its full complement of scientific names.

Two of Eva Melady's exquisite color plates had to be jettisoned for economic reasons, but the rest are here, grouped together in the center of the book for easier reference. Most of the line drawings have been retained but the sprayers and dusters have been redrawn to represent apparatus in current favor.

In the Introduction to the first edition I said, "Probably an apology is in order for a book on entomology written by one who is not a trained entomologist [my academic work was all in plant pathology], and has learned her insects the hard way, through having to subdue them in her own and many other people's gardens." I no longer apologize. I now know that no real entomologist would be fool enough to attempt such a large scope—pests of flowers, fruits, vegetables, trees, shrubs, vines, and grasses in home plantings across the country. The scientist is hesitant to publish even in his own special field, for he is all too cognizant of the many gaps in our knowledge and he seldom ventures an opinion in any field outside his own.

But as a plant doctor, spraying over fifty gardens a week in New Jersey and New York from March to November, checking on problems in most other states during lecture trips, answering countless inquiries from every section, I have to take the broad view. This manual is a combination of my own experience—and I have personally met, if not always conquered, over half of the approximately 1,100 pests presented here—what I have learned in talking with home gardeners and entomologists in nearly every state, and what I am continually learning from books and pamphlets. My house overflows with books, technical and garden, with bulletins, circulars, periodicals, scientific and otherwise. I have done my best to keep up with, and digest, this continuing flood, but in these swiftly changing times many books are partially out of date before they get off the press and even the information in current periodicals will be somewhat outmoded by the time this book gets into print. Descriptions and life histories of insects are reasonably stable; control measures and names are subject to constant revision.

Of the many people who have helped me with insect problems over the years I can name but a few: Irene Dobroscky Van de Water, who was the entomological half of the Plant Doctor until she married an apple farmer; Dr. C. C. Hamilton, of Rutgers University, who has patiently answered my questions for a quarter of a century; Dr. E. O. Essig of the University of California whose writings on western pests have been so very useful; John C. Schread of the Connecticut Experiment Station; Dr. Louis Pyenson, Long Island Agricultural and Technical Institute; Dr. Floyd Smith, entomologist, Entomology Research Branch, U. S. Department of Agriculture. I particularly thank Dr. Reece I. Sailer and his colleagues at the U. S. National Museum for help with names of insects, and M. Truman Fossum, Agricultural Marketing Service, for many statistics. I continue to be grateful to

Eva Melady and Ellen Edmonson for the fine illustrations, and I hereby express appreciation to Clara Claasen of Doubleday & Company, for encouragement in preparing this revision, a task that proved to be somewhat more arduous than the original version.

CYNTHIA WESTCOTT

Glen Ridge, New Jersey
August 1955

INTRODUCTION TO THE FIRST EDITION

This is the book I have worked on for a long time, because I needed it on my own desk to answer your many questions. Maybe if it is on *your* desk you will be able to find the answers to most of your own questions, and my own neglected garden will get a few more spare moments of attention.

Probably an apology is in order for a book on entomology written by one who is not a trained entomologist, and has learned her insects the hard way, through having to subdue them in her own and in many other people's gardens. About half of the pests considered here are personal enemies, if "enemies" is the right word for creatures who provide me with a livelihood as a plant doctor. Some of the rest I have met in garden visits across the country. I have not personally sprayed camellias for tea scale, nor azaleas for peony scale, nor pittosporum for cottonycushion scale, nor crape myrtle for aphids; but I have stayed long enough in the South to see these insects, and many, many more, and to realize the need for action by gardeners.

I have never sprayed California Christmasberries for lacebugs, but I have met them in that year-round garden state; and I have also seen, out there, whiteflies on fuchsias, Diabroticas devouring roses, webworms spoiling lawns, and more slugs and snails than an eastern gardener ever dreams of.

Once, when I was lecturing in Iowa on a below-zero winter day, I remarked that I had never met a boxelder bug face to face. Whereupon the amused garden club members told me to look down at the rug I was standing on! But those Iowa gardeners had never met a Japanese beetle, so we were even.

The one comforting thing in pest control is that injurious insects are pretty well divided up around the country. No one section has more than its fair share. When you bewail the fate that seems to have sent bugs just to your personal address, keep in mind that others are wailing over a lot you don't have, so you're not without company.

You also have some company when you set out to subdue those bugs; although the number of bewailers will always be larger than the number of subduers.

This book, then, is written largely from face-to-face combat with insects known intimately in day-by-day contests; partly from insects known casually in passing; and partly from insects met in books—many, many books, and many, many articles in periodicals, bulletins, and circulars, to the authors of which I express my profound appreciation. It has been said that getting all your material from one author is plagiarism, while getting it from many authors is research. On that basis much of this book might properly be termed research.

In order to acknowledge my debts properly, and hoping to start some gardeners at least on a little research of their own, I have listed elsewhere in this volume some of the books in my library which show the thumbprints of frequent consultation.

My grateful thanks go to Eva Melady for the inspiration of her lovely color plates, and to both Miss Melady and Ellen Edmonson for the many fine line drawings.

CYNTHIA WESTCOTT

Glen Ridge, New Jersey
May 1946

CONTENTS

LIST OF COLOR PLATES

LIST OF LINE DRAWINGS

HOW TO USE THIS BOOK

The Gardener's Bug Book is not designed to be swallowed whole. It is not meant to floor you with so many pests that you decide not to garden at all. It is a reference manual to be consulted as problems arise. You will never have, in one place, all the pests presented here, but you will have your fair share and after you have gardened long enough to know that insects are facts of life not to be completely ignored, you will start trying to identify them and to keep them at a minimum with the least effort.

Before using this book as a manual, before attempting to look up information on any specific pest, please read Chapter I for a general picture of insects in gardens and types of control measures.

Next read the first part of Chapter II, on garden chemicals, carefully and thoroughly. Skim through the alphabetical list of insecticides, acaricides, attractants, et al., so that you will know the types of chemicals available and their general functions, but don't worry about the long chemical names. Common names or trade names will be sufficient for most of you. Plan to return to this list of chemicals before using any particular one. No one expects you to remember the specific information. Be sure to read, most attentively, the words under Stop, Look, and Listen, *before* opening any package and *before* using any material on any plant at any time.

Chapter III helps you in choosing, manipulating, and cleaning a sprayer, in making up spray mixtures. If you prefer dusting, check its advantages and disadvantages, the types of dusters available.

Chapter IV orients insects in the animal kingdom, tells how they are made and grow, how they are named, prerequisites to later identification.

With this background information there are two methods by which you can locate the information you need about a plant enemy.

(1) If you know the common name of the insect or other pest,

look it up directly in Chapter V, "Garden Pests (and a Few Friends)." Here groups are in alphabetical order under common names: ANTLIONS, ANTS, APHIDS, ARMYWORMS, BAGWORMS, BEES, BEETLES, and so on. Consult the table of contents for the complete list of 68 such groups. Under each heading a general discussion of group characteristics is followed by specific insects arranged alphabetically by their common names. For instance, if you want information on the rhododendron lace bug, turn to BUGS for characters common to all true bugs and distinguishing family characteristics and then thumb your way along to R for **Rhododendron Lace Bug*** for detailed information. The common name is given in boldface type, marked with an asterisk if it is one presently accepted by the Entomological Society of America, followed by the scientific name in italics. If there is another name in rather common use it is also given, and capitalized. For example, the **Mourningcloak Butterfly***, *Nymphalis antiopa* (Linnaeus), is treated under BUTTERFLIES because that is the approved common name. Linnaeus first named the species and so his name is given as the author, but put in parentheses because some later scientist transferred it to a different genus. This insect, however, may be more familiar to you as the Spiny Elm Caterpillar and so this name is also given, both in the description and in the Index.

(2) If you do not know the name of the pest, look up, in the alphabetical treatment of Host Plants, Chapter VI, the plant or plants attacked and note the most likely prospect—Borer or Caterpillar, Mealybug or Aphid. There may be only a few listed, so that checking back is simple. There may be many kinds of aphids or borers in the check list and so you will have to skim through the description of each one to find yours. Your particular species may not be in this book at all, for the nearly 2,000 pests included are still less than 20 per cent of those that might possibly be damaging. But you can find its type described and you can probably control it without knowing its full name. In a few cases an insect is listed under a host and is not specifically described in Chapter V. If it is not in the Index, don't waste time hunting for it.

The color plates are numbered. The plate number is referred to in the description of the pest and in the Index. Line drawings are indicated by boldface in the Index. Insect size is indicated by a line on the color plate.

THE GARDENER'S BUG BOOK

Chapter I

INSECTS IN THE GARDEN

Insects are not new! They have been around for three hundred million years according to one estimate; at least fifty million years are quoted by another authority. Either figure far surpasses the less than one million years during which man has evolved. Insects, therefore, are well ahead of man in the race for survival and ever since the beginning of his existence man has had to try to tip the balance of nature in his favor.

There is a lament in the Bible (Joel 1:4, King James version) which sounds very modern: "That which the palmerworm hath left hath the locust eaten; and that which the locust hath left hath the cankerworm eaten; and that which the cankerworm hath left hath the caterpillar eaten." Sometimes, however, the locust leaves nothing for either the cankerworm or man, for insects may appear in incredible numbers. In some countries vast swarms of locusts, measuring several hundred square miles and containing three hundred million individuals (weighing five tons) per mile, devour every bit of edible vegetation.

Chemicals for pest control are not new! Homer wrote of "pest-averting sulfur" around 1000 B.C. But *organized* chemical warfare against insects is relatively new. The year 1954 marked the centennial of professional entomology in the United States. Our public fight began in 1854, when the New York State Legislature appropriated funds and Dr. Asa Fitch was employed to study injurious insects and their control. The next month Townend Glover was appointed as the first federal entomologist.

In 1971, the Entomological Society of America had 6,230 members, distributed in federal and state departments of agriculture, in state experiment stations, in public health services, in the armed forces, or working as pest-control operators or conducting research for industry. Some of these are listed in the American Registry of Certified Entomologists now maintained by the Society. This really small number of entomologists means that not too much individual help is available to the more than thirty million gardeners in this country. Many gardeners take their problems to the clerks in seed stores or garden centers. These usually have no professional training and their advice may or may not be helpful. This book is planned so that each gardener may learn for himself enough about insects to profit from the investigations made by professionals. It also provides finger-tip reference for those who advise the gardener or are engaged in the commercial production or maintenance of ornamentals or food crops.

ARE INSECTS INCREASING?

Gardeners are always complaining about the numbers of insects now compared to the good old days. They say our forefathers did not have to be continually concerned with pests. Great-grandfather, however, was not accustomed to the unblemished fruits and vegetables of today's market and he did not worry too much about holes in the foliage of ornamentals. But he had plenty of insect problems! Many of the pests we fear today are mentioned in a book, *Insects Injurious to Vegetation,* published in 1841 by T. W. Harris in Massachusetts. As far back as 1833 the plum curculio could totally destroy plum, apricot, and nectarine crops. The codling moth, first mentioned by name in 1868, was recorded in 1898 as causing an annual loss of one fourth to one half of our apple crop. Serious codling-moth invasions in the West have occurred since 1922. Our native eastern grape phylloxera became a major pest in California in 1863. The cottonycushion scale from Australia nearly wrecked the citrus industry in the 1870s.

It is, however, quite true that insects are increasing. One reason is that we continue to introduce new insects along with foreign plants. Despite the Plant Quarantine Act, created in 1912 to regulate the movement of nursery stock, insects still sneak through quarantine and inspection, often aided by unthinking gardeners who want a plant souvenir of their travels. Every thirteen minutes around the clock a foreign pest is intercepted at quarantine, but occasionally one escapes detection.

Within our own country our present rapid transportation greatly facilitates insect spread. Despite precautions, Japanese beetles do get a foothold in a new area near an airport. And despite the Federal Plant Pest Act of 1957, which prohibits the movement of plant pests into or through the country, gardeners continue to exchange and to transport plants and unnoticed insects, mites, and nematodes.

Mechanized farming, with large areas devoted to a single crop, has vastly increased insect populations, and so has our habit of planting streets or other areas with large numbers of a single ornamental species. Both the farmer and the home gardener have, paradoxically, increased some pests by the too generous use of broad-spectrum insecticides, thereby killing many insect parasites and predators as well as the pest species.

INSECTS AS FRIENDS OF MAN

No one knows exactly how many kinds of insects there are, and figures vary widely even on the number already described. The fourth (1962) edition of *Destructive and Useful Insects* by Metcalf, Flint, and Metcalf gives 686,000 as the estimated number of living described species of true insects with perhaps 100,000 of these in North America. A *Field Guide to the Insects* by Borror and White (1970) gives 88,600 as the number of species in North America north of Mexico and estimates that perhaps a thousand insects may be found in any fair-sized backyard. Relatively few insects—probably not more than a tenth of the total number—can be designated as public enemies. The rest are either harmless or decidedly beneficial. Without insects, life as we know it today would not exist. We depend on insects for pollination of 85 per cent of our fruits and many of our vegetables. They play a large role as scavengers. They provide food for birds and fishes. They give us honey and wax, shellac, cochineal, and silk; they have a minor role in surgery and medicine. Practically every insect order contains some useful species that live on destructive insects. It is only within the last thirty years, when some chemicals have reached such a high degree of nonselective efficiency, that we have learned the extent of the role played by parasites and predators in reducing harmful insects and mites.

INSECTS AS ENEMIES OF MAN

In 1868 our crop loss due to insects was figured at 300 million. Today the annual figure is over 4 billion and without control measures the figure would be astronomical. In general, we feed about ⅒ of our crops each year to insects, but this can vary, with the crop and the location and the season, from 0 to 100 per cent. The newer chemicals have, in many cases, drastically reduced losses. Greenhouse operators who used to average 15 per cent have, with proper methods, cut that loss to 1 or 3 per cent. Used outdoors, many of the new chemicals have caused environmental problems and there is agitation for decreased use. Figures are not available for home-

garden losses, but some of the nurseryman's profit comes from plants
sold to replace those killed by insects in home plantings.

Besides their direct effect on plants, insects may be even more injurious as disseminators of plant disease. Leafhoppers spread the
viruses causing curly top, aster yellows, peach yellows, cranberry false
blossom, elm phloem necrosis, peach X disease, and Pierce's disease of
grape. Aphids transmit viruses causing bean, cucumber, and crucifer
mosaics, potato leaf roll, onion yellow dwarf, citrus tristeza. Several
species of thrips carry the virus of tomato spotted wilt and a mite is
the vector of peach mosaic. Bark beetles spread the Dutch-elm-
disease fungus; the peach tree borer helps to distribute the plum-wilt
fungus; the plum curculio aids the fungus causing brown rot of
peach, plum, and cherry; and the cabbage maggot spreads the blackleg disease of that host. Flies, bees, and aphids are all vectors of
bacterial fire blight and the iris borer is intimately connected with
vile-smelling soft rot. Cucumber beetles transmit the bacteria of
cucurbit wilt, and flea beetles those causing Stewart's disease of corn.
Insects are also, of course, enormously important as vectors of human
diseases, but these are outside the scope of this garden manual.

WAYS OF CONTROLLING INSECT PESTS

Control of plant pests has never been limited to spraying and dusting operations, but the multitude of modern chemicals has, in recent
years, made some overlook the fact that chemical control is only one
facet of an integrated program. Now the pendulum is swinging back
with perhaps too much emphasis on the possible adverse effects of
chemicals and a tendency to believe that if we let Nature alone
everything will be all right. Maybe so, but that depends on whose side
you are on. The much-quoted "balance of nature" is merely a continuing struggle to the death, and if man does not use all resources
at his command, including chemicals, the insects will certainly come
out on top. To keep our exploding population fed, clothed, and
housed chemicals are an absolute necessity. They must, however, be
used with restraint and discretion, and fitted into a program that
also makes full use of natural, biological, legal, mechanical and cultural measures.

Natural control comes from the climate and physical characteristics
of a region and the presence there of natural enemies. Not many insects live in all climatic zones—arctic, temperate, and tropical. Winter
temperatures restrict the range of some; summer heat limits others.
Some insects prefer a warm, moist climate; others like it warm and
dry. Some insects can fly or be carried by the wind long distances;

others can crawl only a short distance. Large lakes, rivers, and mountain ranges check the natural spread of insects. The character of the soil limits certain pests, wireworms flourishing in poorly drained soil, nematodes in sandy soil.

Birds, moles, shrews, skunks, snakes, lizards, newts, salamanders, and toads eat many insects. Birds consume more than enough to pay for the cherries, strawberries, grapes, and corn that they also eat. Skunks eat a lot of grubs, compensation for the rather conspicuous holes they leave in lawns.

Biological control is a sort of artificial restoration of the balance of nature, bringing in insect predators and parasites, encouraging birds and useful animals, introducing nematodes, bacteria, fungi, or viruses that will work on undesirable insects.

When, despite quarantines and inspection, a foreign pest gets established in this country, we send scientists abroad, often to many countries, in a search for its natural enemies. When such enemies are brought to this country, under strict security, exhaustive tests must be made to ensure that they will not themselves become pests. Then methods must be found for mass rearing in quantities and for effective distribution, often by repeated releases at suitable colonization sites under proper conditions of temperature and humidity.

There are many failures, with perhaps less than a fourth of the attempted introductions established. There have been a few spectacular successes, such as the complete control of cottonycushion scale on California citrus by Vedalia, an Australian lady beetle, and a fairly large number of partial successes where biological control is used along with other methods. Almost all insect orders include some beneficial members, and these are particularly important for forage crops where chemical residues are undesirable.

Microbial insecticides are coming into wider use as potent weapons for biological control. Spores of the bacteria causing milky disease of the Japanese beetle, applied to sod as a powder at frequent intervals, will in time give an excellent kill of grubs but it may take several years. Commercial preparations of *Bacillus thuringiensis* are applied with an ordinary sprayer for the control of cabbage loopers and similar caterpillars and have some effect on gypsy moths and other tree pests. The action is essentially chemical in nature, the toxin coming from crystals formed in the bacterial cells, and the same precautions are necessary.

Macerated bodies of cabbage caterpillars infected with a polyhedrosis virus can be disseminated by airplane at the low rate of 5 to 10 larvae per acre for good control. Another virus, also dispensed from planes, takes care of sawflies on pines around reservoirs where chemicals may not be used. There are 254 viruses now known to affect insects with about ten, including one for the corn earworm, feasible for use. So far as we know at this time, such virus diseases offer no harm to man or wildlife, but there is always the possibility of future complications.

Fungi also have a place in biological control. At least fifteen species of Entomophthora attack aphids; one species has markedly decreased brown-tail moths and another is the most important natural control of the grape leafhopper. Some fungi trap nematodes in the soil, but as yet no practical application of this ability has been developed. Most nematodes are pests but some devour other nemas and so may be classed as beneficial.

The most startling new development in biological control is the release of male insects, sterilized by irradiation, to mate with normal females and so render the eggs infertile. This method, used to eradicate screw-worms, a livestock pest in the South, is now being tried along the border between Mexico and California for the control of the Mexican fruit fly. California and Arizona are cooperating in a program using sterile males for control of the pink bollworm, and the technique may work against the boll weevil.

The female insect has a substance, called a pheromone, that attracts the male. Some of these sex attractants have been made synthetically and can be used as baits in traps. We have also developed chemical sterilants that can affect insects attracted to traps. Attractants and sterilants are included in the next chapter on garden chemicals. Another synthesized chemical is a juvenile hormone. Insects treated with this do not develop to the adult stage and so cannot reproduce.

Control by exclusion may be either legal or voluntary. The Plant Quarantine Act of 1912 authorizes the Secretary of Agriculture to impose quarantines and restrictions on plants and plant products and any other articles necessary to prevent the spread of insect infestations or plant diseases. The Act authorizes inspectors of the Department of Agriculture to search, without a warrant, persons coming into the United States and any vehicles coming from any country or moving interstate.

The Insect Pest Act, passed by Congress in 1905, was superseded in 1957 by the Federal Plant Pest Act, prohibiting the movement from any foreign country into the United States, or interstate, of any insect in a live state that is notoriously injurious to cultivated crops.

It is not expected that a quarantine can keep out a pest forever, but the expense of the inspection service is justified if the insect is prohibited for a period sufficiently long to enable us to learn its life history, to develop control measures, and to introduce its parasites.

Home gardeners should make their own voluntary exclusion laws. Why, for instance, borrow trouble by introducing into the garden a delphinium crippled by cyclamen mites, or a Norway spruce with aphid galls, or a juniper covered with scale?

Cultural control, including sanitation, is usually free from expense except for labor costs. Sometimes it does not even require labor, merely a little planning based on life histories of particular insects. Diversified planting is of primary importance; mixing types and species in the garden keeps increase of pests at a minimum. Crop rotation is a fundamental principle in good culture, although it is not always possible in a small garden. Most insects attack a small group of related plants. Cabbage worms chew members of the cabbage family; the squash vine borer sticks to the cucurbit group. Mexican bean beetles don't like much except beans. By switching locations for crops you can either starve out certain pests or keep them from building up huge populations.

Soil cultivation during the season destroys some insects. Spading up the vegetable patch in the fall, leaving the ground rough, exposes some larvae and pupae to death by freezing. Garden sanitation —destruction of crop residues, weeds, and trash—is always important but even this supposedly foolproof method of pest control requires a bit of thought. On land subject to erosion over the winter it may be wiser to let some corn roots remain to anchor the soil even if an occasional borer may hibernate in the old stalk.

Control by mechanical measures depends on barriers erected between the plant and the pest. A cardboard cylinder keeps cutworms away from young transplants; Hotkaps keep cucumber beetles off seedlings; a square of tar paper on the ground keeps the cabbage maggot from depositing eggs too close to young broccoli or cabbage.

Timing of planting is another cultural measure. In Connecticut snap beans planted in early June often mature between broods of Mexican bean beetles. Early summer squash may come along ahead of the squash vine borer; late corn is less apt to be injured by the European corn borer.

In addition to such "escape" methods there is also the possibility of resistant varieties. Long used in disease control, resistance is also becoming a weapon against insect pests, being somewhat successful against corn borers, earworms, rootworms, and a few potato insects. Unfortunately, it may take ten to fifteen years to develop even partially resistant varieties and as soon as one is developed the pest may produce another race or strain to which the host is susceptible.

Advocates of organic gardening claim that plants grown without chemical fertilizer but with proper organic culture are resistant to pests. Vigorous plants may more readily survive the devastating effects of pests, but on the other hand some pests, such as aphids, are attracted to lush, succulent tissue. In a few cases some relation between nutrition and susceptibility to insects or mites has been demonstrated, but this field is largely unexplored. Entomologists looking for insects can usually find them even on plants produced "organically."

Control by chemicals makes up the bulk of this book on garden pests. The list of materials available today is given in the next chapter, and the application of these for the control of specific pests is given in Chapter V.

Chapter II

GARDEN CHEMICALS

Beginning with World War II and the spectacular debut of DDT, there was tremendous activity in the development of chemicals for the control of plant pests. Before the 1940s chemical control was limited and simple; then it became decidedly complex, with some unforeseen effects on the environment. Now we have gone to the other extreme; some chemicals, like DDT, are banned for home-garden use, others are restricted, to be applied only by professionals with permits.

In 1854 tobacco, soap, and sulfur were about the only materials tried as insecticides. In 1865 Paris green, brushed onto vines with a broom to halt the Colorado potato beetle, became the first successful stomach poison. About 1880 kerosene emulsion was tried as a contact insecticide and in another quarter of a century was largely replaced by oil sprays. The proprietary miscible oil Scalecide, which appeared on the market in 1905, is still sold under that brand name. Lead arsenate became available commercially in 1903 and calcium arsenate came into use, chiefly for cotton pests, about ten years later. Rotenone became popular about 1933.

That was the year I started out as a doctor to gardens. I used a miscible oil or lime-sulfur as a dormant spray, lead arsenate for chewing insects, and nicotine sulfate for sucking insects on ornamentals, with rotenone for fruits and vegetables. When I retired from such active pursuits, in 1960, there was a choice of many hydrocarbons besides DDT, including benzene hexachloride, lindane, methoxychlor, TDE, chlordane, toxaphene, aldrin, dieldrin, heptachlor, and endrin; many phosphates, varying from TEPP—so poisonous that a drop of undiluted chemical on your skin can kill you—to safe malathion; nitrophenyl derivatives such as Elgetol; carbamates such as Sevin; and some synthesized botanicals along with pyrethrum and rotenone. There were fumigants of varying degrees of safety, poisonous systemic insecticides, and relatively safe synergists, attractants, and miticides.

There are perhaps a hundred basic chemicals that are now marketed under trade names, in thousands of different formulations and combinations and under prescribed safeguards.

For each new chemical an average of six years has been spent in research and up to six million dollars to get that product tested, registered, and on the market. With broad-spectrum pesticides, that could be recommended for a wide variety of pests, the manufacturer could take a chance of getting his money back. But now that the emphasis is on selective pesticides, that may control only one or two insects apiece, the manufacturer is loath to gamble so much money; it is very likely that sales will not justify the cost of finding a proficient new chemical. So the flood of new pesticides has now been reduced to a trickle, and there are prohibitions and restrictions for many of those already on the market.

In 1938 the Federal Food, Drug and Cosmetic Act made provision for the pesticide residues in food. In 1947 the old Insecticide Act, passed in 1910, became the Federal Insecticide, Fungicide and Rodenticide Act, requiring that economic poisons (pesticides) shipped in interstate commerce be registered with the U. S. Department of Agriculture.

In 1954 the Miller Amendment to the Food, Drug and Cosmetic Act required tolerances for pesticide residues in or on raw agricultural products and made it illegal to sell food products with residues in excess of stipulated tolerances in interstate commerce.

In 1959 an amendment to the Federal Insecticide, Fungicide and Rodenticide Act explanded coverage to include nematocides, defoliants, desiccants, and plant-growth regulators.

Although federal legislation applies only to pesticides in interstate commerce most states have adopted a "Uniform State Act" for controlling distribution and sale of pesticides within their borders.

In 1970 the Environmental Protection Agency was formed and registration of pesticides passed from the U. S. Department of Agriculture to the Pesticides Regulations division of that Agency.

Here are the steps leading to the introduction of a new chemical and its registration:

1. *Preliminary screening.* Controlled greenhouse experiments show whether the new chemical has more or less activity than a standard pesticide for a cross section of insect species.

2. *Secondary screening.* About 5 per cent of the synthesized compounds show promise for additional evaluation. The selected chemical then is tested on rats for acute oral toxicity and for hazards of handling. It is investigated more extensively in the greenhouse and on a wider range of insects. Analytical methods are developed for determining the amount of residue.

3. *Preliminary field testing.* On crops in a few areas of expected insect infestation, with tests on persistence of residue, influence of weather, etc.

4. *Secondary field testing.* The material is screened for cost as compared to standard chemicals and extensive toxicity studies are made on several species of experimental animals.

5. *Large-scale field testing.* This must yield all information necessary to show the safe level of the pesticide as a residue on edible crops. From these data the Food and Drug Administration is requested to set a tolerance for specific crops. This is expressed in parts per million (ppm), a term expressing the weight of the residue in relation to the product weight. This is set at only $\frac{1}{100}$ of the amount that might be harmful under maximum consumption. The amount of permissible residue has been explained as equivalent to a dash of vermouth in a martini made with 20,000 gallons of gin.

6. *Marketing.* The label registered with the Environmental Protection Agency is a legal document. It must spell out the purposes and effects of the chemical as well as necessary precautions, detailed instructions for use, first-aid information, and antidotes.

The label must contain:

a. Name and address of the manufacturer or person for whom manufactured.

b. The name, brand, or trademark under which the article is marketed or distributed.

c. The net weight, volume, or measure of contents.

d. An ingredient statement. Each active ingredient is listed with the correct percentage by weight and the total percentage of inert ingredients.

e. Poison labeling (skull and crossbones) on products highly toxic to man. Antidotes are listed; safety equipment.

f. A warning or caution statement as necessary to prevent injury to man, animals, or plants.

g. Adequate directions for use. The petition presented for label registration must show that the product is useful for the control of specific pests and that it can be handled safely if all directions are followed.

So much for the manufacturer! He has gone through a lot of money, worry, and red tape to get that label on his product so it can be included in the array on the shelves of your local garden-supply store. The next step is yours. If you are like nine out of ten gardeners you will grab the package off the shelf, merely glancing at the brand name and not looking at the fine print on the label. You will take it home, put it on the kitchen table, open it up, scattering some of the contents, and then—possibly—look at the label just enough to learn if the dose is 1 teaspoon or 2 tablespoons per gallon of water. Meanwhile you can inhale enough vapor to kill you, or you can spill enough on your skin to kill you, or you can scatter specks of lethal powder around the kitchen.

As a safety measure everyone should read *every word* on a label before a pesticide container is opened. The material may be so poisonous that it requires respirator, special clothing, and rubber gloves. If so, take it back to the store unopened. Such a product is not for an amateur without experience. If there is no skull and cross-bones, no list of protective clothing, then read all the warning and caution statements and proceed according to directions.

Since the formation of the Environmental Protection Agency there is less likelihood of the home gardener getting hazardous materials. Many chemicals may not now be sold from the open shelf but are restricted to persons with special permits. The chemicals given in this chapter include those presently available to professionals; the home gardener may be able to purchase only a small percentage of these.

INSECTICIDES, ACARICIDES, ATTRACTANTS, CHEMOSTERILANTS, AND SYNERGISTS

The following list of chemicals is in alphabetical order according to approved common name, where such has been designated, otherwise by trade name. Common names are written in lower case; trade names are capitalized. The chemical name is given in parentheses. The LD_{50} values refer to the dosage, in milligrams per kilogram of body weight, lethal to 50 per cent of the white rats used to test oral toxicity. The lower this value, the more precautions should be taken in handling the chemical.

Abate® (o,o-dimethyl phosphorothioate o,o-diester with 4,4'-thiodiphenol). Mosquito and midge larvicide, of low toxicity to mammals, fish, and wildlife. LD_{50} 2,000.

Acaraben®. See chlorobenzilate.

Acaralate®. See chloropropylate.

Akton® (o,o-diethyl o-(2-chloro-1-(2,5-dichlorophenyl)vinyl) phosphorothioate). Nonsystemic soil insecticide for lawn chinch bugs and sod webworms. LD_{50} 146.

aldicarb (2-methyl-2-methylthio) propionaldehyde o-(methylcarbamoyl) oxime. Temik®. Extremely poisonous systemic insecticide and acaricide, to be used only by professional operators. LD_{50} about 1.

aldrin (not less than 95 per cent of 1,2,3,4,10,10-hexachloro-1,4,4a,-5,8,8a-hexahydro-1,4-*endo-exo*-5,8-dimethanonaphthalene). Highly toxic persistent soil insecticide, now being phased out of use. LD_{50} 55.

Alfa-tox®. Combination of diazinon and methoxychlor used for alfalfa pests, spittlebugs, pea aphids, insects on small fruits and vegetables. LD_{50} 2,000.

allethrin (2-allyl-4-hydroxy-3-methyl-2-cyclopenten-1-one ester of 2,2-dimethyl-3-(2-methylpropenyl)-cyclopropanecarboxylic acid). A synthetic pyrethrum, allyl homolog of Cinerin I, contact insecticide of very low toxicity to mammals, leaves no harmful residue on vegetables. LD_{50} 920.

amidithion (o,o-dimethyl-S-(N-methoxyethyl)carbamoylmethyl phosphorodithioate). Thiocron®. Systemic insecticide-acaricide for aphids, mites, thrips, leafhoppers, sawflies, fruit flies on cherries, vegetable crops. LD_{50} 600.

aminocarb (4-(dimethylamino)-*m*-tolyl methylcarbamate). Matacil®. Nonsystemic insecticide useful for cabbage looper and other caterpillars on lettuce and cole crops, for mites, flea beetles, bean beetles, spruce budworm, jack pine budworm, and other pests. LD_{50} 30–50.

Amiphos® (o,o-dimethyl-S-2-(acetylamino)ethyl dithiophosphate). DAEP. Insecticide for aphids, thrips, mites, and scale insects on fruits, vegetables, and ornamentals. LD_{50} 438.

Aphidan® (o,o-diisopropyl-S-ethylsulfinyl methyl dithiophosphate). Systemic insecticide.

Aramite® (2(*p-tert*-butylphenoxy)-1-methylethyl-2-chloroethyl sulfite). Alkyl aryl sulfite acaricide. Excellent for mite control on ornamentals, safe to handle, and with little hazard for wildlife but possibly carcinogenic and not recommended for fruits and vegetables. Not compatible with alkaline materials. LD_{50} 3,900.

Aspon® (o,o,o,o-tetra-*n*-propyl-dithiopyrophosphate). Effective for control of chinch bugs in lawns. LD_{50} 1,200.

azinphosmethyl (o,o-dimethyl S-(4-oxo-1,2,3-benzotriazin-3(4H)-ylmethyl) phosphorodithioate). Guthion®. Highly toxic phosphate insecticide registered for use on many vegetable and fruit crops, trees and other ornamentals. Standard treatment in some places for leafrollers, aphids, and mites on apples. LD_{50} 15.

azobenzene (diphenyl diimide). Acaricide formerly used in greenhouses as a paste on heating pipes.

Azodrin®. See monocrotophos.

Bacillus popilliae. Preparation of bacterial spores causing milky disease of Japanese beetles. Sold as Doom® and Japidemic®.

Bacillus thuringiensis, with varieties *B.t. thuringiensis* and *B.t. galleriae,* bacterial preparations containing a crystalline toxin causing disease in various caterpillars on vegetables and trees. Harmless to humans and animals. Sold as Thuricide, Agritol, Bakthane, Biotrol.

barium fluosilicate. Insecticide for treatment of fruits and vegetables before edible parts are formed.

Baygon®. See propoxur.

benzene hexachloride (1,2,3,4,5,6-hexachlorocyclohexane). BHC. Persistent insecticide, of unpleasant odor, now banned for most uses. LD_{50} 600.

Bidrin®. See dicrotophos.

binapacryl (2-*sec*-butyl-4,6-dinitrophenyl 3-methyl-2-butenoate). Morocide®; Acricid®. Nonsystemic acaricide, effective for mites on fruits and nuts. LD_{50} 120–165.

bromophos (o-(4-bromo-2,5-dichlorophenyl) o,o-dimethyl phosphorothioate). Nexion®. Nonsystemic insecticide-acaricide useful for food crops. LD_{50} 3,700–6,100.

calcium arsenate. Stomach poison dangerous to wildlife, bees, and many beneficial insects; sometimes recommended for potatoes and a few other vegetables, seldom for ornamentals. LD_{50} 35–100.

calcium cyanide. Cyanogas®. Fumigant, with use restricted to persons who understand the dangers and proper handling.

carbaryl (1-naphthyl n-methylcarbamate). Sevin®. Broad-spectrum insecticide replacing DDT on fruits, vegetables, and ornamentals. Relatively safe for mammals and most wildlife but toxic to bees and may increase mites. Do not use on Boston ivy and Virginia-creeper. Effective for Japanese beetles, tent caterpillars, leafminers, lacebugs, bagworms, and sawflies. Usual dosage 2 tablespoons of 50 per cent wettable powder to 1 gallon of water. LD_{50} 500.

carbofuran (2,3-dihydro-2,2-dimethyl-7-benzofuranyl methyl-carbamate). Furadan®. Systemic soil insecticide, also effective for aphids and other pests on apples and walnuts. Oral toxicity very high, LD_{50} only 5, but dermal toxicity 885.

carbon disulfide (carbon bisulfide). Insecticide fumigant, dangerous because of extreme inflammability, poisonous if inhaled. Used for stored grain and sometimes for injecting into borer holes.

carbon tetrachloride. Insecticide fumigant, sometimes combined with carbon disulfide to reduce handling hazards. Poisonous; avoid exposure to vapors.

carbophenothion (S-[(*p*-chlorophenyl thio)methyl]o,o-diethyl phosphorodithioate). Trithion®. Insecticide, acaricide, useful on many fruit, vegetable, and nut crops and on ornamentals. LD_{50} 6–100.

chlorbenside (*p*-chlorobenzyl *p*-chlorophenyl sulfide). Mitox®. Acaricide, safe for use on fruits and ornamentals. LD_{50} 2,000–10,000.

chlordane (1,2,4,5,6,7,8,8-octachloro-2,3,3a,4,7,7a-hexahydro-4,7-methanoindane). Stomach and contact insecticide effective for soil pests such as ants, beetle grubs, chinch bugs, sod webworms, and termites. Very useful but being phased out of home garden use because it is one of the persistent chlorinated hydrocarbons. LD_{50} about 500.

chlorfenethol (4,4'-dichloro-*alpha*-methylbenzhydrol). Dimite®. Acaricide only, for mites on ornamentals; particularly useful for cyclamen mite on delphinium. LD_{50} 500.

chlorfenvinphos (2-chloro-1-(2,4-dichlorophenyl)-vinyl diethylphosphate). Birlane®, Sapecron®, Supona®. Insecticide for control of root maggots, rootworms, cutworms, and potato beetles. LD_{50} 12–56.

chlorobenzilate (ethyl 4,4'-dichlorobenzilate). Acaraben®. Acaricide of low toxicity to warm-blooded animals, used for many species of mites. LD_{50} 700–3,000.

chloropicrin (trichloronitromethane). Larvacide®, Picfume®. Fumigant, used as soil insecticide, fungicide, and nematocide. Tear gas, highly toxic to man and wildlife but leaving no harmful residue.

chloropropylate (isopropyl 4,4'-dichlorobenzilate). Acaralate®. Acaricide, safe to use for mites on apples and pears. LD_{50} 5,000.

Cinerin I and **II**. See pyrethrum.

cue-lure (4-(*p*-hydroxyphenyl)-2-butanone acetate). Attractant, used in bait sprays, especially for melon flies. Of low mammalian toxicity.

cryolite (sodium fluoaluminate). Kryocide®. Protective insecticide currently less popular.

Cygon®. See dimethoate.

Cythion®. Premium grade of malathion, which see.

D-D® Soil Fumigant (1,3-dichloropropene and 1,2-dichloropropane mixture). Dowfume N®. An excellent soil fumigant for wireworms and other soil insects as well as nematodes. Apply only to fallow soil; wait 2 to 4 weeks before planting. Toxic to mammals by ingestion or inhalation but irritating enough to minimize danger; little hazard to wildlife if used as directed. LD_{50} 140.

DDT (1,1,1-trichloro-2-2-bis (*p*-chlorophenyl)ethane). Very effective broad-spectrum insecticide, with long residual action but now banned for home garden use. First synthesized in 1874, by a German chemist, it was 1939 before it was put into practical use—in Switzerland against the Colorado potato beetle. Used as a public health aid during World War II, DDT is credited with saving five million lives and preventing a hundred million illnesses by controlling mosquitoes, lice, flies, and other vectors of human disease. DDT is only mildly toxic to mammals and is less harmful to bees than some other pesticides, but it is toxic to many beneficial insects and may increase spider mites and certain scale insects. It is toxic to fish at low dosage and birds may be killed when DDT is used at more than 2 pounds per acre. It builds up in the food chain and so may cause trouble even used at "safe" dosages. It is persistent and seems to be present in the environment around the world. The decline in bald eagles and some other endangered species is thought by many to be due to thin eggshells caused by DDT. LD$_{50}$ 113–250.

demeton (o,o-diethyl S(and o)-[2-(ethylthio)ethyl]phosphorothiates). Systox®. Highly toxic systemic insecticide and acaricide, not recommended for home garden use. Applied to soil, demeton helps plants resist mites, aphids, and thrips. Do not use without respirator and protective clothing. LD$_{50}$ 2–12.

diazinon (o,o-diethyl o-(2-isopropyl-4-methyl-6-pyrimidinyl)phosphorothioate). Spectracide®, Gardentox®. Effective for resistant soil insects and for pests of fruits, vegetables, and ornamentals. Highly toxic to honey bees but relatively safe for mammals. LD$_{50}$ 108.

Dibrom. See naled.

dichloroethyl ether (bis(2-chloroethyl)ether). A soil fumigant sometimes used for sod webworms, also in corn earworm oils. Strongly irritating. LD$_{50}$ 105.

dichlorvos (2,2-dichlorovinyl o,o-dimethyl phosphate). DDVP, Vapona®. Contact and stomach poison, also acting as a fumigant. Available as No-Pest® resin strips to be hung in greenhouses for control of thrips and other pests. LD$_{50}$ 62.

dicofol (4,4'dichloro-*alpha*-(trichloromethyl)benzhydrol). Kelthane®. Acaricide safe for home garden use, recommended for cyclamen mite as well as spider mites. LD$_{50}$ 800.

dicrotophos (3-hydroxy-N,N-dimethyl-*cis*-crotonamide, dimethyl phosphate). Bidrin®. Highly toxic systemic insecticide. Injected into trees it has controlled European elm scale and some pine insects. Tested for control of bark beetle vectors of Dutch elm disease, the results have been inconclusive. To be used only by professional operators. LD$_{50}$ 22.

dieldrin (not less than 85 per cent of 1,2,3,4,10,10-hexachloro-6,7-epoxy-1,4,4a,5,6,7,8,8a-octahydro-1,4-*endo-exo*-5,8-dimethanonaphthalene). Octalox®. Contact and stomach insecticide now being banned in some states for its toxicity and persistence in soil. Highly effective for wireworms, white-fringed beetles, black vine weevils, grasshoppers, armyworms, borers, curculios, sawflies, thrips, and other insects. LD_{50} 46.

Dimecron®. See phosphamidon.

dimetan (5,5-dimethyl-3-oxo-1-cyclohexen-1-yl-dimethylcarbamate). Systemic insecticide.

dimethoate (o,o-dimethyl phosphorodithioate 5-ester with 2-mercapto-N-methylacetamide). Cygon®, De-Fend®, Rogor®. Systemic insecticide and acaricide, less hazardous to use than most other phosphates. Controls a wide range of pests on ornamentals, nonbearing fruits and certain vegetables. Especially useful for many scale insects and mealybugs, for aphids and thrips. May be injurious to chrysanthemums, Burford holly and some other plants; use only on plants listed on the label. LD_{50} 215.

dinitrobutylphenol (2-*sec*-butyl-4,6-dinitrophenol). DNBP, Dinoseb®. Insecticide and herbicide. LD_{50} 37–50.

dinitrocresol (4,6-dinitro-*o*-cresol, sodium salt). Elgetol® 30, Sinox®, DNOC. Poisonous insecticide and herbicide, used as a dormant spray for some scale insects and aphid eggs. LD_{50} 10–50.

dinitrocyclohexylphenol (2-cyclohexyl-4,6-dinitrophenol). DN-111®, Dinex®. Insecticide and acaricide for use on tree fruits for certain pests; also a herbicide. LD_{50} 65–330.

dinocap (2-(1-methylheptyl)-4,6-dinitrophenyl)-4,6-dinitrophenyl crotonate). Karathane®. A fungicide, often sold as Mildex® but also of some use as an acaricide. LD_{50} 980.

dioxacarb (*o*-1,3-dioxolan-2-ylphenyl methylcarbamate). Elocron®. Contact and stomach insecticide, effective for aphids, sawflies, some beetles, various caterpillars. LD_{50} 107–156.

dioxathion (2,3-*p*-dioxanedithiol S,S-bis-(o,o-diethyl phosphorodithioate). Delnav®. Insecticide and acaricide, effective for mites on ornamentals and fruits. LD_{50} 19–176.

disparlure (*cis*-7,8-epoxy-2-methyloctadecane). Gypsy moth sex attractant.

disulfoton (o,o-diethyl S-[2-(ethylthio)ethyl]phosphorodithioate). Di-Syston®. Systemic acaricide and insecticide; highly poisonous. Can be applied in seed furrow, broadcast or as a foliar spray, particularly effective for sucking insects. Available as granules, liquid concentrate, or with fertilizer but not recommended for amateur gardeners. LD_{50} 2–12.

Dursban® (o,o-diethyl o-(3,5,6-trichloro-2-pyridyl)phosphorothioate). Broad-spectrum insecticide for control of chinch bugs, sod webworms, aphids, mites, and caterpillars. LD_{50} 163.

Dyfonate® (o-ethyl-S-phenyl ethylphosphonodithioate). Soil insecticide for rootworms, wireworms, cutworms, symphilans. Highly toxic and persistent in soil. LD$_{50}$ 8–17.

Dylox®. See trichlorfon.

endosulfan   (6,7,8,9,10,10-hexachloro-1,5,5a,6,9,9a-hexahydro-6,9-methano-2,4,3-benzodioxathiepin 3-oxide). Thiodan®. Insecticide for pests on potatoes and other vegetables and fruits. LD$_{50}$ 110.

endrin   (1,2,3,4,10,10-hexachloro-6,7-epoxy-1,4,4a,5,6,7,8,8a-octahydro-1,4-*endo-endo*-5,8-dimethanonaphthalene). Highly toxic insecticide for some field crops, controlling cutworms, armyworms, aphids, corn borers, plant bugs, webworms, and other pests, also used to control pine mice. Not for amateur gardeners. LD$_{50}$ 5–45.

EPN (o-ethyl o-*p*-nitrophenylphenylphosphonothioate). Acaricide, insecticide, effective for certain mites, European corn borer, orange tortrix, and grape berry moth. LD$_{50}$ 7–65.

ethion (o,o,o',o'-tetraethyl S,S'-methylenebisphosphorodithioate). Nialate®. Insecticide, acaricide, used with dormant oils for control of mites, aphids, scale insects, also for summer control of pests on fruits and ornamentals. Fatal if swallowed, toxic to fish and wildlife. LD$_{50}$ 13–208.

ethylene dibromide (1,2-dibromoethane). Bromofume®, Dowfume® W-85. Soil fumigant, for insects and nematodes. LD$_{50}$ 146.

ethylene dichloride (1,2-dichloroethane). EDC. Insect fumigant, used around peach trees to control borers. LD$_{50}$ 670–800.

Etrofol® (2-chlorophenyl-N-methylcarbamate). Hopcide®. Insecticide effective for leafhoppers and planthoppers.

eugenol (4-allyl-2-methoxyphenol). Attractant, used in Japanese beetle traps. LD$_{50}$ 500–5,000.

fenitrothion (o,o-dimethyl o-(4-nitro-*m*-tolyl)phosphorothioate). Sumithion®, Folithion®, Accothion®. Contact insecticide and selective acaricide, used for pests on orchard fruits and vegetables. LD$_{50}$ 500.

fenson (*p*-chlorophenyl benzenesulfonate). Acaricide, for mites on orchard fruits, killing eggs as well as nymphs. LD$_{50}$ 1,560–1,740.

formetanate (*m*[[(dimethylamino) methylene]amino]phenyl methylcarbamate). Acaricide, of oral toxicity but safe dermally. LD$_{50}$ 22.

formothion (o,o-dimethyl phosphorodithioate S-ester with N-formyl-2-mercapto-N-methylacetamide). Anthio®. Systemic and contact insecticide-acaricide for spider mites, aphids, woolly aphids, psyllids, mealybugs, whiteflies, scale insects, thrips, leafminers, sawflies. LD$_{50}$ 375–535.

Fundal®   (N'-(4-chloro-o-tolyl)-N,N-dimethylformamidine,hydrochloride). Acaricide for nursery stock and nonbearing apple trees. LD$_{50}$ 295.

Furadan®. See carbofuran.

Galecron® (N-(4-chloro-*o*-tolyl)-N,N-dimethylformamidine). Acaricide effective for resistant mites. LD_{50} 162.

Gardona® (2-chloro-1-(2,4,5-trichlorophenyl)vinyl dimethylphosphate). Phosphate insecticide of very low mammalian toxicity; can be used without protective clothing on a wide range of crops but especially useful for apple pests. LD_{50} 400–5,000.

geraniol (an alcohol closely related to cyclic terpenes). Attractant used in Japanese beetle traps.

Guthion®. See azinphosmethyl.

gyplure (*cis*-9-octadecene-1,12-diol-12-acetate). Gypsy moth attractant; synthetic female scent used in traps to survey infestations.

hellebore. Insecticide prepared from *Veratrum album* and *V. viride,* formerly in common garden use.

hemel (hexamethylmelamine). Experimental insect sterilant.

hempa (hexamethylphosphoric triamide). Experimental insect sterilant.

heptachlor (1,4,5,6,7,8,8-heptachloro-3*a*,4,7,7*a*-tetrahydro-4,7-methanoindene). Soil insecticide, formerly used for control of fire and other ants, grasshoppers, and beetle grubs but toxic to game birds and now banned in many areas. LD_{50} 40–188.

hexalure ((Z)-7-hexadecen-1-ol acetate). Insect attractant.

hydrogen cyanide (hydrocyanic acid). Fumigant extremely toxic to humans, to be used only by professionals.

Imidan® (o,o-dimethyl S-phthalimidomethyl phosphorodithioate). Prolate®. Insecticide-acaricide effective for codling moth and other pests on tree fruits and nuts, also for alfalfa weevil. LD_{50} 216.

jubavione. A hormone-like compound, now synthesized, that prevents insects from developing to the adult stage.

Karathane®. See dinocap.

Kelthane®. See dicofol.

Kepone® (decachloro-octahydro-1,3,4-metheno-2H-cyclobuta(cd) pentalen-2-one). Insecticide for control of ants, mole crickets, armyworms, sod webworms, and citrus rust mite on nonbearing trees. LD_{50} 114–140.

Lannate®. See methomyl.

Lanstan®. See chloronitropropane.

lead arsenate. Stomach poison for chewing insects, highly toxic to mammals if ingested. LD_{50} 100.

Lethane 60® (2-thiocyanatoethyl laurate). Insecticide of low mammalian toxicity. LD_{50} 500.

lime sulfur (calcium polysulfides). Fungicide, acaricide, insecticide, used as a dormant spray for scale insects, especially rose, junipcr, and pine needle scales. Of low mammalian toxicity.

lindane (gamma isomer of 1,2,3,4,5,6-hexaxchlorohexane of 99 per cent purity). Purified form of benzene hexachloride, very effective for lace bugs, aphids, especially woolly aphids, leafrollers, wireworms, and other insects. Being phased out of use because it is one of the persistent chlorinated hydrocarbons. LD_{50} 76–200.

London purple (mixture of calcium arsenite and calcium arsenate). Outmoded as an insecticide.

magnesium arsenate. Formerly used for some insects not controlled by lead or calcium arsenate.

malathion (diethyl mercaptosuccinate, S-ester with 0,0-dimethyl phosphorodithioate). Broad-spectrum phosphate insecticide of low toxicity to mammals and recommended for many home garden uses. Harmful to bees and some beneficial insects; sometimes phytotoxic in certain formulations. The wettable powder is safer than emulsions in hot weather. Cythion® is premium-grade malathion of less unpleasant odor. Controls aphids, scale crawlers, mealybugs, whiteflies, and many chewing insects. Do not use on ferns or crassula. LD_{50} 885–2,800.

Marlate®. See methoxychlor.

mecarbam (S-[(ethoxycarbonyl)methylcarbamoil]methyl 0,0-diethyl phosphorodithioate). Insecticide-acaricide with ovicidal action. Controls scale insects, fruit flies, leafhoppers, and root maggots. LD_{50} 36.

medlure (*sec*-butyl 4(or 5)-chloro-2-methylcyclohexanecarboxylate). Attractant of low mammalian toxicity; used in baits for control of the Mediterranean fruit fly.

menazon (S-[(4,6-diamino-*s*-triazin-2-yl)methyl]o,o-dimethyl phosphorodithioate). Saphos®. Systemic insecticide, particularly for aphids on potatoes and cole crops. LD_{50} 1,200–2,000.

Metacide® (o,o-dimethyl o-*p*-nitrophenyl phosphorothioate, parathion mixture). Mixture of parathion and methyl parathion, highly poisonous but slightly less toxic to mammals than parathion.

metaldehyde (a polymer of acetaldehyde). Molluscicide, used in baits and sprays as an attractant and toxicant for slugs and snails. LD_{50} 630.

Meta-Systox-R. See oxydemetonmethyl.

metepa (tris(2-methyl-1-aziridinyl)phosphine oxide). Insect chemosterilant. LD_{50} 93–277.

methiotepa (tris(2-methyl-1-aziridinyl)phosphine sulfide). Metapside®. Insect chemosterilant.

methomyl (S-methyl N-[(methylcarbamoyl)oxy]thioacetimidate). Lannate®. Broad-spectrum insecticide registered for use on cole crops, lettuce, and certain ornamentals, highly poisonous. LD_{50} 17–24.

methoxychlor (1,1,1-trichloro-2,2-bis(p-methoxyphenyl)ethane). Marlate®. Analog of DDT and replacing it. Much safer for mammals and most wildlife but with about the same effect on bees and beneficial insects. Recommended as a substitute for DDT for controlling bark beetle vectors of Dutch elm disease and for many food crops and ornamentals. Usual dosage is 2 tablespoons of 50 per cent wettable powder to 1 gallon of water. LD_{50} 6,000.

methyl apholate (2,2,4,4,6,6-hexahydro-2,2,4,4,6,6-hexakis(2-methyl-l-aziridinyl)-1,3,5,2,4,6-triazatriphosphorine). Chemosterilant.

methyl bromide (bromomethane). Highly toxic fumigant for soil insects and nematodes; extremely hazardous by inhalation and without special odor to give warning; to be used only by expert operators. Not very phytotoxic and may be used in special chambers to fumigate potted plants and outdoors under special covers. LD_{50} 9.

methyl chloride (chloromethane). Aerosol propellant of rather low mammalian toxicity.

methyl demeton (mixture of o,o-dimethyl S-(and o)-(2-ethylthio)-ethyl phosphorothioates). Meta-Systox®. Another phosphate, slightly less hazardous than demeton. Insecticide and acaricide. LD_{50} 180.

methyl parathion (o,o-dimethyl o-(p-nitrophenyl)phosphorothioate). Slightly less toxic than parathion, effective for many insects.

Methyl Trithion® (o,o-dimethyl S[(p-chlorophenylthio)methyl]phosphorodithioate). Acaricide, insecticide, used for cotton insects and chinch bugs in turf. LD_{50} 200.

mevinphos (methyl 3-hydroxy-*alpha*-crotonate dimethyl phosphate). Phosdrin®. Highly toxic but nonpersistent systemic acaricide-insecticide. Controls aphids, mites, grasshoppers, cutworms, leafhoppers, caterpillars, and other pests. Not for home gardeners. LD_{50} 6-7.

mirex (dodecachlorooctahydro-1,3,4-metheno-2H-cyclobuta(cd)-pentalene). Insecticide with low hazard to humans and wildlife, especially useful in control of imported fire ant, harvester and leaf-cutting ants. LD_{50} 306.

monocrotophos (dimethyl phosphate ester with (E)-3-hydroxy-N-methylcrotonamide). Azodrin®. Highly toxic systemic insecticide-acaricide used on cotton; also controls corn earworm and fall armyworm. LD_{50} 21.

Morestan®. See oxythioquinox.

Morocide®. See binapacryl.

morphothion (o,o-dimethyl S-(morpholinocarbonylmethyl)phosphorodithioate). Ekatin®. Another phosphate insecticide. LD_{50} 40-225.

naled (1,2-dibromo-2,2-dichloroethyl dimethyl phosphate). Dibrom®. Bromex®. Nonsystemic insecticide-acaricide with some fumigant action. Safer than DDT and recommended for various crops. LD$_{50}$ 430.

naphthalene. Insecticidal fumigant of low mammalian toxicity; has been used in greenhouses and for gladiolus thrips.

nicotine (1,3-(methyl-2-pyrrolidyl) pyridine). Nicotine sulfate contains 40 per cent of the alkaloid and, sold as Black Leaf 40, was formerly widely used by home gardeners. Little or no nicotine is now produced in the United States; some is imported from England. Contact insecticide, highly toxic if inhaled, ingested, or spilled on the skin but with little residual effect; not harmful to bees and most beneficial insects. The usual dosage is 1 teaspoon of the sulfate and 1 ounce of soap to 1 gallon of water. LD$_{50}$ 50 to 60.

oils. Sometimes animal or vegetable oils, as fish oil or lemon oil, but usually petroleum products in emulsions, when the oil is broken into fine globules in water, or miscible oils that mix readily with water. Oils are safe for the operator and they are exempt from tolerance but they may be phytotoxic if used when the temperature is below 45° F. or above 85° F. Oil sprays should not be used on sugar and Japanese maples, beech, black walnut, butternut and should be used with caution on magnolia and some evergreens. Superior oils are sometimes combined with ethion for dormant sprays to control scale insects and other overwintering pests.

Omite® (2-(p-tert-butylphenoxy)cyclohexyl 2-propynyl sulfite). Acaricide with residual killing action, registered for control of many mite species on apple, peach, plum, pear, and useful on rose and other ornamentals. Very safe for humans, does not kill bees, and less harmful than other chemicals to beneficial predatory mites. LD$_{50}$ 2,200.

ovex (p-chlorophenyl p-chlorobenzenesulfonate). Ovotran®, chlorfenson. Safe acaricide with long residual effect, used for mites on deciduous fruits, nuts, and ornamentals. LD$_{50}$ 2,000.

oxydemetonmethyl (S-[2-(ethylsulfinyl)ethyl]o,o-dimethyl phosphorothioate). Meta-Systox®. Systemic acaricide-insecticide, applied to soil to render plants toxic to aphids, mites, leafhoppers, leafminers, whiteflies, and other pests. LD$_{50}$ 65–80.

oxythioquinox (cyclic S,S-(6-methyl-2,3-quinoxalinedithiol)dithiocarbonate). Morestan®, chinomethionat. Insecticide-acaricide-fungicide safe for humans. Used for mites, pear psylla, and other pests on fruits, vegetables, and ornamentals. LD$_{50}$ 3,000.

para-dichlorobenzene (1,4-dichlorobenzene). Paracide®, Paradow®. Fumigant used for peach tree borers, applied to soil around trees. LD$_{50}$ 1,000–4,000.

parathion (o,o-diethyl o-p-nitrophenyl phosphorothioate). Extremely toxic insecticide, not to be used by home gardeners. Readily absorbed through skin and lungs; protective clothing required. Used by professionals on many crops, including foods, because it has a short residual effect. LD_{50} 13.

paris green (copper acetoarsenite). An old stomach insecticide, sometimes used in poison baits for cutworms, grasshoppers, and armyworms. LD_{50} 22.

Pentac® (decachlorobis(2,4-cyclopentadien-l-yl). Acaricide, very effective for the two-spotted mite and recommended for indoor floral crops. Slow in initial reaction but with long residual effect. LD_{50} 3,160.

Perthane® (1,1-dichloro-2,2-bis(4-ethylphenyl)ethane). Insecticide of great safety, used for looper control on vegetables and for pear psylla. LD_{50} 6,100–8,170.

Pestox III®. See schradan.

phenothiazine (thiodiphenylamine). Insecticide, fungicide of low toxicity to man but may cause dermatitis. Used for apples, pears, quinces.

phorate (o,o-diethyl S-[(ethylthio)methyl]phosphorodithioate). Thimet®. Extremely toxic systemic acaricide, insecticide, to be used only by professionals. Effective for many pests on vegetables and ornamentals, including aphids and leaf miners. LD_{50} 1–5.

phosalone (o,o-diethyl S-[(6-chloro-2-oxobenzoxazolin-3-yl)-methyl] phosphorodithioate). Zolone®. Insecticide-acaricide approved for grapes, apples, and pears. LD_{50} 100–180.

Phosdrin®. See mevinphos.

phosphamidon (2-chloro-N,N-diethyl-3-hydroxycrotonamide dimethyl phosphate). Dimecron®. Systemic and contact acaricide-insecticide, used for aphids, mites, beetles, plant bugs. LD_{50} 15–33.

Phostex® (mixture of bis(dialkyloxyphosphinothioyl)disulfides). Acaricide-insecticide, used in Pacific states to control pear-bud blister mites and in dormant oil sprays for scale insects. LD_{50} 2,500.

piperonyl butoxide (a-[2-(2-butoxyethoxy)ethoxy]-4,5-(methylenedioxy)-2-propyltoluene). Used as a synergist with pyrethrins and rotenone; of very low mammalian toxicity. LD_{50} 7,500.

Plictran® (tricyclohexylhydroxytin). Acaricide, particularly useful for mites resistant to other chemicals; effective for nymphs and adults but not so good for eggs. LD_{50} 180–820.

promecarb (m-cym-5-yl methylcarbamate). Carbamult®. Nonsystemic contact insecticide used for Colorado potato beetle, some caterpillars and leafminers. LD_{50} 35–248.

propoxur (o-isopropoxyphenyl methylcarbamate). Baygon®. Carbamate insecticide with fast knockdown and long residual effect. Used for insect pests of man and animals and also for soil applications to control rootworms and root maggots, with systemic action against aphids, thrips, leafminers, leafhoppers, and scales. LD_{50} 95–175.

propyl isome (dipropyl 5,6,7,8-tetrahydro-7-methylnaphtho(2,3-d)-1,3-dioxole-5,6-dicarboxylate). Synergist of very low mammalian toxicity, used with pyrethrins. LD_{50} 1,500.

Pyrethrin I (ester of chrysanthemum monocarboxylic acid and the alcohol pyrethrolone). Active principle in pyrethrum.

Pyrethrin II (ester of chrysanthemum dicarboxylic acid and the alcohol pyrethrolone). A constituent of pyrethrum.

pyrethrum. From dried flower heads of *Chrysanthemum cineraefolium* and some other members of this genus, active principles being Cinerin I and II (esters of chrysanthemum monocarboxylic acid and dicarboxylic acid with the alcohol cinerolone) and Pyrethrins I and II. Contact insecticide of very low mammalian toxicity, with little hazard to bees and beneficial insects but toxic to fish. LD_{50} 200–2,600.

rotenone (1,2,12,12a-tetrahydro-2-isopropenyl-8,9-dimethoxy(1) benzopyrano(3,4-b) furo(2,3-h) (1) benzopyran-6(6aH)-one). Contact and stomach insecticide derived from plants, species of *Derris* and *Lonchocarpus,* the latter found in Central and South America, a principal source. Highly toxic to fish but of low toxicity to most mammals. In the form of ground derris it may kill nesting birds. LD_{50} 60–1,500.

ryania. From ground stem and root of *Ryania speciosa,* a South American shrub. Contact and stomach poison relatively safe for mammals. Used for corn borers and some other pests of food crops, including codling moths on apple. LD_{50} 750–1,200.

sabadilla. From seeds of *Schoenocaulon officinale,* a South American plant of the lily family. Irritating to the eyes and respiratory tract, but less toxic than rotenone when inhaled or ingested. Used for squash bugs, stink bugs, and similar insects. LD_{50} 4,000.

schradan (octamethylpyrophosphoramide). Pestox III®, OMPA. Systemic acaricide-insecticide; highly poisonous, requiring extreme care. Used mainly for mites and aphids on ornamentals, walnuts, and some nonfood crops. LD_{50} 8–25.

sesamex (2-(2-ethoxyethoxy)ethyl 3,4-(methylenedioxy)phenyl acetal of acetaldehyde). Sesoxane®. Synergist for pyrethrins and allethrin. LD_{50} 2,000.

sesamin (2,6-bis[3,4-(methylenedioxy)phenyl]3,7-dioxabicyclo-(3,3,0)octaine). Synergist for pyrethrins. A component of sesame oil.

sesamolin (6-[3,4-(methylenedioxyphenoxy)-2-(3,4-(methylene-dioxy)phenyl]-3,7-dioxabicyclo(3,3,0)octane). Synergist.

Sevin®. See carbaryl.

siglure (sec-butyl 6-methyl-3-cyclohexane-1-carboxylate). Insect attractant of low mammalian toxicity, used for the Mediterranean fruit fly.

sodium arsenate. Highly toxic insecticide and herbicide, sometimes used in ant baits.

sodium arsenite. Insecticide and herbicide now out of favor because of its extreme toxicity. Formerly used in baits as well as a weed-killer. LD_{50} 10–50.

sodium selenate. One of the first systemic insecticides. Of high mammalian toxicity; must not be applied to land later to be used for food crops. Now in less common use, it has been available in 2 per cent concentration, form P-40, for control of chrysanthemum leaf nematode and as capsules (Kapsulate) for cyclamen mite on African violets.

sulfotepp (o,o,o',o'-tetraethyl dithiopyrophosphate). Bladafume®, Dithione®, Sulfatep. Highly toxic acaricide-insecticide used in greenhouse aerosols for aphids, mites, whiteflies, and thrips. LD_{50} 7–10.

sulfoxide (1,2-(methylenedioxy)-4-[2-(octylsulfinyl)propyl] benzene). Synergist of very low mammalian toxicity, used with pyrethrins and allethrin. LD_{50} 2,000–2,500.

sulfur. A fungicide acting also as an acaricide, controlling some mites and fleahoppers. Incompatible with oils and dinitro sprays; phytotoxic to Viburnum carlesi; may burn foliage in hot weather.

Spectracide®. See diazinon.

Systox®. See demeton.

TDE (1,1-dichloro-2,2-bis(p-chlorophenyl)ethane). DDD, Rhothane®. Insecticide relative of DDT but of much lower mammalian toxicity; used on many fruits and vegetables but toxic to fish. LD_{50} 400–3,400.

Tedion®. See tetradifon.

Temik®. See aldicarb.

tepa (tris(1-aziridinyl)phospine oxide). Aphoxide. Insect chemosterilant.

tepp (ethyl pyrophosphate). Vapotone®. Highly toxic to warm-blooded animals, quickly absorbed through skin. Effective for mites and soft-bodied insects; vanishes quickly after application so that it can be used on food crops up to 3 days of harvest. Not recommended for amateur gardeners; to be used only with protective clothing and gas mask. LD_{50} 0.5–2.

tetradifon (*p*-chlorophenyl 2,4,5-trichlorophenyl sulfone). Tedion®. Very safe acaricide, killing mites in all stages of development; used on fruits, vegetables, and ornamentals. LD_{50} 14,700.

tetrasul (*p*-chlorophenyl 2,4,5-trichlorophenyl sulfide). Animert®. Acaricide, related to tetradifon, killing mites during hatching of eggs. LD_{50} 6,810.

Thimet®. See phorate.

Thiodan®. See endosulfan.

thioquinox (cyclic 2,3-quinoxalinedithiol trithiocarbonate). Eradex®. Acaricide used on ornamentals to kill spider mites and their eggs. LD_{50} 3,400.

Thuricide®. See *Bacillus thuringiensis*.

toxaphene (chlorinated camphene containing 67–69 per cent of chlorine). Stomach and contact insecticide that does not accumulate in tissues as much as DDT. Widely used on cotton, also effective for control of chinch bugs, armyworms, and some other insects; may injure cucurbits. LD_{50} 40–283.

trichlorfon (dimethyl(2,2,2-tri-chloro-1-hydroxyethyl)phosphonate). Dylox®, Dipterex®. Insecticide registered for use on a wide variety of field crops, vegetables, and ornamentals for many different species of insects. Applied by airplane, it is promising for gypsy moth control. LD_{50} 500.

trimedlure (*tert*-butyl 4(or 5)-chloro-2-methylcyclohexanecarboxylate). Attractant for the Mediterranean fruit fly.

Trithion®. See carbophenothion.

Vapona®. See dichlorvos.

Vapotone®. See tepp.

Viron/H®. Biotrol®. Experimental virus insecticide (Heliothis polyhedrosis virus) for control of tussock moths, corn earworms, and some other pests.

Viron/T®. Trichoplusia virus for control of cabbage looper and similar pests.

Zectran® (4-dimethylamino-3,5-xylyl-n-methylcarbamate). Controls a wide variety of pests, including foliage insects and mites, slugs and snails. Highly toxic in acute oral tests but with rapid degradation and low dermal toxicity; has been proposed for spruce budworm control with aerial sprays. LD_{50} 15–63.

Zinophos® (o,o-diethyl-o-2-pyrazinyl phosphorothioate). Cynem®, thionazin. Insecticide for soil application on mint, corn, vegetables, strawberries (West Coast only), and nursery stock; also dip for flower bulbs and nursery stock. Highly toxic, LD_{50} 12.

Zytron® (o-(2-4-dichlorophenyl)o-methyl-n-isopropylphosphoramidothioate). Dowco® 118. Herbicide also effective for ants, chinch bugs, and grubs in turf. LD_{50} 270.

CHEMICALS IN COMBINATION

There are thousands of all-purpose sprays and dusts now on the market that combine several different chemicals. A fungicide (sulfur, copper, captan, Benlate, dichlone, ferbam, folpet (Phaltan) glyodin, maneb, zineb, or ziram) is usually included to take care of plant diseases in the same application as that intended for insects and mites. It is seldom possible to solve all problems with one mixture, but usually you can find one that will do fairly well for ornamentals, another for vegetables, and another for fruit trees, with a few supplementary treatments for special pests.

In choosing the right combination you must make sure that the active ingredients and the diluents used in making up the mixture are safe on the plants you want to protect. Rotenone is nontoxic to most plants but sometimes sulfur is combined with it, both as a diluent and as a fungicide, and sulfur is decidedly toxic to most melon varieties and to some other cucurbits.

While we were allowed to use it, DDT was very useful on many plants but it did markedly reduce squash yields and it could kill or seriously injure some varieties of camellias, though others were little affected. DDT in a rose spray or dust without a miticide encouraged so many spider mites that the results were worse than no treatment. When DDT was formulated for mosquito control it sometimes caused injury to foliage, not from the DDT itself but from the kerosene or other oil solvent.

A spray containing lead arsenate planned for shade trees is not usually safe on the tender foliage of peaches and other stone fruits, or for flowering cherries or ornamental plums. For these, lead arsenate is used at a weaker strength and lime or zinc sulfate is added as a safener.

Dimethoate (Cygon) is an excellent insecticide for camellias but it may injure chrysanthemums or Burford holly.

The mixing of incompatible chemicals may cause injury to a plant that would be safe with either one alone, or one chemical may inactivate another so that the spray loses its potency. Until recently, gardeners were almost always urged to add a good spreader-sticker to their spray mixture, but now we know that that may be bad advice. Some additives seem to increase plant injury, perhaps by increasing plant absorption, and some seem to decrease efficiency, perhaps by increasing runoff, perhaps by actual chemical change. Unless a manufacturer directs that a specific spreader-sticker be added to his product, it might be wise to use it without an additive.

STOP, LOOK, AND LISTEN!

Before using any chemical or combination, in any form, at any time, on any plant, ask yourself these questions:

1. *Is it safe for me?* Before opening any package or bottle READ THE LABEL. See if you are to take special precautions against inhalation or skin contact. The very moment of opening a bag or can of toxic dust presents the grave danger of getting poison into your lungs. The moment of opening a bottle presents a chance of spilling concentrated liquid on your skin.

If you are an amateur gardener, avoid using chemicals that require respirator and protective clothing and that come with directions to wash clothing after each use. But after using *any* chemical wash your face and hands. Never smoke while spraying or dusting. You get the chemical from your hands to the cigarette and thence into your mouth. Avoid use of chemicals on a windy day; work so that the spray or dust blows away from you.

2. *Have I safeguarded my neighbor's children and pets?* Children do trespass and they sometimes find discarded containers with a trace of poison left inside. There have been tragic fatal accidents. It is not easy to dispose of leftover poisons and their containers. In fact, this is one of the biggest problems at the moment in regard to pesticides and the environment. Some authorities recommend holding some of the more hazardous materials until the government can work out some satisfactory method. Burning containers is no longer recommended; it may itself create a hazard. Nor should liquids be flushed down a drain or the toilet because eventually the poisons may get to rivers. Deep burial is one answer, but few of us have waste land to use in this fashion. If you have a municipal trash collection which is used for a land-fill operation it may be possible to wrap containers in several thicknesses of newspaper and put them out with the garbage. It is important to figure closely how much material will be needed in a season and to purchase only that amount.

At the end of any spraying operation there is some unused liquid. This can be poured into a gravel drive where it will be absorbed instantly, but not down a drain nor where it might stand in gutters or hollows long enough for birds or a dog to take a drink.

Under no circumstances should a chemical be divided and part given away without the original label with all its warnings.

3. *Do I know the active ingredient in this material and is it for-*

mulated for use on plants? Is there any danger of injuring my plants at the dilution needed to kill the insect? Sometimes there is a narrow limit between an effective dosage and one that is phytotoxic.

4. *Is there any diluent in this dust or spreader in this spray that may harm my plant?*

5. *Is it specifically recommended for the pest I want to kill?*

6. *Are the weather conditions right for this chemical on this plant at this time?* Oil sprays injure all plants somewhat and evergreens severely if used when it is too cold; copper puts red spots on rose leaves in cold weather; sulfur and malathion may burn tender foliage in too hot weather.

7. *Have I used anything on this plant in the recent past that would either inactivate this chemical or be injurious to the plant when mixed with this chemical?* Don't lime your lawn the same spring you use chlordane for pest control; don't follow summer oils with sulfur.

8. *Have I used any other material in this sprayer recently and forgotten to clean it out?* The sprayer should be rinsed between different chemical mixtures and at the end of each day. Weed killers, however, should be used in a separate sprayer, for it is almost impossible to clean a sprayer that has been used for 2,4-D sufficiently for protective spraying.

9. *Have I measured or weighed the amounts correctly?* If you need only 1 teaspoon and spill enough more to make 2, you are doubling the dosage and vastly increasing the chance of injury. Worse yet, that amount you may remember as 1 tablespoon is only 1 teaspoon in the manufacturer's directions and so you are tripling the dose and perhaps killing your plants. Always reread the label just before mixing up a pesticide.

10. *Have I compensated for possible harm from this chemical?* Have you added a miticide to take care of the red spiders that Sevin may encourage? Are you remembering to save the bees by not spraying fruit trees in full bloom? Are you leaving some of your garden unsprayed as a haven for beneficial insects?

If you can answer these questions, go ahead and apply your chemical. If you don't know the answers, stop and think again before spraying or dusting. You can do more harm in ten thoughtless minutes than the bugs can do in a whole season. If you don't know *what* you are doing and *why* you are doing it, don't do anything in the line of chemicals. Stick to sanitary and cultural measures and encourage the beneficial insects and birds to work for you.

Chapter III

SPRAYING AND DUSTING

THE ART OF SPRAYING

Spraying is a fine art and one which all too few gardeners ever acquire. It takes a lot of common sense and a modicum of brains. It takes a sense of timing and a sense of responsibility to plants. It takes a little mechanical skill but not necessarily too much brawn. We used to be able to hire the brawn but with the scarcity and present cost of garden help some of us are turning thankfully to hose-end sprayers and letting water pressure take the place of hand pumping. And a few others are using a small mist blower, known as Atomist, with an electric cord plugged into an outdoor outlet. Of course, we have long had gasoline-powered sprayers for the larger estates. Lack of common sense in selecting and applying chemicals (which includes neglecting to read labels) and inability or unwillingness to keep up regular treatments throughout the growing season are the chief obstacles to maintaining a vigorous, reasonably pest-free garden.

CHOOSING A SPRAYER

Sprayers vary in size and type from those suitable for a few house plants to large trucks for farmers and shade-tree experts and airplanes for large-scale operations.

Aerosol "Bombs." True aerosols are air suspensions of solid or liquid particles of ultramicroscopic size. They remain suspended in air for hours and are very effective in fogging operations for mosquitoes but are not so useful for plant pests. The so-called aerosol sprays have somewhat larger particles, which deposit readily on foliage. The insecticide is dissolved in liquefied gas and held under pressure in a metal container known as a bomb. When a valve is opened (by pushing a button), the chemical is dispersed in a fine

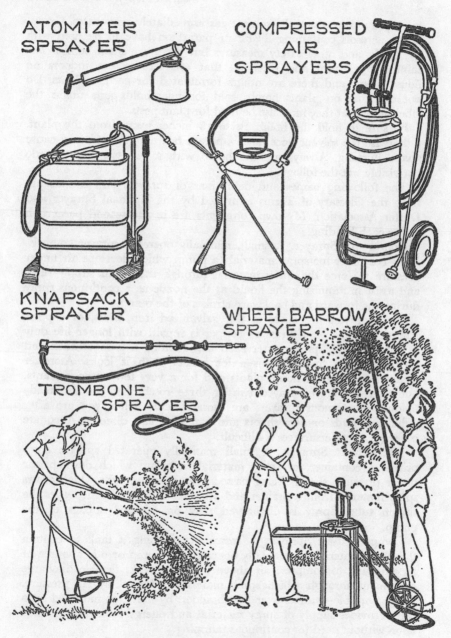

ATOMIZER SPRAYER

COMPRESSED AIR SPRAYERS

KNAPSACK SPRAYER

WHEELBARROW SPRAYER

TROMBONE SPRAYER

1. Sprayers of assorted sizes and types.

mist spray from which the solvent gas immediately evaporates. Greenhouse aerosols containing TEPP or parathion have to be used with gas masks and other safety measures but there are small bombs containing pyrethrum and rotenone that are safe to use indoors on house plants and there are others formulated for garden plants. Do not ever use on plants bombs sold for household pests unless the label states that they may also be used for plant pests.

Be sure to hold the bomb 12 to 18 inches away from the plant. Otherwise the solvent does not evaporate fast enough and may cause severe burning. Always use the bomb with a sweeping motion; do not visibly wet the foliage.

The following names and definitions of sprayers and dusters are from the Glossary of Terms approved by the National Sprayer and Duster Association. My own comments are in the second paragraph under each heading.

Continuous Sprayer. A small, manually operated sprayer comprising a container for spray material; a pump which develops air under pressure to force the spray material through the liquid supply tube, and assist in atomizing the liquid at the nozzle as a continuous spray during the forward and backward strokes of the pump.

Such sprayers are made of tin, galvanized iron, brass, or copper. The extra expense of brass or copper is repaid with longer life only if you clean the sprayer after each use. Pushing a plunger back and forth to get a fine spray is a lot harder than it looks. Atomizer sprayers are fine for house plants and for a very few outdoor plants, but after you have sprayed two or three rosebushes you are ready to quit. Continuous sprayers are most effective when you are after aphids on buds or new shoots and can hit them directly. Adequate coverage of undersurfaces is difficult.

Intermittent Sprayer. A small manually operated sprayer comprising a container for spray material; a pump which develops air under pressure, the air being passed over a siphon tube which draws spray material from container and atomizes the liquid as it leaves the siphon tube. Spray is discharged only on forward strokes of the pump.

Compressed-air Sprayer. A sprayer comprising a tank to contain the spray material; a manually operated air pump or other source of air pressure, to compress air above liquid in tank; flexible discharge equipment through which spray material is forced by air pressure. Easily portable—carries over the shoulder, by hand, or mounted on a cart. Provides supply of spray material and energy for constant operation without need for continuous pumping.

This sprayer, varying in capacity from 1½ to 4 gallons, is as good

POWER SPRAYERS

HOSE
SPRAYER

HOUSE PLANT
INSECT BOMB

2. More sprayers and ways to treat plants.

as your ability to pump it up. I am no longer adequate to the task. The short hose and spray rod with a curved or swivel nozzle make it possible to reach underside of foliage without much difficulty. There is no agitator, so the tank must be shaken occasionally to keep the chemicals from settling out.

Knapsack Sprayer. A sprayer carried on the operator's back, knapsack style. Comprises a tank to contain unpressurized spray material; a manually operated pump which develops hydraulic pressure within the pump; flexible discharge equipment through which spray material is forced by hydraulic pressure.

This is a fine sprayer for a man, but rather heavy for a woman to carry on her back, although I used one for several years with a good deal of satisfaction. The pressure is continuous, maintained by an effortless moving up and down of a lever on the right side of the operator while the left hand is free to hold the spray rod, which can send spray to the top of fairly tall bushes or underneath low plants. The spray mixture is kept agitated and comes out in fine droplets.

Slide Sprayer (Trombone Sprayer). A manually operated hydraulic sprayer with telescoping plunger, operated by two hands. Draws material from attached or separate container and discharges it as a spray under pressure on either forward and back strokes of the plunger or on forward strokes only.

This type allows you to send a stream of spray up into small trees, but it is a nuisance to keep moving the bucket around, and working the slide back and forth is fairly arduous.

Bucket Pump (Barrel Pump). A manually operated hydraulic piston-type pump which may be held or mounted in a container holding the spray material. Draws spray material into the pump when plunger is operated and discharges it into a continuous spray through the discharge equipment. Provides flexibility in size and type of container and high pressures.

Wheelbarrow Sprayer. A manually operated hydraulic sprayer mounted on frame with wheelbarrow-type handles and one or two wheels. Comprises a container holding spray material, a manually operated barrel pump, mounted within, which draws spray material into the pump when plunger is operated and discharges it in a continuous spray through the discharge equipment. Provides portability, large capacity, and high pressures.

I used a sprayer of this general type (12-gallon Paragon) in spraying other people's gardens, all day, every day, for over a quarter of a century. In those days my chief requirement of an assistant was that he have a strong right arm, and the chief disadvantage of this type of sprayer is that it takes two people to operate it efficiently. My helper did the pumping and pushed the heavy truck around the garden; I concentrated on operating the spray rod. This comes in 3 sections and for trees all are put together, but for most garden work 2 sections are best. A 10-foot hose comes with the sprayer, but I had this replaced with a 25-foot length of heavy-duty spray hose to reach easily all sides of shrubbery and to get into garden beds at some distance from paths. This type of sprayer is quite easily cleaned and costs little more than a good knapsack sprayer. It provides a fine mist with little visible residue to mar the beauty of ornamentals.

Hose-end Sprayer. An applicator attached to garden hose, operated by water pressure, which mixes liquid or solid spray materials in water stream and discharges the mixture.

Now that I no longer doctor other gardens and no longer have an assistant to help in my own, I have adopted the lazy hose method and find it surprisingly effective with the right equipment. I use the *Hayes 6 Spray Gun* (also sold as the *Ortho Queen Size Sprayette*). This type has an extension tube as deflector which allows good coverage of underleaf surfaces, and it also has a shutoff at the jar. The type of sprayer used for applying fertilizers and weed killers to lawns, where you have to keep your thumb over an air vent, is not adequate for pest control on flowers and shrubs. A single mixing will serve for 1 to 6 gallons of spray. I use wettable powders or liquids with equal success, but I do make my mixtures in a separate jar and then strain into the hose jar through a wire tea strainer.

Power Sprayer, Hydraulic Type. A sprayer with hydraulic pump (piston, gear, roller, etc.) driven by gasoline engine or electric motor. Comprises a tank or other container for spray material; a power-driven pump which draws spray material into the pump and discharges the spray material under pressure into the discharge system.

Power sprayers are available now in all sizes, from the 5-gallon affair, which seems to me too small to be worth the cost, to the large 300-gallon tank on a truck which delivers from 5 to 50 gallons a minute under 200 to 800 pounds pressure. For estates, sprayers of 15-, 25-, or 50-gallon capacity are practical if you can afford the initial investment and will keep them clean so they last long enough to give adequate return on that investment. Power spraying usually takes more spray solution than hand spraying for the same amount of protection.

Mist Blowers. Low-gallonage sprayers, often used by commercial operators in addition to hydraulic equipment but seldom entirely replacing it. The spray mixture is very concentrated; air instead of water is used as the carrier so that a foglike mist comes out of the machine. Mist blowers may be fairly large power machines or small enough to be carried. One sold as the *Atomist* is now popular with some home gardeners. It is powered by electricity.

Airplanes and **Helicopters.** Used for custom spraying of large-acreage farms, for the routine spraying of field crops, or forests, for control of outbreaks of spruce budworm, gypsy moth, and other pests of great economic importance.

MAKING UP SPRAY MIXTURES

Measurements must be exact. Keep with your spray materials a set of plastic measuring spoons and a glass measuring cup marked in ounces. Remember your household measurements:

> 3 level teaspoons are 1 level tablespoon.
> 2 tablespoons are 1 fluid ounce.
> 16 tablespoons are 1 cup (8 fluid ounces).
> 2 cups are 1 pint.
> 4 cups are 1 quart.
> 16 cups (4 quarts) are 1 gallon.

By a little figuring you can save much time in measuring. If direction calls for 1⅔ tablespoons, you can be exact by measuring 1 tablespoon and 2 teaspoons. But if you need 8 tablespoons, it is a lot quicker to measure out ½ cup. If you are making up dormant spray oil at 1 to 15 dilution, put in 1 cup of oil and add water to make 1 gallon. But if you want a summer spray of about 1 to 50 dilution, you add 3 gallons (48 cups) of water to 1 cup of oil. The actual dilution is then 1 to 49 but that is near enough at such a great dilution.

If directions in bulletins call for 1 pint in 100 gallons, just figure that that means 1 pint to 800 pints or a 1 to 800 dilution; 1 quart to 100 gallons is a 1 to 400 dilution. The following table will help in transposing figures for any amount of spray you wish.

DILUTION TABLE FOR SPRAYS

Desired Amount of Finished Spray	Amount of Concentrated Spray for Dilution			
	1–200	1–400	1–600	1–800
1 quart	1 tsp.	½ tsp.	⅓ tsp.	¼ tsp.
1 gallon	4 tsps.	2 tsps.	1½ tsps.	1 tsp.
5 gallons	6 tbsps.	3 tbsps.	2¼ tbsps.	1½ tbsps.
50 gallons	1 quart	1 pint	1½ cups	1 cup
100 gallons	2 quarts	1 quart	1½ pints	1 pint

When it comes to mixing sprays from dry materials, directions usually are given in pounds of chemical per 100 gallons of water—e.g.

3 pounds lead arsenate to 100; ½ pound actual carbaryl (which means 1 pound of the 50 per cent wettable powder) to 100. Translating pounds to tablespoons for small amounts of spray is difficult because of the difference in weight of various compounds. One ounce of lead arsenate is 5½ tablespoons but 1 ounce of calomel is only 1¾ tablespoons; wettable sulfur is about 3 tablespoons to an ounce; hydrated lime 4 to 5 tablespoons; and 50 per cent carbaryl (Sevin) about 6. The measurement also varies according to whether the material is fluffed up or packed down hard.

Chemicals marketed in small packages for home gardeners usually give the dosage per gallon in teaspoons or tablespoons. In purchasing commercial amounts for garden use, I read the label to see how many pounds are recommended to 100 gallons of water and then I figure how many grams or ounces that means for 1 gallon. I weigh that amount out and then see how many tablespoons it fills and mark the figure on the package for subsequent use. My small scales weigh in grams but it is easy to transpose from the metric system by knowing that 28.35 grams equal 1 ounce; 453.6 grams equal 1 pound.

In making up sprays the usual method is to make a slurry by adding water very slowly to the dry material, stirring constantly, but some chemicals work better sprinkled on top of the pail of water. The directions on the package sometimes tell you; sometimes you find it out by trial and error. Some compounds work better if a spreader, such as Household Dreft, or DuPont Spreader-sticker, or Triton B-1956, is added to the diluted spray. But in some instances such additives are harmful, so manufacturer's directions should be carefully noted. Dry mixes usually have some inert materials which do not go into solution, so the diluted spray should always be strained into the tank through cheesecloth or a special strainer.

MANIPULATING THE SPRAY ROD

Handling the spray rod to get complete coverage, yet not to drench the plants so the spray runs off or builds up too much residue, is where the fine art of spraying comes in.

The type of spray droplets and the amount of unsightly residue depend somewhat on the hole in the nozzle. A very small hole is required for the fine spray we usually want for ornamentals. Since almost all chemicals have an abrasive action which constantly enlarges the hole, a new nozzle should replace the old whenever the droplets get larger, or it takes more spray to cover the same number of plants.

In spraying, work from several different positions—first from one side, then the other, then around from the back, keeping the rod constantly in motion and sending the spray from the underside of the lowest leaves up through the bush. You can end up with a swipe over the top of plants to get aphids on buds and new shoots but ordinarily if you do a good job from underneath, with the nozzle turned up, enough spray falls back on top of the leaves to take care of that surface. Work rapidly; don't stay in one place long enough for water to run off the leaves or collect at the tip of the leaves to produce burning. Apply a fine, even mist.

If possible, wait until the foliage is dry in the morning before spraying, but if it rains every few hours get out and do the best you can between showers. With an even distribution of droplets you don't have to worry about spraying in full sun, even in hot weather, unless the chemical you are using, like sulfur or oil, is one that is injurious at high temperatures. For beetles chewing flowers or thrips inside petals, you have to direct the full force of the spray into the flower. For such purposes it is wiser not to have an ingredient in the spray that will leave a dark residue.

There is a widespread belief that rain washes off the spray and the application must be repeated after the shower. That is seldom true. Modern pesticides are formulated to stand a good bit of weathering, and the important thing is to have the protective spray in place before the insect pest or the disease pathogen arrives. So I always advise spraying roses and other plants with continuing problems more or less regularly every week. This means that there is always sufficient residue to take care of the enemy regardless of weather.

TIMING THE SPRAY

Exact timing may be somewhat more important in applying fungicides than in dealing with insects, but it does play a large part in the successful use of all pesticides. The life histories given under the specific pests often suggest the proper timing of control measures. Scale insects must be killed when plants are dormant or with a summer spray during the brief period when vulnerable young crawlers are moving. To be effective, the spray for boxwood leafminer should be in place before the orange fly emerges. The most important time to spray apples for codling moth is when most of the petals have fallen but before the calyx closes. Japanese beetle sprays on roses have to be repeated weekly to keep the new growth protected. Unless you plan an early spray for roseslugs and pine sawflies, most of the damage will be done before you know the pests are out. On the other hand, it is foolish to waste money spraying for pests that have already finished their season. If there is only one brood, as with cankerworms, and the caterpillars chew for only a month or so, a spray near the end of that month is scarcely justified, whereas one near the beginning of the period would be highly desirable.

CLEANING THE SPRAYER

The best way to clean a sprayer is to *keep it clean*. Strain all mixtures into the spray tank through close-mesh cheesecloth to avoid clogging nozzles and thoroughly rinse the sprayer at the end of *every operation*. This is necessary for the longevity of the plants as well as for the apparatus. Leftover solutions have unpredictable and often injurious results. Never, never put away a sprayer without discarding all liquid left in the tank and pumping at least two changes of water through the entire system. Don't just dump water in and pour it out again; keep on pumping until water comes out of the nozzle crystal-clear.

Once or twice during the season, and at the end before putting away for winter, more strenuous cleaning is indicated. Pour a pail of warm water with a handful of trisodium phosphate (available at hardware stores) into the tank; let it soak, then scrub with a stiff brush. Soak the small metal parts—nozzle, strainer, etc.—in kerosene; poke wire through the rods. Reassemble, rinse with water containing a cupful or two of vinegar, and finally rinse with pure water.

If the sprayer has been used for killing weeds with 2,4-D it is next to impossible to clean it sufficiently for general spraying. If you want to try, rinse spray tank and hose with water; fill tank with water containing 2 teaspoons household ammonia per quart; stir and pump a little into hose and nozzle; let stand at least 18 hours; drain, rinse at least twice, pumping water through hose and nozzle. Rinse again, pumping water through the whole system, immediately before putting in a spray mixture, for faint traces of 2,4-D will still be present.

DUSTING PREFERRED?

Dusting has a place in every garden. In my own, I have dusted vegetables and ornamentals I care little about and guinea-pig plants, which get all kinds of combinations tried out on them, but I much prefer spraying for roses and other flowers that are too glowingly beautiful to have their colors dimmed by even the finest film of dust.

I don't subscribe to the theory that you do not have to wear old clothes for dusting and can do it any time you have a few spare

moments. Dusts are harder on my shoes than sprays; I have to tie
up my hair and cover up my arms and clothes. If I use sulfur I have
to cry myself to sleep at night to get the particles washed off my
eyeballs. Of course I should wear goggles but I dislike them more
than the sulfur.

There is also a theory that you can dust plants between showers if
necessary, and so get protection from a dust when there would be
no chance to spray. But for ornamentals I believe just the opposite.
If you dust a rose when the leaves are wet with either rain or dew,
the dust goes on in lumps and stays in unsightly blotches that are
an eyesore all summer. If you spray a rose when it is wet, you may
not get the best control and you may have to make a second application a little sooner than usual but you have not spoiled the beauty
of that rosebush for the rest of the season. If, however, dust can be
applied to a dry plant and can be blown up through the foliage from
underneath, so that only a fine film settles on the upper surface,
then dusts need not be too unsightly for the majority of plants.

In very early days dusts were sometimes applied by beating a
cheesecloth bag with a stick. The modern cans or cartons, with
holes punched in the top to be used like salt shakers, and the con-
traptions where you purchase the dust inside one cardboard cylinder
telescoped within another are not even as good as the cheesecloth
bag. If you want to dust, by all means purchase a reliable duster.

Plunger Duster. Dust Gun. A small, manually operated duster
comprising a container for the dust material; a plunger pump which
develops a current of air at each forward stroke which picks up dust
from the dust container and discharges it through the discharge
equipment. Volume of dust discharged and range of carry controlled
by size of pump and speed of stroking.

Plunger dusters are satisfactory for small gardens if the dust is
discharged through an extension tube having a deflector which can
send the dust up through the foliage.

Crank Duster. A manually operated duster which comprises a
hopper or container for the dust; an agitating device; a high-
velocity, gear-driven fan, driven by a hand-operated crank which
develops a continuous current of air which carries the dust through
the discharge equipment. Volume of dust discharged controlled by
regulating device, and range of carry by speed of fan.

In addition to the large crank dusters used by market gardeners
there is a **midget rotary duster**, made of lightweight aluminum, that
is delightfully easy to operate. Used with an extension tube, it provides adequate coverage and I can highly recommend it from personal experience. Another type, which supplies only its own very fine

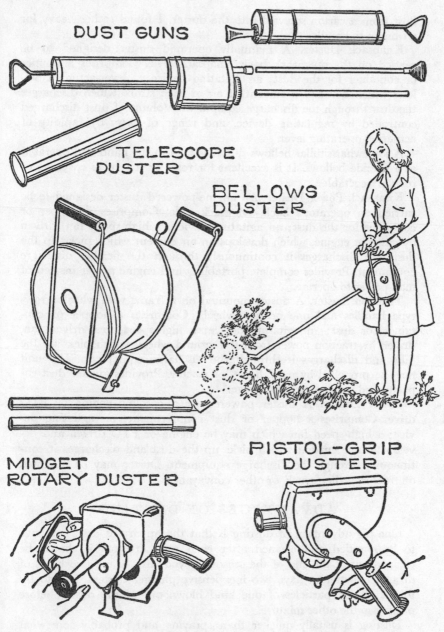

DUST GUNS

TELESCOPE DUSTER

BELLOWS DUSTER

MIDGET ROTARY DUSTER

PISTOL-GRIP DUSTER

3. *Various types of dusters.*

dust from a carton screwed into the duster, I found rather heavy for a woman to handle.

Knapsack Duster. A manually operated duster designed to be carried on the operator's back, knapsack style. Comprises a hopper or container for the dust; an agitating device; a lever-actuated bellows which develops a current of air at each stroke which discharges the dust through the discharge equipment. Volume of dust discharged controlled by regulating device, and range of carry by rapidity of actuating operating lever.

A somewhat similar bellows duster is held in the hand and operated as a fireside bellows. It is excellent for roses or for quick coverage of rows of vegetables.

Knapsack Power Duster. An engine-powered duster designed to be carried on operator's back, knapsack style. Comprises a hopper or container for the dust; an agitating device; a high-speed fan, driven by gasoline engine, which develops an air current which picks up the dust and discharges it continuously through the flexible discharge equipment. Provides complete portability and engine power instead of man power to operate.

Traction Duster. A duster mounted on a frame with wheelbarrow-type handles and one or two wheels. Comprises a hopper or container for dust; an agitating device; a high-speed, gear-driven fan, driven by traction power from the ground wheel, which picks up the dust and discharges it through the discharge equipment. The unit may be propelled by man, horse, or tractor. Provides greater dust capacity and wider area of coverage.

Power Duster. A duster powered by a gasoline engine or PTO drive. Comprises a hopper or dust compartment; an agitating device; a high-speed fan which may be engine or PTO driven and develops an air current which picks up the dust and discharges it continuously through the discharge equipment. Duster may be mounted on tractor, trailer, truck, or other conveyance.

ADVANTAGES OF DUSTING

One big advantage of dusting is that the apparatus does not have to be emptied and cleaned after each use, although it should be cleaned out at the end of the season. If you wish to use two kinds of dust, it is better to have two inexpensive plunger dusters than to try to get all the particles of one kind blown out of the duster before putting in the other mixture.

Dusting is usually quicker than spraying and probably somewhat more foolproof, if you use prepared mixtures and don't try to roll your own. I mean that "roll" literally, for in making dust mixtures at home, you put the ingredients in a tin with some round stones and roll back and forth, round and round. However, it is difficult to do a good job of mixing and few of us know enough about compatibility and diluents and fluxers to make our own mixtures.

Chapter IV

INSECTS IN ORDER

The entomologist says an insect is a very special creature with body divided into three sections, only three pairs of legs, and usually with wings. He also says that a bug is a very special kind of sucking insect. The layman says that any small crawling or flying animal is an insect and any insect is a bug. The dictionary says both are right. In the first edition of this *Bug Book* we stretched several points to include rabbits, dogs, squirrels, mice, moles, and other creatures in one alphabetical treatment of garden pests. Now we are devoting all the space available to animals that the layman might consider a "bug."

Exact figures are unobtainable, but there are probably a million different species of animals in the world that have already been classified, and many more unclassified. These are divided into a few main groups known as Phyla and then subdivided into Classes, Orders, Families, Genera, and Species. Man belongs in the phylum Chordata, which includes all the vertebrates (creatures with a backbone), in the class Mammalia, which includes animals with hair and mammary glands, in the order Primates, which also includes monkeys, in the family Hominidae, which does not include monkeys, the genus *Homo*, and the species *sapiens*. Man is not always as wise as his species name would indicate, and I definitely include him among the garden pests. This subject is considered in detail in my book *Are You Your Garden's Worst Pest?* (Doubleday, 1961). Unfortunately, this is now out-of-print but your library may have a copy.

Slugs and snails are in the phylum Mollusca, along with clams and oysters. Earthworms, which are not often pests, are in the phylum Annelida and roundworms are in the phylum Nemathelminthes. Nematodes have been included here but have now become so important that many nematologists put them in a separate phylum, Nematoda. Nematodes are animals but they usually cause diseases in plants, rather than injury. In some universities, nematology is studied in the zoology department, in others it comes under plant pathology. Nematodes were included in previous editions of this book but are omitted in the present edition, both because we needed space for more insects and because they have been extensively treated in the third edition of my *Plant Disease Handbook* (Van Nostrand Reinhold, 1971).

At least three fourths of all animals are in the phylum Arthropoda, which means they have segmented bodies, bilateral symmetry, paired jointed appendages usually terminating in claws, chitinous exoskeleton, ventral nervous system, and heart dorsal when present. The classes listed below have members that are garden pests.

CLASSES OF THE PHYLUM ARTHROPODA

Insecta (Hexapoda). All true insects, about 90 per cent of all species in the Arthropoda. They have only 3 pairs of legs.

Arachnida. The spiders, ticks, and mites, with only 4 pairs of legs.

Crustacea. Crayfish, lobsters, crabs, and sowbugs, with 5 to 7 pairs of legs; most species aquatic in habitat.

Chilopoda. Centipedes, "hundred-legged worms," but not quite literally. They have 1 pair of legs on each segment.

Diplopoda. Millipedes, "thousand-legged worms," with 2 pairs of legs on each segment.

Symphyla. Symphylans, garden centipedes, with 12 pairs of legs.

INSECT MORPHOLOGY

Insects have an exoskeleton—a protective shell on the outside of soft body parts—rather than the internal skeleton of higher animals. The chief chemical in the outer covering is chitin. The surface of the body consists of a number of hardened plates, separated by membranous areas.

The segmented body is divided into 3 main sections—head, thorax, and abdomen. Six of the body segments are fused into the head, which is usually hard, heavily sclerotized. Most insects have a pair of large compound eyes made up of hexagonal facets. They also usually have 3 simple eyes, *ocelli,* located on the upper part of the head between the compound eyes. The head also bears a pair of *antennae,* feelers, which arise in front of the compound eyes. In chewing insects with biting mouth parts we have a *labrum,* upper lip, just below a plate called the *clypeus; mandibles,* the first pair of jaws; *maxillae,* the second pair of jaws; and *labium,* lower lip. The mandibles act as teeth, cutting or tearing off leaf portions and then masticating the food. In sucking insects there is a long slender beak with the labium on the outside and inside, 4 sharp *stylets* which

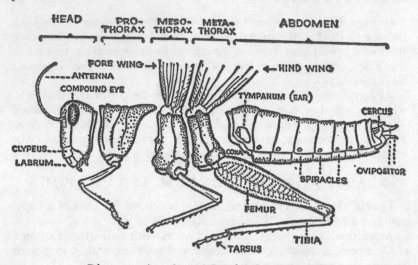

4. Diagram of an insect showing important parts.

pierce the plant and draw out the sap. These stylets are the mandibles and maxillae greatly modified. The labrum in this case is merely a short flap covering the groove in the labium.

The middle section of an insect is the *thorax.* This is further sub-divided into *prothorax,* just back of the head, *mesothorax,* bearing the fore wings; and *metathorax,* bearing the hind wings. Each tho-racic segments bears 1 pair of legs. The total of 6 legs is the chief diagnostic characteristic separating insects from other arthropods.

The word arthropod means jointed leg or foot; insects are able

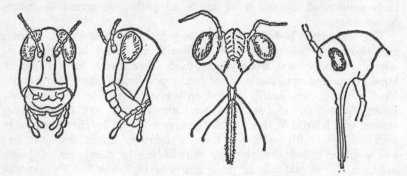

5. Mouth parts, front and side views: left, chewing insect; right, suck-ing insect.

to jump and hop about because of the way their legs are jointed. The first heavy leg section, corresponding to the thigh, is called the *femur,* the next, the *tibia.* The segmented foot is known as the *tarsus,* and insects are differentiated from each other by the number of segments in the tarsus, usually 2 to 5, and the claws and pads on the pretarsus, the last segment. The femur is joined to the thorax by 2 small segments called the *coxa* and the *trochanter.*

Insects are the only winged invertebrates; their wings are always attached to the thorax. When only 1 pair of wings is present, as in flies, it is the fore wings, attached to the mesothorax. The wings are thin sheets of parchmentlike cuticle with ribs known as *veins.* The number, branching, and arrangement of the veins are very important to entomologists classifying insects but are of little import to laymen.

The third section of the insect, the *abdomen,* typically has 11 segments, but the last is much reduced so that there appear to be but 10. The apex of the abdomen often bears a pair of structures called *cerci* (singular: *cercus*), and the female usually has an *ovipositor,* the egg-laying apparatus. In wasps and bees this is modified into a stinger and drawn up into the body when not in use. The abdomen never has true legs but may have fleshy, jointed appendages known as *pro-legs.*

Insects breathe by means of *spiracles,* pores along the side of the body opening into tubes called *tracheae.* The number of tracheae varies, but there is usually a pair on the mesothorax, one on the metathorax, and a pair on each of the first 7 or 8 abdominal segments. Contact poisons work largely because of the way they affect this respiratory system.

Insects do not have a true ear but have various organs for the perception of sound waves. In grasshoppers there is an oval plate, *tympanum,* on each side of the first segment of the abdomen, which serves as an ear. In crickets the "ears" are on the front tibiae.

HOW INSECTS GROW

Because insects live inside a chitinous exoskeleton which cannot be expanded as they grow, they progress by a series of molts, splitting and casting off the old shell or *cuticulum.* Such discard shells are known as *exuviae,* which means clothes. Between the time the insect pulls free from the old covering and before the new form is heavily chitinized there is a chance for expansion in size. The stages between molts are called *instars.* The egg hatches into the first instar, terminated by the first molt; this molt produces the second instar when the young insect is larger and sometimes of different appearance. There may be 3, 4, 5, or even 20 molts, depending on the species.

The adult insect never increases in size; growth is always in the life stage that follows directly from the egg. Some insects have a simple or *gradual metamorphosis,* with the young resembling adults except for size and possession of wings. Such young are called *nymphs* during their growing period. Figure 6 shows insect metamorphosis in diagrammatic form. The bug hatches from an egg into a nymph and grows in size through different instars (the number shown here does not represent the exact number for each species), acquires external wing pads, and then, without any prolonged resting stage, molts again into the adult form with wings, never growing after that.

Other insects have a complete metamorphosis with the adult totally different from the young insect, often living in a different habitat. In the life stage following the egg the immature insect, usually wormlike, is called a *larva.* The wings, if any, are developed internally during the immature stages and there is a resting or pupal stage before the final molt.

The larva of a beetle is known as a grub. It increases in size in different instars but does not change much in appearance. In the resting stage the pupa is naked with the form of the legs showing on the outside of the pupa case.

The larva of a moth or butterfly is a *caterpillar* and may change considerably in appearance during different instars. The pupa may be a *chrysalid* attached to a twig by a strand of silk, or it may be enclosed in a *cocoon,* or it may be a naked pupa in the soil.

The larva of a fly is known as a *maggot,* and it transforms to the adult stage in a *puparium.*

INSECT ORDERS

The orders of insects whose individuals are commonly found in gardens, either as friends or enemies, are:

Collembola. Springtails: wingless; without metamorphosis; chewing mouth parts.

Orthoptera. Crickets, mole crickets, grasshoppers, katydids, mantids, walkingsticks: gradual metamorphosis; 4 wings; nymphs with compound eyes; chewing mouth parts.

Dermaptera. Earwigs: beetle-like but with simple metamorphosis; 4 wings; nymphs with compound eyes; chewing mouth parts.

Isoptera. Termites, "white ants": gradual metamorphosis; chewing mouth parts.

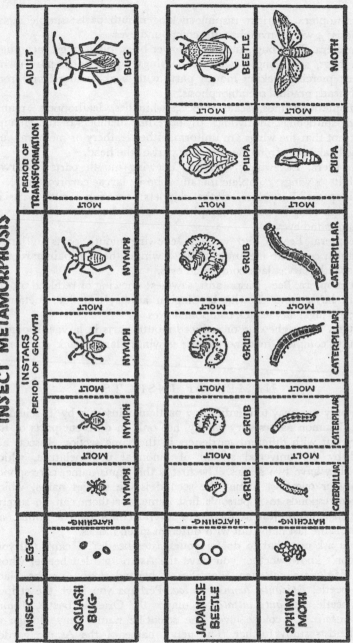

6. Metamorphosis or growth stages of a sucking insect (squash bug) with gradual metamorphosis; and of a beetle and a moth (chewing insects) with complete metamorphosis.

Thysanoptera. Thrips: rasping-sucking mouth parts; simple metamorphosis; 4 wings; nymphs with compound eyes.

Hemiptera. True bugs, including flower bugs, plant bugs, lace bugs, chinch bugs, stink bugs: with "half wings," part hard, part membranous; piercing-sucking mouth parts with beak arising from front part of head; gradual metamorphosis.

Homoptera. Aphids, scale insects, whiteflies, leafhoppers, planthoppers, spittlebugs, mealybugs, psyllids: like members of the Hemiptera except that the wings are uniform, either leathery or membranous, and the beak arises from the posterior part of the head.

Neuroptera. Lacewings, antlions: chewing mouth parts in larvae and adults; 4 wings; complete metamorphosis; larvae carnivorous.

Lepidoptera. Butterflies, moths, skippers: chewing mouth parts in larvae, siphoning in adults; complete metamorphosis; 4 wings; larvae lack compound eyes.

Coleoptera. Beetles and weevils: chewing mouth parts in larvae and adults; complete metamorphosis; 4 wings; the fore pair hardened into a sheath; larvae lack compound eyes.

Hymenoptera. Bees, wasps, ants, sawflies: chewing or reduced mouth parts in larvae and chewing-lapping in adults; complete metamorphosis; 4 wings; larvae lack compound eyes.

Diptera. Flies: chewing or reduced mouth parts in larvae, sponging in adults; complete metamorphosis; 2 wings; larvae lack compound eyes.

NAMES OF INSECTS

The only sure way to identify any particular insect is by its scientific name. Common names vary widely, not only in different parts of the country but with different gardeners in the same section. Insects are named by the universal system of binomial nomenclature, which means they have two names. The first is the genus name, corresponding to your own last name; the second is the species name, which really corresponds to a person's first name, for there can be several species in a genus just as there are several children in a family, all with the same last name but with different given names.

If you ask me what to do for your "aster beetles" I can't tell you, for I don't know whether you have the Asiatic garden beetle, whose name, *Maladera castanea,* identifies it beyond doubt, or the black blister beetle, *Epicauta pennsylvanica.* Perhaps you have the striped blister beetle, *Epicauta vittata,* or maybe the Oriental beetle, *Anomala orientalis.* Of course, even the scientific names may change as the scientists study further. The genus name of the Asiatic garden beetle was Anomala in previous editions of this book; now it is Maladera.

You will notice in these examples that the species name is usually descriptive. *Castanea* refers to the lovely chestnut color; *orientalis* and *pennsylvanica* refer to places of origin; while *vittata* means striped. In fact, the names often tell you a great deal about the insects, and you often need the scientific name to get more information from books and other sources.

In citing insects by scientific names, the species is usually followed by the name of the author who first described it. In the first two editions of the *Bug Book* authors were omitted because they have little import for the backyard gardener. They have been included since then to aid the professionals who, apparently, also turn to this manual for quick reference.

Unfortunately, with insects as with plants, names get shifted around a bit. A species is put into another genus, or the original name for a genus is revived, or one genus is split in two and so on. Where such changes have been made the name of the original author is put in parentheses.

In compiling this revision I have used the latest (1970) compilation of "Common Names of Insects" approved by the Entomological Society of America, revising some of the scientific names to accord with recent taxonomic studies, and using my own best judgment where a pest has no approved common name. Approved names are marked with an asterisk.

Chapter V

GARDEN PESTS (AND A FEW FRIENDS)

Here are the bugs and other insects, the slugs, snails, sowbugs, millipedes, and mites, in alphabetical order according to their common names.

A borer may be either a moth or a beetle but if it is commonly called a borer it is discussed under Borers. For instance, the shothole borer is a beetle (*Scolytus rugulosus*). You will find it by looking under Borers and then thumbing your way along to S—shothole. But it is sometimes called the Fruittree Bark Beetle and so you will find a cross reference to it under Beetles, in the F section. The adult of the rhododendron borer is a moth, but because it is not commonly called by its adult name, it is listed only under Borers without any cross reference.

With the aid of the Index you can probably find the pest you want quite quickly if you know some common name for it, even if it is not the one presently approved by the Entomological Society of America. So far as possible, insects are treated under their "official" common names, but other names are given in the text and in the Index. The scientific names, brought up-to-date so far as I am able, are given in italics, after the common names printed in boldface. The name of the author first describing a species is given with the Latin name. If the genus name has later been changed the author's name is given in parentheses.

You may not, however, recognize an insect enough to guess at a common name. If all you know is that you have a caterpillar on a cherry, turn to Chapter VI, "Host Plants and Their Pests," and look up Cherry. There you will find a long list of pests with a few brief comments on some of the more important. If your caterpillar is officially known as a caterpillar, you will find it in the list of insects following the word "Caterpillar" in boldface. Then you can turn back to the section on caterpillars in this chapter and look up the ones you think might be your specimen. If you live in New Jersey you obviously do not have the Western Tent Caterpillar but you may have the Eastern Tent Caterpillar.

Your caterpillar, however, may be better known by its adult form—perhaps codling moth, found under Moths, or a bud moth, found under Budworms (Bud Moths). Or it may be called a Cankerworm, Leaf Crumpler, or Leafroller. Perhaps it isn't a caterpillar at all but the larval stage of a Sawfly, or the maggot of a Fly or the grub of a Beetle. You may have to explore several possibilities before you can, by a process of elimination, arrive at the probable classification of your caterpillar.

I have given a rather involved example. Under many hosts you will find very few possibilities listed and will not have to do so much checking back and forth. Although we have fairly good lists for common fruits and vegetables and some other economic plants, for many ornamentals the readily available information is rather sketchy and so my lists of known possibilities is quite short.

ANTLIONS

Antlion, *Myrmeleon* sp. The larva of an adult similar to a dragonfly, in the order Neuroptera, family Myrmeleontidae. The adults have

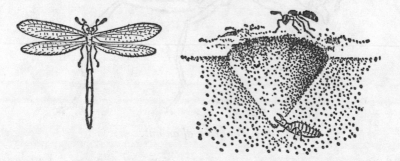

7. *Antlion larva waiting at the bottom of a pit dug for its ant victim, and winged adult antlion.*

4 long, slender wings, about equal in size, marked with many small branching veins and cross veins, a long, narrow, very soft abdomen, and short, threadlike antennae knobbed at the tip. The larvae, queer creatures with sickle-shaped jaws, are called doodlebugs in the South. They dig conical pits in sandy soil, up to 2 inches across and nearly as deep, and there lie in wait for ants and other victims to fall in. Sand adheres to the hairs covering the broad abdomen of the doodle-

bug and helps to conceal it from its prey. It is definitely not a garden pest although its useful role may be rather minor.

Spottedwinged Antlion, *Dendroleon obsoletus* (Say).

ANTS

Ants belong to the order Hymenoptera, along with bees and wasps, and are in the family Formicidae. They are social insects, living in colonies all over the world, outnumbering almost all other terrestrial animals and comprising some 6,000 kinds.

The body of an ant is sharply constricted into its 3 divisions—head, thorax, and abdomen. The antennae, 6-to-13-segmented with

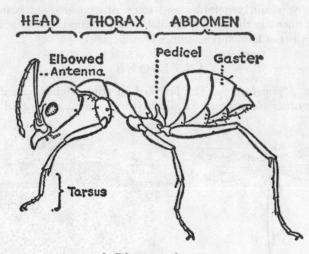

8. Diagram of an ant.

the first segment very long, are hinged like an elbow and have a club at the tip. The gaster, soft part of the abdomen, is attached to the thorax by a pedicel—a movable link which, in the subfamily Formicinae, has only 1 segment but in the Myrmicinae has 2 parts. Besides the digestive organs, the abdomen contains a device for releasing poison. Species in the Myrmicinae have a real stinger like that of a bee. This releases poison in the wound, causing considerable burning and pain. Members of the Formicinae have a poison bladder; they first bite their enemy, then squirt poison into the bites. Some ants eject a foul-smelling secretion from the anus.

Each ant colony has 3 castes—males, queens, and wingless, sterile workers. After mating, the males die and the queens shed their wings to form new colonies or to enter an established colony. The queen is larger than the other ants and does all the egg-laying. She raises the first brood of workers, feeding them with her saliva; after that the workers feed the queen and tend the young, maggot-like larvae. They build new galleries for the nest and forage for food. Some ants live on household sweets or greasy proteins, some on honeydew of aphids, mealybugs, or scale insects; some feed on seeds, grains, or vegetable roots, some on fungi cultivated in their nests, and some on other insects.

Some ants make disfiguring mounds, disturb plant roots, and occasionally act as vectors of plant disease. Fire-blight bacteria may be disseminated by ants, and they probably distribute spores of the fungus causing Botrytis blight of peonies. Ants are attracted to the sticky secretion on peony buds but do no direct harm. Many ants are useful as scavengers and pollinators and some as predators. The first known application of biological control, antedating recorded history, was the practice in the Orient of placing bamboo poles between trees to facilitate movement of a predatory ant feeding on citrus pests.

Allegheny Mound Ant*, *Formica exsectoides* Forel. The mound-building ant common in eastern U.S., particularly damaging to forest stands. The large mounds, 2 to 3 feet high, up to 8 feet across, contain thousands of individual ants. Small trees and shrubs within 35 feet of such mounds are killed by the injection of formic acid into the tissues near the ground, resulting in a sunken band girdling the stem. The ants have reddish-brown head and thorax, blackish-brown abdomen, 1-segmented pedicel; they feed chiefly on insect honeydew. Chlordane is effective in control: 2 ounces of wettable powder for each 2 feet in mound diameter, spread evenly and scratched in with a rake.

Argentine Ant*, *Iridomyrmex humilis* (Mayr). This import, first noted here in 1891, is thought to have come to New Orleans with coffee from Brazil. It spread in commerce through the South and Southwest and is now a house and garden problem in Arizona, Arkansas, California, Florida, Georgia, Louisiana, Mississippi, North and South Carolina, Tennessee, and Texas. The workers are slender, $1/12$ to $1/8$ inch long, brown, with 1 segment in the pedicel, and a musty, greasy odor when crushed. They nest in large colonies in dark, moist places and travel in definite trails. They are very injurious to citrus and other fruits and to shade trees, attacking blossoms and distributing aphids, mealybugs, and scale insects.

Control. A 2 to 5 per cent solution of chlordane in deodorized kerosene can be used around houses. In citrus groves dieldrin has been sprayed on tree trunks and litter underneath once a year in spring or summer but dieldrin is now frowned upon. A special Argentine Ant Bait, distributed in small containers on a community-wide basis has eliminated the pest in some towns. This bait contained sodium arsenite and is now seldom used because of its extreme toxicity. Some commercial ant baits contain sodium arsenate.

Bigheaded Ant*, *Pheidole megacephala* (Fabricius). Common in warmer areas, sometimes a nuisance in seedbeds. Similar to fire ants but with 12-jointed antennae and 3-jointed antennal club.

Black Carpenter Ant*, *Camponotus pennyslvanicus* (De Geer). A large native species, ¼ to ½ inch long, dark brown to black, nesting entirely in wood—trees, buildings, stumps, and telephone poles—in the eastern half of the country. It makes honeycomb galleries and signals its presence by sawdust protruding from the holes. In this species the tip of the abdomen has a circlet of hairs, the pedicel is 1-segmented, and a freshly crushed worker has a formic acid odor. It is fond of sweets and can bite but not sting. Control by injecting chlordane or malathion into the holes, preferably with an oil gun of the type used for automobiles. Keep ants from entering trees by pruning carefully and painting the cuts.

California Harvester Ant*, *Pogonomyrmex californicus* (Buckley). The most common agricultural ant in California, clearing large areas around nests. Widespread in Texas, Arizona, New Mexico, and Nevada, reported from Utah. This pale red ant, ¼ inch long, bites and stings severely, collects seeds, and interferes with planting operations. See Red Harvester Ant for habits and control.

Cornfield Ant*, *Lasius alienus* (Foerster). A native species, present in much of the U.S., nesting in soil or rotten wood, making objectionable nests (small mounds) in lawns, especially in the Northeast. It is small, ½₁₂ to ¹⁄₁₀ inch long, stout, soft-bodied, light to dark brown; the anal opening is surrounded by a fringe of hairs; the pedicel is 1-segmented; there is no antennal club; there is a formic acid odor. The sweets-loving workers caress root aphids to stimulate the production of honeydew, protect them in their nests over the winter, and ward off their enemies. See also Corn Root Aphid. Treat nests in lawns with diazinon, chlordane, or carbaryl.

Crazy Ant*, *Paratrechina longicornis* (Latreille). A household pest.

Fire Ant*, *Solenopsis geminata* (Fabricius). Formerly called tropical fire ant. This is a yard ant entering houses to feed on meat, milk, sweets, and cereals. The workers have a larger head than other species. The bite and sting are painful. Mounds may be numerous in Texas peanut fields, hindering harvest. See Imported Fire Ant.

Florida Carpenter Ant*, *Camponotus abdominalis floridanus* (Buckley). Common in Florida, similar to the Black Carpenter Ant.

Florida Harvester Ant*, *Pogonomyrmex badius* (Latreille). An agricultural ant similar to the Red Harvester Ant.

Imported Fire Ant*, *Solenopsis saevissima richteri* Forel. A South American species, first identified in Mobile, Alabama, in 1929 but probably present for some years previously and unnoticed because of its resemblance to native fire ants. Transported on logs in streams, by cars, trucks, trains, airplanes, and in nursery stock, the imported fire ant is now a menace to 10 southern states. Alabama, Arkansas, Florida, Georgia, Louisiana, Mississippi, South Carolina, and Texas are under Federal quarantine. In 1969 there was one suppressive area in Tennessee and several in North Carolina, both being taken care of by state regulations. This ant will probably not survive in colder regions.

The ants feed on young succulent vegetables, may attack and kill ground birds, young quail especially, and newborn animals and may sting people with very painful and sometimes serious results. Their chief damage is from their hard mounds, from 15 inches to 3 feet high, which interfere with farm operations. There may be up to 60 mounds per acre, and an average mound may contain 25,000 to 100,000 ants. The workers are ⅛ to ¼ inch long, reddish to blackish red, with a 2-segmented pedicel and 2-segmented antennal club.

A federal-state eradication program, started in 1957, brought criticism because heptachlor, applied at 2 pounds per acre, seriously injured wildlife. The amount was reduced to ½ pound per acre but there was still criticism and a bait, mirex, was substituted in 1962. The bait was composed of soybean oil, an attractant, mirex, the insecticide, and ground corncob grits. Although some object even to mirex most researchers believe that it has no harmful effect on wildlife, that it results in no harmful residue in milk, meat, or vegetables and that it can be applied to pastures containing dairy or beef cattle without removing the animals. More recently an encapsulated oil bait, prepared with mirex, has been dispensed from airplanes. One year trained veterinarians checked wildlife in the treated areas and found no fatalities from the mirex.

Individual mounds in home gardens can be treated with chlordane (4 tablespoons of 45 per cent emulsion to 3 gallons of water, or 5 per cent dust), first breaking up the hard surface of the mound and treating this and an area 3 feet beyond. A physician should treat the sores or pustules caused by stings. People especially sensitive to fire-ant venom should be inoculated against allergic reactions.

Recent studies show that there are really two species of imported fire ants. One, the black imported fire ant, *Solenopsis richteri* Forel, came to Mobile, Alabama, in the 1920s from Argentina or Uruguay and is now present only in parts of Alabama and Mississippi. The red imported fire ant, *S. invicta* Buren, came from Central America and was found in Alabama about 1945. This is the more vigorous species and is the dominant fire ant in southeastern United States.

Larger Yellow Ant*, *Acanthomyops interjectus* (Mayr). A common soil species fostering mealybugs and aphids on plant roots. The yellow workers, $\frac{1}{10}$ to $\frac{1}{8}$ inch long, have a lemon-verbena odor. See Cornfield Ant.

Little Black Ant*, *Monomorium minimum* (Buckley). A native house pest but usually nesting outdoors in soil. The slender workers are $\frac{1}{12}$ to $\frac{1}{10}$ inch long, jet-black and shiny. They are fond of honeydew and other sweets, fruits, vegetables, meats, and cereals.

Little Fire Ant*, *Wasmannia auropunctata* (Roger). A common house pest in parts of Florida.

Odorous House Ant*, *Tapinoma sessile* (Say). A native species, sometimes making shallow nests outdoors. The workers are deep brown to black, $\frac{1}{10}$ to $\frac{1}{4}$ inch long, soft-bodied, with 1-segmented pedicel, and have a rotten coconut odor when crushed. This species is omnivorous in its food habits and attends honeydew-excreting insects.

Pavement Ant*, *Tetramorium caespitum* (Linnaeus). An imported species, common in lawns along the Atlantic seaboard, nesting under stones or edges of pavements. It is a frequent garden and greenhouse pest, gnawing at roots and tubers and stealing seeds. Treat individual ant hills with chlordane, $\frac{1}{8}$ teaspoon of wettable powder put in the center of a mound and watered in, or use chlordane emulsion, 1 ounce to 1 gallon of water, or 5 per cent dust. Diazinon or malathion may also be used.

Pharaoh Ant*, *Monomorium pharaonis* (Linnaeus). A tiny, slow-moving ant, same genus as the Little Black Ant.

Pyramid Ant*, *Dorymyrmex pyramicus* (Roger). Common in Florida and California, in lawns and houses. This small species, with black abdomen and reddish-black head and thorax, is named for a pyramid-like projection on the thorax.

Red Carpenter Ant*, *Camponotus ferrugineus* (Fabricius).

Red Harvester Ant*, *Pogonomyrmex barbatus* (F. Smith). Also known as Texas Harvester Ant and Agricultural Ant. This species causes heavy losses in cultivated crops in the Southwest, clearing areas 3 to 35 feet in diameter bare of all vegetation. The nest is a deep cone, going down to 10 feet, and is a honeycomb of tunnels and chambers. The colony consists of a queen and innumerable workers, reddish brown, $\frac{1}{4}$ to $\frac{1}{2}$ inch long, vicious if molested. The ant colonies may kill trees and shrubs and there is a direct loss of seeds, either newly planted or ready for harvest. To control, apply a continuous band, 4 to 6 inches wide, of 5 per cent chlordane dust in a circle 5 to 6 feet in diameter, centering on the nest entrance. Rubber boots offer some protection from ant stings while the chemical is being applied.

Silky Ant*, *Formica fusca* Linnaeus.

Smaller Yellow Ant*, *Acanthomyops claviger* (Roger).

Southern Fire Ant*, *Solenopsis xyloni* McCook. A native species common in the Gulf States, found as far north as North Carolina, and with subspecies in California and the Southwest. The workers are variable in size, $\frac{1}{16}$ to $\frac{1}{4}$ inch long, and in color, shining yellowish-red or darker. The body is hard and the pedicel and antennal club are 2-segmented. These ants steal planted seeds, infest houses, and sting severely, killing young quail on hatching. They nest in open places, in loose mounds.

Texas Leafcutting Ant*, *Atta texana* (Buckley). A pest of most species of plants in Texas and Louisiana and a serious defoliator of young pines. Foliage is removed in pieces and carried to subterranean nests as a substrate on which the ants grow a fungus for food, much as we cultivate mushrooms. The soil may be mounded several inches high over the burrows, which extend for many feet below the surface. Adjoining colonies may cover 1,000 square feet or more. The workers are reddish brown, $\frac{1}{16}$ to $\frac{1}{2}$ inch long, with many spines on head and thorax, a 2-segmented pedicel. Methyl bromide is the most effective fumigant, introduced 2 feet or more below soil surface, at the rate of 1 pound to 600 square feet. The use of this hazardous material should be left to professionals. The ant may also be controlled with pelleted mirex bait, minimum dosage being 1 gram per mound.

Another leafcutting ant, *Trachymyrmex septentrionalis,* is found along the Atlantic Coast in open pine woods, making crescent-shaped mounds of sand.

Thief Ant*, *Solenopsis molesta* (Say). A native species, nesting outdoors in soil or wood, and a common house pest, with a preference for protein foods, sometimes injuring germinating corn seeds. The workers are small, $\frac{1}{15}$ to $\frac{1}{10}$ inch long, light yellow to bronze, with 2 segments in the pedicel and in the antennal club.

Western Harvester Ant*, *Pogonomyrmex occidentalis* (Cresson).

Western Thatching Ant*, *Formica obscuripes* Forel.

APHIDS

Aphids, plant lice, are sucking insects in the order Homoptera. (Some entomologists consider Homoptera a suborder in the order

Hemiptera.) There are a great many species of aphids abundant on, and injurious to, all forms of vegetation. At least a few species are inevitable in every home garden, and it is often easier to control aphids than to understand their complicated life histories and to distinguish between species.

True aphids are in the family Aphididae, members of which are viviparous (bearing living young) during part of their life cycle.

Woolly aphids, which feed on bark and roots and sometimes form galls, are put in the family Eriosomatidae by some, are included in a subfamily under the Aphididae by others.

Pine and spruce aphids feed only on conifers, often alternating in their life history between two different conifers, and form galls on the primary host. All the females are oviparous (depositing eggs) and none bear living young. They have been classified in the family Chermidae but recently placed in the subfamily Adelginae in the family Phylloxeridae. The members of the other subfamily—the Phylloxerinae—feed on plants other than conifers and often have a complex life history. The grape phylloxera is a common and important species in this group.

Typical aphids (subfamily Aphinae) are small, soft-bodied, pear-shaped, with a pair of cornicles—wax-secreting tubes—projecting

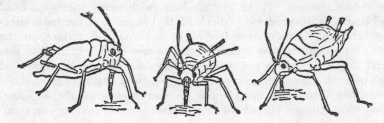

9. Aphid getting ready to feed and in process of sucking sap.

from the 5th or 6th abdominal segment; a cauda, projection from the tip of the abdomen; antennae with 4 to 6 segments; and 2-segmented tarsi (feet). The mouth parts form a hollow beak (rostrum) which arises far back on the underside of the head. The beak encloses 4 needle-like stylets, which pierce plant tissue so that the sap can be sucked out. All aphids secrete honeydew from the anus. This is really plant sap, rich in sugars, attracting ants and forming a medium for the growth of a black fungus known as sooty mold. Wings, when present, are usually clear, with few veins, and are held vertically over the body when at rest. This rooflike position of the wings differentiates aphids from true bugs, whose wings are laid flat over the body.

Aphids are of all colors—black, green, pink, red, yellow, lavender, brown, or grayish—and the young nymphs may differ in color from the wingless adult and the latter may differ from the winged form. Some aphids live out their lives on a single plant; others infest several to many different plant species. Some aphids require an alternate host, wintering on one type of plant, usually woody, then migrating to one or more herbaceous species for the summer.

The life history of an aphid is complicated even for the single-host type. In a typical case, overwintering eggs hatch in spring into wingless females called stem mothers (fundatrix). These are parthenogenetic, viviparous females, reproducing without fertilization by a male and holding eggs in their bodies to give birth to living young. Their progeny are similar females but some develop wings and migrate to other plants of the same species when the colony gets too dense. Many more such generations may be produced during the summer, but toward autumn male and female wingless forms are born. These mate and the oviparous females lay fertilized eggs for wintering. Males may be either winged or wingless; oviparous females are usually wingless. In warm climates living young may be produced continually with no overwintering egg stage.

Alternate host aphids also winter as eggs and hatch into wingless females, but in the third or fourth generation they produce winged females which migrate to the summer food plant. There may be 6 or more generations of wingless females on this host before winged males and females appear for the trek back to the woody winter host. There winged females give birth to wingless females which mate with the winged males and then lay fertilized eggs on the bark. Males thus appear in the life cycle but once a year, at the approach of cold weather.

In the subfamily Eriosomatinae, the woolly and gall-making aphids, cornicles are lacking, or are mere pores, and the cauda is inconspicuous, but abundant wax glands cover the body with white, cottony threads. Many such species have an alternate host, on which the galls are formed. The sexual forms lack mouth parts and the ovipositing female lays a single egg.

Members of the subfamily Adelginae lack cornicles, have a reduced wing venation, and have only egg-laying females. They feed only on conifers, living on needles, twigs, or in galls. Their antennae are 5-segmented in winged forms, 4-segmented in sexual forms, 3-segmented in wingless females. Wings at rest are held rooflike over the body, which is often covered with waxy threads. The Cooley and Eastern Spruce Gall Aphids are important members of the Adelginae.

In the subfamily Phylloxerinae the antennae are 3-segmented in all forms, the wings at rest are held flat over the abdomen, and waxy threads are not produced, although some individuals may be covered with a waxy powder. See Grape Phylloxera for the best example of this group.

Aphids cause loss of plant vigor and sometimes stunting, deformation of buds and flowers, curling or puckering of leaves. The honeydew, substratum for sooty mold, is attractive to ants which herd destructive root aphids. Of chief importance, perhaps, is the role of aphids as vectors (transmitters) of mosaic and other virus diseases, the bacteria of fire blight and other disease-producing organisms.

Most aphids are readily controlled by applying a contact insecticide at the proper time. Nicotine sulfate, sold as Black Leaf 40, was the old reliable spray, used at 1 to 1½ teaspoons with 1 ounce of soap to 1 gallon of water. Nicotine is now rather out-of-date—partly because of its toxicity to humans and partly because it is no longer manufactured in this country but must be imported. Rotenone and pyrethrum are still effective and, because of their low toxicity to people, particularly useful in small aerosols for house plants. Dinitro compounds are sometimes used in a dormant spray to kill aphid eggs. Malathion is currently widely recommended as a safe spray. Lindane is very useful for woolly and gall aphids but its use is restricted, in some states, to operators with permits. Dimethoate, a systemic and reasonably safe phosphate, is of value on many plants but may be phytotoxic on some. TEPP, parathion, and other highly poisonous phosphates are used by commercial growers on vegetables because the residue is

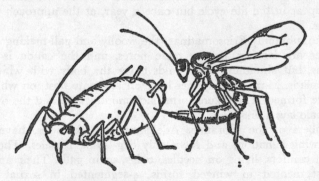

10. Parasitic wasp laying an egg in an aphid.

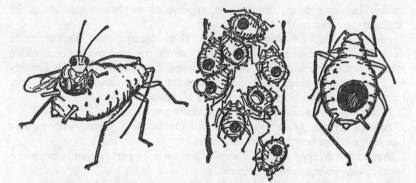

11. Young wasp emerging from parasitized aphid and dead aphids showing emergence holes (greatly enlarged).

quickly dissipated, but they are not for home gardeners. Diazinon, Meta-Systox-R, and endosulfan are other possibilities for aphid control.

Parasites, insects which live part of their lives in or on other insects without killing them, and predators, which kill and devour other insects, are very helpful against aphids. Parasitic wasps are common and whenever you find a dead aphid with a hole in the back you know that it has been parasitized and a young wasp has emerged from that hole. Lady beetles, aphidlions (larvae of lacewings), and the sluglike larvae of syrphid flies all help in reducing aphid populations.

A new and rather effective mechanical control is the use of aluminum as a repellent. Heavy aluminum foil may be stretched along rows of plants, or seedlings may be transplanted into holes made in heavy-duty aluminum. This method is practical for vegetable growers who want to keep these sucking insects off their crops and for gladiolus growers who want to avoid virus diseases carried by aphids.

Repelled by aluminum, aphids may be attracted by certain colors, with yellow preferred by many species. Yellow pans filled with water can be used to trap aphids.

In the following pages aphids are taken up alphabetically under common names, those officially recognized by the Entomological Society of America being marked with an asterisk. Important aphids are treated in some detail, others are dismissed in a line or two. Though the list is long, it includes but a fraction of the thousands of plant lice in the world—a fraction intended to be representative of aphids injuring trees, flowers, or vegetables on home properties in different sections of the United States.

Alder Aphid, *Oestlundiella flava* (Davidson). Pale Yellow with dark brown cornicles and markings, more or less woolly, on alder leaves; not too common. Another species, *Euceraphis gillettei* Davidson, pale, apple-green with pale cornicles, is common on twigs and leaves of alder and birch in the Rocky Mountain region.

Alder Blight Aphid. See Woolly Alder Aphid.

Alfalfa Aphid, *Macrosiphum creelii* Davis. Pale green, with antennae longer than body, on alfalfa leaves.

American Maple Aphid, *Periphyllus americanus* (Baker). Summer forms pale green, on maple leaves.

American Walnut Aphid, *Monelliopsis caryae* (Monell). Yellow with dusky spots, on leaves of walnut and hickory.

Apple Aphid*, *Aphis pomi* De Geer. Green Apple Aphid, common and widespread on apple, sometimes on pear, wild crabapple, hawthorn, and mountain-ash, more injurious to nursery than to orchard trees, but common on sucker growth. Terminals may be entirely covered by aphids in midsummer and growth halted. Leaves may be loosely curled, but not tightly as by the rosy apple aphid; young apples may be deformed; there is a copious amount of honeydew with resultant sooty mold. The apple aphid winters as shiny black eggs on bark and the dark green nymphs appear as buds are swelling in early spring. The adults, yellow green with dark cornicles, head, and legs, remain through the summer, not migrating to an alternate host.

Control. Remove suckers. Commercial growers can spray with parathion, ethion, or Trithion at the ½-inch green stage and with dimethoate at third cover. Home gardeners may use a dormant oil spray with a dinitro added, or malathion or dimethoate later.

Apple Grain Aphid*, *Rhopalosiphum fitchii* (Sanderson). Abundant on small grains and grasses during the summer but not seriously injuring the winter hosts—apple, pear, wild crabapples, and hawthorn. Control measures for apple and rosy apple aphids will take care of this species on apple.

Araucaria Aphid, *Neophyllaphis araucariae* Takahashi. On monkey-puzzle tree, Norfolk-Island pine. First noted in Florida in 1963. Yellow; 5-segmented antennae; females viviparous; males unknown.

Arborvitae Aphid, *Cinara tujafilina* (Del Guercio). Widely distributed, perhaps more important in warmer states, feeding in colonies on twigs, branches, and roots, often seriously weakening arborvitae, Italian cypress, and retinospora, also reported on redcedar. The small, reddish-brown lice with a whitish bloom feed all year on roots, attended by ants, and on aerial parts spring and fall. Treat the soil with chlordane. Lindane is an effective spray but is now restricted; try malathion.

Artemisia Aphid, *Macrosiphum artemisiae* (Fonscolombe). Metallic dark green or blackish, in dense colonies on roots of artemisia, also reported on yarrow, oxeye-daisy, and costmary; in western states. Other species on artemisia include *Macrosiphum coweni* (Hunter), dark brown to blackish green; *Artemisaphis artemiscola* (Williams), shining reddish black; and *Macrosiphum artemisiae* (Gillette), dark brown; and *Pleotrichophorus glandulosus* (Kaltenbach).

Asparagus Aphid, *Brachycolus asparagi* Mordvilko. A Mediterranean insect first noted in the U.S. in 1969, recorded from Delaware, New York, New Jersey, Pennsylvania, and Virginia on asparagus and asparagus fern. Young growth is damaged, internodes shortened, and brush severely rosetted. Spray with malathion.

Aster Aphids, *Dactynotus anomalae* Hottes and Frison, *Macrosiphon asterifoliae* Storm and *M. breviscriptum* Palmer. Green, common on New England aster, particularly *D. anomalae*.

Azalea Aphid, *Vesiculaphis caricis* (Fullaway). Reported on azalea in California and also in Maryland. Another species on this host is *Amphorophora azaleae*.

Bald Strawberry Aphid, *Chaetosiphon minor* (Forbes).

Balsam Twig Aphid*, *Mindarus abietinus* Koch. Pale green, covered with white wax, curling and roughening balsam fir and spruce twigs from New England to the Pacific Coast, with migrants sometimes going to pine. Spray with malathion in late spring. Try dimethoate or Meta-Systox-R on trunk.

Balsam Woolly Aphid*, *Adelges piceae* (Ratzenburg). An introduced species attacking balsam and other firs in New England, New York, New Jersey, North Carolina, Washington, and Oregon. It causes gouty swellings at tip of twigs, abnormal growth of sapwood on main trunks, sometimes death. The very small blue-black body is covered with long, waxy threads. Long slender stylets pierce the bark, injecting a toxin. The wood becomes brittle and reddish, needle growth is reduced, and the foliage gradually dies. There is no alternate host, the aphids wintering as nymphs on bark. Spread is mostly by wind, winged forms being rare.

A predaceous beetle, *Laricobius erichsoni,* has been released in the hope of biological control in forest areas. Spray ornamental trees with malathion or diazinon.

Bamboo Aphid, *Myzocallis arundinariae* Essig. Yellow, with black markings, common on leaves of bamboo in California.

Banana Aphid, *Pentalonia nigronervosa* Coquerel. A tropical species, reddish brown to nearly black with clouded wings and sometimes found in greenhouses, introduced with bananas. Reported on caladium indoors in Oklahoma and Washington, D.C.

Barberry Aphid*, *Liosomaphis berberidis* (Kaltenbach). Small, yellowish green, usually found in groups on underside of leaves and on shoots of barberry and mahonia.

Bean Aphid*, *Aphis fabae* Scopoli. A common and important species, congregating in great numbers on succulent plant parts, causing general debility and yellowing foliage. The young nymphs are green, spotted with white wax, very small; the adults are dark green to dull, sooty black. The winter host is chiefly euonymus, sometimes highbush cranberry, deutzia, and snowball. The summer forms frequent various vegetables—bean, asparagus, globe artichoke, beet, carrot, corn, lettuce, parsnip, rhubarb, spinach, squash, watercress—and many ornamentals. It is practically inevitable on nasturtium, clustering on underside of leaves, and occurs on dahlia, calendula, elderberry, globe thistle, hibiscus, mockorange, oleander, poppy, portulaca, and zinnia.

Control. Spray with malathion, diazinon, or dimethoate. Commercial growers may use more dangerous parathion, Trithion, or Di-Syston.

Beech Aphid, *Phyllaphis fagi* (Linnaeus). Dark green, covered with loose white flocculence, infesting undersides of leaves of practically all species of beech in the Northeast and also important on ornamental plantings in Oregon and California. This aphid is particularly noticeable, and sometimes decorative, on copper beech. Spray with malathion.

Beech Blight Aphid*, *Prociphilus imbricator* (Fitch). Large, bluish, covered with white wool, on underside of branches and sometimes on trunks of beech from New England west to Illinois and south to Georgia, also reported on sycamore. It may be abundant enough to kill twigs or even young trees. Spray with lindane if allowed; if not, use malathion.

Birch Aphids. Several species are rather common and generally distributed. The **European Birch Aphid**, *Euceraphis punctipennis* Zetterstedt, considered one of the most annoying pests of ornamentals in Alaska, appears on various species of birch across the country, particularly on white birch. It is a large green and black species, with a flocculent waxy covering. *E. lineata* Baker is also listed on birch.

A large green aphid with short cornicles and no wax, *Calaphis betulaecolens* (Fitch) and its near relative, *C. betulella* Walsh, produce quantities of honeydew on birch foliage. Spray with malathion, dimethoate, diazinon, or Meta-Systox-R.

Blackberry Aphid, *Aphis rubifolii* (Thomas). Minute, yellowish green, tightly curling leaves of wild and cultivated blackberries in New York; reported on red raspberry in the Rocky Mountain region.

Black Cherry Aphid*, *Myzus cerasi* (Fabricius). Commonly injurious to sweet cherries, occasionally serious on sour cherries, also found on ornamental cherries. Shiny black eggs winter on branches near buds and hatch as buds are opening. The large black aphids reproduce rapidly, curling leaves of terminal shoots and infesting fruit clusters. The fruit is dwarfed and sooty mold growing in the copious honeydew makes it unmarketable.

Control. Commercial growers may spray with parathion in April at shuck fall and/or at first cover. Malathion is safe for home owners. A dinitro spray in fall after leaves have fallen or in spring before buds break helps in control.

Black Citrus Aphid*, *Toxoptera aurantii* (Fonscolombe). Small, $\frac{1}{15}$ inch, reddish brown to nearly black, with long legs, important on citrus in California, Florida, and other warm climates. Camellias are often infested and sometimes ixora, clusia, seagrape, and other tropical ornamentals. This aphid has been found on English holly as far north as Maryland, possibly introduced on nursery stock. Leaves are cupped, curved, and distorted but not tightly curled; they are covered with sooty mold. The species is also a vector of the Tristeza disease virus, though not as efficient as some other aphids.

Control. Normally the black citrus aphid is held in check by predators, parasites, and fungus diseases. Spraying with malathion or rotenone is sometimes necessary. Commercial growers may use phosphates such as parathion or demeton. Control ants which disseminate the aphids.

Blackmargined Aphid*, *Monellia costalis* (Fitch). On hickory, pecan, and walnut; reported important on pecans in New Mexico.

Black Peach Aphid*, *Brachycaudus persicae* (Passerini). Shiny black with immature forms reddish brown, with short wartlike cauda, antennae as long as body. Native in Eastern states and occasionally serious where it has been introduced in the West. This species infests roots, tender shoots, and fruit of peaches, almonds, apricots, sometimes plums. Black wingless forms live on roots through the year, migrating in spring to new growth. Paradichlorobenzene has been used on the root forms. Malathion can be used on foliage.

Black Pecan Aphid*, *Tinocallis caryaefoliae* (Davis). A pest of hickory in the North, destructive to all pecan varieties in the South, causing permanent defoliation and reducing the nut crop. Nymphs are pale green, adults darker green with black spots. Bright yellow spots appear on the leaves, which turn brown and drop by midsummer. There may be 15 generations before eggs are deposited in bark crevices for the winter. Commercial growers should spray as soon as first yellow spots appear, with nicotine sulfate in summer oil or with parathion.

Blackspotted Hickory Aphid, *Monelliopsis nigropunctata* (Granovsky).

Bowlegged Fir Aphid, *Cinara curvipes* Patch. On balsam, white, alpine, noble and Spanish firs, Englemann spruce, and deodar. This species is brownish black with long, curved tibia, the "bowlegs."

Boxelder Aphid*, *Periphyllus negundinis* (Thomas). A pale green species, with long hairs, on leaves and twigs of boxelder and sycamore maple. Another green species, *Drepanosiphum braggii* Gillette, may also infest boxelder foliage. It is larger, with antennae longer than body.

Brown Ambrosia Aphid, *Dactynotus ambrosiae* (Thomas). Brown to dark blood-red, rather large, common, and widespread on a number of plants, including goldenrod, aster, lettuce, endive, eupatorium, rudbeckia, iris, and sunflower. Said to be especially important on lettuce and endive in the West and heavy on iris in New Mexico.

Brown Citrus Aphid*, *Toxoptera citricida* (Kirkaldy).

Buckthorn Aphid*, *Aphis nasturtii* Kaltenbach. One of four common potato aphids, more important in the Northeast. This species winters in the egg stage on buckthorn, winged migrants flying in summer to potatoes, some other vegetables, nasturtium, and a few other ornamentals. The aphid is small, yellow to dark green to nearly black, and is a vector of potato leaf roll and mild mosaic viruses. DDT can no longer be recommended for control. Home gardeners may use malathion; commercial growers may use endosulfon or parathion applied in late July (in the Northeast) or disulfoton applied in the planting furrow or fertilizer band.

Cabbage Aphid*, *Brevicoryne brassicae* (Linnaeus). Common throughout North America on cabbage, broccoli, cauliflower, brussels sprouts, kohlrabi, collards, kale, radish. Small gray-green lice with a powdery, waxy covering congregate in dense clusters on underside of leaves, causing them to cup and curl, and on flower heads. Broccoli in home gardens is frequently infested. Plants are dwarfed, seedlings may be killed. This species winters in the North as small black eggs on stems and old leaves of cabbage and other crucifers. In the South, it continues to produce living young with no sexual stage and with many generations a year.

Control. In home gardens use malathion spray or dust, or rotenone. Commercial growers may use demeton in the transplant water or parathion or Phosdrin as a spray. Dimethoate is a less hazardous possibility.

California-laurel Aphid, *Thoraphis umbellulariae* Essig. On this host.

Canadian Fleabane Aphid, *Dactynotus erigeronensis* (Thomas). Yellowish green on erigeron (fleabane), also reported on goldenrod.

Caragana Aphid*, *Acyrthosiphon caraganae* (Cholodkovsky). On pea-tree.

Ceanothus Aphid, *Amphorophora ceanothi* (Clarke). Reddish brown and black, infesting limbs, twigs, leaves of ceanothus and soapbush in California.

Chokecherry Aphid, *Aphis cerasifoliae* Fitch. Tightly curling terminal leaves of chokecherry (wild cherry). Summer hosts are grains and grasses.

Chrysanthemum Aphid*, *Macrosiphoniella sanborni* (Gillette). Shiny dark brown, almost black, with short cornicles, occurring in great numbers on tender terminal shoots and on underside of chrysanthemum leaves. Growth is stunted, leaves are slightly curled, and plants may die. Common and widespread. If infested cut flowers are brought into the house, the aphids may cause dark stains. Spray with malathion or diazinon. Vapona strips can be used in greenhouses or the chemical (dichlorvos) may be painted on steam pipes.

Clover Aphid*, *Nearctaphis bakeri* (Cowen). Primarily on clover but summering also on related plants, wintering on hawthorn, apple, pear, quince, reported on myrtle. Generally distributed but more serious in the Northwest, where crops are lost because of honeydew causing seeds to stick together. This species may be green with a black patch or pinkish or yellow green mottled with dark green or rusty flecks; it has short cornicles. Seed treatment with demeton before planting is less likely to kill beneficial insects than foliage sprays.

Columbine Aphid, *Pergandeidia trirhoda* (Walker). Small, cream-colored lice appear in late summer; plants may be stunted and covered with honeydew. The Blackbacked Columbine Aphid, *Kakimia essigi* Gillette and Palmer, is small, green and pinkish, with a dark patch on the back.

Cooley Spruce Gall Aphid*, *Adelges cooleyi* (Gillette). Occurring wherever spruces are grown, common on ornamental Colorado blue spruce, also infesting Engelmann, Sitka, and oriental spruces, with Douglas-fir as an alternate host. Immature stem mothers winter on spruce, mature in early spring, and lay eggs in masses of white, cottony wax. On hatching, the nymphs migrate to new growth. Their feeding at the base of needles introduces a toxin, causing the formation of conelike galls, about 2½ inches long, at the tip of twigs.

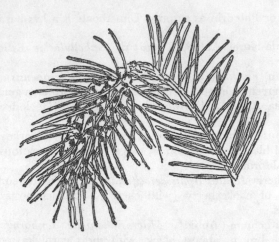

12. Aphid gall on blue spruce.

Each gall contains many chambers with several nymphs in each. The galls open in midsummer (around July 1 in New Jersey) and the aphids migrate to Douglas-fir, there to deposit eggs on needles. The nymphs wintering here are covered with fluffs of cotton. A winged stage in spring takes the aphid back to spruce, but cycles may continue on either host. No galls are formed on Douglas-fir.

Control. Avoid planting spruce and Douglas-fire together; cut off galls before they open in summer. Spray as new growth starts and in late summer with malathion or Meta-Systox-R. In research tests an April spray with Ethion and Superior oil has been very effective or an application of endosulfan (Thiodan). Lindane has been helpful but is restricted.

Coreopsis Aphid, *Aphis coreopsidis* Thomas. Tupelo Aphid. On coreopsis, eupatorium, cosmos, privet, also reported distorting foliage of sourgum (tupelo) and covering ground with honeydew.

Corn Leaf Aphid*, *Rhopalosiphum maidis* (Fitch). Small, bluish green, densely congregated in the curl of corn leaves, in the upper part of stalk, and in tassels, where the honeydew interferes with pollination and attracts earworm moths. This aphid is common in all corn-growing areas but more abundant in the South, feeding also on sugarcane and wintering on barley.

Lady beetles, lacewings, and other predators are helpful in control. Planting early and fertilizing to hasten maturity is helpful. If necessary, commercial growers can spray with parathion or endosulfan.

Corn Root Aphid*, *Aphis maidiradicis* Forbes. A serious pest, dependent for its existence on ants, especially the cornfield ant. Roots of corn, clover, beet, carrot, cotton, and grasses are infested with myriads of pinhead size, bluish-green powdery lice with short legs. Ants collect the aphid eggs in autumn, store them in their nests over winter, then transport the young in spring to smartweed and grass roots where the stem mothers mature and produce 2 or 3 generations before the ants carry them to corn roots for another 10 to 20 generations. If winged forms are produced to fly to other cornfields, the migrants are seized by the ants and carried back down underground.

The corn root aphid and other species also infest roots of many ornamentals, including aster, browallia, amaranthus, buttercup, calendula, chrysanthemum, cosmos, dahlia, erigeron, eupatorium, portulaca, primrose, sweetpea, and zinnia. Plants turn yellow, stop growing, and wilt in bright sun.

Control. Use chlordane to control the ants and cultivate to break up their nests before planting annuals. If allowed to use lindane, pour 1 to 2 cups of lindane spray (1 tablespoon to 1 gallon of water) into a depression around the stem of growing plants.

Cotton Aphid. See Melon Aphid.

Cowpea Aphid*, *Aphis crassivora* Koch. This species was long considered identical with the European *A. medicaginis,* but the latter is not known in America. The nymphs are slaty gray; the adults shiny black with white legs. They are common on laburnum (goldenchain), locust, rose-acacia, deutzia, honey-locust, and other ornamentals as well as cowpea, beans, clovers, and grape. Spraying with malathion or other aphicide may be necessary to keep the aphids from ruining new growth. Azodrin and Thimet have been recommended as a seed treatment for black locust.

Crapemyrtle Aphid*, *Tinocallis kahawaluokalani* Kirkaldy. Confined to crapemyrtle and abundant wherever this host is grown. Foliage is often covered with sooty mold growing in the copious honeydew. Spray early and thoroughly with malathion.

Crescentmarked Lily Aphid*, *Neomyzus circumflexus* (Buckton). Yellow, with a black U-shaped patch on the back. Common on lily and other ornamentals, including asparagus fern, California-laurel, calla lily, columbine, crocus, cyclamen, ferns, freesia, fuchsia, gladiolus, gloxinia, hydrangea, iris, myrtle, rose, penstemon, snowberry, violet, and wallflower, also celery and potato. This species is important as a vector of mosaic and other virus diseases. Commercial growers often use a systemic insecticide, such as phorate granules, applied in the furrow at time of planting, or demeton applied to the soil when the plants are 6 inches high. Home gardeners must be content with foliage sprays of malathion or other safe aphicide.

Currant Aphid*, *Cryptomyzus ribis* (Linnaeus). Common on currant throughout the United States, occasional on gooseberry, recorded on deutzia and snowball. Leaves curl, crinkle, and hump up into half galls above the portions where the stem mothers are producing their numerous yellow-green progeny. Such humped areas turn red and leaves may drop. Glossy black eggs on twigs hatch into wingless females which continue to reproduce parthenogenetically on currant while winged females migrate to various weeds for the summer. The aphids return to currant in autumn, produce males and females, and overwintering eggs.

Control. Spray with malathion early in the season, being sure to cover underleaf surfaces. A dormant dinitro spray is said to give control.

There are other currant aphids. The **Variable Currant Aphid,** *Aphis varians* Patch, may curl leaves of golden and black currant but is not common. The **Ornamental Currant Aphid,** *Amphorophora ribiella* (Davis), is a pale yellow-green species on leaves and twigs of ornamental (golden) currant. Also green on golden currant is *Aphis ribiensis* Gillette and Palmer. Terminal leaves of currant and gooseberry may be curled by *A. Ribi-gillettei* Allen and Knowlton.

Cypress Aphid, *Siphonatrophia cupressi* (Swain). A rather large green aphid with convex abdomen, large cauda, and short cornicles infesting blue and Monterey cypress in California.

Daylily Aphid, *Myzus hemerocallis.* See also Sand Lily Aphid.

Delphinium Aphid, *Brachycaudus rociadae* (Cockerell). Russet-colored Larkspur Aphid. Common on annual larkspur and perennial delphinium, clustering between buds in the flower spikes or on underside of leaves, which are cupped downward. The shoots are dwarfed, florets fail to open. The aphids, a striking orange red with dull-black head, dusky brown legs and antennae, have been confused by amateurs with the red goldenglow aphid but they are two different species. Spray with malathion, directing it toward underside of foliage and between buds of flower spikes.

Dock Aphid, *Aphis rumicis* Linnaeus. A black aphid heavily infesting dock and apparently confined to this host, although it has been confused with the bean aphid. It has been reported on citrus and avocado in California.

Dogberry Aphid, *Kakimia cynosbati* (Oestlund). Yellow to green, on leaves of currant and gooseberry.

Dogwood Aphid, *Aphis cornifoliae* Fitch. Greenish black, on leaves and stems of dogwood. Another dark-green aphid, *Aphis neogilletti* Palmer, curls dogwood leaves. It is rather rare but, when it occurs, infestations are heavy. *Anoecia corni* Fabricius is also reported on Cornus and the Whitebanded Dogwood Aphid, *A. querci* (Fitch).

Dogwood or Sunflower Aphid, *Aphis helianthi* Monell. Greenish yellow mottled with darker green. It winters on dogwood and migrates to wild and cultivated sunflower for the summer, often seriously curling leaves.

Douglas-fir Aphid, *Cinara pseudotaxifoliae* Palmer. Pale brownish yellow, fairly common on bark of Douglas-fir twigs. Eggs are laid end to end on the needles. A similar species, *Cinara splendens* (Gillette and Palmer), is also reported on twigs of this host.

Dusky-veined Walnut Aphid, *Panaphis juglandis* (Goeze). European Walnut Aphid. A relatively new walnut pest, first noticed in California in 1952. It is larger than the walnut aphid and is clustered in colonies on upper surface of leaves, along midribs. It is yellow with brown to black markings.

Eastern Spruce Gall Aphid*, *Adelges abietis* (Linnaeus). A European insect widely distributed in the Northeast on Norway spruce,

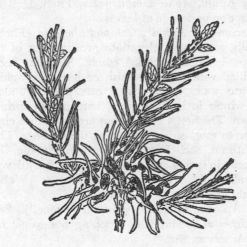

13. Aphid galls on Norway spruce.

also attacking white, red, black, and Engelmann spruce. Pineapple-shaped galls, ½ to 1 inch long, are formed at base of new shoots (Plate II). Greenish immature females hibernate on twigs near terminal buds, feed and mature in spring, then deposit a mass of eggs under a waxy cover. These hatch in a week and the nymphs feed at base of developing needles, their saliva causing the bases to enlarge into bulblike hollows. Fifty such cells may be joined together into a typical gall, each cell holding up to a dozen aphids. New galls are green with the closed mouth of each cell marked with a red or purple line; old galls are brown. The galls open in midsummer, releasing aphids which develop wings at maturity and fly to needles of the same or another spruce tree but not to an alternate host. Eggs deposited at the bases of new growth produce the overwintering females. There are no males in this species. Infested branches often die. Individual trees show a marked difference in susceptibility, some eventually dying, some with retarded growth, and some almost immune from attack.

Control. Propagation from immune individuals is the best long-range control. The galls can seldom be cut out without spoiling the symmetry of the tree. Spray infested trees in spring at start of terminal enlargement and again in late summer with lindane (if allowed to use it), or malathion or Meta-Systox-R. An early April spray of lime sulfur is an older recommendation.

Elaeagnus Aphid. See Russian-olive Aphid.

Elderberry Aphid, *Aphis sambucifoliae* Fitch. Dull blackish green, often abundant on underside of leaves.

Elm Cockscombgall Aphid*, *Colopha ulmicola* (Fitch). General on elm. The galls, a series of elevations growing out of the leaf, green with red tips resembling cocks' combs, ½ inch high by ¾ inch broad, are filled with small greenish or brownish aphids which drip honeydew onto walks, people, and cars parked under trees. Shiny brown eggs winter in bark crevices, hatching in spring when leaves are half grown. The first 3 generations are passed on elm, then winged forms migrate to roots of grasses during the summer. There is a return to elm in autumn, each female laying a single egg. To prevent deformation, spray in spring as soon as leaves are fully developed.

Another gall aphid, *Kaltenbachiella ulmifusa* (Walsh & Riley), is reported on slippery elm.

Elm Leaf Aphid*, *Tinocallis ulmifolii* (Monell). Small, yellow to green, sometimes abundant and dropping honeydew from underside of foliage of American elm.

Elm Sackgall Aphid, *Colopha ulmisacculi* (Patch). Forms bladderlike galls on upper side of leaves of English elm and summers on grass roots, attended by ants.

Eupatorium Aphid, *Macrosiphoniella eupatorii* (Williams). Reddish brown with black head, thorax, and legs.

European Peach Aphid, *Brachycaudus prunicola* (Kaltenbach).

Evening Primrose Aphid, *Aphis oenotherae* Oestlund. Variable in color, green to slate to rusty, on evening primrose and epilobium.

English Grain Aphid*, *Macrosiphum avenae* (Fabricius). Generally distributed on wheat and other grains, on wild and cultivated grasses, and on corn. Grass-green or pink lice on Kentucky bluegrass make this species of interest to home owners. It is usually held in check by natural enemies.

Fern Aphid, *Idiopterus nephrolepidis* Davis. Small, black, with whitish legs and black areas in wings. It infests ferns in houses and greenhouses and outdoors in California. Boston fern is a favorite host. Malathion and perhaps other sprays may injure certain types of ferns; use with caution. Pyrethrins may be helpful.

Filbert Aphid*, *Myzocallis coryli* (Goeze).

Flocculent Fir Aphid, *Cinara occidentalis* (Davidson). Olive green with powdery wax and long hairs on appendages. It infests bark of twigs; eggs are usually only one to a needle.

Fourspotted Hawthorn Aphid, *Macrosiphum crataegi* (Monell). Pale yellow with 4 green spots, common on hawthorn leaves.

Foxglove Aphid*, *Acyrthosiphon solani* (Kaltenbach). An important pest of potatoes but common in the flower garden on acanthopanax, campanula, geranium, gladiolus, lily, pansy, penstemon, physostegia, pyracantha, scarlet sage, verbena, veronica, viburnum, and reported on African-violet indoors. The small aphids, shining light green with a dark patch around the base of the cornicles, winter in the egg stage on foxglove and other hosts, migrating to lower leaves and stems of potato in summer. Feeding on the flower hosts results in yellowed or blanched spots, sometimes leaf curling or a distortion resembling a virus disease. Vegetable hosts besides potato include tomato, cucumber, and turnip. Spray or dust with malathion.

Geranium Aphid, *Acyrthosiphon pelargonii* (Kaltenbach). Grape green, with antennae longer than body, on leaves of geranium (Pelargonium), calceolaria, calla lily, chrysanthemum, cineraria, verbena, and viola.

The **Wild Geranium Aphid**, *Amphorophora geranii* Gillette and Palmer, is found on true geranium, not Pelargonium. It is dull yellow green with sooty markings.

Giant Bark Aphid*, *Longistigma caryae* (Harris). Hickory Aphid. Our largest aphid species, ½ inch long, occurring only on trees—beech, birch, chestnut, elm, hickory, linden, maple, oak, pecan, sycamore, walnut, and willow—in the eastern half of the country, New England to Florida and west to Minnesota. Wingless forms are ash-gray with black spots on the thorax; winged forms have all-black thorax. They feed on bark of twigs and small branches and when abundant may cause injury or death. There are several generations a year. It may pay to have the trees sprayed with malathion when aphids first appear.

Giant Willow Aphid, *Tuberolachnus salignus* Gmelin. Large, blackish but appearing gray from its many hairs, with a conspicuous tubercle on the back. In large colonies on the bark of various willows, often near the ground.

Gillette's Bluegrass Aphid, *Rhopalosiphum poae* Gillette. Dusky brown to black with pale cornicles, infesting lawn and wild grasses, including Kentucky bluegrass. Also common on roots of grasses is a sordid yellow to olive-green species, *Forda olivacea* Rohwer.

Goldenglow Aphid*, *Dactynotus rudbeckiae* (Fitch). Bright red lice with long legs, body ⅙ inch long, are practically inevitable on goldenglow or coneflower (Rudbeckia) wherever grown. They seem to stick straight out from the stems and may also cluster on flower buds. The same species may also appear on chrysanthemum, goldenrod, Fuller's teasel, sunflower, and lettuce. A similar red aphid on larkspur and delphinium is a different species. See Delphinium Aphid.

Goldenrod Aphid, *Aphis solidaginifoliae* Williams. Black to reddish or greenish brown, folding goldenrod leaves along the midrib so they look like pods. See Brown Ambrosia Aphid for another species on goldenrod.

Gooseberry Witchbroom Aphid*, *Kakimia houghtonensis* Troop. Gooseberry leaves are tightly curled by pale yellow-green lice.

Grain Root Aphid, *Forda formicaria* Heyden. On grain roots, also reported on aster.

Grape Phylloxera*, *Phylloxera vitifoliae* (Fitch). A common, injurious, gall-forming species. A native of eastern United States, this is

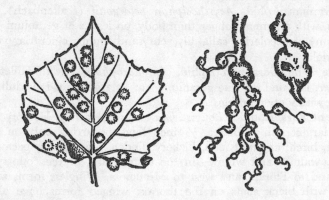

14. Grape phylloxera, showing galls on leaf and roots, and root gall enlarged.

the most destructive grape pest in western America and in Europe. It nearly wrecked the grape industry when introduced into France, and has been devastating in Italy and Germany. In its original home varieties have acquired resistance so that eastern vineyards are seldom seriously injured.

The life history varies according to location. In the East, young lice, hatching from overwintering eggs on canes, settle on grape leaves, producing, by their feeding, pea-shaped galls open on the underside. One female in each gall becomes a stem mother, laying 400 to 600 eggs. Young yellow-green nymphs, hatching from those eggs in 7 to 10 days, migrate to form new galls on other leaves. Several such generations occur during the season but about every third generation some of the aphids move down to the roots to form nodules there. There may be 5 or more generations of the root-gall type, but finally some of the root forms acquire wings and migrate to vines where they deposit 2 kinds of eggs. The small eggs produce males, the larger eggs, females; both are wingless. They mate and each female deposits a single overwintering egg under bark of the cane.

In California vineyards the leaf form is extremely rare and the sex forms seldom mature. Nymphs winter on grape roots and summer generations succeed each other on the roots, although winged migrants may appear to establish new colonies or wingless individuals may crawl to other vines. Feeding roots are destroyed; plants frequently die.

Control. The most practical control is the grafting of desirable European varieties onto resistant native rootstock. Where European rootstocks are used, as in parts of California, the vineyards may be flooded at certain times to kill the root forms or the soil fumigated before new vines are set. Lindane has controlled phylloxera on leaves; endosulfan may be used postbloom.

Grapevine Aphid*, *Aphis illinoisensis* Shiner. Very small, dark brown, common east of the Mississippi River. The lice may be abundant in dry weather, covering new shoots. They also infest fruit clusters, causing some drop, but often disappear after a heavy rain. In autumn the aphids migrate to black haw, returning to grapes in early summer. Nicotine sulfate formerly gave control; commercial growers may use parathion.

Greenbug*, *Schizaphis graminum* (Rondani). A small green aphid of general distribution, more important to farmers than home gardeners but occurring in bluegrass lawns. Greenbugs may be disastrous to wheat and other grains and may also feed on rice, corn, and sorghum. Outbreaks are dependent on weather conditions, being favored by a mild winter and cool spring. In warm weather this aphid is held in check by a parasitic wasp, but this stops reproducing below 65° F.

Green Citrus Aphid. See Spirea Aphid.

Green Gooseberry Aphid, *Aphis sanborni* Patch. Alternating between *Ribes* sp. and epilobium, also reported on elderberry.

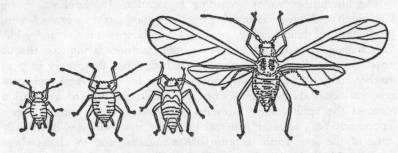

15. Stages in development of the green peach aphid.

Green Peach Aphid*, *Myzus persicae* (Sulzer). A native of Europe, known there as greenfly, this species is now distributed all over North America. Often called the Spinach Aphid, it is most injurious to spinach, and to potatoes and peaches, but it also infests beet, celery, eggplant, lettuce, tomato, pepper, crucifers, cucurbits; and many ornamentals, including aster, calendula, catalpa, carnation, crocus, chrysanthemum, dahlia, dianthus, English ivy, forget-me-not, freesia, iris, lily, nasturtium, pansy, poppy, primrose, rose, snapdragon, sunflower, tulip, verbena, and violet; and some fruits—citrus, apricot, cherry, plum, and prune—besides peach. The green peach aphid is a dangerous vector of tomato and tobacco mosaic, beet yellows, lettuce, dahlia and canna mosaics, leaf roll of potatoes and other virus diseases.

Shiny black eggs winter on bark of fruit trees and hatch into pale, yellowish green aphids, with 3 dark lines on the back, about the time peaches come into bloom. Living young are produced for 2 or 3 generations and these suck sap from twigs; migrants then go to garden plants. In autumn winged females return to peach and give birth to true sexual females which mate with males flying over from spinach and other summer hosts.

Control. Use malathion, diazinon, or dimethoate in home gardens. Commercial growers may prefer parathion or Phosdrin.

Green and Pink Willow Aphid, *Aphis saliceti* Kaltenbach. Various forms are apple green, pink or rust-red, with long, pale cornicles, on willow leaves and twigs.

Green Spruce Aphid*, *Cinara fornacula* Hottes. Light green, with some white powder, on Colorado spruce.

Grindelia Aphid, *Atarsos grindelliae* Gillette. Pale yellow to green, without feet (tarsi), on gumweed and aster.

Hawthorn Aphid, *Brachycaudus crataegifoliae* (Fitch). Long-beaked Clover Aphid. On hawthorn from New England to Illinois, also on Japanese quince, pyracantha, apple, pear, with clover and other legumes as summer hosts. The aphids are pinkish to yellowish green and their sucking causes young hawthorn leaves to curl tightly, older leaves to crinkle. Spray with malathion when leaves are first unfolding. See also Fourspotted Hawthorn Aphid.

Hemlock Woolly Aphid, *Adelges tsugae* (Annand). White tufts on bark and needles of western hemlock, sometimes killing ornamentals in the Pacific Northwest. Reported on eastern hemlock in Virginia in 1951 and from Pennsylvania in 1969.

Hickory Aphid. See Giant Bark Aphid.

Hickory Leaf Aphid. See Black Pecan Aphid.

Hollyhock Aphid, *Macrosiphum eoessigi* Knowlton. Reddish brown with black appendages, on hollyhock.

Honeysuckle and Parsnip Aphid, *Hydaphis foeniculi* (Passerini). Yellowish, on honeysuckle and snowberry as winter hosts, migrating to dill, celery, carrot, and parsnip for the summer.

Other species on honeysuckle include *Amphorophora crystleae* Smith and Knowlton, pale green on leaves; and *Amphicercidus flocculosus* Gillette and Palmer, yellow brown covered with powder, on leaves and twigs of honeysuckle and snowberry.

Hop Aphid*, *Phorodon humuli* (Schrank). This is one of the plum aphids, wintering in the egg stage on plum, prune, sometimes apple, cherry, peach, raspberry, or alder. Pale yellowish-green nymphs may nearly cover underside of foliage before green-and-black winged forms, with long cornicles, appear for the summer migration to hops, sometimes sunflower. A few stay on the winter host. Use a dormant oil or dinitro spray or malathion as the leaves unfold.

Horsemint Aphid, *Myzus monardi* (Davis). Yellow brown, tightly rolling leaves of horsemint.

Impatiens Aphids, *Aphis impatientis* Thomas, and *Macrosiphum impatiensicolens* Patch, *M. impatientis* Williams.

Iris Root Aphid. See Tulip Bulb Aphid.

Ivy Aphid, *Aphis hederae* Kaltenbach. A dark purplish-green, brown or black species common on growing tips of English ivy; also reported on euonymus, viburnum, and aralia. Also known as the Ivy Aphid, but less common, is *Aphis pseudohederae* Theobald, which is dark maroon-brown.

Outdoors, the ivy aphid is often heavily parasitized and may be attended by numerous ants. Indoor ivy can usually be kept pest-free with a weekly bath or with an aerosol containing pyrethrins.

Juniper Aphids. There are several species. The **Rocky Mountain Juniper Aphid,** *Cinara sabinae* (Gillette and Palmer), is commonly injurious. It is light yellow brown marked with black and appears in colonies on bark, often killing twigs. The **Powdery Juniper Aphid,** *Cinara pulverulens* (Gillette and Palmer), is also yellow brown, on bark. *C. junipivora* (Wilson) is reported from foliage of redcedar. The **Hemispherical Juniper Aphid,** *Siphonatrophia gravida* (Knowlton), appears as a minute green drop on upper side of needles.

Larch Aphid*, *Cinara laricis* (Hartig). Dark brown to black, with brown spots on abdomen, infesting twigs and needle bases.

Larch is also the alternate host for two spruce gall aphids. See Spruce Aphid.

Larkspur Aphid. See Delphinium Aphid.

Latania Aphid, *Cerataphis lataniae* (Boisduval). Frequently called the Lantana Aphid, but that is a perpetuation of an old mistake. This Latania or palm species is rather rare and may not even occur in the United States. It has been confused with *C. orchidearum,* which infests orchids, and *C. variabilis,* confined to palms. The latter two are common here and are similar to the latania aphid. The nymphs are dark, disklike, with a white fringe; the winged forms are dull brown to black. See also Orchid Aphid and Palm Aphid.

Leafcurl Ash Aphid, *Prociphilus fraxinifolii* Riley. Leaves are tightly folded and curled into a mass, a pseudo-gall, at tips of twigs. The species is common on white, red, and Modesto ash, especially in California.

Leafcurl Plum Aphid, *Brachycaudus helichrysi* (Kaltenbach). Pest of plum and prune, the winter hosts, especially in western states. Summer hosts include aster, carrot, celery, chrysanthemum, cynoglossum, cineraria, eupatorium, gerbera, heliotrope, lobelia, marguerite, mertensia, sunflower. The summer forms are pale green to lemon yellow, the others are dark green to brownish. Plum leaves are tightly curled. A dormant spray is the best preventive.

Lettuce Aphids. The Brown Ambrosia Aphid, which see, is important on lettuce and endive in some western and southern states. A green aphid, *Acyrthosiphon barri* (Essig), damages lettuce in Arizona, California, and other western states.

Lettuce Root Aphid*, *Pemphigus bursarius* (Linnaeus). Yellowish white or dull green with wax glands. Wintering in petiole galls on poplar, summering on roots of lettuce, carrot, grasses, aster, and goldenrod.

Another lettuce root aphid, *Pemphigus brevicornis* Hart, is a very small, oval, white to pale yellow species, with dusky legs and white powder. Other hosts include aster, erigeron, achillea, euphorbia. Also on lettuce, with galls on poplar, is *P. longicornis* Maxon.

Lily Aphids. See Crescentmarked Lily Aphid and Purplespotted Lily Aphid for the more common species, also Western Lily Aphid.

Linden Aphid, *Eucallipterus tiliae* (Linnaeus). A yellow-and-black species, with clouded wings, often abundant on linden leaves.

Little Blackveined Aster Aphid, *Aphis asterensis* Gillette and Palmer. Mottled greenish yellow, in heads of New England aster, reported in New York, and on leaves and stems of heath aster in Colorado; rather rare.

Little Hickory Aphid, *Monellia caryella* (Fitch).

Locust Aphid, *Myzocallis robiniae* (Gillette). Yellow to greenish with long antennae, on locust leaves.

Lupine Aphid, *Macrosiphum albifrons* Essig. Also called Essig's Lupine Aphid. A large green species entirely covered with white powdery wax, with long legs and cornicles. It infests tips of annual and perennial lupines in spring and early summer.

Malaheb Cherry Aphid, *Myzus lythri* (Schrank). Green, on leaves and stems of *Prunus malaheb,* also on pear and plum, as winter hosts, on epilobium and lythrum as summer hosts.

Manzanita Leafgall Aphid, *Tamalia coweni* (Cockerell). Dull yellow to blackish, marked with dark green, on manzanita and bearberry. Found inside pod-shaped galls formed by one third of the leaf being folded lengthwise on the rest. Galls are green or red.

Maple Aphids. See Norway Maple Aphid and Painted Maple Aphid. Other species include *Drepanaphis carolinensis* Smith, which may cause defoliation, *D. kansensis* Smith, *D. keshenae* Granovsky, *Periphyllus* spp., *Prociphilus* spp.

Mealy Plum Aphid*, *Hyalopterus pruni* (Geoffroy). An alternate-host aphid wintering in the egg stage on plum and prune twigs, migrating to reed grass or cattails. This is a pale-green aphid with a mealy or powdery coating, native of Europe, especially important in the West. It may infest apple, apricot, and peach as well as plum, curling foliage, causing general stunting, fruit splitting, and spoilage by excrement and sooty mold. Use a dormant dinitro or oil spray or malathion or parathion (commercial growers only) when aphids appear.

Melon Aphid*, Cotton Aphid*, *Aphis gossypii* Glover. One of our most destructive species, distributed throughout the country but more serious in the South where there are many generations. In a Texas experiment 51 generations were reared in a single year; in nature there might be about half that, with perhaps 80 offspring per female. There are upward of 100 possible hosts. A partial list includes, besides melon and cotton, asparagus, avocado, bean, beet, celery, cucumber, pumpkin, squash, spinach for vegetables; citrus fruits, pomegranate, strawberry, loquat; and aster, ailanthus, begonia, buckthorn, catalpa, chrysanthemum, cineraria, cyclamen, gardenia, dogwood, gourd, hibiscus, hydrangea, ironwood, ilex, lily, nemesia, rose, seagrape, sunflower, syringa, tabebuia, thistle, verbena, weigela, and wisteria.

The aphid is very small, usually dark green but varying from pale yellow to brown or nearly black, with black cornicles. In the South, living young are produced throughout the year. When a colony gets too dense, winged forms migrate to start another. In the North, there is an egg stage on live-forever and other weeds with migration to garden plants in early summer.

The first sign of aphid infestation in the melon or cucumber patch is the wilting and curling of leaves (Plate I) accompanied by visits of ants, bees, wasps, and flies to get the honeydew. This aphid is a vector of cucumber and melon mosaic, a strain of which is responsible for the serious mosaic disease of lilies. On cucurbits, the mosaic shows as mottled dark- and light-green foliage with stunting of vines. The melon aphid is the worst watermelon pest in Florida, large acreages often being destroyed before the melons can be shipped. On orange, grapefruit, and other citrus trees the aphids distort and curl young twigs. They are vectors of tristeza, a virus disease of citrus.

Control. This is difficult after the leaves and tender tips start curling. Aluminum foil stretched on the ground as a mulch will repel aphids. Home owners may use a malathion dust on vegetables but this may be injurious if applied to wet foliage. Commercial growers may use Meta-Systox-R (though not more than once or twice a season), parathion, diazinon, or Trithion (but not on pumpkin) or endosulfan. Lily growers may treat seed before planting with a systemic phosphate or spray with demeton when plants are 6 inches high. In normal seasons natural parasites and predators are quite efficient in keeping this aphid in check, but if a cool, wet spring, unfavorable for beneficial insects, is followed by a hot dry summer, favorable for aphid reproduction, there may be trouble.

Mint Aphid, *Ovatus crataegarius* (Walker). Yellow green mottled with dark green, on mint foliage; also reported on bergamot.

Monell's Sumac Aphid, *Rhopalosiphum rhois* (Monell). Light rusty brown to greenish yellow, common on terminal shoots and leaves of sumac.

Monterey Pine Aphid, *Essigella californica* Essig. Green, slender, with long hind legs, on needles of Monterey pine; also reported on lodgepole and white pine.

Norway Maple Aphid*, *Periphyllus lyropictus* (Kessler). A nuisance to large numbers of people, most of whom have never seen or heard of it. This is a large, hairy, green to brown aphid infesting underside of Norway, and sometimes sugar, maple foliage through the summer, dropping copious quantities of honeydew to smear windshields and bodies of automobiles parked under street trees. Heavy maple infestations may be followed by heavy summer leaf drop and a sticky mess on sidewalks. The aphid may be more abundant on trees that have been sprayed with carbaryl. Spray early in summer with malathion. Nurserymen may use endosulfan. Wet the undersurface of leaves thoroughly.

Oak Aphids. There are many species. The **Eastern Duskywinged Oak Aphid**, *Myzocallis discolor* (Monell), is reported common on white oaks. It is small, greenish or yellowish with dark spots and dusky bands on wings. Related forms are the **Clearwinged Oak Aphid**, *M. punctata* (Monell), and *M. walshii*, and *M. boerneri*. *Hoplochaitophorus quercicola* (Monell) is yellowish with black hairs, sometimes injurious to foliage of young oaks. *Therioaphis bellus* (Walsh) is small, bright yellow, with cloudy wings, infesting many eastern oaks and live oak in California. *Stegophila quercicola* (Monell), green to yellow or brown with flocculent wax, lives exposed on oak leaves or in galls on edges of leaves. *S. quercifoliae* (Gillette), the **Woolly Oak Aphid**, is common on scrub oaks in the Rocky Mountain region. An oak Phylloxera, *Phylloxera similans,* has been recently recorded from Pennsylvania.

Oat Bird Cherry Aphid, *Rhopalosiphum padi* (Linnaeus). Nymph green with posterior orange, adult blackish green, similar to the apple grain aphid.

Oenothera Aphid. See Evening Primrose Aphid.

Oleander Aphid, *Aphis nerii* Fonscolombe. A pretty yellow-and-black species common in Florida and California and occurring in other states. It appears in spring on young oleander shoots and later migrates to milkweed, although it can stay on oleander the entire year.

Oleaster Thistle Aphid, *Capitophorus elaeagni* (Del Guerico). Also called Artichoke Aphid. Pale yellow and green with darker markings, often abundant on globe artichoke in California and Louisiana. It winters on elaeagnus (Russian olive) and shepherdia. Various thistles are summer hosts.

Orchid Aphid, *Cerataphis orchidearum* (Westwood). On orchids. See also Latania Aphid.

Ornate Aphid, *Myzus ornatus* Laing. A pest of fuchsia in California.

Ornamental Currant Aphid, *Amphorophora ribiella* (Davis). Pale yellow-green, on golden and black currant.

Painted Maple Aphid*, *Drepanaphis acerifoliae* (Thomas). Greenish or brownish with dark borders on wings; on leaves of various species of maple.

Pale Chrysanthemum Aphid, *Amphorophora rufomaculata* (Wilson). Reported on chrysanthemum and artemisia.

Palm Aphid, *Cerataphis variabilis* Hille Ris Lambers. On palms. See also Latania Aphid.

Pea Aphid*, *Acyrthosiphon pisi* (Harris). A smooth pale-green species with black tarsi, generally distributed but of special importance to large growers and the pea-canning industry. In large pea fields, aphids may be so abundant that plants and ground appear white from cast skins; vines wilt and die. Even when less abundant the quality of the peas is affected. The aphid is also a vector of the virus causing pea enation and yellow bean mosaic. It winters on clovers and alfalfa, migrating to peas, including sweetpea, about May 1, there to produce 7 to 20 generations, depending on the weather. There is some migration to other legumes in summer but aphids are again abundant on the fall crop of peas.

Control. Phosphate sprays or dusts are recommended for peas— malathion, dimethoate, diazinon, or parathion. Some pea varieties are resistant but there are several biological races of the pea aphid so that maintaining plant resistance is difficult. On forage crops control is largely by beneficial insects—lady beetles, lacewings, and larvae of syrphid flies.

Pecan Leaf Phylloxera*, *Phylloxera notabilis* Pergande. Galls on pecan leaves.

Pecan Phylloxera*, *Phylloxera devastatrix* Pergande. Galls on pecan stems.

Pine Bark Aphid*, *Pineus strobi* (Hartig). Principally on white pine, occasionally on Scotch, Austrian, and other pines over most of the country. This is a small, dark louse covered with wax, congregating in conspicuous white, flocculent colonies on underside of larger limbs or on main trunk, giving a whitewashed appearance. The immature forms winter under the felty masses or under the bark, maturing and laying eggs in April or May, from which come both winged and wingless forms. Most of the former migrate to other pines; the latter lay eggs for a brood of adults appearing in August and September, whose young are the hibernating nymphs. This aphid is more unsightly than injurious on older trees but may damage unthrifty young trees in ornamental plantings.

Control. A dormant spray, miscible oil or lime sulfur, has been recommended. Spraying with lindane in late April has given excellent control but its use is restricted. Malathion may be substituted, repeating if necessary later in the season.

Pine Leaf Chermid*, *Pineus pinifoliae* (Fitch). On white and lodgepole pines and red, Engelmann, black and Sitka spruces. The woolly nymphs winter on pine, migrate to spruce in spring where they produce compact terminal galls with only 1 or 2 aphids per chamber. The galls open in June and the aphids migrate back to old pine needles, where they give birth to nymphs which move to the new growth and are covered with white wax for the winter. Needles may turn yellow and new growth appear sickly. Spray pines with lindane or malathion. Break the galls off ornamental spruces and destroy them before the cells open.

Other Pine Aphids. Many other species are listed on pine. Among those infesting needles are the **Woolly Pine Needle Aphid**, *Schizolachnus pini-radiatae* (Davidson), on Scotch, red, and yellow pine and a sister species, *S. pineti* (Fabricius) on Scotch and mugho pines; the **Powdery Pine Needle Aphid**, *Eulachnus rileyi* (Williams) on longleaf and yellow pine; *E. agilus* (Kaltenbach), sometimes serious in Scotch pine plantations for Christmas trees, also on red pine; the **Green and Brown Pine Needle Aphid**, *Essigella fusca* Gillette and Palmer, common on piñon pine; and *E. pini* Wilson, the **Speckled Pine Needle Aphid.**

Oxydemetonmethyl has controlled pine needle aphids in Christmastree plantations. Azodrin is also effective without killing predators.

On bark of various pines there are a dozen or more species of *Cinara*, mostly brown or black, covered with a white powder and with short antennae. See also White Pine Aphid.

Podocarpus Aphid, *Neophyllaphis podocarpi* Takahashi. Reported from California in 1954 and from Louisiana in 1966. May be dense on lower surface of Podocarpus leaves, causing them to curl. The species is pulverulent (powdery) reddish brown to purple. Plants may be covered with sooty mold growing in the honeydew.

Polygonum Aphid*, *Capitophorus hippophaes* (Walker). Greenish yellow with reddish streaks; winters on sea-buckthorn and Russian-olive; summers on polygonum.

Poplar Petiolegall Aphid*, *Pemphigus populitransversus* Riley. Turnip Root Aphid. Globular galls on leaf stems have transverse mouths. The greenish yellow, small, stout aphids have poplar as a winter host and summer on roots of cruciferous plants. This species

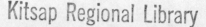

is important on Lombardy poplar. Diazinon granules are suggested for soil treatment of turnips.

Poplar Twiggall Aphid*, *Pemphigus populiramulorum* Riley. Dark-green aphids causing globular galls with transverse mouths on twigs.

Poplar Vagabond Aphid*, *Mordwilkoja vagabunda* (Walsh). Green powdery aphids live clustered together in a bladder-like leaf gall composed of crumpled leaves of a terminal bud.

Other Poplar Aphids. Among the numerous other species on aspen, cottonwood, and poplar are: **Poplar Bulletgall Aphid**, *Pemphigus populicaulis* Fitch; **Foldedleaf Poplar Aphid**, *Thecabius populicon-duplifolius* (Cowen), which winters in a folded pseudo-gall but summers on leaf bases of ranunculus; **Poplar Leafpurse Aphid**, *Asiphum pseudobyrsum* (Walsh) with leaf folded downward on midrib; **Poplar Leafpetiole Gall Aphid**, *Pemphigus populicaulis* Fitch, with the gall formed at the leaf base; **Poplar Sugarbeet Root Aphid**, *Pemphigus balsamiferae* Williams, wintering in yellow-green to reddish pocket galls on underside of leaves, summering on roots of beet, aster, and other plants; the **Reddish Brown Poplar Aphid**, *Pterocomma populifoliae* (Fitch) on bark; the **Crescentgall Poplar Aphid**, *Cornaphis populi* Gillette, in crescent-shaped galls composed of folded edges of leaves; the **Clearwinged Aspen Aphid**, *Chaitophorus populifoliae* Davis, green and black with hyaline wings, on aspen leaves and twigs; the **Clearwinged Cottonwood Leaf Aphid**, *C. populellus* Gillette and Palmer, light green to yellowish, on leaves; the **Black Cloudywinged Poplar Leaf Aphid**, *Periphyllus bruneri* (Williams), having wings with black borders, on leaves and twigs; the **Cloudywinged Cottonwood Leaf Aphid**, *P. populicola* (Thomas); the **Spotted Poplar Aphid**, *Aphis maculatae* Oestlund, black with white patches, on leaves and twigs; and the **American Poplar Bark Aphid**, *Pterocomma pseudopopulea* Palmer, yellow to olive brown, on bark.

A systemic, Meta-Systox-R, injected into the tree through roots or trunk, has effectively controlled some cottonwood leaf aphids.

Potato Aphid*, *Macrosiphum euphorbiae* (Thomas). Common throughout North America (Plate II). This aphid is a menace as a vector of mosaic and other virus diseases of potato and tomato. Years of great abundance, when the aphid is present in epidemic proportions, are followed by lean years. Rose is the winter host, occasionally apple, agrimonia, and potentilla. Black eggs on rose canes hatch into glistening pink-and-green lice, about ⅙ inch long, with long cornicles. These feed on rose buds and succulent young leaves but in early summer migrates fly or crawl to potatoes and other summer hosts, including amaranthus, asparagus, aster, bean, cineraria, citrus, columbine, corn, cotoneaster, currant, eggplant, euphorbia, fuchsia, geranium, gladiolus, groundcherry, hibiscus, iris, Jerusalem-cherry, lettuce, oxalis, pea, penstemon, pepper, poppy, petunia, pumpkin, raspberry, squash, strawberry, sunflower, sweetpotato, tomato, tulip, turnip, and many weeds.

Potato foliage is curled and distorted by aphid feeding; the vines often turn brown and die. On tomatoes the blossom clusters are so devitalized that no fruit is set. Generations develop every 2 or 3 weeks, with vines rapidly covered with lice. On a single tomato plant 24,688 aphids were once counted. In September and October the aphids return to roses, there to produce egg-laying females which mate with males flying over from summer hosts.

Control. Commercial growers may use dimethoate, diazinon, or the more toxic Phosdrin or Phosphamidon. Aerosol bombs with pyrethrins may be used for aphids on rose buds between regular combination-spray applications. Malathion is safe for the operator.

Privet Aphid*, *Myzus ligustri* (Mosley). Privet (Ligustrum) sometimes has new leaves tightly curled lengthwise. The aphids leave in midsummer but return in autumn to lay eggs.

Purplespotted Lily Aphid*, *Macrosiphum lilii* (Monell). Yellow with a purple patch on the back, 1/8 inch long, common in eastern United States. It feeds on underside of lower leaves, on stems, buds, and seed pods of regal, formosanum, speciosum, and other late-flowering garden lilies, causing yellowed foliage, sometimes premature death. Spray or dust with malathion; cut off and burn infested stems in early fall before females deposit eggs. Endosulfan or parathion are possibilities for commercial growers.

Raspberry Aphids. The large green **European Raspberry Aphid,** *Amphorophora agathonica* Hottes, is rather common on underside of leaves of red and black raspberries, and loganberries. It is important as a vector of raspberry mosaic. The **Spottedwinged Raspberry Aphid,** *A. rubicola* (Oestlund), is occasional on leaves of red raspberry. It is greenish with a dusky spot on tip of fore wings. Also rather rare is *A. sensoriata* Mason. A small, greenish aphid, *Aphis rubicola* (Oestlund), sometimes appears on leaves and tips of red and black raspberries, and a small pale-yellow relative, *A. rubifolii* (Thomas), is infrequent on red raspberry.

Use malathion as necessary for control. Parathion or Guthion are suggested for commercial growers.

Red and Black Cherry Aphid, *Aphis feminea* Hottes. Red, with black head, clustering on cherry, wild cherry. Rather rare, reported from Massachusetts, New York, Illinois, and District of Columbia.

Rhododendron Aphid, *Macrosiphum rhododendri* Wilson. Pale pink-and-green species infesting this host in the Pacific Northwest.

Rose Aphid*, *Macrosiphum rosae* (Linnaeus). A large, green species with black appendages, with a pink form in some areas. Common and widespread on cultivated roses, reported as sometimes injurious to pyracantha, found also on ilex. This is a single-host species, continuing to breed on roses through the season. It injures tender leaves, stems, and buds, and deposits eggs for the winter on canes. There are several predators and parasites and when the lady-beetle larvae or aphidlions are at work it is sometimes better to stop spraying temporarily and give the beneficial insects a chance. Malathion, Meta-Systox-R, dimethoate, or pyrethrins will control.

Other Rose Aphids. The **Small Green Rose Aphid,** *Myzaphis rosarum* (Kaltenbach), is smaller than the rose aphid, has no pink forms, and is not restricted to succulent new growth. The **Black and Red Rose Aphid,** *Macrosiphum nigromaculosum* MacDougall, may infest rose leaves and stems but is rather rare. Another species, *M. pseudodirhodum* Patch, has been reported on greenhouse roses. The **Rose and Bearberry Aphid,** *Amphorophora nervata* (Gillette) is found on leaves and twigs of cultivated roses and on bearberry. The **Hairy Rose Aphid,** *Lachnus rosae* Cholodkovsky, a dark species with hairs, is occasional on canes of wild roses. *Myzaphis bucktoni,* found on swamp rose in Maine, is a new record for North America.

Rose Grass Aphid, *Metapolophium dirhodum* (Walker). Yellow to pale green, wintering on twigs and leaves of rose, summering on celery, oats, and various grasses.

Rosy Apple Aphid*, *Dysaphis plantaginea* (Passerini). An important apple pest, curling leaves and deforming young fruit, producing "aphis apples" (Plate II). This species is present throughout apple-growing sections and may also feed on pear, hawthorn, and mountain-ash. It winters as dark-green shiny eggs attached to twigs or in bark crevices, hatching over a period of 2 weeks when buds are opening. The stem mothers, purplish or rose with a waxy coating, feed on the outside of buds until leaves start to unfold, then work their way down into the cluster. When their sucking makes the leaves curl around them they are well protected from sprays. Stem mothers continue to produce living young through spring and early summer, but around July winged forms, rosy with black head and thorax, migrate to stems of narrow-leaved plantain. The aphids return to apple and deposit eggs from October to November.

Control. Dormant dinitro sprays have been recommended to kill overwintering eggs but a current program for farmers calls for parathion, Trithion or Ethion at the half-inch green stage. Malathion or diazinon may prevent curling on hawthorn if applied early enough. Syrphid flies, lady beetles, lacewings, and parasitic wasps are very helpful in warm seasons but when the weather is cold and wet, aphids get the upper hand unless man steps in.

Russetcolored Larkspur Aphid. See Delphinium Aphid.

Russian-olive Aphid, *Capitophorus elaeagni* (Del Guercio). Yellow-green, marked with darker green, on Russian-olive, sea-buckthorn, and buffaloberry.

Rusty Plum Aphid*, *Hysteroneura setariae* (Thomas). A rust-brown aphid common on plums in the East and west to Colorado. It also feeds on corn, grasses, sugarcane, and Virginia-creeper. Use a dormant spray or malathion later.

Sand Lily Aphid, *Myzus leucocrini* Gillette and Palmer. Nymphs are light green, adults are brownish green with 2 rust-orange blotches. On leucocrinum, sand lily, and recorded as injurious to daylilies in Florida.

Sedum Aphid, *Aphis sedi* Kaltenbach. On various species of sedum; similar to the melon aphid.

Shallot Aphid*, *Myzus ascalonicus* Doncaster. On shallot and violet.

Snowball Aphid*, *Neoceruraphis viburnicola* (Gillette). Cause of the familiar curling and deforming of new leaves of common snow-

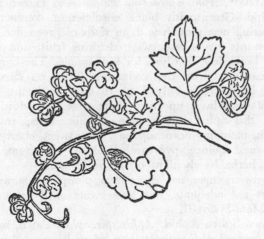

16. Snowball leaves curled by aphids.

ball (*Viburnum opulis*) and some other species in early spring (Plate II). The aphids vary in color from ash-gray to dark green and start curling the leaves long before they are expanded. Control is difficult because the lice are protected almost from the beginning

inside the curled portions. Spray or dust with malathion, starting as
the leaf buds break or apply a systemic insecticide to the soil. It may
be easier to replace the common snowball with resistant *Viburnum
tomentosum.* See also Viburnum Aphid.

Snowberry Aphid, *Brevicoryne symphoricarpi* (Thomas). Yellow,
maturing to black or dusky green with white, powdery patches;
curling snowberry leaves. Another species, *Aphis incognita* Hottes
and Frison, yellowish green, less common but sometimes found with
the snowberry aphid, lives on leaves in summer, on roots spring and
winter. The **Pulverulent Snowberry Aphid,** *Amphicercidus pulverulens* (Gillette), is sordid brown or green, powdery, on bark at base
of stems.

Solanum Root Louse, *Smynthurodes betae* (Westwood). Pale pinkish yellow with brown head and appendages, powdery. On roots of
potato, bean, sweetpea, beet, carrot, aster, goldenrod, vinca, grasses,
and other plants.

Sowthistle Aphid, *Nasonovia lactucae* (Linnaeus). Greenish, with
pale appendages. Winter hosts, leaves of golden and black currant;
summer hosts, celery, sowthistle, and wild lettuce.

Spinach Aphid. See Green Peach Aphid.

Spirea Aphid*, *Aphis spiraecola* Patch. Also known as the Green
Citrus Aphid. Green with black cornicles, a common species on
spirea, covering new growth with myriads of green lice. On citrus it
curls and stunts leaves and twigs, deforms fruit, and covers everything with honeydew, medium for sooty mold. The eggs and sexual
forms appear on spirea, the viviparous forms on citrus and other
hosts. The life cycle is only 6 to 10 days, with the possibility of
large populations built up in a short time. In addition to spirea
and citrus this aphid infests many shrubs, trees, and herbaceous
ornamentals, including acanthopanax, bittersweet, cherry-laurel, hawthorn, Japanese quince, pyracantha, phlox, viburnum, apple, pear,
and various herbs. Newly planted trees suffer most.

Citrus growers may use dangerous phosphate sprays if natural
enemies are not adequate, but homeowners will use malathion, diazinon, or Meta-Systox-R.

The **Brown Spirea Aphid,** *Aphis spiraephila* Patch, hazel to chestnut green, covered with powder, also infests leaves and twigs of spirea
but is less common than the green species.

Spotted Alfalfa Aphid*, *Therioaphis maculata* (Buckton). An import from the Middle East, first noted in New Mexico in 1954. By
1957 it had spread from coast to coast, a serious menace to forage
crops, alfalfa, and clovers. The aphid is small, pale yellow or grayish
with dark spots. It reproduces rapidly, killing foliage by its sucking,

and clogging baling machinery with sticky honeydew. The introduction of imported parasites and the action of native predators and entomophagous fungi has brought this pest largely under control, although chemicals may be necessary on young seedlings.

Spruce Aphid*, *Elatobium abietinum* (Walker). Present in California, Oregon, and Washington, mostly near the coast, reported from North Carolina in 1970, the first record in the East. A small, dark green species living on older needles of Norway, white, and Sitka spruces in spring and early summer, often causing the needles to turn yellow and drop. The lice disappear in summer, the alternate host being unknown. Spray ornamentals with diazinon, malathion, or Meta-Systox-R.

Other **Spruce Aphids**. Many species of Cinara infest spruce. The **Powdery Spruce Aphid**, *Cinara braggi* (Gillette), yellowish, marked with dark brown and lightly covered with powder, is rather common on bark of ornamental blue spruce in parks; the honeydew may damage automobiles in the vicinity. The **Black Polished Spruce Aphid**, *C. coloradensis* (Gillette), is also fairly common in parks on blue and Engelmann spruce, as is the **Spotted Spruce Aphid**, *C. palmerae* (Gillette), dark brown with a spotted pattern of pulverulence. The **Dark Brown Spruce Aphid**, *C. piceicola* (Cholodkovsky) is reported on twigs of spruce nursery stock. The **Light Brown Spruce Aphid**, *C. engelmanniensis* (Gillette and Palmer), is rather rare on Engelmann spruce. *C. pilicornis* (Hartig) is reported on spruce and hemlock.

Gall aphids on spruce include *Pineus similis* (Gillette), which produces loose terminal galls on current year's growth, from New England to Minnesota, and *P. floccus* Patch, which galls the entire new growth on spruce and goes to pine as an alternate host. Larch is the alternate host for *Adelges* (*Chermes*) *strobilobius* Kaltenbach and *A. lariciatus* Patch, which stimulates galls with very short needles.

See Cooley Spruce Gall Aphid and Eastern Spruce Gall Aphid for the most important gall formers on this host.

Strawberry Aphid*, *Chaetosiphon fragaefolii* (Cockerell). A small, pale-yellow species occurring in dense populations on strawberry leaves and stems, but with a marked preference for younger leaves. A pale-green form of this species occurs on leaves and stems of wild rose and another on potentilla. Winged forms migrate from rose to strawberry and reproduce abundantly on the latter. This aphid is particularly important as a vector of strawberry yellows, crinkle, and other virus diseases.

Diazinon may be used by home gardeners, Thiodan, Guthion, or parathion by commercial growers. Malathion is a safe aphicide but should not be used on strawberries if cyclamen mite is present.

Strawberry Root Aphid*, *Aphis forbesi* Weed. On roots and crowns of strawberries, particularly injurious in Central Atlantic States. Black, shiny eggs, overwintered on leaves and stems, hatch in early spring into dark, bluish-green aphids which feed on new leaves. They are found there by the little brown cornfield ant and carried to strawberry roots. There are several generations, keeping the ants in honeydew, but in autumn winged forms fly to the leaves and give birth to sexual males and females which mate and provide overwintering eggs. In mild winters the root forms also persist. Strawberry plants lack vigor, have pale foliage; the fruit dries up or fails to mature properly.

Control. Phosphate sprays are recommended for the leaf forms. In preparing new beds, cultivate the ground deeply in early spring to drive out the ants and set uninfested plants. Treat the soil before planting with diazinon, spray, or granules, and disk in thoroughly.

Sugarbeet Root Aphid*, *Pemphigus populivenae* Fitch. Found in the western half of the country on roots of sugar beets, beets, mangels, and many weeds. The aphids are yellow, with a mass of white waxy cotton toward the rear of the abdomen. They appear as bits of white mold on roots. A winged form, black with a white waxy covering, migrates to poplar for the winter, depositing eggs on the bark, and returns to beet in July, after feeding on poplar leaves during the spring. When beets are grown on irrigated land, root aphids can be reduced by irrigation at 10-day intervals.

Sumac Gall Aphid, *Melaphis rhois* Fitch. Red ball-like galls on sumac leaves.

Sunflower Aphid, *Aphis debilicornis* (Gillette and Palmer). Dark olive-buff on curled leaves and stems of sunflower and Jerusalem artichoke. See also Dogwood or Sunflower Aphid.

Sweetclover Aphid*, *Therioaphis riehmi* (Börner). A European species that recently appeared in North America and is now present from the Atlantic to the Pacific, from Canada to the Gulf of Mexico. It does not injure other legumes. It is pale yellow with black spots, somewhat resembling the spotted alfalfa aphid.

Sycamore Maple Aphid, *Drepanosiphum platanoides* (Schrank). A large, common aphid in various shades of yellow, red, or green, with black markings; on Norway, English, and sycamore maples.

Thistle Aphid*, *Brachycaudus cardui* (Linnaeus). A large, shiny green to yellowish species, with a black patch and bands, long cornicles; summering on thistles, chrysanthemum, and weeds; wintering on apricot, prune, and plum.

Tulip Bulb Aphid*, *Dysaphis tulipae* (Fonscolombe). Also called Iris Root Aphid. A white powdery species with the wingless form pinkish or green with dusky markings. The winged form has black head and thorax, yellow or green body, short cauda and cornicles, is $\frac{1}{10}$ inch long. The aphids infest bases of plants at or below ground level and hide in flower stems, under leaf sheaths, or in seed pods. They attack all varieties of bearded and beardless iris and continue to feed on stored rhizomes. They are common and abundant on stored bulbs or corms of tulip, lily, freesia, crocus, gladiolus, and are reported on roots of celery, carrot, and blackberry-lily. Plants are stunted, distorted, or killed.

Placing tulip bulbs in bags with the inside dusted with 4 per cent malathion has given control. Greenhouse operators can treat iris and tulips with endosulfan before planting for forcing. Dusting bulbs with lindane also controls aphids.

Tulip Leaf Aphid, *Rhopalosiphoninus tulipaella* (Theobald). Very small, green, clustering on leaves and shoots of iris and tulip. Leaves and flowers may fail to open and plants may die. This aphid also winters on dormant bulbs. Another species, *R. staphyleae* Koch, also occurs on iris and tulip in storage. Dust with malathion.

Tuliptree Aphid*, *Macrosiphum liriodendri* (Monell). A small green species abundant on underside of leaves and secreting copious quantities of honeydew. Leaves of tuliptrees and foliage of broad-leaved evergreens growing underneath are often densely coated with black sooty mold. This aphid is also reported on magnolia. Lady beetles are common predators but seldom prevent damage; spray with malathion when aphids appear.

Turf Aphid, *Acyrthosiphon festucae*. New in North America, reported from California in 1971 on fescue turf.

Turnip Aphid*, *Hydaphis pseudobrassicae* (Davis). Also called False Cabbage Aphid and Turnip Louse. It resembles the common cabbage aphid but does not have the waxy body covering. It is pale green and the winged form has black spots, a black head, and transparent wings marked with black veins. This species is generally distributed but causes more serious losses in the South. It feeds chiefly on turnip, mustard, and radish but may infest other crucifers—cabbage, cauliflowers, collards, kale, kohlrabi, rutabaga—and is reported on lettuce. Full-grown females give birth to 50 to 100 living young during a period of 20 to 30 days, and in the Gulf States a great many generations have been observed in a single year. Spray or dust with malathion or diazinon; commercial growers may use more toxic phosphate sprays.

Turnip Root Aphid. See Poplar Petiolegall Aphid.

Vetch Aphid, *Aphis craccae* Linnaeus. Newly discovered in Maine and New York, apparently only on vetch. Black, covered with gray or whitish secretion as an adult.

Viburnum Aphid*, *Aphis viburniphila* Patch. Reddish brown, mottled, with black head and hairy legs. Fairly common on leaves and stems of *Viburnum opulis* and *var. sterile*. See also Snowball Aphid.

Violet Aphid*, *Myzus violae* (Pergande). A wine-red species, with clouded wing veins and swollen cornicles. Infests shoots, buds, and leaves of wild and cultivated violets in California and is present in greenhouses elsewhere.

Walnut Aphid*, *Chromaphis juglandicola* (Kaltenbach). On English walnut; abundant and serious in Pacific States in summer. The color varies from lemon-yellow to salmon-pink to brown. Injury comes from loss of sap from aphids feeding on underside of leaves, and from sooty mold growing in the honeydew. Phosphate sprays are usually used by orchardists, the first application in spring, the second in July or August. Malathion dust is also used. A braconid wasp parasite (*Troxys pallidus*), introduced from Europe in 1959, has spread rapidly over coastal areas and is promising for control.

The **European Walnut Aphid**, *Panaphis juglandis* (Goeze), is yellow with brown to black markings and occurs on upper surface of walnut leaves. See also American Walnut Aphid.

Waterlily Aphid*, *Rhopalosiphum nymphaeae* (Linnaeus). Small, olive-green to golden-brown, on waterlily, lotus, water plantain, cattail, pondweed, and knotweed for summer hosts. On its winter fruit-tree hosts—almond, apricot, cherry, plum—the aphid is larger and covered with white powder. Waterlily leaves are disfigured and decayed, flowers discolored and stems distorted. Japanese cherry grown near waterlily ponds may be injured.

Control. In pools with fish, remove fish, lower water level to expose foliage, and spray with malathion or pyrethrum. Change water before replacing the fish. If fish cannot be removed, fill pool to overflowing and wash aphids onto lawn with the hose. Spray plums with malathion in spring, before aphids migrate to waterlilies.

Western Aster Root Aphid, *Aphis armoraciae* Cowen. Pale to olive green, with powder, common on roots of aster, erigeron, salsify, parsley, horseradish, and other plants. For control see Corn Root Aphid.

Western Lily Aphid*, *Macrosiphum scoliopi* Essig. On Easter lilies in California.

Western Wheat Aphid*, *Brachycolus tritici* Gillette. Pale yellowish or greenish, powdery, on leaves of wheat.

Whitebanded Dogwood Aphid, *Anoecia querci* (Fitch). Of various colors with cross bands and covered with powder, on dogwood and occasional migrants on oak. Grasses are summer hosts.

White Pine Aphid*, *Cinara strobi* (Fitch). Found on eastern white pine from New England to Illinois and south to the Carolinas, feeding on twigs and branches. Small trees may be heavily damaged or killed. Eggs are laid in lines on needles with sooty mold developing in the honeydew. Spray with a superior type dormant oil in spring and with malathion later; or wash off the aphids with a strong stream of water from the hose.

White Aster Root Aphid, *Prociphilus erigeronensis*. Yellow-buff, woolly; on roots of aster, China aster, primrose, lettuce, evening primrose, sunflower; winter host is unknown.

Wild Parsnip Aphid, *Aphis heraclella* Davis. Deep green mottled with yellowish green, on leaves and stems of celery, carrot, and parsnip.

Willow Aphids. Many species are recorded, some quite common. *Periphyllus salicorticis* (Essig) is greenish yellow or rust-brown with darker spots. It occurs on bark of older limbs and often at or beneath surface of the ground. The **Black Willow Aphid**, *Pterocomma smithiae* (Monell), pink or salmon as a nymph, rusty brown with bluish powder as an adult, commonly infests bark of twigs of willow and poplar. The related **Reddishbrown Willow Bark Aphid**, *P. bicolor* (Oestlund), reddish brown with powdery markings, is likewise common on willow bark. The **Flocculent Willow Aphid**, *P. flocculosa* (Weed), reddish brown covered with bluish "wool," is found on leaves and bark. Willow is winter host to two green aphids, *Cavariella aegopodii* (Scopoli) and *C. essigi* (Gillette and Bragg). The former summers on dill, celery, caraway, carrot, and parsnip; the latter goes to cow parsnips. The **Little Black-and-green Willow Aphid**, *Chaitophorus viminalis* Monell, commonly infests willow leaves in large colonies.

See also Giant Willow Aphid.

Witch-hazel Leafgall Aphid, *Hormaphis hamamelidis* (Fitch). Forming conical galls on upper surface of leaves, found from New England to North Carolina and Illinois. Birch is an alternate host. The **Spiny Witch-hazel Budgall Aphid**, *Hamamelistes spinosus* Shimer, forms galls on stem buds of witch-hazel and goes on to birch.

Woolly Alder Aphid*, *Prociphilus tessellatus* (Fitch). Also known as Alder Blight Aphid and Maple Leaf Aphid. Widely distributed, with maple considered the primary host, alder the secondary. Leaves are folded downward over large woolly masses covering blue-black aphids. In early fall males and females, the latter small and orange, migrate from alder to maple to mate and lay eggs on the bark. At the same time a wingless hibernating form on alder crawls down the trunk to spend the winter under leaves on the ground. Lady beetles and the sluglike caterpillar of an orange butterfly (*Feniseca tarquinius*) feed on these aphids, but ants protect them in exchange for honeydew.

Woolly Apple Aphid*, *Erisosoma lanigerum* (Hausmann). Of world-wide distribution, wherever apples are grown, also attacking pear, hawthorn, mountain-ash, elm, sometimes rose and other ornamentals. It covers trunk and branches with white cottony masses enclosing purplish-brown lice and forms knots on the roots, causing many fibrous roots, stunting, and sometimes death of young apple trees (Plate II). It may also transport the fungus causing perennial canker of apple.

The life history is complicated. This woolly aphid winters in several forms—eggs on the bark of elm trees, immature nymphs on apple roots, or, in warm climates, as egg-laying females on apple bark. The eggs on elm hatch in spring into wingless forms which feed on elm buds and leaves for 2 generations, turning young leaves into curled rosettes that protect the aphids. The next generation has wings and migrates to apple, hawthorn, and mountain-ash, where some of the lice feed in wounds on trunk and branches and others work their way down to the roots, where the most important injury is produced. In autumn winged migrants return to elm while other, wingless aphids remain to produce living young on apple roots.

Control. An effective parasite, *Aphelinus mali*, has been distributed to many countries, but it works best at fairly high temperatures and is killed when methoxychlor is used in the spray schedule. However, its numbers are not decreased by parathion and TEPP, which are effective for the aphids. Orchardists also use diazinon, Guthion, or malathion. Root forms may be killed on nursery stock by dipping in a strong nicotine solution before planting. Home gardeners may use malathion on ornamentals.

Woolly Beech Aphid. See Beech Blight Aphid.

Woolly Elm Aphid*, *Eriosoma americanum* (Riley). Attacks American elm with roots of shadbush or serviceberry the alternate host. One side of the leaf is rolled under to enclose woolly dark-green to black lice. Another species, the **Woolly Elm Bark Aphid**, *Eriosoma rileyi* Thomas, powdery flesh-colored to brownish, is found on bark of trunk and roots of American and slippery elm, also in curled leaves. No alternate host is know.

Woolly Hawthorn Aphid, *Eriosoma crataegi* (Oestlund). A large black species with wax in 2 long white filaments, on bark of hawthorn and curling leaves of elm, also reported on flowering crab and pyracantha. It has been confused with the woolly apple aphid and is parasitized by the same wasp.

Another **Woolly Hawthorn Aphid,** *Prociphilus corrugatans* (Sirrine), is less common. It is olive-green and lives inside curled leaves of hawthorn and shadbush. The summer host is not known.

Woolly Honeysuckle Aphid, *Prociphilus xylostei* (De Geer). Yellow, with black head and thorax, woolly; inside partly curled honeysuckle leaves.

Woolly Larch Aphid, *Adelges strobilobius* Kaltenbach. On larch, appearing as white woolly masses on needles and as dark aphids on underside of twigs and clustered at base of needles. It migrates to spruce, forming small galls at tip of current growth. Spray with malathion or lindane.

Woolly Pear Aphid*, *Eriosoma pyricola* Baker and Davidson. Similar to the woolly apple aphid, established on the Pacific Coast and in limited locations farther east. The life cycle is completed on elm, where leaf galls are formed.

Woolly Pine Needle Aphid. See under Pine Aphids.

Yellow Clover Aphid*, *Therioaphis trifolii* (Monell). Fairly common but not often significant on clovers.

Yellow Rose Aphid, *Acyrthosiphon porosum* (Sanderson). Pale, on rose, wild and cultivated, and strawberry.

Yellow Sugarcane Aphid*, *Sipha flava* (Forbes). On sorghum, corn, and grasses.

ARMYWORMS

Armyworms are related to cutworms, in the family Noctuidae, order Lepidoptera. They are the larvae of night-flying moths and work in armies, devouring everything in their paths.

Armyworm*, *Pseudaletia unipuncta* (Haworth). Common in all parts of the country, especially injurious east of the Rocky Mountains, and an ancient native pest. The Pilgrim fathers reported damage to corn as early as 1632, and this species has been intermittently disastrous ever since. It reaches epidemic proportions at varying intervals of years, usually being more serious after a cold spring. The caterpillars are 1½ inches long, smooth, greenish, with dark stripes and with a fine, broken, light-colored stripe down the back. They travel in dense armies, devouring all crops along the line of march, wheat, corn, oats, and rye being favorite food plants. They winter mainly as larvae, then form dark-brown pupae in the soil, whence emerge brownish-gray moths. These "millers" have a small white dot in the center of each front wing; they are 1½ inches across the wings. The moths fly only at night; they are attracted to lights and decaying fruits. The females deposit greenish-white eggs in long rows on lower leaves of grasses. There may be 2 or 3 generations a year, with the first most injurious.

Control. Spraying or dusting with methoxychlor or malathion has been suggested for corn. Poison baits, same as for grasshoppers, may be used across the line of march. Many insects, especially tachinid flies and wasplike egg parasites, are helpful in control. The caterpillars are also eaten by birds, skunks, and toads.

Beet Armyworm*, *Spodoptera exigua* (Hübner). Also known as the Asparagus Fern Caterpillar. The larvae are green above, yellow underneath, with a dark stripe on the back and yellowish stripes on each side. They eat corn, cotton, peas, peppers, spinach, tomatoes, as well as beets and asparagus fern, carnation, geranium, gladiolus, and primrose. Adults are a mottled gray. Sevin may be used on ornamentals but it will kill bees.

Bertha Armyworm*, *Mamestra configurata* Walker. Reported on apple buds.

Fall Armyworm*, *Spodoptera frugiperda* (J. E. Smith). So named because it does not appear before fall in northern states. It is a trop-

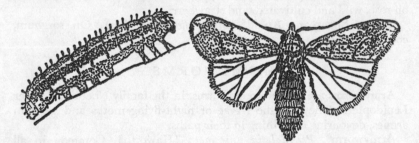

17. Fall armyworm, larva and adult moth.

ical insect, wintering in southern Florida and along the Gulf Coast, migrating north in summer as far as New England and Michigan. Called the Southern Grassworm in Florida, it eats all grass in easy range (lawns as well as meadows) before moving to corn, second choice. On corn, it is sometimes called budworm and acts like the corn earworm. It is particularly injurious following a cold wet spring and may feed on many vegetables—bean, cabbage, cowpea, cucumber, peanut, potato, sweetpotato, spinach, tomato, turnip—as well as on grass, corn, clover, and grains.

The caterpillars are light tan to green or black, with 3 yellowish hairlines down the back, then a darker stripe next to a waxy yellow stripe splotched with red. They have a conspicuous V-shaped white mark on the head. When they have eaten all the food in one garden, they start a forced march on the next. Because they start feeding near the ground they do a lot of damage before being noticed.

The moths—1½ inches across, with grayish-white hind wings, dark mottled fore wings with a whitish spot at the tip—fly northward in swarms, mostly at night. A single female may deposit up to 1,000 eggs, in clusters of 150 each, on green plants. There may be 5 or 6 generations in the South but only 1 that is important in the North.

Control. In Florida tests with sweet corn the most insect-free ears have been in plots treated with Gardona, parathion plus methyl parathion, Lannate, and carbofuran. Toxaphene has been recommended. Cultivate soil in home garden to expose pupae to their many natural enemies.

Lawn Armyworm*, *Spodoptera mauritia* (Boisduval). Reported on Bermuda grass in Hawaii.

Nutgrass Armyworm*, *Spodoptera exempta* (Walker).

Southern Armyworm*, *Spodoptera eridania* (Cramer). Also called Semitropical Armyworm. This species is prevalent in Florida and has been noted as far north as South Carolina. It is a major pest of celery and sweetpotato, attacks cotton and some other plants. The larvae are black, or yellow with black markings.

Western Yellowstriped Armyworm*, *Spodoptera praefica* (Grote). A problem in western states on alfalfa, also damaging tomato, rhubarb, melons, grapevines, and a variety of plants. The caterpillars are velvety black with yellow stripes; the moths have mottled fore wings, silvery hind wings.

Yellowstriped Armyworm*, *Spodoptera ornithogalli* (Guenée). Also known as Sweetpotato Caterpillar or Cotton Cutworm. A sweetpotato pest in Florida, often defoliating fields in July and August, it may also be serious on soybeans. The caterpillars are day-feeding, olive-green to brown, with a double row of green or black spots on the back and usually a bright orange stripe outside the spots. The moths have mottled gray or brown fore wings, pale hind wings.

BAGWORMS

Bagworms are caterpillars that carry their baglike houses around with them. They are larvae of moths, family Psychidae, order Lepidoptera, with wingless, almost legless females that practically never leave their bags. Of the 20 species in this country only one is commonly mentioned.

Bagworm*, *Thyridopteryx ephemeraeformis* (Haworth). Distributed from Vermont to Florida and west into New Mexico. Although called the Evergreen Bagworm and a frequent pest of conifers, it is a general feeder, sometimes defoliating sycamores, Norway and soft maples, locust, boxelder, linden, citrus trees, as well as arborvitae, juniper, hemlock, larch, and pine. It continues to be the most common pest of ornamental evergreens in Missouri and is recorded on rose, as well as arborvitae, throughout South Carolina. It seems to be more devastating in the South. I have seen miles of redcedars in Virginia and many arborvitae in Texas killed by bagworms but never such total destruction in northern states.

The spindle-shaped bag, 1 to 2 inches long, of unbelievably tough silk, is covered with bits of leaves and twigs from the host plant, a bag hanging on a juniper being of quite different appearance from one on pine (Plate III). The eggs winter in the bag and the larvae hatch in late spring—perhaps April in Florida, May in Tennessee, late May and early June in New Jersey. The larvae, dark brown to black with white to yellowish head and thorax spotted with black, immediately set about making new cases as they feed, enlarging at the top as they grow, thus accounting for the spindle shape. The caterpillar, ¾ to 1 inch long when grown, moves freely about with this bag. When it wants to eat, or to molt, which it does 4 times, it fastens the bag to a twig with a silken thread. The bagworm pupates in late summer and the black male moth, with furry body and feathered antennae, wingspread about 1 inch, flies to mate with the maggot-like yellowish female through an opening at the base of the bag. The female lays 500 to 1,000 eggs in the pupal case inside the bag and then dies.

Control. When there is a light infestation, picking off the bags in winter or spring is the easiest control. Some recommend destroying these; others suggest placing the bags in deep open containers near the infested trees. The larvae, unable to crawl for food, will die but their beneficial parasites will be liberated. For heavy infestations spray in late spring, as soon as the caterpillars start feeding. Use carbaryl plus malathion, or diazinon, dimethoate, carbophenothion, or Zectran. Sometimes woodpeckers and sapsuckers help to reduce bagworms.

BEES

Bees, of the order Hymenoptera, superfamily Apoidea, are tremendously important for pollination in orchard and garden. Apples rarely set fruit unless they are fertilized by pollen from some other variety. Honeybees accomplish 90 per cent of the pollen transfer in apple orchards, but bumblebees, solitary bees, and other insects also help. Pears, cherries, plums, peaches, strawberries, and some vegetables need bees for a good crop or to set seed. Commercial orchardists frequently rent hives of bees for the flowering period. Broad-spectrum insecticides such as carbaryl (Sevin) used in the vicinity may poison the bees. In one section of California there is a warning system, and when there is to be large-scale spraying, owners have time to remove the hives.

Even older insecticides such as lead arsenate may kill bees, and that is one reason why fruit-spray schedules are so carefully timed. The pre-pink spray is put on before blossoms open, and the calyx spray is applied when most of the petals have fallen. No poison should be used while the bees are coming to flowers for nectar.

A few bees have injurious as well as beneficial habits. Leafcutter bees, family Megachilidae, and carpenter bees, family Apidae, are among these.

Alfalfa Leafcutter Bee*, *Megachile rotundata* (Fabricius).

Carpenter Bee*, *Xylocopa virginica* (Linnaeus). Often called large carpenter bee. Large, robust, about 1 inch long, similar to a bumblebee but with the upper part of the abdomen largely bare. This species excavates galleries in solid wood.

Leafcutter Bees, *Megachile* spp. Moderate-sized, stout-bodied, solitary bees, often nesting in wood or hollow stems of woody plants or in the ground. The bees are hairy, black or metallic blue, green or

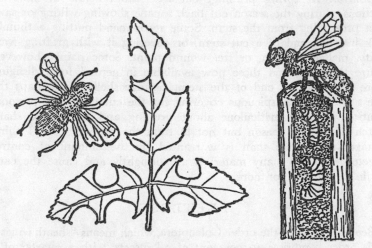

18. Leafcutter bee, left; small carpenter bee, right.

purple, with short, elbowed antennae. The long legs are not equipped with pollen baskets, the pollen being carried on brushes under the abdomen. All members of this group are important pollinators and many are particularly useful with alfalfa, clovers, and other forage crops. The female cuts very precise ovals and circles from margins of leaves, frequently rose leaves. The ovals line the bottom and side of her nest; the circles cap each cell after an egg has been laid inside. These nests are in cavities of dead twigs, in broken ends of branches, or in the pithy stem of plants such as dahlia. There is no control except to cut out wilted or dying shoots containing the nests. And although rose foliage all over the country may be disfigured somewhat by these bees, one should not begrudge a few leaf portions required by this primarily beneficial insect. It is better to admire the perfection of its tailoring.

Small Carpenter Bees, *Ceratina* spp. These bees are known to most rose lovers as pith borers and are a source of great concern, but they are not entirely bad. There are several species, most of them black, with faint metallic highlights, and small, seldom more than 1/3 inch long. They nest in tunnels in the pith of various woody shrubs, with rose a special favorite. When the cut stem shows a hole in the pith, slitting it lengthwise usually reveals a half dozen or so yellowish, curved maggots, lined up in cavities. An egg has been deposited in each of a series of cells and hatching starts at the bottom, so that all leave the twig together.

Control. At spring pruning, cut rose canes below the infested portions; during the season cut back a cane showing wilting or sawdust protruding from the stem. Some recommend putting a thumbtack into the end of a cut stem, or covering it with grafting wax, putty, melted paraffin, or tree-wound paint. Some paints, however, injure the cane, and those now available in aerosol form disfigure more than the cut end of the stem. Orange shellac is perhaps the safest and least conspicuous covering for the cut cane. My personal solution is to be meticulous about pruning and to keep a sharp watch during the season but not to treat the pruning cuts. I think it takes more time than is warranted by the amount of control effected, and too many materials are unsightly and cause the cane to die back an inch or more.

BEETLES

Beetles belong to the order Coleoptera, which means "sheath wings." This order comprises 40 per cent of all insects, with a quarter of a million species already described. It is claimed that one out of every five species of living things is a beetle and that there are about 28,000 species in the United States. Some beetles are predaceous, preying on other insects, some are scavengers, cleaning up rotting animal and plant refuse, but many feed on healthy plant tissue. They are doubly injurious because both larvae and adults have chewing mouth parts.

The chief characteristic of members of the order Coleoptera is the modification of the first pair of wings into hard, tough, or horny

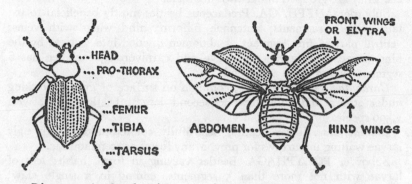

19. Diagram of a beetle with wings in normal position and spread for flight.

sheaths (elytra) commonly called wing covers. These meet, in most cases, in a straight line down the middle of the back and in flight are held stiffly out at the sides. All movement is by the membranous hind wings, which are folded transversely under the elytra when at rest. Some running ground beetles and some weevils lack hind wings and have the hard elytra grown together down the back.

Beetles have complete metamorphosis. The egg hatches into a soft grub, mostly with 6 legs, occasionally legless, then turns into a pupa with the sacs holding the appendages freely movable, and finally transforms into the adult beetle. The mouth parts often indicate beetle habits. Short, chunky mandibles usually belong to a plant-eating species, while a predator more often has long, pointed jaws right for grasping other insects. If the mandibles lack distinct teeth and are covered with stiff hairs, the beetle is likely a harmless pollen feeder. Snout beetles and weevils have the head prolonged forward and downward into a cylindrical snout that may be shorter than the head or much longer than the body. Beetles called curculios have a long curved snout with the mouth parts at the tip of this projection.

Adult beetles have compound eyes but no ocelli (simple eyes), while the larvae have a small group of ocelli on each side of the head but no compound eyes. The antennae have 10 to 11 segments, the tarsi 3 to 5.

There are 122 beetle families reported in the United States, divided by many technical taxonomic characters such as structure of antennae, form of legs, number of tarsal segments, mouth parts. The relatively few families considered here are those containing individuals injurious to garden plants or predators especially helpful to gardeners. They are grouped under two suborders.

Suborder ADEPHAGA. Predaceous beetles mostly beneficial to us; tarsi with 5 segments; antennae filiform; hind wings with veins; ventral part of first segment of abdomen divided into 2 areas by the hind coxae. The larvae are active and carnivorous; each leg has 6 segments with 2 claws at the end.

Carabidae. Ground beetles; common on surface of ground, lurking under stones and rubbish. The second largest beetle family, with 2,500 species.

Cicindellidae. Tiger beetles, beautifully colored adults with ugly larvae waiting in burrows for prey. Many forms are semiaquatic.

Suborder POLYPHAGA. Beetles varying in form, habit; legs of larvae with not more than 5 segments, ending in a single claw; hind wings with reduced venation; first ventral segment of abdomen in a single piece.

Anthicidae. Antlike flower beetles. With small, antlike bodies; occasional on flowers and foliage.

Bostrichidae. False powder post beetles. Wood borers; in branches and twigs. Elongate, somewhat cylindrical, with deflexed head; 1/8 to 1/2 inch long; antennal club 3-segmented; abdominal sternites (segments) of about equal length.

Brentidae. Brentid beetles. Primitive weevils with long narrow body, sides almost parallel, and prothorax almost as long as the elytra; females smaller than males but with a more elongate snout, projecting straight forward.

Bruchidae. Seed beetles. Bean and pea weevils. Short, stout-bodied, mostly less than 1/4 inch long; short elytra not covering tip of abdomen; short broad snouts; prominent eyes, usually gray or brown.

Buprestidae. Flatheaded or metallic wood borers. Hard-bodied, flat, with striking iridescent blue or bronze coloring; head very short; eyes large; antennae short; tarsi 5-segmented. Larvae long, legless, with small head and very broad, flat thorax; working beneath bark of various trees and shrubs.

Byturidae. Fruitworm beetles. Small, hairy, with clubbed antennae and 5-segmented tarsi; reddish yellow, brown or black. Adults feed on raspberry or blackberry flowers; larvae damage berries.

Cantharidae. Soldier beetles. Elongate, soft-bodied, similar to lightning beetles but without light-producing organs; adults often found on flowers; larvae predaceous on other insects.

Cerambycidae. Long-horned beetles or roundheaded wood borers. Very large family with all species feeding on plants, adults on flowers, foliage, or bark, larvae boring in wood. Adults are elongate, cylindrical, mostly over ½ inch long; very long filiform antennae; tarsi apparently 4-segmented, the 5th segment being small and concealed.

Chrysomelidae. Leaf beetles. Feeding mostly on flowers and foliage; closely related to Cerambycidae but with shorter antennae; smaller, more oval in shape. Some larvae feed on foliage, others mine inside leaves, some bore in stems or feed on roots. This family includes many serious plant pests—flea beetles, Colorado potato beetle, asparagus and cucumber beetles.

Cleridae. Checkered beetles. Brightly marked, densely covered with short hairs, ⅛ to ½ inch long; predaceous as larvae and adults, preying on wood borers and on small insects in flowers.

Coccinellidae. Lady beetles. Very useful predators, feeding mostly on aphids. Small, oval, convex, often bright-colored; antennae club-shaped; tarsi 3-segmented. Larvae elongate, somewhat flattened, covered with tubercles or spines, often with colored spots.

Crytophagidae. Silken fungus beetles. Very small, yellowish brown with silky hairs, found under bark or in flowers but feeding on decaying matter.

Cucujidae. Flat bark beetles. Very flat, reddish, brownish, or yellow, found under bark; predaceous on mites and other small insects.

Curculionidae. Snout beetles, curculios, or weevils. Head prolonged into a long or short snout; clubbed and elbowed antennae arising from the snout; tarsi apparently 4-segmented. Adults drill holes in fruits, nuts, or other plant tissue; larvae feed inside fruits, buds, nuts, seeds, or stems.

Dermestidae. Dermestid or skin beetles. Feeding on leather, silk, rugs, etc., but many species feeding on flowers. Small, oval, convex, with short, clubbed antennae, ¹⁄₁₆ to ½ inch long, usually hairy or covered with scales; larvae brownish with long hairs.

Elateridae. Click beetles, wireworms. Having a special joint at union of prothorax and mesothorax, enabling them to snap back into position when placed on their backs. Body elongate, usually parallel-sided, rounded at each end; eyes large; antennae serrate; tarsi 5-segmented; mostly black or brown; feeding on flowers or foliage. The slender, hard wireworm larvae work on seeds and roots.

Histeridae. Hister beetles. Scavengers on dung, fungi, decaying matter but also predaceous on other insects. Small, broadly oval, usually shiny black; cut off square at the apex, exposing 1 or 2 abdominal segments.

Lampyridae. Fireflies, lightning bugs. Soft-bodied, elongate, with pronotum extending over the head; flattish, with luminous segments near end of the abdomen; antennae slender; tarsi 5-segmented. Larvae (glowworms) are predaceous on smaller insects, slugs, and snails.

Languriidae. Lizard beetles. Narrow, elongate, with reddish pronotum and black elytra; feeding on leaves and stems of goldenrod, clovers, various other common plants and weeds. Larvae are stem borers.

Lucanidae. Stag beetles, pinching bugs. Large, brownish, with mandibles on the male half as long as the body and branched like antlers; antennae elbowed; attracted to lights at night. Larvae live in decaying wood.

Lycidae. Net-winged beetles. Elongate, soft-winged, with network of raised lines on the elytra; often found in woods on trunks and foliage but feeding on decaying matter and other insects. Larvae are predaceous.

Lyctidae. Powder post beetles. So named because they bore into dry wood and reduce it to powder, occurring also in woody fungi and dead limbs of trees. Similar to members of Bostrichidae.

Meloidae. Blister beetles. Elongate, soft-bodied, usually cylindrical; large head, set off from thorax; fairly short filiform antennae; 5 segments in tarsi of front and middle legs, 4 in hind tarsi; body fluid containing cantharidin, causing blisters. Adults are injurious, larvae somewhat beneficial.

Mordellidae. Tumbling flower beetles. Usually small, with wedge-shaped, humpback body, head bent down, abdomen pointed and extending beyond tip of elytra; black, covered with dense white hairs sometimes making a white pattern. Often found in flowers and some forms predaceous on small insects; tumbling when disturbed.

Nitidulidae. Feeding on dried fruit and sap; usually small, elongate or oval, active; elytra shorter than abdomen; head large; eyes conspicuous; antennae club-shaped, 11-segmented; tarsi 5-segmented. Attracted to fermenting or souring fluids.

Oedermeridae. Oedermerid beetles. Slender, soft-bodied, occasional on flowers and foliage; eastern forms yellow-brown with tip of elytra black; western forms bright blue with red pronotum, common on ceanothus.

Ostomidae. Grain and bark-gnawing beetles. Head and pronotum

large, and union between pronotum and elytra narrow; larvae feed
on grain and also other insects in grain.

Phalacridae. Shiny flower beetles. Minute, round, shiny, convex,
very small, mostly dark brown. Quite common on flowers of goldenrod and other composites. Larvae develop in heads of flowers.

Scarabaeidae. Scarabs. A very large family with some dung beetles
beneficial as scavengers but with many plant feeders—chafers, June
beetles, Japanese beetle, etc. Adults are oval, robust, with short,
usually elbowed antennae, having clubs made of several thin plates
pressed together; tarsi 5-segmented. Larvae are plump, whitish, usually C-shaped.

Scolytidae. Bark beetles, engraver beetles. Mining on the surface
of hardwood and making patterns under the bark. Small, cylindrical
beetles, brownish or black, with a small head and large first-thoracic
segment; antennae short, with a club; tarsi apparently 4-segmented.
This family also includes ambrosia or timber beetles which penetrate sapwood and heartwood of dead trees and feed on fungi
growing on the walls of their tunnels.

Silphidae. Carrion beetles. Beneficial insects working on bodies of
dead animals, sometimes burying small mice by excavating under the
body. Large, often brightly colored, soft, somewhat flattened; antennae clubbed; tarsi 5-segmented.

Staphylinidae. Rove beetles. A group of predators, the largest family in the beetle group, with 2,900 species. Rather flat, elongate, head
as wide as thorax; fore wings much shortened; tip of abdomen elevated when disturbed; mandibles long, slender, sharp, sometimes crossing in front of the head. Active insects, flying or running rapidly.

Stylopidae. Twisted-winged insects, placed by some in a separate
order, Strepsiptera. Minute parasites on other insects, mostly bees,
sometimes wasps. Females wingless, often legless, males free-living,
winged; tarsi 4-segmented, without claws.

Tenebrionidae. Darkling beetles. Similar to ground beetles, more
common in arid areas. Found under stones and rubbish, under bark
or in rotting wood. Some species are destructive pests of stored
grain and flour, the larvae being called mealworms. Usually brown
or black; antennae usually 11-segmented; eyes notched.

In considering the specific beetles, I am following the entirely
artificial system set up for this book as a whole—i.e., treating them
alphabetically under approved common names. If a beetle is officially named a borer, from its larval state, then it is discussed under
Borers; if its approved name is curculio, then it is considered under
Curculios; and if it is called a weevil, it is treated under Weevils.

Alaska Spruce Beetle. See Spruce Beetle.

Alder Bark Beetle*, *Alniphagus aspericollis* (LeConte). Commonly destructive to western alders, attacking weakened or dying trees. Small, black, robust beetles, ⅛ inch long, bore through bark in pairs, usually at base of branches, and construct longitudinal egg galleries 2 to 5 inches long. Larvae pupate in the soft inner bark. There are 2 generations a year.

Alder Flea Beetle*, *Altica ambiens* LeConte. Feeding on foliage of alders, also poplar and willow, from Maine to New Mexico, and also on West Coast, normally scarce but periodically epidemic and defoliating the host. Color cobalt to greenish blue, shiny; ⅕ inch long; elytra wider at the base, finely punctate. Adults hibernate in protected places, lay orange eggs on leaves in spring. Larvae, dark brown with black heads, eat everything but veins in July and August. Pupation is in the ground. There is 1 generation in Maine, sometimes 2 farther south. Spray with Sevin.

Alfalfa Snout Beetle*, *Otiorhyncus ligustici* (Linnaeus). A European pest first noted in this country near Oswego, New York, in 1933 feeding on raspberries. Since then it has been found on rhubarb and strawberry, as well as alfalfa, its chief host.

Allegheny Spruce Beetle*, *Dendroctonus punctatus* LeConte. A bark beetle.

Ambrosia Beetles, Xyleborus, Platypus, and other genera. Small, cylindrical, brown to black insects resembling bark beetles, making pinholes in dead wood, occasionally in weakened or dying fruit and shade trees, including avocado. The beetles live on fungi cultured in their tunnels.

American Aspen Beetle*, *Gonioctena americana* (Schaeffer). A leaf beetle.

Apple Twig Beetle*, *Hypothenemus obscurus* (Fabricius). A bark beetle, boring in dying apple bark or dead twigs.

Argus Tortoise Beetle*, *Chelymorpha cassidea* (Fabricius). A tortoise-shaped, yellow to bright-red beetle with black spots, very convex, ⅓ inch long, with long marginal spines holding a mass of excrement. This species is present throughout the East and as far west as New Mexico, feeding on morning-glory, moonflower, sweetpotato, and related plants. Spray or dust with malathion.

Arizona Five-spined Ips, *Ips lecontei*. Destroying ponderosa pine in Arizona.

Arizona Pine Beetle. See Southern Pine Beetle.

Ash Bark Beetle, *Leperisinus aculeatus* Say. Common wherever ash grows but attacking only weakened and dying trees. The beetle is very small, dark brown, with tan scales. The **Whitebanded Ash Bark**

Beetle, *L. fasciatus* (LeConte), also small, is black with white markings.

Ashgray Blister Beetle*, *Epicauta fabricii* (LeConte). A common eastern species but abundant as far west as Arizona and New Mexico. Destructive to forest and forage crops and to young trees in nurseries; reported defoliating small honeylocust trees in Virginia. The larvae feed on grasshopper eggs. See Black Blister Beetle for life history and control.

Asiatic Beetle. See Oriental Beetle.

Asiatic Garden Beetle*, *Maladera castanea* (Arrow). Native of the Orient, first found in New Jersey in 1921 and now serious along the Atlantic seaboard from Massachusetts through South Carolina, also present in Ohio and West Virginia. Apparently this beetle does not survive in regions of low summer rainfall. It resembles the Japanese beetle in shape and size but it is a uniform cinnamon-brown and comes out to feed *only at night.*

It is attracted to lights, bangs into screens, flies into automobiles. About 80 plants are attacked including: flowers, aster, azalea, chrysanthemum, dahlia, delphinium, rose, strawflower, sunflower, viburnum, zinnia; vegetables, beet, carrot, corn, eggplant, kohlrabi, parsnip, pepper, and turnip; fruits, cherry, peach, and strawberry. The beetles strip the foliage, especially that near the ground, sometimes severely damaging nursery seedlings of pine, hemlock, yew, barberry, and others. The larvae cut grass roots by their feeding, causing brown patches in lawns, and may feed on roots of many garden plants.

There is only 1 generation a year. Eggs are laid in the soil, at depths to 4 inches, from mid-July to mid-August. They hatch in about 10 days and the grubs start feeding on roots. In mid-October they move down several more inches in the soil for the winter, becoming active again, in the top 5 inches, in mid-April. The grubs pupate in June and the adults emerge in about 10 days, being most abundant between mid-July and mid-August. Full-grown larvae are grayish with light-brown heads, ¾ inch long, found in a curved position. They differ from Japanese beetle grubs chiefly in having the spines at the tip of the abdomen arranged in a semicircle rather than a V.

Control. Grubproof lawns, as for Japanese beetles, with chlordane, applied spring or fall. The bacterial milky disease has some effect on this species as well as on Japanese-beetle grubs. Spray foliage with carbaryl (Sevin).

Asparagus Beetle*, *Crioceris asparagi* (Linnaeus). Introduced from Europe about 1856 and now present in most asparagus regions. The beetles are slender, ¼ inch long, metallic blue-black with 3 yellow squares along each wing cover; reddish margins, prothorax, and head (Plate IV). Adults winter in protected places around the garden, feed on asparagus shoots when they come up in spring, and lay dark-brown eggs attached at one end. These hatch into olive-green or dark-gray, soft, wrinkled larvae with black heads, ½ inch long, which gnaw stems and leaves for 10 to 12 days. Asparagus can be defoliated and is often stained by a dark fluid. The larvae pupate in cells in the soil. The life cycle takes 3 to 8 weeks and there are at least 2 generations in the North, 3 or more in the South.

Control. Use rotenone, malathion, or carbaryl during the cutting season. Spray brush with carbaryl in late summer or early fall to keep beetles from overwintering. Lady-beetle larvae and predaceous plant bugs keep this beetle in bounds; a chalcid wasp is a parasite. See also Spotted Asparagus Beetle.

Aspen Leaf Beetle*, *Chrysomela crotchi* Brown. On cottonwood.

Bamboo Powderpost Beetle*, *Dinoderus minutus* (Fabricius).

Banded Cucumber Beetle*, *Diabrotica balteata* LeConte. A southern pest, from South Carolina around to California, primarily on beans, also on soybeans, and not so important on cucumbers. The adult is light green with 3 bands of darker green.

BARK BEETLES. Members of the family Scolytidae, small cylindrical beetles, usually brown or black, with the head partially concealed from above, a spine or projection at the apex of the front tibia, clubbed antennae, working under the bark of living or dead trees. The female excavates a gallery for egglaying and the larvae tunnel away from this brood gallery, thus making engravings on the wood under the bark. Some species, mostly in the genus Ips, are called engraver beetles. Many species are in the genus Dendroctonus and there has been some confusion in names, some now being reduced to synonymy.

Bark beetles are very important in forestry. They take one-fourth of all the timber harvested each year and are responsible for 90 per cent of the insect-caused mortality of saw timber in the United States. They are also important as disease-vectors, the European and native elm bark beetles transmitting the fungus causing Dutch elm disease.

Methoxychlor is not as effective as DDT for bark-beetle control on living trees but it must now be substituted. Synthetic sex attractants are used to trap some bark beetles and treating felled trees with cacodylic acid serves both to attract and kill the beetles, thus saving the timber. Woodpeckers, mites, predaceous beetles, parasitic wasps, bacteria, and fungi all help in biological control.

Bean Leaf Beetle*, *Cerotoma trifurcata* (Forster). Abundant in southeastern states, occasional elsewhere. The beetle is yellow buff to dull red, ¼ inch long, with 3 or 4 spots on the inner edge of wing covers and a black band near outer margins. The adults chew holes in leaves, feeding from the underside, but slender white larvae feed on roots and nodules, chewing stems under the soil line, sometimes gir-dling them. There are 1 to 2 broods a year on beans, peas, cowpeas, soybeans, and various weeds. See Mexican Bean Beetle for control.

Beet Leaf Beetle*, *Erynephala puncticollis* (Say). A western pest now extending east to the Atlantic States, injuring table and sugar beets, spinach, clovers, and other legumes. The adult is ⅓ inch long, dull yellow with black margins and black spots on the thorax. The grayish or olive-brown larvae are marked with raised tubercles and yellow spots resembling those of lady beetles. Both larvae and adults feed on foliage, with the former more injurious. Destroying weed hosts and cleaning up winter shelters may be sufficient control.

Birch Bark Beetle*, *Dryocoetes betulae* Hopkins. Breeding in beech, wild cherry, and red gum as well as birch, with irregular egg galleries.

Blackbellied Clerid*, *Enocleris lecontei* (Wolcott). One of the checkered beetle predators of bark beetles.

Black Blister Beetle*, *Epicauta pennsylvanica* (De Geer). An all-black species common in the East. A special pest of asters and Jap-

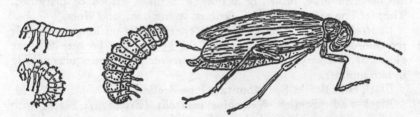

20. Black blister beetle: triungulin, instars 2 and 6, and adult.

anese anemone in late summer but also feeding on flowers and foliage of calendula, chrysanthemum, gladiolus, clematis, dahlia, dianthus, delphinium, ivy, phlox, zinnia; and may be abundant on corn. This species is typical of all blister beetles. They are rather long, ½ to ¾ inch, slender, with the prothorax narrower than the soft and flexible wing covers. The name comes from the cantharidin in their bodies; this will blister the skin if beetles are crushed upon it. This powerful agent, obtained from the "Spanish Fly," a European blister beetle, was formerly used in much the same fashion as a mustard plaster and also as an aphrodisiac. Cantharidin still has a few uses in modern medicine and animal breeding.

Other names for blister beetles are Old-fashioned Potato Bug and

Yankee Bug. Their life history is peculiar, to say the least. They differ from most beetles by being predaceous, and therefore helpful, in the larval state, but plant-eating as adults. The beetle winters as a partly transformed larva, pseudopupa, in a cell in the soil. More than one winter may be spent in this suspended state, but some spring the pseudopupa molts, acquires functional legs, moves about for a while, then goes into the true pupal state, which lasts about 2 weeks. The beetles appear in swarms in June or July or later and feed gregariously. The females lay yellow eggs in clusters of about 100 in holes in the soil. In 10 to 21 days active, strong-jawed larvae start burrowing through the soil until they find the egg mass of a grasshopper. They gnaw into the egg pod and eat the eggs. The larvae molt 4 times, going through a series of changes in form. The first larval stage is called a triungulin and the active triungulins specialize in eating eggs of the two-striped and differential grasshoppers. Some ascend to flowers and may be carried thence by bees to their nests. When the triungulin sheds its skin after the first molt, it looks more like a grub. After the last molt the larva burrows into the soil to form the cell in which it turns into the hard-shelled, immobile pseudopupa.

There are about 250 species of blister beetles in this country. They are black or gray, brown or yellow, sometimes striped or margined. They feed on many vegetables, flowers, young trees, and vines.

Control. DDT, the most effective chemical, is no longer allowed; try chlordane or cryolite. Handpick the beetles, but be sure to wear gloves. If necessary, cover valuable ornamentals with mosquito netting in late summer.

Black Hills Beetle. See Mountain Pine Beetle.

Black Lady Beetle*, *Rhizobius ventralis* (Erichson). Black, with reddish abdomen, ⅛ inch long, found in egg masses of mealybugs and under shells of scales. Introduced from Australia in 1892; a valuable destroyer of black scale.

Blacklegged Tortoise Beetle*, *Jonthonota nigripes* (Olivier). Golden yellow with 3 black dots arranged in a triangle on each wing cover. Larvae are straw yellow with 2 dark spots behind the head (Plate XI). See Tortoise Beetles.

Black Turpentine Beetle*, *Dendroctonus terebrans* (Olivier). An eastern bark beetle working near the base of pine and spruce, especially on pitch pine. In some areas 10 to 25 per cent of trees are killed in a year. Very broad (½ to 1 inch) egg galleries extend downward from entrance holes a few inches to several feet. Beetles are ⅕ to ⅜ inch long, robust, reddish brown to black. The larvae have prominent spines on 8th and 9th abdominal segments. Salvage attacked trees as soon as possible. See Bark Beetles.

Blueberry Case Beetle*, *Chlamisus cribripennis* (LeConte). A leaf beetle, with larvae crawling around dragging a case of their own excrement.

Blueberry Flea Beetle*, *Altica sylvia* Malloch. Reported as causing heavy damage in Maine. See also Flea Beetles.

Bumble Flower Beetle*, *Euphoria inda* (Linnaeus). An eastern species ranging west into New Mexico. The adult resembles a bumblebee, is ½ inch long, broadly oval, yellowish brown mottled with black. It feeds on ears of ripening corn, sometimes on apples, grapes, and peaches. Larvae develop in dung and rotting fruit, which should be cleaned up.

Cabbage Flea Beetle, *Phyllotreta cruciferae* (Goeze). An introduced beetle recorded on cabbage in Delaware and Wisconsin.

California Fivespined Ips*, *Ips confusus* (LeConte). Small engraver beetle on pines.

Caragana Blister Beetle*, *Epicauta subglabra* (Fall). Defoliating caragana stock in nurseries. See also Black Blister Beetle.

Carrot Beetle*, *Bothynus gibbosus* (De Geer). Occuring over most of the country except for southern states. The beetles, ½ inch long, broad, reddish brown with stout legs, gouge out roots and base of stems of amaranthus, carrot, beet, celery, corn, cotton, dahlia, elm, Japanese iris, lily, oak, parsnip, potato, sunflower, and weeds. The nocturnal adults winter in the soil, laying eggs there in spring. The larvae, bluish white, curved, with brown heads, feed on roots of grasses and other plants. There is only one generation. Clean up decaying plant material. Use chlordane dust in soil for grubs, 4 pounds of 6 per cent dust to each 1,000 square feet, and work it into the top 3 inches.

Cedar Bark Beetle, *Phloeosinus cupressi* Hopkins. Cypress Bark Beetle. Mining inner bark and girdling twigs of weakened Monterey and other cypresses and oriental and incense cedar, and redcedar. Another species, *P. dentatus* (Say), injures western juniper, Alaska cedar, and redcedar, making larval galleries at right angles to egg galleries. The **Western Cedar Bark Beetle***, *P. punctatus* LeConte, infests normal, injured, and dead cedars and giant arborvitae in the Pacific Northwest.

Cereal Leaf Beetle*, *Oulema melanopa* (Linnaeus). A European pest, very destructive, reported first from Michigan in 1962 and now present in Wisconsin, Illinois, Indiana, Ohio, Kentucky, New York, Pennsylvania, Maryland, Virginia, and West Virginia. Known areas are under quarantine and everyone is asked to watch for this beetle, which has caused 50 per cent loss in Europe. The adult is ¼ inch long, with black head, reddish brown midsection, and metallic blue back. The larvae, dark brown, shaped like potato bugs, pupate in the soil. This beetle feeds heavily on corn and grains. It is forbidden to move from quarantined areas grains, grass, hay, or straw fodder. Early planting may help in preventing injury and malathion may help in control. Some parasites have been released in infested areas.

Charcoal Beetle*, *Melanophila consputa* LeConte. One of the metallic wood borers.

Cherry Leaf Beetle*, *Pyrrhalta cavicollis* (LeConte). Present in the East in large numbers at intervals of several years. Adults are small red beetles, less than ¼ inch long, feeding on foliage of cherry and peach, sometimes plum, occasionally apple. Brown larvae with yellow and black spots feed only on wild cherry. There is only one generation a year and attacks are so sudden that protective sprays are usually too late.

Chinese Rose Beetle*, *Adoretus sinicus* Burmeister. A Hawaiian pest, frequently intercepted in shipments destined for California; in flowers, including orchids, in stems, and plant cuttings. One of the scarab beetles.

Claycolored Leaf Beetle*, *Anomoea laticlavia* (Forster). One of the chrysomelid beetles, reported on pine, locust, and other trees.

Clematis Blister Beetle*, *Epicauta cinerea* (Forster). Gray, with a yellowish tinge, found on clematis, sometimes aster, verbena, and other ornamentals and on potatoes. See also Black Blister Beetle.

Colorado Cabbage Flea Beetle, *Phyllotreta albionica* (LeConte). Small, black, with a slight brassy luster, infesting cabbage and other crucifers, also beet, from New Mexico into California.

Colorado Pine Beetle. See Mexican Pine Beetle.

Colorado Potato Beetle*, *Leptinotarsa decemlineata* (Say). An example of a native insect which suddenly became dangerous to cultivated plants (Plate IV). For many years this beetle lived on the sandbur weed on high plateaus at the base of the Rocky Mountains. It was described in 1824 and had probably been around as an obscure beetle for a long time. But the pioneer settlers of the West brought with them the potato, which the beetle found much to its taste. In a short time this almost unknown insect became, under the title of "potato bug," the best-known insect in America. It migrated eastward at the rate of about 85 miles a year, following potato plantings, appearing in Nebraska in 1859, Illinois in 1864, Ohio in 1869, reaching the Atlantic coast by 1874. Eventually it made its way to Europe, where it is well established in France, Holland, Belgium, Spain, parts of Italy, and in other countries. It appeared in England but was eradicated there. It is now a problem throughout the United States except in parts of Florida, Nevada, and California.

The Colorado potato beetle is hard-shelled, very broad (⅜ by ¼

inch), very convex, yellow with 10 longitudinal lines on the elytra
and black spots on the thorax. It winters as an adult in the ground,
emerging as soon as potatoes are up to deposit bright orange-yellow
eggs in small clusters on undersurface of leaves. These hatch in 4 to
7 days into very humpbacked, fat red grubs which feed for 2 or 3
weeks, then pupate in the ground. Beetles emerge in another week or
two to lay eggs for the second generation. Adults appear early in autumn to feed for a time, then to enter the soil for hibernation. In the
South, there may be 3 generations, in the extreme North, only 1. Both
beetles and larvae completely ravage potato foliage, often destroying
whole fields. Although potato is preferred, the beetles may go to other
members of the nightshade family, such as eggplant, tomato, pepper,
petunia, nicotiana, groundcherry.

Control. Handpicking was the first control measure tried, and most
farm boys a century or more ago had to pick their quota of potato
bugs. Paris green was the first poison, developed in 1865 specifically
for this pest. This was followed by London purple, calcium or lead
arsenate, and sometimes cryolite. DDT marked a great advance in
control but is now banned. Home gardeners may dust with Sevin,
starting when the beetles first appear and repeating every 10 days to
harvest. Farmers may use Guthion, Thiodan, or Phosphamidon.

Columbian Timber Beetle*, *Corthylus columbianus* Hopkins. One
of the ambrosia beetles, boring in the bark of living hardwoods, including red and silver maples. A stain, produced by the fungi on
which the beetles feed, extends 3 to 6 inches above and below each
egg gallery.

Convergent Lady Beetle. See under Lady Beetles.

Corn Flea Beetle*, *Chaetocnema pulicaria* Melsheimer. A small,
brassy beetle, more dangerous for its ability to disseminate bacterial
wilt of corn (Stewart's disease) than for its feeding on corn foliage,
which results in small perforations. The beetles inoculate the corn
with bacteria which have overwintered in their alimentary tracts. Control with carbaryl (Sevin) or malathion.

Corn Sap Beetle*, *Carpophilus dimidiatus* (Fabricius). A very
small, brown scavenger beetle that eats corn kernels, getting into the
ear when the husk is loosened by birds, or following after earworms.
It is also a pest of dates and other dried fruit. Spray corn with malathion 6 days after silks appear and repeat 10 days later.

Corn Silk Beetle*, *Calomicrus brunneus* (Crotch). A chrysomelid
(leaf beetle) feeding on corn silks.

Cottonwood Leaf Beetle*, *Chrysomela scripta* Fabricius. Occurring
from coast to coast, often more injurious to willows than to cottonwood and other poplars. The beetle, ¼ inch long, has black head and

thorax, the latter bordered with orange red, and gold wing covers with a purplish line at the inner edge, each bearing 7 purple-black spots. The larvae are black when young, later dirty yellow, with black legs, brown heads. They emit drops of pungent milky fluid when disturbed. They skeletonize leaves and may partially defoliate trees, especially in the West. Basket willows are particularly subject to attack. The pupae hang downward from the trees. Spray with carbaryl or malathion.

Similar species on poplar and willow are *Chrysomela knabi* Brown and *C. lineatopunctata* Forster. See also Aspen Leaf Beetle.

Cranberry Beetle, *Lichnanthe vulpina* (Hentz). One of several beetle grubs working on cranberry roots, this species causes a serious annual crop reduction in Massachusetts. Grubs have been killed by treating bogs with dieldrin after harvest; Sevin might be used.

Cuban May Beetle, *Phyllophaga bruneri* Chapin. A scarab beetle from Cuba, first found in Florida in 1959 and now common on 22 species of host plants in the vicinity of Miami. A survey in 1969 showed no northward movement beyond the city and the southernmost infestation was at Homestead. The adults are smaller than most May beetles, under ½ inch; light golden tan with a slight metallic luster; antennae with 9 segments (other Phyllophaga species in the U.S. have 10-segmented antennae; strictly nocturnal. The larvae are C-shaped white grubs feeding on roots of grasses, especially St. Augustine grass. Preferred host of the adult is Florida trema (*Trema micrantha*). It also infests satinwood and mahogany, two other Florida natives, and shaving-brush tree, pecan, bauhinia, golden shower, senna, royal poinciana, coral bean, madre, Chinese hibiscus, Spanish lime, and sapote.

Darkling Beetles. Black or brown nocturnal beetles, common in the West, acting as scavengers, but sometimes becoming serious pests. The **Small Darkling Ground Beetle,** *Metoponium abnorme* (LeConte), is smooth, black or dark brown, ⅓ inch long, with legs slightly reddish. It may injure grapevine buds, bark of young citrus trees, fruit of strawberries and tomatoes. Another species, *Coniontis subpubescens* LeConte, shining black and brown, ⅓ inch long, flies into sugar-beet fields and sometimes attacks young avocado.

Dendrobium Beetle, *Xylosandrus compactus* (Eichh.). A small, dark brown beetle, about ⅟₁₈ inch long, one of the most abundant bark beetles in tropical Florida. It bores into the canes of Dendrobium orchids and attacks pseudobulbs of Cattleya species. Plants have small shot-holes surrounded by yellowish areas and a rot may follow the attack on Cattleya. The food of both larvae and adults consists of the ambrosia fungi grown on walls of the galleries. The beetle may infest a number of other hosts beside orchids. Spray with diazinon or lindane.

Desert Corn Flea Beetle*, *Chaetocnema ectypa* Horn. Very small, metallic bronze, injuring corn, sorghum, small grains in the arid Southwest, breeding on wild grasses. The adults feed on foliage, the grubs on roots.

Diabrotica Beetles. The name popularly given to spotted species of cucumber beetles when they infest flowers in the garden. See Spotted Cucumber Beetle and Western Spotted Cucumber Beetle.

Douglas Fir Beetle*, *Dendroctonus pseudotsugae* Hopkins. The most important bark beetle enemy of Douglas-fir, also attacking western larch and big-cone spruce. The small, reddish to dark-brown beetle, ⅕ inch long, covered with hairs, usually works in injured or dying trees but may feed on healthy specimens. Keep trees growing vigorously; cut down seriously weakened trees. In forests, fire-injured timber should be salvaged rapidly to avoid build-up of beetle populations.

Douglas Fir Engraver*, *Scolytus unispinosus* LeConte. Present in the West on weakened Douglas-fir and big-cone spruce. This beetle is very small, shiny black, with a stout spine.

Driedfruit Beetle*, *Carpophilus hemipterus* (Linnaeus). A small, broad, flat beetle, brown with pale spots, elytra shorter than body. This is one of the scavenger beetles, a special pest of dried fruit, figs, and dates, found on any fermenting tree fruit in orchards, distributing fig smut and other diseases, reported on orange blossoms. Found chiefly in warm climates—California and the Gulf States. Dusting with 5 per cent malathion helps to control the beetles, as does prompt collection of all fallen fruit and destruction of culls. Many beetles can be attracted to traps baited with fermenting fruit. Packages of dried fruits can be fumigated.

Dusky Sap Beetle*, *Carpophilus lugubris* Murray. In corn ears and tassels, sometimes damaging uninjured sweet corn but usually associated with damage by other insects.

Eastern Larch Beetle*, *Dendroctonus simplex* LeConte. A small, dark red to brown beetle infesting dying or injured living larches; no other host. The bark galleries are long, longitudinal, and slightly winding.

Eastern Hercules Beetle*, *Dynastes tityus* (Linnaeus). Unicorn Beetle. A large rhinoceros beetle, 2 to 2½ inches long, greenish gray mottled with black, the male with a horn extending forward over the head.

Eastern Spruce Beetle. See Spruce Beetle.

Eggplant Flea Beetle*, *Epitrix fuscula* Crotch. Very small, 1/16 inch, riddling foliage of eggplant. Spray with Sevin.

Elm Calligrapha*, *Calligrapha scalaris* (LeConte). Also known as Linden Leaf Beetle. The beautifully colored adults feed in elm, linden,

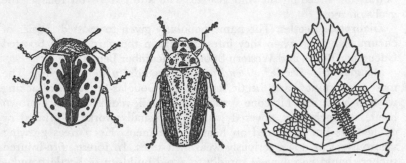

21. Elm calligrapha, left; elm leaf beetle, right.

alder, and willow. It is oval, convex, 3/8 inch long; head and thorax dark coppery green; wing covers yellowish with a pattern of 2 branched stripes down the inside and 11 green dots. The larvae are dirty white with yellow heads, humped like the Colorado potato beetle. Both larvae and adults feed on foliage. Spray with Sevin or arsenate of lead.

Elm Flea Beetle*, *Altica carinata* Germar. Very small, metallic blue or green; larvae and adults feeding on elm foliage in eastern states to Florida.

Elm Leaf Beetle*, *Pyrrhalta luteola* (Muller). A very serious elm pest, import from Europe, first found near Baltimore, Maryland, in 1838, apparently having arrived here some years before that. The beetle attacks American, English, Scotch, Chinese, and Camperdown elms but does not much bother slippery, rock, and winged elms. It is present throughout the United States, but some areas are more heavily infested than others.

The beetles are about 1/4 inch long, rather slender, yellow to olive-green with a dark line near the outer edge of each wing cover (Plate VI). As they grow older and get ready to hibernate, they darken so that the lines are scarcely visible. Hordes of sluggish beetles crawl into houses in late summer, often through cracks around cellar windows and doors. The elm leaf beetle is chiefly a pest in towns and cities where buildings offer dry winter hiding places.

The adults come out from attics and cellars in early spring, mate, and start eating small holes in elm leaves as they unfold. During late May and early June (in the vicinity of New York City) they lay clusters of lemon-shaped yellow eggs, 5 to 25 in a cluster, on under-side of leaves. The egglaying period may last several weeks, until 500 or more eggs have been deposited. These hatch in 5 or 6 days into ½-inch-long larvae. They are yellow but so striped and spotted with black that they appear dark. The larvae skeletonize the leaves, eating everything but veins and upper cuticle. Maturing in 15 to 20 days, each larva drops or crawls to the ground and transforms into a yellow pupa at the base of the tree. Beetles emerge in 6 to 10 days to lay eggs for a second generation. The number of generations depends on the season and locality. There are usually 2, sometimes 1 and a partial 2nd, or 2 and a partial 3rd. In California, where this beetle is a most important pest, there may be 3 or 4 generations.

Unsprayed trees are covered with brown leaves which look like lace or are completely defoliated by midsummer, becoming a terrible eyesore. Often the elms put out new leaves in late summer, a devitaliz-ing process. Complete defoliation for 3 consecutive years may result in death. Weakened trees are host to elm bark beetles carrying spores of the Dutch elm disease fungus, so neglect of the leaf beetle may have tragic results.

Control. DDT, which may no longer be used, was a very effective spray. The older lead arsenate, 4 pounds per 100 gallons of water, plus 1 pint of fish oil or other suitable sticker, is also effective but arsenicals are now frowned upon. Sevin is currently recommended, applied when the leaves are expanding and overwintering beetles are starting to feed, and again about 3 weeks later, when the eggs are hatching. If only 1 spray is possible it should be in late May or early June (in the New York area). Because Sevin may increase mite popu-lations it is well to include an acaricide in the spray mixture.

A fair amount of experimental work has been done with systemic insecticides applied to the soil or injected into the trunk of trees. Bidrin, which is very poisonous, and Meta-Systox-R, which is safer to handle, have controlled the beetle for several weeks when applied with a Mauget tree injector. Soil drenches of dimethoate and oxy-demetonmethyl (Meta-Systox-R) have also given control. There are many insect predators on the elm leaf beetle.

Elongate Flea Beetle*, *Systena elongata* (Fabricius). On sweet-potato.

Engelmann Spruce Beetle. See Spruce Beetle.

European Chafer*, *Amphimallon majalis* (Razoumowsky). A Eu-ropean beetle first noted in New York in 1940, now present in Massachusetts, Rhode Island, Connecticut, New Jersey, Pennsylvania, Ohio, and West Virginia, despite quarantines against it. This chafer causes a turf injury similar to that of Japanese beetles and it has a similar life history. The adult, a typical scarab, is light brown or tan, with dark bands at the inner edge of wing covers, oval, ½ inch long. It feeds on leaves of some trees at dusk but this injury is negligible. Chief damage is from grubs, which prefer grass roots but also feed on roots of chrysanthemum, strawberry, gladiolus, and evergreen seedlings. The grubs—C-shaped, white with brown head, ¾ inch long when grown—burrow below the frost line for winter, resuming feeding before pupation in spring. The beetles start emerging from soil in mid-June.

Control. Federal and state quarantines have restricted movements of plants, sod, soil, and other material that might harbor the beetles; but the federal quarantine was revoked in 1971. The beetles can fly up to 2 miles so peripheral spread from infested areas is to be expected. Turf can be treated with diazinon or chlordane as for Japanese beetle grubs.

European Ground Beetle, *Calosoma sycophanta* Linnaeus. Imported from Europe to aid in control of gypsy and browntail moths. It is a brilliant iridescent golden green with a dark-blue thorax, about 1¼ inches long. Adults hibernate in cells in the ground, emerging in late spring. Eggs are laid in the soil in June and July. The active larvae— elongate, dark, chitinized—run over the ground or climb trees in search of caterpillars or pupae. Do not destroy this beautiful friend.

European Potato Flea Beetle, *Psylliodes affinis* (Paykull). Found in 1968 in New York on bitter nightshade but sometimes damaging potatoes and other solanaceous crops in Europe. The beetle is small, light tan, and makes round holes in leaves; larvae attack roots.

European Spruce Beetle*, *Dendroctonus micans* (Kugelann).

Eyed Click Beetle*, *Alaus oculatus* (Linnaeus). A very large, shiny black beetle with 2 conspicuous eyelike spots on the thorax, some-times called the Owl Beetle. Like all click beetles, this can snap itself upright when placed on its back. The larval stage is a wireworm. The adult is carnivorous and is often found on trunks of old apple trees.

False Potato Beetle*, *Leptinotarsa juncta* (Germar). Plentiful on potatoes in Alabama; related to the Colorado potato beetle.

False Powder Post Beetle. See Branch and Twig Borer.

Fiery Hunter*, *Calosoma calidum* (Fabricius). A friend; a black ground beetle with 3 rows of large copper-colored pits in each wing cover. It is often seen searching for cutworms, potato beetle grubs, and other succulent larvae. It secretes a fiery, burning acid.

Fig Beetle, *Cotinis mutabilis* Gory and Percheron (*C. texana* Casey). Also called Green Fruit or Peach Beetle. A large, flat, broad beetle over 1 inch long, usually green, varying to copper and violet; a fruit pest in Arizona, New Mexico, and Texas. It prefers figs, peaches, and grapes but also feeds on apricot, apple, muskmelon, nectarine, pear, tomato, fruit of cacti, and has been reported on rose. The larvae breed in dung of old corrals, which should be thoroughly cleaned in late winter and early spring.

Fir Engraver*, *Scolytus ventralis* LeConte. On all true firs in the West, also Douglas-fir, Engelmann spruce, and mountain hemlock but especially destructive to white fir in California. Mature trees are infested, mostly in the upper part of the bole, by typical brownish bark beetles, ⅛ inch long. Narrow egg galleries extend across the grain.

FIREFLIES. Lightning Bugs or Glowworms, family Lampyridae, known for their luminescence at night. They are a delight to see and are equally delightful to gardeners for their predilection for slugs and snails, sometimes cutworms. Adults, larvae, and eggs are all luminous in some species. True nocturnal fireflies are found chiefly east of the Rockies. In the West the forms are of the glowworm type; the female is like the larva but emits light; the male has wings but is not phosphorescent.

Fireflies are soft-bodied beetles of medium size, with loose-fitting elytra and the prothorax expanded to cover the head. The light-producing organs are in the last 2 or 3 abdominal segments. According to Fabre, the contortions of the female which result in flashes of light are signals for the male. The light is produced by oxidation of a substance called luciferin in a heatless reaction. The flashing is regulated by controlling the supply of oxygen and each species has its own flashing rhythm.

FLEA BEETLES. A very large group of very small leaf beetles, family Chrysomelidae, named for their habit of jumping like fleas

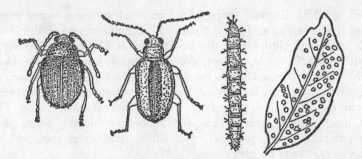

22. Potato flea beetle, left; pale-striped flea beetle, right, and leaf showing typical shot holes.

when disturbed. They usually feed on plants early in the season, often on seedlings set out from greenhouses, sometimes on ornamentals like forget-me-not, perforating foliage with tiny shot holes. The various species go under such names as corn, eggplant, grape, horseradish, mint, pale-striped, potato, sinuate-striped, spinach, strawberry, and sweetpotato flea beetles, some of which are treated separately in this section. Spray or dust with carbaryl (Sevin) or possibly endosulfan.

Some flea beetles have been released as beneficial insects to fight weeds. In Wisconsin flea beetles are used against Canada thistles and in Florida they help control alligator weed.

Fruittree Bark Beetle. See Shothole Borer, under Borers.

Fuller Rose Beetle*, *Pantomorus cervinus* (Boheman). A weevil, probably from South America, ⅓ inch long with a short, broad

23. Fuller rose beetle and feeding pattern on leaf.

snout, a white diagonal stripe across each wing cover, eating ragged areas from margins of leaves at night. A greenhouse pest in the North, it is numerous outdoors in the South and in California, feeding on abutilon, acacia, apple, apricot, avocado, azalea, bean, begonia, blackberry, camellia, canna, cape jasmine, carnation, chrysanthemum, cissus, citron, crapemyrtle, currant, deutzia, dracaena, fuchsia, gardenia, geranium, goldenglow, grapefruit, hibiscus, honeysuckle, lemon, lilies, oak, orange, palms, peach, pear, penstemon, persimmon, plum, plumbago, potato, prune, primrose, pyracantha, raspberry, rose, scabiosa, strawberry, tangerine, and vinca.

The larvae are white or yellowish legless grubs, with a brown head, feeding on roots of young citrus trees and other plants, causing the foliage to turn yellow. Pupation is in the soil and the wingless parthenogenetic females lay eggs in late summer in crevices of tree bark or under buttons of citrus fruit or at the base of plants.

Control. Formerly dusting with cryolite and applying a sticky band around young trees were the chief control measures. Now dusting with malathion or chlordane is easier and quite effective. For potted greenhouse plants, soil can be treated with dieldrin.

Giant Stag Beetle*, *Lucanus elaphus* Fabricius. A very large, dark scavenger beetle, 2 or more inches long, with mandibles, in the male, taking a third of this length and formed like antlers of a stag.

Golden Buprestid*, *Buprestis aurulenta* Linnaeus. Throughout western North America on injured, dying, and dead Douglas-fir, redcedar, spruces, pines, especially in the mountains. The beetle is ½ to ⅞ inch long, metallic, iridescent yellow to green or blue-green; edges of wing covers copper colored, with 4 ridges on each. The larva is a flatheaded borer, 1½ inches long. The life cycle is 2 to 4 or more years.

Golden Tortoise Beetle*, *Metriona bicolor* (Fabricius). A small, tortoise-shaped beetle, looking like a drop of burnished gold, sometimes called a gold bug. The larvae are dull brown, spiny, and carry their excrement and cast skins in a mass on their backs. They feed on morning-glory, sweetpotato, and bindweed. Spray or dust with malathion.

Goldsmith Beetle, *Cotalpa lanigera* (Linnaeus). Related to June beetles, feeding on leaves of aspen or cottonwood, willow, oak, and other hardwoods. The beetle is large, about 1 inch, lemon-yellow above, bronzed underneath, with gold head and thorax. The underside of the body is covered with white hairs. The larvae, resembling white grubs, feed at roots of rose, chrysanthemum, canna, sometimes young conifers. The life cycle takes 2 or 3 years.

Grape Bud Beetle, *Glyptoscelis squamulata* Crotch. Light gray, ¼ inch long, found on grape buds in California vineyards, usually at dusk in early spring. The larvae feed on grape roots. Canes may be smeared with tanglefoot for control.

Grape Colaspis*, *Colaspis brunnea* (Fabricius). The Clover Rootworm, distributed from eastern states into Arizona. The adults are very small, pale brown, elliptical beetles covered with rows of punctures. They are general feeders, making long, curved feeding marks, sometimes in a zigzag pattern, on apple, bean, cowpea, clover, dahlia, grape, melons, okra, potato, rose, or strawberry. In summer eggs are laid at roots of timothy, grape, clover, sometimes other plants; the larvae—small, fat, short-legged grubs—winter there. There is only 1 generation a year. Most severe injury occurs on corn planted in clover sod, larvae at the roots often causing wilting when plants are 6 to 10 inches high. Plow or spade in fall rather than spring; do not plant corn after clover.

Grape Flea Beetle*, *Altica chalybea* (Illiger). A small, metallic dark-blue beetle feeding on unfolding leaves of grape in spring. Light brown, black-spotted grubs also feed on buds and chew foliage ragged. Distributed through the eastern two-thirds of the country, the beetles also feed on apple, beech, elm, plum, quince, and Virginia-creeper. The adults hibernate near vineyards; the larvae pupate in soil. To control adults, spray or dust with Sevin as buds are swelling; repeat when shoots are 6 to 8 inches long to kill grubs.

Gray Willow Leaf Beetle*, *Pyrrhalta decora decora* (Say). Relative of elm leaf beetle, common on willows and poplars. The eastern form is pale, the western is dark.

Green June Beetle*, *Cotinis nitida* (Linnaeus). An eastern species related to the fig beetle of the Southwest, occurring east of the Mississippi and from Long Island south. The adult is rather flat, green with bronze or yellow margins, nearly an inch long and half as broad. The beetles feed on foliage of various trees and shrubs and many fruits—fig, peach, various berries, apple, apricot, nectarine, pear, plum, prune—sometimes on corn and other vegetables. The thick, dirty-white grubs feed on roots of grasses in lawns and golf courses and various ornamentals. The adults are around in July and August and lay eggs in decaying vegetable matter. Avoid piles of grass clippings or manure near lawn or orchard.

Green Rose Chafer*, *Dichelonyx backi* (Kirby). One of several greenish species feeding largely on conifers. This one is reported as causing heavy damage to Douglas-fir Christmas-tree stock in Montana.

GROUND BEETLES. Members of the family Carabidae; feeding chiefly on insects, sometimes on earthworms and snails. One or two

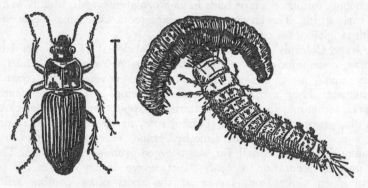

24. Ground beetle: adult and larva working on a caterpillar.

species may be injurious to plants—e.g., *Harpalus pennsylvanicus,* which may be abundant in soil around grapevines and may attack strawberries. By and large, however, ground beetles are decidedly worthwhile additions to the garden, and it ill behooves the gardener to step on one. Ground beetles are found most often lurking under stones; they do not fly but they can run very fast, and many climb trees in search of prey.

The shield-shaped elytra are hard, with fine longitudinal ridges and rows of punctures and are grown together down the back. A common native species, *Calosoma frigidum* (Fabricius), is black but some, like *C. scrutator* (Fabricius), are beautifully iridescent. See also European Ground Beetle and Fiery Hunter. All are large, with ferocious-looking jaws and a very definite indentation between thorax and elytra. Many secrete an offensive liquid for defense.

Ground beetles hibernate in the soil, some passing through 2 winters there, although the cycle is usually 1 year. Eggs are laid in soil. Larvae are flat, heavily chitinized, black and white, with sharp, projecting jaws and a pair of bristly appendages at the posterior end of the body. They are shy, less frequently seen than the adults, but equally predaceous. Ground beetles sometimes scurry into buildings in search of their prey, especially those with stone floors. DON'T STEP ON GROUND BEETLES; THEY ARE YOUR FRIENDS.

Hackberry Engraver*, *Scolytus muticus* Say. A bark beetle breeding in dying hackberry limbs; black, with long ashen hairs on the elytra. Clean up infested material.

Helenium Snout Beetle*, *Baris confinis* (LeConte). A very small, (to $\frac{3}{16}$ inch) black snout beetle, commonly found on growing tips of helenium (sneezeweed) in May and June, sometimes later in the season. White grubs with brown heads bore into stems, killing plants or preventing flowering. A weekly spray or dust of DDT gave control; Sevin may help now.

Hickory Bark Beetle*, *Scolytus quadrispinosus* Say. The most injurious pest of hickories, found from Quebec to Georgia, Mississippi, and Texas. Breeding normally in broken or weakened trees, the beetles will attack and kill healthy trees in epidemics, which may come after droughts. The beetle is small, $\frac{1}{8}$ to $\frac{1}{4}$ inch, dark brown, with 4 spines on abdomen of the male. The grub is white, legless, $\frac{1}{4}$ inch. The grubs mine in sapwood and inner bark, sometimes girdling trunk and branches. Adults bore into bases of leaf stems, terminal buds, or green nuts. Infested trees lose leaves early in summer; tops and branches may die back. The bark is covered with perforations, exit holes of the beetles.

Larvae hibernate in the bark, pupate in wood in spring. The

beetles, emerging in early summer, fly to living hickories, feeding on young twigs. The female bores through the bark to sapwood and makes her longitudinal egg galley, with eggs deposited in niches along the sides of the straight tunnel. Grubs burrow out at right angles. There is 1 generation a year in the North, often 2 in the South.

Control. Because injury is more severe in a dry summer, trees kept well watered are more resistant. Spraying with lead arsenate or Sevin or methoxychlor while beetles are feeding may give some control. It is helpful to cut and burn badly infested trees between October and May, while the larvae are in their burrows, in order to keep the beetles from invading other hickories, but burning is now outlawed in many areas. There are several hymenopterus parasites.

Hickory Saperda, *Saperda discoidea* Fabricius. In eastern and central states. The female is ¾ inch long with brownish wing covers, yellow hairs, and a crescent-shaped marking. The male is smaller, blackish, with 3 lines of gray hairs on the thorax. Large grubs bore in the sapwood of weakened hickories and butternut, often following bark beetles.

Hop Flea Beetle*, *Psylliodes punctulatus* Melsheimer. Small, elongate-oval, shining metallic black or dull green. On hops but also on beets, cabbage, cucumber, potato, radish, rhubarb, tomato, turnip, and watermelon. Feeding by adults injures young plants; larvae feed on roots.

Hoplia Beetles, *Hoplia oregona* LeConte, and other species. Grape-vine Hoplia. Robust scarab beetles, to ⅓ inch, reddish brown with dark head, silvery underside, a problem on the West Coast. The adults feed on blossoms, favoring white, of rose, lily, ceanothus, azalea, orange, peach, and grape and on tender grape foliage. The grubs, resembling Japanese-beetle larvae, feed on roots of roses and lawn grasses. There is only 1 generation. Lindane dust has given control; carbaryl may help.

Horned Passalus*, *Popilius disjunctus* (Illiger). Elongate-robust, black and shiny, with a forward-directed horn on the head. This is the eastern species; there are 2 more in Texas. Passalids are social insects, occurring in colonies in decaying logs but not a menace to healthy trees.

Horseradish Flea Beetle*, *Phyllotreta armoraciae* (Koch). Small, ⅛ inch long, black with a yellow stripe on the wing cover. It deposits eggs in clusters on leaf petioles and larvae burrow into petioles on hatching. It attacks mustard as well as horseradish.

Imbricated Snout Beetle*, *Epicaerus imbricatus* (Say). A brownish gray weevil about ½ inch long, with 2 pale zigzag lines across the wing covers, occurring over most of the United States. It is a general feeder on apple, blackberry, cabbage, cherry, clover, corn, cucumber, gooseberry, muskmelon, onion, pea, potato, raspberry, squash, sugar beet, and watermelon. It injures apples by eating out the buds or cutting off young fruit and leaves. Strawberries may be defoliated. Eggs are laid on foliage and larvae live in roots or stems of legumes and other field crops. Adults appear on apples in late May or June, feeding for about a month; there is 1 generation a year. A general fruit spray schedule should take care of this pest. The beetles can also be jarred from young trees onto a sheet laid underneath.

Imported Willow Leaf Beetle*, *Plagiodera versicolora* (Laicharteg). First recorded in this country in 1915 and now abundant in the Northeast from Washington, D.C., to Maine. It is common on weeping willow but all willows are attacked, the smooth-leaf types most severely, and Lombardy poplar occasionally. The shining metallic blue adult, ³⁄₁₆ inch long, resembles a flea beetle. The larvae are bluish-black, sluglike, with abdomen tapering toward the end. The beetles eat holes in leaves but the larvae rapidly skeletonize them, feeding from the underside. Adults hibernate under bark, emerge in late April or May to lay clusters of lemon-yellow eggs on underside of leaves. They hatch in 4 to 8 days, then the larvae feed for 2 weeks or so before pupating on the leaf. There may be 2 to 4 broods a season.

Control. Spray in late May with lead arsenate or Sevin. Repeat if necessary the first of July.

Iris Blister Beetle, *Lytta cyanipennis* (LeConte). Reported as damaging commercially grown iris in Idaho.

Japanese Beetle*, *Popillia japonica* Newman. A horrible example of an introduced pest which has cost untold millions for lack of a little money and prompt eradication measures when it was first discovered. It probably came from Japan as a grub in soil around plant roots prior to 1912, the year when earth balls around imported plants were prohibited. It was first noticed in 1916, in a nursery near Riverton, New Jersey. The next year it had covered 3 square miles with a half mile heavily infested; in 1918 the infested area was 48 square miles. Now the Japanese beetle has taken over nearly half the country. It is present in Alabama, Connecticut, Delaware, Georgia, Illinois, Indiana, Iowa, Kentucky, Maine, Maryland, Massachusetts, Michigan, Missouri, New Hampshire, New Jersey, New York, North Carolina, Ohio, Pennsylvania, Rhode Island, South Carolina, Tennessee, Vermont, Virginia, and West Virginia. It has been taken in traps near airfields in other areas. It became es-

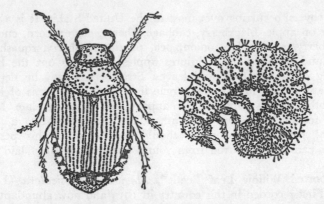

25. Japanese beetle: adult and grub.

tablished near Sacramento, California, in 1961 but eradication measures were immediately started.

Adult Japanese beetles feed on about 275 kinds of deciduous fruits, shade trees, shrubs, and garden flowers, but only a few vegetables— chiefly asparagus, corn, rhubarb, and soybeans. The beetles are exceedingly fond of Boston ivy and Virginia-creeper, birch, canna, chestnut, elm, hollyhock, horsechestnut, linden, kerria, mallow, marigold (African but not French), grape, peach, plum, quince, Japanese quince, rose, rose-of-Sharon, sassafras, turquoise vine, zinnia, to name a mere handful of ornamentals on which the beetles can be expected. They feed on apple and cherry but not as severely as on grape, raspberry, and peach, massing on ripening fruit as well as eating foliage. Evergreens are seldom ravaged and phlox, chrysanthemum, gladiolus, iris, and some other flowers are not favored. Lawns are often wrecked by grubs feeding on roots.

A Japanese beetle is a most beautiful insect, until you see it hanging in a cluster of 100 or so around a peach or over a rose bloom (Plate VIII). It is oval, just under ½ inch long, a gorgeous metallic green with coppery wing covers which are striated with fine longitudinal lines. There are 2 patches of white hairs at the tip of the abdomen and 5 tufts of white hairs projecting from under the wing covers on each side. The adult beetles feed from late June to late October (vicinity of New York) with peak abundance usually in July and a rather sharp falling off in numbers after Labor Day. They feed only in the daytime and are most active on warm, sunny days. Flowers are devoured and leaf tissue eaten between veins, so the foliage looks like lace. Succulent young foliage is preferred. The beetles are gregarious, a whole group demolishing one rose, sometimes in a very short time, before trying the next.

Each female lives from 30 to 45 days, lays 40 to 60 eggs, mostly under grass roots in lawns and golf courses. The grubs hatch in 10 to 12 days, feed on grass roots until cold weather, then move down 8 to 10 inches in the soil to avoid freezing. They move upward in spring, feed on grass roots again until pupation in the soil in late May. The grubs are grayish white with brown heads, ¾ to 1 inch long when full-grown, usually found in a curved position and distinguished from similar white grubs by a V-shaped row of spines on the underside of the last segment of the body. They chew off grass roots so that the turf can be rolled back like a carpet.

Control of Adults. In regions of serious beetle infestation, summer spraying or dusting is almost obligatory. Sevin has been even more effective than DDT and can be used at 1 pound 50 per cent wettable powder per 100 gallons or 1 tablespoon per gallon. Sevin is a broad-spectrum insecticide that may kill the beneficial insects keeping mites under control so be sure to add a miticide to the spray. Malathion is sometimes used with Sevin for beetle control but this is not a good miticide. For vegetables and fruits methoxychlor or rotenone sprays or dusts are possible; commercial growers may use parathion or other phosphate sprays.

Weekly treatment is necessary to protect rose foliage but nothing will keep beetles from feeding on flowers opening between sprays. Some confirmed rosarians cover the bloom with cellophane protectors or erect a frame over the plants. Most of us cut our best buds in the morning and enjoy them in the house during the peak beetle season. The finest roses bloom before and after the Japanese beetles are active, so they need be no deterrent to planting roses. In areas where the beetles have been present for many years they are much less devastating than in more recent infestations.

Some use beetle traps to reduce beetle hordes. Yellow seems the most effective color and they are baited with a mixture of geraniol and eugenol. Traps, however, attract more beetles than they catch and are not recommended near rose beds. Traps are more useful in checking areas of new infestation and in these synthetic sex attractants are used.

Control of Larvae. Lawns may be grubproofed with chlordane, 5 pounds of 5 per cent granules per 1,000 square feet or 4 ounces of 75 per cent emulsion in 25 gallons of water as a spray. Aldrin, heptachlor, and dieldrin have been used in eradication campaigns but with some harm to wildlife. Turf may be treated in either spring or fall.

Insect parasites have been brought from Asia; two Tiphia wasps have become established and are quite effective. The most promising natural control is a bacterial milky disease, disseminated by applying a spore-dust mixture made from inoculated grubs. This is available under trade names, such as *Doom* or *Japidemic,* and is applied at 3-to-5-foot intervals, about a teaspoon per dose. It takes about 3 years to effect much control and there must be a sufficient number of grubs in the soil for the bacteria to live on, but the results are good.

All plants leaving nurseries in beetle areas must be certified. Special control measures are taken around airports; planes departing in summer months are treated to avoid unwelcome hitchhikers. Once in a while a plane does transport a live beetle to uninfested areas, and undoubtedly private automobiles are responsible for some spread. There are many traps to check such infestations; eradicant measures are necessary immediately to prevent the beetle from getting established in yet another state.

Jeffrey Pine Beetle*, *Dendroctonus jeffreyi* Hopkins. Dark brown or black beetles, ⅓ inch long, in dying Jeffrey, sugar, and yellow pines in mountains along the Pacific Coast.

June Beetles. *Phyllaphaga* spp. Familiar large, reddish brown or black beetles, an inch or more long, also known as May Beetles, June Bugs, or Daw Bugs, and as White Grubs in the larval state. There are about 200 species, not to be distinguished by the layman, with similar life histories. They are distributed over the country, probably more serious in the Middle West and South than in the East. The life cycle takes from 1 to 4 years, with a 3-year cycle more common in the North. Adults appear in May, June, or July—earlier in the South—and fly at night, feeding on foliage of ash, birch, butternut, elm, hickory, poplar, oaks, tuliptree, willow, and other ornamentals. Most species prefer hardwoods, but some southern forms feed on pine and cypress and some infest roses. The beetles are attracted to lights and try to enter houses; during the day they remain hidden under grass or in debris. The females enter the soil for egglaying, depositing each egg in a separate ball of earth 1 to several inches below the surface of sod land. The eggs hatch in 2 or 3 weeks and the young grubs feed on roots and underground plant parts until fall, when they burrow downward. The next spring they move up to feed on roots of grass, corn, cereals, potatoes, and other crops. That autumn they again move down in the soil, coming up to feed for a short time in spring prior to forming a pupal cell in the soil. The adults are formed but stay in the cell until the next spring when they emerge to feed as beetles. Most grub damage comes the year after heavy beetle flights. The grubs look like Japanese beetle

grubs but are larger, ½ to 1½ inches, and the spines on the underside of the tip of the abdomen are in the pattern of an elongated
diamond.

Control. Valuable shade trees can be sprayed with Sevin during beetle years. Previous records in a locality show when to expect injury.
Lawns and golf courses can be treated as for Japanese beetles. Avoid
larval injury to roots by not planting susceptible crops like corn or
strawberries in land recently taken over from sod. Summer or fall plowing or spading kills some larvae and pupae, exposes others to birds.

Khapra Beetle*, *Trogoderma granarium* Everts. Not a garden pest
but an imported and important grain problem. A native of India,
this small, oval, brownish-black beetle, noted in stored grain in
California in 1953, spread to New Mexico and Arizona. It has apparently been eradicated but is frequently intercepted by quarantine officials checking on plant material, bagging, and cargo coming
from many countries. People should still be on the watch for yellow-
brown fuzzy larvae and cast skins.

Klamathweed Beetle*, *Chrysolina quadrigemina* (Rossie). One of
the leaf beetles. On July 12, 1948, at Fortuna, California, a monument
was unveiled to this Australian beetle. Since it was first released in
1946 it had cleared more than 100,000 acres of the Klamath weed, a
species of Hypericum poisonous to livestock, and replacing desirable
range plants. The beetle is still dispersing and continuing its useful
existence with the Klamath weed reduced to about 1 per cent of its
former abundance and the land returned to productive grazing. Land
values of rangeland have gone up and cattle have gained weight.

LADY BEETLES. Ladybird Beetles, Ladybugs, members of the
large family Coccinellidae, which means scarlet red. With the ex-
ception of one genus, containing the Mexican bean beetle and the
somewhat less infamous squash beetle, all members of this family are
beneficial, preying on aphids or scale insects or mealybugs in both
their larval and beetle states. In recent years they have had a hard
time staying alive because DDT and some other new insecticides
were as harmful to them as to injurious insects.

Lady beetles are small, ⅙ to ¼ inch long, red or sometimes tan
with black spots, or black with red spots. They are broadly oval
and can be distinguished from destructive leaf beetles by having
only 3 segments in the tarsus (foot). The larvae have flat, carrot-
shaped bodies, broad at the head end and tapering at the other,
with a rather warty back spotted with blue or orange on a grayish
black background. The eggs are usually orange and stand on end in
a cluster of a dozen or so. The pupae, exposed on the leaf, are
cemented to it by one end.

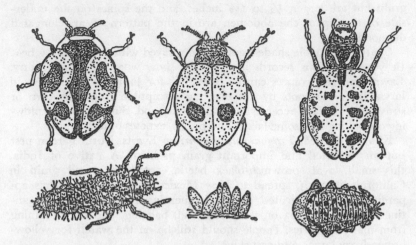

26. *Lady beetles: left to right, Vedalia, two-spotted, and convergent,
with detail of larva, eggs, pupa.*

The progeny and potential usefulness of a single female lady
beetle are enormous. Depending on her species, she may lay up to
1,500 eggs over a period of 2 months, although the normal period
is 1 month. The life cycle may take 12 days in warm weather, 20
to 35 days in cool weather. As full-grown larvae lady beetles average
about 25 aphids a day, and when they change to adults the daily
quota goes up to 50. But they may do more than that. A single
larva has been known to consume 90 adult and 3,000 larval scale
insects during its lifetime. In an average season the aphid population
may be reduced enough so that spraying is unnecessary, but in a
cool wet season the beetles reproduce less rapidly and the gardener
has to spray a bit.

The aphid-eating species of lady beetles require a lot of plant lice
around to maintain themselves. When the aphids are reduced too
far, most of the beetles starve to death, so the species gradually
disappears until a large aphid colony is built up again. Some lady
beetles feeding on scales and mealybugs can, however, survive when
they have reduced harmful insects to a minimum.

Vedalia*, the Australian Lady Beetle, *Rodolia cardinalis* (Mulsant), is one of these. This small beetle, ⅛ inch long, red with black
markings, represents the first successful use of an imported predator
to control an injurious insect, the classic example of biological control. The cottonycushion scale arrived in California from Australia
about 1868 on acacia. By the early eighties it had overrun citrus

orchards, killing hundreds of thousands of orange trees, threatening the entire citrus industry. So the United States Government and the State of California sent Albert Koebele to Australia to look up some native parasites. In the shipment home of collected parasites he also included a predator, Vedalia. There were only 29 specimens of this lady beetle in the first lot and only 514 all together. But Vedalia thrived and within 2 years had the scale under complete control. A trip which cost less than $5,000 saved millions for the citrus industry. Vedalia, as larva and as adult, feeds only on cottonycushion scale, but she manages to survive even when the scale is reduced to low numbers and comes out of her hiding place to check incipient outbreaks. The advent of DDT almost meant the end of Vedalia and a terrific upsurge of cottonycushion scale. But when the havoc was realized, spray schedules in California were revised, Vedalia was reintroduced into orchards and resumed her highly efficient operations.

Black Lady Beetle*, *Rhizobius ventralis* (Erichson). Small, shiny or velvety black, with reddish abdomen, found in egg masses of mealybugs or under shells of various scales. Introduced from Australia in 1892 and valuable as a destroyer of black scale in California.

Convergent Lady Beetle*, *Hippodamia convergens* Guérin-Méneville. The most common species in North America and the one sold by the gallon to farmers and home gardeners for aphid control. The adult has 12 small black spots on reddish wing covers and 2 convergent white lines on the thorax. The larvae are flat, velvety black or grayish with orange spots. This species hibernates in huge masses in western mountains and is collected there for distribution. Unfortunately, the beetles have an urge to migrate when released so that importing them by mail may benefit some garden other than your own.

Thirteenspotted Lady Beetle*, *Hippodamia tredecimpunctata tibialis* (Say).

Transverse Lady Beetle*, *Coccinella transversoguttata* Falderman. Very convex, plain red or with 3 long transverse black spots; common through most of North America.

Twicestabbed Lady Beetle*, *Chilocorus stigma* (Say). Black with 2 red spots, dining on scale insects. The female hides her eggs under the scale shell or in bark crevices; the larvae are grayish with black spines. The adults hibernate under bark or in other protected places in trees.

Twospotted Lady Beetle*, *Adalia bipunctata* (Linnaeus). Very common in eastern gardens and sometimes winters in houses. It has red elytra with 2 round black spots. I find it hunting for aphids on rose canes as early as spring pruning.

Another Australian lady beetle, the **Mealybug Destroyer***, *Cryp-*

tolaemus montrouzieri Mulsant, eats itself out of business. This blackish, hairy beetle with reddish thorax and wing-cover tips was introduced into California to prey on mealybugs infesting citrus. A way was found to keep it alive by maintaining colonies on potato sprouts in insectaries. Millions have been produced and released in citrus areas but the beetle is being somewhat replaced by internal parasites.

Some very small lady beetles, *Stethorus* spp., feed on spider mites. They lay small, oval, cream-colored eggs among mite colonies on underside of leaves. The larvae are hairy, brownish with black markings; the adults are black. The genus *Scymnus* contains many species of small black, brown, mottled, or spotted beetles that feed on mealybugs, scale insects, aphids, and red spiders. The larvae are usually covered with wax and may be mistaken for mealybugs.

There are a great many more helpful lady beetles but space does not permit their enumeration and description.

Larger Elm Leaf Beetle*, *Monocesta coryli* (Say). A large, yellowish beetle with 9 blue-black patches. It appears occasionally in large numbers on slippery or red elm, sometimes on American elm, and it is known to feed on dogwood, hazel, and hawthorn. First described from Illinois, in 1824, it has since been a pest in Arkansas, Florida, Kansas, Maryland, Mississippi, Missouri, North Carolina, Pennsylvania, Virginia, and West Virginia. It appears suddenly in a locality, does a great deal of damage in a small area, completely defoliating trees for a year or so, and then disappears for an indefinite period. The yellow to orange larvae feed in groups. They hibernate in soil, pupate in spring, with adults appearing in late May. Owing to the sporadic nature of outbreaks, control measures are not often attempted.

Lined Click Beetle*, *Agriotes lineatus* (Linnaeus). See Click Beetles.

Lion Beetle*, *Ulochaetes leoninus* LeConte. Large, black, tipped with yellow and resembling a bumble bee; breeding in pines, fir, hemlock in mountains in the West.

Lodgepole Cone Beetle*, *Conophthorus contortae* Hopkins. Adults and larvae bore in small, immature pinecones, causing them to wither and die, with masses of resin on the stem. Almost all pines are attacked by various species of Conophthorus.

Lodgepole Pine Beetle*, *Dendroctonus murrayanae* Hopkins. A black bark beetle, with reddish wing covers, infesting healthy trees, entering near the base and excavating long egg galleries with pitch tubes at the entrance holes. Mostly on lodgepole pine but recorded on Engelmann spruce.

Margined Blister Beetle*, *Epicauta pestifera* Werner. Black with a

BEETLES   135

narrow gray or yellow margin around the wing covers; may be
abundant on various ornamentals. See Black Blister Beetle for life
history and control.

May Beetles. See June Beetles.

Mexican Bean Beetle*, *Epilachna varivestis* Mulsant. Doubtless
the worst enemy of eastern home vegetable gardens (Plate IX).
Like the Colorado potato beetle, this is an example of an insect
long present suddenly assuming great importance. Probably originally
from Mexico, the beetle has been known in the Southwest since
about 1850, but it did not become really dangerous until it reached
Alabama about 1920. Since then it has spread to all of the states
east of the Mississippi. This gangster member of the ordinarily
beneficial lady-beetle family has the typical convex shape but is
somewhat larger, up to ⅓ inch, and is coppery yellow with 16
black dots, 8 on each wing cover. It infests all kinds of garden
beans and cowpeas. It likes lima beans particularly but does not
care much for soybeans, although it will attack them. Larvae and
adults feed on pods and stems as well as foliage.

Mexican bean beetles winter as adults in rubbish or weeds, appearing in bean fields late in March in the South, June in New York.
After feeding for a week or two, the females lay groups of orange-
yellow eggs on underside of leaves. These hatch in 5 to 14 days.
Soft yellow larvae, ⅓ inch long and half as wide, with black-
tipped spines on the back, skeletonize the leaves, always working
from underneath and eating out very regular areas in a lacy pattern.
When full grown, the larvae cement their hind ends to an uninjured
leaf and the pupae push out of crushed larval skins, adults emerging in 10 days or less. A complete cycle takes about a month. Near
New York City there are usually 2 generations, farther north 1 and a
partial 2nd, farther south, 3 or 4.

Control. In home gardens spray or dust with rotenone, methoxychlor, carbaryl (Sevin), or malathion. Commercial growers may use
less safe phosphate sprays. Be sure to cover underside of foliage and
treat at first sign of injury; repeat 10 days later. Time of planting is
one means of control. Near New York City snap beans planted in
early June will mature in July between beetle broods. Discourage
hibernating beetles by cleaning up all plant debris after harvest.
Some bean varieties are rather resistant to this beetle.

Mexican Pine Beetle*, *Dendroctonus parallelocollis* Chapius. Also
known as Larger Mexican Pine Beetle and Colorado Pine Beetle.
Roundheaded, shining reddish-brown, ⅓ inch long. On pines in
the Southwest, attacking injured trees and preventing recovery.

Mint Flea Beetle, *Longitarus waterhousei* Kutsch. Reported as active in untreated mint fields in Oregon; roots may be damaged as well as foliage.

Monterey Pine Cone Beetle*, *Conophthorus radiatae* Hopkins. Small, infesting cones of Monterey pine.

Monterey Pine Engraver, *Ips mexicanus* (Hopkins). Small bark beetle attacking weakened Monterey pine in California, working from the crown downward.

Mottled Tortoise Beetle*, *Deloyala guttata* (Olivier). Golden around the margins of the elytra, the rest mottled black and yellow. The larvae are dull green, bluish along the back, covered with broad, branching masses of excrement. On sweetpotato and morning-glory.

Mountain Pine Beetle*, *Dendroctonus ponderosae* Hopkins. Under the name of Black Hills Beetle this is the worst enemy of ponderosa pine in the Rocky Mountain region, attacking other pines when epidemic. As the Mountain Pine Beetle this is a very serious pest of pines in the Northwest, attacking lodgepole as well as ponderosa and other pines. Although normally infesting only weakened trees in epidemics, it kills trees of all sizes and conditions. The beetle varies from brown to black, is ¼ inch long. Egg galleries are longitudinal and straight; the larval mines are either short and broad or long and at right angles to the egg galleries. See also Bark Beetles.

Native Elm Bark Beetle*, *Hylurgopinus rufipes* (Eichoff). Widely distributed throughout the eastern states on elms and basswood. It is chiefly important because, along with the smaller European elm bark beetle, it may spread the Dutch elm disease fungus. This is a small, brownish black beetle, ⅒ inch long, not so shiny as its European cousin. It works under the bark, making its egg gallery transversely across the wood with larval tunnels coming out at right angles. There are 1 or more generations a year, with the winter passed either as larvae or adults. Often adults of this species emerge in the fall and burrow into the bark of living elm trees. See the Smaller European Elm Bark Beetle for control.

Northeastern Sawyer*, *Monochamus notatus* (Drury). Also called Pine Sawyer, common in northeastern states, attacking white spruce and various pines. The larvae usually burrow extensively in dead or dying trees but many injure apparently healthy trees. The large beetles, ½ to 1½ inches long, blackish with a white or gray pubescence, have very long legs and antennae, a prolonged and flattened head, and a spiny projection from each side of the thorax.

Northern Cedar Bark Beetle, *Phloeosinus canadensis* Swaine. Occurring in the Northeast, breeding mostly in northern white cedar and arborvitae. Twigs in ornamental hedges may break or wilt. The injury is unsightly but not serious.

Northern Masked Chafer*, *Cyclocephala borealis* Arrow. Another lawn pest, similar to white grubs. Damage to turf is frequently reported, from Maryland particularly, and the injury is often compounded by skunks going after the grubs. The **Southern Masked Chafer***, *C. immaculata* (Olivier), is its counterpart in South Carolina, Kansas, and other states.

Nuttall Blister Beetle*, *Lytta nuttalli* Say. A large (1 inch long or more) metallic green or purplish beetle, prevalent in the Rocky Mountains. It feeds on legumes and grasshopper eggs.

Obtuse Sawyer, *Monochamus obtusus* Casey. Brown beetle with gray markings, ½ to ¾ inch, larva 1 to 1½ inches, injuring pine, Douglas-fir, and fir in Pacific Coast States and Idaho.

Odd Beetle*, *Thylodrias contractus* Motschulsky. One of the scavenger dermestid beetles. This one is unusual in having the antennae filiform and the female wingless and larviform.

Olive Bark Beetle, *Leperisinus californicus* Swaine. A very small, robust beetle, black with whitish scales, with exit holes giving a "shot-hole" appearance to bark of olive trees. It prefers sickly trees but may work over into healthy trees. Prune off and burn infested twigs and branches; promote general vigor.

Oregon Fir Sawyer*, *Monochamus oregonensis* (LeConte). A stout black beetle, ½ to 1½ inches long, with gray markings, antennae twice as long as body, and a toothlike projection on each side of the thorax. The larvae, 1 to 1¾ inches, are destructive to scorched, injured, or dying Douglas-firs, true firs, and pines in the West.

Oriental Beetle*, *Anomala orientalis* Waterhouse. Also called Asiatic Beetle and a close relative of Asiatic garden and Japanese beetles. It was first discovered at New Haven, Connecticut, in 1920, is now present in New York, New Jersey, Rhode Island, Pennsylvania, and North Carolina, and has been intercepted in Florida in airplanes arriving from New England. Presumably a native of Japan, this beetle nearly destroyed sugarcane in Hawaii before a parasitic wasp was introduced from the Philippines.

Here on the mainland grasses are preferred host, but this species is also reported on ageratum, cyclamen, iris, hollyhock, phlox, rose, and beet, bean, onion, rhubarb, and strawberry.

Adults are straw-colored with varying dark markings. They emerge from the soil throughout July and August, are active day and night, but eat much less than Japanese and Asiatic garden beetles. Females deposit eggs singly 1 to 9 inches below soil surface and these hatch in 17 to 27 days. Larval feeding on grass roots continues to mid-

October when the grubs move down a foot or more for winter. Root injury starts again in late April with pupation in an earthen cell in early June. The grubs cannot be distinguished from Japanese beetle grubs except by the arrangement of spines in 2 parallel lines on the underside of the abdomen. Grubproof turf as for Japanese beetles.

Pacific Willow Leaf Beetle*, *Pyrrhalta decora carbo* (LeConte). A relative of the elm leaf beetle. It is dull yellow, brown, or black, with short pubescence, common on willows and poplars.

Palestriped Flea Beetle*, *Systena blanda* Melsheimer. Generally distributed, probably a native. The adult is ⅙ inch long, with a broad white stripe down the center of each pale to dark-brown wing cover. It perforates leaves of many different plants—alfalfa, bean, beet, clovers, corn, cotton, eggplant, grasses, lettuce, melon, parsnip, pea, peanut, pear, pumpkin, radish, sunflower, strawberry, turnip— and many weeds. The larvae, just over ¼ inch long, are slender, white, with light-brown heads. They feed on roots of many plants and on corn seed, causing failure to sprout or sickly plants. Spray for adults with carbaryl, methoxychlor, malathion, or rotenone. Keep down weeds; starve out larvae by early and late spading or plowing.

Peach Bark Beetle*, *Phloeotribus liminaris* (Harris). A native pest found in eastern states, attacking mainly peach, sometimes cherry. The small brownish beetle, similar to the shot-hole borer, only ¹⁄₁₀ inch long, winters as an adult in dead or dying wood or in special cells cut in the bark of a healthy tree. The egg gallery runs across the wood rather than lengthwise, as with most bark beetles. Keep trees vigorous by proper cultural methods. Destroy peach prunings and dying trees.

Peppergrass Beetle*, *Galeruca browni* Blake. One of the leaf beetles.

Pine Chafer*, *Anomala oblivia* Horn. Relative of the Oriental beetle. Adults may defoliate Scotch, loblolly, and other pines. Reported as quite damaging in Pennsylvania and North Carolina.

Pine Colaspis*, *Colaspis pini* Barber. Feeding on pines, sometimes spruce, cypress, deodar, in the South, being particularly abundant in Louisiana. It is a small beetle, ¹⁄₁₆ to ⅛ inch long, gregarious, feeding on green needles, often leaving them hanging by one edge with tips turning brown. Young pines may die. Spray or dust ornamental conifers with Sevin or lead arsenate.

Another species, *Colaspis favosa,* is reported damaging to many ornamentals in Florida—crapemyrtle, cuphea, ixora, waxmyrtle, punek tree, with severe injury to ixora.

Pine Engraver*, *Ips pini* (Say). Common through northern United

States, attacking all kinds of pines, though favoring white pine, and sometimes killing spruce (Plate X). This bark beetle often infests small white pines that have been transplanted, its presence told by small, circular holes on branches or trunk. It has also been a frequent visitor to pitch pine after New England hurricanes. The beetle varies from brown to black, is ⅛ inch long; it burrows in sapwood. Long galleries radiate from a circular brood chamber.

A closely related species, *Ips calligraphus* Germar, called the **Coarsewriting Bark Beetle**, is larger and more of a pest in the South. It is the first to attack pines suffering from drought. There are many other species of engraver beetles not described in this manual.

Piñon Cone Beetle*, *Conophthorus edulis* Hopkins. On piñon pine in Colorado, Arizona, and New Mexico. Cones dry and wither before they are half grown. Beetles are very small, dark, shiny, cylindrical.

Pitted Ambrosia Beetle, *Corthylus punctatissimus* Zimmerman. From Massachusetts to Colorado and southward on rhododendron, dogwood, blueberry, mountain-mahogany, sometimes hazel, ironwood, sassafras, water birch. The beetle, dark brown to black, stout, ⅛ inch long, makes horizontal galleries in the wood at the base of the stem, causing it to wilt and break over. Shrubs that are heavily mulched are more likely to be attacked. Cut out wilted stems below point of entrance of beetles. Remove excess mulch.

Plum Gouger*, *Coccotorus scutellaris* (LeConte). A reddish brown beetle, living on wild plum and occasionally going over to domestic plums, prunes, apricots, sometimes peaches and cherries. It resembles the plum curculio but lacks the characteristic humps. The gouger emerges from hibernation earlier than the curculio, and the larvae bore into the fruit to pupate. Spray before blossoms open and then follow the curculio schedule. See Plum Curculio.

Ponderosa Pine Cone Beetle*, *Conophthorus ponderosae* Hopkins. Infesting cones of yellow pine in the West.

Potato Flea Beetle*, *Epitrix cucumeris* (Harris). A common and very destructive small, black, jumping flea beetle (Plate VII). It feeds on potato and related solanaceous plants such as eggplant, groundcherry, pepper, petunia, tomato, and also on apple, arbutus, ash, bean, beet, cabbage, carrot, celery, corn, clover, cucumber, dogbane, elder, forget-me-not, holly, honeysuckle, horsechestnut, lettuce, maple, muskmelon, phlox, primrose, pumpkin, radish, raspberry, rhubarb, spinach, sumac, sunflower, sweetpotato, viburnum, violet, and watermelon. It is present throughout the country. Very tiny, 1⁄16 inch long, it winters as an adult, in spring going first to weeds, sometimes tree leaves. As soon as potatoes or tomatoes appear in the garden, the beetles descend on young plants in hordes, completely riddling the foliage. Eggs are laid in the soil and the larvae feed on roots and tubers. They may be quite destructive, causing scurfy or pimply potatoes, and they are also dangerous as a vector of potato virus diseases. There are usually two broods.

Control. Spray or dust with carbaryl. Commercial growers may use endosulfan or Guthion.

POWDER POST BEETLES. A group of beetles belonging to the families Lyctidae and Bostrichidae, whose larvae burrow into hard, dry wood and reduce it to fine powder. Some species may also bore in living shade or fruit trees, killing twigs or branches.

Prairie Flea Beetle*, *Altica canadensis* Gentner.

Redheaded Flea Beetle, *Systena frontalis* (Fabricius). On corn, smartweed, and other weeds.

Redlegged Flea Beetle*, *Derocrepis erythropus* (Melsheimer). On fruit trees, reported as damaging peach in Pennsylvania.

Red Milkweed Beetle*, *Tetraopes tetrophthalmus* (Forster). Fairly large, red; larvae boring in stems and roots of milkweed.

Red Pine Cone Beetle*, *Conophthorus resinosae* Hopkins.

Red Turnip Beetle*, *Entomoscelis americana* Brown. More of a pest in the Northwest. The beetles are bright red with black patches on the head and three black lines on the elytra, ¼ inch long. Bright-red eggs, orange to black larvae, and bright-orange pupae complete the colorful cycle. Feeding is at night, on alyssum, cabbage, radish, turnip, wallflower, sometimes beans. Spray with carbaryl.

Red Turpentine Beetle*, *Dendroctonus valens* LeConte. Found in pine forests through the country, also injuring ornamental pines in the Atlantic States and Monterey pine in California; sometimes infesting Englemann spruce. This is a comparatively large bark beetle, ¼ to ⅜ inch long, reddish, sometimes nearly black. Egg galleries are longitudinal, somewhat winding. Trees are attacked near the base and reddish pitch tubes are formed; girdled trees may die. When the pitch tubes are noticed, it may be possible to cut out the beetles with a knife or to fumigate them by injecting carbon bisulfide into the galleries.

Red Spider Destroyer, *Somatium oviformis* (Casey). One of the beneficial rove beetles, very small, slender, black, elevating the tip of the abdomen. It deposits orange eggs on the surface of leaves, and the yellow larvae, ⅛ inch long, may daily consume 20 mites apiece. Adults can be numerous on foliage of deciduous fruit and citrus trees infested with various species of mites. See under Lady Beetles for other mite destroyers.

Redwinged Pine Beetle. See Spruce Beetle.

Rhabdopterus Beetles. Several species feed on young foliage of camellias and other ornamentals. *Rhabdopterus deceptor* Barker is found in Texas on camellia, Chinese holly, lychee, redbud, pyracantha, guava, mango, photinia, rose, yaupon, and other plants. *R. bowditchi* Barber is known only in subtropical Florida, infesting avocado as well as ornamentals. *R. picipes* (Olivier), also known as the Cranberry Rootworm, appears in coastal lowland areas from New England to the Mississippi on blueberry, cranberry, and other bog plants. *R. praetextus* (Say) is found inland from Canada to the Rio Grande River and is probably the common species in northern Florida. It injures all camellias, redbud, rhododendron, ampelopsis, rose, loblolly bay, aronia, myrica, and other plants. The beetles are small, compact, elongate-oval in outline, shining blackish bronze, ¼ inch long by ⅛ inch wide. They feed only at night, on buds and tender new leaves, leaving long, rather narrow, usually curved holes or slits in the foliage.

Redwood Bark Beetle, *Phloeosinus sequoiae* Hopkins. Mines inner bark of redwood and redcedar; on injured or dead trees.

Rhinoceros Beetle*, *Xyloryctes jamaicensis* (Drury). Member of a group of very large beetles, subfamily Dynastinae, with a projection like a rhinoceros, mostly southern but this species found as far north as Connecticut. The male is very dark brown, practically black, very broad, over an inch long, with horn curving back from its head (Plate XI). The female is similar but has a small, flat tubercle instead of a horn. The larvae, looking like large white grubs, attack lilacs and sometimes other shrubs just under the surface of the ground, girdling and often killing the bushes. The beetles come out at dusk but their life history is not well known. Chlordane dust or liquid, injected into holes made by the grubs and the entrance then closed, is suggested for control.

Elephant Beetles, *Strategus* spp., are other giant members of this subfamily, found from Rhode Island to Kansas and Texas. They are brown scarabs, 1½ to 2 inches long; they have 3 horns on the head. See also Eastern Hercules Beetle.

Rose Chafer*, *Macrodactylus subspinosus* (Fabricius). Familiar to most gardeners as the "Rose Bug" even though it is a beetle. It is probably called a bug because its wing covers are not as hard and horny as are those of most beetles. The adult is tan, with a reddish-brown head, rather slender, ⅓ to ½ inch long, with prominent long spiny legs (Plate XI). The rose chafer is distributed through the Northeast and may be found as far west as Colorado and Texas. Particularly injurious to roses, peonies, and grapes, it feeds on many other plants—apple, bean, beet, blackberry, cabbage, corn, cherry, dahlia, elder, elm, foxglove, geranium, hollyhock, hydrangea, iris,

New Jersey tea, peach, pear, pepper, poppy, raspberry, strawberry, Virginia-creeper, wisteria, small grains and grasses. It is more troublesome in sandy areas and seems to increase in importance as one goes north from New York City. Rose chafers are also more abundant in areas where Japanese beetles are waning.

The chafers appear in swarms in late May or early June and feed first on flowers, especially roses and peonies, sometimes iris, then go to newly set fruit, being very injurious to grape blossoms, foliage, and young berries. In some areas elm foliage is rather severely damaged. There is only 1 generation, the feeding period lasting 3 to 4 weeks. The eggs, laid in sandy soil, hatch in 1 to 2 weeks. The larvae, resembling white grubs but thinner and smaller, up to 3/4 inch long, feed on roots of grasses and sometimes nursery seedlings, moving down into the soil for winter.

Control. DDT was more effective than earlier pesticides but must now be replaced by methoxychlor or carbaryl. Handpicking helps to keep chafers off roses and some gardeners protect their best bushes with a temporary cheesecloth fence, stretching somewhat higher than the plants. Even if it is open on top the beetles seem not to fly over the barrier. Chickens are poisoned by eating rose chafers.

Rose Leaf Beetle*, *Nodonota puncticollis* (Say). A small, shiny, green to blue beetle, 1/8 inch long, resembling a flea beetle, though not so active. It is distributed from New England south and west to Arizona and Montana. Besides feeding on buds, blossoms, and foliage of rose, peony, and iris, it favors blackberry, raspberry, strawberry, pear, peach, plum, apple (scarring the fruit), and willow. It feeds in spring on clover and other meadow plants before migrating to roses and fruits. Spray or dust with malathion or carbaryl; clean up wasteland breeding places.

Roundheaded Pine Beetle*, *Dendroctonus adjunctus* Blandford. Preventing recovery of injured ponderosa and other pines in Arizona, New Mexico, Colorado, Utah, Nevada, and California. Shiny reddish brown, 1/4 inch long, with long hairs at tip of wing covers.

Sap Beetles. Members of the family Nitidulidae, found usually where plant fluids are fermenting, as in decaying fruits. Usually small, with short elytra and antennae ending in a 3-segmented club. *Glischrochilus fasiatus* (Olivier) is reported in home gardens.

Say Blister Beetle*, *Pomphopoea sayi* (LeConte).

Seedcorn Beetle*, *Agonoderus lecontei* Chaudoir. Sometimes the cause of corn's failing to sprout. This species is dark brown, striped, 1/4 to 1/3 inch long. Corn damage is worse in cold, wet springs when germination is slow or seed is of low vitality. Use good seed; plant late to ensure quick germination. Treating seed with 5 per cent chlordane dust before planting has been helpful. This is one of the ground beetles and primarily a beneficial insect, feeding mostly on other insects. See also Slender Seedcorn Beetle.

Silver Fir Beetles, *Pseudohylesinus granulatus* (LeConte) and *P. grandis* Swaine on grand and silver firs and Douglas-fir. These are bark beetles, ⅛ to ¼ inch, dull, variegated, covered with scales; antennae have a dense plume of hairs; egg galleries are bored transversely.

Sinuatestriped Flea Beetle, *Phyllotreta zimmermanni* (Crotch). Much like the cabbage flea beetle but with a wavy yellowish stripe on each wing cover; 1/12 inch long. The eggs are laid singly on leaves of cabbage, turnip, and radish; the larvae mine inside.

Sitka Spruce Beetle. See Spruce Beetle.

Slender Seedcorn Beetle*, *Clivina impressifrons* LeConte. Like the seedcorn beetle but chestnut brown, also feeding on corn seed. Diazinon and Dursban are promising as seed treatments.

Smaller European Elm Bark Beetle*, *Scolytus multistriatus* (Marsham). Most famous as the vector of the fungus causing a fatal wilt of elms, widely known as the Dutch elm disease. This is a misnomer; the disease did not originate in Holland, although it was first seriously investigated there. This bark beetle (Plate X) was reported in Massachusetts in 1919 and probably arrived from Europe several years before that. It is now known in most states, all except Florida, Georgia, and South Carolina in the Southeast and Washington, Montana, and North Dakota in the Northwest. Although the fungus disease is not present in California, the beetle itself has killed many elms there.

The adult is shiny, brown to black, 1/10 to ⅛ inch long, the female slightly larger than the male. Both sexes have a toothlike projection from the undersurface of the abdomen, serving to distinguish this species from other bark beetles. The grub is white, legless, ¼ inch long, much larger at the head, somewhat curved in its natural position. The beetles attack sickly, dying and recently dead elms and logs, boring small holes through the bark to the sapwood, throwing out sawdust. Each female tunnels out a brood gallery running 1 to 2 inches longitudinally in the wood, and lays from 80 to 100 eggs along this. The grubs make tunnels going out at right angles from the egg gallery, so that characteristic engravings are made in the wood and inner surface of the bark. If many beetles enter, the bark may be separated from the wood all around the trunk or limb.

The grubs transform to beetles in the larval galleries, then exit through small holes, looking like shotholes, in the bark. After emergence the beetles fly to healthy trees and feed by gnawing at the crotches of small twigs before making brood chambers in the older wood. The spores of the Dutch elm disease fungus, formed along the galleries of infected trees, cling to the beetles when they emerge. As they feed, they inoculate healthy elms with the fungus. There are normally 2 broods, beetles of the first brood appearing in May or June, adults of the second about 2 months later.

The fungus, *Ceratocystis ulmi,* came to this country about 1930 on beetles concealed in elm burls imported for furniture veneer and in elm wood used for crates. It has since killed thousands and thousands of trees in most of the states now inhabited by the beetle.

Control of the disease depends on control of its vector. Dead and dying trees should be removed or treated before beetles emerge in spring. A single annual dormant spray will protect healthy elms from bark beetles if enough material is used and complete coverage obtained. This spray was originally a heavy dosage of DDT but this caused bird mortality and other environmental problems. Methoxychlor is the current recommendation. It is less effective than DDT but much less hazardous to wildlife. For mist blowers, the dormant spray is a 12.5 per cent methoxychlor emulsion, with 2 to 3 gallons necessary to cover an average 50-foot tree. For hydraulic sprayers, 2 per cent methoxychlor is used with 20 to 30 gallons required per tree.

Chemotherapy, injection of a chemical that will inactivate the fungus or kill the beetle vector, has been a promising line of research for many years but nothing really practical is yet available. The very poisonous Bidrin has given conflicting results and, if not used in exact dosage, may injure the tree. A parasitic European wasp is being reared by the millions for release against the bark beetles.

Smaller Mexican Pine Beetle. See Southern Pine Beetle.

Southern Masked Chafer*. See under Northern Masked Chafer.

Southern Pine Beetle*, *Dendroctonus frontalis* Zimmerman. Includes Arizona Pine Beetle and Smaller Mexican Pine Beetle. A small, native bark beetle, the most serious forest pest of pine in its range, and occasionally attacking spruce. Epidemics develop with great rapidity, with trees of all sizes attacked but those with trunks larger than 6 inches first, and in the middle and upper parts. The beetle is brown to black, $\frac{3}{16}$ inch long, and it makes winding or S-shaped galleries in the inner bark. There may be 3 to 5 generations a year, with hibernation more commonly as larvae. Feeding begins in early spring, about the time plants start growth, and continues to early summer. Epidemics start in groups of trees, which are more often killed after they have been weakened by flooding, windstorms, or drought.

Control. Trees that can be kept growing rapidly are most resistant to beetle attack. Many natural enemies help in control. Dying trees should be salvaged quickly; where this is impossible, beetles can be killed in felled trees by spraying bark. Benzene hexachloride in fuel oil has been used; cacodylic acid treatment now eliminates the hazard of beetle build-up.

Southern Pine Sawyer*, *Monochamus titillator* (Fabricius). A secondary beetle, boring in wood killed by bark beetles or other agency in eastern and southern states. Galleries are mostly in the inner bark but sometimes score the wood. The borings contain much coarse material. Legless larvae with rounded tubercles on the back make U-shaped galleries. The adult, ⅝ to 1 inch long, reddish brown marbled with white and brown, has a small spine at the end of each wing cover and very long antennae. All dying, killed, or felled timber should be promptly utilized.

Southwestern Hercules Beetle*, *Dynastes granti* Horn. Slightly larger than the eastern hercules beetle and with a longer pronotal horn.

Southwestern Pine Beetle. See Western Pine Beetle.

Spanishfly*, *Lytta vesicatoria* (Linnaeus). A European blister beetle, containing a substance used in drugs.

Spinach Carrion Beetle, *Silpha bituberosa* LeConte. Black, with 3 longitudinal ridges on each elytron, which is short. A scavenger beetle of the Northwest and east to Kansas. Eggs are laid in soil and black-and-white larvae feed at night on edges of leaves of beets, spinach, squash, pumpkin, and some other vegetables.

Spinach Flea Beetle*, *Disonycha xanthomelas* (Dalman). The largest of the common flea beetles, ⅕ inch long, with greenish-black wing covers, yellow thorax, and black head. It feeds exposed on leaves of spinach, beet, and various weeds, lays eggs in clusters on leaves. The larva is a gray-to-purple, warty, wrinkled grub about ¼ inch long. Pupation is in the soil, and there are usually 2 generations a year. Spray with malathion.

Spotted Asparagus Beetle*, *Crioceris duodecimpunctata* (Linnaeus). Introduced from Europe a few years after the common asparagus beetle, first seen near Baltimore in 1881, now distributed over much of the same territory east of the Mississippi. Confined to this host, the beetles can be quite destructive but the larvae feed only on berries. The adult is reddish orange or tan, with 6 prominent black spots on each wing cover (Plate IV). Greenish eggs are glued singly by their sides to leaves just before the berries form. Orange larvae appear in a week or two, bore into the developing berry, eat pulp and seeds. Each larva destroys 3 or 4 berries before pupating in soil. Beetles of the new brood emerge in July and lay eggs for the overwintering generation appearing in September. Control measures are the same as for the asparagus beetle, but collecting and destroying berries may be sufficient.

Spotted Blister Beetle*, *Epicauta maculata* (Say). Black, covered with fine white hairs except in spots where the black shows through. Feeding on many vegetables and field crops in western states.

Spotted Cucumber Beetle*, *Diabrotica undecimpunctata howardi* Barber. Also known as Southern Corn Rootworm. This species occurs

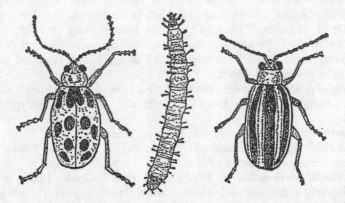

27. Spotted cucumber beetle, left; striped cucumber beetle, right.

anywhere east of the Rockies but it is more destructive in southern states. West of the Rocky Mountains it is replaced by the Western Spotted Cucumber Beetle. The adult is greenish yellow, rather slender, with 12 black spots, a black head, ¼ inch long. It is prevalent on many flowers and vegetables besides cucumber. Vegetables include snap and lima beans early in the season, later all of the cucurbits—cucumber, melon, squash, gourds—and asparagus, beet, cabbage, eggplant, peas, potato, and tomato.

Although the spotted cucumber beetle eats the foliage of many ornamentals, it seems to prefer petals of late summer flowers with light colors, such as aster, calendula, canna, chrysanthemum, coreopsis, cosmos, dahlia, garden balsam, rose, Shasta daisy, sweetpea, and zinnia.

The beetle hibernates as an adult at the base of weeds or other overwintering plants and starts flying when the temperature nears 70° F. in spring. Females lay eggs just below soil level, on or near young corn plants, beans, or weeds. The larvae, which feed on such roots, are more wormlike than most beetle grubs, ½ to ¾ inch long, slender with yellowish-white wrinkled bodies and brown heads (Plate XII). They have been called overflow worms, budworms, and drillworms because they bore out the crown of a corn plant and kill the buds. Corn so injured either breaks off or is dwarfed and yellowish. There are at least 3 generations in the South, 1 and a partial 2nd in the North.

The spotted cucumber beetle is especially important as a vector of plant diseases. It carries the bacteria causing cucumber wilt in its intestines and inoculates plants as it feeds. It also disseminates some viruses.

Control. Avoid damage to corn by planting late in the season, thoroughly cultivating the soil first. Reduce overwintering beetles by cleaning up weeds. Spray or dust with rotenone, methoxychlor, malathion, diazinon, or carbaryl. To prevent bacterial wilt on cucumbers or other cucurbits, spray when seedlings emerge or after transplanting, every 5 days until vines start to run. See also Striped Cucumber Beetle.

Spotted Grapevine Beetle, *Pelidnota punctata* (Linnaeus). A large beetle conspicuous on grape foliage in summer but causing little injury. The adult is over an inch long, very broad, tan, glossy, with 4 black spots on each side. The grubs live in decaying wood— stumps, logs, or roots—and the life cycle takes 2 to 3 years.

Spotted Pine Sawyer*, *Monochamus maculosus* Haldeman. A long, slender dark beetle, with bluish-gray markings and very long antennae. The larvae are destructive to heartwood of dying pine in the West.

Spruce Beetle*, *Dendroctonus rufipennis* (Kirby), formerly *D. obesus* (Mannerheim). Alaska Spruce Beetle, Eastern Spruce Beetle, Engelmann Spruce Beetle, Redwinged Pine Beetle, and Sitka Spruce Beetle are names given to species now considered synonymous with the Spruce Beetle. They attack red, white, black, Sitka, and Engelmann spruce, and also pine, over much of the country and may be very injurious. The adult is black with reddish wing covers; the female makes a 6-inch longitudinal gallery in one tree and may repeat in another. Red boring dust, pitch tubes on the bark, and fading and dropping of needles indicate the presence of beetles.

The beetles breed in forests on windfall trees and may reach epidemic proportions. In 1949 in Colorado the air was full of beetles. A fraction that fell in a small lake formed a drift of dead beetles a foot deep, 6 feet wide, and 2 miles long. The survivors killed 400,000 previously uninfested trees in a mass attack. Large-scale treatment has consisted of spraying the lower 30 to 35 feet of tree boles with orthodichlorobenzene or ethylene dibromide emulsion. A less expensive treatment is the use of a herbicide, cacodylic acid, applied before felling in a frill cut around the tree. Woodpeckers have at times greatly reduced the beetle population. Very low temperatures kill most of the beetles above the snow line. Rapid salvage of wind-thrown or damaged timber is the best prevention.

Squash Beetle*, *Epilachna borealis* (Fabricius). Sharing with the Mexican bean beetle the dubious distinction of being a gangster member of the usually beneficial lady beetle family. It is not as destructive as the bean beetle, but it is fairly common east of the Rocky Mountains on squash, melon, pumpkin, and relatives. It is slightly larger than the Mexican bean beetle, yellow, with 7 black spots on each wing cover. Beetles emerge in June to lay eggs on host plants; these hatch in a week. The spiny larva feeds on foliage for 2 to 4 weeks, then pushes its larval skin down its back while it pupates. The adults hibernate under trash. Control is seldom necessary; methoxychlor, rotenone, or malathion would help if needed.

Steelblue Flea Beetle, *Altica torquata* LeConte. A small metallic-blue or purple beetle, abundant on grapes in New Mexico, Arizona, and southern California. Native hosts are desert and evening primroses.

Steelblue Lady Beetle*, *Orcus chalybeus* (Boisduval). Metallic steelblue or emerald green, introduced from Australia to California in 1892 to prey on black, red, and purple scales.

Stink Beetle*, *Nomius pygmaeus* (Dejean). One of the beneficial ground beetles, sometimes called the malodorous carabid. It has a very offensive smell, is present in California and Oregon.

Strawberry Flea Beetle, *Altica ignita* Illiger. Metallic green, golden bronze, or purple, 3/16 inch long, on strawberry, kalmia, fuchsia, rose, and many other plants; widely distributed. The foliage is riddled with great numbers of small round holes and the leaves often turn brown around the holes. The beetles winter as adults and do most of their damage before strawberries bloom. The beetles feed and breed on evening primrose so practice clean culture. Spray with methoxychlor when necessary.

Striped Ambrosia Beetle*, *Trypodendron lineatum* (Olivier). Infesting conifers; in heartwood of dying trees. Dark with lighter stripes, resembling a bark beetle.

Striped Blister Beetle*, *Epicauta vittata* (Fabricius). Black with a yellow border and median stripe on each wing cover, just over ½ inch long. This very common species, ranging west as far as Montana, is reported occurring in large swarms in Arkansas, both in alfalfa fields and in vegetable gardens. Together with the three-striped blister beetle, this species feeds on bean, soybean, beet, corn, melon, peas, potato, radish, tomato, turnip, and other vegetables. Methoxychlor or rotenone may aid in control.

Striped Cucumber Beetle*, *Acalymma vittata* (Fabricius). A native insect, the most serious cucumber pest east of the Rocky Mountains, a related species taking over cucurbit destruction in the West. The larvae feed only on roots of cucumber, muskmelon, winter squash, and watermelon, about in the order named, but the adults feed also on beans, corn, peas, and blossoms of other plants.

The beetles are yellowish with 3 black stripes, $\frac{1}{5}$ by $\frac{1}{10}$ inch (Plate XII). As unmated adults they winter in woodlands near the vegetable garden, under leaves or rotting logs, in lowland hedgerows, or near wild food plants such as goldenrod and aster, but nearly always keeping in direct contact with the ground. They become active in spring when the temperature gets above 55° F. Before cucurbits are up they feed on pollen, petals or leaves of buckeye, willow, wild plum, hawthorn, elm, syringa, and other plants. They settle on cucumber and related vines as soon as they appear above ground. Mating takes place as they feed on the vine crops. The female lays orange eggs in or on the soil at the base of such plants.

The very slender, white, wormlike larvae, $\frac{1}{3}$ inch long, feed on roots and underground parts of stems for 2 to 6 weeks, often destroying the whole root system with subsequent death of vines. From white pupae in the soil, adults appear in midsummer to feed on cucurbits and legumes for another 6 weeks, often eating into the rind of fruits as well as chewing leaves and flowers. There is 1 generation in the North, 2, 3, or possibly 4 in the South.

The beetles are especially dangerous because they transmit bacterial wilt of cucurbits and cucumber mosaic. In my own garden they have frequently been found in spring on Chinese lantern, the leaves of which are often mottled by the mosaic pattern.

Control. Early feeding by beetles can be avoided by starting seeds under Hotkaps or boxes pushed down into the ground, open at the bottom, covered with mosquito netting or fine wire screening over the top. Unprotected vines should be dusted as soon as they appear and weekly thereafter with methoxychlor, rotenone, malathion, or carbaryl. Insecticide mixtures containing sulfur may injure some squash and melon varieties.

Striped Flea Beetle*, *Phyllotreta striolata* (Fabricius). Widely distributed pest of cabbage; $\frac{1}{12}$ inch long with a crooked yellow stripe on each wing cover. Eggs are laid in small cavities gnawed in the stem. See also Flea Beetles.

Striped Tortoise Beetle, *Agroiconota bivittata* (Say). Dull yellow, with 5 longitudinal black stripes. The larvae are yellowish white with

a median gray line, short marginal spines, and a tail-like projection
bearing cast skins but no excrement. White eggs are laid singly on
leaf stems or vines, each covered with a daub of black pitch. On
sweetpotato, sometimes morning-glory.

Sugarcane Beetle*, *Euetheola rugiceps* (LeConte). Related to rhinoceros beetles, in the subfamily Dynastinae, but smaller. Larvae and
adults feed on sugarcane, corn, cereals, rice.

Sugar Pine Cone Beetle*, *Conophthorus lambertianae* Hopkins.
Hinders seeding of sugar pine in California and Oregon.

Sunflower Beetle*, *Zygogramma exclamationis* (Fabricius). Feeding on wild and cultivated sunflower in the West. Another species,
Galerucella notata (Fabricius), small, dull yellow, also feeds on sunflower and is called the sunflower beetle.

Sweetpotato Flea Beetle*, *Chaetocnema confinis* Crotch. Very
small, $\frac{1}{16}$ inch long, black with a bronzy reflection. It eats narrow
grooves in leaves along the veins. Leaves wilt, plants turn brown.
Besides sweetpotato, the beetle infests morning-glory, sugar beet,
raspberry, boxelder, corn, cereals, grasses. The larvae feed on roots
of bindweed and are reported injuring dichondra lawns. Endosulfan
is suggested for treatment of sweetpotatoes by farmers.

Sweetpotato Leaf Beetle*, *Typophorus nigritus viridicyaneus*
(Crotch). A metallic blue-green, oblong beetle, a little over $\frac{1}{4}$ inch.
It eats tender leaves at the crown of the plant, devouring them
from the margin inward. Pale yellow, plump larvae burrow through
the vine underground.

Syneta Leaf Beetle*, *Syneta albida* LeConte. Western Fruit Beetle.
Common on cherry in the Pacific Northwest, occasional on pear,
prune, apple. The beetles, light gray or yellowish, $\frac{1}{4}$ inch long,
emerge from the ground as the trees bloom and stay near the buds
for about 2 months. They scar and deform young fruit, also feed on
stems, blossoms, leaves. Eggs are dropped to the ground and the
grubs feed in fine fibrous roots. Spraying the trees twice with lead
arsenate, just before blossoms open and just after petals have fallen,
has greatly reduced injury.

Tenlined June Beetle*, *Polyphylla decimlineata* (Say). Robust,
brown, large, covered with yellowish and white scales, arranged to
make 2 stripes on the head, 2 on the thorax, and 4 long stripes and
1 short stripe on each wing cover. Larvae are very large white grubs,
up to 2 inches long. This species occurs primarily in the Rocky
Mountain States and on the Pacific Coast. The larvae may girdle
and destroy roots of ornamental shrubs and nursery trees, including
California privet, black locust, and wisteria.

Threelined Potato Beetle*, *Lema trilineata* (Oliver). In some areas damaging to potato and related plants. The adult is reddish yellow with 3 broad black stripes; the larva plasters granular masses of its own excrement over its body.

Threespotted Flea Beetle*, *Disonycha triangularis* (Say). Related to the spinach flea beetle.

Threestriped Blister Beetle*, *Epicauta lemniscata* (Fabricius). A western version of the Striped Blister Beetle, which see.

Tobacco Flea Beetle*, *Epitrix hirtipennis* (Melsheimer). Distributed through the United States, including Hawaii. In some years the most important pest of tobacco but also feeding heavily on tomato, potato, groundcherry, eggplant, and pepper and on many nonsolanaceous plants and weeds as an adult. The larvae are restricted to roots of solanaceous plants. The beetles are very small, reddish to dark brown, often with a dark transverse band across the elytra. They hibernate as adults, in soil or under trash, migrating to seedbeds in spring, depositing eggs in crevices in soil. The larva is white, threadlike, with chitinized parts light brown. There may be 3 or 4 generations. Use carbaryl or methoxychlor for control, or dimethoate or diazinon.

Toothed Flea Beetle*, *Chaetocnema denticulata* (Illiger). Small, brassy, with face densely punctured, going to corn and beets from wild grasses.

TORTOISE BEETLES. Sometimes called Sweetpotato Beetles or Goldbugs. They comprise several species distributed over the United

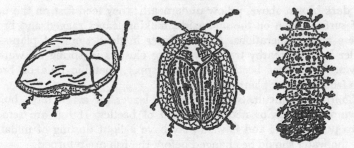

28. Tortoise beetle: adult, two views, and larva carrying its excrement.

States, feeding on sweetpotato, morning-glory and other members of the Convolvulaceae. They are leaf eaters, relatively small, none over ¼ inch, and nearly as wide as long. The margins of the body are extended to hide the head and most of the legs, making the beetles look like tortoises. They eat holes through the leaves or devour entire leaves, sometimes seriously injuring newly set plants. They winter as beetles in protected places, under bark or trash. The larvae, about ⅜ inch long, have conspicuous horny spines with 2 longer ones at the posterior. On these the larva packs its own excrement and cast skins, and curls this over the back like a squirrel's tail (Plate XI). Larvae look like moving pieces of dirt. When full-grown, they fasten themselves to leaves to pupate. Spray with malathion. See also Argus, Blacklegged, Golden, and Mottled Tortoise Beetles.

Tuber Flea Beetle*, *Epitrix tuberis* Gentner. Adults feed on foliage but larvae scar surface of potato tubers and bore into them, often causing severe injury. Spray with carbaryl.

Transverse Lady Beetle*. See Lady Beetles.

Twicestabbed Lady Beetle*. See Lady Beetles.

Twospotted Lady Beetle*. See Lady Beetles.

Tule Beetle*, *Agonum maculicolle* Dejean. One of the ground beetles.

A Turf Beetle, *Serica peregrina*. One of the scarab June beetles, injuring turf.

Unicorn Beetle. See Rhinoceros Beetle.

Vedalia*. See Lady Beetles.

Watercress Leaf Beetle*, *Phaedon viridus* (Melsheimer). Small, bronze black, about ⅛ inch long; larvae brownish black with many tubercles of hairs. There seems to be no practical control.

Waterlily Leaf Beetle*, *Pyrrhalta nymphaeae* (Linnaeus). Dark brown beetle, with dull yellow thorax, ¼ inch long, feeding on leaves and flowers of pond lilies and other water plants. The larvae are dark brown above, yellow underneath; they feed first on the upper leaf surface, then on the underside, making leaves ragged and brown. There are 2 generations. Adults winter in dead stems of plants and under bark of nearby trees, laying egg clusters in spring on waterlily leaves. Other leaf beetles (*Donacia* spp.), metallic blue or brown, also feed on water plants.

Control is difficult. Submerging the leaves for a few days, holding down with hoops or netting gets rid of beetles. If fish are removed from pools, leaves and flowers may have a light dusting of malathion but the water should be changed before the fish are returned.

Western Balsam Bark Beetle*, *Dryocoetes confusus* Swaine. On true firs in the Rocky Mountains, sometimes killing trees. Small, dark, cylindrical beetles, the females with dense, short yellowish hairs on front of the head. Narrow egg galleries radiate out from a central chamber.

Western Black Flea Beetle*, *Phyllotreta pusilla* Horn. Important in the West. The very small, shiny, olive-green to black beetles often appear in swarms on cabbage, cauliflower, horseradish, mustard, cress, radish, watercress, peppergrass, turnip, sugar beet, and corn; also on stock, wallflower, rock cress. The larvae mine in leaves and feed on roots. Spray or dust with rotenone, methoxychlor, or malathion.

Western Cedar Bark Beetle*, *Phloeosinus punctatus* LeConte. Infesting healthy and injured cedar—western, incense, red, Alaska, and Port Orford—and giant arborvitae. Small beetles with toothed projections on male wing covers; egg galleries are short, 1 to 3 inches.

Western Pine Beetle*, *Dendroctonus brevicomis* LeConte. Includes Southwestern Pine Beetle. The most important pest of ponderosa and Coulter pines on the Pacific Coast, responsible for tremendous annual damage to timber. The adults are small, $\frac{1}{8}$ to $\frac{1}{5}$ inch, brown to black bark beetles. They construct a network of winding egg galleries between bark and sapwood. When healthy trees are attacked—seldom those under 6 inches in diameter—resin tubes are formed about the entrance holes. Primarily a forest insect, this beetle may appear in parks and on home grounds. Infested trees should be felled and the bark treated in fall or winter. Woodpeckers and some beetles are natural enemies. Promoting vigorous tree growth is the best preventive measure.

Western Potato Flea Beetle*, *Epitrix subcrinita* (LeConte). Shiny bronze, $\frac{1}{16}$ inch long, injuring potatoes and tomatoes and sometimes any of the hosts listed for the potato flea beetle. This western species is serious in Arizona, California, Colorado, Idaho, Montana, Nevada, Oregon, Utah, and Washington.

Western Spotted Cucumber Beetle*, *Diabrotica undecimpunctata undecimpunctata* Mannerheim. Replacing the spotted cucumber beetle west of the Rocky Mountains. It has the same greenish-yellow wing covers but is slightly smaller with slightly larger black spots. Soon after native grasses dry up in pastures, the adults swarm into the garden, devastating flowers, lawns, ornamental trees and shrubs, truck crops, fruit trees—in fact nearly every green plant except conifers. The pest is called Diabolical Diabrotica by irate gardeners. The larvae feed on roots of corn and sweetpea as well as grasses. Beetles cut holes in ripening fruit, especially in orchards in uncultivated areas, and spread the fungus causing brown rot of apricots, peaches, and other stone fruits.

Control. Spray or dust with malathion, carbaryl, or diazinon.

Western Striped Cucumber Beetle*, *Acalymma trivittata* (Mannerheim). Most abundant and injurious in southern California but ranging into Arizona and Oregon. The adult is like the eastern species, with a yellowish body and 3 black stripes, but the basal portion of the antenna is yellow instead of black. The larvae attack roots of cucumber, melon, pumpkin, squash, and other cucurbits. The adults feed on the tops of these plants and also on bean, beet, corn, pea, sunflower, almond, apple, prune, and other fruits.

Western Striped Flea Beetle*, *Phyllotreta ramosa* (Crotch). Shiny black with a brassy reflection and a conspicuous irregular yellow-white band down each wing cover; $\frac{1}{16}$ inch long. It may be destructive to cabbage, cauliflower, Brussels sprouts, radish, mustard, stock, turnip, wallflower, watercress and other crucifers in California.

Whitefringed Beetles*, *Graphognathus* spp. A complex of species native to South America, first seen in Florida in 1936. Since then

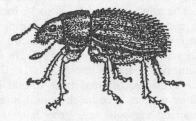

29. Whitefringed beetle.

the beetles have appeared in Alabama, Arkansas, Georgia, Kentucky, Louisiana, Mississippi, Missouri, New Jersey, North Carolina, South Carolina, Tennessee, Texas, and Virginia but some infestations, like that in New Jersey, have been eradicated. The beetles are brownish gray, just under ½ inch long, with a broad, short snout. They are covered with short pale hairs, have margins of wing covers banded with white and two pale lines on head and prothorax. They are gregarious, as many as 200 or 300 beetles being found on one plant eating in from the margins of the leaves or crawling along the ground. The elytra are fused together so they cannot fly. All the adults are parthenogenetic females; no males are known. They feed as adults on about 170 kinds of weeds, vines, trees, shrubs, flowers, and vegetables.

Most damage comes from the larvae, which have been recorded feeding on roots or tubers of nearly 400 plant species. The larvae are yellowish white, curved, legless, up to ½ inch long. Among their numerous hosts are potato, sweetpotato, peanut, cabbage, collards, chufa, turnip, sweet corn, strawberry, blackberry, chrysanthemum, dahlia, daisy, gladiolus, iris, lily, marigold, morning-glory, sunflower, flowering tobacco, violet, and zinnia.

The larvae winter in the soil, usually in the top 9 inches, sometimes lower down, and pupate in a soil cell in spring. The beetles start emerging in May, reaching a peak in June and July. They live for 2 or 3 months, each female averaging 600 to 700 eggs, laid in masses of 11 to 14 at the base of some object—plant, stick, or stone— in contact with the soil. During this time they may crawl ¼ to ¾ mile. The larvae, hatching in 2 weeks to 2 months, eat the soft outer root tissues or may sever the main root. The plants turn yellow, wilt, and die. There is normally 1 generation a year.

Control. Infested areas are under quarantine, and large-scale eradication measures have eliminated the pest in some areas. In home gardens, soil can be treated before planting, using 5 per cent chlordane granules to 1,000 square feet and working this into the top 3 inches of soil. In experiments, potting soil has been treated with disulfoton as a systemic insecticide. Nurseries often fumigate plants with methyl bromide before shipment.

White Pine Cone Beetle*, *Conophthorus coniperda* (Schwartz). A very small, shiny black beetle destructive to cones of white pine from Canada to North Carolina. The adults bore into the stems of young cones to lay their eggs and the larvae feed on scales, seeds, and other tissues of wilting cones that fall to the ground. Gather and destroy infested cones on ornamental plants.

Whitespotted Sawyer*, *Monochamus scutellatus* (Say). Large dark beetles mottled with white; important wood pest through the United States except in the South.

Willow Flea Beetle. See Willow Flea Weevil.

Yellowmargined Leaf Beetle*, *Microtheca ochroloma* (Stål). An introduced pest, from South America, first found in the United States in Alabama in 1947 and since spread to Louisiana, Mississippi, and Florida. It feeds on crucifers—cabbage, collards, mustard, turnip, radish—and also on potato and members of the primrose family. The adult is small and the brown wing covers have a pale-yellow or white margin and 4 rows of deep pits. It feeds on margins of leaves and makes irregular holes in terminal growth.

BILLBUGS

Billbugs are peculiarly shaped snout beetles in the subfamily Rhyncophorinae, present in grasslands and cultivated areas throughout the country but more destructive east of the Great Plains. Adults vary from ⅕ to ¾ inch long, have a cylindrical curved snout (the bill) similar to that of a curculio and hardy body wall and wing covers. They are reddish brown to black, often so covered with mud that their color cannot be told. They gouge out a small hole in a stalk for each white, kidney-shaped egg. When disturbed they "play possum." The grubs are chunky, white, humpbacked, legless, with a hard brown or yellow head. They eat out the pith of stems and then go down to the roots.

Bluegrass Billbug*, *Sphenophorus parvulus* Gyllenhal. Has a body tapered sharply to tip of the abdomen; evenly marked with rounded punctures; ¼ inch long. The grubs excavate stems and eat rootlets of bluegrass and other grasses.

Two other species, *S. sayi* Gyllenhal and *S. phoeniciensis* Chittenden, are also reported infesting lawns. Turf may be treated with diazinon. *S. venatus confluens* Chittenden is a relatively new pest of orchardgrass.

Claycolored Billbug*, *Sphenophorus aequalis aequalis* Gyllenhal. Buff-colored, with fine punctures on upper surface, more than ½ inch long. Adults often kill corn plants and may feed on wheat kernels. Grubs develop in the "nuts" at the ends of roots of rushes, sedges, and reeds.

Cocklebur Billbug. See Cocklebur Weevil, under Weevils.

Maize Billbug*, *Sphenophorus maidis* Chittenden. Broad-bodied, to ⅗ inch long, reddish brown or black, with raised longitudinal lines on wing covers. The billbugs cripple young corn plants, causing excessive suckering.

Palm Billbug, *Rhynchophorus cruentatus* (Fabricius). A very large species on palms and cabbage palmetto.

Southern Corn Billbug, *Sphenophorus callosus* (Olivier). Known as the Curlew Bug; brown with golden reflections, black elevated bumps, ⅜ inch long. It injures rice and peanuts as well as corn and lays eggs in nutgrass.

Timothy Billbug, *Sphenophorus zeae* (Walsh). Working in timothy in the larval stage, causing failure of grass in meadows. The adults attack corn, causing excessive suckering and failure to form ears. The adult is larger than the bluegrass billbug and punctures on the prothorax form a pattern. Do not plant corn on land that has been in sod during the preceding season; avoid reclaimed swampland.

Zoysia Billbug, *Sphenophorus venatus vestitus* Chittenden. Sometimes called the Hunting Billbug; found on zoysia and other lawns. Spraying with Baygon has given some control.

BOLLWORMS

Bollworm is the name given to the larva of a moth devouring unripe pods or bolls of cotton. The true bollworm (*Heliothis zea*) is better known to gardeners as the corn earworm or tomato fruitworm. It is discussed under Earworms.

Pink Bollworm*, *Pectinophora gossypiella* (Saunders). Considered one of the 6 most destructive insects in the world, capable of taking up to 50 per cent of a cotton crop. Probably a native of India, it came to Mexico from Egypt in 1911 and by 1917 had reached Texas. The regulated area now includes Texas, Oklahoma, Arizona, New Mexico, California, with some distribution in Arkansas and Louisiana. Occasionally bollworms are taken from wild cotton or hibiscus blossoms in the Florida Keys or the Everglades. Mallow, rose-of-Sharon, hollyhock, abutilon are sometimes hosts and the bollworm may be spread on okra pods.

The caterpillars are cylindrical, pinkish, about ½ inch long. They eat holes in the bolls, then drop to the ground to pupate. The moth, dark brown, ¾ inch across the narrow fringed wings, emerges in 9 days and deposits eggs anywhere on the cotton plant, concentrating on terminals. The eggs hatch in 3 to 5 days and the larvae bore into the squares, eat the developing flowers, and work in the bolls, consuming lint and seed.

Control. Millions have been spent in containing and eradicating the pink bollworm in this country. Federal and state quarantines regulate the movement of cotton and cotton products and require the treatment of seeds and lint before shipment. Traps are baited with hexalure, a synthetic sex attractant, and millions and millions of sterile moths have been released. Spraying or dusting with carbaryl reduces crop losses.

BORERS

Borers are grubs or caterpillars, larvae of beetles or moths, working in woody tissues or herbaceous stems. There are a great many borers affecting shade and fruit trees, ornamental shrubs, herbaceous annuals and perennials. The proportion selected for inclusion in this manual is small compared to the total number. Borers are particularly destructive to newly set trees and to those weakened from various causes. Some of the factors predisposing trees to borer attack are listed here.

1. *Drought* is a primary factor in making trees susceptible to borer attack; the rootlets dry out, the roots are injured, and the whole tree is systemically weakened. Two or three seasons with deficient rainfall are usually followed by large numbers of borers. Newly transplanted trees are subject to attack before they get their root systems established.

2. *Sunscald* is important with newly transplanted trees and also on established trees suddenly exposed to the sun by removal of another tree, hedge, or building which had previously kept the trunks shaded.

3. *Injuries* from hurricanes, ice storms, frost cracks, bonfires, lawn mowers, etc., provide easy entrance for borers.

4. *Defoliation by leaf-eating insects* produces a weakened condition highly inviting to borers.

5. *Construction activities* with change of grade, lowering or raising of water tables, mechanical injuries from excavations in ditch digging, pipe laying, road building may gravely weaken established trees.

6. *Chemical injuries* from leaking illuminating gas in the soil, chlorides applied to roads to lay dust or to melt ice in winter, or fumes from factories are conducive to poor health and borer attack.

The best control measure is the promotion of good health and vigor by proper watering, especially of newly transplanted trees, fertilizing where necessary, and spraying to control leaf-eating insects.

Wrapping tree trunks the first year or two after transplanting prevents drying out and sunscald and provides a mechanical barrier to borer attack. The wrapping may be done with strips of burlap, newspaper, commercial borer wrap (double-thickness kraft paper with a layer of asphaltum in between) or aluminum foil. Start at the first branch and wind spirally downward, overlapping half the width at each spiral. Tie firmly with twine wound spirally in the opposite direction. The trunk should be sprayed with an insecticide (see below) before covering. The wrapping should be removed in a year, to make sure no borers have gotten underneath and gone to work, but then it can be replaced for a second year. Spraying transplanted young trees and shrubs with an antidesiccant such as Wiltpruf helps to prevent borer attack and may replace wrapping.

For borer prevention on established trees and shrubs, spray or paint trunk and branches at the time eggs on the bark are due to hatch. This is spring for many species, late summer for a few. Repeat at monthly intervals to prevent egg laying by the adult. Effective materials have been DDT, dieldrin, and lindane. The first two may no longer be recommended and the third is restricted. Present possibilities include dimethoate, malathion, methoxychlor, and endosulfan (Thiodan), though the last may be limited to professionals. Dimethoate granules applied to the soil kill some small-tree borers.

If, despite all precautions, holes and sawdust or pitch tubes on the bark indicate borers already at work, there are still remedies. Hand-worming is first, cutting out borers in the cambium beneath the bark, but a sharp knife should be used with caution lest it injure the wood. Treat exposed wood with a good wound paint. Borers in wood can sometimes be killed by probing with a flexible wire, cleaning out the tunnel, and then injecting malathion or carbon disulfide into the hole, then sealing the opening with mud, putty, or calking compound to contain the fumes. Some of the commercial preparations marketed for such injections used to contain nicotine, later lindane.

It is always important to trim injured trees promptly, making smooth cuts flush with the bark, and to cut out all infested wood before the borers can emerge to attack other trees. Tree-wound dressings are now available as aerosols, making prompt treatment of the cut surface easy.

American Plum Borer*, *Euzophera semifuneralis* (Walker). Larva of a small, inconspicuous moth, family Pyralidae, with long, threadlike antennae. Most members of this family are pests of stored products but this plum borer, widely distributed, bores under the bark and sometimes kills shade trees, including maple, sycamore, linden, mountain-ash, as well as plum, almond, apple, apricot, peach, pear, cherry, pecan. It is also a pest of stored sweetpotatoes.

Apple Bark Borer*, *Synanthedon pyri* (Harris). Also known as Pear Borer, but it more commonly infests apple. It may likewise infest pecan, hawthorn, mountain-ash, and shadbush from Maine to Texas. Larvae of a clearwing moth, family Aegeriidae, the borers are found in crotches and in rough bark of neglected trees.

Apple Twig Borer*, *Amphicerus bicaudatus* (Say). Larva of a false powder beetle, family Bostrichidae, attacking twigs of apple, cherry, pear, grape, osage-orange, pecan, ash, and other trees in various parts of North America.

Ash Borer*, *Podosesia syringae fraxini* Lugger. Generally distributed but apparently limited to ash and mountain-ash, more serious in prairie states. The adult is a clearwing moth, family Aegeriidae. The front wings are opaque blackish brown with a violet reflection and red crossbar; hind wings are transparent with a narrow black border; the abdomen is black with yellow bands. The larvae—white worms 1½ inches long, with brown heads—bore in the tree just below ground level or near the base, making so many burrows that the tree easily breaks over in a wind. Cut out infested parts; spray trunks with methoxychlor. See also Lilac Borer for a species just as common on ash.

Australianpine Borer*, *Chrysobothris tranquebarica* (Gmelin). Also called Mangrove Borer. This borer attacks living red mangrove and casuarina trees planted as ornamentals and windbreaks in Florida. The adult beetles, family Buprestidae, are greenish bronze, ½ to ¾ inch long, with 3 lighter impressions on each wing cover. They appear in April, laying eggs under the bark. The flatheaded larvae bore through the back and into the wood to construct pupal cells.

Methoxychlor sprays may help but the best control is to cut out beetle-infested branches or trees in fall or winter.

Azalea Stem Borer, *Oberea myops* Haldeman. A longhorned beetle, family Cerambycidae, girdling tips of stems of azalea, rhododendron, blueberry, mountain-laurel, and perhaps other plants in spring. The beetle is slender, ½ inch across, with yellow head and thorax, the latter with 3 black spots, and grayish-yellow punctate wing covers. Twigs are girdled in 2 places, ½ inch apart, and a yellow egg is thrust through the bark halfway between. The tip dies and the yellow, legless grub, ½ inch or more long, bores down the twig and into the trunk, pushing out sawdust from holes near the ground. It winters in a cell in the crown of the plant, below ground, pupates in spring, and the adults emerge in June (in New Jersey). Infested bushes have dying tips and readily break over from borings in the lower part of the stems.

Control. Cut out and destroy dead and dying tips as soon as noticed. Inject borer paste into holes. Spray stems with methoxychlor in May and June.

Banana Root Borer*, *Cosmopolites sordidus* (Germar). A snout beetle.

Banded Alder Borer*, *Rosalia funebris* Motschulsky. Also known as California-laurel Borer, a longhorned beetle, family Cerambycidae. The larvae mine California-laurel, Oregon ash, willow as well as alder.

Banded Hickory Borer*, *Cerasphorus cinctus* (Drury).

Beet Petiole Borer, *Cosmobaris americana* Casey. A weevil attacking sugar beets and other betaceous crops, soybeans, kochia, and various weeds, interfering with the translocation process. The adult is slender, long-legged, long-beaked, shining dark brown with brown to white hairs. The larva is white to greenish, slightly crescent-shaped when young, then yellow. They bore in petioles.

Bidens Borer*, *Epiblema otiosanum* (Clemens). An olethreutid moth.

Blueberry Tip Borer, *Hendecaneura shawiana.* In stems of cultivated blueberry.

Blackhorned Pine Borer*, *Callidium antennatum hesperum* Casey. Flattened blackish-blue beetles. The larvae have tough, shiny skins, wide heads, and feed beneath bark and in sapwood of dead pines, spruces, hemlocks, junipers, and cedars.

Blue Cactus Borer*, *Melitara dentata* (Grote). A pyralid moth.

Boxelder Twig Borer*, *Proteoteras willingana* (Kearfott). A moth, family Olethreutidae. The larvae attack boxelder twigs and are also reported on maple.

Branch and Twig Borer, *Polycaon confertus* (LeConte). A cylindrical beetle, about ½ inch long, black with brown elytra, burrowing into twig crotches or buds of apricot, olive, avocado, citrus, and fig trees, sometimes grapevines. The large, whitish larvae, with fine hairs, work in dead heartwood of many ornamental trees in California and Oregon. Often there is rather extensive killing of twigs and branches. A sporadic but sometimes severe pest of avocado, this borer indicates its presence by the sugary sap, turning white and flaky, exuding from the entrance burrows.

Prune out infested twigs on small fruit trees. Destroy dead brush and orchard prunings.

Broadnecked Root Borer*, *Prionus laticollis* (Drury). A brownish black beetle with long, serrated antennae, 1 to 1¾ inches, another member of the Cerambycidae. The large, legless, yellowish grub, 2½ to 3 inches, excavates a burrow in roots of oaks, sometimes poplar, chestnut, apple, pine, and grape. Rhododendrons growing near such roots may also be attacked, infested stems being broken off at ground level. The life cycle may take 3 years. There is no reliable method of control.

Bronze Birch Borer*, *Agrilus anxius* Gory. A native beetle, family Buprestidae, the flatheaded borers. Distributed through northern United States as far west as Colorado and Idaho, this species attacks white, gray, black, and canoe birches, poplar, quaking aspen, cottonwood, and willow. It is more injurious to ornamental trees grown in the open than to forest trees, and flourishes on decadent rather than vigorous trees.

The beetle is slender, olive-bronze, with a blunt head, tapering body, nearly 1 inch long. The grub is white, slender, with the region just back of the head enlarged, and with a horny, forceps-like appendage at the tip of the abdomen. It mines in irregular winding galleries just under the bark, which is loosened. The first sign of injury is the dying back of trees at the top, by which time it is rather late for control measures. This is a serious pest, the entire tree usually dying eventually.

Control. DDT and dieldrin may no longer be recommended. Try spraying trunk and branches heavily and foliage lightly with methoxychlor or dimethoate in June (New York) at time of beetle emergence and repeat two weeks later. Keep white and other ornamental birches fertilized and well watered in times of drought.

Bronze Poplar Borer*, *Agrilus liragus* Barter & Brown. Similar to the bronze birch borer, olivaceous-bronze in color, infesting poplars through northern North America.

Brown Wood Borer, *Parandra brunnea* Fabricius. Also called Pole

Borer, a native beetle occurring east of the Rocky Mountains in dead wood and sometimes in cavities in living trees. It may infest almost all hardwood shade trees, some conifers, and apple, pear, and cherry. The beetle is glossy chestnut brown, ¾ inch long, one of the Cerambycidae, the longhorned group, but with antennae no longer than the elytra. Because this borer enters living trees only through wounds, careful pruning, leaving no broken projecting branch stubs, is a preventive.

Burdock Borer*, *Papaipema cataphracta* (Grote). A smooth, pale-brown caterpillar, with a white stripe down the back and along each side, sometimes infesting stalks of delphinium, dahlia, hollyhock, goldenglow, and iris. The adult is an owlet or cutworm moth, family Noctuidae.

California Flatheaded Borer*, *Melanophila californica* Van Dyke. Larva of a Buprestid beetle, infesting pines in the far West and the northern Rockies. Small, tortuous galleries are formed in slow-growing trees.

California Prionus*, *Prionus californicus* Motschulsky. Also called Giant Apple Borer. This very large, 1½ to 2½ inches, shiny, reddish-brown beetle, family Cerambycidae, is common along the Pacific Coast from Alaska through California and eastward into the Rocky Mountain region and the Southwest. The larvae, grubs 2 to 3 inches long, bore in dead or living roots of oak, alder, poplar, and other hardwoods, and in pine, redwood, Douglas-fir, and fir. Fruit trees are sometimes killed. The adults fly at night, midsummer to fall. They are attracted to lights and may hit windows with great force. The females lay their eggs on roots and the resulting larvae bore for 4 or 5 years before they mature. It may be possible to probe for and destroy them with a knife or wire.

Caribbean Pod Borer*, *Fundella pellucens* Zeller. One of the Pyralid moths.

Carpenterworm*, *Prionoxystus robiniae* (Peck). Widely distributed through the country, attacking many shade trees—ash, elm, locust, maple, oak, poplar, willow, and others—sometimes apricot and pear. It is particularly injurious to live oaks and elm on the Pacific Coast. The name comes from the large tunnels—as much as ½ to 1 inch in diameter—which the caterpillar excavates in solid wood of trees. The borer is white, tinted with rose, with small, brown tubercles over the body and a dark-brown head; 1 to 2½ inches long. The larvae feed in sapwood when young, later through heartwood; the trunk may be riddled with burrows. The life cycle may take 3 years or more. The moth, family Cossidae, comes out in June and July, leaving the pupal skin protruding from the burrow. The female is 2½ to 3 inches

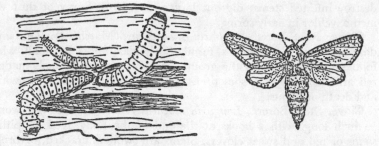

30. Carpenterworm: borer and adult moth.

across the wings, with a stout body, mottled gray fore wings, smaller, smoky hind wings. The male is similar but smaller, with an orange margin on hind wings. Greenish-white sticky eggs are laid in bark crevices, wounds, and old burrows.

Control. Keep all wounds painted. Inject carbon disulfide into openings, about 1 tablespoon to each, and close with putty or grafting wax. Arborists may use calcium cyanide in place of carbon disulfide, or a commercial borer paste.

Cedartree Borer*, *Semanotis ligneus* (Fabricius). A western beetle, family Cerambycidae, working in bark and wood of cedars, arborvitae, redwood, Douglas-fir, and Monterey pine. The adult is black, ½ inch long, with orange or red markings on elytra. The larvae make winding burrows in inner bark and sapwood, girdling and killing trees.

Chestnutbark Borer, *Anoplodera nitens* Forster. An elongate, robust beetle, velvety black with golden bands, breeding in moist bark of chestnut and oak trees in eastern states. Adults are found in tree flowers, and they lay eggs in bark at base of tree and in crotches of living branches. Wounds caused by this borer, allowing entrance to disease spores, played a part in the rapid spread of chestnut blight through North America.

Chestnut Timberworm*, *Melittoma sericeum* (Harris). A pest of our old chestnuts and now one of oak trees in eastern states. The beetle, family Lymexilidae, is chestnut brown, ½ inch long. The larva is slender, white shading to dark brown at the rear. It bores galleries in sapwood and heartwood of dead and living trees. It probably enters through wounds.

Clematis Borer, *Alcathoe caudata* (Harris). The dull-white larva, ⅔ inch long, of a clearwing moth, fore wings black to violet, rear wings transparent with dark margins. The borer works in fleshy roots and crown of clematis and virgins-bower and may hollow out base of stems. Vines are stunted and branches die. Cut out and destroy infested stems; dig out larvae in crowns. Spray or dust with methoxychlor in early spring.

Clover Root Borer*, *Hylastinus obscurus* (Marsham). The small, dark-brown to black beetles, family Scolytidae, and very small, white, footless grubs winter in the ground in clover roots. Tunnels made in red and other clovers, sometimes pea roots, cause wilting, browning, and death of plants.

Clover Stem Borer*, *Languria mozardi* Latreille. Yellowish worms, 1/2 inch long, with 2 hooks at the end of the body, feed on pith in stems of red and sweet clovers. Stems are swollen, cracked, or broken off. The adult is one of the lizard beetles, family Languriidae. It is small, narrow, elongate, with blue wing covers and red head and thorax.

Columbine Borer*, *Papaipema purpurifascia* (Grote & Robinson). Larva of a moth, family Noctuidae, restricted to stems and fleshy roots of wild and cultivated columbine wherever the host is grown. The large reddish-brown moth scatters its eggs on the ground near the plant and the larvae hatch in late April or early May. The salmon caterpillar has a pale stripe down the back, may be up to 1 1/2 inches long. Sawdust-like castings on the ground and dying back of the plant indicate borers at work. Cut off infested stems or destroy plants. Scrape surface of soil in spring to kill eggs. Dust with methoxychlor or spray with Sevin at weekly intervals in late April and May.

Cottonwood Borer*, *Plectrodera scalator* (Fabricius). A large longhorned beetle distributed from Maryland to Louisiana and Texas, particularly injurious in the central and southern states to cottonwood, poplar, and willow. The adult is black, mottled, with a white pubescence; 1 1/2 inches, deeply constricted into segments. It tunnels beneath bark and into wood at base of trunks, infested trees readily blowing over. Sawdust and shredded wood mark its presence. The borer feeds as a larva for 2 years before transforming into a beetle to lay eggs at base of trees. Larvae can be killed by injecting carbon disulfide or borer paste into holes. Spray lower trunks with methoxychlor or endosulfan.

Cottonwood Twig Borer*, *Gypsonoma haimbachiana* (Kearfott). Larva of a small moth, family Olethreutidae.

Cranberry Girdler*, *Chrysoteuchia topiaria* (Zeller). One of the sod webworms or grass moths, family Crambidae, injurious to bluegrass as well as cranberry. An aerial spray of parathion is suggested for commercial cranberry growers.

Currant Borer*, *Synanthedon tipuliformis* (Clerck). A yellowish caterpillar, 1/2 inch long, larva of a small black-and-yellow clearwing moth that looks like a wasp. It is distributed through North America, attacks red and black currants, being more destructive on the latter, and also goooseberry, black elder, and sumac. The larva hibernates in a tunnel in the wood, pupates in spring; the moths emerge in June and July to lay eggs on bark of canes. Cut out and destroy yellowing unthrifty canes before the moths emerge.

Currant Stem Girdler*, *Janus integer* (Norton). One of the stem sawflies, family Cephidae, with adults looking like delicate wasps. The female lays an egg in spring, girdling the stem so the tip hangs down. Legless larvae bore in currant stems. Cut off and destroy infested tips.

Dogwood Borer*, *Synanthedon scitula* (Harris). Sometimes called the Pecan Borer. A whitish caterpillar with brown head, $\frac{1}{2}$ inch long, working in cambium of flowering dogwood and sometimes pecan. The infested areas may be 2 feet or more long and contain up to 50 borers. Small trees or branches may be girdled and die. Small moths, family Aegeriidae, with blue-black margins to their clear wings, emerge from late spring to midsummer to lay eggs in roughened places on the bark.

Control. Spray trunk and branches with endosulfan and repeat a month or so later; or brush ethion over infested areas; or treat soil with 10 per cent dimethoate granules. Avoid mechanical injuries with lawn mowers by placing a guard around the trunk; protect pruning cuts with tree-wound dressing.

Dogwood Cambium Borer*, *Agrilus cephalicus* LeConte. The flat-headed larva of a beetle, working in soft wood; widely distributed but only rarely injurious. Wrap newly transplanted trees; water them properly.

Dogwood Twig Borer*, *Oberea tripunctata* (Swederus). Also known as Elm Twig Girdler and Viburnum Borer. A lemon-yellow grub, larva of a longhorned beetle, boring in center of twigs, making a series of closely placed holes for protrusion of frass. The adult is a slender beetle, to $\frac{5}{8}$ inch long; yellow-tan wing covers, with a black line down the center and black outer margins; three black spots on the thorax and dark head. It emerges in early summer and lays eggs in live twigs. Larvae tunnel down the twig, which may break off as they progress. This borer infests viburnum, elm, and many fruit trees in addition to dogwood. Cut out and destroy infested twigs. Treat soil with dimethoate granules.

Eastern Pineshoot Borer*, *Eucosma gloriola* Heinrich. White Pine Shoot Borer. First reported from Connecticut in 1930 and since then often confused with Nantucket pine moth. Chiefly injuring white and Scotch pine, sometimes on Austrian and red pine, rarely on Douglas-fir, in the Northeast, present also in Michigan. The dirty-white larvae tunnel in pith of new shoots, laterals or leaders, cutting the wood at base of the tunnel. Shoots break off in wind. Moths, family Olethreutidae, copper red with gray scales, appear at end of April or early May, blending with pine-bud scales, to lay eggs on needles or buds.

Elder Borer, *Desmocerus palliatus* (Forster). Cloaked Knotty Horn. A dark-blue beetle with a yellow "cloak" thrown over upper portion of the elytra. The borer is creamy white, an inch long. It riddles base of stems of wild and cultivated elders. The burrows cause dying back of branches, sometimes death of whole shrubs. The beetles sometimes eat notches out of foliage.

Elder Shoot Borer*, *Achatodes zeae* (Harris). The Spindleworm of corn, working in tassel or spindle, found near golden elder. The larva is yellowish-white with a double row of black dots across each segment and a black head. The moth, family Noctuidae, has rusty fore wings mottled with gray, and yellowish-gray hind wings. Cut out dead elder wood in autumn to destroy eggs.

Elm Borer*, *Saperda tridentata* Olivier. Roundheaded larvae of a longhorned beetle, family Cerambycidae. The adult is gray with orange-red bands across the elytra; occurring in eastern states. Park and shade trees are often severely injured, particularly those weakened from defoliation by elm leaf beetles. Eggs are laid in cracks in bark, and grubs work in the inner bark and sapwood, cutting off much of the sap flow. Escaping sap and frass appear as moist spots on the bark. The borers are reddish at first, later creamy white, an inch long when grown. Keep trees growing vigorously with plenty of water; watch for signs of injury and dig out borers; protect bark with methoxychlor.

European Corn Borer*, *Ostrinia nubilalis* (Hübner). One of the most destructive corn pests (Plate XIII). It probably arrived in shipments of broomcorn from Italy or Hungary about 1909 but was not recorded until 1917, in Massachusetts. It has since spread throughout the East and West into Montana, Wyoming, and Utah. It has edged very slightly into Texas. The borer goes south as far as Florida but is not present in that state. It is chiefly a stalk pest, not only in corn but in aster, cosmos, dahlia, gladiolus, hollyhock, chrysanthemum, zinnia, and other flowers as well as in beans, beets, celery, pepper, and potatoes. The corn borer is recorded on about 200 species of plants with stems large enough for the worms to enter.

The larvae, flesh-colored caterpillars with rows of small, round, dark-brown spots, up to 1 inch long, winter in old stalks left around the garden; they pupate in spring. The female moth (family Pyralidae) is yellow-brown with wavy dark bands; the male is somewhat darker. They have a wingspread of 1 inch, fly mostly at night. Eggs are laid in flat masses on underside of corn leaves over a period of 3 to 4 weeks, each female averaging about 400 eggs. These hatch in early June, young larvae working down into the stalks and into the base of ears. Broken tassels, bent stalks, sawdust castings outside small holes signify borers at work. They are occasionally found in fruit or flowers as well as stalks.

The borers predominating in the eastern and southern portions of the corn-borer area are of a multiple-generation strain, varying with the climate. There is 1 generation in northern states, 2 around New Jersey, perhaps 3 in Virginia. A single-generation strain predominates in the North Central States. Despite control measures this pest costs millions of dollars in crop losses each year.

Control. Sanitation is important—cleaning up all stalks (corn, dahlia, or weed) capable of harboring borers over the winter. In regions where there are 2 generations, corn planted the latter half of May usually matures between broods. Early and late corn should be treated. Spray with Sevin, starting when tassels are barely discernible and repeating at 5-day intervals for 3 or 5 applications. Sevin increases mites and kills bees. Include a miticide in the spray and treat in late afternoon when fewer bees are present. Spray thoroughly, especially into the whorl of leaves. Spray ornamentals with Sevin at weekly intervals during July and August.

Of 24 parasites introduced into the United States for corn borer control, 6 have become established. A fungus disease and a protozoan are also helpful.

Firtree Borer*, *Semanotus litigiosus* (Casey). A longhorned beetle.

Flatheaded Apple Tree Borer*, *Chrysobothris femorata* (Olivier). A common pest throughout North America (Plate XIV). The larvae

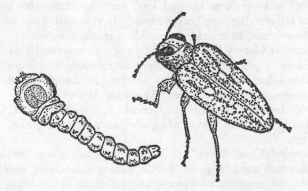

31. Flatheaded apple tree borer and adult beetle.

mine the inner bark, cambium, sapwood, and heartwood of healthy, injured, or dying deciduous fruit and shade trees, including apple, apricot, ash, mountain-ash, beech, boxelder, cherry, chestnut, cottonwood, currant, dogwood, elm, hickory, horsechestnut, linden, maple, oak, peach, pear, pecan, plum, poplar, prune, sycamore, willow, and also raspberry and rose. In the West, oak is often the preferred host; in the East maples and fruits are frequently attacked. This borer kills many trees and shrubs in the nursery and many trees the first season after transplanting. Injury is worse in dry seasons and to tree trunks exposed to too much sun through excessive pruning.

The winter is passed as a grub, up to 1¼ inches long, yellowish white, rather slender, with a broad, flat enlargement just behind the head, usually lying with the body curved to one side, sometimes rather U-shaped. The grub burrows under the bark until full-sized, then bores deeper into the wood. The tunnels, filled with dry frass, run 6 inches or more down the trunk of a small tree or may go around the trunk to girdle it. Overlying bark is discolored, often slightly sunken, and may die, but the injury is not marked by castings, as with other borers.

The beetles, family Buprestidae, are dark olive-gray to brown with a metallic luster, blunt at the head end, tapering at the posterior, ½ inch long. They emerge in May or June and hang around the sunny side of trees or logs. They deposit eggs in bark cracks or some portion of the trunk injured by sunscald or bruising. There is a one-year cycle.

Control. Preventive measures are best. Wrap newly transplanted trees from ground to lower limbs to prevent egg-laying. Shade exposed trunks of young fruit trees by placing an upright board about 6 inches wide close to the trunk on the south side. Prune young fruit trees to keep them headed low. Fertilize and water to promote vigorous growth. Remove borers already in tree with knife or wire and paint the wounds. Insecticides are seldom recommended.

Flatheaded Cherry Tree Borer, *Dicerca divaricata* (Say). An elongate bronze or grayish beetle, widely distributed, infesting cherry and many dying hardwoods. Another species, *D. horni* Crotch, is commonly destructive in the West. The long larvae mine in weakened trees and shrubs, including ornamentals such as ceanothus, California coffee berry, madrona, mountain-mahogany, snowberry elm, sycamore, and others.

Flatheaded Cone Borer*, *Chrysophana placida* var. *conicola* Van Dyke. A small metallic-green beetle mining cones and wood of various pines, firs, mountain hemlock, and redcedar in the West. It injures the seed crop.

Flatheaded Fir Borer*, *Melanophila drummondi* (Kirby). Present but not important in the East; infesting normal or injured firs, Douglas-fir, hemlock, larch, yellow pine, and spruce in the West. Adults are metallic black or bronze beetles, ⅜ to ½ inch long, some with golden spots in wing covers. Curved, flatheaded larvae excavate shallow, winding burrows.

Gallmaking Maple Borer*, *Xylotrechis aceris* Fisher. A small brown beetle attacking red, silver, Norway, and sugar maples. The cream-colored, roundheaded larvae mine in trunks of small trees and in branches of larger trees so extensively that the branch is broken off by wind. New wood produced to heal the wound makes a conspicuous gall.

Grape Cane Gallmaker*, *Ampeloglypter sesostris* (LeConte). A small, reddish-brown, stout-bodied snout beetle making galls on grape shoots.

Grape Cane Girdler, *Ampeloglypter ater* LeConte. Small larvae tunnel in canes causing death of terminal portion. Eggs are laid by a small black snout beetle.

Grape Root Borer*, *Vitacea polistiformis* (Harris). Larva of a brown and orange clearwing moth. Eggs are laid on grape foliage and the round, whitish caterpillars, up to 1¾ inches long, drop to the ground and bore into roots, remaining there for 2 years before pupation in soil outside roots. Cultivate soil to destroy pupae.

Grape Trunk Borer*, *Clytolepus albofasiatus* (LaPorte & Gory). A longhorned beetle.

Hemlock Borer*, *Melanophila fulvoguttata* (Harris). Also called Spotted Hemlock Borer and Eastern Flatheaded Hemlock Borer. It ranges from Maine to North Carolina, attacks hemlock and, more rarely, spruce. The beetle is flat, ½ inch long, dark bronze with wing covers marked with yellow spots. The larva is small, white, with the same type of enlargement behind the head as the flatheaded apple tree borer. The larvae separate the bark from the wood with wide, shallow galleries, often killing trees in parks and on estates as well as those in forests. The beetles emerge in May, June, and July; there is only 1 generation. Drought is most conducive to injury from this borer. Be sure trees have enough water. Prune off infested branches; cut down fatally injured trees; remove and destroy the bark before storing wood. There are several parasites.

Honeylocust Borer, *Agrilus difficilis* Gory. A flatheaded borer on living honeylocust, more important west of the Mississippi River in trees weakened by drought. First symptoms are wet, gummy spots around the nodes.

Iris Borer*, *Macronoctua onusta* Grote. The most destructive pest of iris—German, Japanese, and native blue flag—recorded also on blackberry lily (Belamcanda). The borer winters in the egg stage on old iris leaves and debris and particularly at the base of old iris stalks. The larvae, hatching in April or early May, crawl up the iris leaves and make pinpoint holes as they enter. They gnaw out soft leaf tissue between leaf surfaces and work their way slowly down toward the rhizomes, leaving a water-soaked (due to exuding drops of sap) and ragged appearance to the leaf fans. While in the leaves, the larvae are slender and about 1 inch long, but after reaching the rhizomes, usually in early July, they become fat and repulsive, 1½ to 2 inches long, flesh-colored to pink with chestnut-brown heads. After eating out the interior of the rhizome, the borer pupates in a brown pupa case loose in the soil. The moths, family Noctuidae, have dark purplish fore wings and yellow-brown hind wings. They appear from late August into October, flying only at night. The eggs are flattened and elaborately sculptured, first creamy white with a green tinge, later lavender. In a laboratory test eggs were deposited in groups of 100 or more, with a single female averaging 1,000 eggs, but outdoors in iris foliage the eggs occurred singly or in groups of 3 to 5 together. There is only 1 brood a year.

Control. Clean up all old iris foliage, stalks, and other debris in late autumn to eliminate borer eggs. Young borers can sometimes be killed in place by pressing the leaf between thumb and finger. If iris is to be divided, do it as soon as possible after flowering, cutting out all infested portions.

The chief harm done by iris borers is not so much from their own chewing, devastating as that is, but from their introducing into the plants the bacteria causing the vile-smelling soft rot. This disease was extremely common in gardens before DDT provided an adequate control of borers. Now we must get along without DDT. Spraying in April with endosulfan (Thiodan) has given control but its use may be restricted to professionals. Sevin spray and malathion spray or dust, applied in April when the fans first start to grow, may be effective.

Larger Shothole Borer*, *Scolytus mali* (Beckstein). Sometimes a pest of fruit trees growing near woodpiles. Leaf and fruit spurs may wilt and brown if the beetle feeds in the crotch between spur and twig. This species is recorded from Connecticut, New York, New Jersey, and Ohio.

Leafstalk Borer, *Nepticula sercoptera* (Zeller). Larvae of a small moth bore in leaf petioles, causing drop, and feed in seeds of Norway maple.

Lesser Cornstalk Borer*, *Elasmopalpus lignosellus* (Zeller). Found almost anywhere but only injurious in the South. Slender, greenish, brown-striped worms bore into lower part of stalk, not more than 2 inches from the soil surface, causing distortion and curling of stalks of young corn, often failure to produce ears. The borer feeds also on bean, soybean, pea, cowpea, turnip, even strawberries, and has caused heavy losses in peanuts. The larvae spin their cocoons on the ground under trash. The moths, family Pyralidae, brownish-yellow with gray margins and black spots, appear in 2 or 3 weeks to lay eggs on leaves or stalks. There are 2 generations. Early planting, fall and winter cleanup of land, and rotating corn with a resistant crop are recommended control measures. Aldrin in a band over the seed furrow has given effective control.

Lesser Peach Tree Borer*, *Synanthedon pictipes* (Grote & Robinson). Nearly as important as the peach tree borer, attacking stone fruits, peach, plum, cherry, in all peach-growing sections except the West; most abundant in the South. Masses of gum mixed with brown sawdust exude from upper trunk and branches, especially at forks. Caterpillars ¾ inch long, white with brown heads, work in bark under gum masses. They pupate inside the burrows but close to the openings, which are covered with silk webs. Metallic, blue-black, yellow-marked moths, family Aegeriidae, emerge in May in the South, June in Connecticut, to lay eggs in bark crevices, around crotches or wounds. They are very active on sunny days.

Control. Orchardists should spray with parathion or endosulfan (Thiodan) on June 15, July 1, and September 1 (New Jersey dates), thoroughly soaking all limbs. The home gardener can try malathion but should put most faith in digging out borers by hand, keeping trees properly fed and watered, preventing cultivator damage, prompt treatment of wounds, and choosing trees with wide-angle crotches.

Lilac Borer*, *Podosesia syringae syringae* (Harris). Also known as the Ash Borer and more important on that host than the species officially named the Ash Borer. The lilac borer attacks lilacs, mountain-ash, occasionally privet, through the eastern states to Colorado and Texas. Surely every gardener is familiar with old lilac trunks full of holes and protruding sawdust. On ash there are large scarlike outgrowths where the caterpillars have burrowed in the trunk (Plate XV).

The white borer, ¾ to 1½ inches long, with a brown head, winters in the wood, usually near the ground, feeds again in spring, pushing its burrow nearly through the bark, and then pupates. There are conflicting dates given for emergences, and more than one race may be involved. New England reports late April and May (not until June, 1 year in Connecticut); Illinois reports emergence from May to July and in Virginia it occurs in August and September. The adult is a wasplike clearwing moth with brown fore wings, transparent hind wings with a dark border, wing expanse 1½ inches. It is an active flier. The females lay their eggs in masses at the base of lilac stems or in roughened or wounded places on the bark.

Control. We may no longer spray trunks with DDT or dieldrin. Endosulfan gives fair control, better when applied in summer than in spring, and drenching the bark with dimethoate is quite effective; methoxychlor is another possibility. Borers can be killed in their burrows by injecting borer paste or by inserting a flexible wire. Wounds should be trimmed smooth and painted with shellac or tree-wound dressing.

Limabean Pod Borer*, *Etiella zinckenella* (Treischke). White to greenish or reddish caterpillar, 1 inch long, attacks seeds, in their green pods, of peas, beans, vetch, lupines, and locust trees. The adult is a pyralid moth, small, gray, with ocher markings and a broad white band. Crop rotation is suggested.

Limabean Vine Borer*, *Monoptilota pergratialis* (Hulst). Larva of a pyralid moth, reported as causing some damage to lima beans in Delaware and North Carolina.

Linden Borer*, *Saperda vestita* Say. Principally a linden pest, although it may attack poplars. The beetles (family Cerambycidae) are up to ¾ inch long, dark reddish-brown with olive-yellow pubescence, 3 dark spots on each wing cover. They feed on growing shoots, leaf petioles, and large veins of leaves, often killing tips of branches. Eggs are laid in incisions in trunk and branches. Larvae, white, slender, 1 inch long, mine in bark and wood. Old, unthrifty trees are rather frequently attacked but die slowly, the larger branches first. Worming by hand seems to be the most feasible control but spraying the base of trunks with methoxychlor may help.

Lined Stalk Borer*, *Oligia fractilinea* (Grote). Larva of a noctuid moth.

Little Carpenterworm*, *Prionoxystus macmurtrei* (Guérin). Present throughout eastern United States and west to Minnesota, often more injurious to oaks than the carpenterworm but similar to it in habit and character of damage. Red oaks are favored, especially young trees in street plantings. The female is pepper-and-salt gray, with black, vein-like markings on fore wings, which spread to 2 or 2½ inches; hind wings are clear. The larvae, 2½ inches long, are greenish white with light-brown heads. See carpenterworm for best control.

Liveoak Root Borer, *Archodontes melanopis* Linnaeus. A very large beetle working on eastern live oak, pecan, and hackberry, from Virginia to Florida and along the Gulf Coast. The adult is dark brown, flat, broad, 1¾ to 2¼ inches long, with prominent body segments. The female lays eggs in a collar on young trees just below ground level, and the larvae bore into roots of young oaks, enlarging the root into a huge gall and preventing formation of new roots. New suckers around old stumps make for shrub-oak barrens rather than stately live-oak forests. Digging out the worms by hand is the best control.

Locust Borer*, *Megacyllene robiniae* (Forster). Common wherever black or yellow locust is grown and especially injurious to locusts used as street trees. It is a black longhorned beetle, ½ to ¾ inch long, with bright-yellow crossbands on thorax and wing covers and a conspicuous W-shaped mark at the base of the latter. It feeds on pollen of goldenrod and other composites in autumn. The larvae— white, cylindrical, widest just behind the head—mine in inner bark and sapwood, later burrow into solid wood. Infested trees may be full of longitudinal burrows a half inch in diameter, up to 3 inches long. The trunk may have swollen areas with the bark cracked open. Pupation is in burrows, beetles emerging in August and September to lay eggs in bark scars and crevices. These hatch within 2 weeks and the larvae bore through the corky layer of bark to fashion a small cell for winter. Trees under 6 inches in diameter are more likely to be attacked.

Control. Insert borer paste into the holes and seal the openings. Spray bark of trunk and large branches in late August or early September with lindane (if still allowed). Maintain vigor by proper watering, feeding, and pruning.

Locust Twig Borer*, *Ecdytolopha insiticiana* Zeller. Causes elongate galls, up to 3 inches long, in twigs of black locust. The caterpillar is reddish to yellow, ½ to ¾ inch long. The adult is a small moth (family Olethreutidae) with brown fore wings, gray hind wings. Cut out and burn infested twigs.

Maple Borer, *Xiphydria maculata* Say. One of the wood wasps, family Xiphydriidae, similar to a horntail but lacking the horny plate at the apex of the abdomen. The larvae—cylindrical, whitish, ¾ inch long—make galleries in dead or dying maple wood.

Maple Callus Borer*, *Sylvora acerni* (Clemens). Also known as Maple Sesian. A clearwing moth seriously injuring hard and soft maples in New England and west to Illinois and Nebraska. It is responsible for rough, enlarged scars and deformities on trunks and branches. The trees have difficulty healing wounds because the larvae—white, ½ inch long with brown heads—work in new callus tissue, enlarging small wounds so that young trees are girdled and killed. The moths are amber, with yellow heads and yellow bands on the abdomen,

1-inch wingspread. They appear in late May or June to deposit eggs around old scars and other rough places. Smooth off roughened bark areas; dig out borers under bark in spring; keep wounds painted.

Maple Petiole Borer*, *Caulocampus acericaulis* (MacGillivray). A sawfly fairly common on maple. The larvae, ⅓ inch long, yellow with brown heads, tunnel in leaf petioles in May and June, causing leaf drop. Defoliation seldom exceeds a third of the total foliage so the effect is not too serious. There is only 1 generation a year.

Mulberry Borer, *Dorcaschema wildii* Uhler. One of the most destructive mulberry pests in the South, but found from Ohio to Mississippi, also attacking Osage-orange. The adult is a moderately robust, elongate longhorned beetle, black, covered with gray hairs, and with a narrow light-brown stripe along outer margin. The larvae mine large areas of the cambium and tunnel into wood, girdling and killing branches, sometimes entire trees. In Arkansas adults emerge in May and June, feed for a week or two, and oviposit in niches between bark and wood. The life cycle takes 1 to 2 years.

Nautical Borer, *Xylotrechus nauticus* Mannerheim. Stout, cylindrical beetles (family Cerambycidae), ½ to ⅝ inch long, dark brown with lighter, zigzag markings. The larvae bore in heartwood of dead oak, madrona, and eucalyptus but may attack living trees, including English walnut and peach. Reported from California, Oregon, and Montana.

Neotropical Corn Borer, *Diatraea lineolata* Walker. Small Cornstalk Borer. Bores in stalks of corn and sorghum in Arizona, Texas, and New Mexico.

Oak Sapling Borer*, *Goes tesselatus* (Haldeman). Kills many oaks by cutting them off at the base, weakens others with mines so they break in wind or ice storm. The larva is yellow-white, fleshy. The beetle (family Cerambycidae) is longhorned with yellow-brown wing covers mottled with yellow. The life cycle may last 2 or 3 years.

Oak Timberworm*, *Arrhenodes minutus* (Drury). Also known as Northern Brenthian, a slender beetle with a very long snout (family Brentidae). The shiny brown female, marked with yellow spots, bores a hole in the bark with her snout and pushes an egg to the bottom of the tunnel. The long, slender larvae bore in solid wood of elm, beech, chestnut, and oak, usually in felled timber, sometimes entering living trees through wounds.

Orchid Bulb Borer, *Metamasius graphipterus* (Champion). Blackish beetles, slightly over ½ inch long, with pale-yellow blotches on wing covers, feed on leaves and other parts of orchids. The larvae feed inside bulbs and open the way for fungus rots. Remove and destroy infested bulbs, detected by pressing between the fingers.

Pacific Flatheaded Borer*, *Chrysobothris mali* Horn. Distributed throughout the western states. The adult is a dark-brown to reddish-copper beetle, ¼ to ½ inch long. The larva is similar to the flat-headed apple tree borer and mines normal and injured trees, preferring sunny limbs. Ceanothus is preferred host but alder, apricot, ash, mountain-ash, beech, blackberry, boxelder, California coffee-berry, Catalina cherry, currant, elm, eucalyptus, gooseberry, loquat, manzanita, maple, mesquite, mountain-mahogany, oak, peach, pear, plum, poplar, prune, rose, sycamore, and willow may be attacked. Control measures are the same as for the flatheaded apple tree borer.

Painted Hickory Borer*, *Megacyllene caryae* (Gahan). Distributed from New England to Texas wherever hickory is grown, chiefly a pest of cut timber. It is partial to shagbark hickory but may also infest black walnut, butternut, elm, honeylocust, Osage-orange, and hackberry. The adult is similar to the locust borer, with long antennae, yellow transverse bands, and a yellow W on dark-brown elytra.

Peachtree Borer*, *Sanninoidea exitiosa* (Say). A native moth, the most important enemy of peach trees, also attacking plum, wild and cultivated cherry, prune, nectarine, apricot, and some ornamental shrubs in the genus Prunus (Plate XVI). First sign of injury is usually a mass of gum and brown frass at the base of the trunk, indicating that the white, brown-headed worms are at work in the bark anywhere from 2 to 3 inches below ground to 10 inches above. They winter as larvae of all sizes in the burrows, finish feeding in spring, when they are about 1 inch long, then pupate in brown silk cocoons in soil near the base of the tree. Just before the moth emerges the pupa is forced out of the cocoon.

In the North, most of the moths (family Aegeriidae) emerge during July and August; in the South, during August and September. The female is blue-black with clear hind wings and narrow yellow bands on the abdomen. Each female lays several hundred eggs near the base of the tree trunk, the young worms hatching in 10 days to bore inside the bark. Peaches seldom survive repeated borer attacks.

Control. For many years the standard remedy was a ring of para-dichlorobenzene crystals placed on the soil around the tree 1 inch away from the trunk, and then mounded with 2 to 3 shovelfuls of earth to hold in the fumes. Treating the trunks with DDT largely replaced fumigation and now that DDT is banned commercial orchardists are turning to endosulfan (Thiodan). Spray trunk and scaffold limbs in late September (New Jersey area) using 1½ pounds of 50 per cent WP Thiodan to 100 gallons of water. This is a toxic material with some restrictions for home gardeners. Growers may protect young trees before planting with a Thiodan root dip, 1 pound to 10 gallons of water. This must be used with great caution, wearing rubber gloves, and disposing of excess dip where it will not harm people, pets, or wildlife. Treat several days before planting. Probing out the borers with a knife or flexible wire is helpful but it is seldom possible to find all the worms.

In warmer climates, such as Virginia, more than one application of endosulfan may be necessary. Spraying trunks and lower limbs on May 1, June 1, July 15, and August 15 is suggested for dual control of the peachtree borer and the lesser peachtree borer.

Peach Twig Borer*, *Anarsia lineatella* Zeller. A small, reddish-brown larva, under ½ inch, boring in and killing tips of twigs, infesting fruit later in the season. The borer, a minor pest in the East but quite injurious on the West Coast, infests plums, prunes, nectarines, almonds, apricots, as well as peaches. The grayish moth (family Gelechiidae) is so small that it is seldom noticed. A dormant lime-sulfur spray, 1 to 15 dilution, is helpful, as is spraying with lead arsenate before the blossoms reach the pink stage and after petal fall.

Pecan Borer. See Dogwood Borer. This species attacks pecan in the Southeast, being worse on recently top-worked trees. Protect scions from borer injury by covering all graft wounds with grafting wax which will not crack.

Pecan Carpenterworm*, *Cossula magnifica* (Strecker). Also known as Oak or Hickory Cossid. It bores into trunk and larger branches of pecan, oak, and hickory in southern states. Reddish pellets of wood at the base of the tree indicate that the pinkish larva, 1½ inches long with fine short hairs, is boring within. The moth (family Cossidae) is gray, mottled with brown and black.

Persimmon Borer*, *Sannina uroceriformis* Walker. The larva of a clearwing moth bores into solid wood and taproot of persimmon in southern states, often causing severe damage to trees.

Pigeon Tremex*, *Tremex columba* (Linnaeus). A native wasplike insect, one of the horntails (family Siricidae, order Hymenoptera). The cylindrical white larva, up to 3 inches long, with a short horn at the tip of the abdomen, bores tunnels in diseased and dying trees, most commonly elm and sugar maple, sometimes beech, apple, pear, sycamore, and oak. The female adult, with a 2-inch body and wing-spread, has a reddish head and thorax, black abdomen with yellow bands, smoky brown wings, and a horned tail at the end of the body which is a sheath for a long ovipositor. For control, squirt carbon disulfide into the burrows. The ichneumon wasp is a helpful parasite; the female lays her eggs right through wood into the horntail larva in its burrow.

Pitch Mass Borer*, *Vespamima pini* (Kellicott). Larva of a clear-wing moth, body black and orange, fore wings opaque, blackish, with metallic sheen, found from Georgia to Canada and west to Wisconsin on pitch pine, white pine, and spruce. Eggs are deposited on bark or near a wound and the larvae bore for 2 or 3 years in inner bark and sapwood, causing a great exudation of pitch. Pupation takes place in this pitch mass.

Plum Gouger. See under Beetles.

Ponderosa Pine Bark Borer*, *Acanthocinus princeps* (Walker). A large white grub commonly found in ponderosa pines killed by the western pine beetle, but not injurious to living trees. Adults are large, speckled gray beetles with very long antennae (family Cerambycidae).

Poplar Borer*, *Saperda calcarata* Say. A large native beetle, distributed through the country, attacking Lombardy and other poplars, cottonwood (except for a resistant form in the Mississippi Valley), aspen, and willows. It severely injures ornamental shade trees, marring them with blackened swollen scars on the outside of wood honeycombed with irregular galleries. The beetle is reddish-brown with gray and yellow pubescence, yellow stripes on thorax and elytra, 1⅛ inches long. Adults, appearing from July to September, feed on bark of young twigs and lay eggs in slits in the bark. The larvae—yellow grubs up to 1½ inches—work in the bark the first year, tunneling into the wood in the second year, sending out frass to the openings. This accumulates at the base of trees.

Control. Destroy seriously infested trees before beetles emerge in spring. Nurserymen may spray with endosulfan in July (New Jersey date), repeating 2 weeks later; methoxychlor is another recommendation. Probe borers with a wire or fumigate with carbon disulfide, injected from an oilcan, closing the opening with putty or wax. Painting egg scars with wood-preserving creosote kills young grubs.

Poplar-and-Willow Borer*, *Cryptorhynchus lapathi* (Linnaeus). Also called Mottled Willow Borer. This is a small European weevil which has spread from Maine to Wisconsin and North Dakota since it was first noticed in New York in 1882. It has also been reported in the Northwest. The borer attacks willow, poplar, alder, and birch, with serious injury to poplars and willows over a year old. It winters as partly grown larvae. The grubs—thick, legless, ½ inch long—make burrows around the trunk in the cambium, girdling the tree. As they mature, they enter hardwood and honeycomb it with galleries. Smaller limbs and branches have swollen knotty areas; foliage may wilt. The dark-brown beetles, ⅓ inch long, are covered with light-brown and gray scales in a mottled effect. They are present in July and August feeding on young shoots. They lay eggs in slits cut in the corky bark, often in scar tissue. Spray trunks with endosulfan in late August and repeat in 2 weeks.

Potato Stalk Borer*, *Trichobaris trinotata* (Say). Injures potatoes, early varieties in particular, and may attack eggplant, tomato, groundcherry, and related weeds. It is present in most sections of the country and, when abundant, may destroy whole fields of potatoes. It hibernates as an adult, a bluish-gray snout beetle ⅕ inch long, with 3 black spots at the base of the wing covers. It eats deep holes in stems of new plants in spring and deposits eggs singly in such cavities in stems or leaf petioles. The very small, yellow-white, wrinkled grubs hollow out the stems for several inches, causing wilting and death of plants. Before pupating, the larva packs its burrow with "excelsior"—scrapings from the stem—and chews an exit passage for the adult to use in spring. There is 1 generation a year. Clean up and bury deeply all potato vines after harvest; destroy nearby weeds with stalks large enough to harbor borers.

Potato Stem Borer*, *Hydroecia micacea* (Esper). A noctuid moth.

Potato Tuberworm*, *Phthorimaea operculella* (Zeller). Sometimes called Tuber Moth, destructive to potatoes from Florida north to Virginia and west to California. Eggplant, tobacco, and related weeds may also be attacked. The small moths (family Gelechiidae), narrow-winged, gray-brown mottled with darker brown, ½ inch across the wings, escape from storehouses in spring and lay eggs, singly, on underside of leaves or in eyes of potato tubers. The ¾-inch-long larvae, pinkish white with brown heads, burrow in stems or petioles or mine in leaves. Maturing in 2 or 3 weeks, they pupate inside dirt-covered silk cocoons in trash on the ground, appearing as adults in 7 to 10 days. The entire life cycle takes only a month and there may be 5 or 6 generations a season, with most injury in hot, dry summers. Adults of late broods work down through cracks in soil to lay eggs in tubers, the larvae making dirty, silk-lined burrows through the flesh. They come out of the tubers to pupate in odd corners around the storage room.

Control. Plant uninfested seed pieces; keep potatoes well cultivated and deeply hilled during growth. Spray foliage with endosulfan or azinphosmethyl. Cut and destroy infested vines a few days before digging; do not leave newly dug potatoes exposed to egg-laying by moths during late afternoon or night; destroy culls. Screen storage places in warm weather. Burlap potato bags should be treated with an insecticide to prevent reinfestation or to kill larvae in already infested tubers.

Ragweed Borer*, *Epiblema strenuanum* (Walker). An olethreutid moth.

Raspberry Cane Borer*, *Oberea maculata* (Olivier). A longhorned beetle, generally distributed from Kansas eastward, a pest of raspberry and blackberry, sometimes rose, reported on azalea. The slender black-and-yellow-striped female, with 2 black dots on a yellow thorax, makes a double row of punctures around the stem near the tip and lays an egg between the girdles. The tip wilts and the grub, when it hatches in summer, bores down the cane 1 or 2 inches before hibernating. The next season it continues to bore down inside the cane and pupates inside this burrow; the cane dies. Cut out and destroy wilting tips as soon as noticed, pruning 6 inches below the punctured area. Cut out wilted or dead fruiting canes.

Raspberry Crown Borer*, *Bembecia marginata* (Harris). Also called Raspberry Root Borer, causing wilting and dying of fruiting canes of blackberry, raspberry, loganberry, salmonberry, and wild thimbleberry in early summer, often when berries are ripening. The adult is a clearwing moth, with a black body crossed with 4 yellow bands. Eggs—oval, reddish brown, the size of mustard seed—are deposited on the underside of leaves, near the edge, in late summer. Small white caterpillars hibernate the first winter in blister-like elevations of bark just under soil level or at the base of stems. The borers make extensive galleries in spring, and by the second summer the whole crown may be hollowed out.

Control. Dig out and destroy infested canes and crowns in late fall or early spring. Drench crowns and lower 2 feet of canes with diazinon (4 teaspoons diazinon 2E per gallon water) between October 1 and March 1; repeat a year later. This recommendation is given to home owners in the state of Washington. For commercial growers in New Jersey the current suggestion is parathion applied during egg-laying (about September 10) and repeated 2 weeks later. In serious cases crowns are drenched with diazinon in spring.

Redheaded Ash Borer*, *Neoclytus acuminatus* (Fabricius). Attacking felled hardwoods—ash, oak, hickory, persimmon, mesquite. The adults, working in living trees, are elongate longhorned beetles, reddish-brown marked with yellow crossbands.

Rednecked Cane Borer*, *Agrilus ruficollis* (Fabricius). In eastern United States, causing cigar-shaped swellings in raspberry, blackberry, or dewberry canes, which may die or break off at the swollen joint. Bluish-black beetles (family Buprestidae) with a coppery thorax, 1/3 inch long, lay eggs in bark of canes, usually near a leaf, which may be eaten and appear ragged. The young, flatheaded larvae bore upward in sapwood and several times around the canes, girdling them. The easiest remedy is to cut out swollen canes. Some varieties are rather resistant to attack.

Red Oak Borer*, *Enaphalodes rufulus* (Haldeman). A longhorned beetle.

Rhododendron Borer*, *Synanthedon rhododendri* Beutenmüller. A small, native clearwing moth, injuring rhododendrons and sometimes adjacent mountain-laurel and azalea in eastern United States, also reported on blueberry in Michigan. The moths, black with 3 yellow transverse bands on the abdomen, only ⅜ to ½ inch wingspread, lay eggs in May and June on twigs. The yellow-white larvae, ½ inch long, bore in sapwood under the bark, causing branches to wilt or break off. Injury in the same shrubs increases year to year, with leaves turning brown, main trunks filled with holes and protruding fine sawdust. Cut and destroy infested portions whenever noticed. New Jersey suggests that nurserymen spray bark with endosulfan, starting in mid-May and repeating 3 times at 10-day intervals, and that home owners should substitute lindane for endosulfan. In New York, however, lindane is restricted and not sold without a permit. In a Connecticut test paradichlorobenzene crystals dissolved in xylene were painted on bark of trunk and branches; all borers were killed.

Root Collar Borer, *Euzophera ostricolorella* Hulst. Reported from New York to Florida and Tennessee, Kentucky and Indiana on yellow-poplar (tuliptree) and magnolia. The larvae, 1 inch long when mature, bore near the root collar and lower part of trunk, mostly in an area from 2 inches below the duff to 5 inches above. Trees of all sizes may die.

Rose Stem Girdler*, *Agrilus aurichalceus* Redtenbacher. Similar to the rednecked cane borer, with the same life history, primarily a rose pest but also infesting blackberry. Distribution is mostly east of the Mississippi, but this greenish beetle is also reported on raspberry in Utah. Eggs are laid under bark, and the grubs make 1 or 2 spiral mines around the canes, which swell and sometimes split at such points. This girdler is common on species roses, particularly *Rosa rugosa* and *R. hugonis,* but is rare on garden roses. Cut out swollen canes early in spring.

Roundheaded Appletree Borer*, *Saperda candida* Fabricius. A native beetle distributed generally east of the Rocky Mountains (Plate XIV). It is best known as an apple pest but may be injurious to quince, pear, plum, peach, mountain-ash, hawthorn, wild crab, shadbush, and chokecherry. It usually works in tree trunks at ground level, or just above or below, killing young trees, seriously injuring older specimens. The life cycle is normally completed in 3 years in the North, 2 in the South. The young grub, first brownish red, later creamy white, with a rounded thickening just behind the head, starts to work in the bark, producing brown sap stains, then tunnels in the sapwood for a year or two, ejecting conspicuous coils of rusty-brown frass. The next season it bores into the heartwood, tunneling outward in fall to prepare a winter chamber near the bark. The upper end of the chamber, curved out so that it almost touches the bark, is filled with sawdust-like frass; the lower end is packed with coase wood cuttings. The larva pupates here in May; the beetle emerges from late May to July.

The adults—just under an inch long, yellow or reddish brown above, white underneath—have 2 conspicuous white stripes the length of the body and prominent gray antennae. They crawl over the tree, feeding somewhat on foliage and fruit, and lay eggs in slits in the bark near ground level. In New York egg laying lasts from late June to late August, in Maryland from late May to mid-July.

Control. Examine trees carefully, scooping away an inch or two of earth near the base, for brown castings or stained areas in bark. Cut out borers in shallow tunnels with the tip of a knife; probe for deep-seated borers with a wire with a hooked tip. Worm the trees in early fall and check again in spring. Examine nearby wild host trees for borer infestation. A fumigant for injecting into borer holes is prepared by dissolving 10 grams of paradichlorobenzene in 10 cc of carbon disulfide. The ordinary apple-spray schedule helps to control the beetles on foliage.

Roundheaded Cone Borer*, *Paratimia conicola* Fisher. A rusty reddish-brown beetle, longhorned. The larva tunnels in cones of knobcone and shore pine in California.

Roundheaded Fir Borer*, *Tetropium abietis* Fall. A velvety brown, longhorned beetle, ¾ inch long, pest of western conifers. The grubs work under the bark of felled and standing firs.

Rustic Borer*, *Xylotrechus colonus* (Fabricius). A very common eastern beetle (family Cerambycidae), dark brown with irregular white or yellowish markings. The larvae are found under bark of almost all dead hardwoods.

Sapwood Timberworm*, *Hylecoetus lugubris* Say. One of the ship-timber beetles (family Lymexylidae), slender, elongate with serrated antennae, reddish brown or black. The grubs, with a barbed spine on the 9th segment, make round mines in sapwood of poplar, birch, and tuliptree.

Saskatoon Borer*, *Saperda bipunctata* R. Hopping. A longhorned beetle.

Sculptured Pine Borer*, *Chalcophora angulicollis* (LeConte). Largest of the western flatheaded borers. Adults are over 1 inch long, dark brown to black, with an iridescent bronze luster, and the wing covers are marked with irregularly sculptured areas. Larvae feed in dead pine, firs, and Douglas-fir.

Seagrape Borer, *Hexeris enhydris* Grote. Larva of a moth, abundant on this host in southern Florida.

Shothole Borer*, *Scolytus rugulosus* (Ratzeburg). Equally well known as the Fruit Tree Bark Beetle, a European insect generally

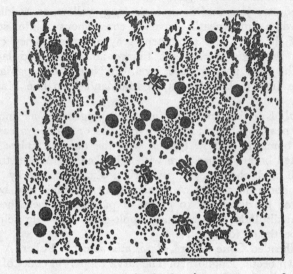

32. Shothole borer: section of bark showing emergence holes, small beetles.

distributed over the country. It makes small holes like shot holes in the bark of twigs of healthy trees and in branches and trunks of weakened trees. In addition to fruit trees—almond, apple, apricot, cherry, loquat, peach, nectarine, pear, plum, and prune—it may attack mountain-ash, elm, hawthorn, and Juneberry. On stone fruits the shot holes are usually covered with gum. If borers are abundant the foliage yellows, wilts, and the tree may die. The pinkish white grub, ⅛ inch long, winters in the inner bark. The larval galleries are winding, sawdust-filled, leading out from a shorter central gallery. The black, blunt beetles, 1/10 inch long, emerge in early summer. The females fly to unhealthy trees to excavate an egg gallery in branch or twig, depositing eggs on each side of this. There may be 1 to 3 generations, depending on climate.

Control. Keep trees in vigorous condition with nitrogenous fertilizers and sufficient water; remove and destroy prunings and dying trees.

Egg-laying can be somewhat prevented by coating trunk and lower branches with whitewash, applying in early spring, in mid-summer, and in the fall. Table salt added to each pail of whitewash will make it stick better. Commercial orchards can be sprayed with parathion, when adult beetles are present in maximum numbers.

Sinuate Peartree Borer*, *Agrilus sinuatus* (Olivier). A European beetle first noticed in New Jersey in 1894, now known in New England, New York, and Ohio. It is primarily a pest of pear but may injure hawthorn, mountain-ash, and cotoneaster. The beetles are slender, very flat, ⅓ inch long, purplish bronze, and feed on foliage. The grubs are long, slender, flat, and make sinuate galleries in trunk and branches during the winter, with swelling or cracking of bark. Clean up dead or dying trees or branches during the winter. Spray foliage with lead arsenate or methoxychlor when beetles emerge (May or June) and repeat 2 weeks later.

Smartweed Borer*, *Ostrinia obumbratalis* (Lederer). Larva of a pyralid moth, related to the European corn borer.

Southern Cornstalk Borer*, *Diatraea crambidoides* (Grote). A southern insect, found from Kansas south, principally on corn. Infested stalks are twisted and stunted, with an enlargement near the ground. Leaves are ragged, showing holes eaten out while still in the whorl. Borers are dirty gray-white, with many dark-brown spots, 1 inch long. They pupate in stalks near the ground. Straw-colored moths emerge in late spring to lay many overlapping eggs on underside of leaves. The borers may move from one plant to another; there are 1 to 3 generations. Control by sanitation, cleaning up corn stubble and refuse right after harvest; by late fall or winter spading or plowing; and by rotation with some other crop.

Southwestern Corn Borer*, *Diatraea grandiosella* (Dyar). Found mostly west of the Mississippi River. A corn pest resembling the southern cornstalk borer in appearance and injury. Treatment with azodrin, carbofuran, or endosulfan has increased yield.

Spotted Limb Borer, *Psoa maculata* (LeConte). A dark bronzy beetle, with grayish hairs, and 4 or more white, yellow, or reddish spots on black or bluish green wing covers. Breeding in dead wood of oak, apple, grapevines, white sage, and other trees and shrubs in California.

Squash Vine Borer*, *Melittia cucurbitae* (Harris). A native pest, present east of the Rocky Mountains, often spoiling 25 per cent of the commerical squash crop and even more injurious in home gardens. Injuring pumpkin, gourd, cucumber, and muskmelon, in that order (Plate XVI). The borer winters as larva or pupa inside a silk-lined cocoon an inch or two below soil level. The clearwing moth—wasplike with copper-green fore wings, orange-and-black abdomen, 1 to 1½ inches across the wings—appears when vine crops start to run. It glues small, oval, flat brown eggs singly on stems and leaf stalks. Young borers hatch in about a week, tunnel into the stem to feed. The first sign of their presence is a sudden wilting of the vine, then masses of greenish yellow excrement protruding from holes in the stem. The borer, a wrinkled white caterpillar up to 1 inch long with brown head, can be found by slitting the stem with a knife. Later in the season it is present in fruits as well as stems. After feeding for 4 to 6 weeks it goes into the soil to make its cocoon. There are 2 generations in the Gulf States, normally 1 in the North, sometimes a partial 2nd.

Control is difficult. Dusting with rotenone or methoxychlor at weekly intervals, starting when vines start to run, kills some larvae before they enter the stems. Farmers may use endosulfan, sprayed on the bases of plants 4 times at 7-day intervals. If the vine begins to wilt, kill the borer with a knife and heap earth over the stem joints to start new roots. Make a second planting of summer squash to mature after the borers are through feeding. Pull up and destroy vines immediately after harvest.

Stalk Borer*, *Papaipema nebris* (Guenée). A universal feeder, occurring everywhere east of the Rocky Mountains. The slender, striped caterpillar, ¾ to 1½ inches long, works in the stem of any plant large enough and soft enough for its operations, although it favors giant ragweed and corn in later stages. The stalk borer is a frequent pest of dahlia and iris and is often found on aster, goldenglow, hollyhock, lily, rhubarb, pepper, tomato, and potato. It winters as grayish, ridged eggs on grasses and weeds. These hatch very early in spring with the borers working first in grasses before going over to herbaceous stalks, entering at the side and burrowing up. The young larva has a dark-brown or purple band around the cream-colored body and several brown or purple lengthwise stripes, but these almost disappear and the full-grown caterpillar is grayish or light purple. The borers are very restless, often changing one host for another. They pupate in late summer just under the soil surface, or, rarely, inside stalks. The moths (family Noctuidae) are grayish brown with white spots on the fore wings, which spread to 1 inch. They appear in August and September to lay upward of 2,000 eggs per female. There is only 1 generation a year.

Control. By the time injury is noted, it is usually too late to save the plant, but sometimes it is possible to slit a stem, kill the borer with a knife, and then bind the stem together. Spray or dust plants with methoxychlor to destroy borers on the move. Clean up weeds in the vicinity.

Strawberry Crown Borer*, *Tyloderma fragariae* (Riley). Rather general east of the Rocky Mountains, especially important in Kentucky, Tennessee, and Arkansas. The adult is a small brown snout beetle less than ⅕ inch long, shaped like a grape seed, each wing cover marked with 3 black bars. The grub is small and yellow, taking on a pinkish tinge as it feeds on strawberry tissues. The adults, which cannot fly, winter under trash in beds and appear about blossomtime to lay eggs—glistening white, elliptical—in shallow holes in crowns and at base of leaf stalks. The grubs hatch in about a week and burrow downward into the center of the crown, killing or stunting the plants. They pupate in the burrow in late summer and the beetles feed on strawberry foliage in early fall, making characteristic small feeding holes. There is 1 generation.

Control. Because the insects cannot crawl very far, locate new strawberry beds more than 300 feet from old strawberry fields. Set certified new plants or those that have been treated with hot water as for the cyclamen mite. Plow up old plantings immediately after harvest. Farmers may treat infested strawberry fields with chlordane or toxaphene but not after fruit is formed.

Sugarbeet Crown Borer*, *Hulstia undulatella* (Clemens). A pyralid moth, gray marked with black, with a red spot near base of fore wings. The caterpillars, transparent green to yellow, attack sugar beets just below the base of the leaves, bore into the crown and down into the root. Silken tubes in the soil extend from beet to beet.

Sugarcane Borer*, *Diatraea saccharalis* (Fabricius). Causing an average annual loss of 10 million dollars in sugarcane and also attacking corn in Florida, Mississippi, Louisiana, and Texas. Related to the southern cornstalk borer, the larva is yellowish white, the moth straw-colored with black dots.

Sugar Maple Borer*, *Glycobius speciosus* (Say). A native longhorned beetle, dangerous to sugar maples in the Northeast and apparently confined to them. The striking adult is black with yellow bands and yellow tips to the elytra, the yellow coloration near the base forming a W; it is 1 inch long. The roundheaded larva is 2 inches long, somewhat flattened, rose-white. It bores a wide channel several feet long in inner bark and sapwood, often going halfway around the tree. The bark over this section cracks, producing an ugly scar to which other insects are attracted. There is a 2-year cycle, adults laying eggs in summer. Remove dead branches before June 1. Cut out grubs where possible. Spray bark in August, wetting it thoroughly with lindane or methoxychlor.

Sweetclover Root Borer*, *Walshia miscecolorella* (Chambers). Larva of a moth, family Walshiidae.

Sweetpotato Vine Borer*, *Omphisa anastomosalis* (Guenée). Larva of a pyralid moth.

Sycamore Borer, *Ramosia resplendens* (Hy. Edwards). A burrowing moth injuring sycamores and live oaks in California.

Tiger Hickory Borer. See White Oak Borer.

Tilehorned Prionus*, *Prionus imbricornis* (Linnaeus). Common on oaks and chestnut in the Southeast, boring in roots of living trees. The adult is a large, brownish black beetle; the larva is elongate, tapering posteriorly, with a wide head.

Tobacco Stalk Borer*, *Trichobaris mucorea* (LeConte). Similar to the potato stalk borer, attacking potatoes in the Southwest.

Turpentine Borer*, *Buprestis apricans* Herbst. On long leaf and slash pines from North Carolina to Texas. The beetles are large, gray-bronze with a greenish metallic luster and longitudinal rows of large punctures on each wing cover. They feed on needles in the tops of trees before laying eggs. The larvae—flatheaded, 1½ inches long—mine the sapwood and heartwood for 3 years.

Twig Girdler*, *Oncideres cingulata* (Say). Twigs and small branches up to several feet long are found neatly cut off and lying on the ground under hickory, pecan, persimmon, oak, poplar, sourgum, honeylocust, and other trees in eastern states, also in Oklahoma. Grayish, hard-shelled beetles, with antennae longer than body, girdle the twigs by cutting round and round from the bark inward. In young trees there may be appreciable injury. Pecans may be deformed and the nut crop reduced. In persimmon the beetle wounds afford entrance to the deadly wilt fungus. Gather and destroy all severed branches in late fall when eggs and grubs are inside.

Twig Pruner*, *Elaphidionoides villosus* (Fabricius). Also called Oak Twig Pruner, found west to Michigan and south to the Gulf States, attacking oak, hickory, pecan, maple, locust, hackberry, elm, walnut, sweetgum, and some fruit trees. Shade trees are often so severely pruned by larvae burrowing in twigs that their shape is ruined. The ground may be thickly strewn with twigs. The adults, (family Cerambycidae), brownish elongate beetles about ½ inch long, appear when oak leaves unfold and lay eggs in leaf axils near tips of twigs. Clean up all severed twigs.

Twolined Chestnut Borer*, *Agrilus bilineatus* (Weber). A native beetle distributed from Maine to Texas. It attacks apparently normal but actually weakened oaks, chestnut, beech, ironwood. The beetle is slender, ⅓ inch long, greenish black, covered with golden hairs and with a golden stripe down each wing cover. It emerges in May or June, feeds on foliage for some time, then lays eggs under bark scales. The larvae are slender, white, flat, with an enlargement behind the head. They mine in cambium, girdling trunk and branches and working from 40 to 50 feet in the air down to the ground. Weakened trees die rapidly. Methoxychlor applied to trunk and branches in early July may help protect valuable shade trees. Water and fertilizer will aid in recovery.

Western Cedar Borer*, *Trachykele blondeli* Marsuel. Bright emerald-green sculptured beetles, ⅝ inch long, destructive to western redcedar, cypress, California incense cedar, and related species. Flathead larvae mine in sapwood and heartwood of living and dying trees.

Western Larch Roundheaded Borer*, *Tetropium velutinum* LeConte. On larch, hemlock, sometimes Douglas-fir, spruce, and pine in Rocky Mountain and Pacific Coast regions. Adults are elongated velvety brown beetles. Larvae construct winding mines between bark and wood and may girdle trees.

Western Peachtree Borer*, *Sanninoidea exitiosa graefi* (Hy. Edwards). A western variety of the peachtree borer, also injuring plum, prune, apricot, sometimes apple and almond. See Peachtree Borer for control.

West Indian Sugarcane Root Borer, *Diaprepes abbreviatus* (Linnaeus). A West Indian pest found infesting a Florida nursery in 1968 and by the next year had spread over 600 acres. The larvae cause severe damage to citrus roots, girdling them, and the adult weevils feed on foliage. The infested areas are regulated by the state to prevent spread.

White Oak Borer*, *Goes tigrinus* (De Geer). Also known as Tiger Hickory Borer. A longhorned beetle attacking hickory, oak, preferably white oak, and walnut. The adult is a brown beetle with a dark band, covered with fine gray hairs, and with pinkish antennae. The larva is 1 inch long, lemon yellow, with prominent segments. It excavates large burrows in sapwood and inner bark. The life cycle may take 3 to 5 years.

White Pine Shoot Borer. See Eastern Pineshoot Borer.

BUDWORMS (BUD MOTHS)

Budworms are small caterpillars that feed in or on opening buds. Sometimes the common name is that of the adult state, bud moth.

Eastern Blackheaded Budworm*, *Acleris variana* (Fernald). An important defoliator of hemlock, true firs, and spruce in northern United States and Canada, often reported from Alaska. Small moths (family Tortricidae), gray or dappled, wingspread ¾ inch, lay eggs in August and September on underside of needles. In spring, bright-green caterpillars with black heads feed on new foliage or opening buds, webbing the needles together. There are several natural parasites and a virus that aid in control.

Eyespotted Bud Moth*, *Spilonota ocellana* (Denis & Schiffer-müller). An apple pest through northern apple sections but also infesting blackberry, hawthorn, larch, laurel, oak, pear, plum, cherry, and occasionally some forest trees. It is recorded as serious on cherry in Wisconsin. The larvae, small brown worms with black heads, winter in small silken cases attached to twigs or bud axils. They eat out the buds as they open in spring or tie leaves together with silken threads. They pupate in early summer in their silken nests. Small brown moths (family Olethreutidae), with a light band on each wing, lay eggs on underside of leaves for the summer brood. Control by spraying with malathion or parathion at the delayed dormant stage.

Green Budworm*, *Hedia variegana* (Hübner). An olethreutid moth.

Holly Bud Moth, *Rhopobota naevana ilicifoliana* (Kearfott). An important pest of holly in the Pacific Northwest for more than 40 years. It was accidentally introduced from British Columbia and spread through Washington and Oregon. Overwintering in the egg stage, the larvae appear as buds are opening and feed on new leaves inside a web. The caterpillars drop to the ground to pupate. Moths emerge and lay eggs during July and August. These are deposited singly on leaves and twigs. There is 1 generation a year and holly is the only known host. Spray with malathion, diazinon, or carbaryl just after new growth starts but before blossoming.

Jack Pine Budworm*, *Choristoneura pinus* Freeman. Causing serious damage to jack pine and some injury to white and red pine in the Lakes States. Defoliation in Wisconsin, Michigan, and Minnesota is often severe enough to require spraying to reduce epidemic populations. The larvae are similar to those of the spruce budworm. The moths are slightly smaller, wingspread under 1 inch, with reddish tan, mottled fore wings.

Larch Bud Moth, *Zeiraphera griseana* (Hübner). A European species causing heavy defoliation of larch and white fir, sometimes Englemann spruce and Douglas-fir in Washington, Oregon, Idaho, and Montana. The larvae feed on tender new growth, crawling into opening buds and webbing new needles together. The moths, wingspread ½ to ¾ inch, have grayish white wings splotched with brown and black.

Lesser Bud Moth*, *Recurvaria nanella* (Hübner). Similar in appearance and habit to the eyespotted bud moth, but mining leaves to some extent.

Pecan Bud Moth*, *Gretchena bolliana* (Slingerland). Primarily a bud feeder; sometimes causes excessive branching or stunting. Young larvae are black, older caterpillars yellow-green with brown heads, just over ½ inch long. Eggs are laid on foliage, or, early in the season, on twigs.

Raspberry Bud Moth*, *Lampronia rubiella* (Bjerkand). A moth in the family Incurvariidae.

Rhododendron Bud Moth, *Euchordylea huntella*. Small pinkish white larvae make blotch mines covered with silk and debris in rhododendron leaves; later mine midrib and bore into twigs and buds. Spray with methoxychlor.

Rose Budworm, *Pyrrhia umbra* Hufnagel. On buds of rose, columbine, and other garden flowers. There are 2 kinds of caterpillars. One is green, spotted with black tubercles and with prominent, dark, longitudinal stripes; the other has whitish orange markings on the back. The adult is the bordered sallow moth. Remove infested buds as soon as noticed. Spray or dust with methoxychlor or malathion.

Spruce Bud Moth*, *Zeiraphera canadensis* Mutsuura & Freeman. An introduced pest established in the Pacific Northwest and Alaska. Very small light-brown moths, with darker diagonal markings, lay eggs on spruce needles. Each young caterpillar crawls into an opening bud, webbing new needles together as it feeds. On Sitka spruce in Washington and Oregon all new tips may be killed; trees are branched excessively.

Spruce Budworm*, *Choristoneura fumiferana* (Clemens). A serious enemy of forest trees, distributed all over northern United States and

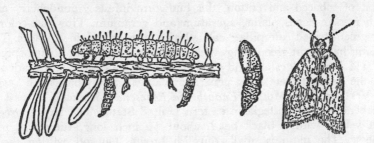

33. Spruce budworm: larva, empty pupa cases hanging from twig, tortricid moth adult.

Canada. It has ranked third in importance of all our insects, next to the cotton boll weevil and the corn earworm. It has cycles of enormous abundance in spruce and balsam fir forests and may injure ornamental spruce, fir, Douglas-fir. When attacks are heavy, entire trees are stripped of foliage and killed; whole forests appear as if scorched by fire. When defoliation is not complete, terminals are killed.

The moths (family Tortricidae)—mottled, buff to gray, only ⅞ inch across the wings—appear from late June through July, being most active in the evening. They lay oval, flattened, greenish eggs in 2 overlapping rows along the needles, and the young larvae feed for a while before hibernating in silken cases on branches. When full-grown the caterpillars are up to 1 inch long, brown with a yellow stripe along the side and yellow tubercles. They start activity when buds break in spring, tunneling first in old needles, then in the center of opening buds, feeding also on pollen of staminate flowers. They eat mostly the base of needles and web the rest together with silk, pupating inside this webbing.

Control. Spray ornamentals with lead arsenate or Sevin just as new growth is starting. Large-scale forest spraying by airplane, using DDT, has been quite effective but subject to criticism. Efforts are now being made for effective substitutes with less adverse effect on the environment. Zectran has given good results but is a highly toxic material. Adverse weather conditions, birds, insect parasites and predators combine to reduce outbreaks. Forest management to reduce the proportion of pollen-bearing firs is a possibility.

Sugarcane Bud Moth*, *Ereunetis flavistriata* (Walsingham).

Tobacco Budworm*, *Heliothis virescens* (Fabricius). Distributed from Missouri, Ohio, and Connecticut southward, most injurious in the Gulf States, reported on ornamentals in California. Primarily a pest of tobacco and cotton, this budworm infests groundcherry and other solanaceous plants, ageratum and geranium. Tiny rust-colored or green-striped caterpillars eat holes in buds or unfolded leaves. The moths have light green wings with 4 oblique light bands, a wing-spread of 1½ inches. Eggs are laid singly on underside of leaves. Pupation is in the soil and there are 2 generations a year. Spray buds with Sevin.

Verbena Bud Moth*, *Endothenia hebesana* (Walker). A pest of verbena and physostegia in eastern United States. The larvae, greenish yellow with a black head, about ½ inch long, tunnel in new shoots. The moth is small, purplish brown. Cut off wilting shoots containing the caterpillars.

Western Blackheaded Budworm*, *Acleris gloverana* (Walsingham). Similar to the eastern blackheaded spruce budworm, which see.

Western Spruce Budworm*, *Choristoneura occidentalis* Freeman. A serious defoliator of various conifers in western North America and recently reported as damaging Douglas-fir cones and seed.

BUGS

To a layman almost any insect is a bug. To an entomologist the word "bug" means a member of the insect order Hemiptera (Heteroptera to some). In this group most of the species have the basal part of the front wing thickened and leathery, the lower half thin and membranous. The hind wings are entirely membranous and slightly shorter than the front wings. True bugs have their wings folded flat over the abdomen, instead of being held in a rooflike position like those of leafhoppers and aphids in the order Homoptera. Bugs have piercing, sucking mouth parts but the beak arises from the front part of the head instead of the posterior. Bugs have a gradual metamorphosis, nymphs resembling adults except for size and possession of wings. Some adult bugs have short wings and a few are wingless. The antennae have no more than 5 segments.

The water bugs—water boatmen, backswimmers, water scorpions, water striders, and giant water bugs—are of little importance to gardeners and are omitted here, along with bedbugs, household pests. Mealybugs and Spittlebugs, not true bugs, are listed under those headings.

Anthocoridae. Flower Bugs or Minute Pirate Bugs, found on flowers or under loose bark, in leaf litter, or in decaying fungi. Most species are black with white markings, very small, less than ⅛ inch. This is a beneficial family, the members feeding on small insects, mites, or insect eggs.

Aradidae. Flat Bugs or Fungus Bugs, found under loose bark or in crevices of dead and decaying trees. They are small, dark brown, very flat. They feed on the sap of fungi or moist, rotting wood and so may be considered scavengers.

Berytidae. Stilt Bugs, feeding on plants in dense herbaceous vegetation. They are slender, long-legged, brownish, rather sluggish.

Coreidae. Coreid Bugs. These are squash bugs, leaffooted bugs and allies, some plant-eating, some predaceous. They are small to large, with rather large compound eyes and 4-segmented antennae. The membranous portion of the fore wings is transversed by numerous parallel longitudinal veins. Some species have conspicuously enlarged legs; some have an offensive odor.

Cydnidae. Negro Bugs, fairly common on grasses, weeds, berries, and flowers. They are small, mostly black, broadly oval, convex, with 5-segmented antennae and spiny tibiae.

Lygaeidae. Lygaeid Bugs, Seed Bugs. A large family, with most members plant-eating, chinch bugs being a destructive example, but with some predaceous members. These are very small bugs, with beak and antennae 4-segmented and only a few simple veins in the wing membranes. Ocelli (simple eyes) are present.

Miridae. Plant Bugs, Leaf Buds. A very large group with almost all members injurious, a few predaceous on other insects. This family includes tarnished plant bug, fourlined plant bug, and apple red bug, also garden fleahoppers. Members possess a cuneus, the apex of the thickened portion of the front wing set apart by a groove. Antennae and beak are 4-segmented.

Nabidae. Damsel Bugs. Wholly predaceous. They are small, brown or black, soft-bodied, with front legs modified for grasping small insects. The beak is long, usually 4-segmented, antennae are 4- or 5-segmented; head and first segment of the thorax are narrow; eyes are large; ocelli are present.

Pentatomidae. Stink Bugs. Small to medium in size, body shield-shaped; antennae 5-segmented; eyes small, 2 ocelli; glands at side of thorax emit strong odor. Some species are plant-eating; some are predaceous on Colorado potato beetles and various caterpillars; some are both.

Phymatidae. Ambush Bugs. Predaceous insects waiting for their prey on flowers, particularly goldenrod. They are small, less than ½ inch long, stout-bodied but with odd shapes, spiny armor, and camouflaging color patterns. The front legs are modified for grasping and they feed principally on bees, wasps, and flies.

Pyrrhocoridae. Red Bugs and Stainers. Plant-eating and gregarious oval bugs marked with red and black. Some members, like the cotton stainer, stain tissue as they feed. Some are antlike in appearance.

Reduviidae. Assassin Bugs. Predators with large eyes midway or far back on long, narrow heads. Ocelli, when present, only 2; antennae with 4 segments, beaks with 3. The abdomen is often widened beyond the margin of the wings. These are beneficial bugs, preying on caterpillars, Japanese beetles, and other harmful insects, but they are also injurious when they dine on honeybees or bite people. Some are called "kissing bugs."

Tingidae. Lace Bugs. Exclusively plant feeders, sucking sap from underside of leaves, which they cover with brown specks of excrement. The family name means "ornamented" and the beautiful small, flat bugs, oval or rectangular in shape, have transparent wings reticulated or netted in a lacelike effect and the head covered with a sort of hood. The nymphs are dark and spiny. Some entomologists separate out the ash-gray lace bugs in a separate family, *Piesmatidae*. They are more slender than other lace bugs, have less sculpturing, and feed on weeds and trees.

Alder Lace Bug, *Corythucha pergandei* Heidemann. Infesting alder, occasionally birch, crabapple, elm, and hazel.

Alfalfa Plant Bug*, *Adelphocoris lineolatus* (Goeze). A European pest, probably introduced here as eggs in packing materials, first recorded in Iowa in 1929. Very destructive to alfalfa and sweetclover but also feeding on other legumes, chrysanthemum, thistle, beet, castorbean, potato, and other plants. Now present from Montana to the East Coast. Yellowish green nymphs and pale yellow adults, with a tinge of brown, feed on flower buds and newly formed seeds. The feeding injury is apparently phytotoxic.

Andromeda Lace Bug, *Stephanitis takeyai* Drake & Maa. A relatively new pest, probably from Japan, seriously damaging *Pieris japonica*. First reported from Connecticut in 1946, it soon spread to New York and New Jersey, appeared in Rhode Island in 1965, and since then has become established in Delaware and Pennsylvania. The upper leaf surface is mottled gray or entirely blanched; the undersurface is stained with dark, molasses-like spots of excrement. Inflorescence is poor and plants may die in a few years from repeated loss of vitality. The adults are ⅛ by ¹⁄₁₆ inch, with intensely black hood and wing veins. Overwintering eggs are imbedded at random over underside of leaves on the lower part of the plant. These hatch much earlier than most lace bugs, sometimes late April in New Jersey, mid-May in Connecticut. There may be nearly 60 dark, spiny nymphs on a single leaf, and they go through 5 molts to adult form in 2 or 3 weeks. There may be 4 or 5 generations a season, with some adults still alive in December. Eggs for summer generations are located in new foliage near top of the plants.

Control. Spray or dust with dimethoate, diazinon, carbaryl, or malathion, starting soon after first nymphs hatch and repeating as necessary for later broods. Reinfestation may come from untreated gardens within several hundred feet. Dimethoate granules applied to the soil have given effective control in Connecticut tests.

Apple Red Bug*, *Lygidea mendax* Reuter. Distributed east of the Mississippi River, more destructive in New York and New England. Injurious to nearly all varieties of apples, the red bug may also attack pear, hawthorn, and wild crab. The active bright red bugs, ¼ inch long, fly readily from tree to tree. Leaves are curled and there are numerous small sunken spots, each marking where the insect beak has punctured the surface. The fruit is deformed, pitted in a dimpled effect, sometimes russeted; the texture is woody. The bugs winter in the egg stage, in lenticels on the bark of smaller branches, and the nymphs appear in the early pink stage of apple bloom, puncturing leaves as they unfold, feeding on their fruit as soon as it reaches ¼ inch in diameter. Adults appear in June; there is only 1 generation. Use a delayed dormant spray of superior oil.

Another species, the **Dark Apple Red Bug**, *Heterocordylus malinus* Reuter, may be present along with the apple red bug. It is reddish black, covered on the upper surface with white, flattened hairs. It has a similar life history and causes the same injury.

Ashgray Leaf Bug, *Piesma cinerea* (Say). More slender than most lace bugs, feeding on trees and weeds.

Ash Lace Bug, *Leptophya minor* McAtee. Also called Ash Tingid, serious on Arizona ash and Modesto ash in California, also reported on poplars in Arizona. This species differs from other lace bugs in having a brown, compact body, with darker dorsal markings, but no lacy lateral lobes. Adults hibernate in or near trees, lay eggs in April, and generations follow at monthly intervals until October. The leaves are whitened and the undersurface covered with black specks, the injury increasing during the summer. Try carbaryl or malathion for control.

Ash Plant Bug*, *Tropidosteptes amoenus* Reuter. This is the eastern species. A western form, **California Ash Mirid**, *T. illitus* (Van Duzee), is more important, being the worst ash pest in California. A third species, *T. pacificus* (Van Duzee), is also reported from the West Coast. Small, oval adults, black or brown with yellow markings, lay eggs in stems of new growth. There is only 1 generation a year, the eggs hatching the next February or March when leaves are developing. Young leaves wilt and brown; older leaves have large white areas with black spots of excrement. Trees may be defoliated. DDT and lindane, both effective, may no longer be recommended. Try malathion, carbaryl, or dimethoate.

Azalea Lace Bug*, *Stephanitis pyrioides* Scott. A major pest of azaleas wherever they are grown. Nymphs and adults suck sap from underside of leaves, resulting in a grayish, splotched, stippled, or blanched appearance of the upper surface. The injury is most unsightly and the plant vitality greatly reduced. The small adult, ⅛ inch long, has lacy wings with brown-and-black markings, light-brown legs and antennae. The nymphs are nearly colorless at first, later black and spiny. Elongate eggs laid in leaf tissues along the veins hatch in 20 to 25 days, the life cycle being completed in 35 to 45 days. There are 2 or more generations. The rusty color of underside of leaves, due to excrement, is a diagnostic sign of lace bugs.

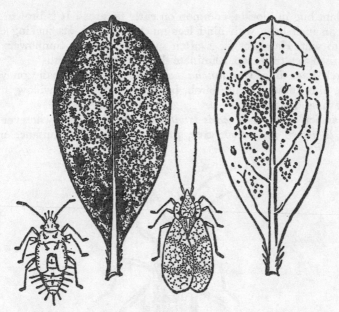

*34. Azalea lace bug, showing loss of color from upper leaf surface, ex-
crement and nymphs on lower surface; nymph and adult greatly enlarged.*

In Alabama overwintered eggs start hatching in February, building
up to a dense population during March, April, and May. Another
brood comes along in July, August, and September. In New Jersey
eggs start hatching in late May or early June, slightly later than
rhododendron lace bugs. The second brood builds up a heavy population in August and September and even later, with evergreen
azaleas of the *amoena* or *hinodegiri* type appearing entirely coffee-
colored, and foliage of deciduous azaleas stippled grayish.

Control. Lindane gives highly satisfactory control but is being replaced by dimethoate (Cygon), diazinon, or malathion. It is important
to spray thoroughly undersurfaces of leaves. A second application may
be required to take care of late-hatching nymphs or infestations from
neighboring bushes. If effective control is not obtained on the first
generation, spray in late summer for the second generation. Dimethoate granules applied to the soil around each bush is said to give seasonal control.

Basswood Lace Bug*, *Gargaphia tiliae* (Walsh).

Biglegged Plant Bug, *Acanthocephala femorata* Fabricius. The largest plant bug in Florida, common on early potatoes. It is brown, more than an inch long, with hind legs much enlarged. Its sucking causes tops to wilt. Handpicking is often sufficient control. Sunflowers have been used as a trap crop. Eliminate thistles, the weed host.

Birch Lace Bug, *Corythucha pallipes* Parsh. Principally on yellow birch, also infesting white birch, beech, hophornbeam, willow, mountain-ash, and maple.

Boxelder Bug*, *Leptocoris trivittatus* (Say). A pest wherever boxelder is grown as a shade tree, probably more of a nuisance in the

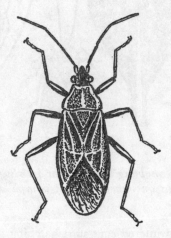

35. Boxelder bug.

Mississippi Valley. The nymphs are bright red; the adults are brownish black with 3 red stripes on the thorax and red veins on the wings, flat, narrowly oval, ½ inch long. They feed on female pistillate flowers, fruits, foliage, and tender twigs of boxelder, sometimes ash, maple, and fruit trees. They are as much a household as an outdoor pest because they swarm inside to hibernate in autumn or else congregate in great numbers on porches, walls, and walks. They do not eat food or clothing but they may feed on house plants.

Control. Spray tree trunks and sunny walls where bugs congregate with chlordane, malathion, or diazinon. For houses, try one of the bombs containing pyrethrum and rotenone. If bugs continue to be too much of a nuisance, remove pistillate boxelder trees near the house.

Brown Stink Bug*, *Euschistus servus* (Say). Broad, flat, shield-shaped, buff to greenish, ½ inch long, sucking on tobacco stems, petioles, or veins. It is also a serious pest of soybean in southern states and may attack other legumes and peaches.

Burrowing Stink Bug, *Pangaeus bilineatus* (Say). Has appeared as a house pest in Pennsylvania and, together with *Tominotus communis*, has damaged peanuts in Alabama and Texas.

Capsus Bugs. Leaf bugs, family Miridae, on forage crops. *Capsus simulans* (Stål) causes silver top of bluegrass. Burn fields after harvest or spray with malathion.

Caragana Plant Bug*, *Lopidea dakota* Knight. On pea-tree.

Ceanothus Lace Bug, *Corythucha obliqua* Osborn & Drake. Common on ceanothus in California, Oregon, and Idaho. The body is black, the hood dark brown, and the wings pale with brown specks and bands.

Chinch Bug*, *Blissus leucopterus leucopterus* (Say). Distributed throughout the United States, but especially injurious in the Mississippi, Ohio, and Missouri River valleys, and in Texas and Oklahoma. See Hairy Chinch Bug for the species common in eastern lawns. The chinch bug is a grain pest and has caused enormous damage to corn and grain crops for more than a century and a half, losses in a single state in one year running up to 40 million dollars.

This very small bug, $\frac{1}{16}$ inch long, black with white wings, which have a triangular black patch in the middle of the outer margins, and red legs, gives off a distinctive vile odor when crushed. It hibernates as an adult in hedgerows, stubble, and clumps of prairie grasses. When the days warm up to 70° F., the bugs fly to grain fields, feed by sucking sap, mate and lay eggs behind lower leaf sheaths of the plants, on the roots, or on the ground. One female lays several hundred eggs, at the rate of 15 or 20 a day. They hatch in 2 weeks into minute, brick-red nymphs with a white band across the middle. The nymphs darken as they grow older, acquiring wings and the black-and-white color at the last molt. As the grain ripens and plants dry up, the chinch bugs migrate, usually while still wingless, crawling to a field of young corn or sorghum. There they mature, mate, and lay eggs for a second generation on corn or grasses. The adults of this brood fly to winter quarters for hibernation. In the Southwest there may be 3 generations instead of 2.

Control. Farmers can reduce food supply of chinch bugs by not growing small grains in an area where corn is the main crop or by substituting legumes for corn in an area where small grains are of chief importance. Ample fertilizer and early planting reduce chinch-bug injury; some corn strains are resistant. Barriers to prevent crawling bugs from reaching the new crop are used effectively—a ridge of earth turned up with a plow and a line of coal-tar creosote applied along the top or a band of insecticide dust between grain and cornfields.

Chrysanthemum Lace Bug*, *Corythucha marmorata* (Uhler). Distributed through the United States where chrysanthemums are grown, blanching foliage and stems of chrysanthemum, aster, and scabiosa. The spiny nymphs resemble azalea lace bugs; the adults have lacy wings and hood. They leave dark, resinous spots of excrement on underside of leaves. They breed on weeds, frequently goldenrod. Spray or dust with malathion.

Clouded Plant Bug*, *Neurocolpus nubilis* (Say). A leaf bug.

Conchuela*, *Chlorochroa ligata* (Say). A large dark olive-green stink bug in the Southwest, feeding on cotton, alfalfa, asparagus, soybean, hemlock, grape, and other plants.

Consperse Stink Bug, *Euschistus conspersus* Uhler. A Pacific Coast pest of fruit—strawberry, raspberry, blackberry, loganberry—and recorded on pear. The bug is small, pale-brown, covered with small black specks, and has red antennae. It gives a disagreeable odor to fruit.

Cotton Lace Bug*, *Corythucha gossypii* (Fabricius). Reported on Datura in Florida.

Cotton Stainer*, *Dysdercus suturellus* (Herrich-Schäffer). A southern cotton insect also injurious to hibiscus, sometimes staining eggplant and orange fruit. The bugs are narrow, long-legged, up to ⅗ inch long, with a bright-red thorax and brown wings crossed with yellow. They stain the lint red or yellow when puncturing the seeds in cotton bolls. Control nymphs with strong contact insecticides; handpick adults.

Dusky Stink Bug*, *Euschistus tristigmus* (Say). One of several stink bugs catfacing peaches, frequently reported from Ohio and Indiana.

Eggplant Lace Bug*, *Gargaphia solani* Heidemann. Dark brown and yellow, relatively large. In southern states ranging west to New Mexico and Arizona on eggplant, tomato, potato, and cassia.

Elm Lace Bug*, *Corythucha ulmi* Osborn & Drake. Found only on American elm but wherever this grows. Foliage may lose color as early as mid-June; new leaves sometimes die. Adults winter in leaves on ground. Spray with malathion or Sevin when young bugs appear.

False Chinch Bug*, *Nysius ericae* (Schilling). Similar to, but even smaller than, the chinch bug. A pest of avocado, sometimes killing young trees, of beets, especially sugar beets, cabbage and other crucifers, sometimes corn. It is more important in semiarid areas. The nymphs feed on weeds and grasses, only the adults on cultivated plants. See also Southern False Chinch Bug.

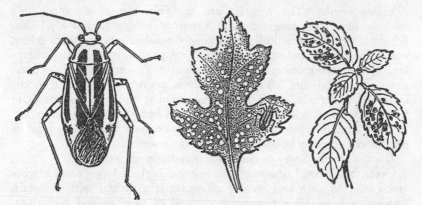

36. Fourlined plant bug, and injury to chrysanthemum and mint.

Fourlined Plant Bug*, *Poecilocapsus lineatus* Fabricius. A general plant pest east of the Rocky Mountains, attacking fruits, chiefly currant and gooseberry, mint, and many ornamentals, with chrysanthemum most injured. The sucking causes round, depressed spots, usually tan, sometimes nearly white or almost black on foliage of acanthopanax, aconite, aster, Chinese lantern, chrysanthemum, coreopsis, dahlia, delphinium, forsythia, gaillardia, globe thistle, goldenglow, heliopsis, heliotrope, honeysuckle, lavender, lupine, morning-glory, peony, phlox, poppy, rose, snapdragon, Shasta daisy, sunflower, sweetpea, weigela, zinnia, and other flowers and shrubs. The injury varies somewhat with the plant, aconite showing dark spots and chrysanthemums many round, light-tan areas on new leaves, with sometimes the whole tip wilting. This is one of the few enemies of mint, young leaves often being covered with black, rather angular spots.

Slender white eggs winter in slits of canes of currant and other plants. They hatch in May or June into bright-red nymphs with black dots on the thorax, but when they change to adults they are greenish yellow with 4 wide black stripes down the wings. There is only 1 generation a year, with feeding injury to plants lasting about 6 weeks. Usually these bugs stop feeding about the time Japanese beetles begin.

Control. Ornamentals can be sprayed or dusted with malathion; use rotenone for mint and other edibles. Start treatment early, as soon as the first nymphs appear; repeat in a week.

Garden Fleahopper*, *Halticus bractatus* (Say). General except in the far western states. The small bugs look something like aphids and suck sap from stems and foliage in the same manner, but they jump like flea beetles. The nymphs are greenish, the adults black, $\frac{1}{10}$ inch or less, with long legs and antennae longer than body. Flea-hoppers appear sporadically on many vegetables—bean, beet, celery, corn, cowpea, cucumber, eggplant, lettuce, pea, pepper, potato, pump-kin, squash, sweetpotato, tomato—and on various ornamentals—chyrs-anthemum, gladiolus, helianthis, heliopsis, portulaca, marigold, morn-ing-glory, rudbeckia, scabiosa, verbena, zinnia, and many others. The foliage has small pale or whitish spots and heavily infested leaves are killed. Plants in shade are preferred. Fleahoppers winter as adults in trash and there may be up to 5 generations a season.

Control weeds. Spray or dust with malathion or Sevin.

Green Stink Bug*, *Acrosternum hilare* (Say). A large, oval, bright-green bug, $\frac{5}{8}$ inch long, bad-smelling. It is a special pest of beans, causing pods to fall, distorting seeds, and of peaches and nectarines, which are catfaced by the feeding punctures. It is found occasionally on apple, boxelder, cabbage, catalpa, corn, dogwood, eggplant, elder-berry, linden, maple, mustard, okra, orange, pea, tomato, and turnip. Control weeds. Spray or dust with naled (Dibrom) or carbaryl (Sevin).

Hackberry Lace Bug*, *Corythucha celtidis* (Osborn & Drake). On this host.

Hairy Chinch Bug*, *Blissus leucopterus hirtus* Montandon. A lawn pest in the Northeast, killing the grass in brown patches similar to fungus brown patch or Japanese beetle damage. The hairy chinch bug differs from the chinch bug in that the adults are predominately short-winged. They winter in tall grass and weeds, migrating to the lawn in April or May to lay eggs at grass roots. When the soil tem-perature is high enough, usually in June, the bright-red nymphs, with a white crossband, start sucking at the base of grass blades. They darken and grow a little larger as they go through various molts, with a brownish stage before they change to black adults, mostly with short white wings. The females lay eggs for a second and more dis-astrous brood which appears in August, with nymphs and adults con-tinuing to feed into October. In November the nymphs either settle down in the lawn or, more often, migrate to tall grasses for the winter.

Injury is most serious in hot dry weather and where the grass is in full sun. Chinch bugs show a preference for bent grasses but are not limited to them. Grass blades are punctured close to the roots and are often stained reddish. The brown, more or less circular areas in turf are usually surrounded by a sickly yellow margin where the bugs have just started feeding. When you cannot roll the grass back like a carpet you can suspect chinch bugs rather than beetle grubs as the cause, but you must see them to be sure. This is difficult unless you get nearly flat on the ground, part the grass blades, and gaze intently at one area for a few minutes. Flooding part of the lawn with warm water and covering it with a white cloth is said to bring the bugs onto the underside of the cloth.

Control. Treat lawns with granular formulations of diazinon, carbaryl, or Dursban, watering well after application. If using wettable powders of diazinon or carbaryl, water the lawn before application and apply with 25 to 30 gallons of water to 1,000 square feet. Make the first treatment in June, when the bugs start action, and repeat, if necessary, in August.

Harlequin Bug*, *Murgantia histrionica* (Hahn). In the stink bug family, the most important pest of cabbage and related crops in the southern half of the United States. Crucifers—cabbage, cauliflower, collards, cress, mustard, Brussels sprouts, turnip, kohlrabi, radish, horseradish—are favored food plants but the bugs may wander over to as-

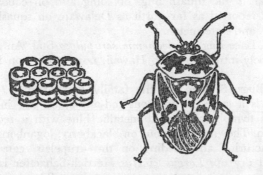

37. Harlequin bug and eggs.

paragus, bean, citrus, cherry, chrysanthemum, corn, eggplant, grape, lettuce, locust, loquat, okra, plum, potato, rose, squash and sunflower. The bugs are black with bright-red markings, flat, ⅜ inch long. They winter around old cabbage stalks and other garden refuse and lay distinctive eggs on underside of leaves of early garden crops. The eggs look like tiny white barrels with black hoops, and they stand on end in a double row. They hatch in 4 to 7 days, and the nymphs suck so much sap that the cabbages wilt, turn brown, and die. Whole crops may be lost but infestations are localized. There are usually 3 generations a season.

Control. Spray or dust with naled (Dibrom). Handpick bugs and crush egg masses.

Hawthorn Lace Bug*, *Corythucha cydoniae* (Fitch). Found on

English hawthorn and other thorns, cotoneaster, pyracantha, Japanese quince. I find this small, dark lace bug, with spiny nymphs, very common on English hawthorn in New Jersey, prevalent in midsummer. In the mid-South it is more serious on pyracantha, with the first brood at work by April and a late brood still going strong in October. The upper surface of leaves loses color in a speckled fashion, while the undersurface is colored with dark bits of excrement. This species winters as an adult and the eggs are laid on new leaves in clusters, each standing on end and covered with a black conical mass. Spray when nymphs are first noticed with diazinon or carbaryl, covering underside of leaves thoroughly.

Hickory Plant Bug*, *Lygocoris caryae* (Knight).

Hollyhock Plant Bug*, *Orthotylus althaeae* Hussey.

Hop Plant Bug*, *Taedia hawleyi* (Knight).

Horned Squash Bug*, *Anasa armigera* (Say). Southern Squash Bug, similar to the squash bug, breeding also on cabbage and collards. It is reported as far north as Delaware on squash, cucumber, cantaloupe, and watermelon.

Lantana Lace Bug*, *Teleonemia scrupulosa* Stål. An American insect purposely introduced into Hawaii, now feeding on Myoprium, a native plant.

Largid Bugs. Stainers, in the family Pyrrhocoridae. *Largus convivus* Stål is a large, conspicuous red-and-black bug in the western states. The nymphs are bright metallic blue with a red spot at tip of abdomen. They are numerous on blackberry, loganberry, and strawberry, puncturing and feeding on the drupelets, causing them to shrivel and dry up. *Largus cinctus* Herrich-Schaeffer is pale tan to orange-brown and is listed as an avocado pest. The variety *L. cinctus californicus* is reported on strawberries in California.

Leaffooted Bug*, *Leptoglossus phyllopus* (Linnaeus). Present in the South and as far west as Arizona, a common pest of vegetables and fruits. The bug is dark brown with a yellow band across the body, ¾ inch long, and with hind legs expanded like a leaf. It attacks pecans, potatoes, beans, cowpeas, tomatoes, and many other garden crops. It likes sunflower, may swarm on Satsuma oranges and tangerines, may be abundant on peaches, and breeds on thistle. Quantities of keg-shaped eggs are depositd on leaves; the young nymphs resemble the adult bug. Spray potatoes with malathion, or, if you are a farmer, with endosulfan or parathion. Hand-picking is helpful.

Lygus Bugs, *Lygus hesperis* Knight, *L. elisus* Van Duzee, other species. Small, flat bugs, greenish to yellowish brown, somewhat mottled, ¼ inch long, relatives of the tarnished plant bug. They are pests of peaches, pears, and apples in the Pacific Southwest, in-

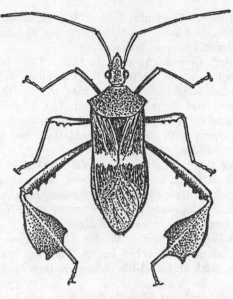

38. Leaffooted bug.

festing leaf buds, puncturing young fruit. Lygus bugs are common on forage legumes and may injure various ornamentals throughout the Rocky Mountain and Pacific States.

Another lygaeid, *Crophius bohemani,* is recorded as heavily infesting eucalyptus trunks in California.

Masked Hunter*, *Reduvius personatus* (Linnaeus). One of the assassin or "kissing bugs" which can painfully bite people but which mostly suck blood of insects, entering houses in search of bedbugs and other pests. It is brownish black and accumulates lint on its head which forms the mask.

Meadow Plant Bug*, *Leptoterna dolabrata* (Linnaeus). On orchard grasses and bluegrass.

Mullein Plant Bug, *Campylomma verbasci* (Meyer). Common in eastern states, both phytophagous, feeding on apple and pear, and predaceous, feeding on mites and aphids.

Negro Bug*, *Corimelaena pulicaria* (Germar). Distributed generally east of the Rocky Mountains. The bugs are short, black, oval, $\frac{1}{10}$ inch long, with an enlarged hard thoracic shield that makes them look like small beetles. They winter as adults and lay eggs singly on leaves. They hatch in 2 weeks and congregate in great numbers, sporadically, on corn, wheat, celery, and other crops, causing wilting and death. They also feed on lobelia, cardinal-flower, and other ornamentals, and some fruits, imparting a bad taste to raspberries and blackberries. Spray with malathion.

Oak Lace Bug*, *Corythucha arcuata* (Say). On various species of oak through eastern states north of the Carolinas, feeding in great numbers on underside of leaves and turning them white. Leaves may curl, turn brown, and drop prematurely. The lace bugs winter as adults or eggs, and there are 2 generations, with damage conspicuous in midsummer. Spray with carbaryl or malathion but include a miticide to prevent a build-up of spider mites.

Onespot Stink Bug*, *Euschistus variolarius* (Palisot de Beauvois). Also called Spined Stink Bug. It is brown, shield-shaped, about ¾ inch long. It feeds on fruit of eggplant, tomato, on garden beans and other plants, causing depressed blemishes known as catfacing.

Onion Plant Bug*, *Labopidea allii* Knight.

Orchid Plant Bug, *Tenthecoris bicolor*. Causes irregular white stippled spots on underside of orchid leaves. The bug has an orange to black body with black and steel-blue wings, ⅛ inch long. Spray or dust with malathion.

Pameras, *Pachybrachyius bilobata* Say. Very small bugs, related to chinch bugs, often destructive to strawberries in Florida. Nymphs look like yellow ants; adults are black with yellow markings, about ⅕ inch long. They appear in strawberry beds toward the end of the season, turning young berries into hard buttons; plants wither. Destroy wild spurge, the weed host; spray into crown of plant with force, using malathion.

Pear Plant Bug*, *Lygocoris communis* (Knight). Also called Green Apple Bug or False Tarnished Plant Bug. The pear bug resembles the tarnished plant bug but it is smaller and darker except at tips of wings. It winters on bark. Nymphs hatching in early spring injure young fruits by feeding punctures, causing drop or deformities. This bug has periodic outbreaks, appearing in 1971 in most of New York pear orchards.

Phlox Plant Bug*, *Lopidea davisi* Knight. A pest of perennial phlox. The active bugs, dull orange or reddish with a black stripe down the back, feed on the upper surface of the more tender leaves and on buds, causing white or pale-green spots. The plant may be stunted, occasionally killed; the blossom head loses its symmetry. There are 2 or more generations. Eggs are laid in fall on phlox stems behind leaf petioles and begin to hatch early in May. Cut down old stalks after first frost; rake up all debris in bed. Dust or spray with malathion.

Ragweed Plant Bug*, *Chlamydatus associatus* (Uhler).

Rapid Plant Bug*, *Adelphocoris rapidus* (Say). One of the small plant bugs similar to lygus bugs and the tarnished plant bug, common on alfalfa and other forage crops, sometimes on potato, beans, soybeans, carrot, even asparagus fern.

Redandblack Stink Bug. *Cosmopepla bimaculata* (Thomas). A small, shiny, black-and-red bug, ⅓ inch long, with a disagreeable odor. It sucks on snapdragon, beard-tongue, columbine, verbascum, and other flowering plants, wintering in protected places.

Rhododendron Lace Bug*, *Stephanitis rhododendri* Horvath. A European insect important from New England to Ohio and south to the Carolinas; also present, though not so injurious, in the Pacific Northwest. The injury is prominent when plants are growing in full sun, the whole shrub having a yellow cast. The individual leaves are mottled with a fine stippling of creamy white or grayish dots, each indicating where the bug has inserted its beak on the underside. The small, ⅛-inch, spined nymphs, with light and dark areas on their flat bodies, hatch in late spring—mid-May near Philadelphia, late May or early June near New York City. They start as a group of dark specks, and the undersurface of leaves is covered with bits of excrement looking like dots of dark molasses when fresh, later giving the leaf a mottled, rusty appearance on the underside. This is an excellent sign of lace-bug injury even when the bugs themselves cannot be seen.

The nymphs move about very little, and then with a peculiar sidewise motion. They turn into adults during June, acquiring beautiful wings, twice as long as the body, rounded at the apex, with veins in a lacy pattern (Plate XVII). They insert eggs, covered with brownish scabs, in irregular rows along the midrib. There are 2 generations a year, the second brood appearing in July, maturing in August, and depositing overwintering eggs in the leaves. Rhododendrons are rarely killed by lace bugs, but infestations unchecked result in yellowed sickly bushes and a gradual decline in vigor.

Control. Several insecticides applied with pressure to the undersurface of leaves soon after nymphs hatch will be effective. Try diazinon or carbaryl or dimethoate or malathion. A second spray 2 weeks after the first is often advisable to take care of late-hatching nymphs and possibly a third for the second brood in July. In some experimental work dimethoate granules applied to the soil around the bush have given seasonal control of lace bugs.

Royal Palm Bug, *Xylastodoris luteolus* Barber. Feeding on royal palms in Florida; small, flattened, oval, pale yellow with reddish eyes.

Say Stink Bug*, *Chlorochroa sayi* Stål. A western plant bug dis-

tributed east to Kansas. Flat, bright green with 3 orange spots and
minute white specks, ½ inch long. It destroys wheat, wilts potato
shoots, feeds on asparagus, bean, pea, sunflower, grains, grasses, and
weeds.

Small Milkweed Bug*, *Lygaeus kalmii* Stål. In western North
America on Asclepias, various species of milkweed. The nymphs are
red and black, the wings of adults black with white margins. Another
species, known as Common Milkweed Bug (*L. reclivatus* Say), is
similar but has 2 white spots on the wings.

Southern Chinch Bug*, *Blissus insularis* Barber. Similar to the hairy
chinch bug, a pest of lawns in warm climates, very important on St.
Augustine grass in Florida and California, sometimes injuring centipede grass in the Gulf States. Considered the most serious lawn pest in
southern Florida, it has been reported as far north as North Carolina
but decreased in severity. Home gardeners may use diazinon for control. Commercial operators who service lawns may prefer ethion, Ak-
ton or Dursban. In California tests a single application in June has
given adequate control for 2 to 3 months. Granular materials are used
against the nymph stage.

Southern False Chinch Bug, *Nysius raphanus*. In southern states
to California, a pest of tobacco but also infesting peas, beans and
other vegetables.

Southern Green Stink Bug*, *Nezara viridula* (Linnaeus). One of
the more important southern pests; found in Virginia, North and
South Carolina, Georgia, Florida, Alabama, Mississippi, Louisiana,
Texas, Arkansas, and Tennessee. The host range includes cucurbits,
crucifers, legumes, citrus fruits, pecan, peach, potato, sweetpotato,
tomato, pepper, okra, corn, sunflower, hackberry, and mulberry. All
plant parts are attacked, but particularly young tender growth and
fruit. The latter is severely distorted, with hard calluses formed
around the feeding punctures. The adult is large, light green, shield-
shaped. The female deposits eggs on underside of leaves about mid-
April, and the nymphs, bluish with red markings, hatch in about 6
days. There are usually 4 generations, adults from the last generation
hibernating in any secluded place.

Control. To protect orchards, avoid a legume crop in summer and
clean up weeds. Spray with carbaryl (Sevin) or naled (Dibrom).

Spined Soldier Bug*, *Podisus maculiventris* (Say). One of the
stink bugs but this one is predatory on Colorado potato beetles and
other pests and so beneficial to man. This species is broad and flat
like other stink bugs, but the pronotum is extended into a sharp
spine on each side.

Squash Bug*, *Anasa tristis* (De Geer). Distributed throughout the country, attacking all vine crops, with preference for squash and pumpkin, gourds and melons next in favor (Plate XII). During the feeding process the squash bug apparently injects a toxic substance into the vines, causing a wilting known as Anasa wilt of cucurbits, closely resembling bacterial wilt, a true disease. After wilting, the vines turn black and crisp; small plants are killed entirely; larger vines have several runners affected. The bugs may be so numerous that no squashes are formed, or they may congregate in dense clusters on unripe fruits.

The adult is dark brown, sometimes mottled with gray or light brown; hard-shelled, ⅝ inch long. It gives off such a disagreeable odor when crushed it is commonly called a stink bug, but it belongs in the family Coreidae while true stink bugs are in the Pentatomidae. Unmated adults hibernate in shelter of dead leaves, vines, boards, or buildings and fly to cucurbits when vines start to run. Mating takes place at that time. Clusters of brick-red eggs are laid in angles between veins on underside of leaves and hatch in 7 to 14 days into nymphs with green abdomen, crimson head, thorax and legs. Older nymphs are a somber grayish white, with dark legs. There are 5 molts before the winged adult. There is usually but 1 generation.

Control. Sanitation is the primary control measure. Remove all rubbish offering winter protection; stimulate plant growth with fertilizer; handpick adults and leaves bearing eggs. Spray or dust the vines with carbaryl. A tachinid fly is an effective parasite.

Superb Plant Bug*, *Adelphocoris superbus* (Uhler). Another of the small plant bugs infesting alfalfa and forage crops. The adult is blackish with orange or yellow sides; the nymph is green with brown markings.

Sycamore Lace Bug*, *Corythucha ciliata* (Say). Widely distributed and common on sycamore, recorded occasionally on ash, hickory, and mulberry. The adults are small, ⅛ inch long, but with wide, flat, white, lacelike wings and prominent lacy projections from the thorax. They winter under bark, and in spring glue black eggs along ribs on underside of leaves. The nymphs are light-colored, spiny; the foliage turns white from their sucking. There are 2 generations and injury resulting in defoliation may be severe on street and shade trees. Spray in early June, or when nymphs appear, with malathion or carbaryl; repeat 2 weeks later.

Sycamore Plant Bug, *Plagiognathus albatus* Van Duzee. Recorded from Connecticut, New Jersey, New York, Delaware, Pennsylvania, and District of Columbia. Nymphs are tan or brown with dark eyes and brown spots on wings, ⅛ inch long. Their feeding produces small, irregular yellowish or reddish spots over the leaves, and sometimes holes where dead tissue drops out. Spray with malathion in early May, repeating 2 weeks later.

Tarnished Plant Bug*, *Lygus lineolaris* (Palisot de Beauvois). Found throughout the country, injurious to more than 50 economic crops (Plate V). Vegetables include bean, beet, cauliflower, cabbage, chard, celery, cucumber, potato, turnip; fruits include apple, peach, pear, strawberry, occasionally citrus. Among flowers, dahlias and asters are frequent victims and the bug sometimes injures calendula, chrysanthemum, cosmos, gladiolus, garden balsam, marigold, poppy, salvia, Shasta daisy, sunflower, verbena, zinnia, and others. The toxin liberated in the plant by the feeding process causes deformed beet and chard leaves, black joints of celery, blackened terminal shoots and dwarfed pitted fruit of peach, buds dying or opening to imperfect flowers on dahlia.

The adult is small, ¼ inch long, flattened, oval, irregularly mottled with white, yellow, and black blotches. These give it a generally tarnished appearance, but there is a clear yellow triangle, marked with a black dot, on the lower third of each side. Adults hibernate among weeds, under leaves, stones, or bark, flying early in spring to feed on fruit-tree buds, then migrating to other plants to lay eggs in leaves or flowers. Nymphs are very small, greenish yellow, marked with 4 black dots on the thorax and 1 on the abdomen. The cycle takes 3 to 4 weeks and there are 3 to 5 generations a season. In the South, feeding and breeding continue through the winter.

Control. Remove weeds and trash to prevent overwintering. Spray with malathion or carbaryl as flower buds start to form and repeat just before they open.

Toyon Lace Bug, *Corythucha incurvata* Uhler. A most disfiguring pest of the lovely red-berried photinia or toyon, the California Christmasberry, in California and Arizona. The nymphs are dirty brown with spines; adults are yellowish brown. Eggs are inserted in underside of leaves and covered with a brown, sticky, cone-shaped mass. Nymphs and adults secrete quantities of honeydew, a medium for black sooty mold. There are several broods a year, with adults hibernating under bark and leaves. Spray with malathion or carbaryl.

Twospotted Stink Bug*, *Perillus bioculatus* (Fabricius). A useful insect, predaceous on armyworms, cutworms, other caterpillars and larvae of various beetles. The bug is small, black with reddish markings.

Walnut Lace Bug*, *Corythucha juglandis* (Fitch). Occasionally abundant on walnut, butternut, basswood, and linden. It is yellow or pale brown with brown bands.

Western Boxelder Bug*, *Leptocoris rubrolineatus* Barber.

Western Brown Stink Bug*, *Euschistus impictiventris* Stål. A small, dark brown bug common on cotton in the Southwest, also on olive, deciduous fruit trees, and sorghum.

Western Chinch Bug*, *Blissus occiduus* Barber. Black, with short wings, even smaller than the chinch bug; found in some western states.

Western Leaffooted Bug*, *Leptoglossus zonatus* (Dallas). Large, nearly flat, brown, with yellow markings and leaflike enlargements of the hind legs. The nymphs are bright red and black. Ranging through Arizona and California, this species breeds on pomegranate where it is thought to spread heart-rot disease. It may also damage olive trees, peach and other deciduous fruits, citrus, dates, and pecan.

Wheel Bug*, *Arilus cristatus* (Linnaeus). One of the predaceous assassin bugs, living in trees and preying on caterpillars and other insects. This species is common in eastern states north to New York, overwintering as bottle-shaped eggs cemented together. The adult has a semicircular crest on the pronotum, resembling half of a wheel, and is unusually large.

Willow Lace Bug, *Corythucha mollicula* Osborn & Drake. Found through the East on willow, its only host; causing serious injury when present in large numbers.

Yucca Plant Bug*, *Halticotoma valida* Reuter. Present wherever yucca is grown, more prevalent in southwestern and southeastern states. The leaves are stippled, covered with black specks of excrement, and turn yellowish. The adult, ⅛ inch long, rather stout, is blue-black with reddish head and thorax. It does not fly readily but runs fast. The nymphs are bright scarlet and may be numerous on leaves. Spray or dust with malathion.

BUTTERFLIES

Butterflies, along with moths, belong to the order Lepidoptera. Their wings, usually large and beautiful, are covered with tiny overlapping scales that rub off like dust on the fingers. Their brilliant iridescent coloring comes from light refracted by many fine ridges on these scales and not from actual pigmentation. Antennae of butterflies usually end in knobs, while those of moths are feathery. Butterflies are day fliers, moths mostly nocturnal. Their mouth parts, adapted for getting nectar out of the throats of flowers, are formed into a long tube, proboscis or tongue, which is coiled beneath the head like a watch spring when not in use. Eggs are laid in exposed places singly or in small groups. Larvae are caterpillars, sometimes called worms. The pupae—chrysalids—of butterflies are not enclosed in cocoons but are attached to the surface of a leaf or stem by a silken pad, sometimes also by a girdle, a silken band around the middle. Only the larval stage is destructive to living plant tissue. The adults do no harm as they sip nectar and many are beneficial pollinators. Some of the caterpillars, too, are beneficial, acting as scavengers or eating other insects and serving as food for birds.

Only those families of interest to gardeners are discussed here, followed by descriptions of a few species named for their adult stage. Those named for the larval stage are discussed under Caterpillars.

Danaidae. Milkweed Butterflies and Monarchs. These are large and brightly colored; the larvae feed on members of the milkweed family.

Hesperiidae. Skippers. These form a connecting link between true butterflies and moths. They are mostly small, wingspread seldom more than 1½ inches, and they are named for their erratic close-to-the-ground flight habit, a kind of skipping. The antennae are not knobbed but have a short hook pointed backward. At rest, the fore wings are held vertically, the hind wings partially spread. The bodies are more robust than those of most butterflies. The larva has a large bulbous head, separated from the rest of the body by a narrowly constricted neck. Larvae tie leaves together with silk for their nests.

Libytheidae. Snout Butterflies. Small brownish butterflies with long projecting palps. Only one species is common.

Lycaenidae. Blues, Coppers, Hairstreaks, and Harvesters. Small delicate, often brightly colored, very common; antennae usually tinged with white and there is a line of white scales encircling the eyes. The caterpillars are flattened, sluglike, with short legs and head bent down beneath the thorax. Many species secrete honeydew, attracting ants, and some live in ant nests.

Nymphalidae. Fourfooted or Brushfooted Butterflies. The fore legs are much reduced and not fitted for walking; antennae are very distinctly knobbed; coloring, patterns, and wing outlines vary greatly. The caterpillars are often quite spiny, with horns on the head. This is the largest family of butterflies and includes some of the best-known species, such as Painted Lady, Mourningcloak, Red Admiral, Viceroy.

Papilionidae. Swallowtails. Our largest butterflies, brightly colored, most with tail-like extension of their hind wings. The caterpillars are large, smooth-skinned, with a forked, malodorous retractile organ that can be thrust out from an opening in the first thoracic segment just back of the head.

Pieridae. Whites, Sulfurs, and Orangetips. These are strong fliers of average size, frequenting open fields and roadsides. Fore and hind wings are nearly the same size but the latter are rounded. The larvae are slender, greenish. Adult whites are white with black markings. The common cabbage butterfly is in this group. The sulfurs are yellow or orange in color and have the wings margined in black. The orangetips, mainly western, are small, white with dark markings and front wings tipped with orange.

Satyridae. Wood Nymphs and Satyrs. Usually of medium size, dull color, flying low, with bases of main veins in the wings swollen and hollow. The caterpillars are inconspicuous brown or green, almost hairless. Many feed on grasses, many are mountain forms.

Black Swallowtail*, *Papilio polyxenes asterius* Stoll. Largely black, with two rows of yellow dots around the wings. The larvae feed on parsley, carrots, and related plants. See Parsleyworm under Caterpillars.

Cabbage Butterfly. See Imported Cabbageworm under Caterpillars.

California Tortoiseshell*, *Nymphalis californica* (Boisduval). A western species feeding on ceanothus, manzanita, amelanchier, sometimes other native shrubs and fruit trees. The caterpillars are black with branched spines and yellow dots. The butterflies are brown and orange, marked with black.

Checkerspot Butterfly, *Euphydryas chalcedona.* Chaldecon. Adults have black wings covered with many yellow spots. Caterpillars are large, bluish black with small orange markings and numerous black compound spines. They feed on aster, buddleia, chrysanthemum, Shasta daisy, monkeyflower, penstemon, veronica, and other plants. They often web foliage as they feed and are quite a garden pest in the Rocky Mountain and Pacific States.

Clouded Sulfur*, *Colias philodice* Latreille. A roadside butterfly, yellow with black wing margins. The larvae feed on clovers.

Columbine Skipper, *Erynnis lucillus* (Scudder & Burgess). The caterpillar, ¾ inch long, velvety green, rather stout with small black head, chews holes in columbine leaves and hides in a rolled-up leaf. The adult is a typical skipper with purplish wings.

Gray Hairstreak, *Strymon melinus* (Hübner). Butterflies have a swift darting flight and are found in meadows and along roadsides. The larvae feed in fruits and seeds of legumes and other plants.

Great Purple Hairstreak, *Atlides halesus* Cramer. Iridescent blue, purple, and black, wingspread over 1 inch, found in southern states.

Hackberry Empress, *Asterocampa celtis* Boisduval & LeConte. The larva of this nymphalid butterfly is bright green with yellow spots and lines, 2 prominent branched horns on a broad head, just over 1 inch long.

Harvester, *Feniseca tarquinius* (Fabricius). Small brownish butterfly with a larval stage predaceous on aphids; not very common.

Monarch Butterfly*, *Danaus plexippus* (Linnaeus). This milkweed butterfly is common throughout America. It is orange-brown with wings bordered and tipped with black, with small white spots in the black border. This species migrates south in large numbers each fall, roosting in trees at night like a flock of birds, reappearing in the North each spring. The caterpillar is yellowish green banded with black, with 2 threadlike appendages at either end of the body. The pale-green chrysalid is held by a belt spotted with gold.

Mourningcloak Butterfly*, *Nymphalis antiopa* (Linnaeus). Spiny Elm Caterpillar. This common species occurs all over America on

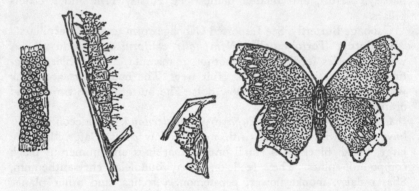

39. Mourningcloak butterfly: eggs, larva (spiny elm caterpillar), pupa, and adult.

elm, especially Chinese elm, also on poplar and willow. The adults have purplish brown wings bordered with a wide yellow stripe, inside of which is a row of blue or purple spots; wingspread is 2½ to 3½ inches. They hide in autumn in nooks and crannies, including tree cavities, fly on sunny March days, but wait until May to deposit sculptured eggs in masses of 300 to 450 around a small branch. The larvae feed in groups on elm, poplar, willow, often defoliating branches. They are black, covered with small white dots and a row of orange or red spots along the back, and lengthwise rows of black, branched spines. They transform to chrysalids in late June or early July, with butterflies emerging in a few days to lay eggs for a second brood in August.

Control. Spray with carbaryl when larvae are young; cut out infested twigs and small branches. Several wasps are parasites; yellow-billed cuckoos and some bugs are predators.

Orange Sulfur Butterfly, *Colias eurytheme* Boisduval. Alfalfa Caterpillar. Mostly orange with black wing margins but some females white. The larvae feed on alfalfa and clovers.

Painted Beauty*, *Vanessa virginiensis* (Drury). Hunter's Butterfly. Ranging throughout North America. The caterpillars are banded dark purple, yellow, and green, with a short row of silver spots on each side of the back. They feed on everlasting, thistles, hollyhock, mallow, forget-me-not, peony, senecio, sunflower. The adults are orange-brown and black with white spots on the front wings and 2 large eye spots on the underside of each hind wing.

Painted Lady*, *Vanessa cardui* (Linnaeus). Thistle Butterfly, said to be the most widely distributed butterfly in the world; often abundant in the West, sometimes in great migratory flights. The adult is large, 2½ inches across the wings, orange-red with black and white markings. The caterpillar varies from green to brown mottled with black, has a light dorsal stripe and a light yellow stripe along each side, grayish spines; 1¼ to 1½ inches long. It feeds on calendula, hollyhock, lupine, sunflower, as well as thistles, mallows, and weeds, often tying together terminal portions. The iridescent chrysalids seem to have been dipped in gold. There are at least 2 broods a year, with butterflies in evidence from early spring to late fall. Spray ornamentals with malathion. Remove infested tips.

Pine Butterfly*, *Neophasia menapia* (Felder & Felder). Chiefly a past of coniferous forests in the West, where great areas of yellow pine and Douglas-fir are defoliated, followed by death of trees, but present also in the East. Adults are white, marked with black; larvae are green with white stripes. A wasplike parasite is effective in bringing outbreaks under control in about 3 years.

Pipevine Swallowtail*, *Battus philenor* (Linnaeus). Feeding on and defoliating Dutchmans-pipe. Caterpillars are dark brown with 4 rows of orange to coral spots and soft hornlike projections; 2 inches long. Adults are blue-green butterflies with white spots on under margins of fore wings and yellow and orange spots on hind wings. Spray or dust with malathion.

Red Admiral*, *Vanessa atalanta* (Linnaeus). Adults are velvety deep brown or black with a red or orange oblique stripe on the fore wings and a margin of the same color on the hind wings. The caterpillars are purplish brown or black, covered with minute white specks, with a continuous row of yellow spots along each side and branching spines. They feed in groups in webs. The chrysalids are brown with golden tubercles and a grayish bloom. The caterpillars are not important as garden pests, feeding mostly on hops and thistles.

Silverspotted Skipper*, *Epargyreus clarus* (Cramer). One of the largest of the skipper butterflies, feeding on locust and wisteria, sometimes causing serious defoliation. The caterpillar is leaf green with a dull-red head. It fastens together several leaflets, feeding inside this case. The butterfly is brown and yellow with triangular white spots on the fore wings.

Spicebush Swallowtail*, *Papilio troilus* Linnaeus. Feeding on spicebush and sassafras, not too serious. The larva is 1½ inches long, largest at the third thoracic segment, pea-green on top with yellow sides, pink head and undersurface, 4 large and 10 small orange spots. The adult is blackish, with a row of small yellow spots along the margins of the front wings and extensive blue-black areas on the hind wings.

Tiger Swallowtail*, *Papilio glaucus*, Linnaeus. Not very important but feeding on apple, ash, birch, cherry, lilac, poplar, and other trees. The larva is dark green, 1½ inches long, the third thoracic segment enlarged and marked with a large yellow spot enclosing a purple spot on each side. The adult is a large yellow swallowtail with black stripes on the front wings and black wing margins.

Viceroy*, *Limenitis archippus* (Cramer). Like the monarch butterfly, feeding on poplar and willow. The head of the larva is green, bilobed, and grooved vertically. The body segments are pink, brown, and green, with tubercles. It overwinters in a shelter made by tying leaves together with silk.

Western Parsley Swallowtail, *Papilio zelicaon* Lucas. On members of the parsley family, including carrot, celery, parsnip, and also a problem of young citrus in Pacific Coast states. The butterfly is yellow or orange and black. The caterpillar, sometimes called California Orange Dog, is bright yellow-green with black bands, orange spots, and an orange scent horn.

Western Swallowtail, *Papilio rutulus* Boisduval. Yellow with black markings, similar to the tiger swallowtail, common in the West. The larvae—pale green with purplish brown head, orange tubercles—feed on alder, willow, apricot, apple, avocado, cherry, and prune.

Zebra Butterfly, *Heliconius charitonius* (Linnaeus). Black, striped with yellow, occurring in the Gulf States, most common in Florida. The caterpillars feed on passion-flower and are protected by toxic secretions. The chrysalid wriggles when disturbed and makes a creaking sound.

Zebra Swallowtail, *Graphium marcellus* (Cramer). Striped with

black and greenish white, with relatively long tails. The larvae feed
on pawpaw.

CANKERWORMS

Cankerworms, often called inchworms or measuring worms, are
larvae of small moths, family Geometridae. Some species in this
group are obnoxious pests of fruit and shade trees and are known
as cankerworms; the others are called loopers or spanworms. They
all move by a series of looping movements, drawing up the abdomen
to the thorax in a loop, grasping the support by their prolegs (false
legs at the end of the body), loosening the thoracic legs, stretching
the body forward, and so on in rapid succession. They also have a
habit of letting themselves down on a thread of silk.

Fall Cankerworm*, *Alsophila pometaria* (Harris). Distributed generally across the United States from North Carolina northward, a

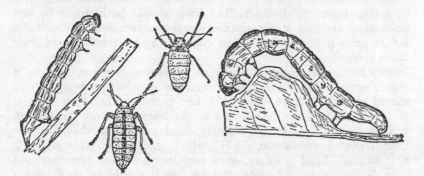

40. Cankerworms: spring, left; fall, right.

threat to fruit trees, apple preferred, but also feeding on apricot,
cherry, plum, prune, and other fruits, and to shade trees, especially
oak and elm, sometimes basswood or linden, birch, and maple. They
even feed on rose bushes near apple trees.

The moths emerge from pupae in the ground in late fall, after
there have been freezing temperatures. The males are brownish gray
with a 1¼-inch wingspread; females have wingless gray bodies, ½
inch long (Plate XVIII). They crawl up tree trunks to deposit
eggs—grayish, shaped like a flowerpot—in a compact, single-layered
mass on main trunk or branches or around smaller twigs. The eggs
hatch in spring about the time leaves unfold, and the larvae feed on
foliage until June.

The caterpillars are brownish above, green below, with 3 narrow stripes along the body above the spiracles and a yellow stripe below. They have 3 pairs of prolegs. They often drop down from trees on a silken thread, climbing up again to resume feeding. There is only 1 generation a year. Toward the end of their season cankerworms may eat conspicuous holes in leaves of rhododendron and other shrubs growing under or near their favored food plants. When full-grown they drop to the ground and pupate in a silken cocoon, 1 to 4 inches deep in the soil.

Control. Banding trees with a sticky material such as Tree Tangle-foot, to prevent the wingless female from crawling up the tree to lay eggs, is a practice less popular now than some years ago, for it has been determined that young cankerworms balloon over, via their silken threads, from unbanded trees nearby. Actual foliage damage is only slightly reduced by this method. Also, unless properly applied to a band of paper or Balsam Wool around the trunk so that the Tanglefoot does not come in direct contact with the bark, there may be serious injury to the bark. The band should be in place by late September and the sticky surface scraped or renewed through the fall to prevent late arrivals from crawling up on the backs of their fallen comrades.

Spraying is far more effective as a control measure, and in a season when a heavy infestation has been forecast, property owners should arrange to have elms, oaks, and perhaps other trees sprayed in late April or early May—as soon as leaves are out far enough to hold a poison. Oaks, particularly, need protection; they may die from repeated defoliation. DDT, which gave excellent control, is now banned. Lead arsenate, once popular, is seldom recommended now. Sevin is safe and quite effective but it should be used with a miticide; it is harmful to beneficial parasites and predators. Methoxy-chlor may be used or the bacterial spray, *Bacillus thuringiensis,* which offers no problems for people or wildlife. There have been conflicting results but some of the recent preparations of the bacteria seem to be quite effective. They are sold under trade names such as Thuricide, Biotrol, Bakthane, Dipel.

Spring Cankerworm*, *Paleocrita vernata* (Peck). Found from Maine to North Carolina, west to Texas and Colorado and in California. Apple and elm are preferred hosts, then oak, hickory, cherry, maple, sometimes other fruit and shade trees. This is one of our oldest pests, a native known in New England for more than 200 years. Along with the fall cankerworm, it appears in cycles, being very abundant for 2 or 3 years, nearly defoliating trees in an area, feeding in such numbers you can actually hear the leaves being crunched, and dropping down on unwary pedestrians from street trees. Then the cankerworms almost disappear for a few years and gradually recruit their armies for another peak of abundance. Trees defoliated for 2 or 3 years in succession may die.

The moths appear in early spring, sometimes on a warm day in February, more often in March. The females are wingless, about the same nondescript gray as the fall cankerworm, but they have a dark stripe down the back and 2 transverse rows of small reddish spines across each abdominal segment on the upper side. The male moths are silky gray with 3 transverse dark lines on the fore wings. They often appear around trees (and even in attics) about the time females are crawling up trunks to lay clusters of oval, brownish-purple eggs under bark scales on main trunk or branches. These hatch in about a month. The caterpillars vary from green to brown to nearly black, usually with a yellowish stripe under the spiracles, up to an inch long. They differ from fall cankerworms in having only 2 pairs of prolegs instead of 3.

Control. Measures are the same as for the fall cankerworm, except that if banding is practiced, the Tanglefoot is applied or renewed in February. In apple orchards the codling moth spray schedule will also control cankerworms.

CASEBEARERS

Casebearers (family Coleophoridae) are moths whose larvae live in portable cases and feed or mine in leaves, fruits, flowers, or seeds. This is a small family and most of the American species belong to the genus Coleophora. Casebearers of the genus Acrobasis (family Pyralidae) secrete their cases between leaves webbed together.

Birch Casebearer*, *Coleophora fuscedinella* Zeller. First found in Maine in 1927 and spreading in that state, attacking all varieties of birch and speckled alder. The moth is very small, grayish brown with a fringe on narrow hind wings. The caterpillar is light yellow to green with a black head, 1/5 inch long. It lives in a small brown cylindrical case, mining and cutting holes in leaves. Badly mined foliage dries and trees appear scorched; buds may be eaten; twigs and limbs die back. There is 1 generation. Larvae hibernate in cases on twigs. Control with a dormant lime-sulfur spray, 1 to 8 dilution, in early spring.

Birch Tubemaker*, *Acrobasis betulella* Hulst. Feeding on black, gray, and paper birch from Maine to Delaware and Pennsylvania, also recorded in Colorado and California. Each larva lives in a frass tube spun between the leaves.

California Casebearer, *Coleophora sacramenta* Heinrich. Willow is the normal host, but the larvae commonly feed on almond, apricot, apple, cherry, peach, plum, prune in the San Francisco Bay regions of California. The moth is bluish white with gray scales, ⅝ inch wingspread; the larva is orange, making a black case widened at the bottom with a winglike projection. There is 1 generation.

Cherry Casebearer*, *Coleophora pruniella* Clemens. Normally feeding on wild cherry but reported injuring cultivated cherries and sometimes apple in the Middle West and Oregon. It winters in its case attached to twigs, moving to young foliage in spring, producing skeletonized and dead areas as it grows and enlarges the case with leaf tissue. Pupation is in late spring. Moths lay eggs on underside of leaves, and new caterpillars are making overwintering cases by late summer. There are several natural parasites. A dormant dinitro spray is effective.

Cigar Casebearer*, *Coleophora serratella* (Linnaeus). General in apple-growing regions, attacking apple, except Jonathan variety, pear, plum, cherry, hawthorn, quince. The light-brown partly grown larva hibernates inside a cigar-shaped, brownish-gray silken case, about ¼ inch long, attached to twigs or branches, and starts feeding as buds unfold in spring. It feeds until July, making blotch mines between the leaf surfaces, then pupates and produces mottled gray moths with narrow, fringed wings, ½-inch wingspread. Eggs are laid on underside of leaves with larvae appearing in late summer to make new cases. The ordinary apple spray schedule should take care of casebearers.

Elm Casebearer*, *Coleophora ulmifoliella* McDunnough. A European insect established in the Northeast, favoring English, Scotch, and American elms in local outbreaks. The moth, buff-colored with gray markings, appears in July. The larvae and their cases are dark brown and the mines are between the principal veins in the leaves. Elms sprayed for cankerworms and leaf beetles will not suffer from this pest.

Larch Casebearer*, *Coleophora laricella* (Hübner). Another European pest, first noticed in Massachusetts in 1886 and now found throughout the range of American and European larch in the eastern half of the country and also in Washington and Oregon. The moth is silver-gray, appears from late May to July. The dark, reddish brown larva feeds as a miner until September, when it constructs its case for winter hibernation. When larvae are abundant the needles turn white and die, growth is checked, and the tree weakened. Spray with lime sulfur, dormant strength, in spring before growth starts. There are many natural enemies but they do not give sufficient control.

Pecan Cigar Casebearer*, *Coleophora laticornella* Clemens. Found from New Hampshire to Florida and Texas on pecan, hickory, and black walnut. The moth is brownish, the larva reddish with a black head, and the case is brown, cigar-shaped, ¼ inch long. Mined areas turn brown and sometimes drop out, leaving holes in foliage. There may also be some defoliation.

Pecan Leaf Casebearer*, *Acrobasis juglandis* (LeBaron). Present in the southern part of the pecan belt, from southern Georgia and northern Florida to Texas, and also reported from Pennsylvania on English walnut. The moths are variable, white, gray, brown or black. The very small larvae feed on young buds and leaves and are damaging chiefly to weakened plants which cannot grow faster than the larvae can eat.

Pecan Nut Casebearer*, *Acrobasis caryae* Grote. A most serious pecan pest, especially in Texas, often damaging in the other Gulf States, destroying a large percentage of the crop. The larva is olive green, ½ inch long; the moth is dark gray with ¾-inch wingspread. The larva winters in a hibernaculum, small cocoon, at the base of a bud. In spring larvae feed on buds and bore into tender shoots, pupating in tunnels. The moths, emerging in May, deposit eggs on the nuts. The young larvae spin a web around several nuts, then enter to feed. This brood pupates inside the nut; moths come out in late June and July. There are 3, possibly 4, generations but the first does the most damage.

Control. If not over 3 per cent of shoots of the previous year are infested with overwintering larvae, control is considered unnecessary. Otherwise, get advice and a spray schedule from your Agricultural Agent or State Experiment Station. DDT, parathion, lead arsenate, and nicotine sulfate are all past recommendations but find out what is recommended now for your particular area. One application before the 1st generation larvae enter the nuts may be sufficient—between April 20 and May 25—but a second spray may be advised for heavy infestations.

Pistol Casebearer*, *Coleophora malivorella* Riley. Found from the Mississippi Valley eastward, a minor pest of apple and other fruits. Similar to the cigar casebearer, but the case, made of silk, bits of leaves and excrement, is bent over like a pistol. The larva winters in the base; buds are injured in spring and leaves mined. Moths appear in summer to lay eggs on leaves and a 2nd generation works in late summer. Control with the regular orchard spray schedule.

41. Pistol casebearer.

Volck's Case Bearer, *Coleophiora volcki* Heinrich. In California apple orchards. The larvae, dark brown, produce large blotch mines and also eat holes in leaves. The brown case is ragged with a tooth-like projection on the back of the anterior end. Hibernation is in cases attached to limbs and twigs and spring feeding occurs on young fruit as well as leaves.

CATERPILLARS

Caterpillars are the wormlike larvae of moths and butterflies. Some are commonly known by the adult form and so are discussed under Butterflies or under Moths. Some have special names—bud-worm, cankerworm, casebearer, cutworm, earworm, fruitworm, horn-worm, leafminer, leaftier, spanworm, webworm—and are treated under such headings. A few of the other thousands of caterpillars are treated in this section.

Caterpillars are of various shapes but the majority have cylindrical soft bodies which are naked, hairy, or adorned with spines. They

TRUE LEGS   PRO LEGS

42. Diagram of a caterpillar.

are composed of 13 segments behind the head with its chewing mouth parts. The first 3 segments each bear a pair of jointed legs terminating in a single claw. In addition to these true legs, abdominal segments 3, 4, 5, and 6 typically have a pair of prolegs, false legs, which are unjointed sucker feet provided with tiny hooks, crotchets, for holding onto a leaf or twig. There is another pair of prolegs on the last abdominal segment. There is also, in many caterpillars, a spinneret near the mouth for making silk.

Control is usually by means of protective spraying with an insecticide on the foliage before the larvae start eating. Sometimes contact sprays are used after the caterpillars are present, and sometimes eradication measures are taken against the egg stage.

Alfalfa Caterpillar*, *Colias eurytheme* Boisduval. A southwestern alfalfa pest occasionally present elsewhere and feeding also on garden peas, beans, and other legumes. The caterpillar is dark green with a pale yellow or white line down the side. The butterflies are sulfur yellow, less frequently white, with wings tipped with wide black bands. Cutting alfalfa low and removing it from the field helps in control, as do some braconid wasps. Microbial insecticides have been successfully used—the polyhedrosis virus and *Bacillus thuringiensis*.

Alfalfa Looper*, *Autographia californica* (Speyer). Causes sporadic damage on the Pacific Coast. This caterpillar is a general feeder, injuring in addition to alfalfa, many cereal and truck crops, fruits, flowers, ornamental trees and shrubs. The looper is about an inch long, dark olive-green with a paler head and 3 dark lines along the back; only 3 pairs of prolegs. The gray moth, with a silver mark on each fore wing, appears at dusk to visit flowers. Control with rotenone or pyrethrum dust on vegetables, carbaryl on ornamentals.

Avocado Caterpillar*, *Amorbia essigana* (Busck). Limited to California and mostly to avocado although it may be a citrus pest. This tortricid or leafroller moth, with reddish brown fore wings an inch across, was first noticed in 1922. The yellowish green larvae skeletonize the leaves or web them together and scar young fruits. There may be 4 or 5 generations. The larvae may also feed on fruit if they can web foliage against the fruit. Tachinid and other parasites help in control.

Azalea Caterpillar, *Datana major* Grote & Robinson. A gregarious caterpillar, feeding in groups, all members raising head and posterior in unison when disturbed. Partly grown larva is reddish to brownish black with white to yellow stripes. The full-grown caterpillar has a red pronotal shield, a black body with longitudinal rows of yellowish spots and sparse white hairs. This is a serious pest of azaleas in the

Southeast—Virginia, the Carolinas, Florida, Alabama, Mississippi, and Louisiana—and is also reported on blueberries in Delaware, on red oak in Maryland, and occasionally on andromeda and apple in Atlantic States.

Banded Woollybear*, *Isia isabella* (J. E. Smith). Generally distributed, our familiar densely hairy "hedgehog" caterpillar, which rolls into a ball when disturbed or for hibernating. It is about 1¼ inches long, black at both ends with a reddish-brown band around the middle. The width of this band is said to forecast the winter; the narrower the band, the colder and longer will be the winter. The adult is the tiger moth, yellow, wing expanse 1½ to 2 inches, a few dusky spots on the wings and black spots on the abdomen (Plate XX). The caterpillars feed on leaves of many garden plants.

Badwing Geometer, *Dyspteris aborivaria* Herrich-Schäffer. A light green moth, front wings large and triangular, hind wings small and rounded. The larva rolls and eats grape leaves.

Barberpole Caterpillar*, *Mimoschinia rufofascialis* (Stephens). A pyralid moth.

Bougainvillea Caterpillar, *Asciodes gordialis* (Guenée). The most persistent and damaging pest of this host. The caterpillar, 1 inch long, green, eats and rolls the leaves, but usually drops to the ground unnoticed when the plant is touched. The moth is brown. During the warmer portions of the year spray or dust with malathion, repeating as necessary.

Cabbage Looper*, *Trichoplusia ni* (Hübner). A native caterpillar common throughout the country. It attacks all members of the cabbage family—broccoli, Brussels sprouts, cabbage, cauliflower, collards, horseradish, kale, kohlrabi, mustard, radish, turnip—and also feeds on beet, celery, lettuce, parsley, pea, potato, spinach, tomato—and on flowers—carnation, chrysanthemum, mignonette, geranium, and others. The looper is said to be a serious lettuce pest. It winters as a green to brown pupa wrapped in a cocoon attached by one side to a plant leaf, and transforms in spring into a moth with mottled brownish fore wings, with a small silvery spot in the middle, and paler brown hind wings; wing expanse is just under 1½ inches.

The females lay many small, round, greenish white eggs, singly, on upper surface of leaves. The larva has a body tapering to the head, greenish, with a thin white line above the spiracles and 2 others down the back; there are 3 pairs of prolegs. After feeding for 2 to 4 weeks, the looper spins a cocoon. There may be 3 or more generations a season.

Control. Microbial insecticides have been effective, either a spray of *Bacillus thuringiensis* or a polyhedrosis virus causing a wilt. Mass

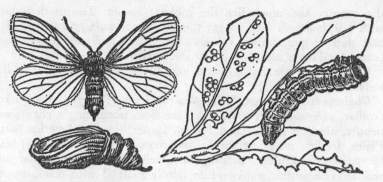

43. California oakworm: moth, pupa, eggs, and larva eating.

releases of the Trichogramma parasite, from eggs carried to tomato fields, have been effective. Spray or dust with malathion or naled (Dibrom).

California Oakworm*, *Phryganidia californica* Packard. On live and other oaks, sometimes on chestnut and eucalyptus in California. It is particularly destructive to live oaks in the San Francisco Bay area, defoliating them periodically in much the same fashion as cankerworms injure eastern oaks. Immature caterpillars feed on live-oak foliage during the winter, but on deciduous trees the oakworm winters in the egg stage. Mature caterpillars are olive-brown with black and yellow longitudinal stripes on back and sides; 1 inch long. After feeding in spring, first by skeletonizing leaves, then by eating holes in foliage, they pupate in May and June in smooth white or yellow chrysalids attached by the rear end to leaves, limbs, or tree trunks. The moths emerge in June and July, lay flattened white eggs for the summer brood on any kind of oak, and the adults appear in October and November. They are uniformly pale brown, with slightly darker antennae and wing veins, 1- to 1¼-inch wing expanse. Although they are abundant enough to cause defoliation only at long and irregular intervals, protective measures should be taken each season.

Control. Various commercial preparations of *Bacillus thuringiensis* have given control. In laboratory tests pyrethrins were more effective than Zectran and that was better than carbaryl or malathion. Spray in March or April, when caterpillars are small. Some parasites and predators normally hold the oakworm in check and a virus wilt disease markedly reduces populations.

California Tent Caterpillar. See Western Tent Caterpillar.

Celery Looper*, *Anagrapha falcifera* (Kirby). General throughout the country and much like the cabbage looper. The moth is large with purple-brown fore wings; the larvae are pale green, with light and dark stripes, up to 1 inch long. They feed on celery, beets, lettuce, and other succulent plants and weeds.

Celeryworm. See Parsleyworm and Black Swallowtail under Butterflies.

Chainspotted Geometer*, *Cingilia catenaria* (Drury). A looper caterpillar, yellowish with spots along the sides resembling a chain; very slender, about 2 inches long. Present in northeastern America to the Plains, feeding on many shrubs and trees, including bayberry, blueberry, sweetfern, alder, balsam, birch, wild cherry, oak, poplar, and willow. The moths, smoky white faintly marked with black, appear from August to September. Eggs hatch late in spring; larvae from June to August.

Clover Head Caterpillar*, *Grapholitha interstinctana* (Clemens). Feeding mainly in heads of red clover, sometimes other clovers, in eastern states. The caterpillars are very small, 1/4 inch, somewhat hairy. The moths, also small, dark brown marked with white, lay eggs on leaves, stems, and heads. The young larvae work their way into the head, destroying half the florets and the seed crop. There are 3 generations with the winter passed as a pupa.

Clover Looper*, *Caenurgina crassiuscula* (Haworth). Reported on clovers and other legumes.

Convict Caterpillar, *Xanthopastis timais*. Also called Spanish Moth, usually found in southeastern states although the recorded range goes to Maine. Spider lily is the natural host but the larvae devour leaves of amaryllis, narcissus, lilies, and tuberose, often eating foliage down to the ground. The caterpillars are brownish or grayish or black, smooth, about 2 inches long, and they have cream-colored bands around the body like convict stripes. The dark-brown pupa is found in the soil near the plants. The moth is pinkish cream to white, with wings spreading almost 2 inches.

Crossstriped Cabbageworm*, *Evergestis rimosalis* (Guenée). The larva has numerous transverse black bands across the green body. The moth is small, mottled yellow-brown. See Imported Cabbageworm for control.

Eastern Tent Caterpillar*, *Malacosoma americanum* (Fabricius). Also called Appletree Tent Caterpillar, present throughout eastern United States and west to the Rocky Mountains. Black cherry, chokecherry, and apple are favored food plants but when these are scarce it makes ugly nests on hawthorn, pear, plum, birch, elm, maple, oak, poplar, willow, and other fruit and ornamental trees. The winter is spent in the egg stage—a dark-brown varnished collar or belt en-

circling the twigs (Plate XVIII). The young larvae hatching early
in March in the South, as leaves start to unfold in the North, gather
in a fork of the limbs to spin their large, webby nest. They leave it
during the day to feed on foliage but return at night or in rainy
weather. They are hairy caterpillars, black with a white stripe down
the back, brown and yellow lines along the sides, and a row of oval
blue spots. They are full-grown, 2 to 2½ inches long, in 4 to 6
weeks, and are often seen in groups crawling down the sides of
houses or feeding on roses and other shrubs before spinning their
dirty-white cocoons on tree trunks or buildings.

The moths, light reddish brown with 2 diagonal stripes across
each fore wing, emerge in about 3 weeks. Each female lays a single
egg collar around a twig, containing 150 to 300 eggs, and covers this
with a sticky substance which hardens and glistens like varnish. There
is only 1 generation a year. The periods of greatest abundance appear
at about 10-year intervals.

Control. Apples are protected by the regular spray schedule used
for codling moths. Wild cherries growing near apple orchards should
be removed. Young caterpillars can be killed by dusting with sulfur
or spraying with *Bacillus thuringiensis* or carbaryl, but if egg masses
are systematically pruned out during the winter and nests wiped
out with a crumpled newspaper when first started, spraying should
not be necessary. The nests themselves can be treated with an aerosol
spray, in the evening when the caterpillars are at home. Burning
out nests with a flaming torch almost always injures the tree and
often starts brush fires.

There are many natural enemies—ground beetles and other predators, egg parasites, a wilt disease—all of which account for the periodic rise and fall in abundance. It sometimes helps to work along with
natural enemies. If egg masses are cut off, encased in fine wire mesh,
and left in the open instead of being burned, it gives the beneficial
parasites a chance to emerge.

False Cabbage Looper. See Soybean Looper.

False Hemlock Looper*, *Nepytia canosaria* (Walker). In northern
United States and Canada on hemlock, spruce, fir, and larch. The
larvae—1 inch long, pale with a yellowish or reddish tinge marked
with black dots, a yellowish lateral stripe and 4 dark wavy hairlines—
feed from June to August. The geometer moths emerge in August
and September.

Filbertworm*, *Melissopus latiferreanus* (Walsingham). Catalina
Cherry Moth, a serious pest of filberts and walnuts in the Pacific
Northwest but distributed through much of the United States. The
small, pinkish caterpillar, ¾ inch long, bores through oak acorns

and galls, hazelnuts, filberts, walnuts, chestnuts, chinquapin, Catalina cherry, and various other fruits and nuts. The moth is pale to dusky with 2 coppery bands near the tip of fore wings. Eggs are laid near nuts or on husks, and worms enter the nuts at the base. They feed for 3 or 4 weeks, then winter in cocoons on the ground.

There is no satisfactory chemical control for nuts. Harvesting at the earliest possible date and drying promptly reduces injury.

Fir Cone Looper*, *Eupithecia spermaphaga* (Dyar). Small, measuringworm caterpillars bore through seeds and cones of Douglas-fir, true firs, and mountain hemlock. The moth is gray with black and red-brown markings, wing expanse 1 inch.

Florida Fern Caterpillar*, *Callopistria floridensis* (Guenée). Native to tropical America and introduced into northern greenhouses on infested plants from Florida. It seems to breed only on ferns, chiefly nephrolepis and adiantum. The caterpillars work at night or on cloudy days, stripping leaflets from old growth, devouring new growth entirely. They are at first pale green, later velvety black, 1½ inches long. During the day they are concealed in the crown of the fern, along the midrib of a frond or in soil. They pupate underground in an oval cocoon. The moth, with brown, patterned wings, emerges in about 2 weeks. There may be a new generation every 7 or 8 weeks. Control by handpicking caterpillars at night or with a pyrethrum dust or spray. Malathion has been suggested but it may injure some ferns.

Forest Tent Caterpillar*, *Malacosoma disstria* Hübner. A native pest of forest, ornamental, and fruit trees, widely distributed from the Atlantic to the Pacific, similar to the eastern tent caterpillar but without a tent. Favorite food plants include maple, oak, poplar, ash, birch, but it may feed on apple, boxelder, cherry, hawthorn, peach, pear, plum, prune, quince, rose, willow and other trees. The caterpillars are gregarious, armyworm style, living in large colonies on a silken mat on larger limbs and tree trunks but not making a nest. The winter egg collars around twigs are cut squarely off at the ends and not rounded down to the twig like those of the eastern tent caterpillar. The larvae, 1½ to 2 inches long, are bluish spattered with black dots and points, with a row of diamond-shaped spots alternating with small white spots down the back. They have pale, longitudinal yellow stripes and are sparsely clothed with soft hair. They eat ravenously in early spring for about 6 weeks. In June or July white cocoons are spun within a leaf or attached to fences or ground objects. The moths emerge in 10 to 14 days to lay about 200 eggs in a band around the twig. They are brownish buff with 2 oblique lines across the fore wings, which expand to 1 to 1½ inches. There is only 1 brood a year.

Control. There are many natural enemies to keep this pest in check, including birds. Inspect ornamental trees for egg bands and cut them off.

Genista Caterpillar*, *Tholeria reversalis* (Guenée). Genista Moth. The caterpillars are orange-green with black-and-white markings and are covered with tubercles. They web foliage of brooms (Genista) and may completely defoliate plants. Adults are snout moths, brown with orange hind wings. Spray or dust with malathion or carbaryl.

Grapevine Looper*, *Lygris diversilineata* (Hübner). Found in northeastern United States to Wisconsin and Missouri, feeding on grape and Virginia-creeper. The slender caterpillar is pale green, often with pink or reddish markings, 1½ inches long. It pupates in loose webs on the foliage. The moth is ocher yellow, marked with rust and purplish brown; wing expanse to 2 inches.

Great Basin Tent Caterpillar, *Malacosoma fragile* (Stretch). Common in the West, especially at high altitudes. The caterpillars have tawny hairs on a black body with blue-and-orange markings. They are omnivorous feeders, webbing orchard trees and ash, aspen, ceanothus, cottonwood, and others. They defoliate bitterbrush, an important browse plant for sheep.

Green Cloverworm*, *Plathypena scabra* (Fabricius). Found in eastern United States to the Plains, on clover, alfalfa, garden beans, soybeans, cowpeas, strawberry, raspberry, and some other plants. The moths are dark brown, black-spotted, wingspread 1¼ inches. They lay eggs on underside of leaves, and the green larvae feed for about a month. There may be 2 to 4 generations but normally they are not abundant enough to justify control measures. There are many parasites.

Greenstriped Mapleworm*, *Anisota rubicunda* (Fabricius). A native eastern caterpillar found west to Kansas and Nebraska, attacking various maples, boxelder and oak. The larvae are pale yellowish-green, striped above with 8 light and 7 dark green lines, with red head, 1½ inches long. They have horns on the thorax, 2 rows of spines on each side of the body, and 4 large spines near the end of the abdomen. They are said to feed more ravenously in the western part of their range, often defoliating maples twice in a season and every tree on an avenue. The moths are pale yellow banded with rose, wing expanse 1½ to 2 inches. They lay pale green eggs in large masses on leaves. The larvae appear in 10 days, feed for a month, pupate in the soil. Moths appear in 2 weeks and caterpillars of the 2nd brood pupate in soil for winter. There may be 3 generations in the South. Several insect parasites and birds aid in control.

Gulf White Cabbageworm, *Ascia monuste* (Linnaeus). The adult looks like the white butterfly of the imported cabbageworm and the larva causes similar injury to crucifers. The caterpillar is yellow with purplish stripes, 1½ inches.

Hemlock Looper*, *Lambdina fiscellaria* (Guenée). Also called a Spanworm, enemy of forest and home plantings from New England to Wisconsin and south to Georgia and a destructive defoliator along the northwestern coast. Hemlock and balsam fir are preferred, but the looper may also feed on arborvitae, beech, birch, blueberry, wild cherry, elm, soft maple, oak, pine, spruce, and willow. The larvae are greenish yellow to gray with a double row of small black dots on the back. Trees may be defoliated and killed or have their symmetry spoiled. Eggs winter on twigs, needles, or in bark crevices and hatch in early June. The larvae feed on needles from the top of the tree downward, dropping on a thread of silk when disturbed. Pupation is under bark or in protected places. Tan to grayish brown moths with purple markings appear at the end of August and fly for several weeks. Spray with carbaryl in late May or early June. Carbofuran has been effective in a Rhode Island nursery.

Another **Hemlock Looper**, *Lambdina athasaria athasaria* Walker, kills hemlocks, including ornamentals. The moth is smaller than the pine looper but similar to it. The larva is yellowish with dark markings, 1½ inches long. Outbreaks have been reported in Massachusetts, Connecticut, Pennsylvania, and Ohio.

See also Western Hemlock Looper.

Hickory Horned Devil*, *Citheronia regalis* (Fabricius). Our largest native caterpillar, larva of the regal moth. It is found from Massachusetts to Louisiana and Texas, feeding on hickory, black walnut, butternut, sycamore, sweetgum, ash, persimmon, lilac, sassafras, sumac, and cotton. It is seldom abundant enough to do much damage. The caterpillar, 4 to 5 inches long, has a green body with black spines. Just back of the head are the devil's horns, very long reddish spines bending backward and tipped with black. The moth has a wing expanse of 4½ to 6 inches. Fore wings are dusky olive spotted with yellow, the veins bordered with red scales; hind wings are orange-red spotted with yellow. Control measures are usually unnecessary.

Hickory Shuckworm*, *Laspeyresia caryana* (Fitch). Pecan Shuckworm, usually the most destructive pest of pecans, present also on native hickories, with 50 per cent of the crop sometimes destroyed. Inconspicuous dark, small moths deposit eggs on young nuts or leaves; on hatching the larvae gnaw into the green nuts, causing them to drop. There are several generations and the last finds the shells too hard to penetrate and so stays in the shucks. Full-grown larvae winter in the shucks on the ground or in trees. Moths of the first generation emerge in Florida from February to April. There is no very satisfactory control. Keep dropped nuts cleaned up or covered with soil, using a disk tiller.

Hop Looper*, *Hypena humuli* (Harris). A noctuid moth.

Imported Cabbageworm*, *Pieris rapae* (Linnaeus). A pest in North America since 1860. Within 20 years of its arrival in Quebec it had spread over the country east of the Mississippi and is now present practically everywhere. It attacks all of the cabbage family—cabbage, cauliflower, kale, collards, kohlrabi, brussels sprouts, mustard, radish, turnip, horseradish, and related weeds; also nasturtium, sweet alyssum, mignonette, and lettuce.

The adult is the familiar white cabbage butterfly, which has 3 or 4 black spots on wings spreading 1¼ to nearly 2 inches (Plate XXVI). The butterflies are around on sunny days very early in spring, the females alighting frequently to glue an egg on the underside of a leaf until each has deposited several hundred. The eggs are yellow, bullet-shaped, ridged. Velvety smooth green caterpillars, with alternating light and dark longitudinal stripes, start feeding in about a week, depositing repulsive pellets of excrement as they eat huge holes in leaves. When full-grown, about an inch long, they pupate in a naked gray, green, or tan chrysalid, with angular projections, suspended by a belt of silk from some part of the plant or a nearby object, even a building. Adults emerge in a week or so and there may be 5 or 6 generations. Hibernation is in the pupal stage.

Control. Formulations of *Bacillus thuringiensis* provide safe and effective control. Commercial growers sometimes use Lannate, Dibrom, or Phosdrin; home gardeners may prefer rotenone or malathion. Clean up old plant parts after harvest; destroy weeds.

Large Aspen Tortrix*, *Choristoneura conflictana* (Walker). A leafroller present from New York and Utah north to Alaska, serious defoliator of poplar forests. The larva, an inch long, is olive-green with black head and shield. It rolls a leaf more or less funnel-shaped, ties it with silk and feeds inside this protection. The moth is light gray, wing expanse 1¼ inches.

Lesser Appleworm. See under Fruitworms.

Linden Looper*, *Erannis tiliaria* (Harris). Also known as Lime-tree or Basswood Looper, fairly common through eastern states and west to the Rocky Mountains. The larvae feed on forest and shade trees—oak, apple, birch, elm, hickory, basswood, maple—and may cause rather serious defoliation. The loopers are bright yellow with 10 longitudinal wavy black lines down the back, 1½ inches long. The moth is buff, marked with brown, with 1¾-inch wing-spread. Eggs are laid from October to November.

Melonworm*, *Diaphania hyalinata* (Linnaeus). Rarely injurious north of the Gulf States, although it may be seen elsewhere. The day-flying moth has pearly white wings margined with a narrow dark band, spreading to 1¾ inches (Plate XXXVI). The body is brown in front of the wings; the abdomen is silver-white tipped with a bushy tuft of slender, hairlike scales. The caterpillar is slender, greenish, with 2 white stripes along the body in most stages. It feeds chiefly on foliage of muskmelon, cucumber, squash, pumpkin, rarely on water-melon. Spray or dust with carbaryl or rotenone. Do not use mixtures containing sulfur which may prevent fruit formation in some melon varieties.

Monterey Pine Looper, *Nephytis umbrosaria* (Packard). A light-green smooth caterpillar tying needles of young Monterey pines to-gether at tops of branches; in central California. The moth is mottled gray, wing expanses 1½ inches.

Navel Orangeworm*, *Paramyelois transitella* (Walker). Reported burrowing into the navel end of oranges in Arizona in 1921, this insect was first thought to be of little importance. Since that time it has become one of the most important fruit and nut problems in California, infesting crops on the tree and in storage, being serious on almond, walnut, and fig particularly but also present in citrus, pomegranate, and macadamia nuts. The larva is yellow or dark gray with a dark head and thoracic shield and it pupates in a cocoon within the fruit. The moth is pale gray with darker markings on the fore wings and a row of crescent-shaped dots on the outer margin. Control measures include plant and orchard sanitation, early harvest of crops, and fumigation of nuts before storage with methyl bromide. Where walnuts are treated for codling moths, there is little trouble with the orangeworm.

Notchwing Geometer, *Ennomos magnarius* Guenée. The moth has reddish yellow wings, with small brown spots, spreading to 1½ to 2 inches. The larvae feed on trees.

Oleander Caterpillar, *Syntomedia epilais juncundissima* (Dyar). The worst pest of oleander in Florida. The larva is orange with tufts of long black hairs scattered over the body, 1½ inches long. The adult is called Polka Dot Moth because of the white spots scattered over the blue-black body and wings. Its shape resembles that of a wasp. Spray with chlordane.

Omnivorous Looper*, *Sabulodes caberata* Guenée. A native of, and apparently confined to, California. Most serious as an avocado pest, often numerous enough to strip trees of all foliage, it also feeds on acacia, alder, aralia, boxelder, buckeye, California-laurel, California Christmasberry (toyon), cherry, chestnut, clematis, daisy, elm, English ivy, eucalyptus, geranium, ginkgo, grevillea, groundsel, honeysuckle, lemon verbena, magnolia, maple, olive, orange, pear, passion-flower, pecan, peppertree, privet, rose, sumac, sycamore, tecoma, violet, black walnut, willow. It is well named omnivorous!

The moth is dull brown or yellow, with 2 darker transverse bands, wingspread up to 2 inches. It is nocturnal but may be found during the day on underside of leaves, where it lays clusters of eggs. The larva varies from yellow to pale pink or green, with yellow, brown, or green stripes on sides and back, and black markings as well. It is 1½ to 2 inches long in the last instar and can eat an entire avocado leaf in a day. The pupa is usually webbed between 2 leaves or inside a leaf folded over. There may be 5 or 6 generations a year. DDT was an effective control; if you garden in California ask your Experiment Station for their recommendation of a substitute.

Orangedog*, *Papilio cresphontes* Cramer. A common and destructive butterfly attacking citrus in Florida. It is called "dog" because one end of the caterpillar looks like the nose of a dog, 2 black spots on the thorax serving as eyes. It is 2½ inches long, dark brown with blotches of light brown. When disturbed, orange-red horn-like processes are protruded and a strong odor given off. The dogs feed voraciously on foliage, often defoliating a young tree in 2 or 3 days. The adult is a large yellow-and-black butterfly very common in Florida. Eggs, white with a reddish tinge, are laid singly on new shoots about February, hatching in 10 days. The best control is to remove caterpillars by hand from young nursery stock.

Orangehumped Mapleworm*, *Symmerista leucitys* Franclemont. Similar to the redhumped oakworm.

Orangestriped Oakworm*, *Anisota senatoria* (J. E. Smith). A native eastern moth, sometimes found in other states, preferring white and scrub oaks, occasionally feeding on other trees. The adults, appearing in early June, are bright tan, with black dots and a white center spot on the fore wings, which expand to 2½ inches. Females lay white to coral-red eggs in clusters on underside of leaves. The male is smaller and darker. The caterpillar is coal-black with orange-yellow longitudinal stripes and black, hornlike appendages at the end of the body, which is covered with short spines. Local infestations may strip foliage from trees in midsummer. Pupation is in soil. There is usually 1 generation, sometimes 2 in the South. Spray with carbaryl or methoxychlor.

Orange Tortrix*, *Argyrotaenia citrana* (Fernald). An important lemon and orange pest in California and other warm climates, also feeding on avocado, oak, pine, black walnut, willow, acacia, apricot, asparagus, begonia, cineraria, Jobs-tears, eucalyptus, ferns, geranium, Jerusalem-cherry, lantana, lavender, penstemon, rose, and wandering-Jew. It has become a raspberry pest in western Washington. The dirty-white, brown-headed caterpillar webs and rolls the leaves on which it feeds and bores into orange rind, causing premature drop and leaving avenues of infection for decay organisms. Sour oranges are scarred around the buttons. Grapefruit may also be infested, but it is not grown so much where the tortrix is injurious. Moths are fawn or gray with darker mottlings. Eggs are cream-colored, sculptured disks, laid in overlapping masses on both leaf surfaces. There are 2 to 4 generations. Spray with carbaryl. Natural enemies are often able to control the orange tortrix, at least 12 parasites being known.

Another orangeworm, the *Garden Tortrix,* may also be a citrus pest in California. It is similar to the orange tortrix but somewhat smaller.

Pacific Tent Caterpillar*, *Malacosoma constrictum* (Henry Edwards). Bluesided Tent Caterpillar. Similar to the western tent caterpillar, larvae have orange-brown bodies with distinctly blue sides and blue dots. They feed on oaks, shrubs, and fruit in California, Arizona, and Oregon.

Palmerworm*, *Dichomeris ligulella* Hübner. Present from Maine to Texas and occasionally serious on apple in northeastern states, the peak coming only once in 60 years. It may also feed on cherry, hazel, oak, pear, and plum. The very active, translucent greenish caterpillars, ½ inch long, with 2 white stripes along the side and 2 narrow white lines on the back, skeletonize the leaves and sometimes eat into young fruit. The small moths, only ½ inch across the wings, appear in July and later hibernate, laying eggs the next spring. The regular spray schedule for codling moth will control palmerworms.

Parsleyworm*, *Papilio polyxenes asterius* Stoll. Celeryworm, Black Swallowtail. The most important of the swallowtail butterflies, occurring all over the United States east of the Rocky Mountains, feeding on celery, carrot, caraway, dill, parsnip, parsley, but not considered a major pest. The caterpillar is a striking creature, 2 inches long, with a black crossband on each segment and just back of the head an opening for 2 soft, forked orange horns (Plate XIX). When disturbed, the larva protrudes these horns and gives out a sickeningly sweet odor. The butterfly has a spread of 3 or 4 inches, black wings with 2 rows of yellow spots, hind wings with blue shadings between the rows, a black spot bordered with orange on the inner margin, and a projecting lobe, the "swallowtail."

In the North the parsleyworm passes the winter as a tan chrysalid suspended from host plants; in the South the butterflies live over the winter. Eggs are laid singly on leaves of food plants, hatching in 10 days. The larvae feed for 10 days to several weeks, occasionally stripping plants of foliage. Another, but similar, species occurs in the West.

Control. Handpicking may be sufficient. If necessary, spray or dust with malathion.

Phantom Hemlock Looper*, *Nepytia phantasmaria* (Strecker). Feeding on western hemlock in the Pacific Northwest and California, also on spruce and Douglas-fir. The moths are white with numerous black markings. They congregate at dawn and dusk and lay eggs on needles in fall. A polyhedrosis virus has caused heavy mortality.

Phigalia Looper, *Phigalia titea* (Cramer). A geometrid caterpillar sometimes causing complete defoliation of trees in Atlantic States, including maple, oak, cherry, sassafras, and dogwood. The larva is flesh-colored, with many fine longitudinal black lines, 1½ inches long. It feeds from May to July. The male moth is pale ash color, with blackish brown markings, 1½-inch wingspread; the female has only partly developed wings.

Pickleworm*, *Diaphania nitidalis* (Stoll). Especially destructive in the Gulf States, but found as far north as New York and Michigan. Muskmelon, cucumber, and squash may be seriously injured, watermelon rarely, pumpkin not at all. Ripening fruits are bored into by white to green caterpillars up to ¾ inch long, with brown heads. They have black spots across each segment in younger stages, are a uniform green or copper when grown (Plate XXXVI). Masses of green, sawdust-like excrement are pushed out from holes in the fruit, which rots and turns sour. Early in the season the caterpillars work on stems, terminal buds, and in squash blossoms. Late crops may be almost totally destroyed. Hibernation is as a pupa inside a rolled leaf, the moth not coming out until late spring, sometimes early June.

The adult has a long slender body with a prominent brush of long hairlike scales at the end of the abdomen. The wings, yellowish white with a wide yellow-brown margin, spread to just over an inch. The moths fly at night, lay clusters of 2 to 7 eggs on underside of fruits, or on stems, tender buds, or new leaves. The first generation is not large, but moths emerging from pupation in July lay many eggs and the 3rd and 4th broods in August really get down to their devastating business. Each worm may enter several fruits before its growth is completed.

Control. As soon as a crop is harvested, destroy vines, unused fruits, adjoining weeds and trash. Bury pupae by spading or plowing in early fall. Plan for an early crop; use squash as a trap crop to keep worms away from melons but destroy vines before larvae are full-grown in squash blossoms. Spray or dust with carbaryl at first sign of worms in blossoms; repeat weekly.

Pine Looper, *Lambdina athasaria pelluscidaria* (Grote & Robinson). Defoliating pitch pine on Cape Cod, red pine in Connecticut, abundant on shortleaf pine in North Carolina. The moth is smoky to ash gray with fore wings crossed by 2 dusky lines; 1¼-inch wingspread. The larva is 1 to 1½ inches long, pale straw to greenish yellow with black markings.

Pink Scavenger Caterpillar*, *Sathrobrota rileyi* (Walsingham). Scavenger bollworm, often associated with pink bollworm of cotton and a scavenger on a wide range of food plants, from oranges to corn. The larva is about ⅓ inch long, deep wine-red with brown head and thoracic shield. The moth has chestnut-brown wings with straw-colored streaks, edged by irregular black scales. If this becomes a pest, it may be controlled with parathion.

Pinkstriped Oakworm*, *Anisota virginiensis* (Drury). From Maine to Georgia and west to Missouri and Texas on various species of oak but not an important pest. The caterpillars are 2 inches long, greenish or grayish granulated with white, and with pink stripes, 2 slender horns, and short spines. The moths are dark with a lilac tinge; the wings of the male are triangular.

Poplar Tentmaker*, *Ichthyura inclusa* Hübner. Distributed from New England to Colorado, feeding mostly on poplar, sometimes on willow. The caterpillars are black, mottled with gray, striped with yellow and brown. They have a pair of black tubercles on abdominal segments 1 and 8, are about 1¼ inches long. They are gregarious and make silken nests by webbing several leaves together or folding over a leaf. As they feed on the surface, they gradually add other leaves. Pupae winter under leaves; moths appear in early spring. They are brownish gray with 3 irregular white lines bordered with red on the outer edge; wingspread just over an inch. It is usually possible to cut out or wipe out whole colonies. If necessary, spray with carbaryl when larvae are small. There are some natural enemies.

Prairie Tent Caterpillar. See Western Tent Caterpillar.

Pruneworm, *Mineola scitulella* Hulst. Reported as destructive to sour cherry in Wisconsin. Larvae feed on blossoms and leaves in early May, pupate in soil, and adults appear in June.

Pumpkin Caterpillar, *Diaphania indica* (Saunders). A pest of cucurbits and other plants in India and Australia, reported from

Florida in 1959 but apparently present there for some years. Appearance and habits are similar to those of the melonworm and pickleworm.

Purplebacked Cabbageworm*, *Evergestis pallidata* (Hufnagel). Present throughout Maine and in scattered locations in the Northeast, also present in part of Utah, feeding inside a silken web on cabbage and other crucifers.

Puss Caterpillar*, *Megalopyge opercularis* (J. E. Smith). One of the stinging caterpillars, found from Virginia to Texas and southward on oak, citrus, hackberry, elm, plum, maple, rose, sycamore, and other deciduous trees and shrubs and even on English ivy. Gardeners should beware of this inch-long larva, covered with long, soft, reddish yellow hairs interspersed with stinging spines. The adult is a flannel moth, small, covered with dense scales to give it a woolly appearance.

If a caterpillar falls on the neck there may be severe irritation; if on the wrist, the whole arm may swell. Handpicking is possible if you wear thick gloves. A formula to sooth the nettling caused by stinging is: 10 grains menthol, 2 drams zinc oxide, 8 ounces aq. calcis, 15 drops acid carbolici.

Range Caterpillar*, *Hemileuca oliviae* Cockerell. A range pest on wild grasses in New Mexico and Colorado but sometimes infesting corn and other cultivated crops. Larvae are yellow, gray, or black, densely covered with coarse, poisonous spines, and with white spiracles encircled with a black line.

Redhumped Caterpillar*, *Schizura concinna* (J. E. Smith). Also called Redhumped Appleworm, distributed over most of the country. The larvae are black with yellow stripes, with the head and a hump on the first abdominal segment red, and a row of spines projecting from the hump, up to 2 inches long (Plate XX). They rest with the rear end of the abdomen elevated. They feed on both fruit and ornamental trees, stripping foliage of apple, apricot, aspen, bayberry, birch, blackberry, cottonwood, cherry, dogwood, hawthorn, hickory, huckleberry, locust, pear, persimmon, plum, poplar, prune, rose, sweetgum, willow, and walnut. The larva winters in a cocoon on the ground, pupates in late spring or early summer. The moths are brown, about 2 inches across the wings, and lay eggs in masses on underside of leaves. The larvae are gregarious, first skeletonizing foliage, then eating everything but midribs. When disturbed, they raise both ends of their bodies. They defoliate one branch before moving to another.

Control. Collect and destroy young colonies. A regular spray schedule for other apple pests should keep them in bounds in orchards. Other plants can be sprayed with malathion.

Redhumped Oakworm, *Symmerista albifrons* (J. E. Smith), and *S. albicosta* (Hübner). Both species go under this common name. They are found in eastern North America from Canada to Florida and west to Kansas and Minnesota; quite common on oaks, reported also on basswood, beech, elm, and maple. The caterpillars, 1½ to 1¾ inches long, have an orange head, wider than the thorax, a smooth yellowish body and dark lines on the back, and the back of the 8th abdominal segment enlarged to form an orange-red hump. The moths have mottled dark-brown to gray fore wings with an area of white along the forward edge; wingspread 1½ inches. They appear from May to July, the females laying pale green eggs in groups on underside of leaves. The larvae are green at first, with black heads, and in that stage they are gregarious, scattering as they mature to the redhumped form. The winter is passed as pupae inside thin white cocoons in the ground litter.

Rednecked Peanutworm*, *Stegasta bosqueella* (Chambers). Frequently reported from Georgia to Oklahoma, infesting peanut buds and terminals. There may be 4 or 5 generations with nearly 100 per cent infestation in some fields. The adult is a small moth, family Gelechiidae.

Saddleback Caterpillar*, *Sibine stimulea* (Clemens). A stinging caterpillar widely distributed through the Atlantic States. It feeds on oak, cherry, sometimes other trees; may attack azalea, canna, dahlia, holly, lily, magnolia, palm, rose, and other plants. Its appearance is most distinctive: flat underneath, rounded above, reddish but with a pea-green patch (the saddle blanket) in the middle of the back and on that a broad purple-brown patch edged with white (the saddle). There are fascicles of spines along the side and 2 tufts of spines at both ends. The irritation is severe; see Puss Caterpillar for soothing formula.

Saddled Prominent*, *Heterocampa guttivitta* (Walker). Also called Antlered Maple Caterpillar, common in Atlantic States, ranging also to Texas. It prefers beech, with sugar maple and apple next, but it also feeds on other maples, oak, occasionally blackberry, cherry, poplar, spirea, and witch-hazel. The young larva bears 9 pairs of horns, starting at the head with a large branched pair like antlers; the mature caterpillar has no horns. It is green to brown or yellow, with a reddish brown saddle spot in the middle of the back. The moth is olive-gray with darker wavy areas and dark dots. Occasionally New England woodlands may be defoliated by this pest and at such times it also feeds on shade trees but it is not considered a

Melon Aphid

Bean Aphid

E.MELADY

I MELON APHID: (a,1) winged female; (a,2) last nymphal stage; (a,3) eggs and young nymph; (a,4) wingless female or stem mother; (b) cantaloupe leaves starting to curl; (c) aphid-transmitted cucumber mosaic on fruit; (d) cucumber leaf mottled by mosaic. BEAN APHID: (a,1) winged female; (a,2) wingless female; (b) aphids on bean; (c) aphids clustering under nasturtium leaves.

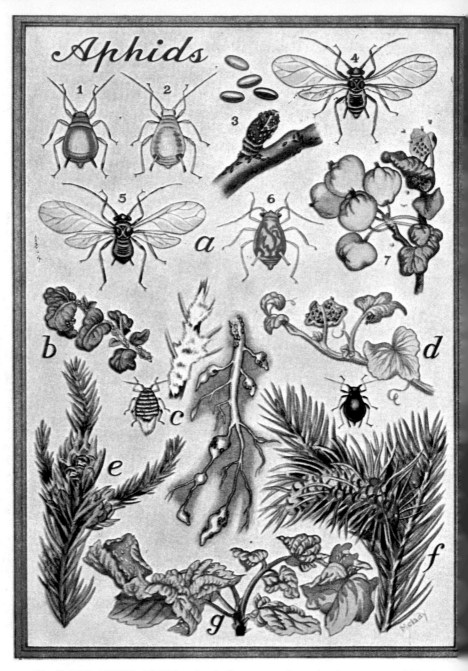

II ROSY APPLE APHID: (a,1) first generation; (a,2) summer aphid; (a,3) eggs, much enlarged, and eggs hatching on apple bud; (a,4) fall aphid, winged female; (a,5) fall aphid, winged male; (a,6) egg-laying female; (a,7) apples distorted, leaves curled. POTATO APHID: (b) injured potato leaves. WOOLLY APPLE APHID: (c) woolly masses on twig, galls on roots. MELON APHID: (d) wingless form and curled leaves. EASTERN SPRUCE GALL APHID: (e) galls on Norway spruce. COOLEY SPRUCE GALL APHID: (f) terminal gall on blue spruce. SNOWBALL APHID: (g) viburnum foliage curled, distorted.

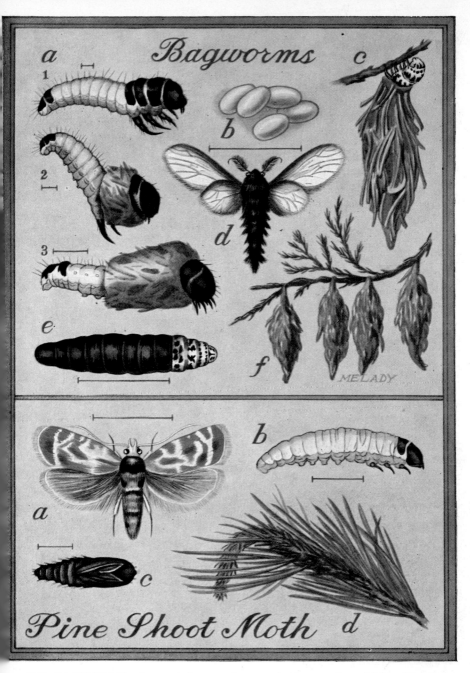

III   BAGWORMS: (a,1,2,3) larva and stages in construction of bag; (b) eggs, highly magnified; (c) female in bag, actual size; (d) winged male moth; (e) wingless female removed from bag; (f) bags in winter. EUROPEAN PINE SHOOT MOTH: (a) moth; (b) larva removed from infested tip; (c) pupa; (d) pine shoot with typical crooking and discoloration.

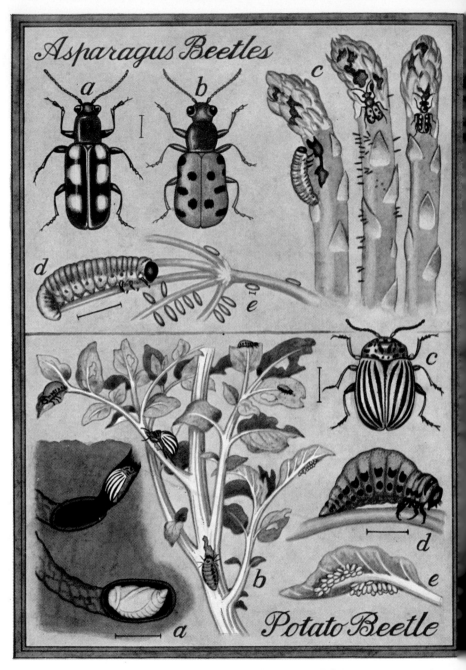

IV ASPARAGUS BEETLE: (a) adult; (c) typical injury to asparagus shoots by grubs and beetles; (d) grub and eggs. SPOTTED ASPARAGUS BEETLE: (b) adult. COLORADO POTATO BEETLE: (a) pupa in soil and adult emerging from soil; (b) portion of potato vine showing larvae, eggs, and beetles; (c) adult beetle; (d) humpbacked grub; (e) egg clusters on underside of potato leaf.

serious pest on ornamentals. Parasites usually take care of the saddled prominent.

Sagebrush Defoliator*, *Aroga websteri* Clarke. Defoliating and killing sagebrush in Oregon, Idaho, Utah, and Nevada.

Saltmarsh Caterpillar*, *Estigmene acrea* (Drury). Generally distributed, one of the woollybears. The caterpillars are very hardy, gray when young, then black with yellow broken lines and cinnamon-red hairs, up to 2 inches long. At times, usually in late summer, they may be as bad as armyworms, eating everything in sight—sugar beets, beans, other vegetables, grapes, carnations, and other flowers. Moths have white wings with black spots and an orange, black-spotted abdomen.

Schizura Caterpillars. Related to Redhumped and Unicorn Caterpillars. *Schizura ipomoeae* Doubleday feeds on rose, apple, wild cherry, willow, and other deciduous shrubs; *S. letonoides* (Grote) on about the same hosts; *S. badia* (Packard) on viburnum.

Sonoran Tent Caterpillar*, *Malacosoma tigris* (Dyar).

Southwestern Tent Caterpillar, *Malacosoma incurvum* (Henry Edwards). Has been controlled with aerial application of a polyhedrosis virus and with *Bacillus thuringiensis.*

Southern Cabbageworm*, *Pieris protodice* Boisduval & LeConte. A southern species resembling the imported cabbageworm, with similar control measures. The butterfly has more black markings on the wings and the caterpillar has longitudinal yellow bands.

Soybean Looper*, *Pseudoplusia includens* (Walker). False Cabbage Looper. On soybean, cabbage, tomato, and also a pest of floricultural crops, especially in southern California. It is important on chrysanthemums, may also feed on carnation, aster, calendula, cineraria, daisy, gerbera, poinsettia, geranium, African-violet, stock, coleus, and hydrangea.

Spiny Oakworm*, *Anisota stigma* (Fabricius). A southern species much like the orangestriped oakworm. The caterpillar is bright tawny orange with a dusky stripe along the back and prominent spines on thoracic segments.

Stinging Rose Caterpillar*, *Parassa indetermina* (Boisduval). A sluglike creature feeding on rose leaves from the underside, also on dogwood, chestnut, oak, wild cherry, hickory, pawpaw, bayberry, plum, apple, and pear. The caterpillar is marked with red, white, and violet stripes and 7 pairs of large, spine-bearing processes; ¾ inch long. It winters in a dark cocoon in refuse. The pale cinnamon-brown moth, wings marked with green and brown, lays eggs in July. Contact with the spines results in a painful burning sensation for several hours.

Striped Garden Caterpillar*, *Polia legitima* (Grote). Generally distributed, more abundant in late summer, a dark, yellow-striped cutworm, similar to the zebra caterpillar. It has some preference for crucifers. The moth is grayish with an irregular pattern. Spray if necessary with malathion; clean up refuse in fall.

Sugar Pine Tortrix, *Choristoneura lambetiana*. A relative of the spruce budworm, found in the Northwest.

Tomato Pinworm*, *Keiferia lycopersicella* (Walsingham). Found outdoors in the South and in southern California, where it is one of the worst tomato pests, and in greenhouses. The larvae, yellow, gray or green with purple spots, only ¼ inch long, make serpentine or blotch mines in leaves which are folded and held together with light webs. Developing buds and ripening fruits have pinholes bored in them with entrance usually at the stem end. Injury to vines is not serious but fruit can be a total loss. The pinworm may also injure eggplant and tomato. Parathion is recommended for commercial growers.

Uglynest Caterpillar*, *Archips cerasivoranus* (Fitch). Cherrytree Tortrix. This leafroller is a northern pest, abundant only at long intervals, mostly on wild cherry, sometimes on cultivated cherry, rarely on apple, sometimes on nursery oaks. The larvae—yellow with black heads, ¾ inch long—tie twigs and leaves together, making a large nest. The moths are yellow with brown spots and blue band, 1-inch wingspread.

Unicorn Caterpillar*, *Schizura unicornis* (J. E. Smith). On apple, wild cherry, willow, and other deciduous trees, defoliating pin oaks in Ohio. The caterpillar is 1⅓ inches long, variegated brown, orange, and green, with a prominent projection on the first abdominal segment. The moth is brownish gray, wingspread to 1⅓ inches. Newly hatched larvae are gregarious, skeletonizing leaves from the undersurface; older larvae consume all but the midrib. They usually defoliate one branch before moving to the next. Full-grown larvae winter in papery cocoons in the ground litter.

Variable Oakleaf Caterpillar*, *Heterocampa manteo* (Doubleday). Distributed from Maine to Alabama, more destructive in the South. The greenish yellow caterpillar, with variable markings, 1½ inches long, devours leaves of oak, especially white oak, basswood, walnut, birch, elm, hawthorn, and persimmon. The moth is pale ash-gray with 3 wavy dark lines crossing the forewings; wingspread 1½ inches.

Velvetbean Caterpillar*, *Anticarsia gemmatalis* Hübner. Found only in the Gulf States on soybeans, velvetbeans, cowpeas, peanuts, kudzu-vine, and young tips of black locust. Soybeans are usually defoliated first. The caterpillars vary from dull green to olive-brown or black with white lines running the length of the body. Nocturnal moths are buff to dark brown or black, with a white diagonal line across the wings. Larvae can be controlled with toxaphene or methoxychlor dust. There is a rather efficient egg parasite and a fungus which attacks the worms.

Walnut Caterpillar*, *Datana integerrima* Grote & Robinson. A native moth found from Maine to Florida and west to Kansas, feeding on walnut, butternut, hickory, and pecan, occasionally on apple, peach, beech, honeylocust, sumac, and willow. The caterpillars are 2 inches long, dull black, reddish when young, covered with long, white hairs. The moths are dark buff with 4 brown transverse lines on the fore wings. Eggs are laid in masses on undersides of leaves. The larvae feed in colonies, crawling to the tree trunk to molt, then going back to feed again. Pupation is in soil. There are 2 generations in the South, 1 in the North. Caterpillar masses can be destroyed or the trees sprayed.

Western Hemlock Looper*, *Lambdina fiscellaria lugulrosa* (Hulst). Destroying spruce-hemlock forests, along the coast of Oregon and Washington, appearing in countless thousands in outbreaks. Western hemlock is the preferred host but the looper may attack Douglas-fir, Sitka spruce, western redcedar, huckleberry, salal, and other broadleaved shrubs and trees. The moths are light buff, fore wings marked with 2 wavy lines, hind wings with 1 line; 1½-inch wingspread. Eggs are laid in September and October, on bark or moss on trunk. Young larvae crawl up tree trunks in spring and feed on young needles. By midsummer a heavily infested forest appears scorched by fire. Full-grown larvae are green to brown with diamond-shaped markings on the back, 1½ inches long. In late summer they clip off small twigs and drop by silken threads to the ground. Outbreaks of this species last about 3 years, then are brought under control by parasites, predators, and a virus disease.

Western Oak Looper*, *Lambdina fiscellaria somniaria* Hulst. Closely related to and resembling the western hemlock looper, periodically destructive to oak in Oregon and Washington. The caterpillars are pale brown mottled with black spots, up to 1¼ inches long. Every few years they get so numerous it is impossible to walk under trees without being covered with them; the trees look as if they had been burned. The moths are yellow to dark brown, dotted with darker scales. In October they cover limbs and branches of trees. Spray with carbaryl, diazinon, or malathion.

Western Tent Caterpillar*, *Malacosoma californicum* (Packard). Includes forms formerly called California Tent Caterpillar, Prairie Tent Caterpillar, and Great Basin Tent Caterpillar. This species constructs large tents like the eastern tent caterpillar. It infests oak in particular but also almond, apple, apricot, ash, toyon, California coffeeberry, ceanothus, cherry, cottonwood, currant, hazel, madroña, plum, prune, redbud, rose, willow, and other fruit and forest trees. The caterpillars are reddish brown or tawny above, pale underneath, with a blue line on each side. Spray with carbaryl, diazinon, or malathion.

There are variations on this species. We have *M. californicum fragile,* with caterpillars having tawny hairs on a black body with blue-and-orange markings; *M. californicum pluviale,* tawny with blue-and-orange spots, living in small, compact nests.

Yellowheaded Fireworm*, *Acleris minuta* (Robinson). Cranberryworm, sometimes injurious on the drier cranberry bogs. The moth, slate-gray, ¾-inch wingspread, lays eggs on leaves in May. Yellowheaded caterpillars web leaves together and feed inside, pupating in their nest in June, producing a second brood to feed in July, and a third in September. Keeping bogs flooded until about May 20 helps to control. Growers use an aerial spray of parathion or Guthion.

Yellownecked Caterpillar*, *Datana ministra* (Drury). General, primarily on fruit trees—apple, apricot, blackberry, blueberry, cherry, peach, pear, plum, quince—also on beech, birch, hazel, hickory, linden, oak, walnut, and other ornamental trees and shrubs. The caterpillar is black with a yellow thorax (the neck), 4 yellow stripes along each side; covered with long white hairs. The larvae work in groups and when disturbed elevate both ends. Young larvae skeletonize leaves, older caterpillars eat all but stem and midrib. The moths have brown fore wings, 1½-inch wingspread. Pupation is in the soil. There is 1 generation a year with chief injury in July and August. Shake caterpillars off small trees and crush them. Spray larger trees with carbaryl when larvae are young.

Yellow Woollybear*, *Diacrisia virginica* (Fabricius). Virginia Tiger Moth. The caterpillars are very hairy, yellow or straw-colored with black lines. They are general feeders, injuring many vegetables and flowers—asparagus, bean, beet, blackberry, cabbage, calendula, calla, canna, carrot, cauliflower, celery, cherry, chrysanthemum, coleus, corn, currant, dahlia, eggplant, fuchsia, gooseberry, grape, hollyhock, lily, melon, morning-glory, parsnip, peanut, pea, petunia, potato, pumpkin, radish, raspberry, rhubarb, rose, Spanish needles, squash, sunflower, sweetpotato, turnip, verbena, and violet. The moths have white wings with black spots and a yellow-brown, black-spotted abdomen. There are 2 broods. Pupae winter inside hairy cocoons. Spray or dust with malathion.

Zebra Caterpillar*, *Ceramica picta* (Harris). General, feeding on cereal, forage, truck, and fruit crops, trees and flowers, including sweetpeas, lilies, and gladiolus, most injurious in late summer. The larvae are velvety black with 2 bright-yellow stripes on each side and many fine yellow transverse lines. The moth is rusty brown. Spray or dust with malathion or carbaryl when larvae are young.

CENTIPEDES AND SYMPHYLANS

Centipedes, "hundred-legged worms," are members of the class Chilopoda, close relatives of true insects. They differ in having only 2 main body parts (they lack a thorax), no wings, and instead of 3 pairs of legs they have 1 pair on each of their many body segments. There are at least 15 pairs of legs but not the hundred that the name implies. Centipedes are like insects in having a single pair of antennae (with 14 or more segments), breathing by tracheae, and with reproductive organs at the posterior end of the body. They look something like worms but are flatter, have a distinct head and jointed legs. They have a pair of poison claws on the first segment behind the head that they use to paralyze their prey. Centipedes usually rest under logs or stones and are swift runners, predaceous on earthworms, snails, and some insects. Their bite is painful to man but not often serious. There are many species and some of the tropical forms go up to 18 inches in length. As a class, they can be considered more beneficial than harmful. True centipedes are not garden pests.

Garden Symphylan*, *Scutigerella immaculata* (Newport). Garden Centipede. Commonly called a centipede because it looks like one,

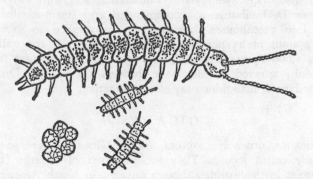

44. Garden centipede or symphylan, showing adult, young, and eggs.

but actually belonging to the class Symphyla. A symphylan is distinguished from a true centipede by having only 12 pairs of legs in the adult form, fewer when young, no poison claws, no eyes, and the genital opening near the anterior end of the body. Symphylans live in damp places rich in organic matter, in leaf mold, manure piles, or peaty soils.

The garden symphylan or centipede is small, ¼ inch long, pure white, very active. It keeps its long antennae constantly moving as it travels through the soil in cracks and tunnels left by decaying plant roots. It is an outdoor pest in warm climates, particularly injurious to asparagus in California, and is a greenhouse pest nearly everywhere. It is considered an important soil pest in 25 of the 31 states reporting its presence. The symphylans eat off fine roots and root hairs and scar underground parts of stems so that plants die or are stunted. Besides asparagus, which has its shoots riddled with tunnels while they are below ground, the garden centipede seriously injures lettuce, radishes, tomatoes, cucumbers, and many ornamentals, including sweetpea, snapdragon, aster, and other flowers.

Small white eggs are laid in clusters of 5 to 20 about a foot deep in soil, any time between April and September; the minute young hatch 7 to 10 days later. At first, they have only 6 pairs of legs, 10 body segments, and very short antennae, but they add another pair of legs and lengthen antennae at each molt. When greenhouse soil is wet down and crops are started in fall, symphylans start feeding on roots; in outdoor gardens they are active in spring. They are rarely seen on the surface of soils, being strongly repelled by light.

Control. Asparagus fields in California have been flooded with water to discourage symphylans. Fumigating soil with ethylene dibromide or D-D mixture is recommended and steam-sterilizing soil brought into greenhouses. Lindane can be applied to greenhouse beds, 3 pounds of 25 per cent wettable powder to 100 gallons of water to 2,000 square feet of bench space. In rose houses this can be forcefully sprayed on the beds through the mulch. Drenching with chlordane or malathion may also be effective.

CICADAS

The cicadas, order Homoptera, family Cicadidae, are sometimes erroneously called locusts. They are members of a large family— 1,500 species in the world, although only 75 in North America—but we commonly distinguish only 2 kinds, the periodical cicada ("17-year locust") and the annual, or dogday, cicada. They are large sucking insects, having front wings of the same texture throughout, and they hold their wings in a roof-like position. They are noted chiefly for their shrill noises—"singing"—produced by special vibratory organs under the base of the abdomen of the male.

Dogday Cicada, *Tibicen linnei* (Smith & Grossbeck). Also called Harvestman and Annual Cicada, but it is not literally annual. It has a 2- to 5-year cycle but the broods overlap, so that some appear every summer. This is larger than the periodical cicada, has a black body with whitish bloom, green margins on the wings, and numerous light markings on thorax and abdomen. The cicadas are around on summer dog days, July and August, but do not cause injury enough to worry about. The cicada-killer, a digger wasp, gets some.

Periodical Cicada*, *Magicicada septendecim* (Linnaeus). A native of North America, named for its regular occurrence at long intervals.

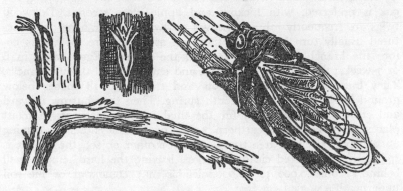

45. Periodical cicada, "seventeen-year locust," laying eggs, and twigs showing bark torn in process.

There are 2 races. The southern race, with its northern boundary Virginia to Oklahoma, has a 13-year cycle; the northern race appears every 17 years and is the one called Seventeen-Year Locust. Both are more abundant east of the Mississippi and both have a number of broods, which appear in different years, so that it may not be 13 or 17 years between cicada swarms in any given locality. The broods are numbered and it is possible to predict accurately when each will appear. Brood II was widespread over the eastern seaboard in 1945, its first appearance since 1928; it came again in 1962 and is expected in 1979. Brood X, the most widespread and abundant of the broods, was serious in Middle Atlantic States in 1953 and came again on schedule in 1970.

The adult periodical cicada has a stout black body about 1 inch long with wings extending well behind the body when at rest. It has reddish orange eyes, legs, and wing veins. It appears from mid-May to early June and is around for 5 or 6 weeks. A town may have cicadas in such abundance that life is made hideous with their shrill, unending song, and people driving through sometimes stop their cars to see what is the matter with their engines. In some gardens tree trunks will be covered with cast shells of the nymphs and the ground under trees literally perforated with holes ½ inch across. The next town, only a mile or so away, may be lucky and have almost no cicadas.

The female has a tough, horny ovipositor and the chief damage is the tearing of twigs as eggs are deposited in rows, the bark being pushed away and the wood raised into bundles of splinters. About 75 trees, shrubs, and herbaceous plants are used for egg laying, but oak is preferred, with hickory and apple close seconds. Dogwood twigs are frequently injured. Leaves on twigs and branches so punctured usually turn brown but hang on as an eyesore for weeks before the branch breaks and falls to the ground. Eggs hatch in 6 or 7 weeks; the antlike young drop and enter the soil through cracks. They burrow down to the roots and stay 6 to 18 inches below ground level until the seventeenth spring. Then they burrow upward and crawl out when ready for the final molt. Sometimes, in moist places, they construct earthern cones or chimneys before coming out. They crawl to a tree trunk, stick, or other object, the thorax is split, and the winged cicada emerges, leaving the hard, empty shell behind. From 20,000 to 40,000 cicadas may come out of the soil underneath a single large tree.

Although we think of the periodical cicada as one species there actually are six, three with the 17-year cycle, *M. cassini* (Fisher) and *M. septendecula* Alexander & Moore, in addition to *M. septendecim*, and three with the 13-year cycle, *M. trecim* Walsh & Riley, *M. tredecassini* Alexander & Moore, and *M. tredecula*, Alexander & Moore. They differ somewhat in color and in song.

Control. The periodical cicada was almost impossible to control sufficiently to prevent egg-laying injury until the advent of carbaryl (Sevin). Now we have something really effective. Use 2 pounds of 50 per cent wettable Sevin to 100 gallons of water (2 tablespoons to 1 gallon) and repeat in 6 or 7 days. Young trees can be protected with mosquito netting. It may be well to avoid setting out a new orchard a year or two before a large cicada brood is expected. Avoid pruning young trees heavily the year before a brood is due. Cut off injured twigs as soon as possible.

Other Cicadas. Several other species of Tibicen and also species of Okanagana appear in western states, some on grass and in rangeland, one on fruit trees. They are somewhat smaller than the eastern annual cicadas but injure plants by their egg laying in the same way. Adults of *Diceroprocta apache* are reported injuring grapevines in California and tips of apricot, peach, plum, ash, bottlebrush, carob, elm, and mimosa in Arizona.

CRICKETS

Crickets are relatives of grasshoppers, order Orthoptera, family Gryllidae, for tree and field crickets, Gryllacrididae for cave and camel crickets, Gryllotalpidae for mole crickets, Tridactylidae for pygmy mole crickets, and family Tettigoniidae for the Mormon cricket, which is really a longhorned grasshopper. Crickets have chewing mouth parts but incomplete metamorphosis. They are noted for the chirping notes produced by the males when they rub together specially modified parts of their front wings. They have long, filiform antennae, a spear-shaped ovipositor, and 2- to 4-segmented tarsi. The hardened horny fore wings are called tegmina; they are flat on the back but bend down abruptly along the sides. Most feed on plants; some are predaceous; some are both.

African Mole Cricket*, *Gryllotalpa africana* Palisot de Beauvois. Frequently intercepted at Quarantine.

Blackhorned Tree Cricket*, *Oecanthus nigricornis* F. Walker. Widely distributed, greenish yellow with head black or with 3 black stripes, destructive in berry-growing regions. It lays eggs in rows in pithy stems of raspberry, blackberry, loganberry, grape, elder, sometimes in woody twigs of maple, elm, peach, apple, and other trees. Canes die above the punctures or split and break off.

Camel Cricket, *Daihinia brevipes* Haldeman. Found in the Great Plains States from North Dakota to northern Texas, reported as injurious in Oklahoma to tomatoes, watermelon, cotton, cowpeas, and other plants in the seedling stage. It feeds at night, is found mostly in sandy areas. Poison bran-mash bait gives satisfactory control.

Changa*, *Scapteriscus vicinus* Scudder. Puerto Rican or West Indian Mole Cricket, an introduced species similar to the southern mole cricket. It is injurious to truck crops, pastures, lawns in the coastal plain of the Southeast. It is 1½ inches long, brown above, light brown underneath. See Northern Mole Cricket for control.

Coulee Cricket*, *Peranabrus scabricollis* (Thomas). More nearly related to katydids than crickets, very destructive in Montana and Washington. Feeding on sagebrush, dung, living and dead animals, it also eats nearly all field and garden crops, fruits, and shrubs. Adults are fat, soft-bodied, 1½ inches long, dark reddish brown.

Females are wingless; males have short, winged stubs. They are active in the daytime and move in migratory hordes, devastating everything in their path. Ditches can be dug to stop migrating swarms, or poison bait can be used as for the Mormon cricket. Western meadowlarks are credited with stopping outbreaks.

Field Crickets, *Gryllus* spp. (complex of species). Common insects in pastures, meadows, and along roadsides, with some entering houses. Most sing day and night. They are black or brown, with a rounded, grasshopper-like body, prominent antennae, ⅗ to 1 inch long. They hide by day under trash, feed at night. They chew foliage, flowers, and tender growth of iris and other flowering plants, and vegetables, especially seedlings. Use chlordane dust or diazinon spray.

Fourspotted Tree Cricket*, *Oecanthus quadripunctatus* Beutenmüller. Like the blackhorned tree cricket except for 2 dark spots in each of the 2 basal antennal segments.

Greenhouse Stone Cricket*, *Tachycines asynamorus* Adelung.

House Cricket*, *Acheta domesticus* (Linnaeus). European brown cricket, the "cricket-on-the-hearth." Introduced from Europe at various ports, this species has been slowly spreading through eastern states. It is pale, yellowish brown, and has dark cross bars on its light head. It may chew book bindings and do other damage in a household.

Jerusalem Cricket*, *Stenopelmatus fuscus* Haldeman. Sand Cricket, a western species with legs adapted for tunneling in sandy soil. It is large, wingless, amber brown, does not have hearing organs on front tibiae. It is a useful predator, injurious to little except potato tubers in newly broken soil.

Mormon Cricket*, *Anabrus simplex* Haldeman. Western Great Plains, Idaho, or Black Cricket, found in most states west of the Rocky Mountains and in some of the Great Plains states. It is very destructive, migrating periodically from native breeding grounds in the hills to devastate garden crops, fruit, and grain. It is of great economic importance as a scourge of range grasses. Eggs are laid in late summer and fall in light, sandy loam, inserted singly just under the surface in bare spots between clumps of grass or sagebrush. Young crickets start hatching early in April and reach maturity in 6 to 8 weeks. There is 1 generation. Adults are 1 inch long, heavy-bodied, with small useless wings but antennae and ovipositor as long as the body; tarsi 4-segmented. They are active during the day and may travel ⅛ to 1 mile a day when they start migration.

Control. Metal barriers or ditches to stop migratory hordes have been used in the past. Now poison bait is used, often applied by airplane. Aldrin baits have been used but may be harmful to wildlife.

One formula calls for 100 pounds of standard bran, 1 pound toxaphene or ½ pound chlordane, and ½ gallon of fuel oil or kerosene, applied at the rate of 10 pounds per acre.

For broadcasting by hand, a wet bait is made of 100 pounds of standard wheat bran, 4 pounds sodium fluosilicate, 12 to 15 gallons of water. This can be reduced proportionately for gardens.

In 1848 flocks of California gulls terminated a terrific outbreak of Mormon crickets in Utah so successfully that a monument was erected to them. The gulls still come to feed on crickets.

Northern Mole Cricket*, *Gryllotalpa hexadactyla* Perty. A native pest, known in damp muddy places from Canada through Florida but a problem only in the South. A European species, *G. gryllotalpa*, has become established in a few places along the eastern coast and threatens nurseries. The only species in the West is *G. cultriger* Uhler. These crickets are large, 1½ inches long, brownish above, paler underneath, covered with velvety hairs. Their front legs are greatly enlarged, adapted for burrowing, and they terminate in 4 strong, blade-like teeth called dactyls (Plate XXI). They live deep in the ground during the day, coming out at night to pulverize a garden bed and the plants growing in it. Most injury comes from their tunnels in the upper inch or two of soil, which cut off roots of seedlings, injure lawns. Mole crickets also eat pits in underground roots and stems, cut off stems above ground, and eat seeds.

Control. Before planting apply a spray or dust of chlordane or diazinon. Use 5 ounces of 40 per cent chlordane wettable powder in 2½ gallons of water and apply to 1,000 square feet of soil surface; work it into the top 6 inches before planting. If mole crickets are damaging established plants use a ready-mixed chlordane bait, applying it to the soil surface in late afternoon following rain or watering.

Snowy Tree Cricket*, *Oecanthus fultoni* T. J. Walker. Widely distributed throughout North America. Tree crickets are generally beneficial, eating aphids, treehoppers, and scales, but they do feed somewhat on flowers, fruit, and leaves; twigs may be broken by their egg punctures. This cricket is pale green, with slender body, ⅝ inch long, with a black spot on the first 2 abdominal segments (Plate XXI). It lays eggs singly in a line down one side of a twig or cane of apple, ash, blackberry, cherry, loganberry, pear, plum, prune, peach, and other fruits and ornamentals. There is only 1 generation and egg laying is in autumn. The songs of the males are short, clear, whistling notes. Temperature regulates the frequency of the chirps. It is said that if you add 39 to the number of chirps made in 15 seconds, the resulting number will give the temperature in degrees Fahrenheit. Control by pruning out infested twigs or canes.

Southern Mole Cricket*, *Scapteriscus acletus* Rehn & Hebard. Recorded from Georgia, Texas, and other southern states. It is much like the northern mole cricket but it has 2 dactyls instead of 4 and is pinkish buff in color.

Twospotted Tree Cricket*, *Neoxabea bipunctata* (De Geer). Like the snowy tree cricket in habit but buff-colored and has hind wings much longer than front wings.

CURCULIOS

Curculios, along with weevils, belong in the order Coleoptera, family Curculionidae. They are beetles with a pronounced snout, the head being prolonged forward with biting mouthparts at the end and elbowed antennae arising midway. Curculios usually have a longer snout with a more pronounced downward curve than weevils. The Curculionidae is one of the largest familes of insects, with more than 2,500 species known in North America. All members eat plants both as larvae and as adults. They are mostly small and dull-colored, with a habit of dropping from bushes and playing dead when disturbed.

Apple Curculio*, *Tachypterellus quadrigibbus* (Say). A native insect found east of the Mississippi River. Preferred hosts are apple, cherry, haw, wild crab, quince, pear, and shadbush. Feeding and egg punctures result in knotty, misshapen, undersized fruit and premature drop. This curculio does not make crescent-shaped marks like the plum curculio but produces a large number of punctures close together. It is brown with 4 humps on the back, and a long, slender snout. It winters in leaves and rubbish on the ground, feeding on buds, fruit spurs, and terminal shoots in spring and attacks fruit as soon as it is set. The larvae develop in June drops and in mummied apples left on trees, pupating inside. Adults emerge from the middle of June to early October.

There are three other curculios on apple: the larger apple curculio, *T. quadrigibbus magnus* List, from Illinois to Texas; *T. consors* Dietz from the Rocky Mountains to the Pacific Coast; and the cherry curculio. Control measures are the same as for the plum curculio.

Black Walnut Curculio, *Conotrachelus retentus* (Say). A common pest of young walnuts in eastern United States. The curculios, pale reddish covered with gray pubescence, hibernate as adults, feeding on young shoots in spring and making crescent-shaped cuts for their eggs in very young walnuts, which drop to the ground half-grown. They pupate in the soil; beetles emerge in August and September to feed on leaf petioles before hibernating. Larvae in dropped nuts can be destroyed by burying deeply or putting nuts in water. Several parasitic wasps and flies aid in control.

Butternut Curculio, *Conotrachelus juglandis* LeConte. Also known as Walnut Weevil, attacking native and Japanese butternuts and young English walnuts. The adult resembles the plum curculio but with white markings; it is ¼ inch long. It punctures nuts, tender tips, and leaf petioles, lays eggs in new growth and, in young nuts, through crescent-shaped slits. The grubs, dirty-white with brown heads, burrow through the nut or down the twig for 4 or 5 weeks, then go below the soil surface to pupate.

Cabbage Curculio*, *Ceutorhynchus rapae* Gyllenhal. An ash-gray weevil, ⅛ inch long, with a short snout. Adults and grubs gouge out stems and adults also work on leaves. They infest seedling cabbage, cauliflower, horseradish, mustard, radish, and turnip. Dust young plants with methoxychlor.

Cabbage Seedstalk Curculio*, *Ceutorhynchus quadridens* (Panzer).

Cambium Curculio, *Conotrachelus anaglypticus* (Say). Common from Massachusetts to Florida and west to Iowa. The larvae feed on cambium and inner bark of many fruit, shade, and forest trees, working around the edges of wounds, retarding healing. They also work in the crowns and roots of columbine, causing wilting and dying, and produce wilting and dieback in young camellia shoots. The snout beetle is small—less than ¼ inch long—reddish brown; the grubs are small, fleshy, legless. Remove and destroy infested plant parts.

Cherry Curculio, *Tachypterellus consors cerasi* List. A variety of an apple curculio.

Clover Root Curculio*, *Sitona hispidula* (Fabricius). A common pest of clover and alfalfa, sometimes feeding on soybeans, cowpeas, and other legumes. Tiny grayish grubs score and furrow roots, nearly girdling them. Small gray or brown beetles with short blunt snouts feed on foliage, sometimes eating off tops of young soybeans entirely. Crop rotation seems the most practical control.

Cowpea Curculio*, *Chalcodermus aeneus* Boheman. Also known as Cowpea Podweevil, injuring cowpeas, seedling cotton, beans, peas, and strawberries. Most important in the cotton states, it occurs as far north as Iowa. Black, humpbacked adults lay eggs in cowpeas or beans in the field and larvae destroy developing seeds.

Grape Curculio*, *Craponius inaequalis* (Say). A native pest of wild grape, injuring berries of cultivated grape in some areas. It is reported as injurious in New England, Florida, Kentucky, Missouri, Ohio, and West Virginia. The small, black beetles, just over 1/10 inch long, winter in sheltered locations and feed for a month or two in spring before laying eggs in cavities under the skin of grape berries. Footless larvae feed on berry flesh and seeds, drop to the ground, and pupate by midsummer. Adults emerge and feed again before hibernation. Control measures are usually unnecessary.

Hickorynut Curculio, *Conotrachelus affinis* Boheman. Confined to hickories, pignut preferred, then shagbark, whiteheart, and butternut. The beetles, reddish brown with a broad band of lighter gray across the back, appear when nuts are half-formed to lay eggs in circular cavities in nuts and shells. Nuts drop in midsummer; larvae stay inside for about a month, then enter the soil to pupate. Bury dropped nuts deeply or put in water to kill larvae.

Plum Curculio*, *Conotrachelus nenuphar* (Herbst). A native snout beetle, found east of the Rocky Mountains, a major pest of stone fruits—plum, peach, cherry, apricot, prune, nectarine—and next to codling moth in importance on apple, sometimes injuring pear and quince. The adult is dark brown with a grayish patch on the back, 4 definite humps on the wing covers, and a long, curved snout which projects forward and downward in an arc $\frac{1}{3}$ the length of the body, which is $\frac{1}{4}$ inch long (Plate XXII). It winters in stone walls, hedgerows, or other protected places, appearing on the trees at blossomtime. The beetles feed on leaves and petals. They injure young fruit by feeding and laying eggs in small circular excavations marked by a crescent-shaped slot underneath. Feeding punctures may result in warts or scars, sometimes misshapen, knotty apples. Grubs in stone fruits render them unmarketable. Also, the punctures on peaches and plums afford entrance to brown-rot spores. Economic losses for the country as a whole run between 8 and 17 million dollars a year.

Eggs hatch, about a week after being inserted in the fruit, into gray-white, legless grubs with brown heads and curved bodies. They feed in the flesh for 2 weeks or more, by which time the fruit has probably fallen to the ground, although most cherries and some peaches remain on the tree until ripe. The larvae leave the fruit and enter the soil to pupate, adults emerging in about a month. There are 2 generations in Virginia, sometimes a partial 2nd in Delaware but only 1 farther north. Temperatures affect activity. Above 70° F. brings beetles out of hibernation, promotes egg laying, and usually results in severe damage.

Control. Guthion or perhaps parathion are recommended to orchardists in some states but they should procure exact schedules from their local agricultural agent. Methoxychlor and malathion are possibilities for home gardeners but they too should obtain schedules tailored for their trees and area. It is always advantageous to pick up dropped fruits and to destroy them by deep burial or soaking in waste oil, and to clean up possible winter shelters. It is also helpful to collect curculios during the season by placing a sheet under a tree and jarring off adults with a stick. There are several parasites and a useful fungus disease.

Quince Curculio*, *Conotrachelus crataegi* Walsh. The most serious pest of quince and confined to this host. It resembles the plum curculio but winters in the soil as a grub. The adult—broad, grayish brown without humps on its back—eats irregular cavities in the fruit, which may be knotty and misshapen. The white legless grubs feed in the fruit during the summer but seldom cause it to drop. They leave the fruit before it drops naturally, so that picking up fallen quinces is no help in control.

Rhubarb Curculio*, *Lixus concavus* Say. Rhubarb Weevil, common from New England south to Florida and west to Idaho. This is one of the largest of the snout beetles, ½ inch long, blackish but covered with a rusty yellow dust. It punctures rhubarb stalks and lays eggs in them, but the larvae develop and feed on common curled dock. Handpick the beetles; destroy all dock plants growing near rhubarb.

Rose Curculio*, *Rhynchites bicolor* (Fabricius). Rose Snout Beetle, bright red with a black undersurface and black curved beak, ¼ inch long (Plate XI). Adults drill holes in buds of wild and cultivated roses, the buds either not opening or producing petals riddled with holes. Small white larvae develop from eggs laid in hips but drop to the ground for pupation and hibernation. This curculio is particularly destructive in cold regions, breeding in wild roses but swarming to cultivated roses in such numbers as to prevent almost all bloom. Western forms vary in color from black and red to black with a greenish luster. DDT was an effective control; now try methoxychlor or carbaryl.

CUTWORMS

High in the ranks of gardening headaches are the cutworms—smooth, fat, soft, repulsive caterpillars, larvae of night-flying moths, family Noctuidae. Different species occur all over the world and injure almost all crops. The solitary or surface cutworms, including black, bronzed, and dingy, are most likely to harass the home gardener. They feed on plants near the surface of the ground, cutting off succulent stems of tomato, bean, cabbage, some other vegetables, and flowers soon after they are set out (Plate XXIII). Climbing cutworms go up the stems of herbaceous plants, shrubs, and vines, sometimes even climbing trees to eat buds, leaves, and fruit. Army cutworms work in large groups and are more prevalent in western gardens. Subterranean cutworms, including pale western and glassy, remain continuously in the soil, feeding on roots and underground stems.

Most surface cutworms have similar habits. They winter as partly grown larvae in cells in the soil, under trash, or in clumps of grass. They start feeding in the spring, working only at night, remaining coiled up in a ball just under the earth surface during the day. When full-grown, they dig down several inches in the soil to make a cell where they pupate from 1 to 8 weeks, or over winter. Southern species have several generations a year, most northern species have but 1, with moths appearing in summer.

Control. In the annual garden, treat the soil before seeding or transplanting with diazinon, working granules or spray into the top

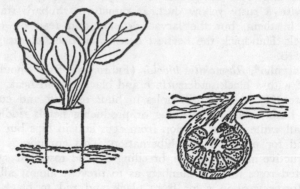

46. Paper collar around a cabbage seedling to foil cutworms; and cutworm in typical position in earth cell.

4 inches of soil; carbaryl may also be used. Many cutworm baits are on the market under brand names. Spread the bait in late afternoon, around the plants but not hitting them.

An old, and still good, method of circumventing cutworms without chemicals is to place a collar of stiff paper or thin cardboard around each plant as it is set out. This should go down an inch or two into the soil to stay in place and to foil worms working just under the surface.

Army Cutworm*, *Euxoa auxiliaris* (Grote). A western species, appearing in armies, attacking all kinds of vegetation in Washington, Oregon, Wyoming, and Utah. Caterpillars are dark with a broad pale line down the back and a dark stripe on each side.

Black Army Cutworm*, *Actebia fennica* (Tauscher). A northern pest, injuring blueberries in Maine, garden vegetables in Alaska.

Black Cutworm*, *Agrotis ipsilon* (Hufnagel). A surface cutworm, known also as the Greasy Cutworm. It is gray to brown to nearly black with a broken yellow line on the back and a pale line on each side, the whole appearance being greasy and shiny. The skin has convex granules, large and small. This species is widely distributed, is very fond of corn and other truck crops, and often cuts off tomatoes in home gardens. It is a restless feeder cutting off many plants to satisfy its appetite. It lays eggs singly or a few together on leaves and stems, often on plants in new land. It winters as a pupa. Moths are reddish to brownish gray with silvery patches at bases and tips of fore wings. There are 2 generations in the North, often 4 in the South.

Bristly Cutworm*, *Lacinipolia renigera* (Stephens). On forage crops, alfalfa and clovers, in the Middle West.

Bronzed Cutworm*, *Nephelodes minians* Guenée. A northern species injurious to corn, grains, and grasses. The larva is dark bronzy brown, striped from head to tail with 5 clear pale lines about half as large as the brown area in between, with a granulate skin. There is 1 generation, the winter being spent as a partly grown larva.

Claybacked Cutworm*, *Agrotis gladiaria* (Morrison). On cotton, corn, and alfalfa. Greenish to dark brown with a broad pale stripe down the back.

Clover Cutworm*, *Scotogramma trifolii* (Rottenburg).

Darksided Cutworm*, *Euxoa messoria* (Harris). A common species that may climb to feed on tree foliage in spring. The dull, pale green larvae attack cultivated crops, wild grasses, and weeds. The moth is silver-gray with dark mottled fore wings. Dursban has been used to control early stages.

Dingy Cutworm*, *Feltia subgothica* (Haworth). A northern species sometimes assuming climbing habit. Larvae are dull dingy brown with a broad buff-gray stripe down the back (divided into triangular areas on each segment), a narrow dark stripe on each side, and coarse skin granules.

Glassy Cutworm*, *Crymodes devastator* (Brace). Widespread, except in the more southern states. It is a subterranean species preferring sod and injurious to crops following sod. The larva is greenish white and rather translucent or glassy with a red head; the skin is not granulated.

Granulate Cutworm*, *Feltia subterranea* (Fabricius). Dusty brown with a rough, granulated skin, on many crops in southern states. It defoliates peanuts in Georgia, infests sweetpotato tubers and dichondra lawns in California, tomatoes and peppers in Louisiana, shade tobacco in Florida, and so on.

Palesided Cutworm*, *Agrotis malefida* Guenée. On cotton, sometimes tomato, pepper, corn.

Pale Western Cutworm*, *Agrotis orthogonia* Morrison. A subterranean form of great economic importance in the West, where it has destroyed millions of dollars worth of small grains, beets, and alfalfa. The body is greenish gray, with brown head and shield and small black spiracles. The moth is mottled gray, nocturnal and diurnal; it appears in late August and September to lay eggs in small batches just under the surface in soft soil. The larvae feed day and night, on cabbage, carrots, and onions as well as grains. Poison baits have no effect; the chemicals have to be washed into the soil. The moths are attracted to light traps.

Redbacked Cutworm*, *Euxoa ochrogaster* (Guenée). Regularly destructive in many northern sections. Larvae are reddish on the back, feed on succulent plants, may be destructive to cereal, forage, and truck crops, including mint and asparagus. They feed both above and below ground, hibernate in the egg stage. They succumb readily to poison bait.

Roughskinned Cutworm*, *Proxenus mindara* Barnes & McDunnough.

Spotted Cutworm*, *Amathes c-nigrum* (Linnaeus). Generally distributed but rather scarce in the South, a surface feeder preferring garden crops. Larvae have wedge-shaped black dashes on each segment, a dark line through the spiracles, and a smooth skin. Eggs are laid singly, or in patches of 100 or more, on leaves. There may be 2 or 3 generations.

Striped Cutworm*, *Euxoa tessellata* (Harris).

Variegated Cutworm*, *Peridroma saucia* (Hübner). A climbing cutworm, perhaps the most widely known and important species, present in many countries, damaging crops in the United States to the tune of several million dollars a year. The larva is ashy or light brown mottled with dark brown, with a distinct yellow dot in the middle of each segment, often a dark W on the 8th segment, a smooth skin. The moth is grayish brown with dark, mottled fore wings and a brassy luster. In early spring it lays small, white ribbed eggs in large irregular masses on foliage and stems of plants or limbs of trees or fences or buildings. The larvae eat foliage, buds, and fruits of garden crops, fruit trees, or vines. They injure flowers outdoors and in the greenhouse. There are 2 generations outdoors, more inside. Handpicking, trapping under boards, poison sprays or dusts are all used in control.

Western Bean Cutworm*, *Loxagrotis albicosta* (Smith). One of the climbing cutworms, first described from Arizona, now present also in Colorado, Idaho, Iowa, Kansas, Nebraska, New Mexico, South Dakota, Utah, and Wyoming. It feeds on foliage, stems, buds, seeds of beans; on leaves, stalks and ears of corn; and is reported on fruits of groundcherry and deadly nightshade. Controls applied to cornfields by airplane include Thiodan, carbaryl, and diazinon.

Western W-marked Cutworm*, *Spaelotis havilae* (Grote). On cereals and corn in western states, also reported on poplar in California.

White Cutworm*, *Euxoa scandens* (Riley).

W-marked Cutworm*, *Spaelotis clandestina* (Harris). Reported on tobacco and hay in the West.

Yellowheaded Cutworm*, *Apamea amputatrix* (Fitch). Reported on vegetables, bluegrass, and other plants.

EARTHWORMS

Earthworms are friends of man! They are not insects but belong to the animal phylum Annelida, meaning rings, and are made up of many round segments. They are usually 2 to 10 inches long with slender, cylindrical, soft bodies, bearing 8 bristle-like projections, setae, on each ring. They are hermaphrodites in that each worm produces ova and sperm cells, but they are not self-fertilized. They mate and the eggs are laid in a round case or capsule which eventually passes off over the head.

Earthworms have been considered by some people the most important of all animals. Charles Darwin estimated that earthworms bring up 7 tons of new soil for every acre of land, that good garden soil normally has about 53,000 worms per acre and poor field soil only half that many. There are earthworm farms raising worms to sell to gardeners with claims made for the wonders worked by so-called "hybrid" worms. However, if your soil has enough organic material to support earthworms, you'll probably have plenty without having to buy them.

Earthworms live in moist soil containing decaying organic matter and crawl out at night to feed, or come out when their burrows are filled with water. They eat the soil and their digestive juices dissolve leafmold and other organic matter; then this digested earth is discharged in the form of castings, soil of the finest quality. Earthworms also drag leaves into their burrows, increasing the organic content of the soil in that way. Strong healthy worms work from 3 to 8 feet underground, making the trip to the surface nightly to deposit castings. Their beneficial action may go much deeper than spade, plow, or rototiller.

Despite the fact that some gardeners want earthworms badly enough to support earthworm farms, others object to lumpy piles of castings on fine front lawns. They can be a nuisance on golf courses and the oriental earthworm (*Peretima hupeiensis*) is definitely a menace. It is known at scattered points from Connecticut to Miami but is concentrated in the Metropolitan New York area. It is light grass-green, has a bad odor when crushed.

Control. Older recommendations called for treating lawns with lead arsenate or Mowrah Meal, later chlordane was recommended with lawns sprayed with 40 per cent wettable chlordane at the rate of ½ pound to 1,000 square feet. DDT had little effect on earthworms. Feeding in leaf litter under sprayed trees they accumulated it in their bodies and so became a hazard for birds.

Earthworms in flower pots are not welcome; they clog up the drainage hole. Limewater is the time-honored remedy, either purchased at the drug store or made at home by stirring 1 pint of freshly slaked lime into 2½ gallons of water and using it as soon as it clarifies. Or water plants with chlordane, using 1½ level teaspoons 40 per cent wettable powder to one gallon of water. Be sure to use chlordane instead of limewater on azaleas and other plants requiring an acid soil.

EARWIGS

Earwigs are beetle-like insects of the order Dermaptera, readily recognized by tail appendages that look like forceps. They have gradual metamorphosis but biting mouth parts, feeding on decayed or living plant material and on other insects. They are largely nocturnal, living under bark or stones or debris on the ground during the day. Their front wings are short, leathery, veinless; hind wings, when present, are membranous, rounded, with radiating veins and are folded up under the front wings when at rest; tarsi are 3-segmented. Some species have scent glands. They were named for the entirely erroneous notion that they crawl into the ears of sleeping persons. The European earwig is the species of most consequence to gardeners.

European Earwig*, *Forficula auricularia* Linnaeus. An introduced species, first discovered at Newport, Rhode Island, in 1911, with another colony appearing at Seattle, Washington, in 1915. Since then it has become widely distributed in Arizona, California, Colorado, Connecticut, Delaware, Idaho, Maine, Massachusetts, New Hampshire, New Jersey, New York, New Mexico, Oregon, Pennsylvania, Utah, Vermont, Washington, and Wyoming. It has also appeared in scat-

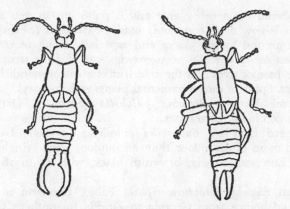

47. European earwig: male, left; female, right.

tered locations in Alabama, Georgia, Illinois, Virginia, and Wisconsin.

The insect is hard, dark reddish brown, up to ⅘ inch long, with a pair of sharp pincers or forceps at the tip of the abdomen, protruding ¼ the length of the body. These structures are longer and more curved in the male than in the female. The front wings are very short and the hind wings are folded up under them, aided by the forceps. Earwigs seldom fly; they run.

The female lays a batch of smooth white eggs in early spring in the soil in any protected place and broods over them until they hatch. She watches over her young until the first molt, then leaves, often to lay another batch of eggs. Young nymphs feed on green plant shoots, eating holes in leaves of many different vegetables and flowers. Older earwigs work on blossoms, eating stamens and bases of petals of roses, dahlias, and many other flowers, and often climb into fruit trees, especially apricot and peach, to dine on ripening fruit. They are quite a pest in houses, crawling over everything in sight, into crevices of various sorts, hiding under cushions, dishes, or clothing.

Earwigs are more important in coastal areas. In California eggs are laid from December through February, and the pest is most destructive from April through July. They are also, however, beneficial as scavengers on decaying matter and in feeding on insect larvae, snails, and other slow-moving animals.

Control. A poison bait was standard control for many years and may still be used. It consisted of 6 pounds of wheat bran mixed with ½ pound sodium fluosilicate and moistened with 1 pint of fish oil. This is scattered toward evening, thinly, over areas frequented by ear-

wigs; it should not touch plants and is poisonous to pets and birds.
Chlordane is now more commonly used, or carbaryl (Sevin), applied
as a dust around hiding places and especially along fences and the
foundations on houses. To keep earwigs out of fruit trees, dust the
soil at the base of trees and the tree trunks about a month before the
fruit ripens. Spray or dust ornamental plants with carbaryl.

Handsome Earwig, *Prolabia pulchella* (Serville). Dark brown,
fairly common in southern states.

Ringlegged Earwig*, *Euborellia annulipes* (Lucas). In southern
states and more of an indoor than an outdoor pest. Wingless, longer
than the European earwig, brownish black, with 15 to 16 antennal
segments.

Southern Earwig, *Labidura riparia* Pallas. Common in southern
gardens and homes, from Georgia to Florida to southern California.
Brown, 1 inch long, mainly a scavenger but eating flowers to some extent.

Striped Earwig, *Labidura bidens* (Olivier). Also southern, and
larger than other earwigs; light brown.

Toothed Earwig, *Spongovostox apicedentatus* (Caudell). Fairly
common among dead leaves and cacti in desert regions of the Southwest.

EARWORMS

Corn Earworm*, *Heliothis zea* (Boddie). Present practically everywhere that corn is grown, the worst corn pest in the United States, although more damaging to sweet corn than to field corn. The claim
has been made that American farmers grow 2 million acres of corn a
year just to feed the earworm. It is damaging to other crops as the
Tomato Fruitworm and the Cotton Bollworm.

The caterpillars, larvae of moths, family Noctuidae, are nearly 2
inches long when full-grown, yellowish or green or brown with
lengthwise light and dark stripes (Plate XIII). In early plantings
they attack buds and feed on unfolding leaves, giving a ragged appearance and possibly some stunting. They feed somewhat on tassels
but most of the damage is to the ear. They feed from the tip, starting
on fresh silk, then working down to the kernels, piling up masses of
moist castings. Feeding on the silk prevents pollination, resulting in
nubbins; feeding on the kernels introduces various mold fungi. Late
season corn may be nearly 100 per cent infested.

As the tomato fruitworm, the larva begins feeding on foliage but
soon works into green fruit, usually burrowing in at the stem end and
sometimes destroying as much as 25 per cent of the tomatoes. They

are restless caterpillars, moving from one fruit to another and over to beans, cabbage, broccoli, and lettuce. As the cotton bollworm, the larva injures green bolls of cotton. Other food plants include alfalfa and clovers, globe artichoke, chickpea, geranium, gladiolus, grape, mignonette, okra, peach, pea, peanut, pear, pepper, pumpkin, rose, squash, strawberry, sunflower, and vetch.

The earworm winters as a pupa 2 to 6 inches below ground; the moths crawl out through exit holes prepared by the larvae. Adults vary in color; the front wings are grayish brown marked with dark lines shading to olive-green; the hind wings are white with dark spots or markings; wingspread 1½ inches. The moths fly at dusk or on warm, cloudy days, feed on nectar of flowers, and lay 500 to 3,000 eggs, yellowish, hemispherical, ridged, singly on host plants. There are 2 or 3 generations a season, and moths of later generations often lay their eggs on corn silk. The newly hatched larva is very small, white with a black head, but grows rapidly, molting every 2 to 5 days. The pupae are seldom able to survive the winter north of Virginia, unless the weather is unusually warm and dry. Most northern infestations come from adults migrating from the South.

Control. There are some corn hybrids on the market partially resistant to corn earworm and there are many natural factors aiding in control, including the fact that one corn earworm will consume another. There are egg parasites; birds feed on earworms, often damaging ears in the process; moles destroy pupae; cold, moist weather reduces infestations. Spray sweet corn with carbaryl (Sevin), starting when silks appear and repeating every 2 to 4 days. To prevent ear damage it is necessary to spray until the silks are thoroughly wet. Use 3 tablespoons of 50 per cent carbaryl wettable powder to 1 gallon of water. In some states malathion is also recommended; diazinon is another possibility. Farmers may use Lannate or Gardona plus parathion.

An older method was the treatment of ears with a special corn earworm oil, applied with a medicine dropper 3 to 7 days after silks first appear, putting the end of the dropper a quarter inch into the mass and squirting in about 20 drops.

On tomatoes, fruitworms can be controlled by spraying or dusting with carbaryl with farmers possibly preferring Guthion.

FLIES

Flies belong to the order Diptera, meaning 2-winged, the order including almost all insects with only 1 pair of wings—mosquitoes, gnats, and midges as well as flies. The second pair of wings is represented, if at all, by threadlike knobbed organs called halteres. There are some wingless flies and some with reduced wings but, in these, halteres are usually present. Fly mouthparts are adapted for piercing-sucking or for lapping. The compound eyes are very large and usually there are 3 simple eyes, ocelli. The tarsi are 5-segmented. The larvae, called maggots, are footless, grublike creatures, usually soft, white or yellowish, with the head reduced. There is complete metamorphosis, with the pupal stage ordinarily passed inside the last larval skin, called a puparium.

There are a great many species of flies. Some are dangerous to man as carriers of human diseases and a few are vectors of plant disease; some are destructive to crops. But some flies are useful scavengers, cleaning up dead animals and plant wastes, and others are insect destroyers, with predators like the syrphid flies, or they are parasites, living in or on harmful insects.

The families listed here contain members of interest to gardeners.

Agromyzidae. Leafminer Flies. Small, yellow or black, the larvae making mines in leaves. See under Leafminers.

Anthomyiidae. Resemble houseflies. Some species are serious pests of garden crops. Many are scavengers.

Apioceridae. Flower-Loving Flies. Rather large, elongate, found on flowers in arid regions of the West but rather rare.

Asilidae. Robber Flies. A beneficial group, adults being predaceous on a variety of insects. Body usually hairy, head hollowed out between the eyes.

Bombyliidae. Bee Flies. Mostly stout-bodied, densely hairy flies found on flowers and grass. The larvae are parasites on caterpillars, grubs, and eggs of grasshoppers.

Cecidomyiidae. Gall Midges. Minute delicate flies or gnats with relatively long antennae and legs, reduced wing venation, many living in plants and causing galls, some not gall-forming, a few predaceous.

Chamaemyiidae. Aphid Flies. Small, usually grayish with black spots on abdomen; larvae are predaceous on aphids, scale insects, and mealybugs.

Chloropidae. Frit Flies. Small, rather bare flies, some brightly colored with yellow and black, common in meadows and other grassy areas. Some are cereal pests, some scavengers, and a few are parasitic or predaceous.

Dolichopodidae. Longlegged Flies. Small to minute, with metallic coloring; abundant in swamps, woodlands, meadows; some members are predaceous on bark beetles and other insects.

Drosophilidae. Vinegar Flies, Pomace Flies, Fruit Flies. Found

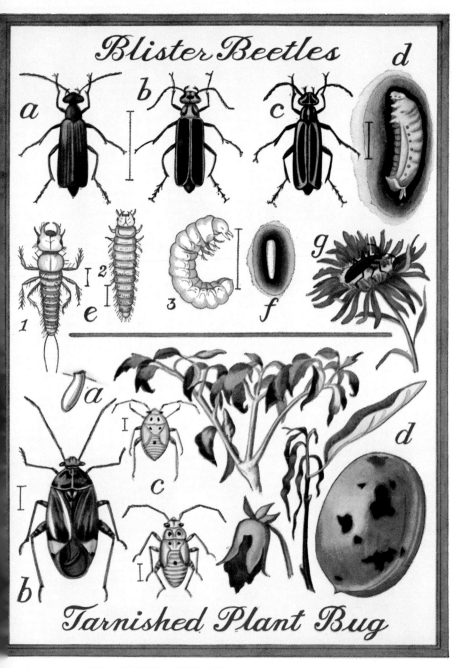

V CLEMATIS BLISTER BEETLE: (a) adult. MARGINED BLISTER
BEETLE: (b) adult. STRIPED BLISTER BEETLE: (c) adult; (d) pseudopupa
in soil; (e,1) triungulin or first larval stage; (e,2) second larval stage; (e,3) third
larval stage; (f) egg in soil, much enlarged; (g) adult feeding on aster. TARNISHED
PLANT BUG: (a) egg, enlarged, inserted in stem; (b) adult bug; (c) nymph in two
instars; (d) injury to fruit, bug, terminal shoot, leaves.

Gypsy Moth

Elm Leaf Beetle

VI GYPSY MOTH: (a) large female moth; (b) small dark male moth; (c)
pupa inside scanty thread cocoon; (d) pupa enlarged; (e) full-grown hairy caterpillar; (f) egg mass. ELM LEAF BEETLE: (a) adult; (b) pupa; (c) grub; (d)
egg cluster on underside of leaf and single egg, much magnified; (e) elm leaves
skeletonized by larvae and with holes eaten by adults.

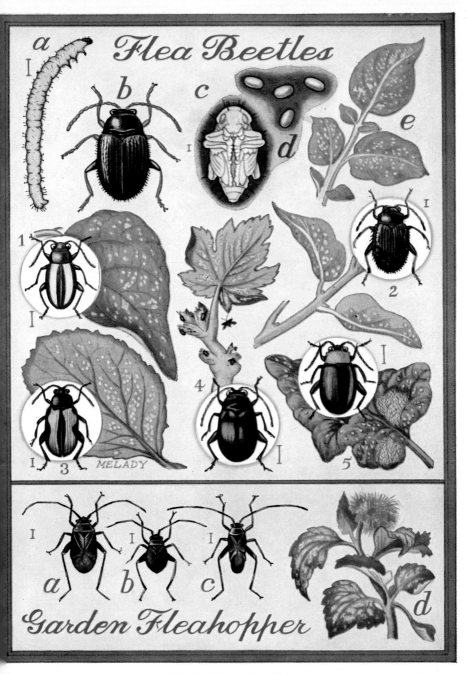

VII POTATO FLEA BEETLE: (a) grub; (b) adult; (c) pupa in soil; (d) eggs in soil; (e) "shot-hole" injury to potato leaf. PALE-STRIPED FLEA BEETLE: (1) adult and injury on bean. EGGPLANT FLEA BEETLE: (2) adult and riddled foliage. STRIPED FLEA BEETLE: (3) adult and injured cabbage leaf. GRAPE FLEA BEETLE: (4) adult and injury to grape leaf. SPINACH FLEA BEETLE: (5) adult, and spinach leaf skeletonized by grubs, riddled by beetles. GARDEN FLEAHOPPER: (a) long-winged female; (b) short-winged female; (c) male; (d) ageratum with foliage yellowed by loss of sap.

VIII JAPANESE BEETLE: (a) adult, with injury on peach, rose, corn; (b) egg in soil, much enlarged; (c) pupa in soil; (d) grub; (e) turf damage from grubs. JUNE BEETLE: (a) white grub actual size; (b) egg, enlarged, and young larva; (c) pupa; (d) adult.

mostly on decaying fruit and vegetation, very small, usually yellow; very useful in studies of heredity.

Mycetophilidae. Fungus Gnats. Slender, delicate, mosquitolike, found in damp places with decaying vegetation or fungi; a few species feed on flowers.

Psilidae. Rust Flies. Slender with long antennae, small to medium, with a ridge across the basal third of the wing; living in roots or galls of plants.

Sciaridae. Darkwinged Fungus Gnats, Root Gnats. Similar to the Mycetophilidae but with eyes meeting above the bases of the antennae. Small, dark, in moist shady places, larvae feeding on fungi, and decaying plant material but some feeding on plant roots.

Stratiomyidae. Soldier Flies. Medium or large, dark or brightly colored, wasplike adults; found on flowers. Some larvae are aquatic, some live in decaying matter, some under bark.

Syrphidae. Flower Flies, Syrphid Flies. Adults hover around flowers and are found almost everywhere. Many are brightly colored and resemble bees or wasps. Many syrphid larvae are highly beneficial, predaceous on aphids and other insects; some live in decaying vegetation; a very few feed on growing plants.

Tachinidae. Tachinid Flies. The most beneficial family of Diptera with 1,300 North American species parasitic on other insects. The flies resemble bristly houseflies, the abdomen usually with large bristles in addition to smaller ones all over the body.

Tephritidae. Fruit Flies. A large group of small to medium flies, usually with spotted or banded wings. The adults are found on flowers or vegetation. The larvae are maggots in fruit and a few are leafminers.

Tipulidae. Craneflies. The largest family in the Diptera, with over 1,450 species in this country. Most resemble overgrown mosquitoes with very long legs, which are easily broken off. Many are aquatic, but a few feed on cultivated plants and some are predaceous.

Australian Sod Fly, *Altermetoponia rubriceps* Macq. Introduced into California some years ago. The maggots have become a serious pest of lawns and golf courses in the San Francisco area.

Black Cherry Fruit Fly*, *Rhagoletis fausta* (Osten Sacken). Distributed through northern United States on cherry, wild cherry, pear, and plum. Except that the abdomen is entirely black and that it prefers sour cherries, this species is like the cherry fruit fly.

Bumelia Fruit Fly*, *Pseudodacus pallens* (Coquillett).

Caribbean Fruit Fly, *Anastrepha suspensa* (Loew). Normally present in Cuba, Puerto Rico, and Jamaica, this fruit fly was found at Key West, Florida, in 1930 and caused little trouble until 1965, when it started spreading as a pest of dooryard fruits. Hosts include avocado, calamondin, Barbados and Surinam cherry, carissa, grapefruit, guava, kumquat, loquat, mango, orange, peach, roseapple, sapodilla, and tomato and pepper. It is not a pest of commercial citrus groves.

Carrot Rust Fly*, *Psila rosae* (Fabricius). A European pest first noticed in Ottawa in 1885, now rather generally present in the Northeast and along the West Coast and found also in parts of Idaho, Utah, Wyoming, and Colorado. It is quite important in Washington and Oregon. Carrot is the most important host but there may also be serious injury to celery, parsnip, celeriac, and parsley and some feeding on coriander, caraway, fennel, and dill. The damage is caused by maggots feeding on the roots, producing stunting, dwarfing, or complete destruction of plants. Larval excrement looks like iron rust in the root tunnels, whence the name rust fly. Soft-rot bacteria follow the maggots so that carrots decompose in a soft, vile-smelling mess.

The fly is small, ⅕ inch, shiny green with yellow hairs, legs, and head, black eyes. It lays eggs about the crowns of host plants. The yellowish maggots, ⅓ inch when grown, work down into the soil to the roots. They feed there for a month, then pupate in the soil to produce a second brood of flies in August. Sometimes a partial third brood damages late carrots and celery, and injury may continue in storage. Brown puparia or maggots winter in soil.

Control. Apply diazinon granules in the seed furrow at planting time. Use 2 ounces of 5 per cent granules of their equivalent per 100 feet of row. Or use 1 tablespoon of 25 per cent diazinon emulsion in 1 gallon of water and apply to soil at base of plants at 10-day intervals. Carrots planted after June 1 (in the New York area) and harvested early may escape injury.

Cherry Fruit Fly*, *Rhagoletis cingulata* (Loew). A native, common in northern United States on cherry, wild cherry, pear, and plum; responsible for most of our wormy cherries. Adults are smaller than houseflies, black with yellow margins on the thorax, 2 white crossbands on the abdomen and a dark band across the wings, typical of fruit flies in the family Tephritidae. They emerge from brown puparia in the soil over a period of 5 or 6 weeks, starting in early June (about a week after the black cherry fruit fly). They fly to trees, feed 7 to 10 days by scraping surface of leaves and fruit, sucking up sap, and lay eggs on young fruit through small slits cut in the flesh. The maggots, developing and eating inside the fruit, produce misshapen, undersized cherries, often with one side shrunken or decayed and turning red before maturity. When full-grown, the worms eat their way out of the fruit, fall to the ground, and spend the next 6 months as puparia 2 or 3 inches below the surface.

Control. The only feasible method is to kill the flies before they lay eggs, which may mean using a special trap to determine when the first adults appear. Or spray when sour cherries start to color, repeating twice at 7-day intervals if this is a serious problem. Home gardeners should use methoxychlor or rotenone; commercial growers may use Guthion. Several parasites attack the cherry fruit fly, with a braconid wasp (*Opius ferrugineus*) most important.

Currant Fruit Fly*, *Epochra canadensis* (Loew). Gooseberry Maggot. A native pest in many sections, common on currants and gooseberries in the West. The adult, yellow-bodied with dark-banded wings, about the size of a housefly, emerges from its puparium in the soil in April or May. It lays 100 to 200 eggs singly in fruit. Whitish maggots cause fruit to turn red and drop prematurely. Feeding continues for a few days in fruit on the ground before the maggots enter soil to pupate. There is 1 generation. Early maturing varieties escape most of the damage. Spray or dust with malathion, making first application when blossoms start to wither, and repeating at 1-day intervals.

Eupatorium Gall Fly*, *Procecidochares utilis* Stone.

European Crane Fly*, *Tipula paludosa* Meigen. Moving into western Washington from British Columbia. The adult looks like a large mosquito with a body 1 inch long without including the very long legs. The flies come from soil of lawns and pastures in late summer and gather on sides of houses. Eggs, laid in grass, hatch into small, gray-brown, worm-like larvae which develop a tough skin and are called leatherjackets. They winter in this stage and feed in spring, underground during the day but, on damp, warm nights, on aboveground parts of many plants. They pupate just below the soil surface in July and August. Control by treating lawn areas with chlordane or diazinon, in the fall after eggs have hatched or in spring.

Frit Fly*, *Oscinella frit* (Linnaeus). Small, short-winged bare flies abounding in rank vegetations and on grasses. The larvae may seriously damage lawns and golf courses.

Fungus Gnats, *Sciara* spp. Mushroom Flies. Often troublesome in potted plants in homes and greenhouses. The plants may lose color and lack vigor without visible injury to aboveground parts, although there may be small scars on the roots or fine roots may be eaten off. Adults—very small, sooty gray to black, long-legged, $\frac{1}{8}$ to $\frac{1}{10}$ inch long—deposit eggs in clusters which hatch in 4 to 6 days. The small, active threadlike white maggots feed either in the root tissue or in the soil around plants for 5 to 15 days, then pupate. Adults live about a week and generations follow rapidly. Because they breed in manure and decaying vegetable matter, potting soil rich in humus is very likely to have these flies. They are also present in mushroom beds. Spray potting soil with malathion or chlordane.

Hessian Fly*, *Phytophaga destructor* (Say). One of the most important world pests, causing great losses in wheat and some in barley and oats. The original home of the Hessian fly was probably Russia. It apparently came to this country in straw bedding used by Hessian troops during the Revolutionary War, being noted on Long Island in 1779. The flies are small, frail, black, the maggots greenish white, shiny. They draw sap from stems causing them to break over, resulting in great reduction in yield.

Although the Hessian fly is not a problem in backyard gardens, the method of control should interest all gardeners, for it uses forethought instead of toil and sweat. Entomologists in all wheat states have worked out the life history of the fly so as to give a safe planting date in each location.

Lantana Gall Fly*, *Eutreta xanthochaeta* Aldrich.

Lantana Seed Fly*, *Ophiomyia lantanae* (Froggatt).

Lesser Bulb Fly*, *Eumerus tuberculatus* Rondani. Several small grayish or yellowish wrinkled maggots, up to ½ inch long, may be found in decaying bulbs of narcissus, hyacinth, amaryllis, onion, iris, shallot. The flies are blackish green with white markings on the abdomen, ⅓ inch long. They appear on flowers in late April or May and lay eggs at base of plants. The maggots can injure healthy bulbs but are more often found in sickly or injured stock. They pupate in the bulbs or in soil nearby; there are 2 generations a year. See Narcissus Bulb Fly for control.

Lupine Fly, *Hylemya lupini* (Coquillett). The most important pest of blue lupine used as a green manure crop in the Southeast; also reported from the West on various lupine species. The adult resembles the seedcorn maggot; the larva is whitish, somewhat slimy, ¼ inch long. It feeds on the tender bud, then tunnels into the stem, the entry hole being covered with hardened brown frass. There are 3 or 4 generations.

Mediterranean Fruit Fly*, *Ceratitis capitata* (Wiedemann). The most destructive member of the fruit-fly family, a potential pest of many deciduous and citrus fruits, including apricot, peach, nectarine, plum, grapefruit, orange, tangerine, kumquat, calamondin, papaya, coffee, Surinam cherry, loquat, figs, guava, mango, prickly pear, sapote, grapes, dates, avocado, apple, pear, quince and nearly 100 other wild and cultivated fruits.

The Mediterranean fruit fly was discovered in Florida in 1929, scat-

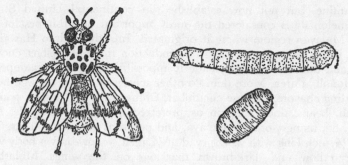

48. Mediterranean fruit fly: larva, pupa, and adult.

tered over an area covering 10 million acres. By a remarkable eradication campaign, providing for a host-free period from May 1 to October 1, prior to which time all ripe fruits had to be shipped or destroyed and during which time no vegetables could be grown which would reach a susceptible stage before October 1, the pest was completely exterminated. Aided doubtless by travelers, it returned in 1956 and spread over 28 counties before it was again eradicated at a cost of 10 million dollars. It came back again in 1962 but was discovered promptly and the proper measures taken. These included a bait spray of a yeast protein with malathion and a sex attractant, medlure, used in traps for determining areas of infestation.

This fruit fly may enter again at any time, in coffeeberries brought in as souvenirs from South America, in an orange carelessly tossed from a ship, or in some other fashion. It is frequently intercepted at quarantine.

The fly became established at Bermuda in 1865, Brazil in 1901, Argentina in 1905, and Hawaii in 1910. It is somewhat smaller than a housefly, has a glistening black thorax with yellowish white lines in a mosaic pattern, yellow abdomen with silver crossbands, and wings banded with yellow, brown, and black. It has sponging mouth parts and takes only liquid food. The female deposits her eggs through a pinprick hole in the rind of fruit, 2 to 10 at a time but totaling up to 800. The eggs hatch in 2 to 20 days and the legless maggots, about ¼ inch long, burrow in the pulp for 10 days to 2 weeks. The life cycle takes 17 days to 3 months, and there may be up to 12 generations a year.

As tourists, please cooperate and don't bring in to this country any material that might possibly harbor fruit-fly maggots.

Melon Fly*, *Dacus cucurbitae* Coquillett. Found in 1956 in a bait trap in California, a pest from Hawaii and frequently intercepted at quarantine, but not now established in continental United States. The melon fly is considered the most important cucurbit pest of the Indo-Malayan region, where it originated. Introduced into Hawaii in 1895, it has seriously curtailed the production there of melons, cucumbers, and tomatoes and has made it impossible to grow cantaloupes in the Honolulu area. More than 80 other species of plants may be hosts, including chayote, Chinese cucumber, Chinese melon, cowpea, gourds, squash, beans, and pumpkin as preferred hosts and bellapple, eggplant, fig, mango, orange, papaya, and peach as occasional hosts. The fly is ¼ inch long with wingspread of ½ inch, yellow-brown body with canary-yellow and dark-brown markings on the wings. Malathion bait sprays have been used for control.

Mexican Fruit Fly*, *Anastrepha ludens* (Loew). A Mexican pest, operating over the border into Texas and a threat to California. This citrus insect is as serious in Mexico as the Mediterranean fruit fly is in Mediterranean countries, but there are fewer host plants and not such wide distribution. It is primarily a pest of citrus fruits and mangoes, but sapotas, peaches, guavas, apples, pears, quinces, plums, apricots, and other fruits are included in quarantine regulations against the Mexican fruit fly. It is larger than a housefly, conspicuously marked in yellow or brown, and lays many white eggs under the skin of fruits. Larvae take 6 weeks for development, first in the rind, later in the pulp. Pupation is in the ground and there are 4 generations a year. By a cooperative agreement the United States conducts eradication measures in adjacent portions of Mexico to keep the flies from crossing the border. Fruit from the regulated area in Texas is treated to kill any possible larvae before being shipped.

Narcissus Bulb Fly*, *Merodon equestris* (Fabricius). A European species introduced here in bulbs. This large, hairy, yellow-and-black fly, about the size and appearance of a small bumblebee, lays eggs on or near crowns of narcissus (preferred host) and amaryllis (much favored). Although hyacinths, lilies, scilla, tulips, and iris are often listed they are merely accidental hosts with larvae failing to mature. The list of true hosts, according to observation in bulb fields, includes cooperia, eurycles, galanthus, galtonia, habranthus, hymenocallis, leucojum, pancratium, sprekelia, vallota, zephyranthes, and cipollini. Ordinarily but one maggot develops in each bulb. It is fat, white to yellow, wrinkled, ½ to ¾ inch long. It soon reduces the bulb contents to a soft, brown mass. Puparia are formed in either bulbs or soil; there is usually 1 generation. Plants with infested bulbs have yellow, stunted foliage or almost no growth. The bulbs feel spongy when squeezed.

Control. In home gardens discard all bulbs that feel soft to the touch. Protect amaryllis put outdoors for the summer with a covering of cheesecloth in early summer, to keep the flies from laying eggs. Or apply 6 per cent chlordane dust to foliage of amaryllis and narcissus in May, getting it into soil cracks and between leaves. Dust bulbs with chlordane before planting and again before covering with soil. Commercial growers have had effective control by soaking bulbs before planting in heptachlor (1 pint to 2 gallons of water, or 4 teaspoons to a gallon). Aldrin and dieldrin have also given good results.

Olive Fruit Fly*, *Dacus oleae* (Gmelin). Present in Hawaii but not yet in continental United States; often intercepted at quarantine.

Onion Bulb Fly*, *Eumerus strigatus* (Fallén). Similar to the lesser bulb fly and apparently confused with it. Reported on onions, sweet-potatoes, and carrots.

Orchidfly*, *Eurytoma orchidearum* (Westwood). Cattleya Fly. This is really a wasp, in the order Hymenoptera, and not a true fly in the order Diptera. It may be a serious orchid pest in greenhouses. The small, black wasp, ⅛ inch long, lays eggs in new growth and sometimes in pseudobulbs, causing swollen places; larvae feed in bulbs, stems, leaves, and buds of many kinds of orchids and continued attacks may kill the plants. Cut out the swollen areas.

Oriental Fruit Fly*, *Dacus dorsalis* Hendel. Not established in continental United States but a few specimens have been found in traps in California. It is frequently intercepted in baggage from Hawaii, where it was established in 1946 to become a very serious pest. It attacks more than 150 kinds of fruits and vegetables, including citrus, guava, mango, papaya, banana, loquat, avocado, tomato, Surinam cherry, rose-apple, passion fruit, peach, pear, apricot, fig, and coffee. The female adult, larger than a housefly, mostly yellow with dark markings, inserts eggs under fruit skin. There has been some control with the use of chemosterilants such as tepa or apholate on the male flies.

Papaya Fruit Fly*, *Toxotrypana curvicauda* Gerstaecker. Common on papayas and also on mangoes in southern Florida dooryards. The female has a very long ovipositor which penetrates through the fruit. The larvae feed on seeds, then eat their way out of the fruit. Remove from the tree all fruits that yellow prematurely; pick up and destroy all dropped fruits. Bait sprays, as for the Mediterranean fruit fly, can be used for control.

Potato Scab Gnat*, *Pnyxia scabiei* (Hopkins). A slender, black-headed maggot, only ⅙ inch long, occasionally infesting tubers in low ground or those stored in damp places. The superficial wounds resemble potato scab.

Range Crane Fly*, *Tipula simplex* Doane. Appearing in large numbers in pastures and grainfields. The adult female is practically wingless, grayish brown and short-legged; the male is winged with long legs. The pale brown rather rough larvae live in round holes, emerging at night and on dull days to feed on green vegetation.

Spanishfly*. See under Beetles.

Syrphid Flies. These are the bright-colored flower flies or hover flies, family Syrphidae. They resemble bees hovering over flowers to feed on nectar and are important in pollination. They are also attracted to tree sap and fermenting fruit. The larvae of a few species, including the narcissus bulb fly, feed on plants and some feed on decaying animals and vegetable matter, but the majority are predaceous on aphids, mealybugs, and other insects and are decidedly friends in the garden. Adults lay white, elongate eggs, singly, among groups of aphids. The larvae are footless, sluglike, tan or greenish; if you see some of them on your rosebuds, withhold sprays for a few days and give the maggots a chance to clean up. They have pointed jaws with which they grasp an aphid, raise it into the air, and suck out all the body contents, leaving the empty skin. A single larva is credited with destroying an aphid a minute over long periods of time and there may be many larvae in a garden.

Tachinid Flies. A most beneficial group, Tachinidae, with all species parasitic on other insects. Most resemble overgrown houseflies; bristly, gray, brown, or black, mottled, without bright colors; usually found resting on foliage or flowers. Eggs are more often glued to the skin of the host insect, sometimes laid on foliage where the insect will eat them along with the leaf. The larvae feed internally on their hosts, which almost always die. Many species have been imported for our benefit. One, brought in to help control gypsy and browntail moths, parasitizes over 100 species of caterpillars. Many are parasitic on cutworms and armyworms.

Walnut Husk Fly*, *Rhagoletis completa* Cresson. Native in the central states on wild black walnuts, injurious to English, black, and other walnuts in California, also a pest in Oregon, Idaho, and Utah, and sometimes attacking peaches as well as walnuts. The adults, a little smaller than houseflies, have transparent wings with dark transverse crossbars. The females deposit eggs in cavities below the surface of the husk; the maggots tunnel through the husks for several weeks, then drop to the ground, or fall with the nuts, to pupate in the soil. Some emerge as flies the next season, others remain in the ground for another year. The decaying husk stains the shell indelibly, making walnuts unsalable even though the kernels are sound.

Control recommendations for California growers call for spraying with malathion or parathion, the first treatment applied when adult flight is regular in late July or early August, and the second 25 days later. A few predators aid slightly in control.

Another walnut husk fly, *Rhagoletis suavis* (Ogten Sacken), is present in eastern states, staining hulls of black walnuts. They become slimy and stick to the nuts. This species is reported in Ohio, Delaware, Maryland, and other states.

Western Cherry Fruit Fly*, *Rhagoletis indifferens* Curran. Similar to the cherry fruit fly but a problem in Oregon, Washington, Idaho, and Montana.

West Indian Fruit Fly*, *Anastrepha mombinpraeoptans* Sein. Sometimes reported caught in traps in Texas; found lightly infesting mangoes in Florida in 1962.

Another species, *Anastrepha nigrifascia,* is present in the Florida Keys with food plants listed as Mimusops and sapodilla. Adults have been taken in traps hanging in a variety of fruit trees.

FRUITWORMS

Fruitworms are caterpillars or grubs infesting fruit.

Cherry Fruitworm*, *Grapholitha packardi* (Zeller). Found throughout deciduous fruit-growing areas of the United States on cherry, blueberry, and wild chokecherry. The full-grown larva winters in a silken cocoon, tunneled in the pruned stub of a dead twig, or under bark, or debris on the ground. Pupation, in May, lasts about 29 days and the moth, dark gray, ⅓-inch wingspread, lays flattened circular eggs on cherry fruit or stems. These hatch in about a week and the larvae, pinkish, about ⅓ inch long, bore into the fruit, often causing serious losses.

Control. Methoxychlor has given control and is safe for home gardeners. Commercial growers may use the more toxic parathion or Guthion. Two treatments will be required, one in late May (in New Jersey) and the second 7 to 10 days later.

Cranberry Fruitworm*, *Acrobasis vaccinii* Riley. Present in nearly every cranberry bog, also seriously infesting blueberries. The moth is ash gray mottled with black, has a ¾-inch wingspread. It lays eggs on berries in July; pale-green larvae eat into berries near the stem, closing the hole with silk. One larva eats out the pulp of 2 or 3 berries before attaining full size, ⅞ inch. There is 1 generation. Infested berries shrivel, and on Cape Cod nearly half the crop may be lost. Spray or dust with ryania or rotenone. Control recommendations include flooding bogs for 10 to 14 days after harvesting and early in May. All infested berries removed by screening should be destroyed.

Methoxychlor has controlled this fruitworm in blueberries but commercial growers may use parathion or Guthion with Sevin in the second application. Be sure to get the proper spray schedule from your local agricultural agent.

Currant Fruitworm, *Carposina fernaldana* Busck. Rather rare; larvae feed on currant fruits, which drop; pupation is in soil.

Eastern Raspberry Fruitworm*, *Byturus rubi* Barber. Most destructive to raspberry and loganberry in northern states. Light-brown beetles, ⅛ to ⅙ inch long, feed on buds, blossoms, and tender leaves, laying eggs on blossoms and young fruits. Slender grubs, white with brown patches, bore into fruits, making them unfit for eating. As the fruit ripens, larvae drop to the ground and pupate in soil. They winter as adults, still in the soil, emerging about mid-April. Spray with malathion when blossoms begin to separate in the cluster and again just before blossoms open. Cultivate the soil thoroughly in late summer.

Gooseberry Fruitworm*, *Zophodia convolutella* (Hübner). Present in northern states on currants and gooseberries. The moth has ashy wings with dark markings; the larva is yellow-green with a pinkish cast, darker lines along the sides. Pupae winter in the ground; moths lay eggs in flowers. Larvae completely hollow out fruit, one worm destroying several berries. Spray with rotenone when webbing is noticed; repeat in 7 to 10 days. Destroy infested berries.

Green Fruitworm*, *Lithophane antennata* (Walker). Generally distributed over eastern states. The larvae feed on foliage of apple,

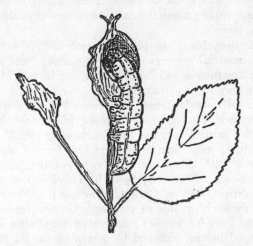

49. Green fruitworm feeding on young apples.

ash, maple, and other deciduous trees and in green fruits of apple, pear, and cherry. The moths emerge in fall, hibernate in woodlands or sheltered nooks in the orchard. They lay eggs in early spring on twigs and branches. The larvae are apple-green with white stripes and slightly raised tubercles, up to 1½ inches long. They eat out the side or one end of young apples, destroying them entirely or making them worthless. DDT and lead arsenate were formerly recommended for control; they might be replaced by methoxychlor or malathion or carbaryl.

Another green fruitworm, *Lithophane laticinerea* (Grote), has been confused with *L. antennata*. It is distributed through the Northeast to North Carolina and west to South Dakota. It feeds on a wide variey of deciduous shade, forest, and fruit trees. It may be a problem in home fruit plantings but is kept in check by the regular spray schedule in commercial orchards. The larva is pale green with a broad yellowish white stripe. The night-flying moth has gray fore wings, hind wings covered with dark brown scales.

Lesser Appleworm*, *Grapholitha prunivora* (Walsh). Closely related to the cherry fruitworm and also a cherry pest, as well as injuring apples, plums, and prunes. Found throughout deciduous fruit-growing areas. The full-grown larva winters in a cocoon under debris on the ground, pupates in spring with the adult moth, resembling the codling moth, emerging in May. Eggs laid on cherry leaves hatch in 5 to 10 days and larvae bore into the fruit, maturing in about 3 weeks and dropping to the ground to pupate. There may be 2 or 3 generations.

Pyramidal Fruitworm, *Amphipyra pyramidoides* (Guenée). Ranging from the Atlantic to the Pacific on a wide range of fruit, forest, and shade trees, with some shrubs and vines, but important only in unsprayed orchards or in home fruit plantings. Overwintered eggs hatch when leaf buds swell and the pale green larvae, with white stripes, feed on tender foliage, later partially eating immature fruit. They pupate in a cocoon on the ground and the moths appear in July. They have brown fore wings variegated with gray or white and coppery orange hind wings. There is only 1 generation.

Sparganothis Fruitworm, *Sparganothis sulphuriana* Fabricius. Cranberry Sparganothis, Blueberry Leafroller. One of the torticid leaf-rolling moths. Usually controlled in cranberry bogs with an aerial spray of parathion plus Guthion.

Speckled Green Fruitworm, *Orthosia hibisci* (Guenée). This was reported in 1970 as a new pest of azaleas, rhododendron, and roses but it is only 1 of the 6 green fruitworms known for nearly a century on fruit and other deciduous trees. This species is distributed through the Northeast and may be present in other states, important only in unsprayed orchards and in home gardens. Hosts include apple, peach, plum, cherry, hawthorn, Japanese quince, Russian almond, strawberry, and many others. The larvae, pale grass-green with white stripes, may deeply excavate rose buds or only nick them and also injure rhododendron and azalea flowers as well as foliage. Hibernation is as pupae in the soil. The ocher-brown and gray moths emerge in early spring and eggs hatch from mid-April to early May. There is one generation. Most damage to ornamentals like roses occurs when they are grown near woodlands. There are some natural parasites.

Tomato Fruitworm. See Corn Earworm under Earworms.

Western Raspberry Fruitworm*, *Byturus bakeri* Barber. Similar to the eastern raspberry fruitworm.

GALLS

Insect galls are swellings or deformities of plant tissues resulting from the irritation caused by feeding of the insect or by a toxin injected during the feeding process. Such plant abnormalities may be blisters or projections on the leaves, swellings on stem or twig, bud galls, flower galls, or root galls. The late Dr. E. P. Felt stated in his book *Plant Galls and Gall Makers* that there were more than 2,000 American insect galls—805 the work of gall wasps, nearly 700 caused by gall midges, 80 by aphids or psyllids, and the rest by sawflies, jointworms, beetles, moths, true bugs, and mites.

Galls are described in this book under the name of the insect producing them: e.g., Eastern Spruce Gall Aphids under Aphids; Chrysanthemum Gall Midge under Midges; Maple Bladdergall Mite under Mites; Mossyrose Gall Wasp under Wasps.

GRASSHOPPERS

Grasshoppers belong to the order Orthoptera and most of them, the shorthorned forms, are in the family Acrididae. They are the locusts of the Bible and the locusts that even in our own time may measure 2,000 square miles in a swarm over the Red Sea. In 1790, when they attacked crops in Massachusetts, the colonists, armed with bundles of brush, drove them into the ocean by the millions. In 1818 grasshoppers destroyed the crops of Montana settlers; in 1877 they halted the covered wagons rolling west. Yearly damages still run into millions but fair control measures have been developed.

Shorthorned grasshoppers are moderately long insects, slightly deeper than wide, usually dark, mottled, with prominent jaws and eyes, antennae always much shorter than the body, and an "ear," hearing organ, or tympanum, on each side of the first abdominal segment. Their hind legs are enlarged for jumping and the abdomen of the female ends in 4 hard, movable prongs which function like a miniature posthole digger when she is inserting her eggs an inch or so into the ground. The eggs are laid in masses of 15 to 50, according to species, and surrounded by a gummy substance which hardens to form a case, the whole being called an egg pod. Grasshoppers feed in the daytime in the sun. They are most numerous in states where the average rainfall is between 10 and 30 inches, attacking cultivated crops and range vegetation, destroying clothing and fabrics in houses, polluting water in wells and reservoirs, presenting a hazard to motorists.

The longhorned grasshoppers, family Tettigonidae, have long hairlike antennae and well-developed stridulating organs with each species having its characteristic song. Katydids and the Mormon Cricket are in this family.

American Grasshopper*, *Schistocerca americana* (Drury). Sometimes damaging field crops and fruits, including citrus, in Alabama, Georgia, Florida, Louisiana, and Mississippi. It is large—2½ inches long, with wingspread of 4 inches; colored tan, white, and pink. Spray with diazinon or malathion, including weed patches around the garden.

Carolina Grasshopper*, *Dissosteira carolina* (Linnaeus). Not very destructive but common through the country, numerous along roadsides in late summer. It is brown, mottled with gray and red, hind wings black with yellow margins; nearly 2 inches long; flies readily when disturbed.

Clearwinged Grasshopper*, *Camnula pellucida* (Scudder). Variable in color, yellow to dark brown with black spots; 1 inch long; migratory habits. Generally distributed but most damaging in Utah, Wyoming, Montana, and Idaho on grains, grasses, garden crops, vineyards, orchards. Egg pods may be numerous in breeding areas and plowing up such areas is quite effective in controlling this particular grasshopper.

Devastating Grasshopper*, *Melanoplus devastator* Scudder. Found west of the Rocky Mountains, migrating periodically from the mountains to the valleys. This species is small, yellow-brown with a row of elongated black spots, with hind tarsi blue at the base, yellow at the tips.

Differential Grasshopper*, *Melanoplus differentialis* (Thomas). Usually yellow with contrasting black markings, clear, glossy outer wings, 1½ inches long; hind thighs with black bars like chevrons. Fairly rare in the East, it feeds on succulent field and garden crops;

in other sections on deciduous fruit trees. In dry years this species persists only in irrigated areas or along streams.

Eastern Lubber Grasshopper*, *Romalea microptera* (Palisot de Beauvois). Sometimes called Florida Lubber, a large, stout, short-winged, clumsy locust attacking grass, flowers, and ornamental trees and shrubs in Florida and other southern states. It is 2½ inches long, with hind wings red with black borders.

Greenstriped Grasshopper*, *Chortophaga viridifasciata* (De Geer). In Nebraska and Wisconsin on forage crops.

High Plains Grasshopper*, *Dissosteira longipennis* (Thomas). Gregarious and migratory, on high ranges and prairies, destroying grasses but not often feeding on cultivated crops. Front wings (tegmina) are long, spotted brown; rear wings are blue at the base, black toward the disk.

Leafrolling Grasshopper, *Camptonotus carolinensis* (Gertstaecker). Small, nocturnal, nesting inside a rolled leaf tied with silk; feeding chiefly on aphids.

Lubber Grasshopper*, *Brachystola magna* (Girard). Ranging east of the Rocky Mountains and in the Great Basin, common and injurious from Montana to New Mexico. It is long, to 2½ inches, with rear wings pinkish and reduced in size.

Migratory Grasshopper*, *Melanoplus sanguinipes* (Fabricius). Found throughout the United States, sometimes migrating in swarms hundreds of miles, destroying crops and range plants wherever it stops. This species is reddish brown, with an irregular black patch on the neck; about 1 inch long.

Nevada Sage Caterpillar*, *Melanoplus rugglesi* Gurney.

Packard Grasshopper*, *Melanoplus packardii* Scudder. Occurring throughout the West, often injurious to pasture grasses. It is yellowish brown with red or blue hind legs, about 1 inch long.

Redlegged Grasshopper*, *Melanoplus femurrubrum* (De Geer). Reddish brown above, sulfur yellow underneath, wings colorless, hind legs red, ¾ inch long. It is common along roadsides and is injurious to legumes, particularly to soybeans in the Middle West, where it cuts through pods, causing seeds to mold. It also feeds on other truck crops, vines, and fruit trees.

Rocky Mountain Grasshopper*, *Melanoplus spretus* (Walsh). Formerly migrating in huge swarms from the Plains east of the Rocky Mountains to the Mississippi Valley and Texas, but its place is now taken by the migratory grasshopper. This species is brown with dark markings, bright-red hind legs; 1¼ inches long.

Twostriped Grasshopper*, *Melanoplus bivittatus* (Say). Common, widely distributed pest of grains, vegetables, fruit trees, all cultivated crops. It is stout, 1¼ inches long, greenish yellow with two light stripes down its back.

Vagrant Grasshopper*, *Schistocerca vaga* (Scudder). In the Southwest. Common on willow, citrus, lettuce, and other cultivated crops. This is a large brown species with numerous black markings and is attracted to lights at night.

Grasshopper Control. Until the advent of chlordane, poison-bran baits were the chief means of fighting grasshoppers, but now dusting or spraying with chemicals is considered more effective and economical. Aldrin, dieldrin, heptachlor and toxaphene have all been used as well as chlordane, applied with ground equipment or by airplane. In home gardens, spray or dust with malathion or use diazinon for ornamentals. Include the weed patches in and around the garden.

GROUND PEARLS

(See under Scale Insects)

HORNTAILS

Horntails are related to wasps, in the order Hymenoptera. Most are in the family Siricidae and are also called wood wasps. A few are stem sawflies, family Cephidae.

True horntails, family Siricidae, are fairly large, an inch or more long, with a horny, spearlike plate on the 1st abdominal segment. The females are thick-waisted, cylindrical, with a long, hornlike ovipositor that resembles a stinger. They alight on freshly felled, injured, or dying trees and insert the ovipositor deeply into the wood to deposit eggs. The larvae are cylindrical, yellowish white, with a small spine

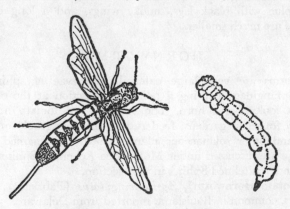

50. A typical horntail with larva.

at the rear of the body, which is often held in the shape of the letter S. They work in solid wood without any opening to the outside. They make circular holes in the wood and pack their boring dust in the tunnels behind them. Pupal cells are constructed near the surface of the wood, and when the adults mature they cut round emergence holes to the surface.

Horntails are more common in the West, being partial to western conifers. An eastern species called Pigeon Tremex is discussed under Borers.

Blue Horntail*, *Sirex cyaneus* Fabricius. Dark metallic blue, attacking many coniferous trees from New England to California.

California Horntail, *Sirex californicus* (Ashmead). Uniformly dark blue with hyaline wings, infesting pines in Pacific Coast states. Another horntail, *Urocerus californicus* (Norton), infests true firs, Douglas-fir, sometimes pine. It is the largest of the western species, the females 1¼ to 2 inches long, black with yellow markings, and an ovipositor only slightly shorter than the body.

Raspberry Horntail, *Hartigia cressoni* (Kirby). One of the stem sawflies, a western species, injuring young shoots of blackberry, loganberry, raspberry, and rose. Bright yellow-and-black females appear in April and May to insert eggs, each with a curved point, under epidermis of tender tips of host plants. The larvae spirally girdle the tips, causing wilting and death. An eastern species, *H. trimaculata,* is known as the Rose Stem Sawfly. See under Sawflies.

Western Horntail, *Sirex areolatus* (Cresson). Yellowish white larvae burrow into sapwood and heartwood of dead Monterey cypress and other cypress, cedar, redwood, pine, Douglas-fir, and related trees from Washington to Colorado. The female adult is large, dark metallic blue with black legs, smoky wings, and a long ovipositor. The males are much smaller.

HORNWORMS

Hornworms are very large caterpillars, larvae of sphinx moths (family Sphingidae) bearing a pointed projection at the end of the body that looks like a horn. The tobacco and tomato hornworms, commonly found in gardens, feed rather interchangeably on tobacco, tomato, and other solanaceous plants. Hornworms named for their adult stage are discussed under Moths. See Achemon Sphinx, Catalpa Sphinx, and Whitelined Sphinx in that section.

Sweetpotato Hornworm*, *Agrius cingulatus* (Fabricius). A southern species, common in Louisiana, reported from Delaware.

Tobacco Hornworm*, *Manduca sexta* (Linnaeus). Sometimes called Southern Hornworm, distributed throughout the Americas. This is an awe-inspiring caterpillar, 3 or 4 inches long, green with 7 oblique white stripes and a red horn projecting at the rear (Plate XIX). It feeds voraciously on tomato, tobacco, eggplant, pepper, potato, groundcherry, and related weeds.

The hornworm winters in soil as a brown, hard-shelled pupa that has a slender tongue projecting down like a pitcher handle. The adult sphinx moth, also called a hawk or hummingbird moth, emerges in May or June to feed at dusk, hovering over petunias and similar flowers to sip nectar with its long tongue. It has a wingspread of 4 or 5 inches, is gray or brown with white and dark mottlings and 6 yellow spots in each side of the abdomen. The female lays greenish yellow eggs singly on underside of leaves. Young larvae hatch in a week, feed for 3 or 4 weeks, molting 5 times, then pupate 3 or 4 inches deep in the soil. There is 1 generation in the North, 2 or more in the South.

Control. Picking off caterpillars by hand is often sufficient control in the small garden. If hornworms are too numerous keep plants dusted with carbaryl. The microbial spray prepared from *Bacillus thuringiensis* is effective against hornworms and leaves no undesirable residue.

Do not destroy caterpillars covered with oval white objects attached to the skin at one end. These are cocoons of a parasitic braconid wasp. The female thrusts her eggs inside the hornworm body; when the larvae hatch they feed for a while inside the caterpillar, then eat their way outside to spin cocoons. If left undisturbed, more wasps will emerge to parasitize other cocoons. See Figure 86.

Tomato Hornworm*, *Manduca quinquemaculata* (Haworth). Almost identical with the tobacco species, feeding on the same plants, controlled in the same way. There are 5 instead of 6 yellow spots on each side of the abdomen of the moth, and 2 narrow stripes extending diagonally across each wing. The larva has 8 instead of 7 diagonal white stripes and they join a horizontal white stripe, forming a series of V's. The horn is green with black sides.

KATYDIDS

Katydids, order Orthoptera, family Tettigoniidae, are longhorned grasshoppers, characterized by long, hairlike antennae; 4-segmented tarsi; auditory organs, when present, at the base of front tibiae (in true grasshoppers the "ear" is on the abdomen); and a swordlike ovipositor in the female. The males sing by rubbing front wings together, each species having a characteristic song. They are mostly

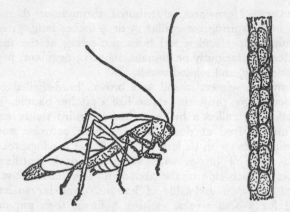

51. Angularwinged katydid and eggs.

plant feeders but cannot always be called garden pests. Control measures are usually unnecessary.

Angularwinged Katydid*, *Microcentrum retinerve* (Burmeister). Like the broadwinged katydid but smaller, found chiefly in the southern part of the United States. It is reported feeding on orange leaves.

Broadwinged Katydid*, *Microcentrum rhombifolium* (Saussure). Widely distributed in the East. Leaf green, about 1½ inches long, this species is best known for its eggs, grayish brown, very flat, ¼ inch long, laid on twigs in double rows, each egg overlapping the next. Gardeners, astonished at such a prominent display of large eggs, often fear they have a new garden menace.

Forktailed Bush Katydid*, *Scudderia furcata* Brunner von Wattenwyl. Widely distributed, taking its name from forked appendages at the tip of the male abdomen. Arboreal in habit, pale green, of medium size, with long narrow tegmina (wing covers). Eggs are laid in the edges of leaves between upper and lower leaf surfaces.

Japanese Broadwinged Katydid*, *Holochlora japonica* (Brunner von Wattenwyl).

Northern Katydid, *Pterophylla camellifolia* (Fabricius). True Katydid, also called Eastern Katydid, heard after dusk in late summer saying, "Katy did, Katy didn't." The song is made by special stridulating organs on the wings of the males, though the females can make faint sounds. The tegmina are dark green, very broad, longer than the hind wings, and entirely enclose the abdomen. This species lives in small colonies in dense foliage of forest and shade trees and is more often heard than seen. Dark, slate-colored eggs are thrust by the female ovipositor into crevices or loose bark or into soft stems of woody plants. The eggs are large, ¼ inch long, pointed at each end. The northern katydid ranges from New England to Georgia and west to Illinois. There is a southern form of this katydid that sings a somewhat longer and faster song.

LACEWINGS

Lacewings are beneficial insects in the order Neuroptera, with membranous front and hind wings held in a rooflike position. Green lacewings are in the family Chrysopidae, brown lacewings in the Hemerobiidae.

Goldeneye Lacewing*, *Chrysopa oculata* Say. The adult has beautiful gauzy green wings, long hairlike antennae, and iridescent red-

52. Goldeneye lacewing: stalked eggs, aphid-lion larva, pupa case, adult.

gold eyes. She lays her oval eggs singly at the end of hairlike stalks so that her cannibalistic offspring cannot eat each other as they hatch. The larvae, called aphidlions, are ugly creatures with double sickle-shaped jaws for capturing prey. The body is flat, tapering at both ends, yellow or gray mottled with red or brown, with projecting hairs or bristles; up to ⅓ inch long. The larvae puncture and suck the juice from aphids, mealybugs, cottonycushion scales, sometimes thrips and mites. They have a habit of carrying the remains of their victims piled up on the back. The larva pupates in a globular white cocoon, often on the underside of a leaf, and the adult cuts out a small lid that swings back as on a hinge as she emerges.

The goldeneye lacewing is the one common in eastern gardens but its place is taken in the West by the **California Green Lacewing**, *Chrysopa californica* Coquillett, which is similar.

Pacific Brown Lacewing, *Hemerobius pacificus* Banks. Important predator on red spiders and other mites, sometimes feeding on aphids. Brown lacewings are smaller than green lacewings and less conspicuous. The adult varies from pale to dark brown and the body is covered with short fine hairs. The larva is spindle-shaped, known as an aphidwolf.

Slender Brown Lacewing, *Sympherobius angustus* (Banks). The adult is very small, slender, brown throughout. The larvae feed on many species of mealybugs, this species being perhaps the most beneficial of western lacewings.

There are many other lacewing species, all useful, particularly on forage crops where chemicals would leave a harmful residue. There are, however, hymenopterus parasites attacking lacewings, which reduce their help.

LEAF CRUMPLER

Leaf Crumpler*, *Acrobasis indigenella* (Zeller). Abundant in Upper Mississippi Valley and some other northern states on apple, prune, plum, crabapple, quince, cherry, wild cherry, wild plum, and pear. It has also been reported on cotoneaster, hawthorn, and pyracantha and as far south as North Carolina. The caterpillar is dark brown, somewhat hairy, ⅓ to ¼ inch long. It winters in cocoons ¾ to 1½ inches long, made by crumpling dead leaves and tightly fastening them to an apple twig. In spring, as apple buds open, the worms loosen their cases and feed on buds, fastening new leaves together with silken thread. They pupate in May and June. The moths, with brown, white-mottled wings, expanding only ¾ inch, lay eggs on new leaves. Young caterpillars, hatching in 2 or 3 weeks, make curved, cornucopia-shaped cases in which they feed for the rest of the season, then use for winter quarters.

Control. If fruit trees are sprayed regularly for codling moths and other pests, leaf crumplers will not be much of a nuisance. Spray ornamentals with malathion, dimethoate, or diazinon. There are several parasitic flies and wasps.

LEAFCUTTERS

Caterpillars that neatly cut out portions of leaves are called leafcutters.

Maple Leafcutter*, *Paraclemensia acerifoliella* (Fitch). Also called

Maple Casebearer, a native pest of sugar maple, sometimes beech, rarely on red maple and birch. The small caterpillar, not over ¼ inch long, dull white with rusty head and thorax, eats as a leafminer for 10 to 14 days, then cuts out oval sections up to ½ inch in size, to make a case for overwintering in leaf litter. Foliage may be nearly destroyed. The moth, with iridescent blue fore wings, fringed, smoky-brown hind wings, emerges in May. Control by raking and destroying fallen leaves in autumn. If necessary, spray with Sevin in June.

Morningglory Leafcutter, *Loxostege obliteralis* (Walker). A greenish caterpillar wih dark spots, ¾ inch long, resembling the garden webworm. It cuts off stalks as leaves wilt and eats large holes in leaves, hiding during the day in shelters made by rolling and folding wilted leaves. The adult is a yellowish moth with faint brown markings. Other hosts include dahlia, mint, sunflower, violet, wandering-Jew, and zinnia. Spray or dust with carbaryl to kill young caterpillars; hand-pick others.

Waterlily Leafcutter*, *Synclita obliteralis* (Walker). The larvae of this moth are aquatic, breathing by means of gills, feeding on water-lily and other plants, often in greenhouses, in boatlike cases made by cutting oval pieces out of leaves and fastening them together with silk. Foliage is reduced to a ragged, rotten mass. Gather and destroy cases. If infestation is severe, lower water in pool and spray or dust with malathion. Fish must be removed before treatment and not returned until water has been changed.

LEAFFOLDERS

Grape Leaffolder*, *Desmia funeralis* (Hübner). Generally distributed east of the Rocky Mountains, also found in California, on wild and cultivated grapes, Virginia-creeper, and evening primrose. The caterpillar is glossy, translucent yellow-green on the sides, darker above, with brown head, 1 inch long. It feeds inside folded leaves. In the East, injury is little more than ragged foliage but in California there may be extensive damage to late maturing grape varieties. Larval attacks are followed by decay of fruit; leaves are rolled tightly instead of being folded over. The moths—black with white markings, wing expanse ¾ to 1 inch—emerge from inside rolled or folded leaves for a summer brood. There are 2 or 3 generations in warm climates but only 1 in New England, where pupation is in soil. In California the 3rd brood larvae may feed in the grape bunches, breaking the berry skins and allowing entrance to spoilage organisms.

Control. A lead arsenate spray is effective if applied before the leaves are folded. Growers sometimes use parathion spray or dust for later broods in California. There are a number of parasites.

Redbud Leaffolder*, *Fascista cercerisella* (Chambers). Larva of a gelechiid moth, found from Maryland to Illinois and Kansas and through the South. The moth is velvety black, with white head and collar, slightly bronzed fore wings, wingspread ⅗ inch. The larva, white with black markings, webs leaves together. There are 2 generations, with moths emerging from May to September.

LEAFHOPPERS

Leafhoppers belong to the insect order Homoptera, family Cicadellidae. There are around 175 genera and 2,000 species in our country.

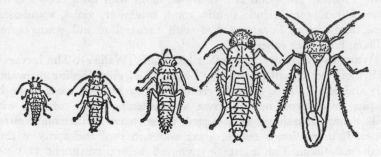

53. Stages in development of the rose leafhopper.

Most of these are quite small, not over ½ inch long, and they feed on foliage of almost all types of plants, usually sucking from the undersurface and hopping away quickly when disturbed. They have piercing-sucking mouth parts and gradual metamorphosis, nymphs resembling adults except for wings. The two pairs of wings are of uniform texture and are held in a rooflike position when at rest. Leafhoppers have a long, wedge-shaped appearance, and the front margin of the head, as seen from above, is either triangular or broadly curved. The large eyes are at the side of the head and small, hairlike antennae arise in front of the eyes. There are 2 ocelli between the eyes and a double row of spines on the underside of the hind tibiae. Most leafhoppers expel honeydew.

Withdrawal of plant sap from the host causes loss of color—often in a stippled pattern—sometimes stunting and general decline in vigor. Some leafhoppers cause a diseased condition in the plant known as hopperburn, which may be due to a toxin injected during the feeding process. Leafhoppers act as vectors of many important virus and similar diseases: aster yellows, blueberry stunt, corn stunt, cranberry false blossom, elm phloem necrosis, curly top of sugar beet, Pierce's disease of grape, little cherry, phony peach, peach X-disease, peach yellows, yellow dwarf of potatoes, tomato big bud, and others.

Leafhoppers have been very effectively controlled by DDT. Now we must turn to malathion, dimethoate, diazinon, or Meta-Systox-R.

Apple Leafhopper*, *Empoasca maligna* (Walsh). Common east of the Rocky Mountains except in the lower Mississippi Valley, also present in the Northwest. During late summer and fall apple foliage turns pale, the green upper surface flecked with many small white spots, the underside covered with dark bits of excrement, often white cast skins. Nymphs and adults are greenish white. There is 1 generation a year and no migration to another type of host, as with the potato leafhopper, but this species may infest roses as well as apples. When roses are grown near apple orchards their foliage is often almost white in late summer and early fall. Hibernation is in the egg stage under loose bark.

Aster Leafhopper*, *Macrosteles fascifrons* (Stål). Sixspotted Leafhopper. This species is tremendously important to gardeners because it transmits the disease known as aster yellows (long thought due to a virus, now attributed to mycoplasma), not only to asters but to many other ornamentals, among them alyssum, anchusa, browallia, capemarigold, cornflower, calendula, chrysanthemum, cineraria, clarkia, coreopsis, cosmos, gaillardia, gypsophila, lobelia, mignonette, petunia, phlox, poppy, rudbeckia, scabiosa, schizanthus, strawflower, sweet-william, vinca, and zinnia. Lettuce and celery are particularly subject to yellows, and the disease may also be transmitted to carrot, parsnip, parsley, and other vegetables as well as alfalfa and grain crops. Symptoms vary with the different plants but there is usually a general yellowing of foliage rather than a mottling or mosaic. There is a clearing of affected veins, plants are always stunted and usually distorted, with excessive branching and shortening of internodes along with virescence (greening) of flower petals. Lettuce develops a condition known as rabbit ear.

The leafhopper responsible for all this trouble is greenish yellow with 6 black spots. It winters in the egg stage on perennial weeds or flowers. The infective material is not carried in the egg and leafhoppers have to hold the mycoplasma 10 to 18 days before it can be transmitted to asters and other garden plants. Nymphs in early instars do not transmit the disease because the period between each molt is shorter than the latent period of the inoculum. At normal summer temperatures the life cycle of the aster leafhopper is about 40 days, so there may be several generations a season.

Control. Carbaryl, malathion, or dimethoate sprays will reduce leafhopper populations but not entirely eliminate them. Commercial growers protect their asters with cheesecloth or muslin, 22 threads to the inch, on wooden frames. In home gardens all diseased plants should be rogued (pulled out) immediately before the disease can be spread.

Beet Leafhopper*, *Circulifer tenellus* (Baker). A western species, found eastward to Illinois and Missouri, dangerous as a vector of curly top, a virus disease (Plate XXIV). The pale greenish or yellowish leafhoppers, ⅛ inch long, are darker toward winter, which they spend as adults on salt bush, Russian thistle, greasewood, filaree, and other wild hosts in arid foothills or desert. Egg laying takes place in March, and the first generation matures on these wild plants. From early May to June, adults of this generation fly in swarms, often hundreds of miles, to sugar-beet fields. As they feed, they introduce the curly-top virus. They are the only known vectors of this disease, which makes the leaf veins warty, petioles kinked, leaves rolled and brittle on the edges, plants stunted and finally killed.

The leafhoppers insert their eggs in veins, leaf petioles, or stems. Nymphs hatch in 2 weeks, become adult in 3 to 8 weeks more. There may be 3 or more generations. When the sugar beets are plowed out, the leafhoppers, carrying the virus, swarm to neighboring gardens, infecting tomato, table beets, cantaloupe, celery, cucumber, pepper, spinach, squash, and other vegetables and many flowers— geranium, nasturtium, pansy, zinnia among others. Symptoms in all plants are the same—curled leaves, stunting—often resulting in death.

Control. Although many leafhoppers can be killed by dusting or spraying with malathion, dimethoate, and other materials they may already have spread the disease. Rogue out plants with curly top as soon as noticed; eliminate Russian thistle and other winter weed hosts so far as possible. The fog belt along the coast of California is fairly free from leafhopper attack and there are a number of natural enemies.

Blackfaced Leafhopper*, *Graminella nigrifrons* (Forbes). A vector of corn stunt disease.

Bluntnosed Cranberry Leafhopper*, *Scleroracus vaccinii* (Van Duzee). Famous as the vector of cranberry false-blossom disease, found from Wisconsin east. The hopper is light brown, short, with a rounded blunt nose. It winters in the egg stage and hatches in May; there is 1 brood a year. Flooding the bogs in late June when young nymphs are present, spraying with carbaryl or parathion, and use of resistant varieties give fair control of the disease and its vector.

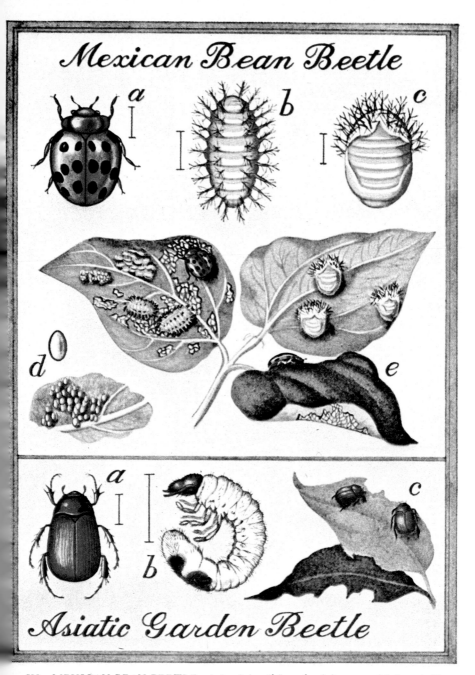

Mexican Bean Beetle

Asiatic Garden Beetle

IX   MEXICAN BEAN BEETLE: (a) adult; (b) grub; (c) pupa with larval skin pushed back at one end; (d) egg cluster on back of leaf and single egg enlarged; (e) bean leaf showing beetle in all stages and feeding pattern. ASIATIC GARDEN BEETLE: (a) adult; (b) grub; (c) beetles, natural size, feeding on foliage.

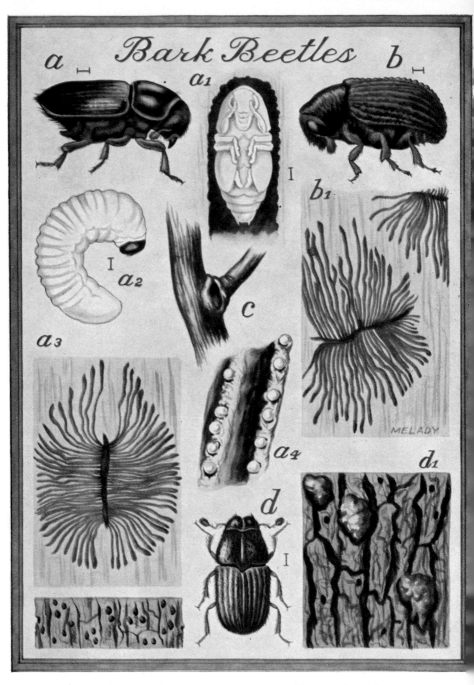

X SMALLER EUROPEAN ELM BARK BEETLE: (a) adult; (a,1) pupa; (a,2) grub; (a.3) characteristic pattern of galleries under bark and exit holes in bark; (a,4) eggs lining gallery, much enlarged; (c) feeding injury at crotch. NATIVE ELM BARK BEETLE: (b) adult; (b,1) galleries in transverse position. WESTERN PINE BEETLE: (d) adult; (d,1) pine bark with resin tubes around entrance holes and small exit holes.

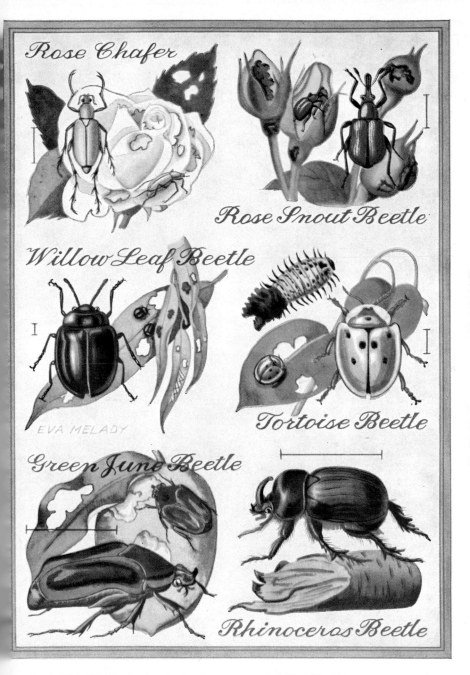

Rose Chafer

Rose Snout Beetle

Willow Leaf Beetle

Tortoise Beetle

EVA MELADY

Green June Beetle

Rhinoceros Beetle

XI   ROSE CHAFER: beetle feeding on rose. ROSE CURCULIO: (Rose Snout Beetle) on rosebuds. IMPORTED WILLOW LEAF BEETLE: willow leaves showing skeletonization by larvae, holes eaten by adults, and single beetle much enlarged. BLACK-LEGGED TORTOISE BEETLE: black-spined larva with excrement on back, adult feeding on leaf, natural size and enlarged. GREEN JUNE BEETLE: feeding on fruit and foliage. RHINOCEROS BEETLE.

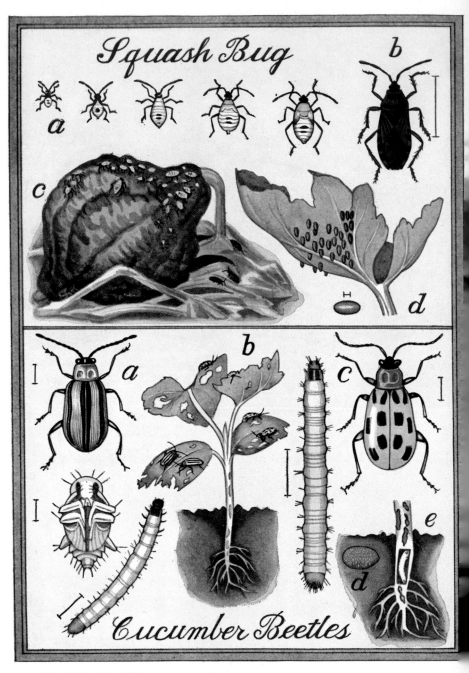

XII SQUASH BUG: (a) nymphs in successive instars; (b) adult; (c) nymphs feeding on squash; (d) eggs grouped on underside of leaf, and single egg, enlarged. STRIPED CUCUMBER BEETLE: (a) adult, pupa, and grub; (b) adults feeding on seedling. SPOTTED CUCUMBER BEETLE: (c) adult and rootworm larva; (d) egg in soil, enlarged; (e) larva in underground corn stem.

Bramble Leafhopper*, *Ribautiana tenerrima* (Herrich Schäffer).

Brambleberry Leafhopper, *Macropsis fuscula* (Zetterstedt). On raspberry, vector of raspberry-rubus stunt.

Clover Leafhopper*, *Aceratagallia sanguinolenta* (Provancher). Prevalent when potatoes are grown next to clover and vector of potato yellow dwarf. The virus winters in the adult leafhopper.

Grape Leafhopper, *Erythroneura elegantula* Osborne in the West, especially in California, and *E. comes* (Say) in Ohio, Michigan, and elsewhere. Adults are slender, about ⅛ inch long, yellow with red markings, active on grape, Virginia-creeper, apple, and other plants. They winter among fallen grape leaves or grasses, feed on developing leaves in spring, inserting eggs in leaf tissue. The nymphs feed almost entirely from underside of leaves. There are 2 or more generations.

A third form, the **Variegated Leafhopper**, *Erythroneura variabilis* Beamer, is common in southern California. It is similar but somewhat darker in color. Home growers should spray or dust with malathion or carbaryl.

Japanese Leafhopper, *Orientus ishidae* (Matsumura). An introduced pest reported in 1919, now well distributed in northern fruit districts, known on apple, aralia, and hazel. It is larger than the apple leafhopper, ⅕ inch long, dark gray, wings milky with brown veins, legs black; nymphs brown with white spots. Leaves turn yellow where nymphs first congregate, often near water sprouts; later, triangular sections of leaves all over tree are killed. Damage may be extensive with weakening of tree. Eggs winter near base of trunk, hatching in late May or early June.

Japanese Maple Leafhopper, *Japanus hyalinus* (Osborne). On Japanese and Norway maples.

Mountain Leafhopper*, *Colladonus montanus* (Van Duzee). A western species—small, brown with a yellow band—common on grasses, carrot, larkspur, goldenrod, apple, prune, peach, and many other plants, being abundant in mint fields. It is a vector of peach X-disease.

Norway Maple Leafhopper, *Alebra albostriella* (Fallén). Causing some injury near New York City. Swollen twigs on Norway maple, looking as if diseased, are produced by eggs laid under bark. Foliage is infested with numerous small, yellowish hoppers. They may also infest alder, birch, elm, and oak.

Painted Leafhopper*, *Endria inimica* (Say). On forage crops, legumes, lawn grasses, wild grapes and brambles, vector of wheat mosaic. Widespread, reported as abundant in Rhode Island and also in Nebraska.

Plum Leafhopper*, *Macropsis trimaculata* (Fitch). An eastern pest important as the vector of peach yellows and little peach, virus diseases affecting peaches, nectarines, plums, almonds, apricots. The leafhoppers, blunt, short, with 3 dark spots, are strong fliers and may travel long distances, although they usually stay near the tree where they were hatched. There is 1 generation, eggs laid on twigs in July and August not hatching until the next May.

Poplar Leafhopper, *Idiocerus scurra* (Germar). Occasionally abundant on Lombardy poplar. *I pallidus* Fitch occurs on poplar and willow.

Potato Leafhopper*, *Empoascus fabae* (Harris). The most injurious potato pest in eastern United States, found in some western states, although there its place is usually taken by other species (intermountain, arid, and western potato leafhoppers). This small, ⅛ inch long, wedge-shaped green leafhopper, with white spots on head and thorax, plays many roles (Plate XIV). Down South, where it shines as a bean pest, it is called the "bean jassid." It is responsible for dahlia stunt, potato tipburn or hopperburn, peanut pouts, and other "diseases" as well as normal leafhopper injury.

Instead of hibernating in the North, the potato leafhopper winters in the Gulf States, breeding on alfalfa and other legumes and weeds. Coming north in spring, it feeds first on apple foliage, possibly maples, moving to beans as soon as the plants are up, often migrating suddenly in swarms. When potatoes are several inches high the hoppers move over to them, laying eggs in main veins and in petioles, each female depositing 2 or 3 eggs a day for 3 or 4 weeks. The eggs hatch in 10 days with nymphs full-grown in about 2 weeks, at the 5th molt. There are 2 generations in the Middle Atlantic States, so that both early and late potatoes are infested.

On potato, eggplant, rhubarb, horsebean, dahlia, and sometimes rose the condition known as hopperburn is prevalent. First a triangular brown spot appears at the tip of the leaf, then similar triangles at the end of each lateral leaflet, after which the entire margin rolls inward and turns brown, often appearing scorched, with only a small part of each leaf along the midrib staying green. The yield of potatoes is cut enormously; dahlias may be so stunted they do not flower. I often find the tipburn effect on rose foliage in August but seldom any rolling. Authorities are not too clear on how this effect is produced. Some state that the potato leafhopper mechanically plugs the phloem and xylem vessels in the leaves so that transport of food materials is impaired.

On bean and apple, leafhopper feeding produces whitening of foliage and sometimes stunting, crinkling, and curling but not the brown, burned effect. In California the potato leafhopper punctures and blemishes the rind of citrus fruit.

Control. Spray or dust with carbaryl, malathion, methoxychlor, or dimethoate starting when potatoes are 4 to 8 inches high and repeat at 10- to 14-day intervals as long as the vines can be kept green. Treat dahlias and other ornamentals as necessary, making sure that the chemical reaches the underside of foliage early, before the margins are burned and rolled.

Privet Leafhopper, *Fieberiella florii* (Stål). A large species, widely distributed, recorded from many plants—privet, quince, peach, plum, cherry, currant, cotoneaster, myrtle, spirea, sometimes on legumes. It is a vector of peach X-disease and western aster yellows. A somewhat smaller leafhopper, *Osbornellus borealis* DeLong and Mohr, is also found on privet and myrtle and is a vector of the yellow leafroll strain of peach western X-disease.

Prune Leafhopper*, *Edwardsiana prunicola* (Edwards).

Redbanded Leafhopper, *Graphocephala coccinea* Foerster. Probably our most conspicuous leafhopper, rather large, with its wings gaudily decorated with alternate bands of magenta and green or blue. It is common on garden flowers, including aster, calendula, gladiolus, hollyhock, marigold, rose, and zinnia but the injury is not serious.

Rose Leafhopper*, *Edwardsiana rosae* (Linnaeus). Imported from Europe, attacking most plants of the rose family but primarily apple and rose, being especially serious on apple in the Northwest and reported also on dogwood, elm, maple, oak, and spirea. It hibernates in the egg stage, usually on rose canes or apple bark. The adults, creamy white to light yellow, ⅛ inch long, produce characteristic light stippling and sometimes a yellowing and slight curling of foliage but no hopperburn. Eggs for the 2nd generation, which defaces rose foliage late into the fall, are laid in July in leaf veins and petioles. Control on roses is especially necessary for the fall brood. Spray with dimethoate, diazinon, malathion, or Meta-Systox-R.

Saddled Leafhopper*, *Colladonus clitellaris* (Say). An important vector of peach X-disease.

Sharpnosed Leafhopper, *Scaphytopius magdalensis* (Provancher). Vector of blueberry stunt, a virus disease.

Sixspotted Leafhopper. See Aster Leafhopper.

Southern Garden Leafhopper*, *Empoasca solana* DeLong. Similar to the potato leafhopper but with a more southern distribution, although occurring in New York. It infests flowers and other ornamentals, including aster, dahlia, willow, amaranthus, tamarix, also potato, peanut, grape, cantaloupe, sweetpotatoes, and other fruits and vegetables.

Sugarcane Leafhopper*, *Perkinsiella saccharicida* Kirkaldy.

Threebanded Leafhopper*, *Erythroneura tricincta* Fitch. On grape,

Virginia-creeper, apple, and other plants. Much like the grape leaf-hopper but more injurious in some states. It makes a very coarse stippling.

Virginiacreeper Leafhopper*, *Erythroneura ziczac* (Walsh). Another species similar to the grape leafhopper, feeding on grape, elm, Boston ivy, and Virginia-creeper, which may have foliage almost completely whitened.

Western Potato Leafhopper*, *Empoasca abrupta* DeLong. Similar to the potato leafhopper.

Whitebanded Elm Leafhopper*, *Scaphoideus luteolus* Van Duzee. Vector of elm phloem necrosis, which has killed so many elms in Ohio and neighboring states and reported in New York in 1971. Eggs wintered on elm bark hatch about May 1; nymphs crawl to leaves and feed on veins; adults move from diseased to healthy trees. Methoxychlor may help to control this leafhopper.

White Apple Leafhopper*, *Typhlocyba pomaria* McAtee. On apple, rose, sometimes currant, gooseberry, and raspberry. Winter is passed in the egg stage underneath bark of small apple branches, and the small greenish nymphs hatch when apple blossoms are in the pink stage. Adults lay eggs in July and 2nd generation nymphs feed in August and early September, adults being most numerous in late September and October. Apple foliage is blanched white and after that the hoppers move in great numbers to nearby rose gardens. The foliage shows a rather coarse stippling and the underside is covered with shiny black dots of fecal deposits. Use malathion, dimethoate, or Meta-Systox-R.

Willow Leafhoppers, *Keonolla* spp. Often abundant on willows and poplars along watercourses in western states, sometimes entering houses.

Yellowheaded Leafhopper*, *Carnocephala flaviceps* (Riley). A western species, small, pale green with yellow head, feeding on grass and grains, also grape, and vector of Pierce's disease of grape.

There are many more species of leafhoppers that are plant problems but they lack the common names needed for inclusion in this reference book.

LEAFMINERS

Leafminers are insects which feed between two leaf surfaces. They may be larvae of flies, moths, sawflies, or beetles. They make blisters or blotch mines or serpentine tunnels and, because they are protected by the host plant most of their lives, control has been difficult, depending on an exact knowledge of the life history of each individual miner.

Now, with the new systemics, there is a little more leeway in timing but detailed knowledge is still required to select the best chemical and method of application.

Apple Barkminer*, *Marmara elotella* (Busck). A moth, family Gracillariidae, leafblotch miners.

Apple Fruitminer*, *Marmara pomonella* Busck. Another leafblotch miner, making a white winding mine under skin of apple fruit.

Apple Leafblotch Miner, *Phyllonorycter crataegella* (Clemens). Widespread, mining leaves of apple, crabapple, hawthorn, and wild cherry. Another species, *P. malifoliella*, may also injure apple leaves, sometimes enough to reduce fruit size.

Appleleaf Trumpet Miner*, *Tischeria malifoliella* Clemens. On apple (preferred), blackberry, raspberry, and hawthorn. Numerous trumpet-shaped mines are made in leaves, pupation taking place there. Very small moths, dark with narrow, fringed wings, emerge through slits in the leaves. There are 2 or more broods. Special control measures are not always needed; parathion is effective.

Arborvitae Leafminer*, *Argyresthia thuiella* (Packard). Distributed from Maine to Missouri, common in home plantings. Very small larvae—⅕ inch long, green with a reddish tinge and black head, short bristles across the back of each segment—mine in the terminal leaves, eating out the inside. The mined tips turn yellow or whitish, finally brown, and stand out prominently against normal green foliage. In the most severe cases all the foliage is mined and the shrubs turn brown all over. Small gray moths, wingspread only ⅓ inch, emerge from mined leaves in May and June to lay eggs which hatch in late June. There is only 1 generation, partly grown larvae wintering in the mines.

Control. For a few plants the easiest control is to cut off and destroy discolored tips. Secin will control the miners but increases the mite problem. Lindane, malathion, and diazinon are possibilities.

Asparagus Miner*, *Ophiomyia simplex* (Loew). Present through the Northeast and in California on asparagus but rather a minor pest. Maggots of a small fly mine in the stalks just below the soil surface. Foliage may turn yellow and die prematurely. Puparia winter in the larval tunnels and the flies appear in late May to lay eggs, with adults of a 2nd generation abroad in July. Pull up old stalks to destroy puparia. Plant rust-resistant strains which are also more resistant to the miner.

Aspen Blotchminer*, *Lithocolletis tremuloidiella* Braun. Present in California, Idaho, Utah, abundant in Wisconsin, making irregular mines in leaves of aspen and other poplars, resulting in premature defoliation. The adult is a small, drab moth.

Aspen Leafminer, *Phyllocnistis populiella* Chambers. Leaving a labyrinthian trail of frass on underside of aspen and poplar leaves. It has caused epidemics in Wyoming and Idaho forests, with trees stunted and many killed.

Azalea Leafminer*, *Gracillaria azaleella* Brants. Azalea Leafroller, found in most states where azaleas are grown but more of a greenhouse than a garden pest in the North; often injurious in southern nurseries and gardens. Eggs are laid in leaves by a small moth, marked with purple and yellow, wing expanse ½ inch. Small yellow caterpillars hatch in 4 days, enter the leaves, and feed between surfaces, causing blisters. When partly grown, the larvae emerge and start to roll leaves at the tip, feeding inside the protection of the roll. A cocoon is made inside a leaf rolled in from the margin. Spray with diazinon or dimethoate.

Basswood Leafminer*, *Baliosus ruber* (Weber). A pest of basswood (linden) throughout its range, known also on oak and apple. The adult is a reddish-yellow, wedge-shaped beetle which winters under leaves and trash, becoming active in May, skeletonizing the foliage. Eggs are laid singly in feeding areas and covered with excrement. The larvae start feeding into the leaves in single mines, then join together in a common mine. Spiny pupae appear in the mines in August; beetles emerge to do more feeding before hibernation. Spray spring or fall, when beetles are feeding, with malathion.

Beet Leafminer*, *Pegomya betae* (Curtis). Maggot of a fly.

Birch Leafminer*, *Fenusa pusilla* (Lepeletier). An imported sawfly, first discovered in Connecticut in 1923 and now a major scourge

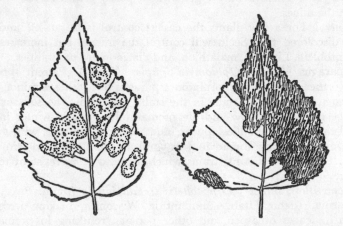

54. Birch leafminer: initial blotch mines and final blighted leaf.

in New England, New York, New Jersey, and Pennsylvania and also in Oregon. Infested trees look as if they had been blighted by a disease. Gray, paper, and European white birches are most favored, in woods and home plantings. The mature larva—½ inch long, rather flat, whitish with black spots on underside of thorax and 1st abdominal segments—winters in a cell in the soil. The black sawfly, ⅟₁₆ inch long, emerges in early May, about the time leaves are half open, and lays eggs in these new leaves. The larvae first make small, gray kidney-shaped blotches in a leaf, but gradually half the leaf turns brown. There are several generations, with flies laying eggs always in newly developing leaves. Hence the first brood is the worst, when all the leaves are new; later broods mostly infest ends of branches or water sprouts.

Control. Lindane has given excellent control of this miner but its use is being curtailed. Spray with dimethoate (Cygon), diazinon, Meta-Systox-R, or malathion in early May, as first leaves are formed, and again in July. Or treat the soil with a systemic, dimethoate granules or Di-Syston 10 per cent granules.

Blackberry Leafminer, *Metallus rubi* Forbes. Sometimes important in the Northeast. Whitish sawfly larvae, with brown heads, make blotch mines between leaf surfaces; plants appear scorched by fire. The adult is blackish, ⅙ inch long. There are 2 broods.

Boxwood Leafminer*, *Monarthropalpus buxi* (Laboulbène). The most commonly destructive boxwood insect. It is a European fly, established in the East in 1910, not as much of a problem in Virginia and the Carolinas as in more northern states. It is not limited to the East; it is a problem on the West Coast as well. The mines are small

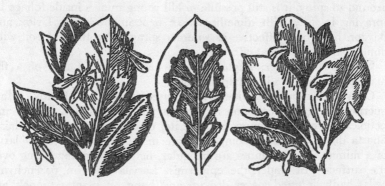

55. *Boxwood leafminer: flies laying eggs, maggots inside blistered surface, pupa cases protruding from mines.*

blotches or blisters in which yellow to orange maggots feed, 2 or 3, sometimes more, to a blister. In spring, some days before emergence, a small opaque window is formed on the underside of the leaf in the middle of the blotch, and if the leaf is torn open, the maggots are found to have pupated and acquired dark heads. Shortly after that the windows are broken, the pupae push part way out of the leaf, and when the small orange midges or flies emerge they leave white pupal skins protruding from the leaves. Appearing in swarms, usually early in the morning, the flies continue to emerge over a period of 10 days to 2 weeks. Each particular female, however, emerges, mates, inserts her eggs through upper epidermis of a new leaf, and dies in about 24 hours.

Time of emergence varies with the location and the season. In Maryland and Cincinnati, Ohio, it is late April. In New Jersey my earliest record was May 8, the latest May 20, with May 14 an average date. New blisters show up in leaves by midsummer, the tiny maggots having started to feed about 2 weeks after egg laying. Infested plants are not killed, at least for several years, but they have a most unthrifty appearance. They are yellow, with sparse foliage, an eyesore in a lovely garden.

Control. The old, and mostly ineffective, molasses-and-nicotine concoction was replaced by DDT, which proved highly satisfactory, with a long residual effect. Now we must substitute methoxychlor, dimethoate, diazinon, or malathion. It is essential, since the fly lays its eggs immediately after emergence, that the spray be on the plant in advance of this event. With proper timing, 1 spray may be sufficient but if there is a long interval after application before emergence a second treatment may be necessary. If emergence occurs before you get around to spray, it is still possible to kill young miners inside foliage by spraying in July with dimethoate. In experimental tests Dylox and Baygon have been effective as summer sprays. Treating the soil with dimethoate is somewhat effective.

Catalpa Leafminer, *Phytobia clara* (Melander). Larva of a fly, making blotch mines in catalpa foliage.

Chrysanthemum Leafminer*, *Phytomyza syngenesiae* (Hardy). Marguerite Fly. Rather common in gardens and greenhouses. Leaves and petioles of chrysanthemum, marguerite, cineraria, eupatorium, daisy, Shasta daisy, and other composites are mined by a pale-yellow larva of a minute fly. The mines are irregular, light-colored, extending over the surface just under the epidermis. Larvae feed on parenchyma cells; badly infested leaves dry up and hang on plants; tunnels are filled with black specks of excrement. Spray with malathion or diazinon.

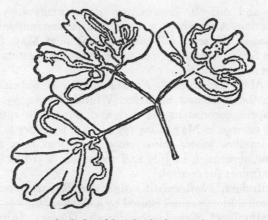

56. Columbine leafminer injury.

Columbine Leafminer*, *Phytomyza aquilegivora* Spencer. Very common in gardens. Striking white, winding tunnels, filled with black bits of excrement, are seen on leaves in almost every clump of columbine. The adult is a pale brownish fly which lays eggs on underside of leaves. When the pale maggots are grown, they emerge through crescent-shaped slits and attach to the leaf brown puparia from which flies emerge in about 2 weeks. There are several generations, with pupation of the last brood in the soil. Spray in spring with malathion; pick off infested leaves.

Corn Blotch Leafminer*, *Agromyza parvicornis* Loew. Wheat Leafminer, an eastern species ranging west to Utah. The adult is a small black fly whose maggots make irregular blotch mines in corn, grasses, and grains, injury being worse in young corn. There are several generations in Florida, with breeding through the winter. Pull up and destroy seriously infested plants. Plant an excess of corn, to have a good stand left after the miners get their share.

Eggplant Leafminer*, *Keiferia inconspicuella* (Murtfeldt). Attacking eggplant and other solanaceous plants in the South. Larvae and moths are like those of the potato tuberworm (see under Borers) but a little smaller. There are several parasites which make this a relatively unimportant pest.

Elm Leafminer*, *Fenusa ulmi* Sundevall. An imported species attacking English, Scotch, and Camperdown elms, sometimes American. Small, shiny black sawflies lay eggs through slits in upper leaf surfaces. In late May white legless larvae, ⅓ inch long, make blotch mines in leaves, often 15 to 20 larvae working in one leaf, which turns brown and shrivels. Leaves may drop prematurely. There is only 1 generation. After about 3 weeks the larvae remain in papery brown cocoons in the soil until pupation the next May. Spray with malathion or Sevin. Treatment for more important insects will probably take care of leafminers.

European Alder Leafminer*, *Fenusa dohrnii* (Tishbein). Distributed through the Northeast on alder. Whitish larvae, ⅓ inch long, winter in papery cocoons in the soil and pupate in spring. Small black sawflies emerge in May to lay eggs in slits in upper leaf surfaces. Ten or more yellow blister mines may be present in a single leaf. There is a 2nd generation in July and sometimes a 3rd in September. See Birch Leafminer for control.

Grape Leafminer, *Phyllocnistis vitigenella*. Reported on culivated grapes in Arizona. Blotch mines caused by a small moth.

Grass Sheathminer*, *Cerodontha dorsalis* (Loew). Injury from a leafminer fly.

Gregarious Oak Leafminer*, *Cameraria cincinnatiella* (Chambers). Making blotch mines on oak, mostly white oak. The larvae are gregarious, 10 or more in a single mine and sometimes several mines in a leaf. There are 2 generations a year with the winter passed in the pupal state. Rake up infested leaves during the winter. Spray in early June (New Jersey) with malathion or carbaryl. See also Solitary Oak Leafminer.

Hard Maple Budminer*, *Obrussa ochrefasciella* (Chambers). A moth, family Nepticulidae.

Holly Leafminer*, *Phytomyza ilicis* (Curtis). A European species very common on our native holly, sometimes on English holly, causing conspicuous blotch mines on upper surface, often several on a leaf. Another species, the American serpentine **Native Holly Leafminer***, *Phytomyza ilicicola* Loew, produces very slender sinuous mines packed with frass. It is not so common, but sometimes the two types of mines are seen in the same leaf. The European miner winters in the mines, a yellow-green larva ⅛ inch long, and pupates there in spring. Small black flies, ¹⁄₁₆ inch long, emerge about the time holly twigs have 3 or 4 new leaves. This may be late April in Maryland, early May in New Jersey, and mid-May in Connecticut. They feed for about 10 days before egg laying. The female makes feeding punctures in foliage with her ovipositor, but both males and females lap the exuding sap. These feeding punctures look like pinpricks, but may be so numerous—up to 50 on a leaf—that the leaf is distorted. Eggs are laid singly in small slits or punctures in lower surface of new leaves. Small larvae start to feed in about a week, but the mines are not noticeable until late summer. There is only one generation a year, emergence taking

57. Work of holly leafminer, left, and native holly miner, right.

place through the upper surface of the leaf the second season after the foliage is mined. The life history of the native holly leafminer is similar but eggs may be deposited in feeding punctures.

Control. Spray as soon as you see black flies around new growth, using dimethoate (Cygon), or diazinon, and spray with Meta-Systox-R or dimethoate in summer to kill the young miners in foliage. The latter may be injurious to Burford holly but this would be unlikely to have leafminers.

There are other holly leafminers. *Phytomyza glabricola* Kulp occurs on *Ilex glabra* and causes yellowish brown to reddish brown linear-blotch mines. *P. opacae* Kulp makes linear yellowish-brown mines traversing the leaf several times; occurs on *Ilex opaca* and *I. cumulicola. P. verticillatae* Kulp makes linear-blotch mines on *Ilex verticillata; P. vomitoriae* Kulp makes irregular linear mines in *I. vomitoria;* and *P. ditmani* Kulp makes blotch mines in leaves of *I. decidua* and *I. serrata.*

Lantana Leafminer*, *Cremastobombycia lantanella* (Schrank). A leafblotch miner.

Larkspur Leafminer*, *Phytomyza* complex, including *aconita* Hendel and *delphinivora* Spencer. Flies common on delphinium, larkspur, aconite. Several larvae feed together to form tan to brown blotch mines filled with dark flecks of excrement. The flies puncture the leaves from the underside, making them turn brown. Foliage often appears blighted by disease. There are several generations, with pupation in summer on the outside of a leaf near a mine. Remove infested leaves. Spray with malathion.

Lilac Leafminer*, *Gracillaria syringella* (Fabricius). Lilac Leafroller. A European moth first known in America in 1925, now widespread, frequently reported injurious to lilac and privet in Rhode Island and in the West—Washington, Oregon, Montana, and Colorado. It has also been reported from ash, deutzia, and euonymus. The brownish moths, with 6 yellow lines on their fore wings, lay eggs in vein axils on underside of leaves. The pale yellow, translucent larvae, $\frac{1}{3}$ inch long, first mine and then roll and skeletonize the leaves. There are 2 generations, larvae of the 2nd hibernating in cocoons in the soil. Moths emerge in May and July. When the miner is abundant, the beauty of lilac and privet is spoiled and there may be injurious defoliation. Spray in May with malathion or diazinon; repeat in July.

Locust Leafminer*, *Xenochalepus dorsalis* (Thunberg). Locust Leaf Beetle, distributed through eastern states south to Mississippi and west to Missouri, feeding primarily on black locust. The beetle, $\frac{1}{4}$ inch long, is orange-yellow with a broad black stripe down the back, black head and appendages. It is active in spring when locusts are coming into leaf; it lays eggs on underside of leaves, 3 to 5 in a pile covered with excrement. The larvae, yellow-white with black heads, burrow from the bottom of this mass into the leaf, making a common circular mine. As it grows older, each larva makes a separate new mine. After feeding for a month, the larvae pupate inside the mines; the leaves turn brown and drop. There may be a second generation of the beetles and it is not uncommon for locusts to lose all their foliage twice in a single season. In most years, the trees make a brown eyesore on hillsides or along roads unless they are sprayed. Spray with malathion.

Lodgepole Needleminer*, *Coleotechnites milleri* (Busck). An important pest of lodgepole pine in California, Idaho, Montana, also mining needles of western white and Jeffrey pine in epidemic areas. In Yosemite National Park and other recreational areas it has killed up to 80 per cent of mature trees in epidemic years. Moths, very small, white or gray, appear every other year to lay eggs behind twig and needle scales and around buds. The greenish larva mines one needle the first year, moves to another for the second year. Lindane-emulsion sprays have been helpful but outbreaks of needleminers are eventually brought under control by parasites and climatic conditions. Use of a malathion-oil spray has reduced the number of parasites.

Morningglory Leafminer*, *Bedellia somnulentella* (Zeller). Convolvulus Leafminer. Small pale caterpillars, larvae of gray moths, make irregular blotch mines in leaves—first serpentine, then widening into blistered blotches. Pupation is in cocoons attached to leaves. This species may be abundant on sweetpotato as well as morning-glory. A parasitic wasp, *Apanteles bedelliae*, is helpful.

Native Holly Leafminer*. See under Holly Leafminer.

Pea Leafminer*, *Liriomyza langei* Frick. Causing large losses in various truck crops in California, injurious to onions in Oregon; also reported on chrysanthemums. Adult is a fly.

Pine Needleminer*, *Exoteleia pinifoliella* (Chambers). Common in eastern states. Sometimes abundant on ornamental pines. Brown larvae, ⅕ inch long, mine tips of needles, entering at some distance from the tip, and then excavate the whole leaf. Injured tips turn yellow, dry up. There is usually 1 generation in the Northeast, with yellow-brown moths, marked with white or gray, laying eggs in June and July. There may be more broods in the South. Spray with methoxychlor.

Pine Needle Sheathminer*, *Zelleria haimbachi* Busck. Jack Pine Needleminer. On jack, lodgepole, ponderosa, and Virginia pines. Small caterpillars mine in the sheath, severing the needles near the base, sometimes webbing them in clusters. The adult is a small gray moth.

Privet Leafminer*, *Gracillaria cuculipennella* (Hübner). A European moth sometimes destructive here. Whitish caterpillars, ⅞ inch long when mature, make blotch mines in leaves, then feed externally in rolled leaves. Spray with malathion.

Serpentine Leafminer*, *Liriomyza brassicae* (Riley). Common throughout the country, more devastating in the South and California. The yellow maggots, larvae of minute black-and-yellow flies, make long, slender, winding white mines under epidermis of bean, beet, cabbage, cowpea, cress, nasturtium, sweetpea, pepper, potato, radish, spinach, turnip, watermelon, and field crops. Pupation is in the mines or in brown puparia in the soil. There are several generations. In addition to decreasing the attractiveness of green vegetables for food, the mines afford entrance to disease and decay organisms. Chlordane, lindane, and diazinon have been helpful in control. Home gardeners should remove infested leaves by hand. There are natural parasites working on this miner.

Solitary Oak Leafminer*, *Cameraria hamadryadella* (Clemens). Disfiguring many species of oak. The pale blotch mines, several on a leaf, contain a single larva each. These are flattened with only rudiments of legs and with the prothoracic segment enlarged. The moth is white with broad irregular bronze bands on the fore wings. There may be 5 or 6 generations in the vicinity of Washington, D.C. The larvae winter in mines in dried leaves so that raking up old leaves is helpful. Spray in spring with malathion or carbaryl.

Rose Barkminer, *Marmara* sp. Leafblotch flies making white winding mines on canes of rose and loganberry.

Spinach Leafminer*, *Pegomya hyoscyami* (Panzer). Generally distributed on spinach, beet, sugar beet, chard, and many weeds, especially lambs-quarters. Slender gray, black-haired flies, ¼ inch long, lay oval white, sculptured eggs, singly or in small groups, on underside of leaves. These hatch in 3 or 4 days into pale-green or whitish maggots which first eat slender, winding mines but then widen these and join them together to make large, light-colored blotches filled with dark excrement. Maggots may migrate from leaf to leaf; they are fullgrown in 1 to 3 weeks and pupate usually in the soil. Adults appear in 2 to 4 weeks and there may be 3 or 4 generations a season. Leaf vegetables are unfit for greens; seed and root development are checked. Remove infested leaves; keep weed hosts destroyed; spray with diazinon, dimethoate, or malathion.

Spotted Tentiform Leafminer, *Phyllonorycter crataegella* Clemens. Rather common in the East, known in the Northwest, damaging in California. Leaves of apple, quince, plum, cherry, wild haw, sweet-scented crab may have up to 15 blotch mines apiece and may be buckled like a tent. The adult is a very small moth with spotted wings. There may be 3 generations, with leaves sometimes losing most of the function, but outbreaks are very irregular, probably due to parasites.

Spruce Needleminer*, *Taniva albolineana* (Kearfott). On blue, Norway, Engelmann, and Sitka spruce from Maine to North Carolina and in Colorado, Idaho, Oregon, and Washington. Dark-brown moths, wingspread ½ inch, lay eggs on needles from mid-May to mid-June. Larvae bore into needles at base and make webs from entrance holes in needles to twigs. Each larva destroys an average of 10 needles. The entire crown of small ornamental spruces can be webbed; on larger trees heaviest infestation is on lower branches. A simple control is to wash off all loose needles and webs with a hose in March and early autumn, cleaning up the trash flushed to the ground.

Two other species mine spruce needles. *Epinotia nanana* Treitman webs dried mined needles together, giving the trees an unsightly, unhealthy appearance. This species, from Europe, occurs from Maine to Ohio and Michigan. A single larva may mine 10 or more needles. The adult is dark smoky brown with $\frac{7}{16}$-inch wingspread. *Recurvaria piceaella* (Kearfott) has a similar life cycle, occurs from Maine to Colorado on blue, Norway, red, and white spruce. The moths—grayish with pale yellow head and thorax—are active in June and July, lay eggs on needles; the larvae mine the needles, then spin them together with silk.

Strawberry Crownminer*, *Aristotelia fragariae* Busck. Reddish larvae, ¼ inch long, burrow in crowns of plants, causing stunting and poor foliage and offering entrance to disease organisms. In the Northwest moths emerge in June and July and lay eggs about the crown. Larvae are full-grown by October. Crop rotation is recommended as well as cleaning up plants.

Sweetpotato Leafminer*, *Bedellia orchilella* Walsingham. Related to the morningglory leafminer.

Sycamore Leafminer, *Phyllonorycter felinella* Heinrich. The moth lays eggs beneath leaf hairs on the lower leaf surface and the larvae— yellowish, ¼ inch long when grown—enter leaf directly. The mines are brownish with black fecal pellets. Raking fallen leaves is helpful.

Tupelo Leafminer*, *Antispila nysaefoliella* Clemens. Sourgum Casecutter. The larvae of this tiny moth mine in the leaves of tupelo, sourgum, and, when mature, cut oval cases out of the leaves, falling with them to the ground. The larva attaches its case to some object by a silken thread and pupates inside. Although it is reported abundant in some years, causing browning of leaves by late summer, my only experience with it was on an estate in Pennsylvania some years ago, when all the gardeners stopped working to wonder at the bits of leaves walking around on the ground. In that instance, every leaf on the ground seemed to have been infested. Spray with malathion in May when adults emerge.

Unspotted Tentiform Leafminer, *Callisto geminatella* Packard. On apple, pear, crabapple, haw, plum, wild cherry. Greenish-gray larvae mine leaves and buckle them, as do those of the spotted tentiform miner. Moths are gray without spots. Hibernation is as a pupa inside folded edges of the leaf. Destroy fallen leaves in autumn.

Vegetable Leafminer*, *Liriomyza munda* Frick.

Verbena Leafminer, *Agromyza artemisiae* (Kaltenbach). Practically inevitable on verbena. Each maggot feeds singly, making a blister or blotch mine, but several mines run together to make the foliage most unsightly. The adult is a tiny midge. Spray with dimethoate, diazinon, or malathion. Rake up plant trash in autumn.

White Fir Needleminer*, *Epinotia meritana* Heinrich. On white fir, reported particularly damaging in Utah, present in California and Arizona. Moths are small, grayish, mottled with black; minute green larvae winter in fir needles, then mine and web them the following spring.

Wild Parsnip Leafminer, *Phytomyza albiceps* (Meigen). A European species generally distributed, making serpentine mines in aster and columbine. The larvae are white, puparia black, flies small, black or metallic blue. Pupation is in the soil.

LEAFROLLERS

Leafrollers are caterpillars which feed protected by the rolled-up leaf of the host plant but not between the two leaf surfaces as do leafminers.

Avocado Leafroller, *Gracillaria perseae* Busck. Serious in Florida. The adult is a small grayish moth, ¼ inch long. The larva feeds on the lower surface of the avocado leaf and rolls it back from the tip, pupating in the rolled portion.

Basswood Leafroller*, *Pantographa limata* Grote & Robinson. General through eastern states. The moths—straw-colored with intricate olive-purple markings, 1½-inch wingspread—emerge in June and July. The larva—1 inch long, bright green with a black head—lives inside the apical half of a leaf rolled into a tube, and feeds from July to September. When full-grown it leaves this nest and makes a small one lined with silk in a fold from one edge of the leaf, spending the winter in fallen leaves inside this protection. Raking up leaves in autumn may be sufficient control.

Bean Leafroller*, *Urbanus proteus* (Linnaeus). A southern pest troublesome to early fall crops of beans, found as far north as Delaware. The 1-inch-long caterpillar is greenish yellow, velvety, with a broad head and contracted neck. It rolls up edges of leaves after cutting slits in them. The adult, a blue skipper butterfly, 2 inches across, with long tails on hind wings, lays eggs on beans in summer. In warm weather larvae take 14 days to mature, a month when it is cooler. Pupation is on plants. By September, beans in Florida may be so heavily infested no pods can be formed.

Boxelder Leafroller*, *Gracillaria negundella* Chambers. Boxelder leaves are mined from the underside, whitened and rolled. Severe injury is reported in Utah and Nevada.

Coconut Leafroller*, *Hedylepta blackburni* (Butler). A pyralid moth.

European Honeysuckle Leafroller*, *Harpipteryx xylostella* (Linnaeus). On Tartarian honeysuckle. Leaves are rolled and ragged. Larvae are leaf-green with 2 brown median stripes outlined with blue-green stripes; ¾ inch long, tapering to a narrow head and tail. The white cocoon, pointed at both ends, is fastened to a leaf. The moth is chestnut-brown with cream-colored markings on fore wings, which expand to ¾ inch. Spray with carbaryl to prevent defoliation.

Fruittree Leafroller*, *Archips argyrospilus* (Walker). Present from coast to coast, capable, in occasional years of abundance, of ruining 90 per cent of an apple crop. This is a general feeder on most deciduous fruits—apricot, blackberry, cherry, currant, gooseberry, loganberry, pear, plum, quince, raspberry—and has been damaging to citrus in California. It may also infest ash, boxelder, elm, horse-chestnut, hickory, locust, oak, osage-orange, poplar, rose, sassafras, English walnut, and willow. It winters in the egg stage, in masses of 30 to 100 plastered on twigs, branches, and tree trunks, covered with a brown or gray varnish. About the time apple buds separate in spring the young worms—pale green with brown heads—crawl to feed on leaves, buds, and small fruits for about a month. They spin a light web around several leaves, roll these together, often enclosing a small cluster of young apples. Cavities eaten in fruit show as deep russeted scars at harvest. When the caterpillars are full-grown, ¾ inch long, they pupate inside rolled leaves or make a flimsy cocoon on trunk or branches. Moths emerge in late June or July. They are brown with gold markings, wing expanse ¾ inch. There is only 1 generation.

Control. A heavy application of a dormant oil spray put on before buds break and applied so as to cover every egg mass has been effective. Growers may spray with Imidan or Guthion at petal fall and 10 to 13 days later. There are many parasites, accounting for the fluctuating abundance of this pest.

Graybanded Leafroller*, *Argyrotaenia mariana* (Fernald).

Hickory Leafroller*, *Argyrotaenia juglandana* (Fernald). Found in the Northeast and west to Wisconsin. The larvae—pale green, semitranslucent, ¾ inch long—roll hickory leaves and feed inside the rolls in May and June. The moths, appearing in June and July, have dark-brown fore wings marked with black and gray hind wings.

Larger Canna Leafroller*, *Calpodes ethlius* (Stoll). Ranging through the South and north to Washington, D.C. The caterpillar, which is up to 1¾ inches long, green, semitransparent with a dark-orange head set off by a narrow neck, cuts off a strip from the margin of a canna leaf and folds it over, feeding above and below from within this protection, eating larger irregular holes as it grows. Damage can be extensive. The adult is a skipper butterfly, brown with white spots. Spray with carbaryl or dimethoate before leaves are rolled. The caterpillars can also be killed by pressing the leaf between thumb and finger.

Lesser Canna Leafroller*, *Geshna cannalis* (Quaintance). Also serious on canna in the South. The caterpillar—yellow-white but with a green tinge after feeding on foliage, 1 inch long when grown—fastens young leaves together before they have unrolled. Foliage is ragged, often turns brown and dies. The moths, uniform light brown, appear in February and March in Florida. It may be possible to kill larvae inside rolled leaves by pressing with your fingers. Clean up dead trash in beds and remove infested plant parts. Spray with carbaryl or dimethoate.

Locust Leafroller*, *Nephopteryx subcaesiella* (Clemens). Found from Maine to West Virginia and Colorado on locust, honeylocust, and wisteria. The larvae, up to 1 inch long, green with faint stripes, black head, feed inside 2 or 3 leaves spun together with silk. They winter as pupae in silken cocoons among leaves on ground. Gray moths, shaded with red, emerge from May to July. In some states there is a 2nd generation with moths again in August and September. The injury is rather common but probably not serious enough to call for control measures.

Mexican Leafroller*, *Amorbia emigratella* Busck. A green caterpillar on avocado in Central America.

Oak Leafroller, *Argyrotoxa semipurpurana* Kearfott. Larva of a tortricid moth seriously defoliating red, pin, scarlet, and scrub oaks in Massachusetts, Connecticut, New York, and Pennsylvania. Several other species occasionally infest oaks.

Obliquebanded Leafroller*, *Choristoneura rosaceana* (Harris). Rose Leaftier. The omnivorous larvae of this moth feed on flowers in greenhouse and garden, chewing holes in rosebuds, rolling up leaves and tying them together, feeding on aster, carnation, geranium, sunflower, verbena. They also feed on vegetables, fruits, ornamental trees and shrubs, including apple, apricot, ash, basswood, bean, birch, blackberry, boxelder, celery, cherry, currant, dewberry, dogwood, gooseberry, hawthorn, holly, honeysuckle, horsechestnut, lilac, loganberry, maple, oak, peach, pear, plum, poplar, prune, raspberry, rose, spirea, strawberry, sumac, and thistle.

The pale-green, black-headed larvae mine the leaves first, then work inside rolled areas, often tying several leaves together. They may also infest fruit. Eggs are laid in overlapping green masses on branches of host plants or on rose leaves in greenhouses.

Control. Parathion aerosols will control in greenhouses. Spray garden plants with carbaryl.

Omnivorous Leafroller, *Platynota stultana* Walsingham. Found on a wide variety of flowers and subtropical fruits in California and Arizona, sometimes serious on citrus. It is truly omnivorous, feeding on alfalfa, celery, cotton, lettuce, sugar beet, melon, strawberry, boysenberry, begonia, oleander, carnation, and rose, to mention only a few hosts. This is a tortricid moth, with dark brown fore wings, the outer half being a lighter yellow-brown. The greenish eggs are laid in flat clusters, overlapping like shingles. The larvae are yellowish or greenish brown with a ragged stripe down the back. This insect has become a persistent rose pest in eastern and midwestern greenhouses. Also present on euonymus. Methomyl and Azodrin have given control, along with *Bacillus thuringiensis.*

Raspberry Leafroller*, *Exartema permundanum* Clemens. An olethreutid moth.

Redbanded Leafroller*, *Argyrotaenia velutinana* (Walker). A native insect widely distributed in the Northeast and ranging to North Carolina and Texas. It feeds on apple, cherry, plum, some small fruits, vegetables, ornamental trees, and flowers, among the latter chrysanthemum, geranium, hollyhock, honeysuckle, lobelia, rose, violet, and zinnia. The moth, brownish with red bands across the wings, which spread only ¾ inch, appears in spring soon after apple buds break. The larva is slender, greenish, just over ½ inch long, and pupates in autumn inside a half cocoon on trees and other objects. There may be 3 generations. Eggs of the 1st are placed on bark, those of the 2nd on foliage or fruits. Early season larvae feed on leaves, spinning light webs, but late season larvae feed on fruits, eating patches off the surface. They roll and tie leaves and terminal growth of ornamentals.

Control. When DDT was used for codling moths this leafroller increased because its parasites were killed; with DDT no longer in use the redbanded leafroller may lose some of its importance. Orchardists may use azinphosmethyl, Imidan, or Guthion. Home gardeners can spray ornamentals with carbaryl or dimethoate.

Strawberry Leafroller*, *Ancylis comptana fragariae* (Walsh & Riley). On strawberry, dewberry, blackberry, and raspberry in northern United States, Louisiana, and Arkansas. The caterpillars, greenish or bronze, up to ½ inch long, fold or roll and tie the leaves into tubes, feeding from within. Plants are weakened, leaves turn brown and die. Fruits are withered and deformed; infested buds appear white or gray from a distance. Small rusty red moths with brown and white markings, ½-inch wingspread, appear in large numbers near the strawberry patch in May to lay eggs on underside of leaves. The larvae feed for 25 to 50 days, first on underside of leaves, then on upper, then pupate inside folded leaves. There are 2 or more generations.

Control. Parasites usually keep this pest under control. If there are more than 1 or 2 larvae per plant dust or spray with malathion or carbaryl.

Sugarcane Leafroller*, *Hedylepta accepta* (Butler).

Sweetpotato Leafroller*, *Pilocrocis tripunctata* (Fabricius). Bluish green caterpillars, up to 1 inch long, feed inside folded leaves, eating holes and skeletonizing.

Threelined Leafroller*, *Pandemis limitata* (Robinson).

Western Strawberry Leafroller, *Anacampsis fragariella* Busck. Occurring in Washington and Oregon along with the strawberry leafroller. The caterpillars are creamy pink, ½ inch long. Leaves are rolled in May and June, moths emerge in July. Hibernation is in the egg stage on old strawberry leaves. There is only 1 generation. Spray with carbaryl; top plants after harvest.

LEAF SKELETONIZERS

Leaf skeletonizers are caterpillars like leafrollers, but they feed more openly, eating out everything except epidermis and veins, without the protection of conspicuously rolled leaves.

Apple-and-thorn Skeletonizer*, *Anthophila pariana* (Clerck). A European pest, first found in New York in 1917, now present from Maine to New Jersey and in the Pacific Northwest, feeding on apple, pear, cherry, and hawthorn. It hibernates as a small, dark-brown moth, lays eggs in spring. The caterpillars—yellow-green with black tubercles, brown heads—feed on underside of leaves first, then make shelters by drawing upper surfaces together with silk, leaves becoming a mass of webbing and frass. There are several generations.

Appleleaf Skeletonizer*, *Psorosina hammondi* (Riley). On apple, sometimes plum and quince, most abundant in central states, where it is of fluctuating importance. The green upper surface of the leaf is eaten off entirely or in part, making the foliage look brown and dead; trees appear to have been struck by fire. Leaves at end of branches may be lightly folded with 2 or 3 lightly webbed together. Brown pupae winter in fallen leaves; dark-brown moths, wings mottled with silver, lay eggs on leaves in late spring. Brownish green caterpillars, ½ inch long, with 4 black tubercles on the back, feed in June and July, then pupate on leaves. The 2nd generation feeds in late August and September. The ordinary spray schedule, if it includes summer sprays for codling moth, will control leaf skeletonizers.

Beanleaf Skeletonizer*, *Autoplusia egena* (Guenée). A noctuid moth.

Birch Skeletonizer*, *Bucculatrix canadensisella* Chambers. General in the Northeast, found as far west as Wisconsin and south to higher altitudes in North Carolina, on gray, paper, yellow, and European white birches. The moths, ⅜ inch across the wings, which are brown crossed with silver, appear in July to lay eggs singly on the leaves. The young larva, yellow-green, bores directly from the bottom of the egg into the leaf, mines it in 2 to 5 weeks, then cuts a crescent-shaped opening through the lower side of the leaf and spins a molting cocoon. After molting, the larva skeletonizes the leaf from the underside, molts again, feeds for another week, then drops to the ground and makes a brown, ribbed pupal cocoon for the winter. There is 1 generation. The pest is serious for 2 or 3 years out of every 10 but the injury comes so late in the season the expense of spraying may not be justified. If necessary, spray with carbaryl about mid-July. There are many parasites.

Cotton Leafperforator*, *Bucculatrix thurberiella* Busck. Hollyhock Leaf Skeletonizer. A cotton pest, larva of a small gray-and-tan moth. It mines in and completely skeletonizes foliage of hollyhocks in California. Spray with carbaryl.

Grapeleaf Skeletonizer*, *Harrisina americana* (Guérin). Common on wild grapes, sometimes injuring cultivated varieties. The larvae feed in groups, side by side across a leaf, eating the upper surface only. Adults are small, smoky black, narrow-fringed moths. The insect is so heavily parasitized no other control is required.

Maple Trumpet Skeletonizer*, *Epinotia aceriella* (Clemens). The leaves of red maple, sometimes sugar maple, are folded loosely in July and August. The small green larva lives inside a long, black, trumpet-like tube near the skeletonized areas. The injury is more spectacular than serious.

Oak Skeletonizer*, *Bucculatrix ainsliella* Murtfeldt. In the Northeast, on red, black, and white oaks, also reported as causing severe injury in Wisconsin. The yellowish green larva is ¼ inch long. The moth is creamy white with brown markings, active in May and late July and August, there being 2 generations. The winter is passed as pupae in cocoons on fallen leaves or debris. Spray in mid-June and early August with carbaryl or malathion.

Palm Leaf Skeletonizer*, *Homaledra sabalella* (Chambers). Palm Leafminer, the major pest of palms in Florida, reported also in South Carolina and Alabama, feeding on saw, cabbage, dwarf, and sabal palmettos, on coconut palm and various date palms. The caterpillars are gregarious, living in colonies of 35 to 100, feeding under a protective web of silk and depositing their excrement in the upper surface of this web. Continued feeding causes dark-brown blotches on leaves, followed by shriveling and death. In heavily infested areas every frond and leaflet may be attacked. The moths, which are rarely seen in the daytime, are attracted to lights at night. They lay eggs on the brown, papery husk which encloses young leaflets. Larvae start to feed directly from the bottom of the eggs on leaf tissue, keeping the eggshells as protection until the silken web is formed. There are often 5 broods, with the winter passed in egg, larval, or pupal stages.

Control. Spray repeatedly, perhaps every 2 months, with carbaryl, lindane, or lead arsenate (if allowed). Cut out infested fronds; remove interleaf husks that may bear eggs.

Western Grapeleaf Skeletonizer*, *Harrisina brillians* Barnes & McDunnough. Occurring in Arizona, California, New Mexico, and Texas. Black-and-yellow larvae feed on leaves of wild and cultivated grapes in late summer. They move in compact colonies as they completely skeletonize leaves. Moths are metallic black or green. Spray with methoxychlor. There are natural parasites and a virus disease helping in control.

LEAFTIERS

Leaftiers are much like leafrollers, tying leaves together with strands of silk and feeding inside that protection.

Aspen Leaftier, *Sciaphila duplex* (Walsingham). Recorded from many states, with sometimes severe outbreaks in Utah, Wyoming, and Idaho on aspen (poplar). Light gray moths, with 2 ragged black bands on fore wings, lay eggs on bark in late summer and young larvae winter in bark crevices. They are dark green to black and feed on new leaves in spring. Larval parasites have been reared from the dark leathery pupae.

Beech Leaftier, *Psilocorsis faginella* (Chambers). Common in the Northeast on beech. The larvae, whitish with pink tint, brown heads, feed in August and September. They winter as pupae with moths appearing in late May and June. The fore wings are light brown with transverse darker streaks. Leaves are tied together, skeletonized, and browned, but the injury is seldom serious enough for control measures.

Celery Leaftier*, *Udea rubigalis* (Guenée). Greenhouse Leaftier. Present throughout North America, a special pest of celery, feeding on a great many garden and greenhouse vegetables and ornamentals—ageratum, anemone, aster, bean, beet, cabbage, carnation, cauliflower, cineraria, chrysanthemum, cucumber, dahlia, daisies, geranium, heliotrope, kale, ivy, lantana, lettuce, lobelia, nasturtium, parsley, passion-flower, pea, sweetpea, rose, spinach, snapdragon, strawberry, thistle, wandering-Jew, to give a partial list.

The moths are brown, fore wings crossed by wavy dark lines, spreading ¾ inch. They are quiet during the day, fly at night. The female lays flattened, scalelike translucent eggs singly or in overlapping groups on underside of leaves, usually close to the soil. They hatch in 5 to 12 days into pale-green caterpillars, turning yellow when grown, ¾ inch long with a white stripe down the back and a dark green line in the center of the white stripe. As they feed, they web foliage together in large masses, filling it with frass, and they mine into soft stems and hearts of plants, especially celery. When disturbed they wiggle violently in their webs or drop to the ground. They pupate in silken cocoons inside the webs. The life cycle takes about 40 days; there may be 7 or 8 generations in greenhouses and 5 or 6 outdoors in warm climates.

Control. Spray or dust with malathion or dimethoate. An older suggestion for celery is to make two applications of pyrethrum dust one hour apart. The first drives the tiers from their webs and the second kills them. Parathion aerosols have been used in greenhouses. Harvest infested outdoor crops early and spade under all crop refuse.

European Clover Leaftier, *Mirificarma formosella* (Hübner). Found in California in 1969 damaging many kinds of clovers. The gelechtiid moth is variegated orange-brown, with smoky hind wings, ¼ inch long. The light-green larvae, ⅜ inch long semiskeletonize the foliage. Two leaf surfaces are folded together by light webbing, followed by discoloration and drying. Pupation is inside folded leaves.

False Celery Leaftier*, *Udea profundalis* (Packard).

Holly Leaftier, *Norma dietsiana* Kearfott. Larvae tie leaves of American holly. Reported in 1961 as a new record for Delaware.

Hydrangea Leaftier, *Exartema ferriferanum* (Walker). A small green caterpillar with a dark head sews terminal leaves of hydrangea

58. Hydrangea leaves fastened together by leaftier, which is eating the enclosed flower bud.

tightly around the flower bud, the effect being that of little pocketbooks. It is often possible to tear open these tied leaves and kill the worm before it destroys the flower. Carbaryl or malathion applied early enough should give control but the leaves are usually tied together before one gets around to spraying.

Oak Leaftier*, *Croesia albicomana* (Clemens). A tortricid (leaf-roller) moth. Other species are also listed as oak leaftiers.

Omnivorous Leaftier*, *Cnephasia longana* (Haworth). Strawberry Fruitworm. A European pest destructive in California and the North-west, first found in Oregon in 1929 on strawberries and Dutch iris. The larvae feed also on flax, peas, and other legumes, and many cultivated plants, including calla lily, bachelors-button, gladiolus, heather, marguerites. Both flowers and foliage are webbed and eaten, and the fruit of strawberries. The moth—tan, with brown spots on fore wings of female, ½ inch long—flies in the evening during June and July. Eggs are laid on rough bark of trees or on rough wood, the young larvae wintering in crevices. In spring, they are carried by the wind on their silken threads to nearby fields. The full-grown larva is cream-colored with a lighter stripe along each side of the back, ⅜ inch long. The pupa is cigar-shaped, brown, found inside strawberry fruits or in webbed foliage.

Control. Avoid planting strawberries near rough-barked trees; do not plant after legumes. Dust with methoxychlor about 15 days after blossoms appear and repeat 3 weeks later.

Sweetgum Leaftier, *Nephoteryx uvinella* (Ragonet). Reported ty-ing and feeding on leaves of sweetgum in Maryland.

MAGGOTS

Maggots are the larvae of flies. Those that are commonly known by their adult name have been treated under Flies; those that nor-mally go under the name of maggot are considered here.

Apple Maggot*, *Rhagoletis pomonella* (Walsh). Also known as Railroad Worm, Apple Fruit Fly, a native pest injurious to apples from the Dakotas east and Arkansas north (Plate XXV). It probably fed originally on wild haws and wild crabs; now it eats apples, blue-berries, plums, cherries, and has been reported on apricot. A smaller variety of this species breeds on snowberry in the West, but there it is not an apple pest. In Connecticut the maggot is considered the primary apple pest, wormy fruit in unsprayed orchards often reaching 100 per cent.

Hibernation takes place inside a small brown puparium buried 1 to 6 inches deep in the soil, but flies do not emerge until summer—late June in some sections, early July in most. They are slightly smaller than houseflies, black, with white bands on the abdomen and conspicuous zigzag black bands on the wings. The females lay their eggs singly through punctures in the apple skin. In 5 to 10 days these hatch into legless white maggots which tunnel through the fruit by

European Corn Borer

Corn Earworm

XIII EUROPEAN CORN BORER: (a) adult moth; (b) larva; (c) pupa and larva inside corn stem, frass protruding from hole; (d) moth laying eggs on corn leaf; (e) borer working in ear; (f) larvae overwintering in old corn stalks. CORN EARWORM: (a) larvae, brown or green striped caterpillars; (b) pupa in soil; (c) moth laying eggs on corn silk and single egg, much enlarged; (d) worm feeding in mass of frass at tip of ear.

XIV ROUNDHEADED APPLE TREE BORER: (a,1) adult beetle; (a,2)
roundheaded grub; (a,3) pupa in wood cell; (c) eggs; (d) section of tree trunk.
showing borer at work, frass protruding. FLATHEADED APPLE TREE BORER:
(b,1) larva with flat enlargement behind head, characteristic curved position;
(b,2) beetle; (b,3) pupa in cell; (e) eggs; (f) larva in winter chamber in tree
trunk. POTATO LEAFHOPPER (Apple Leafhopper): (a) adult; (b,1,2,4,5)
nymphs in different instars; (c) egg in leaf vein.

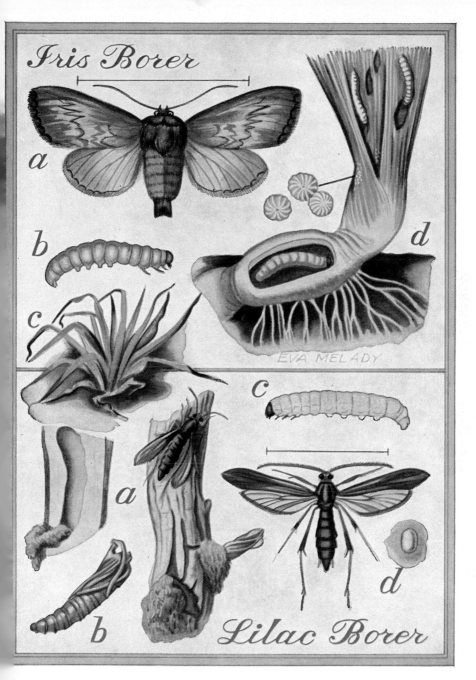

Iris Borer

Lilac Borer

EVA MELADY

XV IRIS BORER: (a) moth, somewhat enlarged; (b) borer, not quite full grown; (c) infested iris; (d) young borers on outside of leaves (usual position is inside fold), older borer in hollow rhizome, and eggs, enlarged. LILAC BORER: (a) lilac stems showing tunnel and protruding sawdust, moth and pupa case; (b) pupa; (c) borer; (d) adult moth and egg (enlarged).

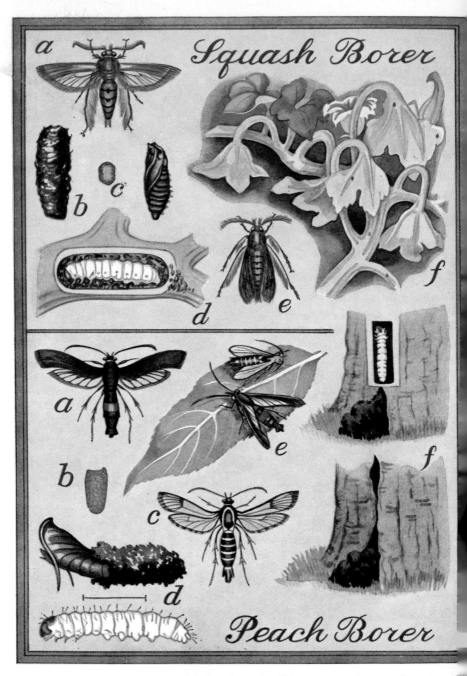

XVI SQUASH BORER: (a) female moth; (b) cocoon; (c) egg, enlarged, and pupa; (d) borer in stem; (e) male moth; (f) vine wilting from borer injury. PEACH TREE BORER: (a) female moth; (b) egg, enlarged; (c) male moth; (d) pupa protruding from cocoon, and borer; (e) adults on peach leaf; (f) section cut in tree trunk to show borer in position, jellylike frass at base.

rasping and tearing the pulp into brown, winding galleries. Early varieties soon become a mass of soft rotting pulp; later varieties have corky streaks through the flesh and a distorted, pitted surface. Completing their growth about a week after apples have fallen to the ground, larvae leave the fruit and burrow in the soil to pupate. Ordinarily pupation continues until the next summer, but in its southern range the apple maggot may have a partial 2nd generation.

Control. Cleaning up and disposing of dropped fruit before the maggots leave the apples to pupate is very important in control. This may mean twice a week for summer varieties. In New Jersey, Imidan or Guthion are suggested for the 3rd, 4th, and 5th cover sprays on apple but these chemicals are not for backyard fruit growers. In Indiana, malathion in a corn protein hydrosylate bait spray has been effective when applied weekly to trunk and scaffold limbs. In Connecticut the flies are attracted to and caught on sticky red spheres on yellow panels.

Blueberry Maggot*, *Rhagoletis mendax* Curran. Malathion is used with a yeast bait for control. Similar to the apple maggot.

Cabbage Maggot*, *Hylemya brassicae* (Bouché). Introduced from Europe more than a century ago; a serious pest in northern states, of little consequence south of Philadelphia. Early cabbage and broccoli after transplanting, late cabbage in the seedbed, early turnips, late spring radishes are most severely injured by maggots but other crucifers, including brussels sprouts, cauliflower, cress, mustard, and sometimes beet, celery, and a few other vegetables, may be attacked (Plate XXVI).

The winter is spent in puparia, 1 to 5 inches deep in the soil. About the time sweet cherries bloom and young cabbage plants are set out, a small fly, ¼ inch long, dark gray with black stripes on thorax and black bristles, crawls out of the soil to lay white, finely ridged eggs at the base of the stems and on adjacent soil. These hatch in 3 to 7 days into small, white, legless maggots, blunt at the rear end, which enter the soil to feast on roots and stems just under the surface, riddling them with brown tunnels. Seedlings wilt, turn yellow, and die. Maggot abundance fluctuates from year to year but often 40 to 80 per cent of young plants are lost. After 3 weeks the maggot forms a puparium from its larval skin, producing another fly in 12 to 18 days. The number of generations is indefinite; ordinarily the first is important on cabbage and its relatives, while late broods menace fall turnips and radishes. In addition to its own feeding injury the maggot is credited with introducing the fungus causing blackleg and spreading bacterial soft rot.

Control. Protect seedbeds with a cheesecloth cover to prevent egg laying. Place a 3- to 4-inch square of tar paper around the stem of each seedling when it is transplanted. Or spray soil before planting with diazinon or apply diazinon granules, working chemical into the top 4 inches of soil. For postplanting control, spray with diazinon when forsythia starts to bloom and repeat 3 times at 10-day intervals.

Carnation Maggot*, *Hylemya brunnescens* (Zetterstedt).

Carnation Tip Maggot*, *Hylemya echinata* Séguy.

Cherry Maggot. See Cherry Fruit Fly under Flies.

Onion Maggot*, *Hylemya antigua* (Meigen). A northern onion pest, rarely injurious in the South. In dry years the onion maggot is of little importance but in a series of wet springs 80 per cent or more of the crop may be destroyed, larvae tunneling in bulb and crown so thoroughly that the onion dies or is worthless. One small maggot can kill a seedling onion; early plantings are most injured.

The winter is spent in chestnut-brown puparia, resembling grains of wheat, several inches deep in soil, or in piles of cull onions or trash. The flies—gray or brown, bristly, ¼ inch long, with large wings and a rather humpbacked appearance—emerge in May or June and lay sausage-shaped white eggs at the base of plants or in bulbs, then pupate in soil. There are 2 or more generations. The 3rd brood often attacks onions just before harvest and causes storage rot.

Control. Destroying all cull onions immediately after harvest is most important. Foliage can be sprayed when flies first appear (as forsythias begin to bloom) with diazinon or malathion.

Pepper Maggot*, *Zonosemata electa* (Say). First noticed in New Jersey in 1921, now present from Massachusetts south to Florida and west to Texas and New Mexico, but mostly in scattered locations. It is serious on pepper, also reported on eggplant, tomato, groundcherry, and weeds of the nightshade family. There is 1 generation a year. Pupae winter in the soil with flies emerging from late June to August. They are yellow with brown bands on clear wings; they deposit large white eggs, the shape of a crookneck squash, in young peppers. The maggots resemble sharp-pointed pegs, translucent white but turning yellow on maturity. The fruits drop or decay. Spray with dimethoate, starting when flies first appear (around June 1 in New Jersey).

Raspberry Cane Maggot*, *Pegomya rubivora* (Coquillett). A northern insect found from coast to coast on blackberry, dewberry, loganberry, raspberry, and rose. The tips of new shoots wilt, sometimes with a purplish discoloration at the base of the wilted part, or are broken off clean as though cut by a knife. Sometimes galls are formed in the canes. The white maggots, ⅓ inch long, tunnel down in the pith after they have girdled the cane and caused the break.

Pupation is in canes. The flies, half the size of houseflies, emerge in spring to lay eggs in leaf axils of tender shoots. Cut off infested tips several inches below wilted portions.

Seedcorn Maggot*, *Hylemya platura* (Meigen). A European insect that arrived in New York more than 100 years ago and is now general over the country. Chief injury is to germinating seed, with peas and beans often more seriously injured than corn. Melon, cucumber, and potato sprouts are often killed; young plants of cabbage, beet, bean, pea, onion, turnip, spinach, radish, sweetpotato are frequent victims, sometimes gladiolus and coniferous seedlings. The maggots transmit the bacteria causing soft rot.

Yellow-white maggots, $\frac{1}{4}$ inch long, sharply pointed at the head end, burrow in seed so that it fails to sprout or produces a weak, sickly plant. Injury is worse in cold, wet seasons on land rich in organic matter. The winter is spent in puparia in soil or as free maggots in manure. Grayish brown flies, $\frac{1}{3}$ inch long, emerge in early July to deposit eggs in rich soil or on seeds or seedlings. There may be 3 to 5 generations.

Control. One method is to wait to plant, or to replant, until the ground is warm enough to allow quick germination and rapid growth. Shallow planting also speeds up germination. Seed can be treated with diazinon or lindane and some seed is already treated with an insecticide and fungicide when purchased. Diazinon granules can be worked into the soil before planting and have been helpful in growing sweetpeas. Gladiolus corms can be treated in the trench at planting time, before covering, with chlordane or lindane.

Sugarbeet Root Maggot*, *Tetanops myopaeformis* (Röder).

Sunflower Maggot*, *Strauzia longipennis* (Wiedemann). Sunflower Peacock Fly, present in many parts of the country, infesting stems of wild and cultivated sunflowers. The flies are a gay yellow; the female has an orange ovipositor and the male a tuft of black spines on the head.

Turnip Maggot*, *Hylemya floralis* (Fallén). Similar to the cabbage maggot and a very serious pest of crucifers in Alaska. Control with diazinon.

MANTIDS

The praying, or preying, mantis and its relatives are very definitely friends in the garden. They belong to the grasshopper order, Orthoptera, and the family Mantidae. They are all predaceous on other insects, capturing their prey with marvelous front legs, long and muscular, fitted with grooves and spines for grasping and holding. While waiting for some unwary insect, they sit in an attitude of prayer. Baby mantids, looking ridiculously like their elders except for wings, are cannibals from the day they are born. They start with aphids, or perhaps one another, going on to larger insects as they grow. A full-grown mantis is not afraid to strike at a frog, a lizard, or a hornet. Of course they are just as likely to eat a harmless or beneficial insect as one that is a pest. There are about 1,800 species but only about 20 species known in North America. Four of these are common in the East.

Carolina Mantid*, *Stagmomantis carolina* (Linnaeus). A southern native, found as far north as southern New Jersey, Pennsylvania, and Ohio. It has uniformly green wings, is about 2½ inches long.

Chinese Mantid*, *Tenodera aridifolia sinensis* Saussure. The common form in the Middle Atlantic States. It was introduced accidentally from Asia about 1895, in nursery stock sent to Philadelphia, and was not imported to fight Japanese beetles, as some believe. In fact, praying mantids don't like Japanese beetles particularly, though they sometimes eat them. The Chinese mantid has spread to Ohio and southern New England and is often seen in gardens in late summer. It is large, 4 or 5 inches long, and the broad front margin of the wings is sharply separated from the larger, brown portion. Its triangular head is highly movable and it has very large eyes that appear highly intelligent. In egg laying the female hangs head down and produces a gummy fluid which she beats into a froth the color of ripe grain to make her egg case (ootheca). This is made up of a series of plates providing chambers for about 200 eggs and is attached to any shrub or tall grass around the garden or in a field. It looks like a short, broad cornucopia of brown-and-tan dried foam.

If you accidentally cut off egg cases during the fall cleanup or spring pruning, simply tie them onto other shrubs and the babies will hatch later. Don't try to keep an egg case in the house; the eggs will hatch too soon and you cannot provide them with their necessary prey. Egg cases can be purchased (3 for $2.50 at this writing) but it is just as much fun to watch for those already present in your garden (I have just passed one on a weigela shrub; around the corner there is one on a rose bush).

European Mantid*, *Mantis religiosa* Linnaeus. Another accidental importation, found near Rochester, New York, in 1899 and established since then through most of New England. It is a little larger than the Carolina mantid, 2 to 4 inches long, but resembles it.

Narrowwinged Mantid*, *Tenodera angustipennis* Saussure. Another Oriental mantid, discovered in Delaware in 1930 and now common around Philadelphia and in much of New Jersey, some parts of New York. It is like the Chinese mantid but somewhat smaller and more slender.

MEALYBUGS

Mealybugs are relatives of scale insects, members of the family Pseudococcidae, order Homoptera. They are really soft scales, with small, oval, soft, segmented bodies covered with a white powdery wax extending in filaments beyond the body. Most mealybugs have these filaments of equal length all around the body, but longtailed mealybugs have longer threads at the posterior end of the body (Plate XXVII). Most species are house or greenhouse pests in the North, garden pests only in subtropical regions, but Comstock and Taxus mealybugs winter out of doors as far north as New York and Connecticut. Mealybugs injure plants by sucking sap and producing copious honeydew, which attracts ants and forms a medium for growth of sooty-mold fungi. Some species cause plant disease, such as pineapple wilt.

The life history of most mealybugs is about the same. The adult female deposits her eggs, 300 to 600, in a compact, waxy sac beneath the rear end of her body. Egg laying continues for a week or two, then the female dies. These conspicuous egg sacs, well known to anyone who has grown house plants, are chiefly at axils of branching stems or leaves but sometimes on other plant parts. Indoors, eggs hatch in about 10 days; the young nymphs remain in the case for a short period, then crawl over the plants. As crawlers, they are oval, light yellow, 6-legged insects with smooth bodies, feeding like aphids by inserting their beaks into plant tissue and sucking out the sap. Soon after feeding begins, waxy filaments start forming, covering the bodies and radiating out in 36 leglike projections. The bugs get more sluggish but do not entirely stop moving. The mature female is much like the nymph, up to ¼ inch long, but the male forms a white case within which it changes to a minute, active 2-winged insect like a fly. It mates with the female and dies soon after, being unable to feed in the winged state. The longtailed mealybug differs by giving birth to living young instead of forming an egg sac.

Malathion sprays have been widely used to control mealybugs, with dimethoate and Meta-Systox-R also possibilities. Outdoors, ethion-oil and carbaryl sprays have been effective for Taxus and similar mealybugs. Soil treatment with systemics may be helpful. There is a good deal of biological control. One of the lady beetles imported from Australia is known as the Mealybug Destroyer and there are a number of parasites.

Apple Mealybug*, *Phenacoccus aceris* (Signoret). On apple in New England, a problem on filberts in Oregon, reported on pyracantha and cotoneaster in California. Sooty mold growing in honeydew smuts apple fruit. On filberts, cottony masses are seen in bark crevices, with winged males abundant.

Azalea Mealybug. See Azalea Bark Scale under Scale Insects.

Citrophilus Mealybug*, *Pseudococcus fragilis* Brain. First observed in California in 1913. It attacks apple, azalea, blackberry, citrus, climbing fig, cherry, columbine, cyclamen, English ivy, eugenia, foxglove, heliotrope, mallow, Mexican-orange (Choisya), mustard, nightshade, peach, pear, pittosporum, plum, prune, potato, pepper-tree, privet, raspberry, rhubarb, rose, grevillea, sunflower, walnut, among others. This species differs from the citrus mealybug in having 2 tapering filaments at the end of the body and ⅓ the length of the body. The body fluid is darker than in other species and the waxy coating is scarce in 4 areas which look like 4 longitudinal lines. For many years it was kept under control by the Australian lady beetle Cryptolaemus, reared on potato sprouts and distributed to growers, but since 1929 a couple of internal parasites from Australia has had this species under commercial control.

Citrus Mealybug*, *Planococcus citri* (Risso). Distributed throughout the world in greenhouses and outdoors in subtropical climates,

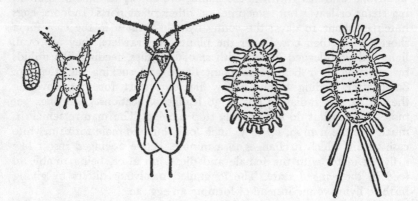

59. Mealybugs: citrus, egg, larva, male and female adults; longtailed (at right).

an omnivorous feeder. As a greenhouse and house-plant pest it is especially troublesome on soft-stemmed plants such as African-violet, coleus, begonia, fern, fuchsia; it is almost always present on gardenia, readily infests amaryllis, avocado, bignonia, camellia, crassula, cineraria, cycas, cactus, chrysanthemum, croton, daphne, dracaena, heliotrope, ivy, lantana, oleander, orchids, poinsettia, rubber plant, umbrella plant, yucca. It is an outdoor pest of citrus trees in California and Florida and in the latter state is numerous on sprouts of spring-grown potatoes kept through the summer for fall planting. In southern California the citrus mealybug is found in the open on most of the plants mentioned above and also on bottle-brush, bouvardia, palms, moonflower, passion-flower, plumbago, strelitzia, and wandering-Jew. It can also live outdoors in Alabama and parts of New Mexico but is not so much of a pest there.

The white powder over the back of the citrus mealybug is very dense, and the filaments are about equal length around the body.

Control. A few mealybugs on house plants can be picked off with a toothpick or killed with a cotton swab dipped in alcohol. Keeping foliage washed or syringed off frequently will prevent mealybug infestations. An aerosol bomb containing rotenone and pyrethrum will keep down light infestations but spraying with malathion is more effective (malathion may injure some ferns and crassula). Dimethoate spray is effective but read the label for plants on which it is safe. Greenhouse operators sometimes use parathion.

Coconut Mealybug*, *Nipaecoccus nipae* (Maskell). Palm or Avocado Mealybug. Common in greenhouses, sometimes in lathhouses, sometimes heavily infesting tree palms in southern California. The brown or yellow body is covered with thick plates of creamy, cottony wax. This mealybug formerly heavily infested avocados, mangoes, sapodillas, and palms in southern Florida but parasites make it no longer a serious pest.

Coleman's Mealybug, *Phenacoccus colemani* Ehrhorn. On wild blackberry, wild strawberry, snowberry, Indian paintbrush, and lizardtail in California; also on grass roots, especially in ant nests.

Comstock Mealybug*, *Pseudococcus comstocki* (Kuwana). Catalpa Mealybug. A Japanese pest distributed from Massachusetts to Florida, known in Ohio, Indiana, Louisiana, and also in California. One of the few mealybugs to winter outdoors in temperate climates, it feeds on apple, boxwood, catalpa, holly, grape, horsechestnut, Japanese honeysuckle, magnolia, maple, mulberry, Osage-orange, peach, pear, Monterey pine, poplar, and weigela. It has long been known as a serious pest of umbrella catalpa but is more recently injurious to apple. In addition to injury from sapsucking, the fruit is greatly disfigured with sooty mold growing in honeydew, often coincident with soft rot. When the mealybugs congregate at a split in the tree or at a pruning scar, knotty galls are formed.

The Comstock mealybug winters in the egg stage in bark crevices, hatching when leaves are about an inch long. There is a 2nd generation maturing in late summer in Connecticut, with 3 broods in Virginia. This is a species with 2 longer filaments at the end of the body.

Control. Chief dependence is on parasites. On catalpa and other ornamentals some control is obtained by cleaning all old leaves from the trees and brushing out mealybugs from crotches and crevices with a stiff brush. Thorough washing of trunk and branches with the hose is helpful. Sometimes a dormant spray of oil or lime-sulfur is used, or a summer spray of malathion or carbaryl.

Cypress Mealybug, *Pseudococcus ryani* Coquillett. Present throughout California, most common on Monterey cypress but feeding also on other cypress, arborvitae, araucaria, Norfolk Island pine, incense cedar, redwood. This species has short lateral filaments and a pair of tail filaments ⅓ to ½ the length of the body.

Fruit Mealybug, *Pseudococcus malacearum* Ferris. On citrus, fig, grapes in California.

Golden Mealybug, *Pseudococcus aurilanatus* (Maskell). Introduced into California from Australia and New Zealand on Norfolk Island pine and the monkeypuzzle tree. It is common in southern California and is found up to San Francisco. The body is reddish purple, covered with yellow wax; eggs are purple in a yellow sac.

Grape Mealybug*, *Pseudococcus maritimus* (Ehrhorn). Baker's Mealybug. Another omnivorous feeder. It was originally found on roots of buckwheat in California and occurs also on roots or tops of clover, elder, buckeye, willow. From these it has gone over to cultivated plants, including apple, century plant, California poppy, coleus, columbine, Canary date palm, carnation, grevillea, lima bean, grape, English ivy, ginkgo, laburnum, lemon, orange, Mexican orange, passion-flower, pear, potato, Japanese quince, strawberry, English walnut, and Japanese yew (taxus).

The grape mealybug is present generally in California, where it is most important on grapes and pears in the Santa Clara Valley, on citrus and English walnut in the coastal section, in Florida where it injures avocado, sweetpotato, and tomato and in Ohio where it infests taxus. It is also recorded from scattered localities in Oregon, Michigan, Missouri, and New York. It may be present in quantity on stored gladiolus corms, is carried over in calla-lily tubers to infest foliage later, and spreads a fungus disease of Texas bluebell.

On grape, the mealybug winters as eggs under loose bark, the spring generation developing on buds, leaves, young fruits. The 2nd generation congregates on grape clusters, where excessive honeydew encourages black sooty mold, making grapes entirely unappetizing. Ants help the mealybugs to get about.

Control. Western growers have used a delayed dormant parathion and oil spray with summer applications of monocrotophos or malathion. Gardeners should use malathion or carbaryl. Chlordane to control ants will indirectly reduce mealybugs. There are efficient natural parasites.

Gray Sugarcane Mealybug*, *Dysmicoccus boninsis* (Kuwana).

Ground Mealybug*, *Rhizoecus falcifer* Künckel d'Herculais. Root Mealybug. A European species living on terminal or outer roots of potted plants, especially cacti. It also feeds outdoors in California on roots of grasses, acacia, boxwood, chrysanthemum, currant, Shasta daisy, gooseberry, grape, larkspur, marguerite, orange, peach, pepper, petunia, plum, California privet, thyme, among others. This mealybug differs in being smaller than average and lacking the wax rods and filaments; it is uniformly covered with white waxy powder. It may be a problem on African-violet.

There are several other ground or root mealybugs. *Rhizoecus americanus* is reported in Florida on Norfolk Island pine. *R. cacticans* is recorded in Washington on African-violet and in California on cacti, echeveria, and sempervivum. *R. kondonis* Kuwana may be a problem in California; it is reported heavy on laurel and on roots of lawn grasses, alfalfa, and prune trees. *R. pritchardi* is listed on African-violet in Pennsylvania. *Geococcus coffeae* Green is a root mealybug on dieffenbachia, philodendron, and citrus.

Control. Greenhouse operators may treat soil of potted plants with highly toxic demeton. Chemical control in vineyards seems to be unnecessary.

Hawthorn Mealybug, *Phenacoccus dearnessi* King. On hawthorn and shadbush in the Southwest, abundant on hawthorn and cotoneaster in Illinois. Wintering on trunks, females migrate to outer branches at the end of April (Illinois), feed at base of leaf buds, migrate back to trunk to mate and lay eggs (up to 1,284 for one female). These hatch in a few minutes and young feed on underside of leaves, then migrate to bark.

Japanese Mealybug, *Pseudococcus krauhniae* (Kuwana). Closely related to the citrus mealybug but with an elongated or serpentine egg sac. It infests orange, wisteria, and Japanese persimmon in the Ojai Valley, California.

Juniper Mealybug, *Pseudococcus juniperi* Ehrhorn. A dark-red mealybug on juniper in the Middle West. Another species, *P. aberrans,* is listed on juniper in California.

Loblolly Mealybug, *Dysmicoccus obesus* Lobdell. Originally described from Mississippi and in 1956 found heavily infesting an ornamental planting of loblolly pines in Delaware. Trees were spindly, with sparse foliage, shorter height, with a white powdery deposit, indicating mealybugs under the bark scales. Ants were numerous. A single thorough application of malathion cleaned up this infestation.

Longtailed Mealybug*, *Pseudococcus longispinus* (Targioni-Tozzetti). Widely distributed in greenhouses and outdoors in warm climates. This species has 2 pencil-like filaments at the tail which are as long as, or longer than, the body. Living young are produced instead of eggs. This is the most important mealybug on avocado, killing the scions after grafting, and infests a long list of other plants. It occurs on citrus—orange, grapefruit, lemon—and on banana, begonia, cactus, calla, cineraria, coleus, croton, dracaena, eucalyptus, ferns, fig, fuchsia, gardenia, guava, pandanus, plum, poinsettia, primrose, rubber plant, sago palm, strelitzia, umbrella plant, carob, zinnia.

Control. On avocado, after grafting, dust top 6 inches with 5 per cent chlordane, or paint the area with a slurry made of 2 pounds 50 per cent wettable powder to 1 gallon of water. This controls ants that bring mealybugs. Spray other plants with malathion. Biological control is fairly efficient, with brown and green lacewings particularly useful. Natural enemies, however, can be upset by ants, insecticides, or heavy road dusts.

Mexican Mealybug*, *Phenacoccus gossypii* Townsend & Cockerell. Introduced from Mexico on cotton and now a general greenhouse pest and an outdoor problem in warm climates. It is often serious on chrysanthemum. Hollyhock, geranium, English ivy, lantana, and stock are other favored food plants. It is not much of a pest on citrus but may infest guava and poinsettia. This is a shorttailed mealybug, blue-gray, covered with a thin powder, with posterior filaments ¼ the length of the body. It attacks leaves, stems, flowers in all stages of growth; it causes stunting of chrysanthemums with distortion of foliage.

Control. Fumigation of greenhouses with hydrogen cyanide is quite effective for this Mexican mealybug, and it has been controlled by low-dosage soil treatment with sodium selenate. Phosphate aerosols are also used commercially. Use malathion in gardens, or home greenhouses.

Orchid Mealybug, *Pseudococcus microcirculans* McKenzie. On orchids in Florida and California. This species is oval, ⅛ to ⅙ inch long, amber, with tail filaments slightly longer than laterals. The sac contains 100 to 200 yellowish eggs which hatch in 2 weeks with the crawlers becoming adult in 6 to 8 weeks. Spray with diazinon, dimethoate, malathion, or Meta-Systox-R.

Pineapple Mealybug*, *Dysmicoccus brevipes* (Cockerell). Chiefly a tropical species, sometimes occurring on pineapple, banana, and sugarcane in Louisiana and Florida. This is a toxicogenic insect which causes, by its feeding on plants, a condition known as pineapple wilt.

Pink Sugarcane Mealybug*, *Saccharicoccus sacchari* (Cockerell).

Redwood Mealybug, *Pseudococcus sequoiae* (Coleman). Common on cypress and redwood, distinguished from the cypress mealybug by anal filaments being very short or lacking.

Root Mealybugs. See Ground Mealybug.

Solanum Mealybug, *Pseudococcus solani* Ferris. On paper-white narcissus bulbs in storage, especially in Florida, migrating to roots of these bulbs from ambrosia, aster, malva, pansy, peanut, potato, tomato, and other plants. The body is pale yellow, sparsely covered with fine white powder. Growers can fumigate with calcium cyanide after harvesting and curing.

Spruce Mealybug*, *Puto sandini* Washburn.

Striped Mealybug*, *Ferrisia virgata* (Cockerell). A tropical species, recorded in Texas in 1895 and in Maryland in 1953, also known in Virginia, Florida, and California. It infests azaleas and many other flowering plants. It is recorded on coconut, wisteria, Japanese privet, fatshedera, codiaeum, oriental plane, and catalpa among other hosts. The nymphs are light yellow; the adults are covered with glassy threads several times as long as the body. They do not secrete honeydew. There are at least 2 generations, with nymphs wintering on seed tassels. Spraying with malathion gives control.

Taxus Mealybug, *Dysmicoccus wistariae* (Green) (=*Pseudococcus cuspidatae* Rau). First reported in a New Jersey nursery in 1915, now common in New Jersey, New York, Connecticut, Massachusetts, and probably present on yew over much of the Northeast. All species of taxus are infested, those with dense foliage, like *Taxus cuspidatae nana* and *T. wardi* being preferred. This species has been collected from apple, basswood, cedar, maple, and rhododendron but probably does not breed on these plants. It is very abundant in home gardens. I have treated a yew hedge 100 feet long with trunks and axils of every plant completely covered with mealybugs. But because the insects are on the interior parts, infestations usually go unnoticed until general poor health causes a close examination.

The female is about ⅜ inch long and half as wide, covered with white wax so distributed that the reddish body shows through in 4 longitudinal lines. There are 15 filaments on each side of the body and tail filaments are about ⅓ body length. This species gives birth to living young. Nymphs winter in bark crevices and are mature by June. There is 1 generation a year; adults disappear in early fall.

Control. I used to have excellent luck with nicotine sulfate, 1 to 400 dilution, spraying with sufficient pressure into the interior of the bushes. Experiments in Connecticut indicate that Ethion-oil and Sevin give excellent control. The New Jersey Extension Service suggests a dormant oil plus ethion in April and melathion or Sevin in mid-May and early June.

There is another form of taxus. *Pseudococcus* sp. which feeds on several kinds of yew but is most abundant on *Taxus capitata.* This one has 2 generations, the young of the first appearing in late June or early July (in Connecticut) and the 2nd in September.

White Sage Mealybug, *Pseudococcus crawi* (Coquillett). Feeding on stems and leaves of white sage, artemisia, greasewood, tan oak, and live oak in California. The body is yellow covered with thick plates of white wax. The lateral filaments are ¼ the width of the body and the tail filaments are ⅓ to ½ as long as the body.

Yucca Mealybug. *Puto yuccae* (Coquillett). Found in California, Arizona, and New Mexico. This large species has a pale body entirely covered with thick plates of white, cottony wax. Besides yucca, food plants include artemisia, aster, banana, black sage, ceanothus, eriophyllum, evening primrose, ice-plant, lantana, lemon, lime, monkeyflower. Roots, crowns, or tops may be infested.

MIDGES

Midges are very small flies, 2-winged insects of the order Diptera. The biting midges, punkies and nosee-ums, are human pests. The gall midges or gall gnats are plant pests in the family Cecidomyiidae but not all species cause galls. The plant midges are very minute delicate flies with body and wings clothed with long hairs that rub off easily. The legs are long and slender and the antennae have loops of hair. The larvae are often brightly colored red, pink, yellow, or orange. Some members of this family are parasites on other insects. DDT was particularly effective for the control of certain midges and in some cases we have not yet found a suitable substitute.

Alfalfa Gall Midge*, *Asphondylia websteri* Felt. A serious pest of alfalfa flowers in the Southwest, causing seeds to be bloated.

Apple Leafcurling Midge, *Dasineura mali* Kieffer. An apple pest in New England and New York. Small orange maggots live inside curled edges of leaves on new shoots. The fly is red with iridescent wings.

Artemisia Gall Midges, *Diarthronomyia artemisiae* Felt and other species. In Utah and Colorado, globose bud, rosette or bladder galls are formed on artemisia. In California, brown or reddish subconical galls form on underside of leaves, or white confluent galls on stems, or small, oval, thin-walled, hairy galls on leaf surfaces.

Balsam Gall Midge*, *Dasineura balsamicola* Lintner. Making small, subglobular swellings at base of needles. Rather widespread but not too serious on balsam and Fraser firs, also on Douglas-fir.

Blueberry Tip Midge*, *Contarinia vaccinii* Felt.

Bromegrass Seed Midge*, *Stenodiplosis bromicola* Marikovsky & Agafonova.

Cactus Fruit Gall Midge, *Asphondylia opuntiae* Felt. A small gray midge with white larvae, often present in great numbers on green and ripening fruit of opuntia cactus, leaving brown pupal skins protruding from exit holes. Common in Colorado, California, New Mexico, Texas.

Catalpa Midge*, *Cecidomyia catalpae* (Comstock). A yellow fly, $\frac{1}{16}$ inch long, appearing in late May or early June, lays eggs on unfolding catalpa leaves. Whitish to orange maggots occur in great numbers close to midrib and large veins on underside of leaves. There are several generations. Maggot injury looks like a fungus disease, with circular dead spots on the leaves and later wilting, browning, crumpling, defoliation. Late in the season maggots enter pods and destroy seeds. Persistent killing of terminal buds stunts and dwarfs trees. The midge winters as pupae in the soil. Cultivate the soil beneath trees to destroy pupae; spray in late May with malathion.

Cattleya Midge, *Parallelodiplosis cattleyae* (Moll). Yellowish maggots, $\frac{1}{8}$ inch long, feed in tips of roots of many kinds of orchids, causing nutlike galls. Cut off and destroy galls.

Chrysanthemum Gall Midge*, *Diarthronomyia chrysanthemi* Ahlberg. Limited to chrysanthemums, all varieties in greenhouse or garden. The frail, long-legged orange gnat, $\frac{1}{14}$ inch long, lays about 100 minute orange eggs on new shoots (Plate XXVIII). Hatching in 3 to 16 days, white, yellow, or orange maggots bore into tissues. The irritation of their feeding causes many cone-shaped galls on upper surface of leaves and on stems, where a number together often form knots. Developing buds are distorted and ruined; stems are twisted. When flies emerge from the galls, usually between midnight and 4 A.M., they leave protruding empty pupal cases. The life cycle is about 35 days with 5 or 6 generations a year on greenhouse chrysanthemums. I usually find 2 in gardens.

Control. Pick off infested foliage. Spray in the evening with lindane; repeat 3 times at 5-day intervals to kill emerging flies and larvae in galls. Parathion is sometimes used in greenhouses by commercial operators.

Clover Leaf Midge*, *Dasineura trifolii* (Loew).

Clover Seed Midge*, *Dasineura leguminicola* (Lintner). Clover Flower Midge. Serious on red clover.

Cranberry Tipworm Midge, *Dasineura vaccinii* Smith. Runners are cupped together, with 1 to 5 maggots in each tip. Growers may use parathion.

Cucurbit Midge*, *Cecidomyia citrulli* (Felt).

Dogwood Clubgall Midge*, *Mycodiplosis clavula* (Beutenmüller). Common on flowering dogwood, a club-shaped gall, ½ to 1 inch long, in twigs. The reddish brown midge attacks young shoots in late May; development of small orange larvae in galls is completed by September when they drop to the ground. Cut off and destroy swollen twigs while larvae are present.

Douglas Fir Cone Midge, *Contarinia oregonensis* Foote. Causes loss of seed in local areas. A dimethoate spray is promising.

False Leafmining Midge, *Cricotopus ornatus*. Sometimes present on waterlily. Larvae of a small fly mine in serpentine tunnels, followed by bacteria. New leaves turn brown and rot.

Gouty Pitchgall Midge, *Cecidomyia piniinopsis* (Osten Sacken). Small orange maggots feeding on tender bark of pine twigs, mostly in the Southeast and Northwest, causing globular masses of resin.

Grape Blossom Midge*, *Contarinia johnsoni* Felt. Sometimes attacking blossoms and buds and preventing fruit development. Eggs are laid in buds, reddish maggots develop, feed, drop to the ground to pupate in a little more than 2 weeks, remaining there until the next spring.

Grape Gall Midge, *Cecidomyia viticola* Osten Sacken. Small conical reddish or greenish leaf galls, ¼ inch long; also on flowers, vines, and tendrils.

Grapevine Tomato Gall Midge, *Lasioptera vitis* Osten Sacken. A green or reddish swelling in new growth, leaf, or tendril, ¼ to ¾ inch long, with pinkish maggots inside.

Holly Berry Midge, *Asphondylia ilicicola* Foote. Reported from Connecticut, Delaware, District of Columbia, Maryland, New Jersey, Virginia, and West Virginia. Holly berries fail to ripen and turn red, remaining green all year. Infested berries are smaller than normal and seeds fail to develop properly. Berries average 1 to 3 lemon-yellow maggots, and these winter in the berry. Adult flies, small, weak fliers, emerge in late May and early June (in Connecticut), and deposit eggs on small fruits, the maggots eating through into the seed. In experimental spraying, lindane, thiodan, and diazinon, applied on June 1 in Connecticut, were effective in control.

Honeylocust Podgall Midge, *Dasineura gleditchiae* Osten Sacken. Widely distributed, important in Indiana, Ohio, Connecticut, and other states, especially in nurseries and on Moraine locust. In severe infestations all leaflets may become podlike galls, dry up and drop prematurely. Adult midges appear in April as new growth starts. Males are black, females have a red abdomen; they are ⅛ inch long. Minute kidney-shaped eggs are inserted in young leaflets; the larvae hatch in a day or two and feed on the inner surface, stopping its development. The outer surface grows normally, thus producing the pod. There may be 5 to 7 broods. Spray with lindane about mid-May and repeat in 10 days.

Juniper Midge, *Contarinia juniperina* Felt. Yellow maggots cause blisters at base of needles which may drop; tips die. Larvae winter in the soil and flies lay eggs on needles in April. Control by pruning dead tips and cultivating soil or treating it with lindane.

Juniper Tip Midge*, *Oligotrophus betheli* Felt.

Maple Leafspot Midge, *Cecidomyia ocellaris* Osten Sacken. Ocellate Leaf Gall. Small galls with cherry-red margins, less than ½ inch in diameter, are formed on red maple. The injury is not important.

Monterey Pine Midge, *Thecodiplosis pini-radiatae* Snow & Mills. A common and serious pest of Monterey pine in California, also present on other pines and Monterey cypress. Minute dark flies lay orange eggs in masses on terminal buds from January to March; orange maggots feed at base of needles until November or December, then pupate in soil. Needles are shortened, yellow, swollen at base. Trees are weakened, look as if swept by fire, and drop needles; some trees die. Cultivate around trees in early winter to destroy pupae.

Monterey Pine Resin Midge*, *Cecidomyia resinicoloides* Williams. A pitch midge living in the resin exudations of Monterey pine but not particularly injurious.

Pear Midge*, *Contarinia pyrivora* (Riley). The fly deposits eggs in pear-blossom buds in late April or May. When full-grown the maggots drop to the ground or remain in fruit, which becomes bloated, lopsided with dark blotches, and drops early.

Pearleaf Midge, *Dasineura pyri* Kieffer. Rolls or folds pear leaves.

Portulaca Gall Midge, *Neolasioptera portulacae* (Cook). Collected in Florida in 1962 as a new North American record.

Rhododendron Tip Midge, *Giardomyia rhododendri* Felt. Young leaves are rolled, swollen, with margin browned by small, whitish maggots. New growth does not develop properly. Spray tips with lindane.

Rose Midge*, *Dasineura rhodophaga* (Coquillett). Confined to roses, a greenhouse pest since 1886, first reported in gardens in 1916 and now found in scattered localities in many states. It arrives in a garden with unbelievable suddenness and works with devastating

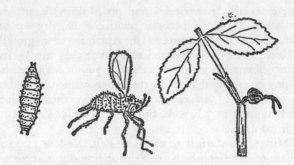

60. Rose midge: maggot, adult, and dead bud.

thoroughness, more often in mid or late summer. A rose flower garden is changed almost overnight into a green garden with every potential bud in a leaf axil black and crisp, every tiny new shoot dead, buds on pedicels twisted, deformed, blackened.

The adult—minute, $\frac{1}{20}$ inch long, reddish or yellow-brown—lays small, yellowish eggs on succulent growth, under sepals of flower buds, in unfolding leaves. In warm weather they hatch in 2 days and young whitish maggots feed at base of flowers, often 20 or 30 in a bud, or on upper side of leaves and leaf petioles, causing them to become distorted, turn brown, and die (XXVIII). They reach maturity, orange, $\frac{1}{12}$ inch long, in about a week. They fall to the ground to pupate in small white cocoons, and new adults appear in 5 to 7 days. The life cycle takes 12 to 16 days in greenhouses, longer out of doors.

Control. The old recommendation of tobacco dust and mulch was largely ineffective. When DDT came along it gave almost complete control when applied thoroughly to bushes and ground. Now that we may no longer use DDT I know of no satisfactory substitute. Various chemicals have been suggested but apparently have not been used in controlled experiments. It may help to prune off into a paper bag for the garbage every infested bud or shoot, visiting the rose garden daily for this purpose.

Sorghum Midge*, *Contarinia sorghicola* (Coquillett).

Spruce Bud Midge*, *Rhapdophaga swainei* Felt.

Spruce Gall Midge, *Phytophaga piceae* Felt. Eggs are laid at base of needles of new shoots or under bud scales. Larvae, up to 100 in a shoot, live in galls similar to those caused by spruce gall aphids.

Sunflower Seed Midge*, *Neolasioptera murtfeldtiana* Felt. Sunflower seeds are infested but the exterior appears normal.

Violet Gall Midge, *Phytophaga violicola* Coquillett. The small fly lays white eggs in curled margins of unfolding new violet leaves. The maggots cause curling, distortion, twisting of leaves, followed by a wet rot. Infested plants are dwarfed; blossoming is rather limited. Clean up fallen leaves frequently.

Willowbeaked Gall Midge*, *Mayetiola rigidae* (Osten Sacken). A fusiform gall, with a beak 1 inch long, near the tip of the stem. Often found on pussy willow.

MILLIPEDES

Millipedes, "thousand-legged worms," class Diplopoda, are long, hard-shelled, cyclindrical, with 2 pairs of legs on each of their many

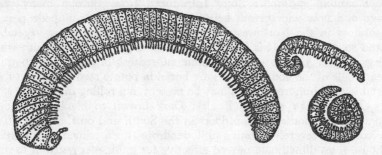

61. Millipede, much enlarged, and in typical positions.

body segments. They are brown or pinkish brown, occasionally grayish, about an inch long, rarely up to 2 inches, and are usually found coiled up like a watch spring. Many gardeners confuse them with wireworms, which are also hard-shelled but these are flat, not round in cross section, have only the 6 legs of a true insect, and do not coil up like a spring (compare Plates XXIII and XXIX). Millipedes have 30 to 400 legs, not 1,000, and short antennae, usually 7-segmented. Some give off an evil-smelling liquid through pores along the body.

Millipedes are useful as scavengers, feeding on decaying vegetable matter and manure, and a few are predaceous, but they may eat small roots or seedlings and bean, corn, or pea seed. They slide into cabbage heads to horrify the cook, tunnel into potato tubers or into carrots, beets, parsnips, or turnips. Fruits that touch damp ground, especially muskmelon, tomatoes, or strawberries, are often entered by these wiry worms. They are frequently found in decaying bulbs but are seldom the original cause of decay. Chief injury is in greenhouses in soil rich in organic matter. They are sometimes found in camellia grafts, injuring young leaves.

Each female deposits about 300 eggs, in clusters of 20 to 100, in soil or on the surface. The eggs are nearly translucent and are covered with a sticky material. They hatch in about 3 weeks. Young millipedes have at first only 3 pairs of legs and fewer segments than the adults. They grow slowly and there is probably only 1 generation a year.

To control millipedes, spray or dust soil with diazinon, Sevin, or malathion, cover all hiding places in greenhouses with the chemical. In gardens, protect ripening fruits with salt hay or other mulch. Destroy refuse.

Millipedes are seldom differentiated by gardeners but species sometimes mentioned in reports include:

Blaniulus guttulatus Bosc. Introduced from Europe many years ago and now widespread, being the most common millipede pest of potatoes in the Northwest. It may also infest many other vegetables and some flowers. It is just over ½ inch long, light brown with white legs—55 to 75 pairs—with prominent reddish-brown ovate spots on each side of the body. Tunnels are bored in potato seed pieces or tubers and several hundred worms may be present in a rolling mass.

Orthomorpha gracilis (Koch). Dark brown to black, a common pest in greenhouses and outdoors in the South and on the West Coast, recorded as severely infesting philodendron. In experiments with greenhouse roses dimethoate proved effective for millipedes resistant to malathion and lindane.

Orthomorpha coearctata (Sauss). Often numerous in lawns in Florida but apparently not very harmful. They may be controlled by spraying the area with chlordane.

Some millipede species, such as *Callipus lactarius* Risso and *Cambala annulata* (Say), are carnivorous, eating insects, and so to be classed as beneficial.

MITES

Mites are not true insects. They belong to the animal class Arachnida, which includes spiders, scorpions, harvestmen (daddy longlegs), and ticks, all grouped together by having 4 pairs of legs instead of the 3 pairs of legs characterizing members of the insect class Insecta. Arachnids also differ from insects in lacking antennae, true jaws, and compound eyes, and in having only 2 body regions, head and thorax being joined together into a cephalothorax. Mites, members of the order Acarina, differ further in having the body seemingly all one piece, without segments. Young mites have only 3 pairs of legs, the 4th pair being added at maturity. Ticks are large members of the order Acarina; mites are the very small, almost microscopic forms.

Many mites are injurious to human beings or to animals. The families listed here include only those having members that are injurious to plants or are beneficial predators on plant pests.

Acaridae. Acarid mites. A large family with members living on all kinds of organic substances, including cheese, dried meats, flour, and seeds. The bulb mite belongs here.

Carpoglyphidae. Driedfruit mites.

Eriophyidae. Gall or blister mites. Very minute, elongate, with only 2 pairs of legs, causing pouch or blister galls on leaves or a rusty appearance to foliage, or bud injury. The pear leaf blister mite and citrus rust mite are prominent examples.

Tarsonemidae. Soft-bodied mites, with the cyclamen mite common and injurious. They are very small, flat, pale, with short legs.

Tenuipalpidae. False spider mites.

Tetranychidae. Red spiders, spider mites. Small, oval, varying from yellow, green, red, or brown; moderately long legs; a few hairs arranged in longitudinal rows on the back; web-spinning.

Trombidiidae. Harvest mites. Resembling red spiders but larger. A bright-red species commonly found in moist leaf litter is a scavenger and not a pest. This family includes chiggers, which attack man.

With the advent of DDT and some other new chemicals mites increased enormously in importance. This has been due to the killing off of beneficial predators and parasites and apparently, in some cases, to a direct effect on the plant tissues—predisposing them in some way to mite injury—and to an effect on the mites themselves—making them more active. Carbaryl (Sevin) has largely replaced DDT for home garden use and this, too, increases the mite problem. It is often necessary to add a miticide to the carbaryl spray. Many excellent miticides have been developed, some very toxic to humans and to be used with caution, others relatively safe. Presently available garden miticides include dimethoate, Kelthane, Meta-Systox-R, Omite, Plictran, and tetradifon. Mites often become resistant to a chemical and another must be substituted.

Apple Rust Mite*, *Aculus schlechtendali* (Nalepa). A western pest, prevalent in Washington; controlled by Thiodan at prebloom. Also reported from Vermont and Indiana.

Ash Flowergall Mite, *Aceria fraxinivorus* (Nalepa). Stamens and flowers of white ash are transformed into galls, ¼ to ¾ inch in diameter, which dry and remain on trees. Spray with Kelthane after buds swell but before new growth begins.

Avocado Brown Mite*, *Oligonychus punicae* (Hirst). On avocado in California, sometimes causing defoliation but not as serious as other mites. It is dark brown, makes light, delicate webbing, has amber eggs. Biological control usually holds this mite in check.

Avocado Red Mite*, *Oligonychus yothersi* (McGregor). The most common pest of avocado in Florida, also attacking mango, camphor, Australian silk oak, and camellias. It has been reported from elm, oak, and pecan in South Carolina. The mites are reddish purple, oval, with immature states greenish. Eggs are laid singly on both leaf surfaces. Leaves are speckled or russeted along the midrib and may drop off. Dusting with sulfur has been quite satisfactory. On avocado, parathion has given a good initial kill but is followed by an increase in mites. Dimethoate may be used on camellias to control mites as well as scale.

Azalea Mite, *Aculus atlantazaleae* Keifer. On terminal buds.

Balsam Root Mite, *Rhizogloephus sagittatae* Faust. Pale-yellow mite on tender leaves of balsam root (Balsamorhiza).

Bamboo Mite, *Schizotetranychus celarius* (Banks). A spider mite known only on bamboo, in Florida, Georgia, California; forming restricted colonies on underside of leaves and living under dense webbing.

Banks Grass Mite*, *Oligonychus pratensis* (Banks). Also known as Date Mite. Common on grasses and grains in western states, occasional on grasses elsewhere. An important pest of date palms in California, also on Washingtonia and Canariensis palms near date gardens, occasional on maple, cypress, and other ornamental trees. The small, pale-yellow mite webs leaves and fruits together; the fruit is scurfy, shriveled, cracked, yellow. The mites winter on grasses and small palm seedlings. Dusting with sulfur is effective.

Beech Mite, *Aceria fagerinea* Keifer.

Beet Mite, *Rhizogloephus torsalis* Banks. On sugar beets and dried figs.

Bermudagrass Mite*, *Aceria cynodoniensis* Sayed. First found on Bermuda grass in an Arizona lawn in 1959, now known in California, Florida, Georgia, New Mexico, Nevada, Oklahoma, and Texas. Mites are most numerous in well-fertilized lawns. The internodes are shortened, resulting in rosetting and tufting of growth; plants are killed, lawns are thinned. Diazinon may control.

Blackberry Bud Mite. See Dryberry Mite.

Blueberry Bud Mite*, *Acalitus vaccinii* (Keifer). Blossom buds may be so deformed they do not set fruit, or the berries have rough, blistered skin. The mites live all year under leaf or fruit-bud scales but can be controlled with a post-harvest spray of a summer oil. Or spray with Thiodan.

Boreal Mite. See Yellow Spider Mite.

Boxwood Mite, *Eurytetranychus buxi* (Garman). Rather general on boxwood. Injury shows as a light mottling of leaves early in the season, followed by a general grayish, dingy, unhealthy appearance. What appear to be minute hen scratches on foliage are an early indication of mites at work. The mites are yellow-green or reddish, $\frac{1}{64}$ inch long. Yellow eggs winter on leaves, hatch in April. The mites breed rapidly with 5 or 6 generations in a summer. Dusting with sulfur has been recommended in the past, or a dormant oil spray before growth starts but spraying with tetradifon, Kelthane, diazinon, or dimethoate may be preferable.

Broad Mite*, *Polyphagotarsonemus latus* (Banks). Often associated with cyclamen mite and causing similar injury in greenhouses and in gardens. The broad mite is pale, almost translucent, slightly smaller and wider than the cyclamen mite. It moves more rapidly and feeds exposed on undersurface of leaves, completing its life cycle in 7 or 8 days. The injury is a blistered and glassy or silvery appearance to the leaf, which may become rather brittle, and sometimes a puckering downward. The broad mite attacks many ornamentals—cyclamen, delphinium, snapdragon, African-violet, begonia, china aster, marguerite, chrysanthemum, fuchsia, lantana, gerbera, geranium, marigold, verbena, zinnia—also avocado, mango, guava, and citrus seedlings in greenhouses. Sulfur dust has given control, or try one of the new miticides.

Brown Mite*, *Bryobia rubrioculus* (Sheuten). Fruittree Mite. Prevalent in western states—California, Colorado, New Mexico, Oregon, Utah, Washington—damaging young foliage of almond, apple, pear, peach, apricot, and cherry; also found on alder.

Bugle Bud Mite, *Aceria ajugae* (Nalepa). Reported from ajuga (bugleweed) in California.

Bulb Mite*, *Rhizoglyphus echinopus* (Fumouze & Robin). Injuring bulbs or corms of amaryllis, crocus, freesia, gladiolus, hyacinth, lily, narcissus, onion, tulip, and underground stems of asparagus, peony, and a few other plants. The mite is whitish, often with 2 brown spots on the body, $\frac{1}{50}$ to $\frac{1}{25}$ inch long, slow-moving, found in colonies. It is abundant on rotting bulbs and decaying plant material but it can also burrow into healthy bulbs and carry bacteria and fungi that produce rots. The mites spread infection from diseased to healthy bulbs in field, greenhouse, and storage.

The mite develops into a 6-legged larva, lasting 3 to 8 days, ending in a quiescent state. It molts into a protonymph with 8 legs, feeds for 2 to 4 days, has a second resting period, and molts into a tritonymph, then finally into the adult form. If conditions are unfavorable after the second molt, the mite goes into a heavily chitinized, nonfeeding but active stage, the hypopus, in which it attaches itself to any moving object, perhaps a mouse or a fly, and so is transported to a new breeding place. The minute, white semitransparent eggs are laid on surface of bulbs or in decaying tissue between the scales.

Control. Discard rotting or soft bulbs containing mites. Immerse others in hot water held at 111° F. for 1 hour. Systox applied as a soil drench to potted bulbs controls mites but at high concentrations causes some plant injury. Daffodil bulbs soaked in 25 W Tedion for 24 and 48 hours had mites killed when ⅛ pound was used in 12 gallons of water. Predaceous mites attack bulb mites.

Bulb Scale Mite*, *Steneotarsonemus laticeps* (Halbert). Related to the cyclamen mite and not associated with rots, as is the bulb mite. These mites feed between leaves and flowers in neck region of the bulb which becomes soft and spongy. Bulbs have yellow-brown, scarlike streaks; flowers and foliage are severely injured. Narcissus and amaryllis are more seriously injured when forced in greenhouses than when grown in fields. Treat by immersing in hot water (111° F.) for 30 minutes.

Carmine Spider Mite*, *Tetranychus cinnabarinus* (Boisduval). Southern Twospotted Mite. One of the red spiders, similar to the twospotted mite but carmine in color; most important in southern states but present elsewhere. This mite is frequently reported as a pest of melons, is common on cotton, and recorded in philodendron, mulberry, sugar beet, and other, widely varying, types of plants.

Camellia Bud Mite, *Aceria camelliae* Keifer. Reported from Alabama, California, and Florida causing a bud drop of camellias with brownish discoloration of tips and edges of young petals; associated with two camellia flower blights caused by fungi. Spraying with dimethoate may be helpful.

Carnation Mite, *Aceria paradianthi* Keifer. On carnations in California.

Citrus Bud Mite*, *Aceria sheldoni* (Ewing). Found on lemon in California in 1937, causing blasted or multiple buds, deformed twigs or leaves, blossoms or fruits, bunched growth, blackening of rind beneath fruit buttons. Also present, but less important, on other citrus varieties in southern California. An oil spray every 6 to 8 months has given good control.

Citrus Flat Mite*, *Brevipalpus lewisi* McGregor. False spider mite, reported also on privet. It can be controlled with sulfur dust or Kelthane.

Another flat mite (*B phoenicis*) is reported severe on Murcott orange in Florida.

Citrus Red Mite*, *Panonychus citri* (McGregor). Purple Mite in Florida, Red Spider to many citrus growers, more serious in arid California than in most Gulf States. Recently reported in Arizona. This mite prefers lemons in California, satsuma oranges along the Gulf, but infests other oranges and grapefruit. Foliage is speckled silver, may turn brown and drop; fruit is gray or yellow and the crop light. Eggs are red, with a vertical stalk, laid on fruit, twigs, leaves. Larvae are at first orange, later dark red; adult females are almost black; males are lighter red but with a dark band around the body. They have red tubercles with white bristles.

Control. Oil sprays applied for scale insects keep down citrus red mites. Specific miticides may be used. Three sprays per year of malathion have been successful in Florida.

Citrus Rust Mite*, *Phyllocoptruta oleivora* (Ashmead). More serious in the Gulf States than in California, injuring orange, grapefruit, lemon, lime, and other citrus fruit. A severe attack starts as faint black areas on green oranges, increasing until the whole fruit looks rusty, dry, rough. Outer cells are killed, size is reduced, rind thickened, quality impaired. The mite is long, wedge-shaped, orange as an adult, only $\frac{1}{150}$ inch long. Yellow eggs are laid in depressions on fruit or on leaves. Cycles are completed in 10 days or less and mites are present through the year in Florida, but least numerous in January and February. Sulfur is a specific for rust-mite. It may be applied as lime-sulfur, 1 to 50 or 1 to 100 dilution, or as a wettable sulfur spray, or as sulfur dust with 3 to 6 applications a year.

Clover Mite*, *Bryobia praetiosa* Koch. On clover, alfalfa, and other forage plants and on lawns and shrubbery around houses. This mite is also a great annoyance indoors, entering houses in large numbers in autumn but not actively injuring furnishings. This mite has been reported on almond and many fruit trees but has probably been confused with the Brown Mite (*B. rubrioculus*). In southern states the mite winters on various clovers and malva but in the North it winters as small red eggs, looking like brick dust. These hatch in early spring. Young mites are red, adults rusty brown, larger than other mites, with front legs longer than others. Their feeding causes foliage to turn yellow and drop.

Control. The luxuriant well-fertilized grass around new dwellings is a factor in the increase of clover mites. Keeping an 18-inch grass-free band around houses and trees will markedly reduce infestations in houses, for the mites migrate between the grass, where they feed, and dwellings or trees where they oviposit and molt. Outside walls of houses and a 10-foot band of grass can be sprayed with diazinon or chlorobenzilate. Indoors use aerosols containing pyrethrins.

Currant Bud Mite*, *Cecidophyopsis ribis* (Westwood). Injurious to black, native, and flowering currants. The buds swell and die before opening, after which mites emerge to infest buds on normally developing canes. Cut out infested shoots; dust with sulfur in early spring.

Cyclamen Mite*, *Steneotarsonemus pallidus* (Banks). Pallid Mite, Strawberry Crown Mite. First noted in New York in 1898 and now present throughout the country as a greenhouse and garden pest. It is particularly injurious to cyclamen, snapdragon, and African-violet indoors, but the greenhouse list includes ageratum, azalea, begonia, gerbera, marguerite, lantana, marigold, verbena, zinnia. Outdoors this mite is probably the worst enemy of delphinium, deforms aconite and snapdragon, is often the limiting factor in strawberry production, may infest peppers and tomatoes.

The mite is too small to see with the naked eye but it can be readily identified by the characteristic reaction of the plants on which it feeds. Cyclamen infested early does not flower; later infestation produces distorted, streaked, or blotched blooms that fall early, with wrinkled, purplish foliage curled into cups (Plate XXX). African-violets are stunted, have twisted stems. Delphinium leaves are thickened, puckered without normal indentations; flower stalks are gnarled, twisted, darkened; buds turn black and seldom open; the whole plant may be stunted to ¼th normal height. Mite injury on delphinium is often known as "blacks" and thought to be a disease caused by a fungus or bacterium. Mites feeding in young, unfolding leaves of strawberries cause stunting, distortion, chlorosis, browning, and shriveling of flowers and no fruit.

The young cyclamen mite is glassy white or transparent pale green, ¹⁄₁₀₀ inch long, slow-moving; the adult is pale brown. The female lays 5 or 6 eggs a day for 2 or 3 weeks at the base of the plant or in crevices about leaves and buds. They hatch in a week into 6-legged larvae which are active for 7 days, then quiescent for 3 days before changing to the 8-legged adults. This is a cool-weather mite, injuring delphinium from early spring to June and in late summer, but seldom active in the heat of midsummer.

Control. Keep this pest out if you can. Purchase only perfect, healthy specimens, whether delphinium for the garden or African-violets for the home. Buy certified strawberries. Space plants indoors so they do not touch; avoid handling clean plants after touching those possibly infested. Discard heavily infested plants. Valuable plants lightly infested can be immersed in hot water at 110° F. for 15 minutes. Strawberry plants can be treated for 20 minutes in water preheated to 100° F. Kelthane is effective for the cyclamen mite and is safe for

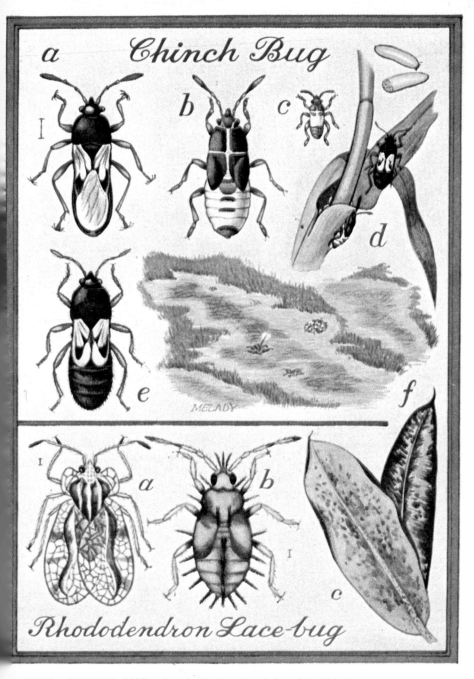

Chinch Bug

Rhododendron Lace-bug

MELADY

XVII CHINCH BUG: (a) long-winged adult; (b) fifth instar; (c) nymph, first instar. HAIRY CHINCH BUG: (d) eggs, much enlarged, and bugs in typical position behind boot of lower grass blade; (e) short-winged adult; (f) turf with brown areas killed by bugs and yellow margins where bugs are working. RHODO-DENDRON LACE BUG: (a) adult; (b) nymph in last stage of development; (c) rhododendron leaves showing browning of lower surface and loss of color on upper surface.

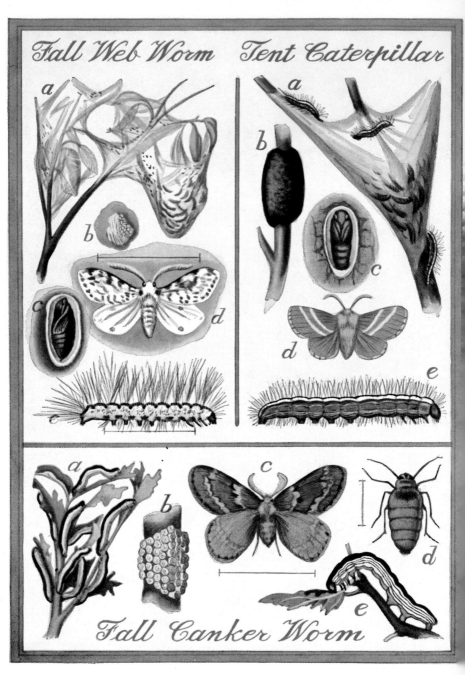

XVIII FALL WEBWORM: (a) web or nest over end of branches; (b) egg mass covered with hairs on underside of leaf; (c) pupa in cocoon in soil; (d) adult moth; (e) full-grown hairy caterpillar. EASTERN TENT CATERPILLAR: (a) nest of caterpillars in tree crotch; (b) egg collar around twig; (c) pupa inside cocoon on bark; (d) adult moth; (e) full-grown caterpillar. FALL CANKER-WORM: (a) larvae ravaging foliage; (b) egg mass on twig; (c) male moth; (d) wingless female moth; (e) full-grown caterpillar with 3 prolegs.

Tomato Hornworm

Celery Caterpillar

XIX TOBACCO HORNWORM, on Tomato: (a) adult moth, natural size; (b) egg on leaflet and egg enlarged; (c) larva with "horn"; (d) pupa in soil. CELERY-WORM: (a) chrysalid; (b) male butterfly, black swallowtail; (c) caterpillar on celery; (d) front view showing forked horn.

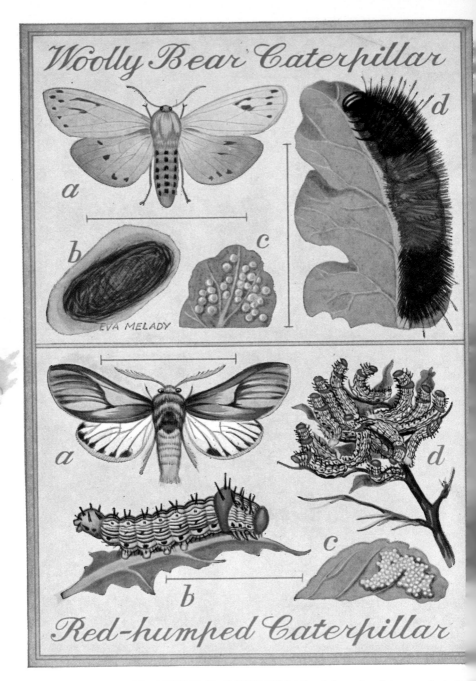

Woolly Bear Caterpillar

Red-humped Caterpillar

XX BANDED WOOLLYBEAR CATERPILLAR: (a) moth; (b) pupa in hair
cocoon; (c) eggs; (d) hairy caterpillar. RED-HUMPED CATERPILLAR: (a
moth; (b) larva with red head and hump; (c) eggs; (d) caterpillars in typica
position.

home garden use. Endosulfan is also satisfactory but needs more caution in use.

Cypress Mites, *Oligonychus coniferarum* (McGregor) and *Eotetranychus libocedri* (McGregor). In western and southwestern states on cypress, Italian cypress, and incense cedar.

Date Mite. See Banks Grass Mite.

Desert Spider Mite*, *Tetranychus desertorum* Banks. Widespread through southern United States on a variety of plants—cactus, carrot, celery, corn, cotton, cucumber, melon, strawberry, and monkeyflower, sweetpea, sunflower, gladiolus, and zinnia.

Driedfruit Mite*, *Carpoglyphus lactis* (Linnaeus). Light-colored, on dried figs, raisins, prunes.

Dryberry Mite*, *Phyllocoptes gracilis* (Nalepa). Blackberry Bud Mite. White, on developing drupelets of Himalaya blackberry.

European Red Mite*, *Panonychus ulmi* (Koch). An imported species first noted in 1911, now serious in the Northeast and Northwest, particularly damaging following use of DDT and perhaps carbaryl in orchards. It is most injurious to apple, pear, plum, prune, but may infest almond, walnut, citrus, and ornamental trees and shrubs, including mountain-ash, elm, black locust, and rose. Bright-red to orange eggs, each with a stalk, winter on twigs and branches, often in crevices of fruit spurs. They hatch in spring just before blooming. The 1st nymphal stage is bright red, the 2nd and 3rd dull green or brown. The adult female is velvety red with 4 rows of curved spines arising from white tubercles; $\frac{1}{50}$ inch long. Foliage is speckled and turns a sickly bronze, looking as if covered with dust, but there is not much webbing. Fruit buds are weakened, many leaves drop. Fruit is undersized, of poor quality. Pearleaf scorch is associated with this mite.

Control. Superior oil applied to apples at the half-inch green stage or earlier is important. Choice of summer acaricides depends on what resistance has been built up. Kelthane and Tedion may be used by home gardeners as well as orchardists. The fungicides Morestan and Karathane seem to markedly reduce mites.

False Spider Mites. There are several species that may be important but do not have common names. *Brevipalpus phoenicis* (Geijskes) which occurs on several plants in Hawaii is common in Florida and Texas in unsprayed citrus groves. It causes swellings on stems, foliar chlorosis, and leaf drop. A single spraying with wettable sulfur or chlorobenziliate is said to eradicate the mite. *B. californicus* (Banks) also occurs on citrus in Florida as well as California. *B australis* (Tucker) may be the cause or the vector of leprosis or Florida scaly bark. *B. lilium* is reported causing azaleas in Alabama to turn rusty brown. *B. essigi* may be a problem on fuchsia in California.

Pentamerismus taxi is a false spider mite recorded as causing extensive damage to yew in Illinois and reported also from Oregon and Maryland.

Fig Mite*, *Aceria ficus* (Cotte). Fig Rust Mite. First reported in California in 1922, now present in Oregon and Florida, probably elsewhere. Eggs are laid in the bud, on leaves, or on branches. The mites are very small, invisible to the naked eye, and are present on terminal buds and young leaves. From 10 to several hundred may infest a single bud, causing defoliation. The fig mite also transmits the virus of fig mosaic and scars the inner surface of fig fruit, causing dead areas for development of sooty mold. Oil sprays are helpful.

Filbert Bud Mite*, *Phytoptus avellanae* Nalepa. Filbert Bigbud. Buds are swollen to 2 or 3 times normal size, with no further development into foliage. In May, when mites leave swollen buds and start crawling to normal buds, some can be killed with an acaricide.

Fourspotted Spider Mite*, *Tetranychus canadensis* (McGregor). Widespread on trees in eastern and southwestern states. Hosts include apple, plum, elm, linden, horsechestnut, Osage-orange, poplar, rose, and umbrellatree.

Fruittree Mite. See Brown Mite.

Gardenia Mite, *Eriophyes gardeniella* Keifer. A pest known in Mexico and Hawaii, reported on gardenia in Florida in 1965.

Garman Spider Mite, *Eotetranychus uncatus* Garman. A fruittree pest in New England, damaging foliage by feeding on undersurface of leaves, causing a crinkled effect. Leaves may be bronzed and, in severe infestations, trees may be completely defoliated and the fruit small. The adult, flesh-colored to lemon-yellow, more elongate than most mites, winters on the tree.

Germander Leafcrinkle Mite, *Aculodes teucrii*. The first report in the United States was from Ohio in 1960, with moderate damage on germander. It is also present in California.

Grape Erineum Mite*, *Eriophyes vitis* (Pagenstecher). A very small mite, overwintering in grape buds and feeding on underside of leaves in spring, causing a superfluous growth of leaf hairs called an erineum, first white, later turning brown. A strain of the erineum mite, called the **Grape Bud Mite,** does not produce erinea. It spends the entire year in buds and leaf axils.

Grape Rust Mite, *Calopitrimerus vitis* (Nalepa). Leaves of white grapes turn yellow, those of black grapes turn red. Sulfur dust controls this eriophyid mite.

Grass Mite, *Siteroptes graminum*. A vector of Fusarium bud rot on carnation and silver top of various grasses.

Grevillea Mite, *Tuckerella pavoniformis* (Ewing). Tuckerellid Mite. On silk-oak in Florida, also reported on redbud and ligustrum.

Hackberry Witchesbroom Mite, *Eriophyes* sp. Associated with a powdery mildew fungus in the formation of witchesbrooms so common on hackberry in eastern states.

Hemlock Mite, *Nalepella tsugifoliae*. Reported on unthrifty hemlock in Michigan, New York, Rhode Island, and Virginia.

Honeylocust Spider Mite, *Eotetranychus multidigituli* (Ewing). Only on honeylocust, *Gleditsia triacanthos*, but widespread, a serious pest in Indiana, Ohio, Illinois, found also in Connecticut, Pennsylvania, North Carolina, Washington, D.C., and Louisiana. The color of the larva changes from pale yellow to dark green as it feeds. The adult is green in summer, orange-red in winter. Infested leaves are stippled yellow and may drop. Spray with Kelthane or Tedion in July; repeat as necessary.

Hydrangea Mite, *Tetranychus hydrangeae*. Reported on hydrangea in California.

Juniper Bud Mite, *Trisetacus quadrisetus* or *T. juniperinus*. Reported in California and Washington as stunting and destroying buds of prostrate juniper.

Lewis Spider Mite, *Eotetranychus lewisi* (McGregor). A citrus pest along the Pacific Coast, causing silvering of lemons and russeting of oranges, recorded also on ceanothus, castor-bean, and olive; a pest of poinsettia in greenhouses in the Northwest and in Florida. The foliage is speckled or peppered, turns pale, and there may be webbing near the flower. Kelthane and parathion have been reported effective in control.

Linden Mite, *Eriophyes tiliae*. On linden in California. A gall mite, *Phytoptus abnormis*, is also reported on linden.

Litchi Mite, *Aceria litchii* Keifer.

Mango Bud Mite, *Aceria mangiferae* (Hassan). A serious pest of mango in Hawaii, reported in Florida in 1960. Terminal buds are dark brown, terminal leaves drop off from some branches; new leaves are deformed.

Maple Bladdergall Mite*, *Vasates quadripedes* Shimer. Bladder-like galls—first red, then green, then black, single or in clusters—appear on upper surface of leaves. They may be thick enough to deform the leaves, injury being more serious on young silver or soft maples. White or pinkish mites winter in bark crevices or bud scales and migrate in late April when the buds break. Spray with dormant oil plus

ethion or malathion at the delayed dormant stage and perhaps Kelthane in May.

McDaniel Spider Mite*, *Tetranychus mcdanieli* McGregor. Reported from Michigan on raspberry in 1931 but more recently
a serious pest of deciduous fruit trees in the Northwest. It has been
collected from apple, plum, prune, cherry, and currant, besides raspberry, from Washington, Oregon, Utah, California, New Mexico,
Montana, North Dakota, Michigan, and New York. It is similar to
the European red mite but a distinct species.

Oak Mite, *Oligonychus bicolor* (Banks). Severe in eastern United
States, important on oak and elm, sometimes on beech, birch, hickory, maple, and other shade trees. It was a problem when DDT was
used for elm bark beetles and may continue to be when carbaryl is
used for cankerworms. The mite is dark green to black with forward
part of the body lighter and brownish; dorsal spines are slender with
no spots at the base; eggs are brown, flat on top. They give the foliage
a very dusty appearance. Add a miticide to caterpillar sprays or apply
a separate spray of Kelthane in June.

Olive Mite, *Oxycenus maxwelli* (Keifer). On buds and stems of
olive in California. This eriphyid mite may cause serious flower drop.

Omnivorous Mite, *Brevipalpus californicus* (Banks). A false spider
mite, serious pest of citrus and of orchids under glass. Intensely red
adults are less than $\frac{1}{100}$ inch long, ovate, flat; eggs are elliptical and
bright red. The mites do not spin webs but feed on upper or lower
leaf surfaces, producing a speckled white appearance. Try Kelthane
or Meta-Systox-R.

Oncidium Mite, *Brevipalpus orchidii* Baker. Another false spider
mite important on Oncidium and Odontoglossum orchids in California.

Pacific Spider Mite*, *Tetranychus pacificus* McGregor. Important
along the Pacific Coast from California to Washington on apple, pear,
cherry, grape, plum, prune, almond, walnut, beans, and various
ornamentals. Since 1954 it has been considered an economic pest of
citrus. Foliage is heavily webbed, turns bronze, and there may be
extensive defoliation; fruit fails to color properly, often with heavy
drop before harvest. This species resembles the twospotted mite and
makes similar webs. Adults winter in trash on ground, migrating to
trees in spring and feeding on lower foliage first. Eggs are laid in
webbing. There are several generations with peak of abundance in
late summer, when mites spin webs at calyx end of fruit. Grapes
turn prematurely red or brown; bean leaves are webbed. Spray with
Kelthane, malathion, or diazinon.

Pallid Mite, *Tydeus californicus* (Banks). Sometimes abundant on avocado. It is white, a little larger than the sixspotted mite, but without spots.

Peach Silver Mite*, *Aculus cornutus* (Banks). Peach Rust Mite. Very small, pinkish, feeding more often on upper surface of leaves, causing silvering. It hibernates under bud scales. It is more of a problem on the Pacific Coast but can be controlled by a dormant lime-sulfur spray.

Pearleaf Blister Mite*, *Eriophyes pyri* (Pagenstecher). Present wherever pears are grown, sometimes on apple, mountain-ash, shadbush, and cotoneaster. Brownish blisters appear on underside of leaves, each about ⅛ inch across but often massed together to nearly cover the leaf. When blisters are opened, small, elongated pinkish or white mites, ¹⁄₁₂₅ inch long, can be seen with a hand lens. Adults winter under scales of fruit and leaf buds, often hundreds in a single bud. They lay eggs in the buds as they swell in spring, and the young burrow in unfolding leaves, feeding entirely inside the blisters. Successive generations develop in the leaves, but they migrate to buds at the approach of cold weather.

Control. Apply a dormant lime-sulfur spray, 1 to 15 dilution, before buds open (but not near painted surfaces); or spray with a superior oil just as buds begin to swell. The weather has to be warm enough for the oil to penetrate.

Pear Rust Mite*, *Epitrimerus pyri* (Nalepa). Bronzing foliage and russeting fruit of pears, sometimes infesting apple, prune, and cherry. A pest on the Pacific Coast and also in New York.

Pecan Leafroll Mite*, *Aceria caryae* (Keifer). Feeds on margins of leaflets, causing them to roll into a thickened gall-like growth parallel to the midvein. Another mite, *Eotetranychus hicoriae* McGregor, seems to be even more important on pecan, causing a scorching of leaves and defoliation. Parathion has given effective control.

Phaelenopsis Mite, *Tenuipalpus pacificus* Baker. A false spider mite, serious pest of Phaelenopsis and other orchids.

Pine Bud Mite*, *Trisetacus pini* (Nalepa). Very minute, yellow blister or gall mite, injuring needles of pine in California and Oregon. Seriously infested pines may have to be removed. A dormant oil spray is helpful.

Pink Citrus Rust Mite, *Aculus pelekassi* (Keifer). A relatively recent pest of citrus in Florida.

Platanus Mite, *Oligonychus platani* (McGregor). A serious pest of sycamore in hot interior valleys of California, also of loquat; present on avocado but under satisfactory natural control. Other hosts include live oak, cork oak, camphor, cotoneaster, cypress, eucalyptus, pyracantha, toyon, walnut, and willow. The mites feed on upper surface of leaves, causing a brownish discoloration.

Plum Rust Mite*, *Aculus fockeui* (Nalepa & Trouessart). Plum Nursery Mite. Causing silvering and longitudinal curling of leaves and, in myrobalan plums, a disease known as necrotic fleck. Present on the Pacific Coast and also in New York.

Pomegranate Leafroll Mite, *Aceria granati* (Canestrini & Massalongo). On pomegranate in California.

Privet Mite*, *Brevipalpus obovatus* Donnadieu. Widely distributed false spider mite, injuring privet, azalea, and other flowering shrubs, palms, ivy, ash, ceropegia, chrysanthemum, coleus, fuchsia. The mite was first described from goldenrod. The egg is elliptical, bright orange-red at first, then darker. The mites are bright orange to dark red with various dark pigmentations. They feed on underside of leaves, on stems, and petioles. Leaves turn bronze underneath and deep red on upper surface of some plants, yellow on others. Privet turns yellow, azalea leaves brown or bronze and drop off. Underside of fuchsia leaves are badly pitted, with heavy leaf drop. Spray with chlorobenzilate, Kelthane, or Omite.

Another mite, *Aculus ligustri*, is common on privet.

Redberry Mite*, *Acalitus essigi* (Hassan). Blackberry Mite. A western species on blackberry, microscopic in size. Mites feed near the base of drupelets, preventing fruit from ripening in whole or in part, causing "redberry disease." Affected fruit stays bright-colored, hard, clings to bushes. Mites winter in buds. Use a dormant lime-surfur spray, 1 to 15 dilution, in March as buds are opening, and a 2nd spray, 1 to 40 dilution, when fruiting arms are about 1 foot long. Or spray with Kelthane in delayed dormant period.

Schoene Spider Mite*, *Tetranychus schoenei* McGregor. Widely distributed in eastern and southwestern states on a wide variety of hosts, including apple, elm, black locust, bean, raspberry, and other brambles.

Sixspotted Mite*, *Eotetranychus sexmaculatus* (Riley). A yellow mite, long a pest of citrus in Florida and southern California, more recently an important pest of avocado in California. Mites occur in colonies on underside of foliage. Such areas, often near veins, are depressed and covered with webs; the upper surface of the leaf has yellowish blisters with a smooth, shiny surface. Oil sprays, DN or sulfur dusts, and parathion have been used for control with malathion and Kelthane more recent possibilities.

Southern Red Mite*, *Oligonychus ilicis* (McGregor). Holly Mite, the Red Spider of the South, also injurious to many shrubs in the North. This mite is most important on holly and azalea but may also damage camellia, camphor, cypress, eucalyptus, loquat, live oak, plane, pyracantha, English walnut, and rose, sometimes other ornamentals. The mites feed on both leaf surfaces, rasping the epidermis. Leaves turn gray or brown as feeding continues. Adult females are nearly black, males and nymphs light red. Both have spiny hairs curving backward. Red eggs are laid on both leaf surfaces, and heavily infested leaves look as if they had been dusted with red pepper. There may be extensive defoliation. There are many generations but in the South most damage is in fall or spring, with low populations in midsummer. In the North, mites start feeding on holly at the end of April, and populations increase rapidly in summer.

Control. In the North, spray in late March or early April with a 2 per cent dormant oil; use Kelthane, Tedion, or chlorobenzilate for later sprays. Nurserymen can treat the soil with a systemic—DiSyston or Thimet—but these are too hazardous for home gardeners.

Southern Twospotted Mite. See Carmine Spider Mite.

Spindlegall Mite, *Vasates aceris-crumena* Riley. The mites feed from the underside of maple leaves, forming hollow galls, and winter under bark scales. A delayed dormant spray of malathion is suggested.

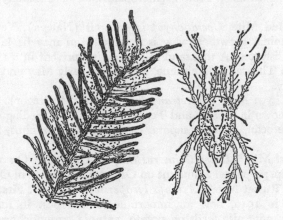

62. *Spruce twig webbed by spruce spider mite and mite as seen under a microscope.*

Spruce Spider Mite*, *Oligonychus ununguis* (Jacobi). A most important evergreen pest. Arborvitae turns brown, spruce grayish, juniper yellow, hemlock nearly white from the sucking of these very small mites. They are dark green to nearly black, with spines on the back and salmon-pink legs. Spherical eggs, wintering at the base of needles, hatch in April or May, complete a generation in 4 or 5 weeks, and go on building up populations until winter eggs are laid in October. The mites spin a quantity of webbing between the needles. Injury is worse in hot, dry seasons and following use of a broad-spectrum insecticide which kills mite predators. Young spruces may die the first season; older trees die progressively, from lower branches upward, over a period of years.

Control. Syringing with the hose to break webs is helpful. Use a dormant spray of lime sulfur or oil, but do not use oil on blue spruce. In mid-May spray with Kelthane or Tedion or chlorobenzilate and repeat in early fall.

Strawberry Spider Mite*, *Tetranychus turkestani* Ugarov & Nikolski. Widely distributed, New York to Florida and California, mostly on low-growing plants but occasionally on pear, peach, apple, walnut, and lemon. This is a serious pest of strawberries, also of beans, soybeans, melon, parsley, eggplant, cotton, clover, alfalfa, and is found on many weeds. The females are straw-colored or greenish with 2 to 4 black spots. They feed in definite colonies on underside of leaves. Plants are stunted with loss of vigor, reduced yield, and sometimes die. Spray with Kelthane, Tedion, chlorobenzilate, or diazinon; repeat as necessary.

Taxus Bud Mite, *Cecidophyopsis psilaspis* (Nalepa). Yew Bigbud Mite. Terminal growth of yew is enlarged and may be killed. New growth is distorted. A thousand mites may be present in a single bud. Spray with Thiodan or Kelthane, starting in early May and repeating as necessary.

Texas Citrus Mite*, *Eotetranychus banksi* (McGregor). A species complex known in Florida and Texas on citrus, also feeding on castorbean, velvetbean, almond, sapota, cassia, croton, zizyphus, flacourtia, and fig.

Tipdwarf Mite*, *Calepiterimerus thujae* (Garman). On arborvitae, dwarfing tips; reported abundant on Oriental arborvitae in Ohio.

Tomato Russet Mite*, *Aculops lycopersici* (Masser). First found in California in 1940, now an important tomato pest in many other states. This mite also feeds on potato, petunia, groundcherry, datura, and other solanaceous hosts. Typical injury is a bronzing or russeting of surface of stems and leaves, with feeding starting at base of the main stalk. Leaves turn brown 3 or 4 weeks later. Fruit is attacked only in severe cases but loss of foliage results in sunburned fruit. Sulfur dust has given good control. Predaceous mites and thrips help out.

Tuckerellid Mite. See Grevillea Mite.

Tumid Spider Mite*, *Tetranychus tumidus* Banks. Common in south-eastern states, in California, and in greenhouses. Destructive to potted ornamentals such as palms, maranta, to pittosporum, and to low-growing vegetable crops, including celery, beans, beet, okra, peas, and sweetpotato.

Twospotted Spider Mite*, *Tetranychus urticae* Koch. A pest in every garden, probably the most common of the mites we call Red Spider. The mites turn rose leaves gray or reddish or yellow or brown, with defoliation by midsummer. Leaves of phlox, hollyhock, primrose, violet, and many other flowers turn yellow, as does the foliage of beans and other vegetables and that of many fruits. Ivy in the house is a sickly gray from red spiders. Nearly all greenhouse plants are subject to infestation. There may be a good deal of webbing over flower buds or between leaves.

Red spiders are very small. The female twospotted mite is less than $\frac{1}{50}$ inch, the male even smaller. The body is oval, yellow or greenish with 2 dark spots on the back, sparsely covered with spines. The young, 6-legged mite feeds for a day or two after hatching, then enters a resting stage; it molts into a 2nd active stage and again rests. The female goes through a 3rd such period before becoming adult, the male only 2 periods. Mating takes place a few minutes after the female reaches adult form and she lays 100 to 200 eggs on underside of leaves in 3 or 4 weeks. Eggs from unmated females develop into males only. The mites make mealy cobwebs on the underside of leaves and from one leaf to another, sometimes entirely covering a new shoot, flower buds and all.

The number of generations increases with the temperature. At 75° F. the adult stage is reached in 5 days; it takes 40 days at 55°. In greenhouses there is a new generation every 20 to 30 days. Outdoors, mites hibernate as adults in soil, on leaves of plants retaining foliage, on weeds, or on tree bark, starting activity quite early in spring but often reaching peak of abundance in July. In situations of high humidity where air is stagnant, mites are always serious. Plants under overhanging eaves, in walled gardens, in dense clumps or thick hedges are most susceptible. Where DDT was used in mist blowers for mosquito control, red spiders built up enormous populations in gardens. Spraying with carbaryl may also increase the mite problem.

Control. There are many excellent miticides. Kelthane and Tedion may be used on both ornamentals and food crops. Dimethoate and Meta-Systox-R have some systemic as well as direct action. The useful Aramite has been replaced by Omite. Plictran is a promising new miticide and Pentac is used in some greenhouses. Syringing plants with the hose is still a good idea, using force enough to break the webs.

Walnut Blister Mite*, *Aceria erinea* (Nalepa). Yellow or brown feltlike galls are formed on underside of leaves but are not very injurious. The mite can be controlled with a dormant lime-sulfur spray, 1 to 10 dilution, when buds swell in spring.

Wheat Curl Mite*, *Aceria tulipae* (Keifer).

Willamette Mite, *Eotetranychus willamettei* (McGregor). Known from southern California to Washington. A serious pest of grape, also present on apple, pear, cherry, raspberry, boxelder, serviceberry, oak, and sycamore. This species is similar to the Pacific spider mite but there is less webbing. In some sections sulfur applied for control of powdery mildew on grapes controls the mite but in other areas it has become resistant to sulfur.

Willow Gall Mite, *Eriophyes salicicola* (Banks). Causing numerous small galls on both surfaces of willow leaves; present in the West.

Yellow Spider Mite*, *Eotetranychus carpini borealis* (Ewing). Boreal Mite. Present from British Columbia to central California, a frequent pest of apple, pear, sometimes cherry, raspberry, blueberry, spirea, alder, and willow. This species is similar to the twospotted mite but is smaller and greenish yellow.

Yuma Spider Mite*, *Eotetranychus yumensis* (McGregor). In California and Arizona on citrus fruits, especially lemon and tangerine.

There are a great many more mite species of possible economic importance but they do not have common names to use for reference. Recently *Tetranychus yusti* McGregor, reported from Louisiana, Delaware, and Florida, was tested on various host plants and found to feed on representatives of legumes, grasses, and composites. It may, however, be suppressed by a predaceous mite. In 1966 a mite identified as *T. marianae* McGregor was found in California on lily-of-the-valley vine and nightshade in a greenhouse and subsequently found outdoors on tomato and eggplant. It was later identified as *T. evansi* Baker & Pritchard but is considered a potential pest.

MOTHS

Moths belong to the insect order Lepidoptera, having wings covered with scales. They differ from butterflies in being mostly night fliers, not holding wings vertical when at rest, in having a heavy, hairy body, antennae that may be feathery but not knobbed, in laying eggs in large clusters often coated with hairs, and with the pupa usually inside a cocoon. There are many families, with different workers not always in agreement. The list below, in alphabetical order, includes only families with members injurious to cultivated plants. Those best known for their caterpillar stage will be found under Borers, Budworms, Cankerworms, Casebearers. Caterpillars, Cutworms, Earworms, Fruitworms, Hornworms, Leaffolders, Leafrollers, Leaf Skeletonizers, Leaftiers, Spanworms, or Webworms.

Aegeriidae. Clearwing moths. Mostly day fliers, wasplike, having wings mostly without scales, the rear edge of fore wings locking over front edge of hind wings. The larvae are borers in woody and herbaceous plants—e.g., peachtree borer, squash borer.

Arctiidae. Tiger moths. Nocturnal, with wings held rooflike over the body when at rest; brightly spotted or banded. The larvae are very hairy—e.g., woollybears, fall webworm.

Citheroniidae. Royal moths. Stout-bodied with large wings. The larvae have horns or spines, feed on trees, pupate in the ground without a cocoon. The hickory horned devil belongs here.

Coleophoridae. Casebearers. Small brown or gray moths, with pointed wings fringed along hind margins. The larvae first mine leaves, then make cases.

Cosmopterygidae. Small moths with long, narrow wings sharply pointed at the apex. The larvae are leafminers or skeletonizers—e.g., palm leaf skeletonizer.

Cossidae. Carpenterworm moths. Large, heavy-bodied, with spotted or mottled wings. The larvae are wood borers.

Crambidae. Grass moths. Common in meadows and lawns, whitish or pale yellowish brown, holding wings close to the body. The larvae are sod webworms.

Dioptidae. Only 1 species in the United States, the California oakworm.

Gelechiidae. Gelechiid moths. Small, dull-colored with narrow fore wings, hind wings often with a curved outer margin, and long, upcurving labial palps—e.g., pink bollworm, potato tuberworm.

Geometridae. Measuring worms, geometrid moths. Small, slender-bodied, some species with wingless females. The larvae have 2 or 3 prolegs at the end of the body and move with a looping motion. They are known as cankerworms, spanworms, or loopers.

Glyphipterygidae. Small moths, similar to tortricid moths. Larvae are usually leaftiers.

Gracillariidae. Leafblotch miners. Very small moths with tapering wings. The larvae make blotch mines.

Heliozelidae. Shield bearers. Small moths with lanceolate wings, the hind wings having no discal cell. The larva of the resplendent shield bearer is a leafminer and casebearer.

Hepialidae. Ghost moths or swifts. Medium to large moths, wingspread 1 to 3 inches, mostly brown or gray with silvery spots. The larvae feed on roots and woody tissues.

Incurvariidae. Small moths with minute spines on wing membranes; female with piercing ovipositor—e.g., maple leafcutter, yucca moth.

Lasiocampidae. Tent caterpillars. Robust, very hairy moths with feathery antennae. The hairy larvae live in webs.

Limacodidae. Slug caterpillars. The larvae are short, fleshy, sluglike, without prolegs.

Lymantriidae. Tussock moths. Medium size, hairy, males with plumose antennae, females wingless in some species. The larvae are hairy, some with tussocks of hairs—e.g., gypsy moth, browntail moth, white-marked tussock moth.

Lyonetiidae. Small moths with very narrow wings. The larvae are leafminers or live in webs between leaves.

Megalopygidae. Flannel moths. Medium-sized with a dense coat of scales mixed with fine curly hairs. The larvae are hairy, sometimes stinging—e.g., puss caterpillar.

Nepticulidae. Minute moths with spinelike hairs on surface of wings. The larvae are leafminers in trees and shrubs.

Noctuidae. Owlet moths and underwings. Largest family in the Lepidoptera, with 2,700 species in this country. Nocturnal, mostly medium size, dull color, heavy-bodied; front wings narrow, hind wings broad. Smooth dull larvae—armyworms, cutworms, loopers—are very destructive.

Notodontidae. Prominents. Brown or yellow with prominently projecting tufts on hind margins of wings. The yellownecked or red-humped larvae have conspicuous tubercles.

Oecophoridae. Webworms. Small, flattened moths, brownish with broad wings rounded apically.

Olethreutidae. Small brown or gray moths, banded or mottled, fore wings rather square-tipped, fringe of long hairs on basal part of hind wings. Smooth-skinned pale larvae feed on foliage, fruits, or nuts—e.g., codling moth, Oriental fruit moth.

Phaloniidae. Web spinners and borers. Moths similar to Tortricids.

Phycitidae. Inconspicuous moths with long, thread-like antennae. The larvae tunnel in fruit, stems, or seeds.

Prodoxidae. Yucca moths. Wing surface with minute spines; females have a piercing ovipositor and pollinate yucca.

Psychidae. Bagworm moths. Females are wingless, larvae live in bag-like cases.

Pterophoridae. Plume moths. Small, slender, gray or brown with wings split into 2 or 3 feather-like divisions; long legs. Larvae are leafrollers and stem borers.

Pyralidae. Pyralid moths. Snout moths. Small, delicate, with front wings elongate or triangular, hind wings broad, labial palpi projecting into a snout. Larvae are various, including European corn borer, grape leaffolder, melonworm.

Saturniidae. Giant silkworm moths. Very large, brightly colored, wings with transparent eyespots.

Scythridae. Related to the Yponomeutidae and with a single genus, *Scythris,* feeding on willow herbs.

Sphingidae. Sphinx or hawk moths. Medium to large, with heavy, spindleshaped body. They feed at dusk and look like hummingbirds. Larvae are hornworms.

Tischeriidae. Small moths with costal margin of front wings strongly arched and hind wings long and narrow. Larvae make blotch mines—e.g., appleleaf trumpet miner.

Tortricidae. Leafroller moths. Small, with front wings square-cut; wings bellshaped at rest.

Yponomeutidae. Ermine moths. Small with narrow fore wings, fringed hind wings. When resting, the wings are tight against the sides of the body, the antennae directed straight forward—e.g., diamondback moth.

Zygaenidae. Leaf skeletonizer moths. Smoky gray or black moths, small. The larvae have tufted hairs.

Abbott's Sphinx, *Sphecodina abbotti* (Swaine). In eastern states and west to Kansas, not abundant but sometimes injuring grape and Virginia-creeper. The caterpillar is 2 inches long, of variable color but basically chocolate or reddish brown. It has a polished eyelike tubercle instead of a caudal horn.

Abutilon Moth, *Anomis erosa* Hübner. Okra Caterpillar. Feeding on abutilon, okra, hollyhock, hibiscus, and mallow. It is a light-green semilooper, similar to the cabbage looper, growing to 1⅜ inches, pupating in a folded leaf. Hand-pick caterpillars or spray with malathion.

Achemon Sphinx*, *Eumorpha achemon* (Drury). A large moth, wings expanding to 3 or 4 inches, fore wings gray with brown marks, hind wings pink; a high flier. The female lays pale eggs on upper surface of leaves; pupation is in mahogany-brown chrysalids in soil. The caterpillars are large, 2 to 3½ inches, green or pinkish, with oblique white bars on the sides; the young larva has a black horn but this disappears with the first molt. Cultivated and wild grapes and Virginia-creeper may be defoliated. There are 2 generations.

American Dagger Moth*, *Acronicta americana* (Harris). Common in the Northeast on apple, basswood, elder, elm, maple, oak, willow, reported on boxelder in Nevada, on birch in Idaho. The larva is 2 inches long, covered with yellowish hairs and with 3 long black pencils of hairs. The body under the hairs is greenish white above, black underneath. It feeds from June to October.

Apple Fruit Moth*, *Argyresthia conjugella* Zeller. A small, dark-gray, night-flying moth, serious in Canadian apple orchards, now a problem in Maine, New Hampshire, New York, California, and Alaska. Hosts include cherry, plum, *Vaccinium* spp., serviceberry, pear, and mountain-ash. The larva—at first white, then pink or flesh-colored with brown spots—feeds in fruit, then pupates in soil.

Artichoke Plume Moth*, *Platyptilia carduidactyla* (Riley). The adult has big, brown, divided (plumed) wings, 1 inch across. Caterpillars feed on new foliage and inside stems, leaf stalks, buds, with noticeable damage to the artichoke head. There are 3 overlapping generations in California, with worst injury in spring. Pick and destroy all wormy artichokes; bury all old plant tops under 10 inches of soil; remove nearby thistles.

Banded Sunflower Moth*, *Phalonia hospes* (Walsingham). Of economic importance on sunflowers in North Dakota. One of the web-spinning moths.

Bella Moth*, *Utetheisa ornatrix bella* (Linnaeus). A tiger moth on peanuts, reported a pest in Alabama.

Black Cherry Scallopshell Moth, *Hydria prunivora* Ferguson. One of the inchworms, attacking only black cherry and sometimes causing serious defoliation in New York in the Adirondacks region. There are 2 generations a year.

Black Witch Moth, *Erebus odora* Linnaeus. Blackish with a wingspread of 4 or 5 inches, breeding in southern states. The larvae feed on various leguminous trees. The noctuid adults sometimes appear in the North in late summer.

Browntail Moth*, *Nygmia phaeorrhoea* (Donovan). Introduced into Massachusetts on nursery stock prior to 1897 and present in all New England States but of less importance in recent years. It may infest apple, cherry, oak, pear, plum, hawthorn, rose, willow, occasionally elm and maple. The caterpillars, 1½ inches long, are reddish brown to nearly black, with a broken stripe along each side, a red tubercle on segments 11 and 12, and are covered with tufts of brown hairs. These are barbed and poisonous, causing a severe rash when they touch the skin, even death if large numbers of small hairs are breathed into the lungs. They winter as young larvae, several hundred webbed together in a nest, feed during the spring, and in June pupate in a cocoon among webbed leaves.

The moths are pure white except for brown scales at the tip of the abdomen, have a 1½-inch wingspread, are active fliers. They appear

MOTHS   347

in July to lay eggs in globular yellow clusters, covered with light-brown hairs, on underside of leaves. There is 1 generation a year.

Control. Cut off and destroy winter webs; spray trees. Spray with Sevin or methoxychlor when leaves come out for overwintering larvae or in August when young caterpillars appear. A fungus disease kills many insects. Browntail moths are included in quarantine regulations for gypsy moths. See Puss Caterpillar for a recipe to sooth the rash.

Buck Moth*, *Hemileuca maia* (Drury). Ranging from southern New Hampshire to Georgia, Oklahoma, and Texas, named because it appears in autumn when deer run. The caterpillars feed gregariously on oak, sometimes on willow. They are brownish black, covered with pale-yellow papillae. Each segment bears 6, 7, or 8 tufts of spines, except segment 11, which has only 5. These irritate the flesh. Moths are brown or blackish except for a wide white band across the wings which encloses ring spots. Eggs, laid in autumn around a branch, hatch in May. Larvae eat enormously until July, when they pupate in the ground. Spray in May as for cankerworms.

Buddleia Moth, *Pyramidobela angelarum* Keifer. In leaf folds of buddleia plants; heavy infestation in some California gardens.

Carnation Tortrix Moth, *Cacoecimorpha pronubana*. Reported from Oregon on viburnum, Portugal-laurel, skimmia, dwarf rhododendron, ivy, ponderosa pine, and other ornamentals.

Ceanothus Clearwing, *Ramosia mellinipennis* (Boisduval). Abundant on ceanothus in California.

Ceanothus Silk Moth*, *Platysamia euryalus* (Fabricius).

Cecropia Moth*, *Platysamia cecropia* (Linnaeus). More conspicuous than destructive, this huge silkworm moth, wing expanse 5 or 6 inches, is dusky brown with a white crossband bordered with red and a red spot near the apex of each fore wing, a white crescent-shaped spot in the center, and coral-red, blue, and yellow tubercles on the body. The caterpillars are pale green, ornamented with blue, red, and yellow tubercles; 4 inches long. They feed on oak, linden, maple, box-elder, elm, birch, willow, poplar, and other trees. Large, gray-brown silk cocoons are conspicuous on bare trees in winter. Control by removing and destroying cocoons.

Codling Moth*, *Carpocapsa pomonella* (Linnaeus). Apple Worm, a European species distributed throughout apple-growing sections of the world (Plate XXV). It came to this country prior to 1819 and is the most serious pest on apple and pear fruit that we have. Crabapples, apricots, cherries, loquats, peaches, plums, haws, and similar fruits are occasionally attacked. Green nuts of English walnut are commonly infested on the Pacific Coast. Unsprayed apples are sure to be 20 to 95 per cent infested. Crop reductions come from wormy fruit, from early drop of immature apples, and from "stings"—small holes surrounded by dead tissue which lower fruit value even though the worms are killed before doing further damage.

The insect winters as a full-grown larva, a pinkish-white caterpillar, 1 inch long, with a brown head, inside a silken cocoon under loose scales on apple bark or in other sheltered places. In spring the worms change to brown pupae and the moths emerge in 2 to 4 weeks. They are grayish brown, with irregular golden-brown lines on the fore wings and paler, fringed hind wings, spreading ½ to ¾ inch. They lay flat white eggs, singly, on upper surface of leaves, on twigs, and on fruit spurs. They work at dusk, when the weather is dry and the temperature fairly high, above 55° F. A cold, wet spring at time of egg laying means less trouble later with wormy apples.

Hatching in 6 to 20 days, small worms crawl to young apples, entering by way of the calyx cup at the blossom end. They tunnel to the core, often eating the seeds, then burrow out through the side of the apple, leaving a mass of brown excrement behind, and crawl to the tree trunk to pupate in cocoons for the next generation. There are usually 2 generations, with the 2nd working from late July to September. Second-brood larvae enter the fruit at any point without preference for the blossom end.

Control. To control codling moths and other apple pests get a spray schedule from your county agricultural agent that is tailored for your particular locality. The recommendations may change from year to year and you should get a schedule planned either for the backyard gardener or the commercial orchardist. In some commercial schedules, Imidan or Guthion is used at petal fall and in cover sprays; in other states azinphosmethyl or Gardona is recommended. In some experimental work the release of males sterilized by cobalt radiation has been quite effective in reducing codling moths.

Cottonwood Dagger Moth*, *Acronicta lepusculina* Guenée. Through northern states on poplar, sometimes on willow. The larva is 1½ inches long, densely clothed with long yellow hairs and with 5 single black hair pencils. It feeds from July to October.

Crinkled Flannel Moth*, *Megalopyge crispata* (Packard). Cream-colored with black and brown markings on wings. The poisonous caterpillar is thick, fleshy, up to 1 inch long, covered with long silky brown hairs which project upward to form a crest along the middle of the back. It feeds on apple, bayberry, birch, cherry, locust, oak, raspberry, and sweetfern in northern states. It is also reported as defoliating many acres of shin-oak in Texas.

Cynthia Moth*, *Samia cynthia* (Drury). One of the giant silkworm moths, ranging from southern Connecticut to Virginia, one of the few pests known to feed on ailanthus and often completely defoliating it. The caterpillars—3½ inches long, green with black dots and blue tubercles—may also feed on wild cherry and plum, have been reported on linden, sycamore, and lilac. They are found mostly near cities. The moth is a beautiful brown with white markings, wing expanse 6 to 8 inches. It was introduced here in the hope of making silk from its cocoons.

Cypress Cone Moth, *Laspeyresia cupressana* (Kearfott). Small grayish-white larvae bore in green-cone clusters and bark of Monterey and other cypress in California. The adult is small, coppery brown with wing expanse of ⅝ inch. It is also reported on arborvitae.

Cypress Moth, *Recurvaria apictripunctella* (Clemens). Found in the Northeast on bald cypress and hemlock. The moth is yellow with black markings, very small, with fringed wings. The larvae mine leaves and web them together in late summer and early fall, hibernate, resume feeding in spring.

Cypress Tip Moth, *Argyresthia cupressella* Walsingham. Common on Monterey and other cypress from California north into Washington. The adult is small, golden with brown markings, only ⅓ inch across. The larva, ¼ inch long, is yellow-green with a brown head. It winters in mined twigs, then makes papery white cocoons on foliage.

Cypress Webber, *Epinotia subviridis* Heinrich. Often found with the cypress tip moth. Brownish green larvae with light tubercles, ⅖ inch long, eat leaves and tie them up with twigs into a nest. Foliage may turn brown; chief injury is in February and May. Arborvitae may be infested along with cypress. Spray with Sevin.

Diamondback Moth*, *Plutella xylostella* (Linnaeus). Considered a minor cabbage pest, although sometimes damaging to any crucifer. It may also attack sweet alyssum, candytuft, stock, and wallflower in gardens and greenhouses. The moths, which winter in cabbage debris, are small, ¾ inch across, with gray or brown wings and white marks making a diamond when the wings are folded; hind wings are fringed. Young larvae, greenish yellow with black hairs, ⅓ inch long, at first mine the leaves, later feed externally. Pupation is inside a lacy cocoon on a leaf; moths emerge in a week. There may be 2 to 6 generations. Spray or dust with malathion or the bacterial *Bacillus thuringiensis* or any treatment used for other cabbage caterpillars.

Douglas Fir Cone Moth*, *Barbara colfaxiana* (Kearfott). On Douglas-fir along the Pacific Coast. Small yellow-white caterpillars mine through scales and seeds. Adults are very small gray moths.

Douglas Fir Pitch Moth*, *Vespamima novaroensis* (Hy. Edwards). Attacking wounds on Douglas-fir, weakened larch, and Sitka spruce.

Larvae are slender, white, 1 to 1½ inches; adults are clearwing moths with orange-red markings on body.

Douglas Fir Tussock Moth*, *Hemerocampa pseudotsugata* McDunnough. Defoliating and killing Douglas-fir and true fir in the Northwest, reported also defoliating willow, ceanothus, and other shrubs. The caterpillars, up to 1 inch long, have bright-colored tufts of hairs and 2 black pencils of hairs at the head and 1 pencil at the posterior. Moths are dull brownish gray; females are wingless. Young larvae are carried by wind and defoliate tops of trees first.

Driedfruit Moth*, *Vitula edmandsae serratilineella* Ragonet.

Eightspotted Forester*, *Alypia octomaculata* (Fabricius). Ranging from New England to Colorado and Texas, feeding on grape, Virginia-creeper, and Boston ivy, sometimes defoliating. The moth is black, wingspread 1½ inches, with 2 yellow spots on each fore wing, 2 white spots on each hind wing. The caterpillar is bluish white, banded with orange, with black lines and dots, orange head with black spots, orange prolegs, black legs; 1½ inches long. Pick off caterpillars by hand.

Elm Sphinx*, *Ceratomia amyntor* (Hübner). Feeding on elm, basswood, and birch through Atlantic states to the Mississippi Valley. The larva, 3 inches long, varies from pale green to reddish brown, with 7 oblique whitish stripes on each side. Adults are sphinx or hawk moths.

Ermine Moth*, *Yponomeuta padella* (Linnaeus). Small moths, with black dots on white front wings. The larvae feed in a web on apple and cherry.

European Pine Shoot Moth*, *Rhyacionia buoliana* (Schiffermüller). First discovered on Long Island in 1914, now present throughout the Northeast south to Tennessee and west to Kansas and Nebraska. It has also appeared in Oregon and Washington where quarantine measures have been in effect. It is a serious problem in home gardens, nurseries, and pine plantations and became so important in southern Wisconsin that pine plantations were discouraged. Red, mugho, Scotch, and Austrian pines are favored, others may be attacked (Plate III). Hibernation is as a partly grown larva, brown with a black head, in a bud or mass of pitch on a bud. Becoming active in warm weather in spring, the caterpillar leaves its winter bud and bores into an uninfested bud on a new shoot. The shoot grows 1 or 2 inches, becomes crooked, straw-colored, dead, usually with a mass of pitch at the larval entrance. Infested shoots are very easy to detect by the color, the crook, or the pitch. Pupation is in the shoot in May and June, with moths starting to emerge in early mid-June and continuing to mid-July.

The moths have reddish brown fore wings marked with silver cross lines, dark-brown hind wings. They are about ¾ inch across. Eggs are laid near tips of twigs, on bark, or in needle sheaths. In 10 days the larva starts boring through needle bases, with needles on terminal shoots turning yellow. At the end of summer the larva moves over to a bud and bores in for the winter.

Control. Infestations in small pines around the house are easily taken care of by breaking off infested shoots in May before moths emerge, making sure the brown caterpillar is inside the part broken off and dropping everything into a paper bag for proper disposal. When pines are too large for this, spray in April and again in late June or early July with carbaryl, dimethoate, or diazinon. Granular phorate and Di-Syston applied to the soil around small red pines have been effective. There are many parasites, 17 being recorded in West Virginia.

Fan Palm Moth, *Litoprosopus coachella* Hill. A problem in residences near fan palms in California.

Filament Bearer*, *Nematocampa filamentaria* Guenée. A geometrid moth.

Fir Seed Moth*, *Laspeyreysia bracteatana* (Fernald). Small pink larvae bore in seeds of white, red, and other firs in Oregon, California, and Colorado. Moths are small, dull.

Geranium Plume Moth, *Platyptilia pica* Walsingham. A California pest that has come east, apparently with cuttings, and is now present on geranium in greenhouses in Ohio, New Jersey, New York, Pennsylvania, and Indiana. The larva bores in flower buds, feeds on flowers and leaves. The small tan moth, 1-inch wingspread, lays 100 to 200 eggs on flower bracts and sepals of buds and these hatch in 1 to 2 weeks. Zectran, parathion, Vapona have been used in control.

Grape Berry Moth*, *Paralobesia viteana* (Clemens). Generally distributed east of the Rocky Mountains on wild and cultivated grapes, most injurious in the Northeast, common in home gardens. Grape berries are webbed together, turn dark purple, drop when about half size. A nearly ripe berry will have a hole and be attached by webbing to a leaf. The moth winters in a cocoon, usually in fallen grape leaves, sometimes attached to loose bark scales. About flowering time the grayish purple adult, ½ inch across the wings, emerges to lay flat, circular, cream-colored eggs on stems, flower clusters, newly forming berries. The larvae, ⅓ to ½ inch long, greenish with brown heads, web parts together as they feed, each worm destroying several berries. When full-grown the larva cuts out a bit of leaf, folds it over, and constructs a cocoon within the fold. These remain on the vine or fall to the ground. Moths of the 2nd generation emerge in July; there may be

3 generations in the South. Cocoons of the 2nd generation are formed on bits of leaves under the trellis.

Control. Spray with Sevin right after bloom and repeat in 10 days. Guthion or malathion may be used for July sprays. Rake up fallen leaves and debris around grapevines in fall and winter.

Great Ash Sphinx*, *Sphinx chersis* (Hübner). On ash and lilac, Canada to Florida and to the West Coast. The larva is light green with 7 oblique yellowish stripes and a pale blue horn at the rear, 3 inches long. The adult is a typical hawk moth.

Gypsy Moth*, *Porthetria dispar* (Linnaeus). An expensive pest of shade, forest, and fruit trees long known in New England and now a threat in many other states. In 1869 a scientist at Medford, Massachusetts, lost, due to a windstorm which broke open screened cages, some caterpillars he had imported for improving the breed of silkworms. About 10 years later these caterpillars were numerous on trees in that vicinity and in 20 years trees in eastern Massachusetts were being defoliated. An appropriation was made for control, but in a year or two the legislature decided to "economize" and stopped the work. By 1905, when control measures were resumed, the gypsy moth covered 4,000 square miles. In 1953 it defoliated a million and a half acres of trees in New England. An infestation that started in New Jersey in 1920 was eradicated within a few years, a small infestation in Ohio was promptly wiped out, and a larger one in Pennsylvania was almost subdued. Discovery in the spring of 1954 of a 10,000-acre infestation near Lansing, Michigan, brought prompt action by state and federal authorities.

The Federal Government enacted quarantine regulations in 1906 and these are still in effect. They provide for inspection and certification of all products—forest, quarry stone, nursery stock, Christmas trees—to which egg clusters may adhere, before shipment out of infested areas. A barrier zone 25 to 30 miles wide was maintained from Canada to Long Island along the Hudson Valley to keep the gypsy moth east of the Hudson River. For many years continuous scouting and clean-up spraying in this zone kept the moth from invading the rest of the country. Eventually this proved insufficient and in 1957 a joint federal-state program was launched to eradicate the moth infestations in New York, New Jersey, and Pennsylvania and to work gradually toward the center in New England. The project was completed satisfactorily in New Jersey and Pennsylvania but in New York outraged citizens brought suit in Federal Court charging invasion of private rights and damage to wildlife, crops, and public health. The judge ruled against the plaintiffs, stating that the injury was minor in view of the results obtained and that the states did have police power for the public good. The atmosphere was such, however, that large-scale control measures have not been resumed and lands that were completely eradicated are being reinfested. Long Island, for instance, receives gypsy-moth larvae wind-blown across the Sound from Connecticut.

At present the generally infested area with quarantine regulations in force includes all of New England and New Jersey, the eastern half of New York and Pennsylvania, with scattered infestations in Delaware, Maryland, and Virginia. (The Michigan infestation seems to be eradicated.) In 1971, about two million acres of trees were defoliated, about double the number in 1970, and a further increase is expected yearly.

Gypsy moths are partial to oak, also apple, alder, basswood, gray and river birch, hawthorn, poplar, and willow, but they also feed on other birches, cherry, elm, black gum, hickory, hornbeam, larch, maple, sassafras. Older larvae eat beech and hemlock, cedar, pine and spruce. Evergreens may be killed by a single season's defoliation; it may take two or three successive years to kill deciduous trees. Some people think there is no real damage if the trees put out a second set of leaves in summer but this permanently weakens the trees and may still lead to death.

The caterpillars are brown, hairy, 2 inches long, with 5 pairs of blue tubercles along the back followed by 6 pairs of red tubercles (Plate VI). They feed at night in June and July, stripping the trees, pupate inside a few threads spun on limb or trunk, and produce moths in 17 or 18 days. The brown, yellow-marked male flies freely. The female is buff-colored with irregular darker markings and she is so heavy she is incapable of sustained flight and can only flutter along the ground. After mating she lays an average of 400 eggs in a cluster, about 1 inch long, oval, the color of chamois skin, and covered with a coating of hair. These are attached to any hard surface near the place of pupation—tree, stone, building, or vehicle. There is 1 generation and the larvae hatch about the first of May. Distribution is by wind dispersal of young larvae, crawling of caterpillars, or the moving of an automobile or trailer, railroad car, quarry stone, nursery stock, Christmas tree, or other object with attached egg cluster. A trailer was found in Florida that had transported gypsy-moth eggs from the infested area.

Control. It is vitally important that individuals cooperate in observing quarantine regulations. Don't try to bring Christmas trees or other plants out of the regulated area without inspection. Check your automobile or trailer if you have vacationed in gypsy-moth country and your home is in an uninvaded area. If the moths are in your own backyard check for egg clusters and destroy them by crushing with a heavy, flat object; or scraping them off into a can containing equal parts of water and turpentine or kerosene; or by painting them with creosote. Catch the caterpillars in a trap made by wrapping a 10-inch band of burlap around the tree trunk. Tie a piece of string around the middle and fold down the upper half. Crush the caterpillars caught under the canopy, wearing heavy gloves.

Spraying is more effective than hand methods and three materials are presently available: carbaryl (Sevin), methoxychlor, and the bacterial *Bacillus thuringiensis*, sold as Thuricide, Biotrol, or Dipel. The last is selective and apparently has no harmful effect on the environment, but it is more expensive and possibly less efficient. Sevin does a very good job on the caterpillars and is safe for man and most wildlife, but it is quite harmful to bees and some other beneficial insects and does increase the mite problem; add a miticide to the spray.*

The United States Department of Agriculture is releasing parasites for control of gypsy moths and also working with a synthetic sex attractant, disparlure, in traps used for checking infested areas.

Hag Moth*, *Phobetron pithecium* (J. E. Smith). One of the slug caterpillars, more interesting than destructive. The larva is brown, with 10 tapering, curved, plume-like processes extending from either side of the back like hanks of hair. It feeds on foliage of various trees and shrubs during the summer but not extensively. It has stinging hairs.

Hickory Tussock Moth*, *Halisidota caryae* (Harris). Hickory Tiger Moth, ranging from New England through North Carolina and west to Missouri, a general feeder on deciduous trees and shrubs, but preferring walnut, butternut, apple, pear, and hickory. It may be abundant locally but seldom causes widespread defoliation. The moth has light-brown fore wings with 3 irregular rows of transparent light spots and thin, pale-yellow hind wings, expanse 2 inches. It appears in June to lay white eggs in patches of 100 or more on underside of leaves. The larvae pass through 8 or 9 instars and feed for 2 or 3 months before spinning cocoons among leaves on the ground. The full-grown caterpillar is 1½ inches long, covered with dense tufts of gray-white hairs and with a row of black tufts along the back; it has a pair of black pencils of hairs on the 1st and 7th abdominal segments. Some parasites, an ichneumon wasp in particular, attack the caterpillars.

Holly Bud Moth. See under Budworms.

Hornet Moth*, *Aegeria apiformis* (Clerck). Rather widely dis-

---

* Imidan is now registered for gypsy moth control.

tributed in northern states, also in California. The moth resembles the giant hornet, with brown abdomen banded with yellow, transparent wings with brown borders. The larvae are borers in roots, trunks, and large limbs of poplar and willow, causing swellings and sometimes death of young trees. They are stout, smooth, white with brown heads and rims around the spiracles; they make extensive burrows. They winter in cocoons in wood borings at the base of trees and pupate in spring. It takes 2 years to complete the life cycle.

Imperial Moth*, *Eacles imperialis* (Drury). A large moth, wing expanse 4 to 6 inches, sulfur-yellow, banded and speckled with purplebrown. The caterpillar is 3 to 4 inches long, green with a brown head and 6-spined yellow horns behind the head. It feeds on many forest and shade trees in eastern United States but is not an important defoliator. Control is seldom necessary.

Io Moth*, *Automeris io* (Fabricius). In eastern states and west to New Mexico, sometimes abundant locally on birch, blackberry, wild cherry, currant, black locust, poplar, willow, and other deciduous trees and shrubs. It is common in Florida on rose, ixora, and other plants and a related species is reported there on azalea. The female moth is purplish red with a large black eyespot on each hind wing; wing expanse 3 inches. The male is smaller, deep yellow. The caterpillar is pale green with a broad brown or reddish stripe, underscored with white along each side of the body, which bears 6 rows of branching green spines tipped with black. The spines are irritating; some people may be poisoned by them.

Juniper Moth, *Periploca nigra*. First noticed in California in 1959, now infesting ornamental junipers over the state.

Lantana Plume Moth*, *Platyptilia pusillodactyla* (Walker).

Lappet Moth*, *Epicnaptera americana* (Harris). In eastern United States on aspen, wild cherry, hickory, oak, and other deciduous trees. The moth is reddish brown with deeply notched wings; expanse 1¼ to 2 inches. The larva is 2½ inches long, flattened, bluish gray with a small lobe or lappet on each side of each segment. Another lappet moth, *Tolype vellida* (Stoll) feeds on apple, poplar, syringa, and is reported on holly in Florida. *T. laricis* (Fitch) appears on larch.

Leopard Moth*, *Zeuzera pyrina* (Linnaeus). A European species first noted in 1879 in a spider's web at Hoboken, New Jersey, now present from southern Massachusetts to Philadelphia. It is recorded on nearly 100 plants. Favored are elm, maple, ash, beech, walnut, oak, chestnut, poplar, willow, lilac, and apple, plum, pear, and other fruits. The moths are white with blue and black spots, the female 3 inches across the wings, the male 2 inches. Adults emerge from May to September. The female has a heavy body, is a feeble

63. Leopard moth.

flier, but lays up to 800 salmon-colored eggs, singly or in small groups, in bark crevices. The young larvae hatch in 10 days and bore into heartwood or enter twigs at base of buds, causing wilting. They make irregular galleries in large limbs and the main trunk, feeding for about 2 years before pupation. The borers are pale yellow or pinkish, spotted with brown or black tubercles of hairs. Small nursery trees and branches of larger trees die; small branches break and hang down; the bark is full of holes with protruding sawdust. Prune off and destroy infested branches; cut down heavily infested trees. Spray trunk and main limbs with malathion or methoxychlor. Kill borers in valuable trees with a wire or carbon disulfide or by injecting commercial borer paste.

Luna Moth*, *Actias luna* (Linnaeus). The lovely adult has delicate green wings expanding to 4 inches, a purple band on front edge of the fore wings and around eyespots, hind wings extending into long, narrow swallowtails. The caterpillar is 3 inches long, green, with 6 pink or green tubercles bearing yellow bristles in each segment. It feeds on hickory and walnut, sometimes on beech, birch, persimmon, sweetgum, willow, and other trees. Control measures are unnecessary.

Madrona Shield Bearer, *Coptodisca arbutiella* Busck. Very small silver gray, gold, and black moths, ranging from California to Washington. The small larvae mine madroña leaves and cut out flattened elliptical sections for pupa cases. Foliage may be entirely riddled with such holes.

Monterey Pine Tip Moth, *Rhyacionia pasadena* (Kearfott). The moth is reddish and silvery gray. The larvae infest terminals of branches of Monterey and other pines along the coast of California.

Nantucket Pine Tip Moth*, *Rhyacionia frustrana* (Comstock). Found from Massachusetts to Florida and west to Texas, injurious

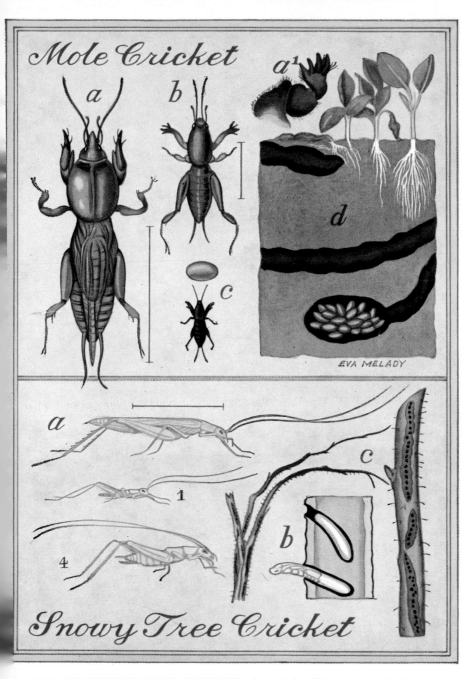

EVA MELADY

XXI NORTHERN MOLE CRICKET: (a) adult, slightly enlarged; (a,1) detail of front leg showing adaptation for digging; (b) nymph; (c) egg, magnified, and first nymphal stage; (d) injury to seedlings from burrows, and eggs in soil pocket. **SNOWY TREE CRICKET:** (a) adult; (a,1) first instar; (a,4) fourth instar, nymphs with wing pads; (b) egg in position in wood and hatching nymph, much enlarged; (c) egg punctures in a row along stem.

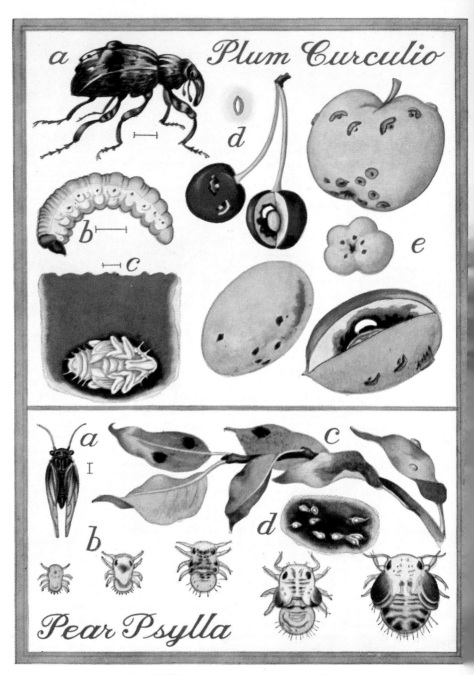

XXII PLUM CURCULIO: (a) adult snout beetle; (b) grub; (c) pupa in soil; (d) egg; (e) typical injury, crescent-shaped scar, on cherry, plum, and apple. PEAR PSYLLA: (a) adult; (b) nymph in different instars; (c) injury to pear leaves; (d) eggs attached to bark by one end.

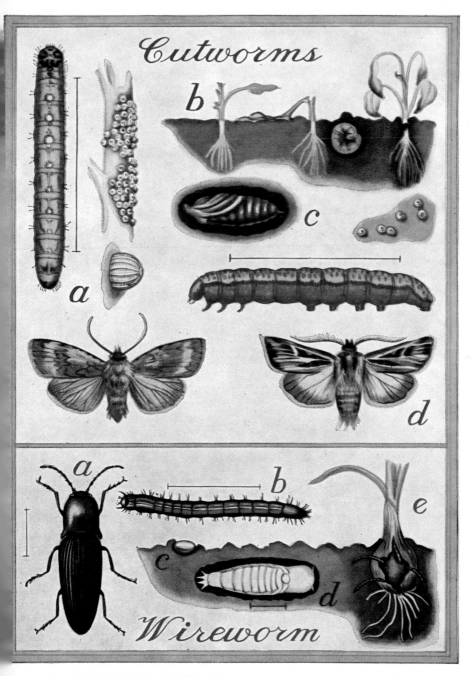

XXIII VARIEGATED CUTWORM: (a) larva, egg cluster, and single egg enlarged, and moth. DINGY CUTWORM: (b) seedlings cut off and cutworm in typical coiled position; (c) pupa in soil, eggs and larva. WIREWORM: (a) click beetle adult; (b) larva; (c) egg; (d) pupa in soil; (e) larvae feeding in bulb.

EVA MELADY

XXIV BEET LEAFHOPPER: (a) curly-top disease of beet, the virus trans mitted by leafhopper, showing clearing of veins, wartlike protuberances, leaf rolling (b) nymph in fifth instar; (c) adult; (d) eggs on leaf and young nymph; (e) disease tomato leaf. SIX-SPOTTED LEAFHOPPER: (a) adult, showing 6 black spots; (b yellows disease of lettuce, transmitted by leafhopper; (c) aster yellows.

to almost all 2- and 3-needle pines. A variety of this species occurs in Minnesota, the Dakotas, Nebraska. There hibernation is in a cocoon in litter on the ground, but usually this moth winters inside the tip of the injured twig. There is 1 generation in Massachusetts, 2 in Delaware and Pennsylvania, 4 in Louisiana and Texas. In Delaware spring-brood moths start emerging the first of April and continue to early June; 2nd brood moths work from early July to August. They are small, ½ inch across the wings, reddish brown with silver-gray markings. They lay yellow, flattened, circular eggs on needles, buds, or shoots. The larvae—yellow to pale brown, ⅜ inch long—mine in needles, then in buds, spinning a web around the needles, often covered with pitch, and then burrow in twigs of new growth to pupate. Young pines are seriously deformed and occasionally die. Loblolly pine is often injured.

Control. Cut off infested tips in late fall or winter (except in central states where larvae are not in tips at that time). Spray with dimethoate or Sevin, starting at the end of April (in Delaware), repeating twice at 14-day intervals.

Nevada Buck Moth, *Hemileuca nevadensis* Stetch. In the Southwest on willow, poplar, and shin-oak. The spiny yellow-and-black larvae feed gregariously.

Northern Pitch Twig Moth*, *Petrova albicapitana* (Busck). Reddish larvae, ½ inch long, bore in twigs, producing pitch on pines in northern states.

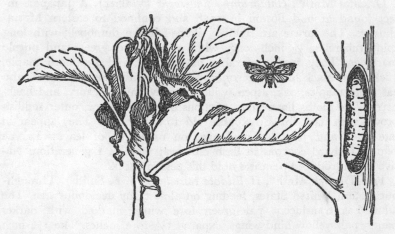

64. Oriental fruit moth injury to peach, and detail of moth and larva.

Oriental Fruit Moth*, *Grapholitha molesta* (Busck). Introduced from the Orient prior to 1915 on nursery stock, established wherever peaches are grown in eastern states and now important in the West. Most serious on peaches, the fruit moth also attacks quince, apple, pear, apricot, plum, cherry, and Chinese hawthorn. First indication in spring is a blackening and dying back of new growth. Fruit injury is similar to that of codling moth in apple but, because the worm enters through the stem, there may be no external sign of injury until breakdown after picking reveals numerous feeding burrows.

Full-grown larvae, pinkish white with brown heads, ½ inch long, winter in cocoons on bark or in rubbish, weeds, or mummified fruit on ground; they pupate in late spring. Moths, gray with chocolate-brown markings, ½ inch across, lay flat white eggs on leaves or twigs shortly after peaches bloom. First-brood larvae attack growing tips, which die, and spin cocoons on bark. Larvae of later broods attack both shoots and fruit. There are 3 or 4 broods in New York, up to 7 farther south.

Control. Orchardists may spray with parathion, Guthion, or Imidan, the last being less toxic to people. Apply at the shuck-split stage and cover stages. Home fruit growers may want to use Sevin. Get an exact spray schedule for your area from the local agricultural agent. Cultivation of soil to a depth of 4 inches in infested orchards 1 to 3 weeks before blooming kills many overwintered pupae. Cull fruits should be promptly destroyed. Some parasites have been released for control.

Oriental Moth*, *Cnidocampa flavescens* (Walker). A Japanese insect found around Boston in 1906 and confined to eastern Massachusetts. The larvae are sluglike, shaped like a dumbbell, with long spiny tubercles, ⅞ inch long, with yellow, blue, green, and purple markings. They feed preferably on Norway and sycamore maple, buckthorn, black birch, cherry, apple, pear, and plum, but may also eat other maples, oak, aspen, willow, honeylocust, hickory, and hackberry. The moths have inner portions of wings yellow, outer reddish brown with dark fringe; expanse 1¼ to 1½ inches. They appear in late June and July, lay oval eggs on underside of leaves. Larvae pupate in hard cocoons in limb crotches; there is 1 generation. Native and introduced parasites hold this pest in check.

Pale Tussock Moth*, *Halisidota tessellaris* (J. E. Smith). Throughout eastern United States, feeding on almost any deciduous tree. The adult has translucent pale-green fore wings marked with darker bands, pale-yellow hind wings, expanse 1½ to 2 inches. The 1¼-inch caterpillar is blackish, sparsely covered with yellow-buff hairs. It also has dense tufts of yellow-gray hairs, 3 pairs of black pencils of hairs, with a white pencil beneath each.

Pandora Moth*, *Coloradia pandora* Blake. Important in western pine belts. Moths have brownish gray fore wings with a spattering of white scales, black lines, and a black spot, hind wings with pinkish hairs, expanse 3 to 4 inches. They lay flattened green eggs in clusters on bark of pine trees in spring. Caterpillars, appearing in August, are dark when young, brown to green with short spines when mature; 2½ to 3 inches long. The life cycle takes 2 years. Large areas of Jeffrey and yellow pines may be defoliated. There are many natural enemies, including a wilt disease, ground squirrels, and chipmunks. Indians have used the caterpillars for food, drying them, then making them into a stew, sometimes roasting the pupae.

Pea Moth*, *Laspeyresia nigricana* (Stephens). A serious pest in northern pea-canning areas, sometimes a garden problem. Present since 1900, the pea moth attacks all field and garden peas, sweetpea, and vetch. Growing pods have irregular cavities eaten out of the side; seeds are spoiled and pods are partly filled with pellets of excrement and caterpillar silk; they turn yellow, ripen prematurely. Inactive larvae winter in silk cocoons covered with soil particles just below the soil surface or in cracks and crevices around barns. They change to brownish pupae in late spring when peas bloom. Small brown moths, marked with black and white lines on fore wings, are active about pea plants in late afternoon, laying minute, flattened white eggs singly on pods, leaves, flowers, stems, or other nearby plants. Young larvae drill into pods. They are yellow-white with dark spots, pale short hairs over the body, dark areas at each end; ½ inch long. They eat their way out of pods and make cocoons in soil until the next spring. Control with cultural measures, sanitation, early planting.

Pepper-and-Salt Moth*, *Biston cognataria* (Guenée). One of the measuring worms.

Pine Cone Moth, *Dioryctria abietella* Dyer & Shannon. An iridescent greenish red caterpillar, ¾ inch long, bores through scales and seed of Douglas-fir, true fir, pine and spruce cones. The moths are gray, mottled with black, 1 inch across the wings.

Pine Tortrix, *Tortrix pallorana* Robinson. On pines, including those in Christmas-tree plantings, also injuring alfalfa and clover.

Pine Tube Moth*, *Argyrotaenia pinatubana* (Kearfott). On white pine through eastern states, lodgepole and whitebark pine in the Rocky Mountain region. Moths have rust-red fore wings, with 2 oblique lines across each, silky gray hind wings, ½-inch wingspread. They emerge in late April and May and the 2nd brood comes in July. Larvae, ⅓ inch long, are greenish yellow with a faint dark line down the back. They make tubes by tying needles together side by side, squarely eating off the free end. The tubes stand erect and may be quite conspicuous; pupation is in the tubes. Control by removing and burning tubes in winter. Parasites are effective.

Pine Tussock Moth*, *Dasychira plagiata* (Walker). On various pines in the Middle West, causing heavy defoliation of jack pine.

Pitch Pine Tip Moth*, *Rhyacionia rigidana* (Fernald).

Pitch Twig Moth*, *Petrova comstockiana* (Fernald). On hard pine from Massachusetts to Virginia, west to Minnesota. The moth is reddish brown mottled with gray, ⅝-inch wingspread; the larva is pale brown with dark-brown head; ½ inch long. It infests small branches and twigs, leaving a thick mass of pitch at the entrance. Cut out such twigs.

Polyphemus Moth*, *Antheraea polyphemus* (Cramer). One of the giant silkworms, feeding on oak, elm, sassafras, wild cherry, ash, sweetgum, maple, poplar, lilac, birch, and other trees but rarely injurious. The moth has brownish yellow wings crossed with a dusky band edged with pink, and a large eyespot on each hind wing. The caterpillar is 3 inches long, light green with an oblique yellow line on sides of each abdominal segment except first and last, 6 small golden tubercles on each segment, with 1 to 3 bristles.

Promethea Moth*, *Callosamia promethea* (Drury). Spicebush Silk Moth. The most common of the giant silkworms, feeding on spicebush, sassafras, lilac, wild cherry, tuliptree, ash, and other plants. The female has light reddish brown wings, crossed near the middle with a white, waxy line and an angular discal spot; wingspread to 3 inches. The male has dark-brown to nearly black wings with light-brown borders and a zigzag line. The caterpillars are 2 inches long, pale bluish green with rows of black, polished warty tubercles, 2 larger coral-red pairs of tubercles on 2nd and 3rd thoracic segments and a yellow pair on the abdominal segment. The cocoon is long, spindle-shaped, enclosed in a leaf.

Redcedar Tortrix, *Tortrix cockerellana* Kearfott. Webbing and defoliating redcedar; reported from Nevada.

Regal Moth*. See Hickory Horned Devil under Caterpillars.

Resplendent Shield Bearer*, *Coptodisca splendoriferella* (Clemens). Small moth with lanceolate wings, gray and yellow marked with brown and silver. The larva makes a linear mine in a leaf of apple, wild cherry, or related tree, and when full-grown makes a case from this mine, lining it with silk and attaching it to limb or trunk.

Rusty Tussock Moth*, *Orgyia antiqua* (Linnaeus). A European species in northern states, a pest of apple, quince, and other fruits, feeding also on beech, mountain-ash, birch, poplar, willow, and other trees. The male moth has rust-brown wings marked with gray lines, a white spot near the hind border of each wing; the female is gray and wingless. The caterpillar is dark gray, 1⅛ inches long, with a pair of black hair pencils from orange tubercles on the 2nd abdominal segment, tufts of white or yellowish hairs on other segments, and a black head.

Satin Moth*, *Stilpnotia salicis* (Linnaeus). First discovered in Massachusetts in 1920, now present in New England, New York, and Oregon, Washington, California, and Idaho, defoliating poplars, feeding also on willow, sometimes on oak. Partly grown larvae winter in small webs in bark crevices, start feeding in late April or May. They are black with conspicuous irregular white blotches down the back and a transverse row of reddish brown tubercles with tan hairs on each segment. They pupate in a cocoon on leaves or on twigs, and the satin-white moths, wing expanse 1½ to 2 inches, emerge in July. They lay eggs in white, glistening clusters on trunk, branches, and leaves. The larvae appear in 2 weeks but grow slowly, finishing their development the next spring. Then they feed ravenously, defoliating trees and often killing them, sometimes migrating to fences, walks, and buildings, annoying people.

Control. Several natural parasites are at work. Spray trees in spring with Sevin, diazinon, or malathion. If egg masses are abundant, paint them with creosote.

Sequoia Pitch Moth*, *Vespamima sequoiae* (Hy. Edwards). Opaque, dirty-white larvae infest branches and trunks, mine the cambium layer of knobcone, lodgepole, Monterey and yellow pine, Douglas-fir, redwood, and other conifers in Montana, Washington, Oregon, and California. The moth looks like a yellow-jacket wasp, black with the last segment of the abdomen bordered with bright yellow. The larvae start working from wounds, and a large mass of gummy pitch covers the point of entrance. They pupate in this mass and the pupa case is protruded so the moth does not touch the pitch on emergence. The species is common but not serious enough to call for control measures.

Silverspotted Tiger Moth*, *Halisidota argentata* Packard. Found from the Atlantic to the Pacific, principally on Douglas-fir but also on true firs, Sitka spruce, shore pine, and other conifers. The moth has reddish brown fore wings, 1½ to 2 inches across, with silvery white dots. The larvae hibernate in webs during the winter, then feed gregariously in spring. They are about 1½ inches long, densely covered with long, brushlike, poisonous brown to black hairs. They spin brown cocoons in June attaching these to needles, bark, or debris on forest floor.

Smeared Dagger Moth*, *Acronicta oblinita* (J. E. Smith). From Maine to Florida and west to the Rocky Mountains, feeding on alder, boxelder, wild cherry, poplar, and willow. The caterpillar is velvety black, dotted and banded with yellow, bearing short reddish hairs.

Snapdragon Plume Moth, *Platyptilia antirrhina* Lange. Small, greenish larvae at first mine leaves, then feed openly on terminal leaves, bore inside developing flowers, seeds, and inside main stems. Mature caterpillars are green or purplish red. Naked pupae are suspended from any part of plants, giving rise to grayish brown moths, ½-inch wingspread. There are 3 generations a year outdoors in California, more in greenhouses.

Snowberry Clearwing, *Hemaris diffinis* (Boisduval). From New England to Georgia and the Great Plains on snowberry and bush honeysuckle. The hornworm larvae, 1½ to 2 inches long, are green to brown or purplish, with dark spiracles. The sphinx moths have clear, transparent wings with dark-brown margins, expanding 1½ to 2 inches, black bodies marked with gold. There are 2 generations; hibernation is as pupae in soil. Handpicking is usually sufficient control.

Southwestern Pine Tip Moth, *Rhyacionia neomexicana.* On ponderosa pine in Arizona.

Spotted Tussock Moth*, *Halisidota maculata* (Harris). Common in the Northeast, ranging through northern states to California, feeding on alder, apple, birch, boxelder, wild cherry, maple, oak, and willow but not a serious defoliator. The moths are about 2 inches across, with dark-yellow fore wings marked by bands and spots, plain, nearly transparent hind wings. Larvae are 1¼ inches long with tufts of yellow hairs in the middle of the body, black hairs at both ends, a line of black spots along the back, and a few, long, whitish pencils of hairs.

Spruce Epizeuxis, *Epizeuxis aemula* (Hübner). Common on ornamental spruce in the Northeast. Small brown larvae, with black tubercles and spiracles, web needles together in large masses and fill them with excrement. They feed on older needles. Moths, brownish gray with wings crossed by narrow bands, emerge in June and July. Eggs hatch in late summer; partly grown larvae winter in webbed masses of dry needles.

Spruce Seed Moth*, *Laspeyresia youngana* Kearfott. Distributed through northern states. The larvae bore into spruce cones, feeding on seeds. The moth is brown, only ⅜ inch across the wings.

Strawberry Crown Moth*, *Synanthedon bibionipennis* (Boisduval). On the Pacific Coast. White to pinkish larvae with brown heads, nearly 1 inch long, bore in the crown, as many as 50 borers sometimes working in a single plant. The foliage turns yellow, recent transplants die; older plants are much weakened. Raspberries and blackberries may be infested as well as strawberries. The clearwing moth, day-flying, resembles a yellow-jacket wasp. Nearly mature larvae winter in strawberry crowns, pupate in May. Moths emerge in June and July, laying eggs on lower leaves; there is 1 generation. Control by sanitary measures; pull and burn infested plants in spring before moths emerge; top plants after harvest; cover beds with straw after topping to prevent egg laying.

Sunflower Moth*, *Homoeosoma electellum* (Hulst). Destructive to cultivated sunflowers, also found on marigold, cosmos, coreopsis, and some other flowers. The moth is gray, lays eggs in florets; the larva is greenish yellow with 5 brown stripes down the back. Larvae feed on the head, in a mass of webbing and frass, destroying the seeds. Pupation is in the head. Spray with diazinon when flowers first appear.

Sycamore Tussock Moth*, *Halisidota harrisii* Walsh. Abundant on sycamore in the Northeast but rarely calling for control measures. The yellow larva has white to yellow hairs with long orange hair pencils. The adult is like the pale tussock moth.

Virginiacreeper Sphinx*, *Darapsa myron* (Cramer). Feeding on grape and Virginia-creeper; resembles the Abbott's sphinx.

Walnut Sphinx*, *Cressonia juglandis* (J. E. Smith). From Canada to Florida and west to the Great Plains on butternut, black walnut, hickories, pecan, and hornbeam. The caterpillar is 2 inches long, from light green to reddish, granulated with white, and with 7 oblique yellowish stripes, a brownish caudal horn.

Western Tussock Moth*, *Hemerocampa vetusta* (Boisduval). California Tussock Moth, on the Pacific Coast from southern California to British Columbia. The female is gray, wingless; the male has brown wings with gray markings. Eggs are laid in felty gray masses on old cocoons or bark of host plants—apple, almond, apricot, blackberry, California Christmasberry, walnut, willows. The caterpillars are gray with red, blue, and yellow spots, 4 tufts of hairs in the middle of the body, 1 white and 1 black tuft at the end, and 2 long black tufts, looking like horns, at the head; ¾ to 1 inch long. They feed on leaves and young fruit. There is only 1 brood. Eggs are deposited in late summer and fall, hatch when leaves unfold in spring.

Control. Remove egg masses in winter; jar caterpillars from trees and prevent return by banding as for cankerworms. Spray with malathion or carbaryl or diazinon.

Whitelined Sphinx*, *Hyles lineata* (Fabricius). Striped Morning Sphinx. Common in the West, occurring throughout the country on apple, azalea, beet, collards, currant, elm, fuchsia, gooseberry, grape, melon, pear, plum, portulaca, prune, tomato, turnip, and other crops.

The hornworm larva is serious on beets and tomatoes in Florida. It is 2½ to 3 inches long, usually green, with yellow head and horn and pale spots bordered with black. Some larvae, however, are black with orange head and horn, 3 yellow spots on the back.

The moths resemble humming birds, with brown bodies marked with white and darker brown; fore wings with white-lined veins and a broad buff stripe; dark hind wings and a rosy band across the middle. They visit flowers at dusk. Pupation is in soil, in shiny dark brown chrysalids. There are 2 broods.

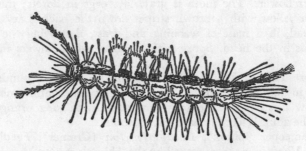

65. Larva of whitemarked tussock moth.

Whitemarked Tussock Moth*, *Hemerocampa leucostigma* (J. E. Smith). A native, common in the East, ranging west to Colorado. This is primarily a city pest, feeding on many deciduous shade trees —elm, linden, maple, horsechestnut, poplar, sycamore, buckeye, willow, and others—and on fruits—apple, pear, quince, plum—but not on evergreens. Foliage is skeletonized and fruits scarred by conspicuous hairy caterpillars, 1½ inches long. These have red heads, 2 pencil-like tufts of long black hairs projecting like horns, with a 3rd tuft at the rear, a black stripe down the middle of the back, bordered with a wide yellow line, 4 white brushes or tussocks of hairs on the first segments of the abdomen.

The female moth is nearly wingless, gray, hairy; the male has brownish wings marked with gray, spreading to 1¼ inches, feathery antennae, legs tufted with white hairs. Eggs are laid in fall in conspicuous masses, about 1 inch long, of 50 to 100, covered with a white lathery substance, on trunk, branches, dead leaves, or on top of the cocoon from which the female emerged. Caterpillars feed from April to June, depending on location, pupate in cocoons on trunk and branches, and the moths emerge to lay eggs for a 2nd generation which feeds in August and September. There are 3 generations in Washington, D.C., and farther south.

Control. A great many parasites work on this insect, but there are also many hyperparasites living on the parasites. Birds eat young larvae. Egg masses can be scraped off or painted with creosote. Spraying with carbaryl or other chemical for cankerworms and elm leaf beetles will also control tussock moths.

Yucca Moth*, *Tegeticula yuccasella* (Riley). A southwestern species responsible for the pollination of yucca plants. The female has specially modified mouth parts with which she scrapes together pollen from the stamens and carries it with her to another flower, where she lays eggs through the wall of the ovary into the seed cavity.

Zimmerman Pine Moth*, *Dioryctria zimmermani* (Grote). On Austrian, pitch, red, Scotch, Swiss, white, and yellow pines over most of their range, reported on other conifers in the West. The moth is reddish gray marked with dark and light lines, 1 to 1½ inches across the wings. It lays eggs on bark, often near wounds, and the larvae, white to reddish yellow or green, ¾ inch long, bore into trunks and branches. Entire tops of trees may break off, or branch tips turn brown. Pitch tubes are formed at the base of injured parts. Prune out infested portions where possible.

ORTHEZIA

Members of this genus are in the order Homoptera, family Ortheziidae. They are close relatives of scale insects and mealybugs and are often called ensign scales or ensign coccids. There are a number of species on wild plants but only one of importance on cultivated plants.

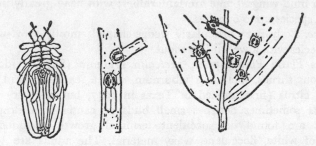

66. *Greenhouse orthezia.*

Greenhouse Orthezia*, *Orthezia insignis* Browne. Infesting 125 or more varieties of greenhouse plants and a garden pest in warm climates. Favored hosts are lantana, coleus, chrysanthemum, cactus, heliotrope, periwinkle, petunia, sage, silver lace-vine, and verbena. This species is called lantana bug for its predilection for that plant and has even been introduced into Hawaii as a beneficial insect to cope with *Lantana camea,* which has become a pest there.

The dark-green wingless nymphs, not much bigger than pinheads, are covered with rows of minute waxy plates. The mature female is pale brown or dark green with a conspicuous waxy fringe around the body and a long, white, fluted egg sac. The total length of adult and sac is only ⅓ inch. Plants become sickly and sometimes die from the constant sucking on leaves, stems, and roots. Spray with malathion; destroy less valuable plants if they are seriously infested.

PLANTHOPPERS

Planthoppers are sucking insects in the order Homoptera, super-family Fulgoroidea. They have been called fulgorids, lightning leaf-hoppers, lanternflies, mealyflata. The tropical species have many grotesque forms and may be 2 inches or more in size. The forms in this country are relatively small, similar to leafhoppers, with the same jumping habit, but a little larger and with the antennae arising below the eyes and with few spurs on the hind tibiae. Some of the families are:

Delphacidae. The largest family of planthoppers, and very common. Hind tibiae have a large apical spur. Most members are quite small and many are short-winged.

Flatidae. Body somewhat wedge-shaped, usually brown or green. Fore wings held almost vertical at rest and with numerous cross veins; hind tibiae with spines on sides.

Fulgoridae. Mostly brown, relatively large, not very common; cross veins on hind wings. Some are lanternflies; with head greatly inflated; tropical species up to 6 inches.

Issidae. Body not particularly wedge-shaped; mostly short-winged; some species with a weevil-like snout.

Citrus Flatid Planthopper, *Metcalfa pruinosa* (Say). Widespread on various shrubs, including viburnum, azalea, camellia, and occurring on citrus (first noticed in Texas in 1947, but not very important). It sometimes destroys small buds or causes fruit drop. The nymphs are found on succulent terminal growth surrounded by masses of white, flocculent, waxy material. The adults are ⅓ inch long, light brownish gray, with very broad wings giving the insect a wedge-shaped appearance. On citrus, parathion has given control.

Corn Planthopper*, *Peregrinus maidis* (Ashmead). Also called Corn Leafhopper, serious in Florida, reported from South Carolina, Texas, and other states. The adult is yellowish green, ⅙ inch long; it has clear wings longer than the body with dark markings near the tip;

antennae with greatly thickened basal portion. Abundant in late August in Florida these delphacid planthoppers collect in large numbers near buds or in axils of leaves; nearly every stalk of young corn may be killed before reaching tasseling stage. It can be controlled with sulfur or pyrethrum dust.

Flatid Planthopper, *Anormenis septentrionalis* (Spinola). Common through most of the United States east of the Great Plains on shrubs and woody vines, viburnum particularly, but also azalea, boxwood, camellia, crapemyrtle, catalpa, Japanese cherry, hawthorn, honeysuckle, wild grape, mulberry, redbud, spirea, dahlia, salvia, lilies, and other plants. Tree trunks and branches are covered with white, flocculent strands concealing the young greenish nymphs, which jump quickly when disturbed. The adults, which are around in August and September in home gardens in the North, are a little larger than the citrus planthopper and have wide bluish green wings. Eggs are laid in slits in bark of twigs and covered with a white, waxy secretion. There is only 1 generation. This species is more conspicuous than injurious and control measures are seldom necessary.

Another flatid planthopper, *Ormenaria rufifascia,* is listed on palms in Florida. A delphacid planthopper, *Delphacodes propinqua,* is recorded as moderate to heavy in Bermuda grass seed plots in Arizona.

PSOCIDS

Psocids, barklice, are small soft-bodied insects with chewing mouth parts in the order Psocoptera, which also includes booklice. They have long, filiform antennae and long legs. If wings are present the fore wings are larger than the hind wings and the two pairs slant rooflike over the body. Barklice are in the family Psocidae, most common, or Pseudocaeciliidae, which includes forms that spin unsightly webs on tree trunks and branches, more often in the South. Although they may be seen outdoors on bark, leaves, fences, and stone walls they are not usually considered pests. They feed on fungi, pollen, lichens, grasses or grains or dead insects. They are not important enough to the gardener to be listed under separate species.

PSYLLIDS

Psyllids belong to the family Psyllidae, order Homoptera. They are related to aphids and are often known as jumping plant lice. They are small sucking insects, usually under ¼ inch, with hind legs enlarged for jumping, and relatively long antennae. Many secrete large amounts of white waxy filaments. Adults are very active, moving quickly when disturbed. Some species are serious pests, some are a nuisance because of copious honeydew and subsequent growth of disfiguring sooty mold, and a western species causes a disease known as psyllid yellows.

Acacia Psyllid, *Psylla uncatoides* (Ferris and Klyver). May be serious on acacia in California, sometimes on albizzia and other shrubs; has been known to enter houses. Also reported in Arizona.

Alder Psyllid, *Psylla floccosa* Patch. Common in the Northeast. The nymphs produce large quantities of wax, and groups of the psyllids look like masses of cotton on stems.

Apple Sucker*, *Psylla mali* (Schmidberger). An introduced species established in Canada. Eggs laid on apple twigs in fall hatch as buds open. Becoming adult in June, psyllids may leave apples for vegetables, returning in autumn for egg laying. Feeding by nymphs injures opening buds, destroys flower clusters, prevents fruit from setting. There is a great amount of honeydew.

Blackberry Psyllid, *Trioza tripunctata* Fitch. A native on wild blackberry in the Northeast, infesting cultivated blackberries and other brambles; reported also in Florida. The adult is ⅙ inch long, yellow-brown, each wing marked with 3 yellow-brown bands. It winters in protected places and soon after growth starts in spring lays eggs in hairs of leaf stems and tender shoots. Nymphs and adults puncture shoots, curl leaves, produce stunting and almost gall-like distortion. There is 1 generation. Spray with malathion, about mid-May and 10 days later.

Boxelder Psyllid, *Psylla negundinis* Mally. On boxelder, similar to the alder psyllid. Spray with malathion in mid-May or early June.

Boxwood Psyllid*, *Psylla buxi* (Linnaeus). Confined to boxwood. Terminal leaves are cupped and young twig growth checked by a small, gray-green nymph covered with a white cottony or waxy material. The adult, a small green "fly" with transparent wings, appears in late May or June and lays eggs in the base of buds. First-instar nymphs winter there and infest terminal leaves as they unfold in spring. Their feeding punctures cause the leaves to curl and form a cup concealing and protecting the nymphs. In Connecticut tests, spraying in early April with diazinon or dimethoate killed overwintering nymphs. This will also control adults; or spray with malathion in mid-May and repeat in 2 weeks.

Fig Psyllid, *Homotoma ficus* Linnaeus. A Mediterranean insect found on figs in California in 1969. Nymphs are soft green, adults either green or brown with transparent wings, large head, protruding eyes. Small, sausage-shaped eggs, first white, then orange, winter in buds.

Hackberry Nipplegall Maker*, *Pachypsylla celtidismamma* (Riley).

67. Boxwood leaves cupped by boxwood psyllid.

Pale to dark reddish brown, forming globular hairy galls on underside of leaves and crater-like depressions on the upper surface. Three other species also form galls on hackberry. Spray with diazinon or carbaryl in early May.

Laurel Psyllid, *Trioza alacris* Flor. A pest of laurel or sweetbay in California and Atlantic States, also on cherry-laurel. Leaves curl and thicken, redden at margins, form galls; plants are unsightly, lose much of their foliage. Nymphs are pale yellow and orange, hidden by long strands of white wax; adults are very small, $\frac{1}{12}$ inch long, greenish yellow to pale brown with light and dark spots. Eggs are white to yellow, covered with fine powdery wax. In New Jersey they are laid in March or April, adults having wintered in or on hosts. Spray with malathion.

Magnolia Psyllid, *Trioza magnoliae.* Reported from Florida. Nymphs and galls appear on stem and leaves of the redbay tree.

Pear Psylla*, *Psylla pyricola* Foerster. An important pest of pear in eastern states since it was first found in Connecticut in 1832, serious in the Pacific Northwest since 1939 and now present in many states in between and as far south as South Carolina. The copious honeydew secreted by pear psyllids covers foliage and fruit; sooty mold growing in this makes brown spots on the leaves, scars and blackens the fruit. There may be partial defoliation, loss of vigor; buds may not develop normally. Bartlett and d'Anjou pears are especially susceptible; quinces are occasionally infested. The adult is dark reddish brown, $\frac{1}{10}$ inch long, and looks like a miniature cicada (Plate XXII). It winters in bark crevices or under leaves on ground and starts in early spring to lay pear-shaped yellow eggs around buds. In 2 weeks these hatch into wingless nymphs, $\frac{1}{80}$ inch long, which broaden and darken through 5 molting periods, becoming adult in a month. There are 3 to 5 generations in a season, with summer eggs laid on leaves or petioles. Nymphs cluster at axils and on underside of leaves, secreting their abundant sticky honeydew. A "decline" in pear trees on the Pacific Coast is laid to the pear psylla. At first it was thought that the symptoms came from a toxin infected by the insect but apparently the psylla is a vector of a virus disease.

Control. A dormant oil spray in early spring kills many adults and eggs. Guthion is now recommended for commercial growers in the East, applied at the cluster-bud stage and in cover sprays. Perthane is effective in Oregon and Washington, applied in very early spring before the overwintering pysllids lay eggs.

Persimmon Psylla*, *Trioza diospyri* (Ashmead). On persimmon in Florida.

Potato Psyllid*, *Paratrioza cockerelli* (Sulc). **Tomato Psyllid***. Present from the Great Plains to the Pacific Coast, chiefly on potato and tomato but also recorded on pepper, eggplant, and tomatillo, causing a disease known as psyllid yellows. Adults are first green, then black with white margins, $\frac{1}{10}$ inch long. The females lay bright-yellow oval eggs, each attached by a stalk to edges of underside of leaves, usually when the temperature is around 80° F. They hatch in 4 to 15 days into flat, scalelike nymphs, first yellow or orange, then green with a fringe of hairs all around the body. During their feeding they inject into the potato plant a substance, probably a virus, that disturbs the proper relation between foliage and tubers. The effect on the potato or tomato varies somewhat with the number of insects present, 10 to 30 being required for full expression of the disease. Even when psyllid nymphs feed on only a few leaves, symptoms appear all over the plant. Basal portions of leaflets turn yellow at margin and roll upward; terminal leaves have a reddish or purple cast; older leaves turn brown and die; stems do not elongate; nodes swell; axillary buds on potatoes develop into aerial tubers or short shoots with swollen bases and small distorted leaves. Feeding by adults does not produce such symptoms; the power is confined to nymphs.

The psyllid winters in southern Texas, New Mexico, and Arizona on wild plants, mostly matrimony vine (*Lycium*), and moves northward to potato and tomato fields in late spring, returning to the southern range in October or November. Other plants of the nightshade family, especially Chinese lantern and groundcherry, may be infested.

Control. Eliminate weed hosts so far as possible, and potatoes sprouting in cull piles. Farmers can treat the soil at planting time with disulfoton granules, applied in bands on both sides of rows. Foliage is sprayed with parathion, starting when 1 adult is found and repeating every 2 weeks for 4 or 5 times.

Sumac Psyllids, *Calophya californica* Schwartz. Black to brown on California sumac in southern California. *C. triozomima* Schwartz, reddish or black with yellow abdomen, occurs in Arizona, Colorado, and California. In the East, *C. flavida* infests smooth sumac. The immature nymphs are dark gray or black with a narrow white fringe; they are found on bark of terminal twigs in winter. *C. nigripennis* infests shining sumac; the adult has black, opaque wings.

Willow Psyllid, *Trioza maura* Foerster. Infesting a large variety of willows throughout North America. It varies in color from bright orange to reddish brown or dark red.

ROOTWORMS

Rootworms are larvae of beetles. They work on the roots of plants and sometimes these are quite different from the plants injured by the adults. For instance, the clover rootworm is the grape colaspis; the southern corn rootworm is the spotted cucumber beetle. Both have been discussed under beetles.

Cranberry Rootworm*, *Rhabdopterus picipes* (Olivier). Important in the beetle stage on rhododendron, camellias, and other ornamentals, not too serious as a root pest of cranberry. It is found along the coast from New England to Florida and along the Gulf to the Mississippi River. The beetles are oval, $\frac{1}{4} \times \frac{1}{8}$ inch, brown to black with a metallic luster. They hide in leaves or rubbish during the day, feed at night or on cloudy days on young foliage as it is opening, making characteristic right-angled holes or crescents. Spray with dimethoate at time new growth starts, repeating in 10 to 14 days. See also Rhabdopterus Beetles under Beetles.

Grape Rootworm*, *Fidia viticida* Walsh. Present in eastern states, except extreme North and far South, on grape and related wild plants. Small, curved, white, brown-headed grubs winter deep in soil, migrating near the surface in spring, changing to soft white pupae in small cells. About 2 weeks after grapes bloom, hairy, chunky, brown beetles, $\frac{1}{4}$ inch long, feed on upper side of leaves, making conspicuous chains of small holes. They lay eggs in clusters on grape canes, often under loose bark. Young grubs drop to the ground, burrow in soil until they reach the roots; they cut off small feeding roots and gouge channels in larger roots until cold weather. Infested vines lack vigor, have little new growth, and yellow foliage.

Control. Spray with carbaryl for the beetle stage as soon as first leaf punctures are noticed. The spray schedule for grape berry moth controls the rootworm.

Northern Corn Rootworm*, *Diabrotica longicornis* (Say). Present from New England to Colorado with scattered infestations in Texas and some other southern states but causing most injury in the Upper Mississippi Valley. The larvae feed only on corn, the adults on many summer-flowering plants, including sunflower heads in South Dakota. Eggs are laid in the ground in fall, around corn roots, and hatch rather late in spring. The larvae, threadlike, wrinkled white worms with brown heads, ½ inch long when grown, burrow in corn roots, making brown tunnels. They leave the roots in July and pupate in soil. Beetles, uniform yellow-green, ⅙ to ¼ inch long, appear in late July and August, feed on corn silk and pollen of other plants, lay eggs in cornfields, and die at first frost.

Control. Rotate corn with another crop. Apply a granular insecticide, such as carbofuran, at planting time in a 6-inch band over rows.

Southern Corn Rootworm. See Spotted Cucumber Beetle under Beetles.

Strawberry Rootworm*, *Paria fragariae* Wilcox. This and other species are found over much of the United States on strawberry, raspberry, blackberry, grape, rose, peach, apple, walnut, butternut, pyracantha, wild crab, mountain-ash, and several other hosts. Rose leaves, in greenhouses or outdoors, may be riddled with small shotholes, bark of new shoots may be gnawed off, buds eaten out. Leaves of strawberries and other fruits may be destroyed. The beetles—very small, ⅛ inch long, oval, shiny dark brown or black—winter as adults among old leaves, straw, or trash. Females lay eggs in spring in soil close to plants or on underside of dead leaves around plants. The small, white, brown-spotted larvae feed on strawberry, rose, or other roots all spring, then pupate in soil, with beetles feeding until frost. In greenhouses or warm climates there may be 2 or more generations.

Control. If necessary, spray or dust strawberries with methoxychlor. Chlordane has been used on roses, applied at first bloom and again in July and August. A phosphate aerosol has been effective in greenhouses.

Western Corn Rootworm*, *Diabrotica virgifera* LeConte. Active in the Middle West on corn, sorghum, alfalfa, and soybeans. Similar to the northern corn rootworm.

Western Grape Rootworm*, *Adoxus obscurus* (Linnaeus). Present on grape, serious in California many years ago, now of minor importance. Fireweed is the native host. The beetle is dark, nearly black, covered with short hairs. It eats chainlike strips in leaves and gouges into young berries. The C-shaped white grubs eat smaller roots entirely and the bark of larger roots. They winter in the soil at a depth of 2 feet or more but in spring burrow up near the soil surface to pupate. Disking the soil at this time destroys many of the pupae.

SAWFLIES

Sawflies belong to the order Hymenoptera, along with bees and wasps. Like other members of that order, the adults have 2 pairs of transparent wings, hooked together. As members of the suborder Symphyta, the females have an ovipositor (egg-laying apparatus) adapted for sawing or boring but not for stinging. It consists of 2 short outer plates and 2 saw-toothed blades which move in opposite directions when the female is slitting a leaf before laying her egg. Almost all sawflies feed on plants in the larval stage. Larvae look like caterpillars but they have more than 5 pairs of prolegs and they do not have crotchets. Most live exposed on foliage, singly or in groups; a few spin webs; some are leafminers. The families given here include those of importance to gardeners.

Argidae. Argid sawflies. Medium to small, stout-bodied, usually dark, antennae 3-segmented with the 3rd segment very long and often U-shaped in males. Larvae feed on various trees and shrubs.

Cephidae. Stem sawflies. Adults slender, compressed; larvae boring in stems of grasses and berries.

Cimbicidae. Cimbicid sawflies. Resembling bumblebees; large, robust, with clubbed antennae. The elm sawfly is the most common species.

Diprionidae. Conifer sawflies. Medium-sized sawflies with 13 or more antennal segments, serrate in the female, comblike in the male. The larvae are very injurious to pine, spruce, and other conifers.

Pamphiliidae. Web-spinning sawflies. Small, stout-bodied, spinning webs, rolling or tying leaves.

Tenthredinidae. Typical sawflies. Small to medium-sized, brightly colored, usually found on foliage or flowers, the larvae highly destructive to trees and shrubs. The family includes birch and elm leafminers, roseslug, pearslug, imported currantworm, larch sawfly.

Xyelidae. A small group of small to medium-sized sawflies, with 3rd antennal segment very long. Larvae feed on hickory, elm, and staminate flowers of pine.

Arborvitae Sawfly, *Monoctenus melliceps* Cresson. In northeastern states, also in Kansas, on arborvitae and juniper. The larvae are ⅝ to ¾ inch, dull green with 3 dark stripes, black legs, and light-brown head.

Balsam Fir Sawfly*, *Neodiprion abietis* (Harris). From New England west to Minnesota and Missouri, defoliating balsam fir, feeding some on spruce. Larvae are green, striped with dark green and brown, with black heads, ¾ inch long when grown. Adults emerge from late June to early September, cut slits in needles for eggs, which hatch in late May or June. Larvae feed gregariously, then spin reddish brown cocoons on twigs or in litter on ground. Spray for young larvae with methoxychlor or carbaryl.

Balsam Shootboring Sawfly*, *Pleroneura brunneicornis* Rohwer.

Birch Sawfly*, *Arge pectoralis* (Leach). On various birches in the Northeast. The larva is fat, yellowish, with rows of black spots, reddish yellow head; ¾ inch long. See Birch Leafminer for the really serious sawfly on this host.

Blackberry Sawfly, *Pamphilius dentatus* MacGillivray. Occasionally blackberry leaves are rolled and webbed by bluish green larvae ¾ inch long, which feed inside the roll. Adults appear in May, lay oval, white eggs end to end on larger veins. Larvae feed until July, then enter soil to remain until the next May.

Blackheaded Ash Sawfly*, *Tethida cordigera* (Palisot de Beauvois). Distribution and habits like the brownheaded ash sawfly. The larva is whitish with a yellow tinge, with shiny black head; ¾ inch when grown.

Bristly Roseslug*, *Cladius isomerus* Norton. Found east of the Mississippi north of Virginia and also in California, a very serious defoliator of wild and cultivated roses. Larvae are sluglike, greenish white, with long, rather stout bristles, ⅝ inch long. They first skeletonize the leaves by feeding from the undersurface, later eat holes clear through. Eggs are laid in slits in upper side of midrib. There may be as many as 5 or 6 generations. Pupation for summer broods is in cocoons on leaves or twigs; overwintering cocoons are in the soil. Almost any insecticide on the foliage *before* larvae start feeding and repeated at frequent intervals will control roseslugs. Try methoxychlor or carbaryl.

Brownheaded Ash Sawfly*, *Tomostethus multicinctus* (Rohwer). A serious defoliator of red and white ash used as shade trees in eastern and central states. Adults emerge when leaf buds show green, and lay eggs in developing leaflets. Yellow-white or greenish white larvae with brown heads eat ravenously until late May or June, then construct cocoon-like cells in the soil where they stay until spring. Spray in May with malathion.

Butternut Woollyworm, *Blennocampa caryae* North. Found on butternut, hickory, and English walnut. The false caterpillars are covered with long white filaments, standing straight up, and when several larvae feed side by side on the undersurface of leaves the foliage seems to be covered with masses of white wool. Underneath the filaments the larvae are pea-green, about an inch long, with 8 pairs of prolegs. They eat from the side of the leaf inward, often leaving nothing but midrib. They pupate near the surface of the ground. The adult is black with reddish thorax. The injury is ordinarily not enough to call for spraying.

California Pear Sawfly*, *Pristiphora abbreviata* (Hartig). Reported from Colorado as well as California, attacking pear blossoms and foliage.

Cedar Cone Sawfly, *Augomonoctenus libocedri* Rohwer. Cones are injured by slug-like larvae. Adults are blue-black with 5 segments of the abdomen brick-red.

Cherry Fruit Sawfly*, *Hoplocampa cookei* (Clarke). A Pacific Coast pest of cherry, plum, prune, sometimes peach and apricot. Adults have black bodies, yellow appendages, are ⅛ inch long. Larvae, white with brown heads, ¼ inch long, work in partly developed fruits and feed on seeds, then leave through a hole in the side to pupate in a silken cocoon for winter. Fruits wither and drop.

Curled Rose Sawfly*, *Allantus cinctus* (Linnaeus). Coiled Rose Worm, found from Maine to Virginia and west to Minnesota on wild and cultivated roses. It curls up like a cutworm, starts in by skeletonizing but ends by devouring entire leaflets except the largest veins. The larva is metallic green above, marked with white dots, grayish white underneath, with yellow-brown head; ¾ inch long when grown. The larvae form cells in the pith of pruned ends of rose canes and pupate there. There are 2 generations in the southern part of the range, 1 in New England. Eggs are laid in upper surface of leaflets. Spray or dust with any stomach poison before larvae start eating.

Cypress Sawfly*, *Susana cupressi* Rohwer & Middleton. Feeding on foliage of Monterey and Italian cypress in California.

Dock Sawfly*, *Ametastegia glabrata* (Fallén). In northern United States on dock, sorrel, and knotweed but burrowing into apple fruit for the winter. The larvae are olive or bluish green with conspicuous white tubercles.

Dogwood Sawflies, *Macremphytus tarsatus* (Say) and *M. varianus* (Norton). Common defoliators of species of Cornus in the Northeast and the Lakes States. The larvae have a shiny black head and body covered with white powder. Spray with methoxychlor or carbaryl.

Dusky Birch Sawfly*, *Croesus latitarsus* Norton. Common in New

England and the Great Lakes area on gray birch, sometimes other birches. The larvae—yellow-green with black markings, black heads, up to 1 inch long—feed in gangs all around the margins of leaves. Saplings may be defoliated. There are 2 overlapping generations, with larvae feeding from early June to late fall. Adults, blue-black with white leg markings, appear in May and June. Spray young trees with malathion or methoxychlor or carbaryl.

68. Elm sawfly larvae (note how the rear end is secured to stem).

Elm Sawfly*, *Cimbex americana* Leach. Giant American Sawfly. Distributed through northern states to Colorado on elm, including Chinese elm. Adults are large, nearly an inch long, steel-blue and black with 3 or 4 yellow spots on each side; long buff antennae with knobbed ends; smoky-brown transparent wings. The larva is pale yellow-green with a black stripe down the back, black spiracles, 8 pairs of prolegs; 1¾ inches when grown. It rests in a coiled position, feeds with its rear end curled around a twig. Eggs are laid in leaf tissue in May, each egg showing as a blister on the underside of the leaf. Young larvae crawl out through a slit in the epidermis, feed for 6 to 8 weeks (from June to October), then spin brown, papery cocoons in soil litter, transforming to true pupae in spring or early summer. Although elm and willow are the principal food plants, alder, basswood, birch, maple, and poplar are sometimes eaten. Adults may injure by gnawing bark of twigs.

Control. Spraying for elm leaf beetles should also control sawflies. Several parasitic wasps and flies are on the job.

European Apple Sawfly*, *Hoplocampa testudinea* (Klug). First discovered on Long Island about 1940, now destructive to apple, crabapple, plum, pear in New England, New York, New Jersey, Delaware, and Pennsylvania. Adults, brown-and-yellow "flies," emerge from puparia in the ground when trees bloom; eggs are inserted in calyx cups. Larvae, white with 7 prolegs, bore into the fruit, leaving a chocolate sawdust on the surface. One larva may damage several fruits. There is 1 generation. Two sprays of rotenone, one at petal fall and the 2nd a week later are suggested for home gardens; or use methoxychlor.

European Pine Sawfly*, *Neodiprion sertifer* (Geoffroy). An introduced species first noted in New Jersey in 1925 and exceedingly troublesome in home gardens, nurseries, watersheds, etc. Now present in all of New England, in New York, New Jersey, Pennsylvania, Ohio, Indiana, Illinois, Michigan, Iowa, and South Dakota. Favored food

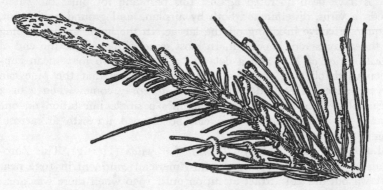

69. Young larvae of European pine sawfly chewing off needles.

plants are red, jack, Swiss mountain, mugho pines, which are seriously defoliated. Eggs are laid in rows in slits in pine needles; just before hatching in late April they look like pine needle scales. The tiny young larvae, green with shiny black heads, join together in gangs but they match the needles so well they are scarcely ever noticed until far too much damage has been done. They feed at first on the side of needles, causing a few tip needles to turn straw-colored and curl slightly, an excellent early diagnostic sign. Several hundred may work together, and after demolishing one twig move on to the next. When disturbed, they move in uncanny unison, elevating their rear ends. Feeding is confined to old needles; infested ornamental pines about the house will show, by the end of May, new green plumes waving at the end of long, naked branches. After 4 or 5 weeks of feeding the full-grown larva is grayish green with a light stripe down the back, 2 white lines bordering a broken stripe of intense green; 7/8 inch long.

Mature larvae drop or crawl to the ground to spin golden-brown cocoons in litter on top of the soil or in protected places on the trunk, sometimes in frass left by pine webworms. Pupae are formed in the cocoons in late summer, adults emerging in September and October to lay their eggs in the current year's growth of needles. They look like small bees or large, fuzzy flies; males are blackish with feathery antennae; females are yellow-brown.

Control. One thorough spraying at the time larvae are hatching should give control for the season. DDT was particularly effective; now we must substitute methoxychlor or carbaryl. In tests, airplane application of malathion or Baygon has given control. Parasitic wasps have been liberated against this pest and for pines on watersheds, a virus, disseminated both by airplane and ground equipment, is quite effective in killing off the larvae. In the home garden timing of the spray is very important. In most seasons this will be the end of April or first of May and a delay of a week or two may mean conspicuous defoliation, resulting in naked branches that the pine can never replace. A reminder of the time to spray comes when 2 or 3 terminal needles turn yellow. Sometimes a single infestation on one branch of an ornamental pine can be cleaned up with an aerosol bomb.

European Spruce Sawfly*, *Diprion hercyniae* (Hartig). This European species was first found on the American continent in 1922 near Ottawa but did not attract attention until 1930 when there was great damage on the Gaspé Peninsula. After that it spread at an alarming rate, and by 1937 was rated the worst enemy of northeastern spruce forests. In Maine it reached its high peak of population in 1939; since then it has declined in numbers due to rodents eating cocoons on the ground, insect predators and parasites, and a wilt disease. This sawfly is now present in all of New England, New York, and New Jersey feeding on white, red, black, and Norway spruces, occasionally others. Trees that are entirely defoliated usually die.

Eggs are laid singly on the needles, with young larvae beginning to feed at the tip. They are light green at first, later dark green with 5 narrow white stripes. They pupate in small brown cocoons beneath trees. The female sawfly is stout-bodied, black with yellow markings; males are rare; reproduction is usually without fertilization. There are 2 or 3 broods. Ornamentals can be sprayed with carbaryl. In forest areas most reliance is on natural controls.

Goldenglow Sawfly, *Macrophya intermedia* (Norton). Light-gray larvae, with a darker-gray median stripe and a row of black spots, occasionally defoliate plants. They rest on leaves in a typical coiled position. There is 1 generation; adults appear in June. Dust or spray with malathion.

Grape Sawfly*, *Erythaspides vitis* (Harris). Sometimes heavy enough on grape to require control.

Grass Sawfly*, *Pachynematus extensicornis* (Norton).

Greenheaded Spruce Sawfly*, *Pikonema dimmockii* (Cresson). On various spruces in northern states, but seldom causing serious defoliation.

Hemlock Sawfly*, *Neodiprion tsugae* Middleton. A western species defoliating hemlock from Oregon northward. Larvae are green, striped when young, 1 inch long when grown. Cocoons are attached to needles or laid in debris on ground. There is 1 generation, with larvae feeding in July and August. A number of parasites keep this sawfly in check.

Hibiscus Sawfly, *Atomacera decepta* Rohwer. Known for more than 50 years but not important in Georgia until increase in plantings of "Henderson's strain" of hibiscus. The adult is very small, black with a red spot, smoky wings. Eggs are laid in tissues of older leaves and larvae skeletonize leaves from lower surface. They are pale green with a dark head. The life cycle is only 28 days with 6 or more generations in a season. Pupation is in soil or leaf litter.

Honeysuckle Sawfly*, *Zaraea inflata* Norton. Climbing and bush honeysuckles may be stripped of leaves by dull-gray, yellow-striped, black-dotted larvae about an inch long. They spin cocoons in the soil. Adults, emerging in spring, are large, with a black abdomen, yellow ring at the base, a line of silver hairs on each segment.

Imported Currantworm*, *Nematus ribesii* (Scopoli). Arrived from Europe about 1857, now general over the United States. It is rare to find a garden with currants or gooseberries without this problem. Larvae or pupae winter in cocoons on the ground; black, yellow-marked adults appear in spring to lay white, flattened, shiny eggs on veins and midribs on underside of leaves. Larvae hatch about the time currants are in full leaf. They feed in from leaf margins in groups, eventually devouring entire leaves. The worms are greeen with black heads and body spots (Plate XXXII). When disturbed they elevate front and rear ends of their bodies. After feeding for 2 or 3 weeks they pupate in the ground. Eggs for the 2nd generation, which is less injurious, are laid in late June and July. Spray or dust with malathion or rotenone.

Introduced Pine Sawfly*, *Diprion similis* (Hartig). Commonly defoliating ornamental pines in the Northeast, first discovered in Connecticut in 1914. White pines and other 5-needled pines are preferred, but others may be eaten. Larvae are yellow-green with a double black stripe the entire length of the back, a broken yellow stripe on each side, and the sides mottled yellow and black; 1 inch long. Adults are black and yellow, wings spreading ¾ inch (Plate XXXI). Adults emerge from pupae on ground in April and May, lay eggs in slits in the edge of needles. There are 1 or 2 generations annually, with most of the larval feeding in May and June and August and September, on new growth as well as older needles. There may be complete defoliation and death of small pines.

Control. Rake up and destroy debris under trees in autumn. Watch for 1st brood and spray with methoxychlor or carbaryl.

Jack Pine Sawfly*, *Neodiprion pratti banksianae* Rohwer. On ponderosa and lodgepole pines in Idaho, Montana, and the Great Lakes region.

Larch Sawfly*, *Pristiphora erichsonii* (Hartig). A serious defoliator of larch, first recorded in Maine and Massachusetts in 1882, in Minnesota in 1909, though apparently present long before that. Outbreaks have been periodic, sometimes defoliating and killing large stands of forest trees or larches in home plantings for 2 or more years in succession. The wasplike yellow-and-black adults, wings expanding ⅘ inch, lay eggs from late May to early July in slits cut in young twigs, causing a twisting. The eggs hatch in about a week, and the larvae feed ravenously in groups of 40 or 50, working the lower branches first. They are dull gray-green above, paler underneath, with black head and legs. There is 1 generation, sometimes a partial 2nd. The larvae winter in tough brown cocoons in duff on the ground.

Control. Birds and mice destroy cocoons; parasitic wasps and flies and a fungus attack larvae. Rake up debris from under ornamental larches in autumn. Spray with carbaryl in June or July if necessary.

Loblolly Pine Sawfly, *Neodiprion americanum* Leach. In Atlantic States, defoliating loblolly pine in Virginia, sometimes feeding on shortleaf pines. The larvae—greenish white with a green line down the back, black spots along the side, reddish brown head, ⅞ inch long—feed from late April to June on old needles. There is 1 generation.

Lodgepole Sawfly*, *Neodiprion burkei* Middleton. Distributed through Oregon, Idaho, Montana, Wyoming, defoliating and killing lodgepole pine. Larvae are green or grayish with lighter stripes, brown heads, 1 inch long.

Monterey Pine Sawfly, *Itycorsia* sp. Attacking and killing only Monterey pine in its native habitat in California. Larvae—dark green or brown with black heads—web needles and excrement into a mass.

Mountain Ash Sawfly*, *Pristiphora geniculata* (Hartig). More or less abundant in New England, New Jersey, and New York on mountain-ash. Winter is passed in cocoons on soil; adults, yellow

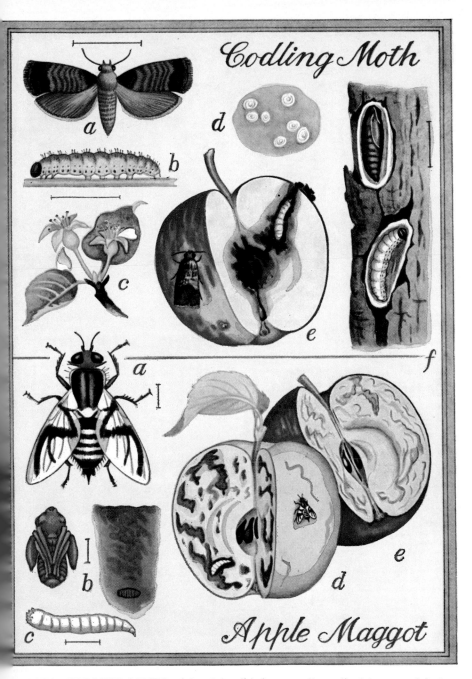

XXV CODLING MOTH: (a) adult; (b) larva or "worm"; (c) stage of fruit
when first worms enter; (d) eggs, enlarged; (e) larva tunneling out, moth on surface
of apple, and sting from second-brood larva entering fruit; (f) larva in winter
position under bark scales and pupa formed in spring. APPLE MAGGOT: (a) adult
fly; (b) pupa, enlarged, and puparium (containing pupa), natural size in soil; (c)
maggot; (d,e) injury to fruit with maggot inside and fly puncturing skin to lay eggs.

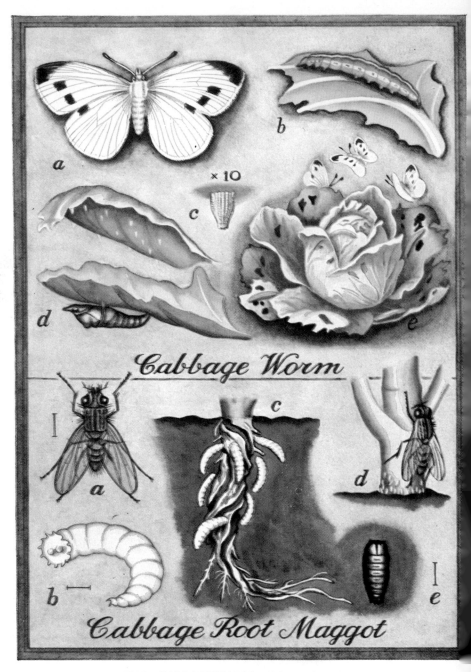

Cabbage Worm

Cabbage Root Maggot

XXVI IMPORTED CABBAGEWORM: (a) adult butterfly; (b) full-grown caterpillar; (c) egg, magnified 10 times; (d) chrysalid attached to leaf; (e) injury to cabbage head by larvae, adults laying eggs. CABBAGE MAGGOT: (a) adult fly; (b) legless maggot (much enlarged); (c) maggots working on roots; (d) fly laying eggs at base of stem; (e) puparium in soil.

XXVII TWO-SPOTTED MITE (Red Spider): (a) adult 8-legged mite, magnified 50 times; (b) young 6-legged larva or nymph; (c) egg enlarged and mites in web on underside of bean leaf; (d) typical mite injury to phlox, juniper, rose, bean, and violet. LONG-TAILED MEALYBUG (a). CITRUS MEALYBUG (b). COCONUT MEALYBUG (c). MEALYBUGS: (d) on begonia; (e) on fuchsia; (f) on coleus; (g) on palm.

XXVIII ROSE MIDGE: (a) adult; (b) larvae on inside of sepal, injury to bud; (c) distortion of young shoot; (d) pupa in cocoon in soil, much enlarged; (e) egg mass on sepal and egg magnified. CHRYSANTHEMUM GALL MIDGE: (a) adult, much enlarged; (b) conical galls on leaf; (c) eggs; (d) stem cut to show pupa and maggot inside galls; (e) shoot with galls on stem and leaves.

with black spots, deposit eggs in slits near edges of leaves in late May. Larvae, green with black dots, work from early June to the middle of July. Often feeding shortly before Japanese beetles appear in New Jersey, their chewing is wrongly attributed to the beetles. They work mostly on the upper foliage, leaving nothing but larger veins and midribs. Occasionally there is a partial 2nd generation. Spray thoroughly with carbaryl as soon as the leaves are fully expanded.

Peach Sawfly, *Pamphilius persicus* MacGillivray. One of the leaf-rolling species. Pale blue-green larvae sometimes eat foliage in June and July. They winter in cocoons in the soil, pupate in spring. Adults, black with yellow markings, emerge in late spring. They are usually controlled by sprays for other peach insects.

Pear Sawfly, *Hoplocampa brevis* (Klug). Feeding on apple and pear and closely related to the European apple sawfly. The adults are very small, mostly brown with yellowish wings.

Pearslug, *Caliroa cerasi* (Linnaeus). On pear, cherry, plum throughout the country, occasionally on hawthorn, Juneberry, mountain-ash, quince. Larvae are dark green to orange, tadpole-shaped, covered with slime, $\frac{1}{2}$ inch long, looking like small slugs. They skeletonize the leaves, eating everything but a network of veins. Black-and-yellow sawflies, slightly larger than houseflies, emerge from cocoons in the earth just after cherries or pears come into full leaf and lay their eggs in leaves. Larvae feed for 2 or 3 weeks from the upper leaf surface, drop to the ground to pupate, with adults coming out in July or August for a 2nd brood, which may completely defoliate young trees. The standard spray program for pears should control slugs. Or apply a separate spray of malathion or carbaryl.

Pine Sawflies. In addition to those treated separately, various other species may infest pine. *Diprion rohweri* Middleton is reported defoliating piñon pine. *D. frutetorum* is recently damaging pine in Indiana. *Neodiprion excitans* Rohwer feeds from the Carolinas to Texas on loblolly, shortleaf, and other pines. *N. nanulus contortae* Ross feeds on lodgepole and ponderosa pine. *N. taedae linearis* Ross is reported heavy on pines in Arkansas. The Nesting Pine Sawfly, *Acantholyda luteomaculata* (Cresson) occurs on white pine in Ohio. This by no means exhausts the list of pine sawflies.

Pin Oak Sawfly, *Caliroa lineata* (Linnaeus). Noted seriously damaging pin oaks in New Jersey in 1946, with widespread infestation in the state the next 2 years, of less importance since then. Reported also from North Carolina and New York. The larvae are similar to pearslugs, up to $\frac{1}{2}$ inch long, yellowish green with black heads, skeletonizing leaves from the upper surface. Infestation starts at top of trees, with the foliage in upper third of trees turning golden brown by late summer, most disfiguring to street trees and those in public parks.

Plum Webspinning Sawfly*, *Neurotoma inconspicua* (Norton). Serious in the Dakotas, present also in northeastern states, on plums and sand cherries. Webs, like those of the fall webworm, enclose ends of branches soon after plums come into full leaf. Smooth, grayish yellow larvae, up to ¾ inch long, feed inside webs, sometimes defoliating branches. Black adults, with red legs, insert eggs in leaf midribs in early spring. Cut off webbed ends of branches. There are several predators attacking larvae.

Poplar Leaffolding Sawfly*, *Phyllocolpa bozemani* (Cooley). From the prairies of Canada south into the United States. Adults lay eggs May to July, injuring leaves so they fold over; injured portions turn black, making foliage unsightly. Larvae eat holes through leaves. When grown, they drop to the ground with the leaves and pupate inside the folds.

Poplar Sawfly, *Trichiocampus viminalis* (Fall). A European species long present in northeastern and southern states, often destructive to ornamental Carolina or Lombardy poplars. The larvae are bright yellow with 2 rows of black spots on the back, 2 rows of small black spots near the spiracles, tufts of short white hairs over the body, black head; ¾ inch long. Larvae arrange themselves side by side on a leaf and eat ravenously; trees may be entirely defoliated. When grown, in 35 to 40 days, they make cocoons in bark crevices or under clods of earth. There may be 2 generations. Spray with carbaryl when larvae are very young.

Raspberry Sawfly*, *Monophadnoides geniculatus* (Hartig). Ranging through northern states but more common on the Pacific Coast, on raspberry, loganberry, dewberry, and blackberry. Adults are black with yellow and reddish markings; larvae are pale green with white spiny tubercles. They feed on underside and on edges of leaves, sometimes stripping the plants. Spray with malathion.

Redheaded Pine Sawfly*, *Neodiprion lecontei* (Fitch). Leconte's Sawfly, injurious to ornamental pines from Maine to Florida and west to Minnesota and Louisiana on Virginia, jack, red, eastern white, Scotch, loblolly, lodgepole, mugho, longleaf, pitch, ponderosa, and Austrian pines, also American larch and deodar. This is the most widespread and destructive of our native sawflies. The larvae live in groups and devour the needles, often defoliating young pines, which either die or are spoiled for ornamental purposes. Young larvae are whitish with brown heads, later yellow with 6 rows of conspicuous black spots and a red head; 1 inch long. In many sections there are 2 overlapping broods, with larvae feeding from May until

70. *Older larvae of redheaded pine sawfly, which have eaten off needles down to the base of the fascicles.*

late fall. Prepupal larvae winter in tough, papery, capsule-shaped cocoons in duff or topsoil under trees. Eggs are laid in slits in needles. The larvae prefer old needles but will eat new growth toward the end of the season, including tender bark of young twigs.

Control. Spray thoroughly with methoxychlor or carbaryl when larvae are young.

Red Oak Sawfly, *Pamphilius phyllisae* Middlekauff. Relatively new, recorded as defoliating red oak in Pennsylvania in 1964. Adults appear in late May, lay eggs along midribs of red-oak leaves in June. Larvae feed from late June to mid-July, rolling and webbing leaves, then drop to the ground.

Red Pine Sawfly*, *Neodiprion nanulus nanulus* Schedl. On red, pitch, and Japanese pine, reported from Maine, Wisconsin, other states.

Roseslug*, *Endelomyia aethiops* (Fabricius). European Roseslug, common on roses east of the Rocky Mountains and also present on the West Coast. This is a yellow-green, rather velvety slug, up to ½ inch long, appearing dark green from the food ingested. It eats the soft part of leaves, which, with nothing left but a network of veins and 1 epidermis, turn brown and crisp, making rose growers think they have "rust." When the leaves are only partly eaten, they appear to have windows in them. When full-grown, the larva enters the soil, constructs a capsule-shaped cell, and stays quiet in this cavity until early spring when the adult lays eggs in pockets in leaf tissue (Plate XXXII). There is only 1 generation of this species; feeding in late summer is due to the bristly roseslug. Control measures are the same and it is important to have carbaryl or malathion on the foliage

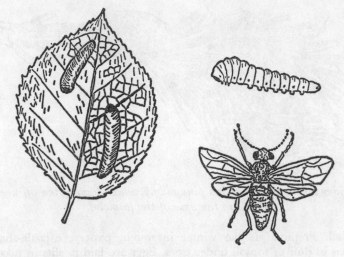

71. Roseslug; larvae skeletonizing leaf, and sawfly adult.

almost as soon as roses come into full leaf to prevent unsightly dis-figuration.

Rose Stem Sawfly, *Hartigia trimaculata* Say. One of the horntails, a wasp-like insect appearing in early summer and laying eggs in punctures made in rose canes. Whitish larvae bore through the canes, 1 to a cane, causing shoots to wilt, stunt, or die back.

Slash Pine Sawfly*, *Neodiprion merkeli* Ross.

Strawberry Sawfly, *Empria maculata.* Reported serious in home gardens in North Dakota.

Striped Alder Sawfly*, *Hemichroa crocea* (Fourcroy). May defoli-ate various species of alder in northeastern and Great Lakes States, oc-casionally feeding on birch. Young larvae are pure white, later yellow with brown stripes, ⅘ inch long. They eat everything except midrib and larger veins. There are 2 generations.

Swaine Jack Pine Sawfly*, *Neodiprion swainei* Middleton. Feeding on jack pine in Canada.

Violet Sawfly*, *Ametastegia pallipes* (Spinola). Often a serious pest of violets and pansies in eastern states, outdoors and in green-houses. Larvae are blue-black or olive-green, smooth, about ½ inch long, marked with white spots on back and sides. They work at night, first skeletonizing lower surface of leaves, later eating holes or feeding from leaf margins to entirely defoliate plants, most often in May and June. Pupation is in stalks of pithy plants; adults, black and yellow, emerge in 2 weeks to blister leaves with eggs inserted in lower side;

foliage may wither. There may be several broods. Spray or dust with malathion or methoxychlor.

White Pine Sawfly*, *Neodiprion pinetum* (Norton).

Willow Redgall Sawfly*, *Pontania proxima* (Lepeletier).

Willow Sawfly*, *Nematus ventralis* Say. Yellowspotted Willowslug, widely distributed in eastern states on willow and poplar, often defoliating willows in ornamental plantings, very injurious to basket willows in the South. The small, dark-brown to black sawfly, marked with yellow spots, lays eggs in leaves, producing blisters. The slugs are black with a greenish tinge and heart-shaped yellow spots along each side of the body. They feed close together in characteristic curved positions for about 3 weeks, then pupate on the ground for a 2nd generation. There may be several overlapping generations in the South. Spray with malathion or carbaryl.

Willow Shoot Sawfly*, *Janus abbreviatus* (Say). The larva is white, without abdominal prolegs but with a prong at the tip of the abdomen. It bores down in the pith. The female adult punctures shoots of poplar and willow for egg laying, causing dieback above the punctures. Cut out infested shoots.

Yellowheaded Spruce Sawfly*, *Pikonema alaskensis* (Rohwer). In the most northern states and New England, on white, red, black, Norway, Colorado blue, and Engelmann spruce. Larvae are yellow-green, striped with gray-green, and have chestnut-brown heads. They prefer new foliage until they are half grown. Eggs are laid in new needles in May or early June, hatching in 6 to 8 days. Larvae feed 30 to 40 days. There is 1 generation, with pupation in spring in cocoons in the soil.

SCALE INSECTS

Scale insects constitute a very large group of plant feeders. Along with mealybugs, which are really soft scales, they belong to the super-family Coccoidea, order Homoptera. The tarsi are usually 1-segmented, with 1 claw, or legs absent. The male is midgelike with 1 pair of wings (rarely wingless) and without a beak. The female is wingless, often legless, and usually with a waxy or scale-like covering. The 1st instar has legs and antennae and is an active insect but subsequent instars are less active and often sessile.

Most scale insects are serious pests of garden and greenhouse plants but a few species are of value because of their secretions. Shellac is made from the wax of a scale insect in India and some cochineal insects have been used as the source of a crimson dye.

Acleridae. A small family with most members on grasses and sedges, feeding from under leaf sheaths. A few species on orchids.

Asterolecaniidae. Pit scales. Females are small and oval, with body covered with a tough waxy film or embedded in a mass of wax. Legs are vestigial or lacking, eyes are lacking, antennae are short, 4- to 9-segmented.

Coccidae. Soft scales, wax scales, tortoise scales. Females are flattened elongate-oval, with a hard, smooth exoskeleton or covered with wax; legs present or absent; antennae absent or much reduced.

Dactylopiidae. Cochineal insects. Resembling mealybugs, the females are red, segmented, covered with waxy plates. The cochineal *Dactylopius coccus* Costa feeds on prickly pear cacti and is the source of a crimson dye, important in olden days.

Diaspididae. Armored scales. The largest family, with many important species. Females are small, soft-bodied, and covered with a shell that is usually free from the insect beneath. It is made of wax together with cast skins (exuviae) of the early stages. Some species are oviparous, others give birth to living young. Eggs are laid under the scale. The first instar young, crawlers, are active and can travel some distance with their 6 legs. Then they settle down, insert their thread-like mouth parts through the epidermis of a leaf, or bark of a stem, and start sucking sap. They molt twice, lose legs and antennae, and remain in one spot the rest of their lives. The males have an elongated body after the 2nd molt and after a 4th molt they have 1 pair of wings, legs, antennae, but no mouth parts. They look like small gnats but have a style-like process at the end of the abdomen.

Kermidae. Gall-like coccids. The females are spherical and resemble tiny galls; legs are absent; antennae are 4- to 6-segmented.

Margarodidae. Giant coccids and Ground Pearls. Females are large, rounded, with a segmented body. Beads are made from some tropical species. The cottonycushion scale is the most important pest in this group.

Some members of the mealybug families Pseudococcidae and Eriococcidae are called scales and included in this section rather than under Mealybugs.

Heavy scale infestations kill branches or entire trees or shrubs. Standard control for armored scales has been a dormant spray, oil or lime sulfur, before growth starts in spring but many scales may now be controlled in the crawling stage with malathion or dimethoate. Summer-oil sprays have been advised for soft or unarmored scales prevalent in greenhouses and warm climates but some commercial growers have replaced these with parathion and some gardeners are using malathion or dimethoate. Sevin and diazinon are registered for control of many scale insects.

Acuminate Scale, *Coccus acuminatus* (Signoret). Serious in Florida on ornamentals, also reported from Georgia, Massachusetts, and New York. It is found on albizzia, apple, banana, bay, bottlebrush, Brazilian peppertree, cajeput, cashew, ceriman, cocculus, cotoneaster, duranta, yellow elder, eugenia, eurya, feijoa, fern, *Ficus* spp., firethorn, flacourtia, frangipani, gallberry, gardenia, gumtree, holly, ixora, jasmine, Java bishopwood, lancewood, loquat, magnolia, mango, marlberry, mountain ebony, myrsine, sweetolive, orchids, persimmon, photinia, osmanthus, sapodilla, sciadophyllus, tabernaemontana, and tevetia. The scale is pale green or yellow, thin, flat. In warm rainy seasons it is controlled by a fungus, *Cephalosporium lecanii*. Oil sprays can be used on mango.

Araucaria Scale, *Eriococcus araucariae* Maskell. Imported into California on Norfolk Island pine; found also in Florida on this host. Oval, white, with wax, this is a soft scale or mealybug.

Artemisia Scale, *Eriococcus artemisiae* Kuwanna. With conspicuous globular white sacs, crowded on twigs of artemisia in California and other western states.

Asiatic Red Scale, *Aonidiella taxus* Leonard. Found on podocarpus in Florida, it was quarantined to prevent dissemination in nursery stock.

Azalea Bark Scale*, *Eriococcus azaleae* Comstock. Azalea Mealybug, a native of Japan. Common on outdoor azaleas in the South, also blueberry, fetterbush, and staggerbush, rather frequent on rhododendrons in the North. White cottony sacs, enclosing dark red females and their eggs, are present in forks of branches and over twigs, sometimes on main stems down to the ground. The males have a similar white covering but are small and more elongate. Foliage and twigs are often covered with black sooty mold growing in secreted honeydew. Azaleas appear yellow and unthrifty.

The winter is spent in the nymph stage, on the plant. There are 2 generations in the South, 1 in the North. In Alabama females mature very early in spring and start to lay eggs in March, with reddish brown crawlers hatching in 3 weeks and maturing in about 100 days. The 2nd brood appears in September. In Connecticut eggs start hatching about June 20, with the young migrants not maturing until the next spring.

Control. Spray with malathion or a summer oil, mid-July in Connecticut. New Jersey suggests a dormant oil in April or malathion or diazinon in late June. In the Deep South, spray with malathion in May and late September.

Bamboo Scale, *Asterolecanium bambusae* Boisduval. Generally distributed where bamboos are grown. Oval, somewhat convex, glossy in appearance, transparent with a yellow or green tinge, marginal fringe of pairs of short, pinkish filaments. On stems and leaves. Another species, *A. bambusicola* has been recently reported from Florida. *Kuanaspis hikosani* was first reported on bamboo in this country in 1960 in South Carolina.

Barberry Scale, *Lecaniodiaspis* sp. Convex, reddish brown, soft scale, sometimes numerous. Spray with miscible oil when plants are dormant or with malathion for crawling stage.

Barnacle Scale*, *Ceroplastes cirripediformis* Comstock. Found in California, Florida, Georgia, Louisiana, Mississippi, and North Carolina on bark or leaves of many plants: ampelopsis, sugar-apple, prickly-ash, California athel, avocado, blueberry, bignonia, Brazilian peppertree, buckthorn, carissa, cherry, citrus, crossandra, golden dewdrop, euonymus, eupatorium, firethorn, fuchsia, gardenia, gaura, guava, holly, inkberry, ixora, jasmine, garbia lily, Spanish lime, litchi, myrtle, parkinsonia, passion-flower, pear, Australian-pine, poinsettia, pomegranate, rockrose, sanchezia, sapodilla, schinus, thornapple, viburnum, and weigela. The female is reddish brown covered with white wax shading to gray or light brown, and with a spine-like process extending through the waxy covering at the anal end of the body.

Beech Scale*, *Cryptococcus fagisuga* Lindinger. A European species first found in Nova Scotia, reported in Massachusetts in 1929 and now present in New England and the Middle Atlantic States, infesting American and European birch. In Massachusetts eggs are laid from mid-June to late July, with hatching starting about August 1 and continuing into September. Young crawlers are abundant during this period. When the pale-yellow nymph settles into a bark crevice, it secretes cottony material which spreads out to cover several individuals. It becomes adult the next spring, nearly circular, $\frac{1}{50}$ to $\frac{1}{20}$ inch across, covered with white wax.

The feeding of the scale kills inner tissue of outer bark, but the most important injury comes from a fungus (*Nectria coccinea* var. *faginata*), which enters the tree through scale wounds. Foliage and twigs die, bark cracks, wood is infected. Apparently the fungus cannot enter until the scale has fed for a year, nor can it reproduce the disease without the scale.

Control. A thorough dormant spray with 5 gallons liquid lime sulfur to 50 gallons of water, or 20 pounds of dry lime sulfur to 100 gallons, is very effective. Miscible oils will kill the scale but may be injurious to beech. Spraying with dimethoate in late May or early

June has killed the beech scale in Connecticut. Spraying with mala-thion in August should kill nymphs.

Bermudagrass Scale, *Odonaspis ruthae* Kotinsky. On grass in Flor-ida, California, Louisiana, Texas, usually found in leaf axils in loose soil at surface of the ground. Oval or nearly circular, mod-erately convex, pure white; exuviae, near end of body, straw-colored and covered with a whitish secretion.

Black Araucaria Scale, *Chrysomphalus rossi* (Maskell). Almost black, much like the Florida red scale. This is a tropical species with a limited distribution on ornamentals in southern California— araucaria, rarely on redwood, sometimes on abutilon, artemisia, banksia, euonymus, hyssop, oleander, olive, orchids, palm, cycad, also on macadamia.

Black Pineleaf Scale*, *Nuculaspis californica* (Coleman). Distrib-uted over most of North America, often associated with pine needle scale on pine, reported also on Douglas-fir, hemlock, and other coni-fers. It may kill young pines. Mature scales are nearly circular, $\frac{1}{16}$ inch across, yellow-brown to black. There are 1 to 3 generations with hibernation as half-grown scales. They can be controlled with lime sulfur. Seedlings sometimes have to be dipped in 1 to 12 lime sulfur be-fore shipping.

Black Scale*, *Saissetia oleae* (Bernard). An unarmored species, pos-sibly the most important economically, present in all citrus-growing regions but not as important in the Gulf States as in California, where it has caused an annual 2-million-dollar loss. The black scale may be a greenhouse pest in the North. Besides orange, grapefruit, and lemon, important food plants include almond, apple, apricot, avocado, beech, fig, grape, oleander, olive, plum, rose, and English walnut. Injury comes not only from the extraction of sap but from the black sooty mold which, growing in honeydew, covers all surfaces of foliage, cutting off light and reducing photosynthesis, coating fruit so it has to be washed.

Overwintered females become adult in spring. They are almost hemispherical, $\frac{1}{5}$ inch across, dark brown to black, with a longitudi-nal ridge and 2 transverse elevations on the back forming the letter H; they deposit an average of 2,000 eggs. These, white at first, later orange, hatch in about 20 days. The young remain under the parent briefly but start crawling and feeding within 3 days, settling on leaves or new growth. They migrate to twigs and branches when partly grown and take 8 to 10 months to mature. There is usually 1 genera-tion, sometimes 2 or a partial 2nd. Males—thin, narrow, flat, semi-transparent—are rare; most reproduction is parthenogenetic.

In addition to the favored food plants mentioned, there are many ornamental hosts—acalypha, allamanda, prickly-ash, artemisia, assonia, banyan, asparagus fern, California mountain-holly, California nutmeg, Brazilian pepper-tree, carissa, cassava, camellia, deodar, ceriman, chinaberry, clerodendron, coral-vine, croton, cypress vine, elder, eugenia, euonymus, feijoa, fuchsia, fern, guava, frangipani, gardenia, golden dewdrop, golden-shower, holly, hibiscus, ixora, jasmine, jacaranda, mountain ebony, mountain-ash, myrtle, orchids, palms, pittosporum, poinciana, poinsettia, pomegranate, Japanese quince, rubber plant, sumac, sapodilla, sapota, sausage-tree, soapberry, strawberry-tree, silk-oak, willow, yucca, and many others.

Control. Originally the black scale was controlled on citrus trees in California by fumigation with hydrogen cyanide under fumigation tents, but the scale in many instances developed a resistance to cyanide. Malathion can be used on ornamentals and either malathion or parathion on citrus. The scale is not so important as formerly because of the highly effective work of *Aphycus helvolus* Compère, a parasite shipped to California from South Africa in 1937. At present it is somewhat less effective but there are other parasites and some predators, although the latter are less efficient.

Black Thread Scale*, *Ischnaspis longirostris* (Signoret). Nearly cosmopolitan, a greenhouse pest in the North, serious on palms, sometimes found on ornamentals including: acacia, agave, andira, bignonia, bottle-brush, Brazilian pepper, camellia, ceriman, coffee, fern, fig, cape-honeysuckle, iris, ixora, jasmine, justicia, lancewood, Indian laurel, Spanish laurel, privet, lily, mahogany, mango, mountain ebony, nolina, sweetolive, palmetto, philodendron, screwpine, randia, strobilanthes. The female is very narrow, threadlike, ⅛ inch long, dark brown to black. Its habit of attaching itself parallel to the ribs keeps it from being observed before palms get abundantly infested. Palms are yellow and stunted, may die if heavily infested. Spray with malathion or dimethoate.

Boisduval's Scale, *Diaspis boisduvalli* Signoret. Circular or somewhat ovate, thin, flat, semitransparent, white to light yellow, exuviae central; male white, narrow, with 3 ridges on the back. Cosmopolitan on palms and orchids; also on palmetto, achemea, anthurium, billbergia, cactus, caladium, dracaena, pineapple, spider-lily, strelitzia, travelers-tree, yucca, zamia. The scales are present on leaf, bark, and fruit. Spray with malathion; dimethoate is also effective but may injure certain orchid varieties.

Bowreyi Scale, *Pseudischnaspis bowreyi* (Targ).

Brown Soft Scale*, *Coccus hesperidum* Linnaeus. Soft Scale, Soft Brown Scale, widely distributed in greenhouses and outdoors in warm climates on ornamentals and fruits. It is rather flat, soft, oval, yellowish green or greenish brown, often with a marbled or ridge effect; ⅛ inch long. It usually resembles the host plant in color and is unnoticed until the infestation is very large. Young are born alive, 1 or 2 daily for a month or two. They are sluggish, settling down near the parent, maturing in about 2 months. A large amount of honeydew is produced, resulting in much smutting of foliage. Plants are weakened, stunted.

This is a rather common pest of gardenia, infesting foliage and tender branches; it is also frequent on fern, camellia, oleander. Other host plants, indoors and out, include acalypha, abutilon, agave, aloe, apple, apricot, anthurium, aralia, ardisia, araucaria, prickly-ash, assonia, avocado, banana, bay, bignonia, bottle-brush, bougainvillea, boxelder, Brazilian pepper-tree, cajeput, cassia, clematis, clerodendron, caladium, calla, camellia, camphor, carnation, century plant, citrus, ceriman, coral-vine, croton, date palm, dracaena, elaeagnus, elder, euonymus, feijoa, fig, grape, seagrape, guava, hawthorn, hibiscus, holly, hollyhock, English ivy, jasmine, ixora, Jupiter tree, lantana, laurel, locust, madroña, magnolia, mango, manzanita, maple, mountain ebony, morning-glory, mulberry, myrtle, peach, pear, phlox, orchids, palms, papaya, parkinsonia, persimmon, Australian, Italian, and Norfolk Island pine, pittosporum, poinsettia, plum, poplar, pothos, quisqualis, redbud, rosary pea, rose-of-Sharon, rose, sage, sapota, snow-on-the-mountain, stephanotis, strobilanthes, sweet-william, strawberry-tree, sycamore, tabernaemontana, viburnum, willow, wisteria, yucca, zephyranthes, and others.

Control. There are a large number of parasites which do an excellent job of controlling this soft scale but many of these are killed when parathion is used in orchards and greenhouses so that the scale flourishes. Azinphosmethyl may be used by commercial growers but others will use malathion, with 2 or 3 applications at 3-week intervals to kill young scales.

Cactus Scale*, *Diaspis echinocacti* (Bouché). On cacti and orchids, common in Florida and the Southwest and on house cacti in the North. The is an armored scale; female gray, circular; $\frac{1}{30}$ inch in diameter; male white, slender. The surface of many cacti may be completely encrusted. Spray with malathion or dimethoate at 2-week intervals. A summer-oil emulsion is effective but may injure some cacti. Try rubbing the scales off with a stiff brush.

Calico Scale*, *Lecanium cerasorum* Cockerell. Found in California on cherry, elm, maple, pear, prune, Boston ivy, Virginia-creeper, English walnut, and since 1964 known in Delaware on cherry, flowering peach, maple, mountain-ash, sweetgum, and other ornamentals; also reported from the District of Columbia. The female—hemispherical, shiny, marked with yellowish areas on a brown background—winters on lower surfaces of larger branches, and the young move to small twigs and branches in spring. Control measures are seldom necessary.

California Red Scale*, *Aonidiella aurantii* (Maskell). The most important citrus pest in California, also serious in Arizona and Texas, less damaging in more humid Gulf States. It probably came from Australia to southern California prior to 1875 on citrus nursery stock. Found in greenhouses in many parts of the country, it occurs outdoors only in warm climates. Ordinarily a pest of citrus—citron, grapefruit, lemon, orange, tangerine—it also infests acacia, aloe, apple, aspidistra, avocado, breadfruit, banana, boxelder, boxwood, chinaberry, coconut, eucalyptus, euonymus, fig, fuchsia, grape, hibiscus, holly, Japanese yew, jasmine, mango, mulberry, oak, olive, palms, passion-flower, pistachio, privet, quince, rose, sago palm, sweetbay, English walnut, willow, yucca. The scales attack leaves, twigs, or fruit, injecting a toxic substance into the tree. Leaves and fruit are spotted with yellow; sometimes the entire foliage turns yellow.

The mature female is pinhead size, $\frac{1}{12}$ inch across, armored, reddish brown, circular. Young scales are born alive; they stay under the parent shell for a few hours, crawl about for a day or two, then settle down and insert their sucking beaks at the places where they will stay the rest of their lives. Cottony secretions are molded into a cap-like covering with a small nipple in the center. After the first molt, in 10 to 15 days, the cast skins (exuviae) are incorporated into the center of the cap which is enlarged at the side. After a second molt and the enlargement, there is a gray margin around the body. The female is fertilized by a small, yellow-winged male and she continues to give birth to 2 or 3 scales a day for 2 or 3 months. There may be 4 generations a year.

Control. Parathion with oil is used by some orchardists. Deciduous ornamentals can have a dormant oil spray from December to February and evergreens a summer oil emulsion, or malathion can be used for crawlers. There are a number of parasites and some effective predators.

Camellia Mining Scale, *Pseudaonidia clavigera* (Cockerell). Reported in Florida in 1962, chiefly a pest of camellia but may also infest azalea, bottle-brush, boxwood, camellia, gardenia, crapemyrtle, cestrum, holly, jasmine, ligustrum, oak, pyracantha, rhododendron, and viburnum.

Camellia Parlatoria, *Parlatoria camelliae* (Comstock). The most common scale on camellia on the Pacific Coast, especially on plants under lath. It is present in Florida, also in Georgia, Louisiana, Mississippi, Oregon, South Carolina, Texas, and Virginia but not very important. It attacks sweetolive as well as camellias. The scale is very small, flat, oval, brownish, found on both leaf surfaces. The female body under the shell is light purple. Parathion has been used effectively by commercial growers.

Camellia Scale*, *Lepidosaphes camelliae* Hoke. Not so important as the tea scale on camellia, present most often on cuttings and on young plants in greenhouses. The female shell is light to dark brown, oyster-shaped, $\frac{1}{10}$ inch long, covering a white to purplish body. The male shell is smaller and narrower. The female starts laying eggs 40 to 50 days after birth, with the life cycle completed in 60 to 70 days. Few crawlers are present during the winter months outdoors because the females do not reproduce then. Foliage is devitalized, drops prematurely, but is not discolored. The camellia scale can be controlled with oil or other sprays applied for tea scale. A parasitic wasp and lady beetles are helpful.

Another armored scale on camellia in California is *Aspidotus degeneratus*.

Camphor Scale*, *Pseudaonidia duplex* (Cockerell). First noted in New Orleans in 1920, now present in Alabama, Mississippi, Louisiana, Florida. This scale is circular, moderately convex, dark blackish brown with orange exuviae, about $\frac{1}{10}$ inch across. It feeds on nearly 200 plants, with preference for the camphor-tree, Japanese persimmon, sweetolive, camellia, azalea, Satsuma orange and other citrus, Japanese honeysuckle, fig, Confederate jasmine, glossy privet, rose. It is sometimes injurious to avocado, elm, grape, hackberry, and pecan. It is so injurious to camphor that just a few scales on a twig can cause defoliation, and a tree can be killed within 6 months of attack. Ants help to disseminate the scale. It has been controlled with an oil spray in winter.

Chaff Scale*, *Parlatoria pergandii* Comstock. A greenhouse pest, infesting some outdoor plants in California, many more in Florida. Food plants include acacia, agave, asparagus fern, assonia, araucaria, aucuba, bay, bignonia, box, cajeput, camellia, camphor, carissa, cinnamon, citrus, cocculus, croton, cycad, currant, eugenia, euonymus, feijoa, fig, guava, holly, honeysuckle, jasmine, mango, magnolia, maple, orchids, lantana, laurel, mountain-laurel, privet, mimosa, silk-oak, oleander, palms, sweetolive, parkinsonia, pepper-tree, persimmon, photinia, pittosporum, screwpine, Confederate rose, smilax, Spanish bayonet, tea, tung-oil, viburnum, wandering-Jew. The female is circular to elongate, smooth, semitransparent, brownish gray with marginal yellow exuviae; found on bark or leaves.

Cassava Scale, *Lepidosaphes alba* (Cockerell). On cassava, tea weed, and *Tunrera ulmifolia* in Florida, also reported from New

Mexico. Oystershell-shaped, straight or curved, rather convex, pale grayish or brownish white; terminal exuviae, slightly darker than shell.

Chinese Obscure Scale*, *Parlatoriopsis chinensis* (Marlatt). Found in Florida, reported also from Missouri, on trunk and branches of *Ficus* spp. but not commercial fig. The shape is variable—short, elliptical to oval, flat or slightly convex; very thin, whitish; exuviae large, light brown to greenish, marginal or submarginal. This scale is covered with bits of bark and is hard to see.

Citricola Scale*, *Coccus pseudomagnoliarum* (Kuwana). A serious citrus pest in parts of California; found also on hackberry, pomegranate, English walnut, and elm. It resembles brown soft scale but is grayer, lays eggs instead of producing living young, has only 1 generation. It feeds on underside of leaves and on smaller twigs during the summer, migrating to branches in late winter or early spring. Most of the parasites of the soft scale also attack this species.

Citrus Snow Scale, *Unaspis citri* (Comstock). Present in southern states and California, limited to citrus. It is somewhat oyster-shaped, moderately convex, brown to blackish brown with brownish yellow exuviae. The numerous males are snow-white, elongate.

Cockerell Scale, *Leucaspis cockerelli* (de Charmoy). On orchids in Florida. *Phenacaspis cockerelli* is reported in Florida on magnolia, ivy, aucuba, elaeagnus, boxwood, and bishopwood.

Coconut Scale*, *Aspidiotus destructor* Signoret. On palms in southern Florida and other tropical climates, also found on almond, annona, Jamaica apple, sugar-apple, asparagus fern, avocado, banana, bottle-brush, box, cajeput, calophyllum, croton, gerbera, eugenia, frangipani, geiger-tree, umbrella grass, gumbo-limbo, honeysuckle, lawsonia, ligustrum, mahogany, mango, silk-oak, palmetto, orchids, papaya, pandanus, screwpine, poinciana, pondapple, wax privet, satinleaf, shore bay, soursop. The scale is very small, circular, thin, faint yellow but transparent, with deeper yellow exuviae. It may be abundant on foliage, may also occur on bark and fruit. It is under control by parasites.

Cottony Bamboo Scale, *Antonina crawi* Cockerell. On bamboo in greenhouses, outdoors in southern California. Oval, dark reddish purple bodies are enclosed in thick, white cottony sacs, often crowded at leaf axils. They may be quite injurious. Spray with malathion or a summer oil.

Cottony Cochineal Scale, *Dactylopius confusus* (Cockerell). A mealybug, on cactus in Florida, Arizona, Colorado, California, New Mexico. Oval, dark red, filled with red fluid, enclosed in a white, cottony mass.

Cottonycushion Scale*, *Icerya purchasi* Maskell. An Australian scale introduced into California on acacia about 1868, soon threatening the entire citrus industry and now present throughout the South and in greenhouses, on a long list of hosts. Food plants include acacia, acalypha, almond, amaranthus, apple, apricot, Aus-

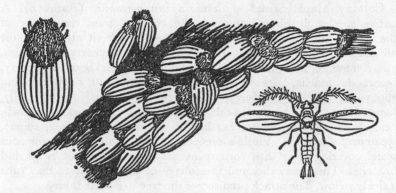

72. Cottonycushion scale; females with fluted egg masses, and winged male.

tralian-pine, boxwood, buckeye, California sage, castor-bean, cedar-of-Lebanon, chrysanthemum, citron, croton, cypress, fig, geranium, grape, grapefruit, sweetgum, Guadalupe palm, hackberry, ironwood, Boston ivy, laurel, lemon, lime, locust, magnolia, maple, mistletoe, oak, orange, peach, pear, pepper, pithecellobium, pine, pittosporum (very commonly infested), poinsettia, pomegranate, potato, quince, rose, sunflower, verbena, veronica, English walnut, willow. Trees may be completely covered with white cushions and sooty mold growing in the honeydew.

The insect itself is reddish brown but the female attaches a large, compact, white, fluted mass, holding from 600 to 800 bright-red eggs. This white egg mass sticks out at an angle from the twig and is very conspicuous. Hatching of eggs in the fluted ovisac occurs in a few days in summer, up to 2 months in winter. Young larvae are red with dark legs, dark antennae, long hairs at the end of the body. Even after molting, this scale keeps its legs and can move about until the egg sac is formed. The males are very tiny, with long white filaments. There are 3 or more generations.

Control. The spectacular control of cottonycushion scale by Vedalia, the Australian lady beetle, marked the first successful subjugation of a pest by the introduction of a natural enemy. Vedalia still keeps this scale from obtaining economic importance on citrus, except where the biological balance has been disturbed by chemicals such as DDT, which has more effect on the predators than on the scale. Where Vedalia is not present or is unable to act, parathion has been effective. Malathion should be substituted on ornamentals in home gardens.

Cottony Maple Scale*, *Pulvinaria innumerabilis* (Rathvon). A native species distributed through the country, most destructive in the North. With some preference for silver maple, it attacks almost all maples, boxelder, linden, black locust, red mulberry, white ash, and sometimes alder, andromeda, apple, beech, blackberry, blueberry, boxwood, bumelia, buckeye, sweetbay, cherry, currant, dogwood, elm, euonymus, grape, gooseberry, hackberry, hawthorn, hickory, holly, honeylocust, lilac, mountain-ash, myrtle, oak, Osage-orange, peach, pear, pecan, plum, poplar, persimmon, quince, rose, spirea, sumac, sycamore, viburnum, Virginia-creeper, willow. This is a conspicuous scale, covering trees with cottony masses on underside of twigs and branches. These may die, and the foliage of the whole tree may turn a sickly yellow. The attack predisposes the tree to border injury.

The scale winters as a small, brown, flattened female, ⅛ inch long, attached to bark. When sap flows in spring, it starts growing rapidly, depositing 1,500 to 3,000 eggs in a cottony mass several times the size of the original scale (Plate XXXIV). Around New York the young hatch in late June or July, crawling from twigs to leaves, where they suck sap along the midrib and veins and secrete honeydew. They mature in August and September and mate; the males die, the females crawl back to twigs for winter. There is only 1 generation.

Control. Former recommendation was to spray before growth starts with a miscible oil, but this may be injurious to soft maples. A current method is to spray with malathion or carbaryl in late June or early July.

Cottony Peach Scale*, *Pulvinaria amygdali* Cockerell. Fruittree Pulvinaria. The scale is flat, oval, yellow or reddish, usually covered with white, cottony wax and with a compact white, cottony egg sac. It feeds on leaves, bark, fruit of peach, prune, plum, apple in California and New Mexico.

Cottony Pine Scale, *Pseudophilippia quaintancii* Cockerell. Reported from Florida, Virginia, and North Carolina on pines, usually at base of needles. The female is oval or hemispherical, yellowish or light brown, covered with fluffy, snow-white secretions.

Cottony Taxus Scale, *Pulvinaria floccifera* (Westwood). Cottony Camellia Scale. A tropical insect reported in Florida and in greenhouses on angels trumpet, ardisia, guava, English ivy and mulberry, camellia, abutilon, and acalypha. In Oregon it infests camellia and holly and was found outdoors on yew (Taxus) in Rhode Island in 1950 and in Connecticut in 1953 where it may also infest dogwood, maple, holly, hydrangea, and other trees or shrubs. It winters as an immature female scale—small, light brown, flattened hemispherical, ⅛ inch long—and resumes feeding in the spring. On maturing, the female produces a long, flat, fluted, white, cottony egg mass extending back 3 or 4 times her length. Eggs hatch during the latter part of June and early July and the young infest underside of taxus leaves and sometimes twigs of previous year's growth. The scale may be abundant enough to coat branches, with severe injury to plants. Spray with a dormant oil in April or malathion in late June and early July.

Cranberry Scale, *Aspidiotus oxycoccus* Woglum.

Cyanophyllum Scale, *Abgrallaspis cyanophylli* (Signoret). Of cosmopolitan distribution on orchids, rubber plant, and many other hosts. The very long list includes acacia, acalypha, allamanda, annona, anthericum, Jamaica apple, sugar-apple, asparagus fern, ardisia, avocado, azalea, banana, bay, bignonia, billbergia, bottlebrush, bougainvillea, calathea, callistemon, camellia, camphor, carissa, cestrum, coconut, coffee, cycas, euphorbia, dogwood, dracaena, elaeagnus, euonymus, fig, flame vine, grape, gerbera, seagrape, guava, sweetgum, hackberry, hibiscus, holly, honeysuckle, ivy, jasmine, cherry-laurel, privet, crapemyrtle, silk-oak, ophiopogon, palms, screwpine, pittosporum, plumeria, pomegranate, quisqualis, smilax, yucca, stephanotis, tabernaemontana, tung-oil, viburnum, Virginia-creeper, zamia.

The female is elongate ovate or triangular; scales are very thin, flat, semitransparent with the yellow body showing through; exuviae are central, yellow. Parasites keep this under control.

Cymbidium Scale, *Lepidosaphes machili* (Maskell). On orchids.

Cypress Bark Scale, *Ehrhornia cupressi* (Ehrhorn). Cottony Cypress Scale. Common on Monterey cypress, also attacking Guadalupe and Arizona cypress and incense cedar in California. Limbs turn yellow, then red or brown. Trees look scraggy; some die, especially those in hedges. The scale has a pink body covered with loose white wax, and is usually found in pits or cracks in bark. Spray with a miscible oil in August and again in late September, or with malathion.

Dictyospermum Scale*, *Chrysomphalus dictyospermi* (Morgan). Spanish Red Scale, widely distributed in subtropics, reported as serious in Connecticut greenhouses on palms in 1905, present outdoors in California, Florida, and other warm states. It is a rather important pest of avocado, a potential threat to citrus, fairly common on acacia, palms, latania, rose, sometimes orchids. It is also recorded on agave, albizzia, allamanda, anthurium, aralia, arborvitae, ardisia, asparagus, aspidistra, bamboo, banana, bauhinia, bay, billbergia, bird-of-paradise, bottle-brush, boxwood, cactus, camellia, camphor, canna, carissa, century plant, Barbados and Surinam cherry, cinnamon, cocculus, cotoneaster, croton, cypress, gerbera, daphne, dracaena, elaeagnus, eucalyptus, euonymus, euphorbia, feijoa, fern, fig, firethorn, gardenia, golddust tree, golden dewdrop, golden-shower, guava, India-hawthorn, holly, honeysuckle, ivy, jasmine, jatropha, juniper, laurel, laurestinus, ligustrum, lily, Spanish lime, liriope, litchi, macadamia, magnolia, mango, mountain ebony, muehlenbeckia, mulberry, myrtle, nolina, silk-oak, oleander, olive, ophiopogon, osmanthus, palmetto, pandanus, parkinsonia, pecan, philodendron, Australian-pine, screwpine, photinia, plum-yew, podocarpus, poinsettia, rose, sapodilla, sparkleberry, tea plant, viburnum, walnut, willow, woodbine, and yew.

Scales infest bark, leaf, and fruit. The female is circular, $\frac{1}{12}$ inch, with dark-brown armor. It deposits eggs and there are 3 or 4 generations in California, 5 or 6 in Florida. Malathion will control this species. Palms in greenhouses should be syringed forcefully and repeatedly with water. Eliminate ants, which carry around young scales.

Dogwood Scale*, *Chionaspis corni* Cooley. A northern species present from Massachusetts to Indiana and Kansas, looking much like scurfy scale on apple. It is occasionally abundant on pagoda, silky, and red-osier dogwood, turning the stems white. A dormant lime-sulfur spray is effective or a miscible oil may be applied just before growth starts in spring. The scales are heavily parasitized.

Elm Scurfy Scale*, *Chionaspis americana* Johnson. Distributed from New England south to Florida and west to Oklahoma and Texas, more serious in the Middle West than in the East. Found most often on American elm, it may attack Camperdown and other elms, killing branches or young trees outright. It also attacks hackberry. The female—pear-shaped, convex, rather thick, $\frac{1}{12}$ to $\frac{1}{8}$ inch long, naturally white but grayish from bark fragments—is found only on bark. The male, white, very small and narrow, is found on both bark and leaves. Purple eggs winter under the female shell. There are 2 generations in the North, more in the South. It can be controlled with a dormant oil spray.

Euonymus Scale*, *Unaspis euonymi* (Comstock). Doubtless known to everyone growing euonymus, though my own observations lead me to believe it is not as prevalent in the Deep South and in California as in cooler climates. It is also common on bittersweet and pachysandra, is sometimes present on ivy and other ground covers growing near euonymus, and has been reported on camellia in Florida. Female scales look like dark-brown oyster shells, $\frac{1}{16}$ inch long; males are almost needle-thin, pure white (Plate XXXIII). Stems and leaves are almost entirely covered with white males, with a scattering of brown females. Leaves turn yellow, drop; vines die back. Climbing euonymus covering walls is more often infested than some of the upright forms; winged cuonymus is usually free from scale. The scale overwinters as a mature fertilized female. Orange-yellow eggs, laid under the female shell, hatch in late spring to crawlers of the same color and are visible in late May and June. A 2nd brood appears in August and September and, in warm climates, a partial 3rd may be present.

Control. Use a dormant oil spray, same strength as for lilacs and other deciduous shrubs, before growth starts in the spring. Nurserymen may use ethion with the oil. The spray may turn old leaves yellow but they are quickly covered with new growth. Spray for crawlers in June and in August with dimethoate or carbaryl.

Another scale, *Lepidosaphes yanagicola* (Kuwalt) has been found on *Euonymus alatus* in Indiana, Ohio, Rhode Island, and West Virginia. It has been reported on pachysandra in Maryland and on butterfly-orchid (Epidendron) in Florida.

European Elm Scale*, *Gossyparia spuria* (Modeer). A soft scale, first found at Rye, New York, in 1884, now spread across the country wherever elms are found, being particularly destructive to ornamental and street elms. Infested trees have yellowed foliage, usually shed prematurely; small branches die, then the larger branches, sometimes the whole tree. Copious honeydew drops to sidewalks and cars and keeps branches black with sooty mold.

Nymphs winter in bark crevices and in very early spring the males form conspicuous white cocoons in which they transform to minute reddish winged or wingless "gnats." Females become adult early in May; $\frac{1}{6}$ to $\frac{3}{8}$ inch long, oval, reddish brown, surrounded with a white fringe. They deposit eggs under their bodies from late May through June, and these hatch within an hour into yellow crawlers which migrate to the leaves, feeding there until fall. Most migrate back to trunk or branches before leaves drop in autumn.

Control. A dormant oil spray plus ethion in April or a foliage spray in summer with carbaryl or diazinon or malathion should be effective. A strong stream of water from the hose will wash off some scales. There are few natural enemies.

European Fiorinia Scale, *Fiorinia fioriniae* (Targ). Similar to the tea scale, found on asparagus fern, avocado, bay, bottle-brush, cajeput, English ivy and palms. The female is brownish yellow to orange.

European Fruit Lecanium*, *Lecanium corni* Bouché. Brown Apricot Scale, distributed through the country, quite injurious on the Pacific Coast. Besides fruit trees—apricot, plum, prune, peach, cherry, apple, persimmon, quince—it may also infest arborvitae, alder, ash, basswood, beech, blackberry, blueberry, black walnut, boxwood, box-elder, butternut, Catalina cherry, cherry-laurel, chinaberry, currant, elm, gooseberry, greasewood, grape, hawthorn, hackberry, hazelnut, hickory, locust, magnolia, maple, mulberry, oak, Osage-orange, pecan, poplar, redbud, rose, sassafras, willow.

The scale has various forms and may represent more than 1 species. Typically the female is large—⅛ inch—hemispherical to oval, and very convex, smooth shiny brown or reddish brown but sometimes covered with a white powder. It winters on twigs and branches, laying eggs under the shell in spring, with hatching from May to July. The males are smaller, flatter, elongated, and almost transparent, with ridges down the back. The nymphs migrate to the leaves and are found mostly among the veins, but they return to bark of twigs and branches for winter. There is 1 generation.

Control. Spray trees when dormant (December to February in California, perhaps March or April elsewhere) with an oil emulsion. The fruit lecanium is heavily parasitized, infected individuals turning black.

European Fruit Scale*, *Quadraspidiotus ostreaeformis* (Curtis). Pear Tree Oyster Scale, on deciduous fruit and ornamental trees.

European Peach Scale*, *Lecanium persicae* (Fabricius). Peach Lecanium. Widely distributed; found on peach, pear, plum, nectarine, also English ivy, ginkgo, gooseberry, grape, holly, Japanese quince, mulberry, rose, and silver thorn but not considered an important pest. Oval, moderately convex; 3 to 7 mm long, light to dark brown, sometimes sprinkled with white wax.

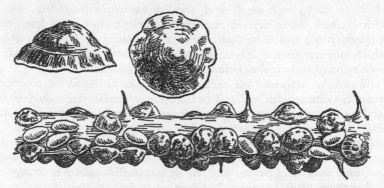

73. European fruit lecanium on blackberry cane.

False Cottony Maple Scale, *Pulvinaria acericola* Walsh & Riley. In eastern United States on soft and sugar maples and on dogwood. Oval, purple, with a medium-brown stripe and a long cottony egg mass. It may cause early dropping of leaves or death of twigs and branches.

False Brown Soft Scale, *Coccus pseudohesperidum* (Cockerell). On orchids.

False Parlatoria Scale. See Parlatorialike Scale.

Fern Scale*, *Pinnaspis aspidistrae* (Signoret). This may be a severe pest of ferns and African-violet in Florida, of ferns and aspidistra in

74. Fern scale, with detail of pear-shaped female, thin male.

homes and greenhouses. It may also infest acacia, bignonia, banana, cajeput, camellia, century plant, cinnamon, citrus, croton, dracaena, fig, geranium, hibiscus, liriope, mountain ebony, mango, ophiopogon, orchids, palms, pepper-tree, screwpine, spiceberry, spleenwort, and violet. This is an armored scale. The males are thin, white, conspicuous, the females ocher-brown, oyster-shaped. Parathion has given good control in greenhouses; malathion should be used in homes, except that it may injure certain ferns.

Fig Scale*, *Lepidosaphes conchiformis* (Gmelin). On figs in California, infesting fruit, leaves, wood up to 2 years old. It is dark brown with a greasy wax coat, similar to the purple scale but smaller. It may be controlled with a dormant oil emulsion, December to March, or a foliage spray of parathion in May. A hymenopterous parasite, *Aphycus*, imported from France, is effective.

Fletcher Scale*, *Lecanium fletcheri* Cockerell. Arborvitae Soft Scale. On arborvitae for many years, now damaging yew and pachysandra and perhaps other plants. Branches and underside of foliage may be covered with scales, with loss of color, vigor, premature defoliation, sooty mold growing in honeydew. Young scales are flat, amber in color; mature females are dark brown, shiny, hemispherical. Immature scales winter on stems and underside of foliage; eggs are deposited under the female in late spring with hatching in June. There is little summer development and most of the feeding and injury occur the next spring. Malathion is effective if applied in August or from April to mid-May.

Florida Red Scale*, *Chrysomphalus aonidum* (Linnaeus). An important pest of citrus in Florida and the Gulf States, also serious on palms, camphor, and roses. It occurs on some nursery plants in California but not on citrus to any extent. This scale is fairly common on

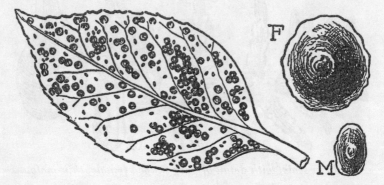

75. Florida red scale on underside of leaf, with detail of male and female.

ivy and other house plants and in greenhouses. Outdoors in warm climates it may infest acacia, acalypha, agave, allamanda, aloe, anisetree, annona, apple, aralia, ardisia, aspidistra, araucaria, avocado, azalea, banana, bay, bird-of-paradise, bottle-brush, bougainvillea, boxwood, cajeput, caladium, calycanthus, camellia, camphor, canna, coconut, carissa, cassia, century plant, cherry, cinnamon, eucalyptus, eugenia, euonymus, feijoa, fern, fig, firethorn, grape, seagrape, guava, gardenia, gladiolus, hawthorn, hibiscus, holly, iris, ivy, ixora, jasmine, laurel, lilac, lily, liriope, litchi, loquat, magnolia, mango, maranta, melaleuca, monkeypuzzle tree, monstera, mountain ebony, muehlenbeckia, mulberry, myrtle, silk-oak, oleander, olive, orchids, ophiopogon, palms, palmetto, pecan, persimmon, photinia, screwpine, pittosporum, plum, plumbago, podocarpus, poinsettia, pothos, pyracantha, rose, satinleaf, sapota, schefflera, soursop, spice plant, spirea, spurge, tabernaemontana, tea plant, ternstroemia, travelers-tree, rubber plant, viburnum, vinca, wisteria, and zamia.

This is an armored scale, small, $\frac{1}{12}$ inch, circular, reddish brown to nearly black with a lighter central portion; often very numerous on leaves, either surface, and on fruit, but not infesting twigs. It deposits eggs which hatch in a few hours, and there can be 5 or more generations in greenhouses. This species does not produce noticeable honeydew.

Control. Florida citrus growers have sprayed with oil from mid-June to mid-July or with parathion, June through August. A parasite, *Aphytis holoxanthus,* has been released for control. Use malathion for plants in homes. Keeping ivy and other house plants frequently bathed with water will reduce scale infestations.

Florida Wax Scale*, *Ceroplastes floridensis* Comstock. Found in Alabama, Florida, Louisiana, Mississippi, North Carolina, and probably other subtropical areas. This species is very important on camellias and may infest many other hosts, including abelia, acacia, apple, ardisia, prickly-ash, avocado, barberry, bay, bear grass, bignonia, blueberry, bottle-brush, boxwood, Brazilian pepper-tree, buckthorn, bumelia, cajeput, carissa, cedar, cherry, cinnamon, citrus, cotoneaster, crapemyrtle, croton, cunninghamia, cuphea, dahlia, duranta, elder, elaeagnus, eugenia, euonymus, feijoa, fern, fig, firethorn, gallberry, gardenia, glory-bush, guava, gumbo-limbo, hawthorn, ixora, jasmine, jessamine, litchi, loquat, magnolia, mango, maple, muehlenbeckia, mulberry, myrtle, oleander, olive, orchids, palms, parkinsonia, peach, pear, periwinkle, persimmon, photinia, pine, pittosporum, plum, podocarpus, poinsettia, pomegranate, quince, raphiolepis, rubber vine, sapodilla, sapota, sassafras, serissa, seagrape, sparkleberry, spirea, strobilanthes, tea plant, tecoma, and viburnum.

The reddish or purple-brown body is covered with a thick, white waxy coating tinted with pink, often with some dark spots; $\frac{3}{16}$ inch across. Red eggs are laid under the body of the scale, which shrinks as they accumulate. Crawlers collect on underside of leaves along midribs; adults cling to twigs. There are 3 generations in Florida. Spray with malathion or dimethoate when young crawlers have settled on twigs, or use a summer oil, 1 to 2 per cent according to host tolerance.

Flyspeck Scale, *Gymnaspis aechmeae* Newstead. On orchids.

Forbes Scale*, *Quadraspidiotus forbesi* (Johnson). Present east of the Rocky Mountains on cherry (especially sour cherry), apple, apricot, pear, plum, quince, currant, almond, peach, and dogwood. This species was increased by the use of DDT in orchards. Scales are grayish, thin, flaky, circular, with a tiny raised reddish area in the center; they are massed on trunk and branches. Partly grown scales winter on bark; young appear in May, born alive and also produced from eggs. There are 1 to 3 generations. Dormant oil sprays may not give complete control; a delayed dormant spray is more effective in some areas. Parathion or malathion can be used in cover sprays.

Frosted Scale, *Lecanium pruinosum* Coquillett. In California and Arizona, increased as a walnut problem when DDT was used for codling moth and infesting about the same list of fruit and ornamental hosts as the European fruit lecanium. It is a large, convex brown scale, covered with a frosty wax. A dormant parathion spray has been used for walnuts, applied in late fall or winter after complete defoliation.

Globose Scale*, *Lecanium prunastri* (Fonscolombe).

Gloomy Scale*, *Melanaspis tenebricosa* (Comstock). Present from Washington, D.C., to Florida and Texas, most injurious to soft maples; also on sugar maple, hackberry, elm, boxelder, buckthorn, sweetgum, gallberry, redbud, mulberry, soapberry. It is dark gray, circular, very convex, melting into the bark in color. It is mostly controlled by natural enemies.

Glover Scale*, *Lepiosaphes gloverii* (Packard). Found in southern states, often associated with purple scale and with a similar life history; more important in Florida than in California. Hosts include arborvitae, boxwood, citrus, cherry, coconut, croton, euonymus, ivy, laurel, ligustrum, mango, magnolia, mulberry, myrtle, cabbage palmetto, orchids, and podocarpus. The female is long and narrow, straight or curved, yellow brown to dark brown. It may infest bark, leaf, or fruit.

Golden Oak Scale*, *Asterolecanium variolosum* (Ratzeburg). Pit-making Oak Scale. Found wherever oaks are grown, often injurious to young ornamental trees and sometimes killing mature trees if they suffer from drought. The scale is circular, slightly convex, polished greenish gold, with a marginal fringe and minute glassy spines. It makes small pits in the bark and lies in these depressions, its feeding producing galls or swellings. It winters as a mature female and, because of its waxy case, is rather resistant to oil sprays, although a dormant oil spray is still recommended in the East, with malathion for summer sprays.

Grape Scale*, *Diaspidiotus uvae* (Comstock). Generally distributed on grape, sometimes on peach, hickory, sycamore, resembling San Jose scale in size and habits. Shells are circular to elliptical, gray or yellow-brown with a pale yellow spot and white nipple at 1 side of center; they are usually present on old canes under loose bark. There is 1 generation. Severe pruning may be sufficient control; if not, apply a dormant spray of oil or lime sulfur.

XXIX MILLIPEDES: (a) millipede enlarged to show 2 pairs of legs on each segment, typical coiled position; (b) seeds injured by millipedes; (c) injury to young seedling; (d) tomato attacked when resting on ground. SPOTTED GARDEN SLUG: (a) slimy trail on cineraria; (b) seedlings eaten; (c) egg cluster; (d) month-old slug; (e) mature slug with spots. SOWBUGS: (a) adult; (b) young sowbug; (c) form known as pillbug, which rolls into a ball; (d) infested seedlings; (e) sow-bugs working at roots; (f) favorite hiding place under moist flowerpot.

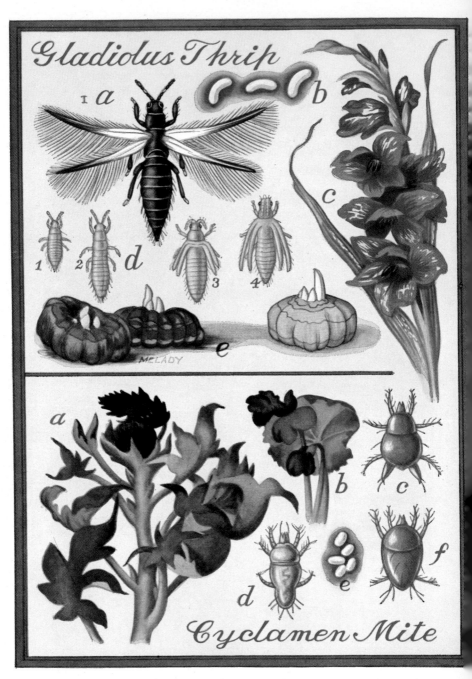

XXX GLADIOLUS THRIPS: (a) adult, showing fringed wings; (b) eggs, much enlarged; (c) typical injury to flowering spike and foliage; (d,1) first-stage larva; (d,2) second-stage larva; (d,3) third-stage (prepupa); (d,4) pupa with wing pads; (e) injured corms at left, healthy corm at right. **CYCLAMEN MITE:** (a) delphinium spike, with typical distortion; (b) injured cyclamen; (c) adult male, highly magnified; (d) young 6-legged larva; (e) eggs; (f) adult female.

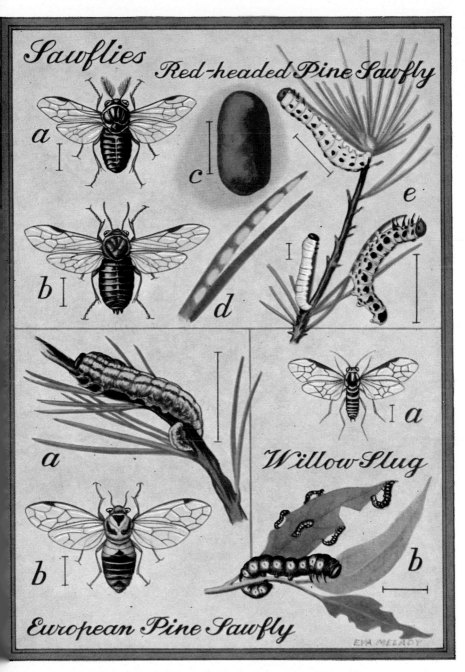

XXXI RED-HEADED PINE SAWFLY: (a) male adult; (b) female sawfly; (c) pupa in papery cocoon on ground; (d) eggs in slits along needle; (e) young and mature larvae feeding on pine. INTRODUCED PINE SAWFLY (labeled European Pine Sawfly): (a) larva in typical position on twig; (b) adult. WILLOW SAWFLY (Willow Slug): (a) adult; (b) larvae feeding on willow leaves.

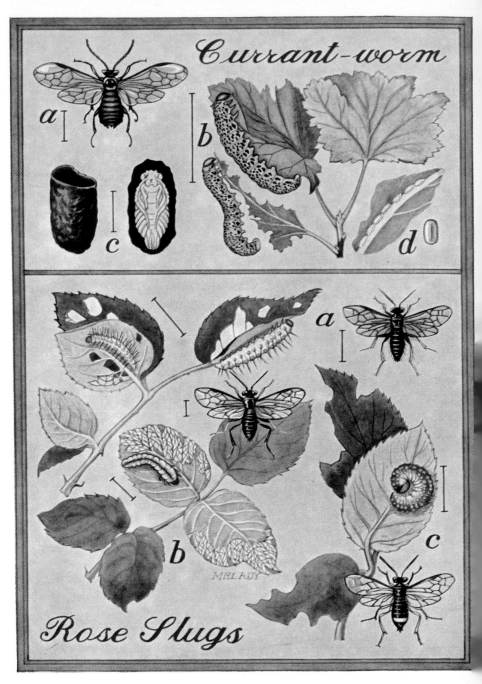

XXXII IMPORTED CURRANTWORM: (a) adult female sawfly; (b) larvae and feeding injury; (c) cocoon and pupa inside cocoon; (d) eggs along vein and single egg, enlarged. BRISTLY ROSE-SLUG: (a) adult sawfly and larvae feeding on leaf. ROSE-SLUG: (b) leaf showing typical skeletonizing but larva and adult enlarged. CURLED ROSE SAWFLY: (c) larva in coiled position, injured leaf, adult.

Greedy Scale*, *Hemiberlesia rapax* (Comstock). A common armored scale attacking ornamentals throughout the country, mostly in greenhouses, outdoors in warm climates. The female is quite convex, elliptical to round, small, gray, with yellow or dark-brown exuviae near one edge. The scales are omnivorous feeders on bark, sometimes leaves and fruit, of acacia, almond, apple, avocado, bay, birch, cactus, camphor, chinaberry, camellia, ceanothus, cherry, cissus, cotoneaster, cottonwood, English holly, English ivy, English walnut, English laurel, eucalyptus, euonymus, fig, fuchsia, genista, guava, grape, heather, mountain-holly, honeysuckle, Japanese quince, California-laurel, lavatera, locust, magnolia, maple, manzanita, mistletoe, myrtle, mulberry, olive, orange, Oregon-grape, oak, palms, passion-flower, pear, pecan, pepper-tree, pittosporum, pomegranate, pyracantha, quince, redbud, rose, sage, sedum, sequoia, strawberry-tree, silver tree, strelitzia, silk-oak, umbrella tree, English walnut, willow.

Control with aerosols in greenhouses and by spraying with malathion or summer white oils in gardens.

Green Scale*, *Coccus viridis* (Green). Found in tropical climates, infesting many types of plants in Florida, including apple, aster, bamboo, banana, blue dawn-flower, button-bush, cabbage palmetto, castorbean, citrus, coffee, eggfruit, elder, ferns, fig, fireweed, frangipani, grape, seagrape, groundsel, guava, iresine, ixora, jasmine, lancewood, lantana, marlberry, sapodilla, sapota, satinleaf, snowberry, soursop, Spanish needle, sumac, tea, thistle, Virginia-creeper, mangrove, willow, and yerbe maté! The female is oval, more or less pointed in front, pale green with 2 black spots. The friendly fungus *Cephalosporium lecanii* keeps the green scale under control.

Green Shield Scale*, *Pulvinaria psidii* Maskell. On ornamentals in Florida. A white cottony egg sac projects from a green shield. Food plants include acalypha, akee, alder, almond, anthurium, apple, aralia, avocado, bay, bignonia, bottle-brush, Brazilian pepper-tree, cajeput, camellia, canna, carissa, ceriman, chalice-vine, chinaberry, citrus, clerodendron, coffee, croton, currant, cypress vine, elder, elm (Chinese), feijoa, fern, fig, frangipani, gardenia, geiger-tree, gerbera, seagrape, groundsel, guava, hackberry, hamelia, holly, honeysuckle, iceplant, ixora, jasmine, laurel, Spanish lime, litchi, mango, marlberry, muehlenbeckia, mulberry, myrtle, crapemyrtle, silk-oak, palm, passion-vine, California pepper, persimmon, pittosporum, plumeria, plum, sapodilla, sapota, snowberry, soapberry, soursop, Spanish needles, tabernaemontana, tecoma, and travelers-tree. This species is mostly in southern Florida and may be serious on species of Ficus and on guava.

Ground Pearls. Scales or mealybugs, family Margarodidae, relatively large, rounded, shining bodies with an iridescent luster found loosely scattered in soil or on roots of plants. Those in the tropics have been used for adornment by the natives. Some species are becoming turf problems in the warmer sections of the United States. The only successful treatment seems to be ample water and fertilizer applied through the growing season.

Margarodes meridionalis Morrison. Cream to silvery, elliptical, with a rather brittle, thin-walled, waxlike shell, varying in size from a grain of sand to 4 mm. Found on centipede grass in Florida and through the Southeast, recorded on St. Augustine grass in California, Bermuda grass in Arizona. It is also present in soil around grapefruit and other citrus trees.

Margarodes rileyi Giard. Riley's Ground Pearl. On plant roots in the Florida Keys. It is nearly globular, 2 to 4 mm, with a thin, wax secretion, color like a pearl.

Eumargarodes laingi Jakubski. A serious pest of Centipede grass in Florida, reported also from North Carolina and infesting roots of St. Augustine grass. It is globular, very small, brownish yellow to light red when the adult is ready to emerge from its waxy covering. The 1st pair of legs in the female is adapted for digging.

Hall Scale*, *Nilotaspis halli* (Green). An almond pest, formerly established in California but an example of an insect that has been successfully eradicated.

Hemispherical Scale*, *Saissetia coffeae* (Walker). A tropical species common in greenhouses and in gardens in mild climates. It is frequently present but not important on citrus and avocado, may be important on cycads, conspicuous on ferns, palms, and other ornamen-

76. Hemispherical scale on fern (note detail showing cushion shape and height).

tals, including allamanda, aloe, almond, amaryllis, annona, anthurium, ardisia, asparagus fern, avocado, banana, bamboo, begonia, bignonia, bergamot, bougainvillea, Brazilian pepper-tree, carissa, cherry, citrus, clerodendron, camellia, chrysanthemum, coffee, coral plant, croton, dracaena, duranta, Dutchmans-pipe, elder, eugenia, ferns, fig, frangipani, gardenia, geiger-tree, gerbera, seagrape, guava, holly, honeysuckle, ixora, jacaranda, jasmine, crapemyrtle, ligustrum, lily, myrtle, nephthytis, oleander, olive, orchids, sago palm, periwinkle, mountainholly, sapodilla, soursop, Spanish-needles, spiceberry, stephanotis, tabernaemontana, Turks-cap, viburnum, willow, and zamia.

The female is a smooth glossy brown, hemispherical with flared margins, about ⅛ inch in diameter. It secretes much honeydew, which attracts ants and is a medium for black sooty mold, making fern fronds an eyesore. Parathion will kill some stages but not nearly mature scales. Malathion may be used on some plants but may be possibly injurious to certain succulents and ferns; dimethoate should be limited to plants listed on the label; carbaryl is satisfactory in some cases.

Hemlock Scale*, *Abgrallaspis ithacae* (Ferris). A native American species, widely distributed, quite common in the West. Scales are circular, nearly black, with a nipple, occurring in great numbers on underside of needles of hemlock, Douglas-fir, Monterey, yellow, knobcone and other pines. They sometimes kill young trees.

Another species, *Fiorinia externa* Ferris, called **Fiorinia Hemlock Scale**, has become even more important on hemlock in the East and sometimes fir, spruce, and yew. It is reported as a problem in New York, Connecticut, Maryland, Massachusetts, New Jersey, Ohio, and Pennsylvania. Hemlocks appear whitewashed from the abundance of insects on the needles, usually on the underside. Trees turn yellow, may be defoliated. The female is elongate, pale yellow to pale brown but it lives inside the cast skin of the last molt so that it appears white. Females continue to reproduce throughout the year in some sections; in Massachusetts there are 2 generations—in late June and September, but eggs continue to hatch through the summer.

Control. Spray with a dormant oil in April and/or with dimethoate in late June and midsummer, perhaps again in September.

Hickory Scale, *Chionaspis caryae* Cooley. On pecan in Florida, on bark of hickory in some other states, but not common. The female is pear-shaped, dirty-white, terminal exuviae pale yellow or brown.

Holly Scale*, *Dynaspidiotus britannicus* (Newstead). On holly in Pacific Coast States. The scales are circular, flat, brown with a yellow center, nearly ⅛ inch across. They occur on leaves, twigs, and berries and when numerous weaken trees. Dimethoate gives some control.

Another holly scale, *Asterolecanium puteanum* Russell, feeds on

American holly, yaupon, and bumelia from Delaware to Alabama. It makes both shallow and deep pits in twigs. A species of *Lecanium* is reported injuring new growth of holly, with sooty mold growing in honeydew. It is convex, amber to reddish brown, with crawlers appearing in late June and July. There is 1 generation and a delayed dormant or a summer oil has given more control than malathion.

Howard Scale, *Abgrallaspis howardi* (Cockerell). A Rocky Mountain species occurring mostly at high altitudes in Colorado and New Mexico. Pear is the preferred host, but it may feed on almond, apple, ash, peach, plum, prune, and other deciduous fruits and on vegetables. Also identified as this species is a scale on yucca in Florida and other southern states. The scale is circular, flat, pale gray wih a reddish tinge. It causes pitting and a reddish stain on fruit. Control is the same as for the San Jose scale.

Irregular Pine Scale, *Toumeyella pinicola* Ferris. An important pest of ornamental pines in California. Trees lose vigor and are covered with sooty mold. The scale is small, of irregular shape, yellowish, and lives at the base of needles of small twigs of Monterey and other pines. There is 1 generation with crawlers in mid or late spring. Spray in summer with carbaryl or malathion.

Italian Pear Scale*, *Epidiaspis leperii* (Signoret). A California pest of pear, plum, prune, apple, Persian walnut, and a special pest of California Christmasberry, which may be killed by it. The female is dark red or purple, covered with a circular, dark-gray, shiny shell with dark-brown exuviae. The male is slender, white with yellow exuviae. Infestations of long duration cause deep depressions in limbs and may hasten death. Lichens usually cover the scales. Spray in winter with a heavy oil emulsion, drenching limbs and trunk, adding 1 ounce of caustic soda to each 2 gallons of spray to remove the lichens protecting the scales.

Japanese Scale, *Leucaspis japonica* Cockerell. Originally considered a pest of maple and privet, now infesting also boxwood, holly, Japanese quince, and rose from Rhode Island to Maryland. The scale resembles a narrow oyster shell, $\frac{1}{16}$ to $\frac{1}{12}$ inch long, dull grayish white, often thickly encrusting trunk and branches. A dormant oil spray gives satisfactory control; or spray with diazinon or dimethoate.

Japanese Wax Scale, *Ceroplastes ceriferus* Anderson. General in Florida and other subtropical climates and found north to Virginia on blueberry, azalea, camellia, Chinese elm, citrus, fig, eugenia, gumbo-limbo, Chinese holly, yaupon, jasmine, mulberry, pear, persimmon, plum, quince, sapodilla, sapota, and Turks-cap. The female is circular, thick, waxy, very convex with surface more or less roughened, white or creamy white, 3 to 8 mm across. Under the shell the body is brown or purplish brown. The scales are found on bark and leaves. Spray with dimethoate or malathion.

Juniper Scale*, *Carulaspis juniperi* (Bouché). On juniper, sometimes arborvitae, incense cedar, and cypress used as ornamentals throughout the United States, not important in forest stands in this country. But after it was introduced into Bermuda it killed off most of the native junipers on that island. Whenever junipers around the house look dingy gray or yellowish or generally unthrifty, examine the needles closely for very small, $\frac{1}{20}$-inch, dirty-white, round scales with a yellow center. These are females; the male is even smaller, white, narrow with a ridge down the back. They winter as nearly grown scales and the young hatch in early June (Plate XXXIII).

Control. Spray with lime sulfur, 1 to 9 dilution, in early April unless the shrubs are too close to painted surfaces. Malathion or diazinon may be used for the crawling stage in June.

Latania Scale, *Hemiberlesia lataniae* (Signoret). Widely distributed in greenhouses and warm climates on palms, orchids, canna, gladiolus, raspberry, rose, tamarisk, and other ornamentals. Florida hosts also include Australian-pine, loquat, and other plants. This is an armored scale, circular, $\frac{1}{16}$ to $\frac{1}{12}$ inch. It lays yellow eggs, and sulfur-yellow crawlers appear on branches, twigs, leaves, or fruit. Malathion is effective in control but natural enemies may suffice.

Lesser Snow Scale, *Pinnaspis strachani* Cooley. A general pest of ornamentals in Florida, sometimes killing hibiscus. The female is pear-shaped, white, semitransparent, sometimes speckled with brown from incorporation of bark fragments. The male is very small, elongate, very white, and is so numerous it looks like salt over the bark. Hosts include abelia, abutilon, acacia, agave, althea, balsam-apple, prickly-ash, asparagus fern, aspidistra, assonia, avocado, bignonia, bird-of-paradise, camphor, candleberry, carissa, carob, cassia, cassava, castor-bean, chinaberry, cinnamon, cissus, seagrape, crassula, croton, cuphea, dracaena, echeveria, elaeagnus, elder, eucalyptus, fern, fig, frangipani, geranium, grape, hackberry, hemlock, hibiscus, hollyhock, honeysuckle, ice-plant, inkberry, ivy, jacaranda, jasmine, jessamine, lantana, ligustrum, lily, liriope, Spanish lime, litchi, magnolia, mango, maple, morning-glory, mountain ebony, oak, silk-oak, oleander, orchids, passion-vine, peach, pepper-tree, persimmon, screwpine, pittosporum, poinciana, poinsettia, rubber, sansevieria, sapodilla, Spanish bayonet, spiceberry, sumac, sunflower, thunbergia, tung-oil, umbrella tree, wisteria, woodbine, and zizyphus.

This species may build up a heavy infestation but it is usually heavily parasitized. It may be controlled if necessary with malathion or summer oils.

Long Soft Scale, *Coccus elongatus* (Signoret). Outdoors in Florida, in greenhouses elsewhere. It is elongate-elliptical, moderately convex, smooth, yellowish or brownish gray with darker mottled areas. It is found on acacia, acalypha, albizzia, annona, assonia, bottle-brush, buckthorn, cassia, ceratonia, croton, dracaena, euphorbia, fern, fig, golden dewdrop, hibiscus, jacaranda, jasmine, Japanese pagoda-tree, litchi, maranta, mountain ebony, myrtle, silk-oak, parkinsonia, Australian-pine, pithecolobium, plum, poinsettia, rose, soursop. It is not considered economically important.

Mackie Scale, *Lepidosaphes mackieana* Mackie.

Magnolia Scale*, *Neolecanium cornuparvum* (Thro). A soft scale, probably a native, distributed through eastern states and also recorded from Nebraska, on various species of magnolia and other trees and shrubs in the magnolia family. This is the largest scale insect in the United States. The female is ½ inch across, notably convex, covered with white wax, under which the body is shiny brown with honeycomb pits and large glands. When the scales are numerous the branches appear to be covered with white cotton, and when the scales are removed, a scar is left on the bark. Trees may be severely injured and appear sickly, leaves remaining small. There is much honeydew with resultant sooty mold over foliage and branches. Young nymphs hibernate on new wood, molt early in spring, again in June, and start secreting white wax. By August or September they are producing living young. There is 1 generation in the North.

Control. A dormant oil spray gives excellent results, especially if it is used with ethion. Or spray in mid-August or early September with carbaryl, diazinon, or malathion. Home gardeners can scrub off many scales with a stiff brush and soap.

Mango Scale, *Leucaspis indica* Marlatt. In Florida and Hawaii on mango, Spanish-needles, and soursop. The female is long, narrow, thin but very convex, white.

Maple Phenacoccus, *Phenacoccus acericola* King. In northeastern states, mostly on sugar maple. It resembles cottony maple scale with its large white cottony masses, but these are always on the underside of leaves and not on the twigs. It is conspicuous but not very important.

Masked Scale, *Chrysomphalus personatus* (Comstock). In Florida (Key West) on bauhinia, Barbados cherry, eugenia, fig, rose, sapodilla, seagrape. Very small, circular or thimble-shaped, gray-brown to nearly black, brittle.

Mexican Wax Scale. See Japanese Wax Scale.

Mimosa Scale, *Chrysomphalus mimosae* (Comstock). In Florida (Key West) on acacia, Spanish jasmine, and hog plum, but not serious. The female is circular or elongated, very small, moderately convex, whitish gray and hard to distinguish from the bark of the host. Another mimosa scale, *Aspidiotus diffinis,* is reported from Florida.

Mining Scale*, *Howardia biclavis* (Comstock). On many ornamental plants in warm climates. The list includes acacia, allamanda, banyan, bignonia, bougainvillea, camellia, Australian-pine, chinquapin, duranta, eggfruit, elder, fig, gardenia, hamelia, heather, honeysuckle, ixora, jacobinia, jasmine, jessamine, lantana, ligustrum, Spanish lime, loquat, mango, mountain ebony, silk-oak, olive, papaya, pepper-tree, pomegranate, quisqualis, sapodilla, sapote, sage, strobilanthes, tabernaemontana, tamarind, tecoma, wisteria, and zizyphus. The scale—circular, moderately convex, white or grayish—mines into bark and epidermis of leaves and twigs. See also Camellia Mining Scale.

Newstead's Scale, *Lepidosaphes newsteadii* (Sulc). Reported in Florida, California, Mississippi on leaves of arborvitae, Florida cedar, cypress, junipers, pine, and retinospora. It is oyster-shaped, moderately convex, light brown with terminal exuviae.

Nigra Scale, *Saissetia nigra* (Nietner). First noted as a citrus pest in California in 1900 and since found on 161 species of plants in that state. This is now general in subtropical regions. Florida hosts include andromeda, sweetbay, guava, hibiscus, mango, myrtle, pandanus, papaya, strobilanthes, Turks-cap, and willow. It may be abundant on hibiscus but it is usually controlled by parasites. The parasite introduced for black scale makes the nigra scale now unimportant in California. The scale is elongate-oval, slightly curved lengthwise, moderately convex or humpbacked, brown to brownish black, shiny.

Oak Eriococcus, *Eriococcus quercus* (Comstock). A mealybug in southern states, clustering on stems and leaves of blueberry, gallberry, ivy, oak, and water oak. It has an oval, fluted sac.

Oak Kermes, *Kermes pubescens* Bogue. Oak Gall Scale. Distributed widely on oak in northern United States but more conspicuous than injurious. The females—globular, mottled light brown, ⅛ inch across—look more like hard galls along the leaf veins and terminal twigs than scales. Leaves are sometimes distorted, puckered, growth checked. The winter is spent on bark but in spring females migrate to leaves. The young are covered at first with a white pubescence.

Oak Lecanium*, *Lecanium quercifex* Fitch. On oak in eastern United States. It is elliptical, quite convex, more or less tapering at ends, light to dark brown.

Oak Scale, *Chionaspis quercus* (Comstock). On oak, reported from Florida, California, New Mexico, and Texas. It is long, narrow at the exuvial end, widened at the posterior, convex, very small, light to dark gray, with yellow-brown exuviae.

Oak Wax Scale, *Cerococcus quercus* Comstock. On oak in California and Arizona. The scales are completely encased in a mass of wax.

Obscure Scale*, *Melanaspis obscura* (Comstock). On pecan, hickory, elm, hackberry, and oak, from Massachusetts to Florida and Arkansas. It is a special pest of pecans from Alabama to Texas and may occur on chestnut, chinquapin, dogwood, grape, plum, maple, soapberry, viburnum, willow, and wild myrtle. The female is roughly circular, grayish, closely resembling tree bark. The male is half her size. On pecans the infestation starts on lower and inner tree parts and gradually spreads up and out, killing many smaller branches, reducing vigor, making the tree more susceptible to attacks of other insects. There is 1 generation a year, with crawlers moving in June. Spray with a dormant oil emulsion (2 per cent for weak trees, 3 per cent for vigorous) in January or February before buds swell.

Oleander Scale*, *Aspidiotus nerii* Bouché. Ivy Scale. Present throughout the warmer states and in houses and greenhouses in the North. As the names imply, it is especially serious on oleander and ivy, but it is an omnivorous feeder with a very long list of host plants, including century plant, cycads, palms, olive, lemon, orange, also acacia, aloe, aucuba, avocado, azalea, bay, blueberry, camellia, cactus, chinaberry, cocculus, dogwood, elaeagnus, fern, hibiscus, genista, holly, jasmine, ligustrum, magnolia, orchids, osmanthus, peppertree, poinsettia, periwinkle, persimmon, rose, redbud, rubber-tree, yucca, tung-oil, verbena. The females are circular, somewhat flattened, pale yellow, sometimes with a purplish tinge, $\frac{1}{10}$ inch across. The males are much smaller, pure white, numerous. Heavily infested plants lose their color and vigor, may die.

Control. Prune out all encrusted branches. In winter, spray with a summer-oil emulsion; in summer, spray with dimethoate or malathion at monthly intervals.

Olive Scale*, *Parlatoria oleae* (Colvée). Olive Parlatoria. An introduced pest established at 3 widely scattered points; near Baltimore, Maryland, on privet, and in California and Arizona. Since it was found in California in 1931 it has become a major agricultural pest, having been reported on 211 plant species including, besides olive, almond, apricot, apple, peach, pear, plum. For many years the insect stayed on a few plants on the university campus at Tucson, Arizona, but after a series of mild winters it became established on many hosts, affecting twigs, leaves, fruits. Ornamental hosts include ash, Brazilian pepper, cotoneaster, elaeagnus, grape, English ivy, jasmine, Kentucky coffee tree, loquat, Chinese lilac, mulberry, oleander, palms, periwinkle, photinia, pomegranate, privet, pyracantha, rose, sage, trumpet-vine, tung-oil, viburnum, Virginia-creeper. The female shell is dirty-gray, ovate, circular, very small; the insect itself is purplish brown. The scales overwinter as adult females, with egg laying starting in late March. Hatching on deciduous fruit trees is in April, on olives in May. There are 2 generations.

Control. The most effective spray for commercial growers seems to be parathion applied with oil. Malathion injures young olive fruit but may be used on ornamental plants. Many natural enemies have been liberated in olive orchards.

Orchid Scale, *Furcaspis biformis* (Cockerell). On orchid leaves and pseudobulbs. The female resembles Florida red scale; it is almost circular, moderately convex, very small ($\frac{1}{18}$ to $\frac{1}{12}$ inch), dark reddish brown with somewhat lighter margin, exuviae central or subcentral. The male is similar and much smaller. Spray with dimethoate, diazinon, malathion, or Meta-Sysox-R.

Orchid Pit Scale, *Asterolecanium epidendri* (Bouché).

Oriental Scale, *Aonidiella orientalis* Newstead. Sometimes a serious pest of coconut palms in Florida, also found on annona, avocado, banana, bay, bird-of-paradise, cactus, canna, carissa, carnation, chinaberry, croton, gerbera, date, elaeagnus, eucalyptus, fig, frangipani, golden-shower, guava, hibiscus, ivy, ixora, jasmine, mango, oleander, olive, orchid, palmetto, palms, persimmon, Natal plum, plumeria, rose, rubber, tabernaemontana, tamarind, tea plant, trumpet plant, and zamia. The scale is circular or oval, rather flat, light yellow-brown with lighter edges, polished, with central exuviae. It is mostly under control by natural enemies.

Osborn's Scale, *Aspidiotus osborni* Newell & Cockerell. In southern states and as far north as Kansas and Ohio on grape and pecan. The shape is irregular, the color dirty-gray, the subcentral exuviae orange but covered with secretion.

Oystershell Scale*, *Lepidosaphes ulmi* (Linnaeus). Generally distributed on deciduous trees and shrubs, known to every gardener and fruit grower. As the name implies, the scales look like miniature oysters encrusted over trunk, limbs, twigs, or on soft stems (Plate XXXIV). There are 3 color races of this scale with different life cycles. The gray race occurs on common lilac, beech, maple, willow, and many ornamentals. The scales are small, $\frac{1}{8}$ inch long by $\frac{1}{16}$ inch wide, broadened at the posterior end, usually curved, with many parallel cross ridges, acquiring a whitish bloom with age. There is only 1 generation, with crawlers appearing in June.

The brown race, the apple oystershell, is common on fruits— apple, apricot, pear, plum, quince, currant, fig, grape, raspberry, almond, and Persian walnut; it is also serious on dogwood, hybrid lilacs, boxwood, mountain-ash, horsechestnut. When old, the scales are very dark, almost black; there are 2 generations. The yellow-brown race has a yellow fringe on the rear portion, is common on birch and poplar, has a 2nd brood in late July. Other plants that may be infested with oystershell scales are peony, ailanthus, alder, aspen, basswood, bittersweet, boxelder, butternut, camellia, camphor, clematis, cotoneaster, elm, ginseng, hackberry, heather, holly, honeysuckle, Juneberry, locust, mountain-holly, New Jersey tea, oak, orchids, pachysandra, sassafras, spirea, sycamore, tamarisk, tuliptree, viburnum, Virginia-creeper, yucca.

The winter is passed as elliptical, nearly white eggs under female shells; they hatch late in spring, late May or June. The young crawlers, whitish with 6 barely visible legs, move about for a few hours, then insert their beaks into the dark and start making the waxy scale covering. The brown and yellow-brown races mature about mid-July, when the tiny yellowish 2-winged males mate with the females. As the female deposits her eggs under the shell, her body gradually shrinks until death. With the brown and yellow-brown races the eggs hatch within 2 weeks; with the gray race, not until the next spring.

Control. Lilacs and other shrubs that almost always have this scale should have a dormant oil spray in spring before buds break, usually late March. The addition of ethion makes this more effective. Spray for crawlers in June with dimethoate or malathion. Remove heavily encrusted and weak branches before spraying. There are many natural enemies—birds, mites, parasitic wasps, and predators.

Palmetto Scale, *Comstockiella sabalis* (Comstock). In Florida on palm and palmetto, also reported from California, Louisiana, Mississippi, and Texas. It is circular, irregular when crowded, snow-white, with central exuviae.

Parlatoria Date Scale*, *Parlatoria blanchardi* (Targioni-Tozzetti). Date Palm Scale, a small gray-and-white scale, introduced from Egypt in 1890, a menace to the date industry of California and Arizona. An eradication campaign, started in 1922, was successfully concluded in 1934. This included destroying some infested trees, pruning others and searing them with a gasoline torch.

Parlatorialike Scale, *Pseudoparlatoria parlatorioides* (Comstock). False Parlatoria Scale. In Florida, California, South Carolina, and Texas, sometimes serious on acalypha, alternanthera, avocado, bay, bignonia, blackberry, blueberry, camellia, camphor, carnation, coleus, fern, fig, flame vine, guava, hamelia, hibiscus, holly, honeysuckle, inkberry, ivy, ixora, jacobinia, jasmine, laurestinus, magnolia, oleander, tea-olive, orchids, palms, palmetto, papaya, pepper-tree, redbud, strawberry bush.

Peach Lecanium. See European Peach Scale.

Peony Scale, *Pseudaonidia paeoniae* (Cockerell). Killing twigs and branches of azaleas and camellias in the South, sometimes present on ligustrum and other shrubs, including shrub peony and rhododendron. The small brown convex shell is very inconspicuous, looking like a slight hump on the bark until the scale is rubbed off, or dies and falls off, leaving a conspicuous white circle on the twig. Crawlers, purple in color, are present in May; there is only 1 brood. Sprays are largely ineffective unless timed for crawlers, usually late May. Parathion is used by some nurserymen but malathion is safer for home gardeners.

Pineapple Scale*, *Diaspis bromeliae* (Kerner). Tropical pineapple pest, also present in greenhouses. It infests cactus, canna, chalice vine, hibiscus, English ivy, jasmine, olive, orchids, palm, sago palm, and various tropical plants, It has a nearly round, thick, white or gray shell over an orange-yellow body with purplish tints.

Pine Needle Scale*, *Phenacaspis pinifoliae* (Fitch). A native, widely distributed, common in home plantings on nearly all species of pine and on various spruces; occasional on hemlock, fir, incense cedar; most prevalent east of the Mississippi River. The female is pure white, $\frac{1}{10}$ inch long, widening toward the lower end, varying in shape according to the needle it is on. The male, $\frac{1}{25}$ inch long, is white, with 4 parallel ridges. Pine branches infested with scale usually turn yellow. On small Austrian and mugho pines every leaf may be white with scales, the needles yellowing, the whole shrub unhealthy, or a single branch may be heavily infested and the rest free from scale (Plate XXXIII). Reddish eggs winter under the scales and start hatching in May, with a 2nd brood appearing in late July.

Control. Spray with lime sulfur, 1 to 9 dilution, or with a dormant oil, evergreen strength, before new growth starts; or spray with dimethoate or malathion in late May and August. When a single branch is infested, it can usually be pruned out without spoiling the shape too much. Lady beetles and some hymenopterous wasps share in control measures.

Pine Scales. Various other scales infest pine, including at least 14 species of the genus Matsucoccus. These are small, oval, yellow to brown, and inconspicuous, half-buried in bark or needles. Some of these are treated separately. See Pinyon Pine Scale, Prescott Scale, Red Pine Scale. *Matsucoccus gallicolus* (Morrison) occurs in many places east of the Mississippi and on many species of pine, often heavily infesting pitch pine, browning needles near tip of branches, sometimes killing limbs. This species can be controlled by spraying with lime sulfur or malathion when crawlers appear on new growth. *Matsucoccus paucicatrices* Morrison injures and sometimes kills sugar pine in California, may also infest western white and limber pines in Oregon, Montana, and Wyoming.

Pine Tortoise Scale*, *Toumeyella numismaticum* Pettit & McDaniel. On Scotch, Austrian, and jack pines in northern states, killing Christmas-tree pines in the Middle West. Females are reddish brown and very convex. Heavily infested pines are coated with black sooty mold; there is heavy foliage drop; needles are shorter than normal; young trees may die. Another species (*T. pini* King) infesting mugho, lodgepole, Scotch, and other pines is reported in Connecticut, Pennsylvania, Michigan, and Florida.

Pinyon Needle Scale, *Matsucoccus acalyptus* Herbert. Credited with killing hundreds of piñon pines in Utah and Nevada, also present in other states.

Pit Scales. Small scales producing pits in bark or leaves. The **Pit-making Pittosporum Scale,** *Asterolecanium arabidis* (Signoret), was first collected in Connecticut in 1925 and had spread to California by 1945. It occurs on pittosporum, English ivy, green ash, and privet. In 1967 it was found on sugar beets, also on broad-leaved cress and phlox. *A. minor* Lindinger lives in pits in bark of oak and has killed many chestnut oaks in Pennsylvania and is also known in North Carolina.

Other pit scales include *Cerococcus kalmiae* reported on azalea in Maryland, *C. deklei* on hibiscus in Florida, and *Lecaniodiaspis prosopodis* on mimosa in Maryland.

Prescott Scale, *Matsucoccus vexillorum* Morrison. Causing extensive killing of branches of ponderosa pine in the Southwest. The females settle on twigs, mainly at nodes, lay eggs, and cover them with fluffy white wax. Larvae feed beneath scales at base of needles and in cracks and crevices in twigs.

A Privet Scale, *Parlatoria pyri*. Reported from Washington, D.C., a recent pest.

Proteus Scale, *Parlatoria proteus* (Curtis). Important on orchids, especially the strapleaf varieties, and present on many other plants. An armored scale, the female is elongate oval, $\frac{1}{25}$ to $\frac{1}{12}$ inch long, slightly convex, brownish or greenish yellow with lighter margins.

Purple Scale*, *Lepidosaphes beckii* (Newman). The most important citrus pest in Florida and the Gulf States, outranked in California only by the California red scale and the black scale. The purple scale appeared in Florida in 1857 on lemons imported from Bermuda; it reached California in 1889 when 2 carloads of Florida orange trees were planted without previous disinfestation. Besides

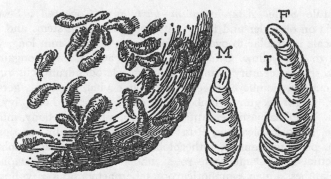

77. Purple scale on citrus fruit, with detail of oyster-shaped male and female.

citrus, purple scale infests allamanda, anise, avocado, banksia, berga-mot, Barbados cherry, beauty bush, carissa, cassia, croton, dogwood, elaeagnus, eucalyptus, fig, magnolia, jessamine, euonymus, feijoa, eugenia, jasmine, jetropha, laurel, ligustrum, lilac, magnolia, mango, myrtle, pachysandra, oak, olive, orchids, passion-flower, pecan, sago palm, pepper-tree, periwinkle, pittosporum, plum, privet, Spanish bayonet, Spanish dagger, silver thorn, thunbergia, walnut, yucca, and other plants.

This is an armored scale, the female shaped like an oystershell, straight or curved, light to dark brown or purple, ⅛ inch long. The male is similar but smaller and narrower. Foliage turns yellow where scales have been feeding, may turn brown and fall out; fruit is stunted, ripening delayed, color and flavor affected; feeding wounds afford entrance to disease fungi. The female deposits from 40 to 80 pearly eggs under her shell which hatch in 2 weeks to 2 months. The pale nymphs crawl for a short time, seek a shaded location on bark or fruit, insert their beaks, and settle down, secreting 2 long protective threads. The females molt twice at 3- to 4-week intervals, becoming thicker and purplish or reddish brown. The male molts 4 times, emerging in 2 months as a 2-winged insect. There are 3 generations. Some sprays, notably those containing copper and zinc, increase populations of purple scale on citrus.

Control. Oil sprays are used in Florida from June 15 to July 15, or parathion is applied during the period from June through August. In California the nymphs are vulnerable to parathion in late July and August. There are many natural enemies, including the twice-stabbed lady beetle. The Australian lady beetle, predaceous mites and hymenopterous parasites.

Pustule Scale, *Asterolecanium pustulans* (Cockerell). Severe in Florida on oleander and fig, in pits and pustules in stems and leaves. The scale is circular to oval, convex, rough, about 2 mm long, yellow-green to pale yellow. Other hosts include acacia, bay, bougainvillea, carissa, cassia, century plant, chinaberry, clerodendrum, clitoria, cork tree, cuphea, dombeya, eugenia, fig, flame vine, gardenia, geranium, grape, seagrape, gumbo-limbo, hackberry, hibiscus, holly, ivy, jacaranda, jacobinia, jasmine, lantana, mango, mountain ebony, mulberry, myrtle, silk-oak, oleander, Russian-olive, orchids, palm, passion-vine, peach, pear, persimmon, pithecolobium, plum, plumbago, poinciana, poinsettia, rose, Confederate rose, rubber-tree, sapodilla, stephanotis, strobilanthes, sumac, symphoricarpos, tabernaemontana, zizyphus.

Putnam Scale*, *Diaspidiotus ancylus* (Putnam). Similar to San Jose scale but not so serious, found over most of the United States. It is circular, dark gray to nearly black, with brick-red exuviae, just off center. Basswood and soft maples are quite susceptible to this scale; it is also found on apple, ash, beech, blueberry, bladdernut, cherry, chestnut, currant, cranberry, dogwood, elm, gooseberry, hackberry, hawthorn, hickory, linden, locust, Osage-orange, oak, peach, pecan, persimmon, pear, plum, quince, snowball, tuliptree, willow, walnut.

Pyriform Scale*, *Protopulvinaria pyriformis* (Cockerell). Distributed generally in Florida on a wide variety of hosts. The scale is broadly triangular or pear-shaped, greenish to brown with a white egg sac appearing as a fringe around the margin. Food plants include acalypha, allamanda, aralia, prickly-ash, aspidistra, avocado, azalea, banana, bay, bignonia, bottlebrush, boxwood, Brazilian peppertree, bumelia, button-bush, cajeput, camellia, camphor, carissa, caryophyllus, ceriman, Barbados cherry, chinaberry, cinnamon, cassia, cocculus, coffee, croton, currant, gerbera, dracaena, elm, eucalyptus, eugenia, euonymus, feijoa, fig, frangipani, gardenia, guava, holly, honeysuckle, ivy, ixora, jasmine, jessamine, lantana, laurel, litchi, loquat, mango, mountain ebony, myrtle, silk-oak, oleander, palm, papaya, paradise-tree, peach, phlox, privet, ricepaper-plant, rubber, sapodilla, sapota, sassafras, schefflera, serissa, soursop, sparkleberry, sumac, trumpet flower, and viburnum.

Quohog-shaped Scale, *Palinaspis quohogiformis* (Merrill). Shape similar to a quohog, very small, brownish, covered with sandlike material, attached at bud axils. Found in Florida but not economically important on acacia, bleeding-heart, bougainvillea, camellia, cotoneaster, croton, elder, fig, gardenia, grape, grevillea, hibiscus, honeysuckle, jacaranda, jasmine, ligustrum, litchi, mango, mignonette-tree, mountain ebony, mulberry, silk-oak, jessamine, pepper-tree, plum, poinciana, sandalwood, sapota, serissa, soapberry, tamarind, tecoma, trumpet creeper.

Red Bay Scale, *Chrysomphalus perseae* (Comstock). In southern states, also recorded in New Jersey. It is circular, flat, dark reddish or chocolate brown, with dark gray central exuviae, very small. Plants infested in Florida include avocado, azalea, bay, blueberry, camphor, white cedar, Arizona and Italian cypress, feijoa, gordonia, hemlock, holly, ivy, Jacobs ladder, juniper, ligustrum, lyonia, magnolia, mangrove, oak, olive, orchids, osmanthus, palm, palmetto, pine, screwpine, retinospora, sparkleberry, yucca.

Red Date Scale*, *Phoenicococcus marlatti* (Cockerell). Common on date palm in California and Arizona but apparently not very injurious. The female is reddish purple, resting in, and somewhat enveloped by, cottony filaments. The male is wingless. Food plants are restricted to 3 species of Phoenix palms.

Red Pine Scale*, *Matsucoccus resinosae* Bean & Goodwin. First discovered in Connecticut in 1946, and on Long Island in 1950, this scale has been killing red pine in parts of New York and Connecticut and has invaded New Jersey. There is first a slight yellowing of needles of current year's growth, then the foliage turns brick-red and the tree dies. Larvae and adults are small, inconspicuous, yellow to brown, hidden in bark or beneath needle fascicles. There are 2 generations, with eggs laid in May and late August. There is no practical control except to cut infested stands.

Red Wax Scale*, *Ceroplastes rubens* Maskell. First collected in Florida in 1955 and considered eradicated but it appeared again. It has infested aralia, agloenama, anthurium, philodendron, frangipani, ivy, ixora, beadfruit, spindletree, and other plants.

Rhodesgrass Scale*, *Antonina graminis* (Maskell). Destructive to lawns and golf courses in Florida and Texas. St. Augustine grass loses color and vigor. The scales are small, dark, covered with a white growth. They usually stay around nodes at base of grass blades; mature adults winter on roots. Crawlers are dark, lively, found on any part of grasses, and on any of 74 grass species, including Bermudagrass. It has been found in California, Arizona, and New Mexico as well as Florida and Texas. Parathion sprays or dusts have been used for control but this is dangerous and there is no easy way to control grass scales.

Rhododendron Scale, *Aspidiotus pseudospinosus* Woglum. A small, circular, dirty-tan scale on rhododendron, covering stems and underside of leaves, with yellow spots appearing on upper leaf surfaces. This came into prominence in New Jersey following spraying of nearby trees with DDT, although present before DDT came into use.

The species is also recorded on ilex in Oklahoma. A dormant oil spray is fairly effective. Use malathion for crawlers in June or July.

Rose Scale*, *Aulacaspis rosae* (Bouché). Widely distributed wherever roses or bramble hosts are grown. The round, flat, white female shells, covering orange or pinkish bodies and red eggs, ½ inch across, are very conspicuous on canes, which often appear whitewashed. The males are small, narrow, snow-white. Blackberry, loganberry, raspberry, dewberry, thimbleberry, and related plants may be infested. Climbing roses and neglected hybrid perpetuals are more likely to be attacked than hybrid trees pruned low each spring. But now that rosarians prefer more moderate pruning, scale may become a problem on hybrid teas also. In New York, eggs hatch in late May or June with a 2nd generation in August.

Control. If roses are sprayed with lime sulfur a 1 to 9 dilution directly after pruning in spring (provided buds have not opened more than ¼ inch) rose scale is readily controlled. For climbers near painted surfaces a dormant oil will have to be substituted or else malathion for crawlers, but in my experience neither is as effective as lime sulfur. Prune out heavily infested canes.

Rose Palaeococcus, *Palaeococcus rosae* R. & H. A kind of mealybug, yellowish with short waxy filaments around the body. Reported from Key West on sugar-apple, Otaheite gooseberry, rose, and sapodilla.

Rufous Scale, *Selenaspidus articulatus* (Morgan). In Florida on acacia, sugar-apple, avocado, banana, bauhinia, citrus, croton, fig, gumbo-limbo, jacaranda, jasmine, ligustrum, Spanish lime, mountain ebony, oleander, palm, pine, hog-plum, pomegranate, rose, rubber, sapodilla, tamarind. The scale is circular, slightly convex, semitransparent, gray to yellow-brown with lighter margin, central copper-colored exuviae.

San Jose Scale*, *Quadraspidiotus perniciosus* (Comstock). Probably from China, first discovered at San Jose, California, in 1880, now present in every state. It is particularly injurious to deciduous fruit trees, often causing death if left unchecked. Fruit hosts include apple, pear, quince, peach, plum, prune, apricot, nectarine, cherry, blackberry, currant, gooseberry. Ash, mountain-ash, poplar, hawthorn, lilac, linden, elm, willow are also subject to injury. Other hosts include acacia, actinidia, akebia, alder, almond, arborvitae, beech, birch, false bittersweet, button-bush, buckthorn, catalpa, ceanothus, chestnut, cotoneaster, dogwood, elder, eucalyptus, euonymus, fig, hackberry, hibiscus, honeysuckle, locust, loquat, maple, mulberry, pecan, orange, Osage-orange, persimmon, photinia, privet, Japanese quince, rose, sassafras, shadbush, silver thorn, smokebush, snowball, snowberry, spirea, sour-gum, strawberry, sumac, Virginia-creeper, English walnut, willow.

The female is yellowish, covered with a gray, circular, waxy shell, $\frac{1}{16}$ inch in diameter, elevated in the center into a nipple surrounded by a yellow ring. Young scales are small and nearly black. The male is oblong-oval, acquires 2 wings. Young scales winter on bark, becoming full-grown when apples bloom. After mating, females give birth to living young, crawlers with 6 legs which move over the bark until they find a suitable place to insert their mouth parts. There are 2 to 6 generations a year, depending on location. The scale is spread by being carried on bodies of birds and larger insects and through shipments of nursery stock. Bark on trees is often reddened around the scales, which may be so numerous they overlap, completely covering a branch. On fruit, they form gray patches at blossom and stem ends; there is often a red, inflamed area around each scale.

Control. Lime sulfur first came into use as a dormant spray for the control of San Jose scale, and it may still be used in some places at a 1 to 9 dilution before buds break in spring. However, as early as 1914 the scale started to show some resistance to lime sulfur so oil sprays have been used. Spray with malathion or carbaryl for crawlers.

Scurfy Scale*, *Chionaspis furfura* (Fitch). A native pest of deciduous fruit and ornamental trees, widely distributed in the United States. The female is grayish white, rounded at one end so it is rather pear-shaped, $\frac{1}{8}$ inch long. The male is small, snow-white, narrow, with 3 longitudinal ridges (Plate XXXIV). Food plants include pear, apple, quince, cherry, gooseberry, currant, black raspberry, peach, and many ornamental trees such as dogwood, mountain-ash, white and prickly-ash, aspen, black walnut, elm, hawthorn, hickory, horsechestnut, maple, willow. The scales are abundant on bark, giving it a scurfy appearance; they infest foliage and may spot fruit. Scurfy scale is most often present on shaded parts of trees in neglected orchards where foliage is too dense. It is not so important on trees receiving good care.

Reddish purple eggs winter on bark under female shells, hatching in late spring, May or June, after trees are in full leaf. Purple crawlers move about for a few hours, then settle down on bark. There are 2 generations in the southern range, with eggs of the summer brood laid in July. There is only 1 brood in the North with overwintering eggs laid in the fall.

Control. A 3 or 4 per cent dormant oil spray is usually effective. Malathion or carbaryl may be used for crawlers.

Soft Azalea Scale, *Pulvinaria ericicola* McConnell. On azalea, rhododendron, and huckleberry, in District of Columbia, Delaware, Maryland, New York, Ohio, and Florida. The elongate, oval, reddish brown body is covered with glassy wax and has a prominent white egg sac.

Soft Scale. See Brown Soft Scale.

Sourgum Scale, *Phenacaspis nyssae* (Comstock). On gums and hornbeam in Florida, Georgia, Indiana, North Carolina, and Texas. The scale is nearly triangular, flat, delicate, snow-white, with light-yellow terminal exuviae.

Spirea Scale, *Eriococcus borealis*. Occasionally infesting spirea. It is a white mealybug in forks of branches; it resembles azalea bark scale.

Spruce Bud Scale*, *Physokermes piceae* (Schrank). A special pest of Norway spruce but present on other spruces, distributed from New England to Maryland and Minnesota, reported in Oregon. Mature scales are ⅛ inch across, round, gall-like, reddish brown with flecks of yellow, dusted with powdery wax, situated in clusters of 3 to 5 at base of branchlets, and so closely resembling spruce buds they are difficult to detect. Infestation is at tips of lower branches. Great quantities of honeydew attract bees and form a medium for black mold. Young insects are born in June or July, winter as partly grown scales. There is 1 generation. Use a dormant oil spray in spring before growth starts or malathion for crawlers.

Sweetgum Scale, *Diaspidiotus liquidambaris* (Kotinsky). On sweetgum, recorded from Florida, Georgia, Mississippi, Louisiana, Texas, Ohio, District of Columbia, and New York. The minute, circular to oval female, lemon-yellow, lives in a pit on lower side of leaf. The area above becomes a small, round, conical mound. The pits are usually near intersection of veins and midrib.

Sycamore Scale, *Stomacoccus platani* Ferris. Occurring naturally on native sycamore in California and now a serious pest of introduced Oriental plane. The female is dark yellow, ¹⁄₁₆ inch long. It winters on bark of trunk and branches, protected by loose cottony threads. Nymphs migrate to leaves and mature there, causing brown spots, sometimes distortion and defoliation, but they return to trunk and limbs for egg laying. There are 3 generations, with young scales becoming active in late January, which is the best time for spraying with a medium oil.

Tea Scale*, *Fiorinia theae* Green. The most important camellia insect in the Deep South, not so serious in California; sometimes found on greenhouse camellias in the North. Although the scales are on the underside of foliage, infested camellias can be told at a

78. Tea scale on camellia, showing brown females and nymphs covered with white cotton on underside of leaf and yellowing of upper leaf surface.

distance by yellow blotches on upper leaf surfaces, generally unhealthy appearance of the whole plant, premature dropping of leaves. Bloom is decreased, cuttings may die before roots develop. The scale is as serious on Chinese holly as on camellias in some parts of the South and may at times infest bottle-brush, dogwood, euonymus, ferns, mango, palms? (perhaps misidentified), figs, Satsuma orange, orchids, teaplant, yaupon.

The female is at first thin, light yellow, later hard, brown, elongate-oval or boat-shaped, $\frac{1}{16}$ inch long, with the residue of the first molt attached at one end. Yellow eggs, 10 to 16, are held under the shell. The male is soft, narrow, with a ridge down the middle. Both scales are held in a conspicuous tangle of white, cottony threads; often the entire undersurface of the leaf is white, dotted with small brown female shells. The eggs hatch in 7 to 21 days, depending on the weather. Flat yellow crawlers move to new growth, attach themselves after 2 or 3 days, secreting first a thin white covering, later the many white threads. The 1st molt is in 18 to 36 days, the 2nd a week later; egg laying starts 41 to 65 days after birth. There are many overlapping generations, so that crawlers and young nymphs are present on foliage at any time between March and November in Alabama.

Control. Spray with a summer oil right after camellia blooms cease and before new growth starts. During the season, spray monthly with malathion or dimethoate. The latter is very effective but may be somewhat injurious to Chinese holly, although safe on camellias. Dimethoate may also be used as a soil drench, 2 tablespoons Cygon to 1 gallon of water for plants up to 6 feet tall.

Terrapin Scale*, *Lecanium nigrofasciatum* Pergande. Blackbanded Scale. A native insect widely distributed over eastern states and Canada. It is a branch-and-twig scale, attacking common fruit trees, many shade trees and shrubs. A partial list of hosts includes maple, sycamore, boxelder, hawthorn as preferred food plants, with occasional infestation on ash, cottonwood, European plane, mulberry, linden, live oak, redbud, willow. Florida hosts include bay, blueberry, buckthorn, bumelia, gum, holly, jasmine, cherry-laurel, lime, maple, saffron-plum, sparkleberry. The soft, unarmored female is nearly hemispherical, ⅛ inch in diameter, dark reddish brown, smooth, shining, with 10 or 12 dark bands radiating from the high center of the back to the fluted edges. Partly grown females winter on twigs, reach full size in June when they give birth to living young. Each nymph leaves the mother in a day or two, migrates to a leaf for 6 weeks, then moves back to a branch, where it is fertilized by a minute winged male. When scales are numerous, twigs are said to give off a putrid odor. The drain on the tree is serious; smaller branches die; foliage is thin; sooty mold grows in quantity in honeydew, covering trunk and branches and dropping to sidewalks.

Control. There are many predaceous and parasitic insect enemies. A dormant miscible oil, applied as late in spring as possible before buds burst, is satisfactory.

Tesselated Scale, *Eucalymnatus tessellatus* (Signoret). Palm Scale. A tropical tortoise species appearing in greenhouses on many kinds of palms, orchids, and other plants, found mostly on leaves, rarely on bark. Plants infested outdoors in Florida include allamanda, avocado, banana, bay, bottle-brush, cactus, cajeput, carissa, Chinese pepper-plant, cinnamon, dracaena, eugenia, feijoa, fig, gardenia, gingerlily, guava, holly, yaupon, ivy, ixora, jasmine, jessamine, laurel, litchi, mango, ribbonbush, myrtle, oleander, palms, sapota, soursop, strobilanthes, tabernaemontana, thunbergia, and viburnum. The scale resembles brown soft scale but it is larger, darker brown, and the surface is marked with pale lines to form a mosaic. In Florida the friendly fungus *Cephalosporium lecanii* helps to keep it under control.

Tesserate Scale, *Duplaspidiotus tesseratus* (de Charmoy). On orchids.

Tuliptree Scale*, *Toumeyella liriodendri* (Gmelin). Liriodendron Scale. Probably a native, noted as injurious in Michigan in 1870. It is distributed over the United States east of the Rocky Mountains, on tuliptrees for the most part, sometimes on magnolia and linden. In Florida it may be serious on magnolia and also infest banana shrub, bay, button-bush, fig, cape-jasmine, and walnut. One of the largest of the soft scales, the female is ⅓ inch across, very convex, hemispherical, a rich dark brown. Scales are usually crowded together and somewhat distorted along the twigs and branches. The winter is spent as small, partly grown nymphs, brown with lighter ridges, clinging tightly to twigs. They grow fast in spring and produce young by August. There is 1 generation. Spray with a dormant oil emulsion in April and with malathion in late August. During the season large scales can be scrubbed off twigs or small trees with a rag or brush and soapy water. Parasites often keep this scale under control.

Utah Cedar Scale, *Aonidia shastae* Coleman. Redwood Scale. Very small, thin, dirty-white, transparent, cone-shaped. Found on redwood leaves in California, on cedar in Kansas and Utah.

Vanda Orchid Scale, *Genaparlatoria pseudaspidiotus* (Lindinger). Oval, ⅟₁₈ to ⅟₁₂ inch in diameter, dark brown with ash-gray margin, often covered with a thin waxy or dusty secretion.

Walnut Scale*, *Quadraspidiotus juglansregiae* (Comstock). A European scale found on a wide variety of trees and shrubs, including English, Persian, and Japanese walnuts, almond, apple, apricot, ash, azalea, bay, boxwood, boxelder, cherry, cherry-laurel, coralberry, cottonwood, currant, dogwood, elderberry, elm, gallberry, sweetgum, gordonia, haw, holly, honeysuckle, hackberry, laurel, horsechestnut, linden, locust, maple, oak, peach, pear, plum, prune, pecan, persimmon, tuliptree, pyracantha, redbud, rose, spirea, sumac, and viburnum. The female is mottled orange, covered with a flat, nearly circular, gray to reddish brown shell, ⅛ inch in diameter. Spraying thoroughly with lime sulfur, 1 to 8 dilution, just before buds expand in spring, has been effective.

White Peach Scale*, *Pseudaulacaspis pentagona* (Targioni-Tozzetti). West Indian Peach Scale. Present from Florida north to Maryland and occasionally farther up the coast. It is an armored scale attacking privet, walnut, flowering peach, lilac, catalpa, and various fruits—peach, plum, cherry, pear, apricot, grape, and persimmon. Other Florida hosts include abelia, allamanda, ash, boxwood, buddleia, chaste-tree, Jerusalem-cherry, chinaberry, cotoneaster, deutzia, dogwood, elaeagnus, Chinese elm, fig, fringe-tree, geranium, golddust tree, goldenrain-tree, holly, honeysuckle, hypericum, cherry-laurel, English laurel, laurestinus, ligustrum, magnolia, mountain ebony, mulberry, sweetolive, orchids, palm, Brazilian pepper, redbud, photinia, Scotch broom, spirea, sumac, tung-oil, and walnut. The female is ⅟₁₀ inch, light gray or dingy white, with yellow exuviae; the male is elongated, pure white. The scales are often clustered at base of branches, which die. There are several generations, on bark, leaf, and fruit. Sometimes serious, it is mostly controlled by parasites. A dormant spray may be advisable.

Woolly Pine Scale. See Cottony Pine Scale.

Willow Scurfy Scale, *Chionaspis salicis-nigrae* (Walsh). A common scale on willow in Middle Atlantic States, also infesting poplar, dogwood, shadbush, tuliptree, alder, ceanothus. The female is large, white, somewhat pearshaped but broadest at the middle; the male is long, narrow, snow-white. Purple eggs winter under the female shell; there are 2 generations. Willow twigs and branches may be coated with scales; branches and young trees may die. Spray with oil just before buds break.

Yellow Scale*, *Aonidiella citrina* (Coquillett). Almost identical with California red scale except for yellow color and for being found only on foliage and smaller twigs.

Yew Scale. See Cottony Taxus Scale.

Yucca Scale, *Aspidiotus yuccae,* reported on yucca in Florida.

Zamia Scale, *Diaspis zamiae* Morgan. Reddish with a prominent convex shield which is waxy with marked radial stripes.

SLUGS AND SNAILS

Slugs and snails are not insects but mollusks, belonging, along with oysters, clams, and other shellfish, to the large animal phylum Mollusca, characterized by individuals which have soft, unsegmented bodies, usually protected by a hard calcareous shell. They are in the class Gastropoda, containing forms that have a univalve shell or none, and in the order Stylommatophora. A slug is merely a snail without a shell, or with a shell reduced and located internally (Plate XXIX).

Snails have 2 pairs of tentacles or feelers, a large pair above, bearing eyes at the tips, and a smaller pair below, used for smelling. The mouth is in the center of the head, below a lower pair of tentacles, and below that is the opening of a large mucous or slime gland. The soft visceral hump contains most of the internal organs. Over this is formed the shell, secreted by the mantle which forms a fold where the shell joins the body or "foot" of the snail. On the right side, under the edge of the mantle, is the breathing pore with the anus immediately in back of that. The foot contains mucous glands and muscles by which the animal crawls. When disturbed it may withdraw entirely into the shell. It can even become dormant under unfavorable circumstances, sealing the opening of the shell with a mucous sheet, the operculum, which soon hardens to a leathery texture. Snails have been known to remain dormant as long as 4 years.

Slugs are much like snails in structure but they lack the visceral hump and shell. The mantle is a smooth area in the anterior 4th or 3rd of the back. Slugs range in length from ¼ inch to 8 or 10 inches, in color from whitish yellow to black, usually mottled. Without the protection of a shell they need damp places and are usually found in the daytime under decaying boards and logs or any debris around the garden. They feed at night by rasping holes in foliage, their mouths being equipped with a horny file, the radula. Although more than 30 species of slugs and several hundred species of snails have been recorded in this country, only a few are of economic importance.

Metaldehyde baits and sometimes dusts and sprays are standard for slug control. Chlordane is also used either as a foliage spray or in a bait with metaldehyde. Zectran is also effective in control. Baits should be put under bits of board to protect birds and pets. Recently it has been found that placing shallow saucers of beer, fresh or stale, attracts slugs and causes them to drown. Fermented grape juice has about the same effect. It is always helpful to clean up the garden and eliminate hiding places for slugs.

An introduced slug, *Arion ater* (Linnaeus), that has not been given an official common name, is now abundant in the Pacific Northwest. Reported in Oregon in 1942, it has become the dominant species in certain areas in Washington, is important in California, and has been recorded from Utah, Michigan, and Kansas. The slugs interfere with commercial production of narcissus bulbs, are a serious strawberry pest, and are generally a nuisance on flowers and vegetables in home gardens, feeding at night. They are hard to control. Metaldehyde baits are somewhat effective and so is a band of metaldehyde dust around a flower bed, so placed that the slugs must cross it in noctural movements.

Banded Wood Snail*, *Cepaea nemoralis* (Linnaeus). In flower gardens in parts of the South, also noted in Utah. The shell is conspicuous, light yellow with longitudinal chocolate-brown striping, 1 inch across.

Brown Garden Snail*, *Helix aspersa* Müller. European Brown Snail, distributed over the world, known in California since 1850, where it is thought to have been deliberatly "planted" for food purposes from stock brought from France. It is now very numerous in citrus orchards, is a pest on avocado. It eats holes in citrus leaves, makes pits or scars on fruit, covers tree trunks with shells. It feeds on avocado foliage, blossoms, and young fruit, scarring the latter. This snail is also important in flower and vegetable gardens, is destructive to grasses, shrubs, and trees. Most serious on the Pacific Coast, it also occurs in many parts of the South.

Full-grown shells have 4½ to 5 whorls, are 1¼ to 1½ inches in diameter. They are grayish yellow with brown applied in 5 bands. The mouth is surrounded by fleshy lips but inside there is a chitinous jaw to cut or scrape off food. White, spherical eggs are laid in a nest in the soil. Young snails have only 1 whorl; they take 2 years to reach maturity.

Control. Hand-pick snails; surround trees with a barrier of lime on the soil which acts as an irritant and keeps snails from walking through it. Broadcast poison baits of metaldehyde around "skirts" of trees, following rains or irrigation, when there is plenty of moisture present.

Citrustree Snail, *Drymaeus dormani* (Binney). Manatee Snail, believed by some Florida growers to be helpful in a biological control program. They may reduce enemies of beneficial insects and they clean up plants by feeding on sooty-mold fungi and algae.

Giant African Snail, *Achatina fulica* Bowditch. Found in Florida in 1969 and a potentially serious agricultural pest. It is a general feeder, observed in its first appearance on Sanchezia, St. Augustine grass, and hibiscus. It is over 5 inches long, sometimes the size of a lemon. Eradication measures were begun immediately and by the end of 1969 the infestation was much reduced and in late 1970 no live snails were found in treated areas. However, in 1971 it was found again. It is said that children spread it by taking it in school buses and that the first snail came from Hawaii, brought in a pocket by a school child.

Grass Snail, *Vallonia pulchella* (Müller).

Gray Field Slug*, *Deroceras laeve* (Müller). Fern Snail. Dark gray or buff to black, ½ to 1 inch long. It is common in lawns and fields and sometimes in greenhouses. There it hides in soil during the day but at night eats parenchyma tissue from the underside of fern leaves.

Gray Garden Slug*, *Deroceras reticulatum* (Müller). True Garden Slug. Very common, small, averaging ¾ inch, never over 1½ inches, hiding in small cracks and crevices. The color varies from white to pale yellow, lavender, purple, or nearly black with brown specks and mottlings. This is one of the worst pests of garden and field crops, especially in humid regions. Grapejuice added to metaldehyde on wheat bran or plastic foam increases the effectiveness of the bait and if beer is placed in shallow vessels the slugs tumble in from the edges.

Greenhouse Slug*, *Milax gagates* (Draparnaud). Widely distributed, very destructive. It is a uniform black to dark gray with a lon-

XXXIII JUNIPER SCALE: (a) round, white, female scale, much enlarged;
(b) male scale, same enlargement; (c,d) scale on juniper twigs. PINE NEEDLE
SCALE: (a) two forms of the female scale; (b) ridged male scale; (c) infested
pine needles. EUONYMUS SCALE: (a) dark, oyster-shaped female; (b) narrow,
white, ridged male; (c) infested euonymus; (d) on bittersweet.

XXXIV SAN JOSE SCALE: (a) round female scale; (b) oblong male scales; (c) young crawler; (d) adult winged male; (f) infested apple twig and fruit. SCURFY SCALE: (a) single female, much enlarged, and branch with male scales; (b) single male and branch with male scales; (e) female scale removed, showing eggs. OYSTERSHELL SCALE: (a) single female and branch with female scales; (c) young crawler; (d) adult male; (e) female turned over to show eggs under the shell. COTTONY MAPLE SCALE: (a) female with cottony egg mass and infested maple twig; (c) young crawler; (e) eggs.

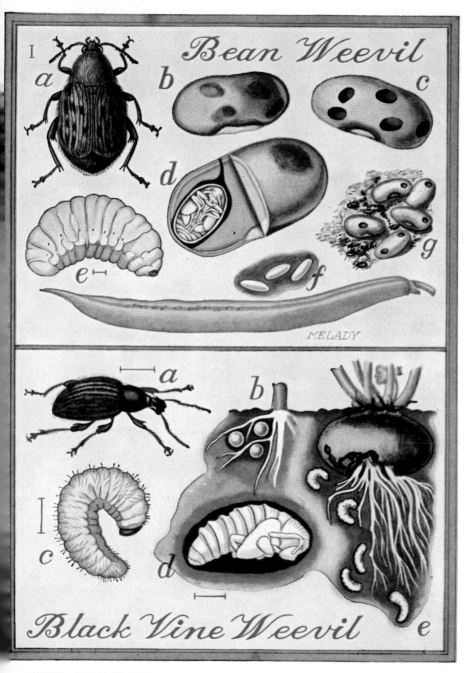

XXXV   BEAN WEEVIL: (a) adult weevil; (b) bean with blemishes indicating weevils inside; (c) exit holes in seed; (d) pupa in position inside seed; (e) grub, much enlarged; (f) eggs, magnified and in position on bean pod; (g) remains of a weevil-infested bag of seeds. **BLACK VINE WEEVIL:** (a) adult; (b) eggs among roots in soil; (c) grub, enlarged; (d) pupa in earthen cell below soil surface; (e) grubs in soil, natural size, and injury to cyclamen corm.

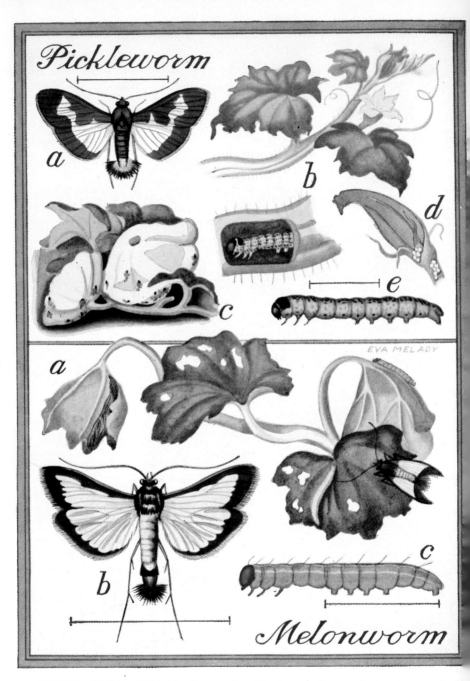

Pickleworm

Melonworm

EVA MELADY

XXXVI PICKLEWORM: (a) moth with characteristic scaly brush at end of abdomen; (b) melon shoot showing feeding injury, and stem cut to show young larva; (c) squash with entrance holes; (d) eggs at base of bud; (e) full-grown larva. MELONWORM: (a) squash vine with feeding holes, pupa in folded leaf, moth; (b) adult moth; (c) full-grown larva.

gitudinal ridge down the body and a diamond-shaped mark in the center, 1½ to 3 inches long. It shows some preference for coleus, cineraria, geranium, marigold, and snapdragon. A 15 per cent metaldehyde dust has been used for floricultural crops.

Greenhouse Snails, *Oxychilus* spp. Four species of snails are common in greenhouses and cellars throughout the United States. The shell is a uniform gray or brown, with a very flat coil, ½ inch in diameter.

Spotted Garden Slug*, *Limax maximus* Linnaeus. Giant Slug. Ranging from 1½ to 7 inches, averaging 3 to 5 inches. The smaller slugs are

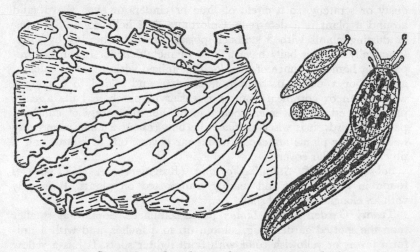

79. Spotted garden slug and injury to hosta leaf.

often a uniform dark gray or black, the larger are yellow-gray or brown mottled with black, usually with 3 rows of black spots extending from the mantle to the rear end of the body; the mantle is yellowish with black spots. The eggs are oval, translucent light yellow with a tough elastic outer membrane. They are laid in masses of 25 or more, held together with a mucilaginous substance, under boards, trash, or flowerpots, in compost piles, under stones or other damp places, any time from spring to fall outdoors, also in winter in greenhouses. The eggs hatch in about 28 days at room temperature, sooner at high temperatures. The young slug is dull white, less than ½ inch long, thin; it darkens and develops slowly. In a month it is an inch long, dark brown, with spots beginning to show. It usually takes more than a year to develop full size.

Working mostly at night, these slugs extend their slimy length over leaves, eating large ragged holes, leaving behind a viscous trail of slime. Slugs are among the earliest pests to start chewing in gardens, and they keep on until late in the autumn. Hollyhock leaves almost always show slug holes in early spring, as do primroses, iris, saxifrage, violets, and many other plants with foliage close to the ground. Slugs also like to hide in cabbage and lettuce heads.

Control. Cleaning up the garden to get rid of hiding places is always effective. Removing old iris leaves after first frost not only outwits borers, it makes slugs homeless. Shingles in the garden will trap slugs, ready for mass execution. They hate to crawl through anything dusty or scratchy, so a circle of lime or cinders or even sharp sand around a plant is a deterrent. Chlordane dust helps some. Spraying or dusting plants with a stomach poison prevents chewing by slugs. Practically all slug baits have a base of metaldehyde. It can be prepared at home (1 ounce of metaldehyde mixed with 2 ounces calcium arsenate or 1 ounce of sodium fluosilicate and added to 2 pounds wheat bran or cornmeal) but it is easier to purchase baits already prepared and in convenient pellet form. For the safety of children, pets, and birds, it is wiser to place the bait (about a tablespoon every few feet near plants attacked) under jar covers, bits of board, half a tin can, or similar cover.

Subulina Snail*, *Subulina octona* (Bruguiere). A small species found in greenhouses and readily transported on plants. It is gray with an elongate, pointed shell.

Tawny Garden Slug*, *Limax flavus* Linnaeus. Somewhat smaller than the spotted garden slug, seldom up to 4 inches, and with a uniform tawny or yellowish color with faint lighter spots. It has a yellow mantle and bluish tentacles.

White Garden Snail*, *Theba pisana* (Müller). One of the species used as food in Europe. It has a white shell with irregular darker mottlings, a little smaller than the brown garden snail. It became established in California in 1914 as an important pest of citrus, but infestations have been eradicated, as they appeared in various counties, by quarantines, inspection, handpicking in residential areas, cutting and burning infested wild vegetation, flaming of rocks and soil, and use of calcium-arsenate-bran bait.

Other food snails may be problems. *Otala vermiculata* was found in Texas in 1970 damaging shrubbery and trees at Waco. It had already been reported from Louisiana, California, and Ohio. This is a common food snail in Mediterranean countries. Another edible snail, *Helix pomatia,* was found in Florida in 1969. This is a pest of succulent plants, including vegetables, and has been damaging in

Michigan and reported in Louisiana but apparently not established there. This species is the escargot of European restaurants.

A West Indian snail, *Bulimulus guadalupensis* (Bruguiere), was found in Florida on dracaena plants in 1969 for a new United States record but this snail feeds on decaying vegetable matter and is not considered very important.

SOWBUGS AND PILLBUGS

The words sowbug and pillbug are used rather interchangeably for soil pests related to crayfish. They are in the class Crustacea, which includes arthropods having 2 pairs of antennae and at least 7 pairs of legs, and in the order Isopoda. They have flat, oval, brown bodies about ½ inch long, with 7 pairs of legs on the thoracic segments and with the abdominal segments fused and compressed (Plate XXIX). One species, the common **Pillbug**, *Armadillidum vulgare* (Latrielle), also called Roly-poly, has a habit of rolling up into a ball like an armadillo, which it resembles in miniature.

The **Dooryard Sowbug**, *Porcellio laevis* Koch, does not roll up when disturbed. The female sowbug has a ventral pouch known as a marsupium. The eggs are laid in it and held for about 2 months, and then the young, 25 to 75 in a brood, stay in the pouch for some time longer. Young sowbugs are similar to adults; they take a year to mature.

Sowbugs and pillbugs breathe by means of gills and prefer damp, protected places. They are found as scavengers on rotting plant parts, under flowerpots, or decayed boards, or in manure, and they may be quite injurious to seedlings—cutting roots, girdling the young stems. They are mostly greenhouse problems, although commonly present in garden soil. Occasionally they damage tender growth of field or garden crops.

Control. A poison bait of 1 part Paris green to 9 parts sugar was long recommended for greenhouses but has been replaced by newer chemicals. Spray soil and greenhouse branches with methoxychlor, malathion, carbaryl, or diazinon or dust with chlordane.

Watercress Sowbug*, *Lirceus brachyurus* (Harger).

SPANWORMS

Spanworms are caterpillars with the looper or measuring-worm habit and some have already been discussed under Caterpillars.

Bruce Spanworm*, *Operophtera bruceata* (Hulst). In northern states on sugar maple, poplar, birch, with serious outbreaks reported in Vermont and Wisconsin. The larva, ¾ inch long, is bright green

with 3 narrow yellowish white stripes. The male moth is gray with
flecks of brown, 1⅛-inch wing expanse; the female is brownish
gray, wingless. She lays eggs in November in bark crevices and these
hatch in early spring. There is 1 generation.

Cleftheaded Spanworm, *Amphidasis cognataria* Guenée. Pepper and
Salt Moth. The larva is about 2 inches long, with deeply cleft head,
greenish to reddish brown, with tubercles, resembling twigs of its
food plant. The adult is dull white, sprinkled with brown or black.
This species occurs in the Atlantic States, feeding on willow, poplar,
wild cherry, sweetfern, apple, locust, and other deciduous trees.

Cranberry Spanworm*, *Anavitrinella pampinaria* (Guenée).

Currant Spanworm*, *Itame ribearia* (Fitch). Present in various
parts of the East and in Colorado, feeding on currants and gooseberries, sometimes blueberries. The worms are light yellow with many
prominent black dots, just over an inch long. Like other loopers, they
drop down on a silken thread when disturbed. Sometimes they are
numerous enough to defoliate bushes. The moths have slender bodies
with broad yellow wings marked with black. Eggs are laid in stems in
summer, hatching the next spring when leaves are out.

Elm Spanworm*, *Ennomos subsignarius* (Hübner). Snowwhite
Linden Moth, Linden Looper. Found from New England to Georgia
and west to Colorado. Before 1880 this species was very abundant
around New York and Philadelphia; about 1910 it was very abundant
in forest areas in the Catskills; there was a major outbreak in Massachusetts in 1914 and in Connecticut in 1938. It is prevalent again
in the 1970s, both in Connecticut and in Westchester County, New
York, a problem along with gypsy moths. The looper is a particular
pest in cities and in outbreak years it defoliates not only elm and
linden but maple, beech, yellow birch, horsechestnut, and other trees.
The worm is about 1½ inches long, brownish black, with head and
anal segments bright red. The moth is frail, pure white, wings expanding to 1¼ to 1½ inches. Eggs are laid about midsummer, in
groups on branches, and do not hatch until the next spring. Larvae
begin at once to devour foliage, grow rapidly, and pupate in a loose
cocoon in a crumpled leaf. When moths appear in late July they
migrate long distances, appearing in cities like a summer snowstorm.

Control. The English sparrow is credited with doing a grand job
of ridding cities of this pest, helped along by at least 2 insect
parasites. In years of peak infestation trees should be sprayed with
carbaryl, or whatever material is being used for cankerworms and
gypsy moths, as they come into full leaf.

Walnut Spanworm*, *Coniodes plumogeraria* (Hulst). Similar to the spring cankerworm, found in Pacific Coast states. The larvae are pinkish gray varied with darker gray, or black and yellow.

SPITTLEBUGS

Spittlebugs are sucking insects of the order Homoptera, family Cercopidae. They are not true bugs but rather closely related to

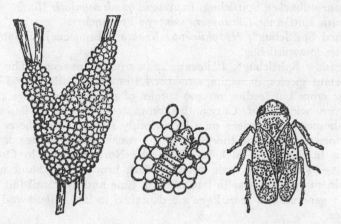

80. Spittlebug on grass blades: frothy "spittle"; nymph in bubbles; adult without protection.

leafhoppers and are sometimes called froghoppers. The adults are drab brown, gray or black, sometimes marked with yellow, and they look rather like short, robust leafhoppers. Antennae and 2 ocelli are situated between the eyes. Hind tibiae are smooth with only 1 or 2 heavy spines on their outer sides and clusters of small ones at the extremities. They hop away but do not fly very much. They insert eggs in plant stems or between stem and leaf sheath in grasses.

The remarkable thing about spittlebugs is the frothy mass (children call it frog spit) enveloping the nymphs. This spittle is a combination of a fluid voided from the anus and a mucilaginous substance secreted by glands on the 7th and 8th abdominal segments, mixed with air drawn in between a pair of plates under the abdomen. The mixture is forced out under pressure, as from a bellows, to make uniform bubbles. The tail, going up and down, operates the bellows and keeps the bubbles coming. As soon as the first bubbles are formed, the nymph reaches back with its legs and hooks onto the globules, dragging them forward to its head. The greenish nymph is soon hidden under a mound of snow-white foam, protected from sun and preying insects. Many spittlebugs are relatively harmless but several are economically injurious to plants. Spray with methoxychlor, malathion, or endosulfan or use systemic insecticides.

Alder Spittlebug*, *Clastoptera obtusa* (Say). Ceanothus Spittlebug. On alder and ceanothus, other hosts.

Cranberry Spittlebug, *Clastoptera vittata* Ball.

Diamondbacked Spittlebug, *Lepyronia quadrangularis* (Say).

Heath Spittlebug, *Clastoptera saintcyri* Provancher.

Lined Spittlebug*, *Neophilaenus lineatus* (Linnaeus). Related to the meadow spittlebug.

Meadow Spittlebug*, *Philaenus spumarius* (Linnaeus). The most important species, damaging strawberries especially, alfalfa and other forage crops but feeding on 400 species of garden and forage plants and very widespread. Chrysanthemums, stock, and other flowers in greenhouses and gardens may be seriously stunted. Strawberry fruit is distorted, small, and the plant greatly weakened. This pest is most serious in regions of high humidity, the Northeast and in Oregon. Adults—¼ inch long, pale straw to dark brown, with blunt heads, prominent eyes—appear in late May or June and live until fall, with only 1 generation a year. Eggs are deposited in late August and September.

Control. Spray alfalfa and other forage crops with methoxychlor as young nymphs hatch and in late summer to prevent oviposition. Spray strawberries and ornamentals with methoxychlor, malathion, or endosulfan.

Pecan Spittlebug*, *Clastoptera achatina* Germar. The frothy mass is found on young nuts and on tender shoots in spring and early summer. Pecan trees have been injured in Illinois, although this species is not considered a serious pest in the South. There are 2 broods, May and July.

Pine Spittlebug*, *Aphrophora parallela* (Say). A native pest of pine from New England to Arkansas, most injurious on Scotch pine but also infesting white, pitch, red, jack, and Virginia pines, and Norway spruce. Eggs are laid at base of terminal buds in July and August, hatch in May, and the young feed on twigs, which are covered with spittle. The insects continually eject undigested sap like light rain, and branches are covered with black sooty mold. Scotch pine may die within 2 or 3 years. Spray with malathion in May and again in July.

Saratoga Spittlebug*, *Aphrophora saratogensis* (Fitch). From New England to Florida and west to the Great Lakes states, seriously damaging jack and red pine. The nymphs live on sweetfern, willow, brambles, and other plants, below the surface of the litter in forests and above the root collar. Adults migrate to pine in late June and July, where they feed until October, extracting large quantities of sap. They are tan with lighter markings forming a diamond pattern. The nymphs have a bright-red abdomen during the first 4 instars, but are brown in the 5th instar.

Malathion, at ½ pound per acre, has been effective in controlling this spittlebug in Michigan pine plantations. Granular systemic insecticides, including propoxur, carbofuran, aldicarb, and phorate, have also been effective.

Sunflower Spittlebug*, *Clastoptera xanthocephala* Germar.

Twolined Spittlebug*, *Prosapia bicincta* (Say). A pest of lawn and field grasses in south and central states but also on other hosts, including sweet corn, sorghum, and holly, and ranging from Massachusetts to Florida and west to Kansas and Texas. The adults, larger than most spittlebugs, are dark brown with 2 lighter bands across the wings. Nymphs feeding on centipede, Bermuda, and St. Augustine grasses cause these to dry out. Adults feeding on holly distort, stunt, or discolor new foliage and cause light blotches on underside of older leaves. Guthion, malathion, endosulfan, and carbaryl sprays are effective in control.

SPRINGTAILS

Springtails belong to the insect order Collembola, a group of small insects less than ¹⁄₁₅ inch long, without wings and with almost no

81. Garden springtail.

metamorphosis. They have chewing or piercing mouth parts and short antennae with few segments, and are of various colors. They can jump incredible distances by means of a forked appendage, the furcula, which is folded forward under the abdomen when at rest. Under the 1st abdominal segment there is a short, tubelike structure believed to have a respiratory function. There are more than 2,000 species distributed from the Arctic to the Antarctic in damp places. About 70 of these attack seeds and seedlings, mushrooms, sugarcane, and invade houses but only 1 species is usually considered in garden literature. Some species congregate on the surface of snow and are called "snowfleas"; others live on surface of ponds or on sea beaches; others are in leaf mold or decaying material. In fact, springtails are around us most of the time, but they are so small we seldom notice them.

Garden Springtail*, *Bourletiella hortensis* (Fitch). A dark, active species found most often on young plants in seedbeds and in outdoor gardens. They have a soft, round body, black to dark purple with yellow spots, and a distinct head. They are very small, ¼₅ inch long. They jump quickly by means of the tail-like appendage. They chew holes in thin leaves such as spinach, and make pits in cotyledon leaves of beans and cucumbers, and may damage any small plant close to the ground. Spray or dust with chlordane or malathion.

SYMPHYLANS

See Centipedes and Symphylans.

TERMITES

Termites are not ants, although they are often called "white ants." They are not even in the order Hymenoptera where true ants belong.

82. *Termites: winged sexual form and nymph; and wood tunneled by termites. Note thick "waist" compared to true ant.*

Termites are in the order Isoptera, meaning equal wings. These are long, narrow, membranous, folded flat over the back when at rest. The best way to tell termites from ants is to look at the "waist." Ants are deeply constricted, while termites have a broad joining between thorax and abdomen. Termites have chewing mouth parts but gradual metamorphosis. They live in galleries in wood or in the ground, except when the winged forms are swarming.

Termites are social insects like ants and have a well-developed caste system with: (1) primary reproductive members, kings and queens, sexual forms which escape from an old colony to found a new one, losing their wings after migrating; (2) secondary reproductive members, mature males and females without wings but with wing buds, which take charge in case the king and queen are killed; (3) ergatoid kings and queens, sexually mature but lacking wings entirely; (4) workers, blind, pale, wingless, nonreproductive, constituting the main population for the colony; (5) soldiers, wingless insects with enlarged heads and mouth parts.

The food of termites is wood or cellulose in some form and they have protozoa in their intestines to enable them to digest this cellulose. Some species live in dry wood above ground but the species important to the householder and gardener are the soil-inhabiting forms, particularly the **Eastern Subterranean Termite***, *Reticulitermes flaviceps* (Kollar), and the **Western Subterranean Termite***, *R. hesperus* Banks. These work on wood on or in the ground or build covered runways to reach wood above the ground. They are not new pests, as some termite-control operators advertise; they have been found in fossils and probably were on this continent before man. Their periods of abundance seem to be in waves, however, with some years when damage to buildings is abnormally high.

Subterranean termites sometimes injure living trees and shrubs, being more harmful in warm climates. In Florida they eat away the bark around the collar of newly transplanted orange trees, sometimes injure apple, peach, pear, cherry, plum, apricot, lemon, guava, pecan, walnut. The injury is usually worse in recently cleared woodland containing old, decaying stumps or in land rich in humus. Fruits which drop and lie on the ground may be invaded. In cities, roots and heartwood of shade trees are entered; seedlings are injured in nurseries.

The **Formosan Subterranean Termite**, *Coptotermes formosanum* Shiraki, was first found in continental United States in 1965 in a warehouse at Houston, Texas, and was later found in Louisiana. Efforts are being made to eradicate it. The **Southern Subterranean Termite** is *Reticulitermes virginicus* (Banks).

The **Desert Dampwood Termite**, *Paraneotermes simplicicornis* (Banks), sometimes injures roots of young citrus trees but the **Drywood Termite**, *Kalotermes minor* Hagen, feeds on wood above ground, usually in dried heartwood, sometimes in living tissue, gaining entrance through wounds or crevices and not via the soil.

Flowering plants, mostly those with woody stems, can be infested in gardens or greenhouses by subterranean termites, which start on decaying wooden stakes or labels or wooden benches in contact with moist earth. Chrysanthemums are rather commonly injured and heliotrope, begonia, geranium, poinsettia, cosmos, jasmine, pansy, oleander, and others have been injured on occasion. Termites reach potted plants through the hole in the bottom of the pot. In southern states field and truck crops may be injured—corn, cotton, sugarcane, rice, grasses, white and sweetpotatoes, artichoke, bean, beet, cabbage, carrot, cranberry, peanut, rhubarb, squash, turnip, cantaloupe, and other melons.

Control. Use resistant wood for garden stakes and posts—redwood is excellent for grape stakes and fence posts—or use wood treated with a commercial preparation containing copper napthenate or similar material. Tree surgery and cleaning up old grapevines and other woody debris around the garden reduce the termite menace. Paint pruning scars with a mixture of 1 part creosote to 3 parts coal tar after shellac has been applied to protect living tissue at edges of the bark. Avoid the use of manure while termites are in soil.

Subterranean termites can be killed in soil around trees by applying carbon disulfide or carbon tetrachloride emulsion. Poke small holes around plants 12 inches apart and pour in about 1 teaspoon in each; more can be used in fallow soil. Chlordane can be worked into the soil around living trees and shrubs and can be mixed with the soil before setting smaller plants. Sap-pine stakes can be used to trap termites; the stakes are then pulled up and drenched with boiling water. When swarming indicates the position of a colony, drench the spot with kerosene. In new greenhouses proper construction keeps termites from entering. Benches in older houses can be cleaned up with kerosene emulsion.

THRIPS

Thrips belong to the insect order Thysanoptera, the name meaning bristle or fringe wings. They are very small, slender insects, about as wide as a fine needle, only just visible to the naked eye. The 2 pairs of long narrow wings, with few or no veins, are edged with long hairs like stiff fringe. The mouth parts are fitted for piercing and rasping; antennae are usually short, 6- to 10-segmented; tarsi (feet) have 1 or 2 segments and end in a bladder-like vescicle instead of claws. Thrips often scar fruit and foliage with their scraping mouth parts and are commonly found on flowers. Some are predaceous on mites and small insects, some eat fungi and decayed vegetable matter but most are very injurious. One species is the vector of tobacco ring-spot virus.

There are 2 suborders, with most of the plant pests belonging to Terebrantia, distinguished by having a sawlike ovipositor, and to only a few families in this suborder.

Aeolothripidae. Broad-winged or banded thrips. Adults are dark, have broad wings with 2 longitudinal veins and several cross veins, usually banded or mottled. The antennae are 9-segmented and the ovipositor of the female curves upward. Most forms are predaceous.

Thripidae. Common thrips. This family contains most of the species of economic importance as plant feeders. Wings are narrow, pointed at the tip; body somewhat flattened; antennae 6- to 9-segmented; ovipositor usually well developed, curved downward.

Heterothripidae. A small family with only 2 genera in the United States—Heterothrips and Oligothrips. Similar to Thripidae but antennae 9-segmented.

Merothripidae. Large-legged thrips. The front and hind tibiae are enlarged, the pronotum has a longitudinal suture on each side, antennae are moniliform, and the ovipositor is much reduced. The common species, *Merothrips morgani* Hood, occurs under bark, in debris, and on fungi.

Phloeothripidae. In the suborder Tubulifera, the female lacking an ovipositor and the last segment tubular. Larger and stouter than most other thrips, usually dark brown or black, often with light-colored or mottled wings. Some are beneficial predators; a few, like the lilybulb thrips, are plant feeders.

DDT was an excellent control for most thrips and this is one case where we really miss it. Malathion, dimethoate, diazinon, or Meta-Systox-R will give brief protection. Some thrips are repelled by aluminum mulches.

A **Banded Thrips**, *Aeolothrips fasciatus* (Linnaeus). Found in flower heads feeding on other thrips, aphids, and mites. Adults are yellow to dark brown with 3 white bands on the wings; larvae are yellow shading to orange.

Banded Greenhouse Thrips*, *Hercinothrips femoralis* (O. M. Reuter). A pest in greenhouses, and of sugar beets, cacti, and date palm outdoors in California and Alabama. The thrips is dark brown or black, with head, prothorax, and end of abdomen reddish yellow, fore wings dusty with white areas. This species may moderately or heavily infest alstroemeria, amaryllis, agapanthus, aralia, buddleia, yellow calla, chrysanthemum, dracaena, rubber plant, gardenia, gerbera, gladiolus, hydrangea, hymenocallis, nerine, philodendron, sprekelia, sweetpea, snapdragon, screwpine, and other greenhouse plants including sweetpotatoes and tomatoes. Control is the same as for the greenhouse thrips.

Bean Thrips*, *Caliothrips fasciatus* (Pergande). Widely distributed, a general feeder on legumes, truck, field, and forage crops, grasses, deciduous and citrus trees, a special pest of beans, avocado, olive, pear, and orange. Nymphs are reddish yellow, adults gray-black, with black-and-white wings. They feed in colonies, making foliage of beans, peas, and other crops bleached or silvered, wilted, covered with black bits of excrement. Eliminate weeds around the garden, especially prickly lettuce and sow thistle.

Another common species on beans, including soybean, is *Sericothrips variabilis* (Black), which causes yellow spotting or browning of foliage.

Blueberry Thrips*, *Frankliniella vaccinii* Morgan. A pest of blueberries in Maine and part of New York. Adults appear when first blueberry leaves separate in the buds, causing a tight curling, reddening and malformation of leaves. The female is light brown with gray head, legs, wings, and 1st antennal segments. Recommended procedure has been a quick burning over of blueberry fields.

Camphor Thrips*, *Liriothrips floridensis* (Watson). Very injurious to camphor-trees in the Gulf States. The adult is black, 1/50 inch long; the young are straw-colored, changing to orange-red at the 2nd molt. The thrips feed on buds and tender tips, causing dieback, and on branches, causing blackening, cracking of bark, deformation of limbs. Breeding is nearly continuous. Injury is worse on nursery trees, or on older trees that have been trimmed and cut back. Shellac pruning cuts.

Chrysanthemum Thrips*, *Thrips nigropilosus* Uzel. Often serious on greenhouse chrysanthemums, sometimes outdoors. Young leaves are flecked whitish from loss of sap and often have a gummy residue. The shoots die back if thrips are numerous. Use malathion or parathion aerosol or spray in greenhouses; outdoors use malathion or Lannate.

Citrus Thrips*, *Scirtothrips citri* (Moulton). Important in the Southwest and probably third in importance of all citrus pests in California. It is a native insect, restricted to the Southwest, not occurring in the Gulf States. It is serious on sweet and mandarin oranges, lemon, lime, grapefruit, pomelo, kumquat, tangerine, sometimes infests pomegranate, grape, umbrella-tree, apricot, rose, rarely occurs on walnut, olive, willow, almond. Pepper-tree is the only host besides citrus on which it overwinters—in the egg state, the nymphs hatching in March. The injury is a very definite ring scar around the fruit at the blossom end, withering and curling of leaves, blossom-drop before fruit is set. The nymphs are yellow to orange, the adults are orange-yellow with black eyes, $\frac{1}{50}$ inch long. There may be 10 to 12 generations a year in the warmer localities.

Control. Consult your experiment station for the best pesticide to replace DDT for your locality. Treat at petal-fall to prevent scarring of fruit and in the summer to protect new growth.

Composite Thrips*, *Microcephalothrips abdominalis* (D. L. Crawford). Frequently found on zinnia, marigold, and other flowers but of minor importance. The entire life cycle is passed in the flower heads. Adults are very small, dark brown; greatest abundance is in autumn, when there may be some injury to flower seeds.

Cuban Laurel Thrips*, *Gynaikothrips ficorum* (Marchal). Recently a problem in California on Indian laurel fig, rubber plant, and other species of Ficus, also known in Florida. Spray with dimethoate.

Daylily Thrips, *Frankliniella hemerocallis* Crawford. On daylily, similar to the tobacco thrips but legs are concolorous with body. Perhaps a native of Japan, possibly native here, present in Florida, Maryland, New York, and Wisconsin. Foliage is flecked or silvery, or scarified brown.

Dogwood Thrips, *Rhopalandrothrips corni* Morison. Present in California.

Dracaena Thrips, *Heliothrips dracaenae* (Heeger). Dusky yellow with abdomen shaded with brown; netted head, thorax, and wings. It is present in California on dracaena, rubber tree, Kentia palm, Sago palm, and century plant.

Florida Flower Thrips, *Frankliniella bispinosa* (Morgan). A southern pest of roses, white-blossomed Spanish needle, and other flowers; of strawberry blossoms, which either drop off or turn into brown, hard berries; of citrus bloom. They are found in tomato blossoms but are only occasionally damaging to them. The adult has an orange head and thorax, lemon-yellow abdomen, which is often curled over the back when disturbed. The larvae are similar but paler in color, lack wings.

Flower Thrips*, *Frankliniella tritici* (Fitch). Wheat Thrips, present in nearly every state but primarily an eastern species. It is an omnivorous feeder on grasses, weeds, flowers, field, forage, and truck crops, fruit and shade trees, berries, vines, but with preference for grasses, legumes, roses, and peonies. Young thrips are lemon-yellow, adults amber or brownish yellow with an orange thorax; $\frac{1}{20}$ inch long They injure only the flowers, not foliage, and come to roses and other ornamentals daily from flowers on trees and grasses, weeds nearby.

Rosebuds turn brown and either ball, petals staying stuck together, or open partway to crippled, distorted blossoms with brown edges on

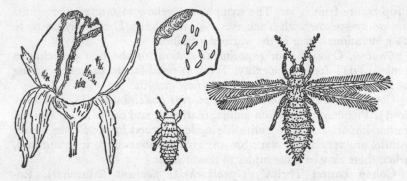

83. Flower thrips: injury to rose; nymph and adult much enlarged.

the petals. The thrips can be seen inside the petals, usually near the base. Flower thrips are color sensitive, preferring some varieties, often yellow or light-colored, over others. Tested on sticky cards this species can even distinguish between 3 kinds of white. The life cycle may be completed in 2 weeks and there can be many generations but they are most abundant on the June bloom of roses, with comparatively little injury to the fall display. There are more thrips in Georgia than in New York and there the population peak comes in mid-May. Peonies are often markedly injured by flower thrips. They may appear on daylilies but there is a special daylily thrips on that host. They are common on Japanese iris, although not so harmful on this host.

Control. This is an exceedingly difficult insect to control because thrips are continuously arriving on rosebuds from tree and grass flowers round about. The old tartar-emetic-brown sugar concoction was given up in favor of DDT but even that was not too satisfactory. Some recommend individual bonnets on selected rose buds, or covering beds with cloth on a frame. Spraying with malathion or dimethoate gives some protection. Diazinon and Meta-Systox-R are also recommended. Infested buds and all blooms as they start to fade should be promptly removed to reduce the thrips population. During the migration period roses and peonies may be cut in tight bud and opened indoors.

Gladiolus Thrips*, *Taeniothrips simplex* (Morison). All too universally present in gardens. A relatively new insect, noticed first in Ohio and Canada in 1929 and rapidly distributed through the country. Of chief importance on gladiolus, it is also a pest of iris—Spanish, Japanese, German, and bulbous—and is known to feed and breed on amaryllis, aster, carnation, delphinium, freesia, hollyhock, narcissus, and poker plant (Plate XXX).

Although one of the larger species of thrips, the adult is only $\frac{1}{16}$ inch or less, black or brownish black with a creamy white band across the base of the wings. Females insert kidney-shaped eggs in growing plant tissues. First-stage larvae, white with red eyes, hatch in about a week, changing soon to pale-yellow 2nd-stage larvae. The next, prepupa, stage is orange; the true pupal stage is light yellow with white antennae, wing pads, and legs; red eyes. The dark adult appears in about 3 days. The complete life cycle takes 2 to 4 weeks, depending on the temperature, the effective range being 50° to 90° F. There are several generations in the garden and breeding may continue on corms in storage. Thrips are killed by low temperatures and do not winter in the ground except in warm climates.

Injury on gladiolus is a silvery appearance of the foliage, due to the many small areas where cell sap has been lost, followed by browning and dying of leaves. Flowers are deformed, with whitish flecks or streaks; spikes may not open. Corms in storage become sticky, corky, russeted, and fail to germinate when planted or produce poor or no flowers.

Control. Until DDT came to the rescue many gardeners had almost given up growing gladiolus; then they learned that by dusting the foliage and treating the corms after harvest with DDT they had almost complete control. Now we must try other methods. Starting when leaves are about 6 inches high, spray or dust every 10 days with dimethoate, diazinon, or carbaryl. After harvest and curing, dust corms with malathion before storage and keep in a cool place (near 40° F.). Experimental work indicated that if Vapona strips are hung in the storeroom and the corms left in open bags there is effective control. If corms appear infested at planting time, soak in Lysol solution for 3 hours ($1\frac{1}{2}$ teaspoons Lysol to 1 gallon of water).

Grape Thrips, *Drepanothrips reuteri* Uzel. A pest of grapes in California. It looks like the flower thrips and causes burning and curling of young leaves, scarring of berries.

Grass Thrips*, *Anaphothrips obscurus* (Müller). Sometimes abundant on grains and grasses, occasionally on corn, destroying softer parts of foliage, flowers, and developing kernels. On grasses it causes silvertop. Destroy old stems and litter where insects hibernate.

Greenhouse Thrips*, *Heliothrips haemorrhoidalis* (Bouché). Practically worldwide, present outdoors in California, Florida, Georgia, and similar warm climates and in greenhouses nearly everywhere. Infested garden plants include avocado, on which this is a major pest, citrus, grape, mango, sapote, cherimoya, guava, and other subtropical fruits and many ornamentals. Among the latter are arbutus, azalea, carissa, croton, cypress, eucalyptus, eugenia, hibbertia, laurestinus, mandevilla, mesembryanthemum, myrtle, rhododendron, rose, statice, toyon, viburnum. In greenhouses there may be serious injury to amaryllis, begonia, chrysanthemum, citrus, croton, cyclamen, dahlia, ferns, fuchsia, gloxinia, nasturtium, orchids, palm, rubber plant, and others.

The greenhouse thrips is distinguished by a deep network of lines over head and central portion of the body, which is blackish brown, with the posterior end lighter; $\frac{1}{24}$ inch long; legs yellow; wings slightly clouded but without bands; antennae slender and needle-like at the tip. Feeding is almost entirely on foliage and fruits, often in concentrated colonies on inner parts of trees and shrubs with all stages present at the same time. Eggs are inserted just under the epidermis of leaves or fruit, producing blisters. Plants look silvery or bleached, leaves papery, wilting, dying, sometimes dropping off. Foliage and fruit are spotted with reddish-black dots of excrement.

Control. Spray or dust with malathion or dimethoate. Greenhouse operators sometimes use parathion.

Hollyhock Thrips, *Liriothrips varicornis* Hood. Apparently limited to a semiarid climate; found in California principally on hollyhock. It resembles the toyon thrips; larvae are brilliant red and black, adults all black. Colonies feed in depressions in leaves, stems, and roots. Water soil around base of plants heavily; destroy all old stalks and volunteer plants during fall and winter.

Iris Thrips*, *Iridothrips iridis* (Watson). Often abundantly infesting Japanese iris, sometimes other types. Larvae—first white, later yellow—rasp folds of inner leaves, causing russeting, blackening, stunting; tops die and turn brown. Adults are dark brown, usually wingless. Spray with dimethoate. Destroy thrips in divisions by immersing in hot water, 110° F. for 30 minutes.

Lily Bulb Thrips*, *Liriothrips vaneecki* Priesner. Confined to lily and orchids; known in New York, North Carolina, California, Oregon, and Washington. This species, shiny black, $\frac{1}{16}$ inch long, with salmon-pink and black larvae and pupae, spends its entire life on bulbs, feeding on epidermis of outer scales near base. Injured areas tend to turn rusty brown and be sunken or flabby but there is no great damage.

Madroña Thrips, *Thrips madroni* Moulton. In Oregon and California on ceanothus, madroña, azalea, elderberry, rhododendron. It is pale yellow to dark brown.

Mullein Thrips*, *Haplothrips verbasci* (Osborn).

Onion Thrips*, *Thrips tabaci* Lindeman. Probably the most widely distributed thrips in the world, found in all onion-growing sections, attacking nearly all garden plants, many field crops and weeds. Many hosts are incidental with little breeding upon them but some of the more important vegetable hosts, besides onions, are: bean, beet, carrot, cabbage, cauliflower, celery, cucumber, melons, peas, squash, tomato, and turnip. Injury to onions shows first as whitish blotches, then blasting and distortion of leaf tips, followed by withering, browning, and falling over on the ground. The bulbs are distorted, undersized. Thrips congregate in great numbers between leaf sheaths and stem, and carry over on bulbs in storage. Peas, cucumbers, and melons have crinkled, curled, dwarfed foliage.

Ornamentals infested by the onion thrips include rose and carnation, which have petals spotted and streaked, asparagus fern, calla, campanula, chrysanthemum, dahlia, gaillardia, gloxinia, mignonette, foxglove, Jerusalem-cherry, sweetpea. This species transmits the spotted-wilt virus to tomatoes, dahlias, and other flowers.

The onion thrips varies in color from pale yellow to dark brown, is $\frac{1}{25}$ inch long. Wings are a uniform dusky gray without bands; larvae are creamy white; pupation is in soil. Eggs are laid in surface tissue and hatch in about 5 days in summer. The 1st molt of the larva is on plants, the 2nd in soil. A generation is completed in a little over 2 weeks and in mild climates like California reproduction continues through the year. Winter hosts elsewhere are weeds and bulbs in storage.

Control. Spray or dust with malathion or diazinon, making 2 or 3 applications at 1- to 2-week intervals, beginning when thrips are numerous enough to scar leaves.

Orchid Thrips, *Chaetanaphothrips orchidii* (Moulton). A Florida species first noted on grapefruit in 1937. It is light yellow, very active, causing a silvery to dark-brown discoloration of immature fruit.

Pear Thrips*, *Taeniothrips inconsequens* (Uzel). An imported species, first noted in California in 1904, now present in Washington, Oregon, New York, Pennsylvania, and Maryland. Prune is injured even more than pear. Other hosts include apple, apricot, cherry, grape, peach, plum, poplar, maple, California-laurel, madroña, willow, and weeds and grasses around orchards. The adult is uniformly dark brown, slender, bluntly pointed at each end, $\frac{1}{25}$ inch long, with grayish wings lighter at the base. It emerges from the ground in spring and feeds in developing buds, causing a bleeding and gumming of pear buds, blackening of prune buds, deformed leaves and blossoms, crop reduction. After feeding for weeks, eggs are laid in stems of fruit and foliage. White larvae appear in 2 weeks and feed under husks of young fruit, causing scarring and distortion. After 3 more weeks, they drop to the ground, burrow into the soil, and construct cells several inches to 3 feet below the surface, where they remain until spring. Spray with malathion.

Privet Thrips*, *Dendrothrips ornatus* (Jablonowski). An eastern species very injurious to privet in some seasons, turning hedges uniformly gray and dusty-looking. The leaves may be somewhat puckered. The larvae are yellow, spindle-shaped, as many as 20 to 25 individuals on underside of a single small leaf. The adults are dark brown to black with a bright-red band. Eggs are deposited on lower surface of leaves and in their petioles and hatch in about a week. There are 3 generations in Connecticut, with overwintering in leaf litter under privet, under the bark of trees and in moss. Spray with malathion, carbaryl, Pyrenone, or Gardona.

Redbanded Thrips*, *Selenothrips rubrocinctus* (Giard). A pest from the West Indies that has invaded Florida, infesting avocado, guava, mango, and reported on orchids. It is dark brown to black with a bright-red band across the body. Injury and life history are similar to that of the greenhouse thrips.

Tobacco Thrips*, *Frankliniella fusca* (Hinds). On tobacco, cotton, and other plants. Nymphs are yellow, adults brown.

Sixspotted Thrips*, *Scolothrips sexmaculatus* (Pergande). Yellow with 3 black spots on each front wing. Predaceous on mites.

Sugarcane Thrips*, *Thrips saccharoni* Moulton.

Toyon Thrips, *Rhyncothrips ilex* (Moulton). On California Christmasberry. The adult—black, glossy, with silvery-white wings—hibernates in curled leaves, mates in early spring, feeds on new unfolding leaves, and lays yellow, waxy eggs loosely on them. The larvae—pale yellow, later reddish—feed with adults on new growth, causing it to be distorted, curled, sometimes killed. When mature, larvae drop to the ground to pupate, rest while the toyon is in bloom, then the new adults feed on the 2nd rush of new growth. Natural spread is slow; most dissemination is on nursery stock. Pick off and destroy curled leaves in fall and winter. Spray for active stages with malathion.

Tubulifera Thrips, *Haplothrips clarisetis* Priesner. An African species, of the suborder Tubulifera, first noticed in this country in 1958 in New Mexico, doing serious damage to young lettuce; also reported from California. It is very dark brown to jet black with silvery wings.

Western Flower Thrips*, *Frankliniella occidentalis* (Pergande). On practically all types of plants. The thrips vary from lemon-yellow to dusky yellow-brown, winter on weeds, and feed in tree blossoms in spring, causing scarring and distortion of fruits. They are more injurious to apricot, peach, plum, and nectarine blossoms in southern

California than farther north, where the blooming season is over before populations build up. They injure grapes in season, beans as they come through the ground. They injure cucurbit vines suffering from lack of water, cause blossom-drop of peas, tomatoes, melons, sometimes strawberries. Blooms of roses, carnations sweetpeas, and gladiolus are streaked. This species spreads spotted wilt disease that infects tomatoes and many other vegetables and ornamentals on the West Coast.

Eggs are laid in tender stems, buds, flowers, and hatch in 5 to 15 days. Larvae feed on succulent portions for 7 to 12 days, molt once on the host, drop to the ground, pupate, molt once during this resting stage and, in cool climates, hibernate in protected spots. Peak of infestation is in late spring. Adults can be carried long distances by wind but migrations are usually local. See Flower Thrips for control.

TREEHOPPERS

Treehoppers are sucking insects in the order Homoptera. They are closely related to leafhoppers but belong to the family Membracidae, which is characterized by having a pronotum (taking the place of the thorax in other insects) greatly enlarged and grotesquely developed into horns, knobs, or other peculiar shapes. Treehoppers have been called the brownies of the insect world. They injure trees and shrubs by their egg laying and the nymphs feed on weeds, grasses, corn, and legumes. One treehopper transmits the disease pseudocurlytop.

Buffalo Treehopper*, *Stictocephala bubalus* (Fabricius). Serious in the Middle West, often damaging in the East to apple, pear, peach,

84. Buffalo treehopper, side view.

quince, cherry, and other fruits, and to rose, elm, locust, cottonwood, and other ornamentals. The injury comes from the wounds made by the female in oviposition. These are double rows of curved slits inside which 6 to 12 elongated yellowish eggs are embedded in the inner bark. Infested trees look rough, scaly, or cracked, and seldom make vigorous growth. Fungi causing rose cankers and other diseases gain entrance through the slits.

Eggs winter in the wood; they hatch in late spring into pale-green spiny nymphs which drop from the tree and feed on sap of various weeds and grasses until mid-July or August, when they become adult. Viewed from above, they are triangles—light green, blunt at the head end but with a short horn at each upper corner, pointed at the rear; ¼ inch long. The female has a knifelike ovipositor to cut slits in twigs for her August egg laying.

Control. Clean cultivation of an orchard, keeping down all weeds and grassy growth, and avoiding summer cover crops for a season or two help in control. A dormant oil spray kills many overwintering eggs. Spray with malathion or dimethoate during June.

Oak Treehoppers, *Platycotis vittata* (Fabricius) and *P. quadrivittata* (Say). Both species feed gregariously on deciduous and evergreen oak and are widely distributed. *P. vittata* is green to bronze, ⅜ inch long, with surface punctures and red dots. *P. quadrivittata* is pale blue with 4 red longitudinal stripes and well-developed pronotal horns. The nymphs are black with red and yellow marking, 2 black spines.

Quince Treehopper*, *Glossonotus crataegi* (Fitch).

Thornbug, *Umbonia crassicornis* A & S. Known in Florida for more than 100 years but a common pest only in the last 20 years. It occurs on calliandra, pithecellobium, tamarind, and various flowering legumes. The hoppers are green with tan to red lines, brownish wings, a high horn at the back; ½ inch long. Eggs are laid in grooves in branches.

Threecornered Alfalfa Hopper*, *Spissistilus festinus* (Say). A western alfalfa pest, also a nuisance in Florida on beans, cowpeas, tomato, watermelon, with adults common on hickory, oak, black locust, viburnum. It is yellow-green with the outline of a triangle when viewed from above.

Twomarked Treehopper*, *Enchenopa binotata* (Say). Frequently found on butternut, sometimes on locust, bittersweet, sycamore, hickory, willow, wild grape, redbud, hoptree, and viburnum. This small treehopper looks much like a bird in side view, with a high, curved horn projecting forward from the thorax. It is dusky brown with 2 lemon-yellow spots on the back. The female lays eggs in butternut buds and in twigs just below the buds. These are uncovered but she also lays eggs in bark of locust and other trees and these she covers with a frothy, waxy material in corrugated layers. Eggs are laid in August and September and hatch the following May into small, white, powdery nymphs which mature in late June and July into very active adults. Butternut buds are often destroyed by the egg laying, and leaves are punctured. Grape stems and bittersweet vines may be punctured. There is no very satisfactory control but a dimethoate or malathion spray might help if applied while nymphs are active.

Widefooted Treehopper, *Campylenchia latipes* (Say). Through the United States on a wide variety of grasses, shrubs, forage plants. It is cinnamon brown, with a deeply keeled pronotal horn, 2 lateral horns, a densely punctured and hairy pronotum.

There are other treehoppers that may be damaging but they have no common names. *Tortistilus albidosparsus* has been reported heavy on grapevines in California. Nymphs of *Vanduzea triguttata* have appeared on sycamore trees in California.

WALKINGSTICKS

Walkingsticks belong to the grasshopper order Orthoptera, and to the family Phasmatidae, a remarkable group of insects that so

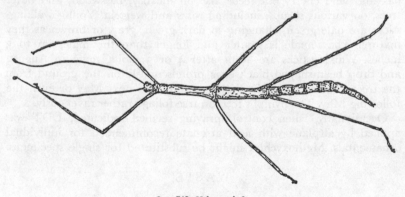

85. Walkingstick.

closely resemble their environment, twig or leaf, that they go unnoticed until they move. Many species are tropical. Those in this country, except for one in Florida, are wingless. They are very long and thin, with the thorax about half body length; they have long legs and antennae. The legs are all alike, the forelegs not being modified for grasping as in the mantids, with which they might be confused. They have the power of partially replacing a lost leg at another molt. They have biting mouth parts and feed on foliage. They emit a foul-smelling substance as a defense weapon.

Giant Walkingstick, *Megaphasma dentricus* (Stoll). Very large, up to 6 inches long, similar to the common walkingstick but not numerous enough to be destructive.

Prairie Walkingstick, *Diapheromera velii* Coquillett. On shrubs and grasses in the Great Plains west of the Mississippi but rarely abundant. It is similar to the common walkingstick but has a more elongate head.

Twostriped Walkingstick*, *Anisomorpha buprestoides* (Stoll). Reported defoliating ornamentals in Alabama and Georgia; doubtless present elsewhere. When its legs are touched or birds come near, it ejects a painful spray from sac-like glands in the thorax.

Another species, *A. ferruginea* Beauvois, feeds on trees and shrubs from Nebraska to the Carolinas and Georgia. It appeared in a widespread outbreak in Kansas in 1961, with black locust and white oak the worst victims.

Walkingstick*, *Diapheromera femorata* (Say). Northern Walkingstick. The common species from New England to the Rocky Mountains, frequently defoliating trees in the Midwest. It prefers black oak and wild cherry but feeds also on hickory, basswood, and other trees, on various shrubs, including roses and weigela. Young walkingsticks are pale green, changing to dark green, gray, or brown as they mature. The female is stouter and longer than the male, up to 3 inches. Walkingsticks are adult after 4 or 5 molts, mate in August, and drop bean-shaped black eggs promiscuously on the ground from the trees. These remain in the litter until the next May or even the following May. The nymphs feed on tree foliage rather ravenously.

Occasionally, when control spraying seemed indicated, DDT was applied by airplane with lead arsenate recommended for individual ornamentals. Methoxychlor might be substituted for single specimens.

WASPS

Most wasps are not garden pests. The few harmful species are far outnumbered by the beneficial forms. Like bees, ants, and sawflies, wasps belong to the order Hymenoptera, characterized by 2 pairs of membranous wings hooked together, and to the suborder Apocrita, having the abdomen joined to the thorax by a slender waist. The mouth parts are adapted for chewing and lapping, and there is complete metamorphosis. The female has a definite ovipositor and in some groups this is used as a stinger, in others not. Many entomologists restrict the term "wasp" to members of the stinging Scolioidea, Vespoidea, and Sphecoidea; others include superfamilies Ichneumonoidea, Chalcidoidea, Cynipodea, and Chrysidoidea. Both types are included in this section of Wasps, with only a fraction of the 90,000 species in the world, in the few families of importance to gardeners.

Agaonidae. Fig wasps, imported to pollinate the Smyrna fig, which bears only female flowers. The wasp develops in galled, infertile flowers on the anther-bearing caprifig and takes pollen to the Smyrna.

Braconidae. Braconids, small insects with a short abdomen; important parasites of aphids (note the many dead aphids with a round

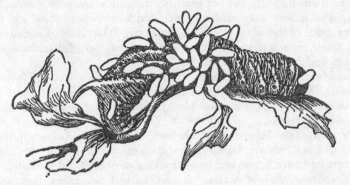

86. Tomato hornworm parasitized by braconid wasp. The white egglike objects are cocoons.

hole in the back), of larvae and pupae of moths and butterflies, and some beetles. Tomato hornworms and catalpa sphinx caterpillars are often covered with white oval objects that look like eggs but are cocoons of braconid wasps.

Chalcididae. Chalcids, minute or very small insects, short-bodied, with head as wide or wider than the thorax; black or brown; wings almost veinless; legs short with hind femora much enlarged. All forms are parasites, chiefly on larvae of beetles, moths, butterflies, and flies, but some are hyperparasites living on other beneficial insects and in that way become harmful.

Chrysididae. Cuckoo or jewel wasps, brilliant green, blue, red, or purple with sculptured body, seldom over ½ inch. They are external parasites of other bees and wasps, lay eggs in other nests.

Cynipidae. Gall wasps, very small, responsible for most of the galls on leaves and twigs of oaks and other plants. There are many species, and the galls may be numerous and unsightly but the hosts are not killed and seldom even weakened.

Encyrtidae. Very small wasps, mostly parasites on aphids, scale insects, and whiteflies, but a few are hyperparasites.

Eulopidae. Small insects, parasites on a number of major crop pests but including some hyperparasites.

Eurytomidae. Seed chalcids, jointworms. Some are parasitic on other insects, some are plant pests. They are usually black, often rather hairy, with thorax coarsely punctate, abdomen rounded or oval and somewhat compressed.

Ichneumonidae. Ichneumons. A large family of slender insects with elongate abdomen (sometimes sickle-shaped), often with an ovipositor longer than the body but not used for stinging man. One species has a body 1½ inches long and a 3-inch hairlike ovipositor which penetrates bark of trees to parasitize horntails. The various members of this family are important natural controls of harmful beetles, caterpillars, and sawflies.

Pelecinidae. Pelecinid wasps. The female has a long filiform abdomen. There is only 1 species in the United States, *Pelecinus polyturator* (Drury). This is shiny black, 2 inches long, a parasite on Japanese-beetle larvae.

Perilampidae. Stout-bodied chalcids, with large, coarsely punctate thorax, small, shiny, triangular abdomen, often found on flowers. Many species are hyperparasites, attacking our beneficial parasites.

Pompilidae. Spider wasps, slender with long, spiny legs, mostly dark-colored, usually feeding on spiders.

Pteromalidae. Minute black or metallic-green or bronze insects, triangular in profile, most species valuable as parasites on crop pests.

Scelionidae. Egg parasites, useful in controlling Mormon crickets and grasshoppers, but sometimes killing mantids, lacewings, and other beneficial insects.

Sphecidae. Solitary wasps, tunneling in soil or wood, stocking their larders with spiders, grasshoppers, caterpillars, aphids, bugs, and flies. This group contains the mud-daubers and the giant cicada killer.

Thysanidae. Small, stout chalcids attacking scale insects and whiteflies.

Tiphiidae. Tiphiid wasps, mostly fair-sized, black, somewhat hairy, parasites on grubs of scarabaeid beetles. One species was introduced to control Japanese beetles and had been very helpful.

Torymidae. Very small, metallic-green parasites, mostly on insects living inside plant tissues, galls, or seeds.

Trichogrammatidae. Very minute parasites inside eggs of other insects, important in the control of various caterpillars. Cards covered with Trichogramma eggs are sometimes sold to farmers and home gardeners.

Vespidae. Social wasps—the hornets, yellow jackets, etc., making nests from wood fiber—and solitary potter wasps. Most are beneficial, feeding their young with injurious caterpillars and acting as pollinators, but the giant hornet is a real pest in the garden.

Alfalfa Seed Chalcid*, *Bruchophagus roddi* (Gussakovsky).

Apple Seed Chalcid*, *Torymus varians* (Walker). The larvae infest seeds of untreated apples.

Blackberry Knotgall Wasp, *Distrophus nebulosus* Osten Sacken. Causing knotty, rounded, or elongate swellings, 2 to 6 inches long, often with deep longitudinal furrows.

Blueberry Stemgall Wasp, *Hemadas nubilipennis* Ashmead. Causing a kidney-shaped gall, first green then reddish brown. Common on blueberry stems.

California Peppertree Chalcid, *Eumegastigmus transvaalensis.* An introduced species, first reported in California in 1960.

Cicada Killer*, *Sphecius speciosus* (Drury). Digger Wasp. A very large wasp, up to 1½ inches long, black with the abdomen banded with yellow, and a wickedly long, curved ovipositor or stinger. Appear-

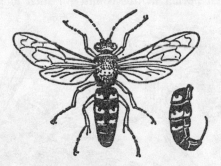

87. Cicada killer, digger wasp, with side view of abdomen showing ovipositor, "stinger."

ing in midsummer or later, this wasp makes a mess of lawns, tunneling far underground and marking the openings of its burrows with little mounds of earth. It also damages paths, banks, and terraces. I have seen it abundant enough to lift and crack concrete sidewalks with its tunnels and mounds, to say nothing of scaring to death all the passers-by. After making her burrow, the wasp goes to look for a cicada in a tree. She darts at it and they both fall to the ground. The wasp stings the cicada to paralyze it and then, straddling her bulky prey, she crawls up a tree to a good launching point to take flight toward her burrow. If she does not make it the first time, she tries another tree and another glide. Arrived at the opening, she drags in the cicada, stores it in a cell, and lays an egg between its legs. Each cell is provided with 1 or 2 cicadas, sealed off before the next cell is filled. The egg hatches in 2 or 3 days and the larva feeds on the cicada contents for about 2 months, then makes a cocoon of silk and rests in it until the next summer, when it pupates and produces the adult.

Control. I used to whack these creatures with a kind of giant flyswatter made of heavy wire mesh on a stick, and squirt carbon disulfide into the holes. Dusting with 5 per cent chlordane or carbaryl into the holes is easier and probably more effective. Dust in the evening, after the wasps are back in their burrows, and cover with a mound of earth. Or spray the area with diazinon.

Clover Seed Chalcid*, *Bruchophagus platyptera* (Walker). A general and important pest of clover and alfalfa seed, but it does not destroy the value of these crops as forage.

Fig Wasp*, *Blastophaga psenes* (Linneaus).

Giant Hornet*, *Vespa crabro germana* (Christ). Vespa Hornet. This is the largest hornet in this country, 1 inch long, dark reddish

88. *Giant hornet, natural size and slightly enlarged, tearing bark from lilac stem for nest.*

brown with orange markings on the abdomen, resembling the cicada killer but stouter and hairier, and without such a terrifying ovipositor. It is a special pest of lilac near New York City, tearing the bark from twigs and branches and girdling them. The result appears to be the work of a squirrel; it seems impossible that an insect could inflict that much damage. The giant hornet may also injure boxwood, birch, willow, poplar, franklinia, rhododendron, and other treees and shrubs and even dahlia. It is found along the Atlantic seaboard from Massachusetts to Georgia and inland to Tennessee, Kentucky, Ohio, and Indiana. The injury comes in August and September, when the wasps tear off the bark to use in making their large, paper nests in hollow trees or suspended from the roof inside barns and other buildings or from the eaves of houses.

Control. Some recommend trying to find the nest and puffing in calcium cyanide dust but this is difficult. Spray trunks and branches of lilacs and susceptible shrubs with carbaryl, chlordane, or diazinon. Prompt treatment is obligatory; the wasps can quickly girdle a branch.

Grape Seed Chalcid*, *Evoxysoma vitis* (Saunders).

Incense Cedar Wasp*, *Syntexis libocedrii* Rohwer. Cedar Horntail. Black with greenish white markings and reddish legs. Larvae bore outer wood of incense cedar in California.

Mossyrose Gall Wasp*, *Diplolepis rosae* (Linnaeus). The galls appear in June and July. Each is a globular mass of mosslike filaments surrounding a cluster of hard cells, each of which contains one larva which remains in the cell until spring. There is no control except removal of galls or infested canes.

Oak Gall Wasps. Hundreds of wasps cause galls on the many species of oaks—on roots, at the crown, in the bark, on branches and twigs, on buds, and on foliage. They are far too numerous to discuss individually. In addition to the many small leaf galls there are the familiar large brown galls known as oak apples, each of which is a leaf deformed by a wasp. An interesting wasp on white, chestnut, and basket oaks is the wool sower, *Callirhytis seminator* Harris, which produces a globular, pink-marked woolly growth, $1\frac{1}{2}$ to 2 inches across, on twigs. There is really nothing the gardener can do about oak galls.

Roseroot Gall Wasp*, *Diplolepis radicum* (Osten Sacken). Causing a large conspicuous swelling, 1 to 2 inches across on roots of cultivated roses. It is not very common.

WEBWORMS

Webworms are caterpillars that feed protected by webs. Some, like the tent caterpillar, have been treated elsewhere; those commonly known as webworms are discussed here.

Ailanthus Webworm*, *Atteva punctella* (Cramer). From New York to Illinois and southward, more common in southern states. Tree-of-heaven (ailanthus) is the preferred host. The adult moths have bright-orange fore wings, marked with 4 crossbands of yellow spots on a dark-blue ground; dusky, nearly transparent hind wings; expanse 1 inch. The caterpillars, olive-brown with fine white lines, feed gregariously in fine webs in August and September, with moths appearing in September and October. Control measures are seldom used, although spraying with carbaryl in August is a possibility.

Alfalfa Webworm*, *Loxostege commixtalis* (Walker). Larvae are green-to-yellow caterpillars with a light stripe down the back; adults are buff-colored moths, irregularly marked with light and dark gray, with a row of spots on underside of hind wings, spreading to 1 or 1¼ inches. Food plants and control are the same as for the beet webworm.

Barberry Webworm, *Omphalocera dentosa* (Grote). Black, white-spotted caterpillars, 1½ inches long, web twigs together and devour leaves of common and Japanese barberry in late summer and fall. The ugly, frass-filled masses remain over ends of shoots during the winter. Spray in summer with carbaryl.

Beet Webworm*, *Loxostege sticticalis* (Linnaeus). Present from the Mississippi Valley west to the Continental Divide. Along with the alfalfa webworm, this small webbing caterpillar is a general and destructive feeder on cabbage, beet, sugar beet, bean, pea, potato, spinach, cucurbits, and other vegetables, alfalfa, and forage crops. The larvae work like armyworms, cleaning up one field, then moving en masse to the next. They are yellow or green to nearly black, with a black stripe down the middle of the back and 3 small black dots bearing bristles at the end of each segment. As they skeletonize and devour leaves, they make a tube several inches long to a hiding place under a clod of earth or other protected spot where they retreat when disturbed. They pupate 2 to 3 weeks in a cell an inch or 2 underground. The night-flying moth is smoky brown with straw-colored spots and lines and a continuous dark line near the margin of the hind wings. White to yellow or green oval eggs are laid on underside of leaves. There may be 3 partial generations.

Control. Use pyrethrum or malathion spray or dust.

Bluegrass Webworm*, *Crambus teterrellus* (Zincken). See Sod Webworms.

Boxwood Webworm, *Galasa nigrinodis.* Larva of a Chrysaugid moth. Forms heavy webs on boxwood; known in Maryland, Pennsylvania, and Virginia.

Buffalograss Webworm*, *Surattha indentella* Kearfott.

Cabbage Webworm*, *Hellula rogatalis* (Hulst). An imported species distributed through the southern states. The caterpillars, grayish yellow with purple stripes, ½ inch long, feed under webbing on inner leaves, hearts, stalks of cabbage, cauliflower, kale, sometimes on beets, collards, horseradish, radish. The moths are grayish, mottled with brown. Spray or dust with malathion or Dibrom as soon as plants appear.

Corn Root Webworm*, *Crambus caliginosellus* Clemens. One of the sod webworms. The caterpillar is whitish, just over ½ inch long; the snout moth is straw-colored with indistinct markings. Walking over the grass stirs up the moths, which move in jerky flights and rest with their wings so tightly folded around their bodies they look like tubes. Eggs are laid in summer; young larvae feed a little, then hibernate in nests in grass and sodland, becoming active in spring. They destroy roots and work from the crown into cornstalks, injuring developing leaves like budworms, and often chew stalks at the surface of the ground like cutworms. Full-grown in July and August, they pupate underground in a silken cocoon. Do not plant corn in land recently taken over from sod. If young corn shows injury, dig it up and plant a substitute crop.

Cotoneaster Webworm, *Cremona cotoneaster* (Busck). Yellow larvae, turning dark when grown, make silken webs from a larger silken refuge at the base of branch junctions. They skeletonize the leaves and make unsightly nests. They winter in the refuge, pupate there in spring, produce grayish black, night-active moths. Small plants die; others are weakened. Spray with malathion or diazinon.

Fall Webworm*, *Hyphantria cunea* (Drury). Widely distributed, feeding on at least 120 varieties of fruit, shade, and woodland trees. Popular hosts are apple, cherry, peach, pecan, English walnut, black walnut, ash, boxelder, birch, chokecherry, elm, hickory, linden, poplar, sycamore, white oak, willow. Roses and other shrubs are sometimes webbed. The webworm acts much like the tent caterpillar but makes its nest over the ends of branches rather than at tree crotches.

Cocoons enclosing brown pupae winter under trash on the ground or under bark. Satiny white moths, often marked with brown spots, wings spreading 1½ to 1¾ inches, emerge over a long period in spring. They lay greenish eggs in masses of 200 to 500, often covered with a woolly layer of scales. The caterpillars are pale green or yellow with a dark stripe down the back and a yellow stripe along each side. The body is covered with very long silky gray hairs arising from black and yellow tubercles. When full-grown, about an inch long after 4 to 6 weeks of feeding, they crawl down trees to form cocoons. There are 2 broods in the Middle Atlantic States, the first feeding in late May and June, the 2nd and more destructive from July through September. The larvae spin a layer of silk over the surface of a leaf as soon as they start feeding, eventually webbing together ends of several branches. The nests are always most unsightly, and one or more branches may be defoliated but seldom the entire tree.

Control. Summer sprays for codling moth will prevent damage by webworms on apples. Ornamentals can, if necessary, be sprayed with carbaryl or diazinon but it is often possible to cut off webbed ends of branches without resorting to spraying. This should be done immediately the webs appear. There are several natural enemies, egg parasites and others.

Garden Webworm*, *Loxostege rantalis* (Guenée). A native, found over most of the country but more of a pest in the Middle West and Southwest. It is much like the alfalfa and beet webworms, attacking alfalfa, clover, and field crops, but also working on garden vegetables such as beans, soybean, cowpeas, beets, and on strawberries, scarlet verbena, and castor-bean. The hairy caterpillars, a little over an inch long, are greenish with dark spots. They spin webs wherever they go and make silken tubes for shelter on the ground. There are up to 5 generations in Texas, 2 or 3 in the North. Dust vegetables near harvest with pyrethrum or rotenone.

Juniper Webworm*, *Dichomeris marginella* (Dennis & Schiffermüller). A European species first recorded in 1910, now present from Maine to North Carolina and west to Missouri, also in California on common and Irish juniper and redcedar. The winter is passed as partly grown larvae in silken cases in webbed foliage. They are light brown with a reddish brown stripe down the back, 2 wider dark-brown stripes along the side, with short white hairs over the body, ½ inch long. They feed in early spring, then pupate in May. The moths, emerging in June and early July, have brown fore wings with white margins, fringed gray hind wings, wingspread only ⅜ inch. They lay eggs in leaf axils of new terminal growth, and the caterpillars web the needles together with silk. The webs enclose a good bit of frass and the needles turn brown and die. Sometimes the whole top of a small juniper is webbed and massed together.

Control. Spray with diazinon or carbaryl in early May and July. If using carbaryl include a miticide. Cut out webbed masses where possible.

Lespedeza Webworm*, *Tetralopha scortealis* (Lederer).

Mimosa Webworm*, *Homadaula anisocentra* Meyrick. Discovered on mimosa in Washington, D.C., in 1940 and now a serious pest of both mimosa (Albizzia) and honeylocust from New Jersey to Florida, around the Gulf into Louisiana and west to Oklahoma, Kansas, and Nebraska. It has also invaded one part of California. The moths— gray with a silver luster, stippled with black spots, ½ inch wingspread —appear in June and lay eggs on mimosa flowers as well as foliage. The larvae—dark brown sometimes diffused with rose or pink, just over ½ inch long—feed first gregariously in a web spun over flowers and leaves, later singly on tender terminal leaves and on green pods of both hosts. The foliage is usually skeletonized, eaten from the underside, with the upper epidermis left intact. Leaves die, turn dull gray on mimosa, brown as if fire-scorched on honeylocust. In midsummer larvae descend to the ground on silken threads and spin cocoons in bark or in the ground cover. There are 2 generations and a partial 3rd. The webbing is most conspicuous in August from the 2nd brood.

Control. Spray with carbaryl or diazinon mid-June, mid-July, and mid-August (New Jersey dates).

Oak Webworm*, *Archips fervidanus* (Clemens). On oak in northeastern states and west to Wisconsin. The gray-green larvae with black heads, ¾ inch long, live gregariously in a web. The moth has yellow-brown fore wings, gray hind wings, is ⅞ inch long. Another species, *Tetralopha asperatella* (Clemens), also occurs on oak in eastern states. The larvae are ¾ inch long, brown with yellow stripes, and live in 2 or 3 leaves webbed together.

Pale Juniper Webworm, *Aethes rutilana* (Hübner). A European species introduced about 1878, now present from Maine to New Jersey and Indiana on juniper. The larvae are brownish yellow; the moths have yellow fore wings marked with red; gray hind wings; wing expanse ⅜ inch. Foliage is webbed and brown.

Parsnip Webworm*, *Depressaria pastinacella* (Duponchel). Present on parsnip, celery, and related weeds in northern states east of the Mississippi River. Flower heads are webbed together and eaten by small yellow, green, or grayish caterpillars with small black spots and short hairs. They interfere with seed production and may mine in stems. The moth is gray, winters under loose bark, lays eggs in spring on developing flowers. Caterpillars pupate in mines in stems, moths coming out in late summer. Cut and destroy infested flower heads.

Pine False Webworm*, *Acantholyda erythrocephala* (Linnaeus). A sawfly found in Connecticut, New York, New Jersey, and Pennsylvania on red and white pines, sometimes other species. The larvae are greenish gray striped with purplish red; up to ⅘ inch long. Adults emerge from earthen cells from mid-April to early May and lay eggs on needles. These hatch the last 3 weeks in May and the larvae feed gregariously in a loose webbing, cutting off the needles and pulling them into the web. There can be extensive defoliation. Older larvae make silken tubes along the twigs, then drop to the ground in late June. There is only 1 generation. Spray with methoxychlor or carbaryl in May before needles are webbed.

Pine Webworm*, *Tetralopha robustella* Zeller. Pine Pyralid, a native present from New England to Florida and west to Wisconsin on pitch, red, white, jack, and loblolly pines, injurious to seedling or small trees, not to larger trees. The moths, with purple-black fore wings with a transverse gray band, smoky black hind wings, spreading to 1 inch, emerge from June to August. The larvae—yellow-brown with 2 dark stripes along each side, ¾ inch long when grown—work near the ends of terminal twigs, producing quantities of brown frass in silken webs. When mature they go into the ground and spin flimsy cocoons for the winter. Spray with methoxychlor or carbaryl before webbing starts.

Sod Webworms, *Crambus* spp. Lawn Moths, small millers that fly up as you walk across the grass. There are many species damaging lawns in different parts of the country, but they are more abundant in warm climates. They usually injure blue or bent grass, sometimes fescue and other grasses. Irregular brown spots in lawns indicate damage.

In California *Crambus bonifatellus* (Hulst) prefers moist lowlands, *C. sperryellus* Klots drier locations. The former is a slender, gray black-spotted larva with a brown head; the moth is creamy buff with small white, brown, or black spots. The latter is a light-gray larva with dark spots on head and body; the moth is golden with fore wings streaked with silver.

The **bluegrass webworm***, *C. teterrellus* (Zincken), is more at home in Kentucky and other parts of the Southeast. It is often accompanied by other species. The predominant species in the East is the **Vagabond crambus***, *C. vulgivagellus* Clemens. This is normally a grass feeder but sometimes attacks corn.

All these moths have snouts, made of labial palps, and they fly slowly over grass at dusk in a zigzag fashion, dropping eggs anywhere. Young larvae skeletonize grass blades; older caterpillars cut them off completely. They make silken tubes between the grass stems, shelters camouflaged with bits of grass and bright-green excrement. Pupation is in silken cocoons just below the surface of the ground; there may be several overlapping generations.

Control. Many chemicals have been suggested for control, applied in the evening at monthly intervals: chlordane, 2½ pounds of 5 per cent granules per 1,000 square feet; diazinon, 2 pounds of 10 per cent granules; carbaryl, 4 pounds of 5 per cent granules. Professionals may also use Baygon or Ethion.

Sorghum Webworm*, *Celama sorghiella* (Riley).

Southern Beet Webworm*, *Herpetogramma bipunctalis* (Fabricius). Sometimes serious on spinach.

Spotted Beet Webworm*, *Hymenia perspectalis* (Hübner). The larva is green with purple dots on its head; the moth is cinnamon-brown with narrow white bands on the fore wings. Eggs are laid on leaves of beet and amaranth. Use pyrethrum dust if the foliage is to be used for greens.

Sweetgum Webworms, *Salebria afflictella* Hulst and *Tetralopha melanogramma* Zeller. Reported damaging to this host in Delaware.

Vagabond Crambus*, *Crambus vulvagellus* Clemens. See under Sod Webworms.

WEEVILS

Weevils are really beetles, of the order Coleoptera, with the head more or less prolonged into a beak or snout, with mouth parts at the end. Most species are in the family Curculionidae and are injurious plant feeders. Weevils infesting fruits and nuts are often called Curculios and have been treated under that heading. See also Billbugs.

Adaleres Weevil, *Adaleres humeralis* Casey. Light to dark brown beetles with grayish mottling, punctate wing covers, feeding on foliage and terminal buds of avocado. Since they cannot fly they can be kept off trees with a sticky band around the trunk.

Alfalfa Weevil*, *Hypera postica* (Gyllenhal). The most important enemy of alfalfa, also infesting clovers, imported from southern Europe about 1900 and first reported from Utah in 1904, now widely distributed and causing annual losses of many million dollars. Grayish brown to black weevils with short gray hairs, ⅛ to ¼ inch long, with medium beak, winter about the crowns of alfalfa or in debris, feed in spring, then lay shiny yellow, oval eggs in cavities in alfalfa stems. The larvae are white at first, then green, with a prominent middorsal stripe. Plants are stunted or eaten to nothing but woody fibers. Careful timing of cutting the crop helps in control. Spray with methoxychlor plus malathion. Several species of parasites have been released.

Annual Bluegrass Weevil, *Hyperodes anthracinus* (Dietz). In recent years causing losses in annual bluegrass in Connecticut and on Long Island. Small, dark brown to almost black weevils, marked with gray, winter under clumps of fescue grass and emerge in April to lay elongate eggs in stems of bluegrass (*Poa annua*), with the larvae killing large areas of turf. In Connecticut experiments dimethoate and diazinon gave a good kill of weevils. On Long Island the most effective chemicals were azinphosmethyl, Supracide, and Dursban.

Apple Flea Weevil*, *Rhynchaenus pallicornis* (Say). Found from Missouri and Illinois east to New York, but more destructive in the western portion of this range, on apple, haw, winged elm, hazelnut, quince, wild crab, and blackberry. The adults, very small black snout beetles, 1/10 inch long, winter in trash or grass under apple trees. In spring they puncture newly opening leaves and buds, lay eggs along midribs. The grubs mine between the upper and lower leaf surfaces, pupate in a cell inside the leaf, emerge as beetles in late May and June. They feed for 2 weeks on foliage, riddling the leaves with tiny shot holes, then go into hibernation. A spray of parathion, at the pre-pink or pink stage, is effective if applied to underside of leaves.

Arborvitae Weevil*, *Phyllobius intrusus* Kono. A Japanese species found in Rhode Island in 1947, now present also in Connecticut, Massachusetts, and New Hampshire, probably elsewhere. The adult, covered with greenish scales and fine short hairs, emerges from the soil in early May and is around until July, laying eggs around roots. The eggs hatch in 13 to 17 days. The larvae, white to light pink with brown heads, feed on roots of arborvitae, retinospora, juniper. They pupate in late spring, 10 inches deep in the soil, and the adults feed in the daytime on the top third of plants, eating tiny, cup-shaped areas from new terminal leaves. Adults can be killed by spraying with lindane. Treating the soil with chlordane in late May or early June may help.

Asiatic Oak Weevil*, *Cyrtepistomus castaneus* (Roelofs). A new and serious pest of oak and chestnut, first found in New Jersey in 1933, now known from Rhode Island to South Carolina and west to Illinois and Arkansas. There is a 1-year cycle with larvae apparently feeding and wintering on roots. They pupate in June with adults emerging in great numbers about a week later. The weevils, black to dark reddish brown, with metallic-green scales, start feeding on sapling oaks and chestnuts, eating everything but midveins of leaves, but by August they move to larger trees and also invade hickory, hazelnut, beech, dogwood, raspberry, and some other trees and shrubs. They enter houses in the fall.

Bean Weevil*, *Acanthoscelides obtectus* (Say). Probably a native American although found around the world. Beans stored for food or seed are almost certain to be devoured by weevils unless precautions are taken. This seed weevil is a small snout beetle, ⅛ inch long, olive-brown mottled with darker brown and gray, with reddish legs and antennae. Escaping from stored beans in the garden, it lays eggs in holes chewed along the seam of a bean pod. Small, hairy white grubs, produced in 3 to 30 days, enter and feed in young seed (Plate XXXV). If the storage room is warm, there may be many generations during the winter, the grubs pupating in cells inside the beans, the weevils eating their way out through the seed coat, leaving conspicuous round holes.

Control. Never plant seed known to be infested. After harvest, dry seeds quickly, fumigate with carbon disulfide in a tight steel bin; or heat, dry, at 135° F. for 3 to 4 hours; or suspend seeds in a bag in water, heat to 140° F. and then dry rapidly. Treat seed beans with lindane before planting.

Bean Stalk Weevil*, *Sternechus paludatus* (Casey).

Black Elm Bark Weevil*, *Magdalis barbita* (Say). A small, jet-black beetle with a prominent snout, found from New York to South Dakota and south to Georgia. The beetles emerge from branches of unhealthy elms in May or June and lay eggs in bark. Grubs burrow to the inner bark and sapwood, making longitudinal galleries 1½ inches long. Maintain tree vigor by fertilizing; water during droughts.

Black Vine Weevil*, (*Otiorhyncus*) *sulcatus* (Fabricius). Cyclamen Grub. A European species now widely distributed here. It is a serious pest of yew (Taxus), rhododendron, azalea, hemlock, retinospora, and some other broad- and narrow-leaved evergreens and is a greenhouse menace. Nearly 80 hosts have been listed, including ampelopsis, begonia, blackberry, cranberry, cyclamen, gloxinia, geranium, gardenia, maidenhair fern, primrose, raspberry, spirea, strawberry (although not as injurious as the strawberry root weevil), wisteria.

The adult is a small weevil, ⅜ inch long, with a short snout. It is black or brownish with fine yellow hairs and a sort of corrugated effect down its hard, wingless body (Plate XXXV). Larvae are small, whitish, curved grubs which remain in soil feeding on small roots, often destroying them completely. Hibernation is usually as partly grown larvae, sometimes as adults in soil. After feeding on roots during April and May, larvae turn into soft white pupae, emerging as weevils in June. They hide in the soil during the day, feed on foliage at night. They feed for a month or more before laying eggs in cracks and crevices in the soil and in trash around plants. The young grubs, hatching in 10 days, feed on fine hair roots and on bark around the crown but their heaviest damage is the next spring.

Specimens of yew newly transplanted from nursery to garden are particularly subject to grub injury. Small roots are eaten off, larger roots girdled. If plants in a yew hedge do not start into new growth at the normal time in spring, if tops turn yellow, then brown, the black vine weevil is probably to blame. Feeding by the adult is from the tip of the needle or along the side. On rhododendrons large irregular holes are eaten in from leaf margins at night. In greenhouses grubs continue to feed during the winter months, causing stunting, death, of cyclamen, primrose, and other plants. Adults appear earlier in spring than outdoors and lay eggs over a longer period.

Control. It is easier to kill adults than grubs in soil. In late June, as adults are emerging, spray or dust soil, base of plants, and foliage with chlordane. Nurserymen may prefer endosulfan (Thiodan). Dieldrin has also been recommended but is being phased out of use. Drenching with carbofuran is helpful.

Boll Weevil*, *Anthonomus grandis* Boheman. Cotton Boll Weevil.

The most notoriously evil insect in the world, yet with such a beneficial influence on methods of agriculture, that in one section of the country it has had a monument erected to it. As home gardeners, you are not directly concerned with controlling the boll weevil but as citizens you are profoundly affected by it. Some years ago it was estimated that every person in the United States paid ten dollars a year more for cotton goods because of the boll weevil. Its arrival in Texas from Mexico in 1892 closed down cotton gin and oil mills, caused banks to fail, depreciated land values, turned wealthy growers into paupers. It still costs us an enormous amount each year. Cotton farmers have spent about $75 million annually just for insecticides to beat the weevil and yet losses have averaged nearly $230 million a year.

If, when the boll weevil was first noted, a barrier zone—an area about 50 miles wide where no cotton was grown—had been instituted, the weevil might have been kept within bounds. But at that time it did not seem possible to live in Texas without growing cotton and, rather than take away the source of livelihood from families in such a barrier zone, the Texas legislature turned thumbs down on that proposal and let the boll weevil go its destructive way.

The weevil is small, ¼ inch long, hard-shelled, yellow, gray, or brown, nearly black with age, covered with grayish fuzz, with a long slender snout. It lays an egg in each of 100 to 400 cotton buds or squares and there may be 8 to 10 generations a year. It also feeds on okra, hollyhock, and hibiscus, plants related to cotton.

When the boll-weevil devastation was at its height, cotton farmers learned to do two things. One was ordinary sanitation, clearing the fields and burning old stalks. The other was diversification of crops. They grew corn, hay, potatoes, sugarcane, and especially peanuts and hogs. One county in Alabama cleared $5 million on its first peanut crop. And so, at Enterprise, Alabama, the citizens of Coffee County erected a fountain in honor of the boll weevil, and put on it this inscription, which I once made a special trip to read:

IN PROFOUND APPRECIATION
OF THE BOLL WEEVIL
AND WHAT IT HAS DONE
AS THE HERALD OF PROSPERITY
THIS MONUMENT WAS ERECTED
BY THE CITIZENS OF
ENTERPRISE, COFFEE COUNTY, ALABAMA

Broadbean Weevil*, *Bruchus rufimanus* Boheman. Confined to the West Coast, attacking broadbeans first, then peas and vetches. It is slightly smaller than the pea weevil and has several individuals in a seed instead of 1, but resembles it otherwise.

Bronze Appletree Weevil*, *Magdalis senescens* LeConte.

Cabbage Seedpod Weevil*, *Ceutorhynchus assimilis* (Paykull). In the Pacific Northwest and California, damaging seeds of crucifers—cabbage, turnip, radish, mustard. Adults are black to gray, ⅛ inch long; they lay eggs in seed pods after making punctures with their snouts. The larvae, small, white, legless, feed on seed embryos for about 3 weeks. Dusting with lindane or parathion has given commercial control.

Carrot Weevil*, *Listronotus oregonensis* (LeConte). A pest of carrot, parsley, celery, feeding also on parsnip, dill, and related wild weeds, from New England to Georgia and west to Colorado. The beetles, dark brown, ¼ inch long, hibernate in grass and debris, lay eggs in May in cavities in leaf stalks. White, legless, curved, brown-headed grubs, up to ⅓ inch long, burrow down into the upper part of the carrot root or into celery hearts. The zigzag feeding destroys much tissue. Mature in about 2 weeks, the grubs leave the roots and pupate in soil. Beetles appear in July to lay eggs for a 2nd brood which is injurious in August. There may be a partial 3rd brood.

Control. Rotation of crops has been standard treatment. Spray with carbaryl, beginning in late May or early April, repeating at 2-week intervals. Or use apple pomace bait—1 part calcium arsenate to 20 parts, by weight, of dried apple pomace moistened with water.

Cattleya Weevil, *Cholus cattleyae* Champion. Adults, just under ½ inch long with white marks on their backs, feed on pseudobulbs and puncture leaves. Larvae also feed on leaves and stems and afford entrance to decay organisms. Handpick.

Citrus Root Weevil*, *Pachnaeus litus* (Germar). Found in southern Florida on citrus, beans, strawberry, avocado, tobacco. Eggs are laid in leaves, larvae drop to the ground and feed on roots. Parathion reduces populations to some extent.

Clover Head Weevil*, *Hypera meles* (Fabricius). Through the East to the Mississippi River, also in Kansas and Utah. A pest of clover, lowering seed production and skeletonizing bean foliage. The adult is black or reddish black, elongate oval, with punctate back covered with gray or brown, sometimes metallic, scales.

Clover Leaf Weevil*, *Hypera punctata* (Fabricius). Chiefly damaging alfalfa and clovers, but with adults feeding on many flowers. They are dark brown with black flecks on the back, paler underneath, with a robust snout. Spray ornamentals with methoxychlor.

Clover Seed Weevil*, *Miccotrogus picirostris* (Fabricius).

Cocklebur Weevil*, *Rhodobaenus tredecimpunctatus* (Illiger).

Cocklebur Billbug. Common on sunflower, evening primrose, and similar plants, sometimes a pest of dahlia and chrysanthemum. The adult is reddish with 13 black spots and a long, curved snout, about ⅓ inch long. It winters in trash, lays eggs on tender stalks in May or June; larvae hollow out the stalk near the base, pupate in August. Hand-pick the weevils; spray with methoxychlor or carbaryl; plant dahlias late to avoid injury and stake them; clean up ragweed, thistle, joe-pye-weed and other weed hosts around the garden.

Corn Stem Weevil, *Hyperodes humilis* (Gyllenhal). First observed as a pest of sweet corn in Florida in 1959, not previously known to injure cultivated crops. Grubs mine the lower stems, causing stunting. The adults, dark brown with white scales, are active at night.

Coffee Bean Weevil*, *Araecerus fasciculatus* (De Geer).

Cowpea Weevil*, *Callosobruchus maculatus* (Fabricius). Present in southern states and California, where there may be 5 or 6 generations a year. Yellowish grubs, ¼ inch long, feed inside seeds in growing cowpea pods. Adults—bronze-black, hump-backed snout beetles, ⅕ inch long—feed on plants and lay eggs in holes eaten into pods.

Cranberry Weevil*, *Anthonomus musculus* Say. Small, black, with reddish wing covers. On cranberry leaves and dormant buds. New shoots are killed; entire crops may be destroyed.

Cribrate Weevil, (*Otiorhyncus*) *cribricollis* Gyllenhal. First reported in California in 1929 as a pest of privet, viburnum, and turf, more recently a pest of globe artichoke and other plants, including blackberry, willow, lilac, pyracantha, ornamental plum, rose, pittosporum, pomegranate, camellia, and olive trees. The larvae feed on roots, the adults on buds and foliage. A fungus, *Beauveria bassiana*, kills adults in the field.

Currant Fruit Weevil*, *Pseudanthonomus validus* Dietz. In western states on currant. The adults, very small, pale reddish brown marked with pale yellow or white pubescence, puncture young fruit near stems in which eggs are inserted; larvae feed on developing seeds; fruits dry up and drop.

Deodar Weevil*, *Pissodes nemorensis* Germar. A native snout beetle present from northern New Jersey to Missouri and throughout the South, injurious to deodar, Lebanon and Atlas cedars, also reported on Scotch and white pine in a weakened condition. The adult, brownish with irregular markings of brown-and-white scales, gnaws through the bark with its slender beak and feeds on the cambium, often girdling a leader or side branch. It lays eggs in small holes in the bark; the grubs, white with brown heads, ⅓ inch long, burrow in wood and kill leaders and terminal twigs which start to die in January. Small trees may be killed. The grubs pupate in March and the beetles feed in April, then disappear in the surface litter to rest until fall. Spray with methoxychlor in April, when beetles are feeding; feed the trees as necessary; water during drought periods.

Douglas Fir Twig Weevil*, *Cylindrocopturus furnissi* Buchanan. Feeding on small branches of Douglas-fir and ponderosa pine in the Pacific Northwest, sometimes killing young trees.

Egyptian Alfalfa Weevil*, *Hypera brunneipennis* Boheman.

Engelmann Spruce Weevil*, *Pissodes engelmanni* Hopkins. Injuring terminals of Englemann spruce in the West, similar to the Sitka spruce weevil.

Filbert Weevil*, *Curculio occidentalis* (Casey). Infesting filbert nuts in New Mexico, Arizona, California, Oregon, Washington, and Utah. Cleaning up and destroying dropped nuts is quite effective in control.

Gorse Weevil, *Apion ulicis* Forster. A seed weevil from France introduced into California and Oregon for the biological control of gorse, a noxious weed. The weevil has been spreading satisfactorily.

Hazelnut Weevil*, *Curculio neocorylus* Gibson. Occasionally injuring the hazelnut seed crop.

Hibiscus Weevil, *Apion hibisci* Fall.

Hollyhock Weevil*, *Apion longirostre* Olivier. Known since 1907 and now distributed over most of the country. The adults are black, covered with gray hairs, and have a long snout. They make small round holes in leaves and lay eggs in flower buds. Small white legless larvae eat the seed embryo and pupate in its place, adults emerging in August. Spray or dust hollyhocks before pods are formed with methoxychlor, lindane, or chlordane. Cut and destroy stalks with infested seed pods.

89. Imported longhorned weevil, showing characteristic long antennae and foliage injury.

Imported Longhorned Weevil, *Calomycterus setarius* Roelofs. Another Japanese pest, first noted in New York in 1929 and reported from Connecticut in 1932. Since then it has spread to Delaware, Kansas, Kentucky, Illinois, Indiana, Massachusetts, Michigan, Minnesota, Missouri, Nebraska, New Hampshire, New York, New Jersey, Ohio, Iowa, Rhode Island, South Carolina, Virginia, West Virginia, and Wisconsin. It is a general feeder, consuming foliage and blossoms of grasses, legumes, flowering garden plants, vegetables, field crops, ornamental shrubs, house plants, vines. It also wanders into houses, crawls over walls and ceilings, gets into food.

Adult, black but appearing gray from their gray scales, ⅜ inch long, with prominent long antennae (the long horns), emerge in late June and are abundant in July and August. They eat irregular areas in from margins of leaves. Eggs are laid in sod and grubs are in the soil until the next June. Adults are wingless and natural spread is slow, but the weevils readily get around by crawling on people and into vehicles. Among the preferred hosts are ivy, lespedeza, African marigold, rose, strawberry, and Virginia-creeper. Dust or spray with chlordane or malathion.

Iris Weevil*, *Mononychus vulpeculus* (Fabricius). Breeds commonly in seed pods of blue flag iris, sometimes punctures ovaries of Japanese and European iris, causing rough, corky scars. Fat grubs feed on the seeds, pupate within the pods. Adults—black, with yellow-and-white scales, ⅕ inch long—emerge when pods burst open. Unless seeds are being saved for breeding, destroy all flower heads as they fade. If seeds are needed, cover blossoms with cheesecloth bags.

Japanese Weevil, *Pseudocneorhinus bifasciatus* Roelofs. First collected near Philadelphia in 1914, now found at scattered locations in Connecticut, Delaware, District of Columbia, Indiana, Maryland, Nebraska, New Jersey, New York, Pennsylvania, South Carolina, and Virginia. It feeds heavily on California privet, sometimes on azalea, camellia, Japanese barberry, chrysanthemum, clematis, fern, forsythia, geranium, honeysuckle, hemlock, lilac, lima bean, mimosa, mountain-laurel, lily-of-the-valley, rhododendron, rose, rose-of-Sharon, oak, strawberry, weigela, and veronica. I met it only once when I doctored gardens, but then the weevils were present on privet by the hundreds, cutting broad, rounded sections from the margins of the leaves, resulting in a crenulated appearance. The adults feed in the daytime. They have fused wing covers so they cannot fly, are dark with a broad abdomen, rather short snout. Spray or dust with chlordane.

Large Chestnut Weevil*, *Curculio caryatrypes* (Boheman). A limiting factor in growing Asiatic chestnuts to replace our lost American species.

Lesser Clover Leaf Weevil*, *Hypera nigrirostris* (Fabricius). One of the more important clover pests, especially of red clover. Adults feed on foliage, lay eggs in stems or buds; plants are stunted, misshapen. They are first brown, then grass-green.

Ligustrum Weevil, *Ochyromera ligustri* Warner. A new species found in North Carolina in 1959, feeding on Japanese privet, reported also from South Carolina on most species of privet, lilac, and on grape leaves. The adult is small, shiny brownish yellow with golden scales. The female lays eggs in seed capsules or fruit in summer and larvae winter in seed, pupating in May. Adults feed on foliage in late June and early July, cutting round or oblong holes; they also feed on pollen.

Lilac Weevil, *Otiorhyncus meridionalis* Gyllenhal. Recorded as damaging lilac, arborvitae, and privet in California and Washington, lilac and strawberries in Nevada, privet in Idaho.

Lily-of-the-Valley Weevil, *Hormorus undulatus* (Uhler). Notches leaves in from the margin in curious fashion. The injury is common but appears after blooming so control measures are seldom attempted.

Lily Weevil*, *Agasphaerops nigra* Horn. Heavy infestations are recorded on lily in California.

Lodgepole Terminal Weevil*, *Pissodes terminalis* Hopping. Mines through pith of terminals and kills them down to the first whorl of branches.

Maize Weevil*, *Sitophilus zeamais* Motschulsky.

Mango Weevil*, *Cryptorhynchus mangiferae* (Fabricius).

Monterey Pine Weevil*, *Pissodes radiatae* Hopkins. Infesting Monterey and other pines on the Pacific Coast. It mines the stems, tops, and bases of young pines above and below ground.

New York Weevil*, *Ithycerus novaboracensis* (Forster). Sometimes injurious to apple trees and young pears near woodlands, also on oak, hickory, beech in the Northeast. Large snout beetles—3/4 inch long, gray, spotted with black—prune off twigs and cut into buds. Control measures are seldom used but the beetles can be jarred from young fruit and shade trees and destroyed.

Northern Pine Weevil*, *Pissodes approximatus* Hopkins.

Obscure Root Weevil, *Sciopithes obscurus* Horn. Adults—grayish-brown with a dark, white-bordered irregular band on elytra—feed on leaves of rhododendron, azalea, viburnum, camellia, rose, yew, and other plants. Larvae feed on roots. This weevil is also a problem on small fruits—strawberries and raspberries in Oregon, Washington, and California.

Spraying with malathion is recommended for home gardeners; nurserymen may use Guthion or carbofuran.

Orchid Weevil, *Diorymerellus laevimargo* Champney. Dendrobium Weevil. On various species of cattleya and dendrobium. The beetles, ⅛ inch long, shiny black with striated (grooved) wing covers, feed on tender leaves or flower petals and lay eggs in root tips, especially in the cattleyas. Small, legless, curved larvae feed on new roots, hollow out old roots, cause tips to blacken.

Another weevil, *Orchidophilus aterrimus* (Waterhouse), is common on orchids in Hawaii.

Pales Weevil*, *Hylobius pales* (Herbst). A native, found from Maine to Florida, west to Minnesota, favoring white pine, often on red, sometimes on Scotch, loblolly, shortleaf pines, American larch, Norway spruce, and other conifers. It is important in Christmas-tree plantings. The adult is reddish brown to black, speckled with gray or yellow scales, black head and thorax, ⅓ inch long. The larva is white with a light-brown head, ½ inch long. The weevils feed, mostly at night, on bark of seedlings, girdling young trees near ground level and killing many; they also feed on twigs of older trees. They hibernate as adults, lay eggs in fresh-cut logs or stumps in May. Grubs burrow beneath bark, grow slowly, pupate under the bark in September. Most damage comes from the young adults after emergence, before winter hibernation.

Control. Spray the bark, especially the lower portion, with lindane in late May.

Pea Leaf Weevil*, *Sitona lineata* (Linnaeus). First noted in British Columbia in 1936, now a menace in Oregon and Washington, present also in California, Idaho, and Montana. The adults—slender, grayish brown with alternating light and dark lines—eat U-shaped notches in from margins of leaves, resulting in a scalloped appearance, but they may go on to complete defoliation. The larvae destroy root nodules in pea fields and are restricted to legumes. The adults feed also on apple, blackberry, raspberry, rose, and strawberry.

Pea Weevil*, *Bruchus pisorum* (Linnaeus). A seed weevil, present throughout the country. The beetles are short, chunky, ⅕ inch long, brown, flecked with white, black, and gray patches. The larva is white with a small brown head. The female lays her eggs on the outside of a pea pod, the larva bores through the wall of the pod and into one of the young peas, growing inside for 5 or 6 weeks, consuming the contents. It pupates inside the pea and the adult emerges in 1 to 3 weeks. Several larvae may enter a pea, but only 1 survives. There is no continuous breeding in storage as with bean weevils. The weevils may remain in stored seed a year or two before emerging, but usually they come out soon after pupation and hibernate in any protected place.

Control. Spray with malathion or methoxychlor when peas start to blossom and continue weekly until pods form. Destroy vines immediately after harvest. Many birds feed on pea weevils.

Pecan Weevil*, *Curculio caryae* (Horn). Hickory Nut Weevil. Found wherever pecans or hickories grow, sometimes causing loss of 80 per cent of the pecan crop. The dark-brown adults, ⅜ inch long, attack newly formed pecans, causing them to shrivel and drop. Early maturing varieties, such as Stuart, Schley, Mahan, and Moneymaker, are most commonly infested. The female has a beak longer than its body (that of the male is slightly shorter) and with it she punctures the nuts and places eggs, usually 3 to a nut, in the kernel as soon as the water stage is passed. Larvae emerge from nuts in late fall, go down 3 to 9 inches deep in the soil, stay there 1 to 2 years, then pupate in September or October, transforming to the adult in 3 weeks. They remain in the soil until the next July or August, when they come out to feed on nuts. Thus the life cycle takes 2 or 3 years.

Control. DDT was very effective. Ask your experiment station for the best present substitute. With only a few trees, weevils can be reduced by jarring the trees with a pole and collecting the weevils on sheets underneath, then dropping them into kerosene. Clean up all dropped nuts.

Pepper Weevil*, *Anthonomus eugenii* Cano. A Mexican insect now important in California, Arizona, New Mexico, Texas, Georgia, and Florida. Small white grubs feed inside buds of bell, sweet, and chili peppers, causing buds and most of pods to drop off. Adults are reddish brown to black with a brassy luster; they have curved beaks, are ⅛ inch long. There are several generations a year. Thiodan gives control. Carbaryl is effective but is followed by build-up of green peach aphids.

Pineapple Weevil*, *Metamasius ritchiei* Marshall.

Pine Gall Weevil*, *Podapion gallicola* Riley. Forming galls on twigs of scrub, pitch, and red pines.

Pine Reproduction Weevil, *Cylindrocopturus eatoni* Buchanan. Killing small ponderosa and Jeffrey reproduction pines in California. Adults puncture needles and bark.

Pine Root Collar Weevil*, *Hylobius radicis* Buchanan. Important in the Northeast on Scotch pine, also on Austrian, red, and jack pines in roadside plantings. The soil around base of stems is blackened and soaked with pitch, larvae being present here or in cambium of root collar. Lindane sprayed on the ground around trees helps in control.

Pitcheating Weevil*, *Pachylobius picivorus* (Germar).

Puncturevine Weevils, *Microlarinus* spp. Beneficial insects feeding on stems and seed pods of puncturevine in California and being released elsewhere.

Red Clover Seed Weevil*, *Tychius stephensi* Schoenherr.

Red Elm Bark Weevil*, *Magdalis armicollis* (Say). A reddish snout beetle infesting weakened elms. Keep trees fed and watered; remove dying or injured limbs.

Sandcherry Weevil*, *Coccotorus hirsutus* Bruner.

Sassafras Weevil*, *Odontopus calceatus* (Say). Found east of the Mississippi injuring sassafras, tuliptree, magnolia, and poplar. Small black snout beetles feed on leaves as buds break, producing many holes. Eggs are laid in midrib of leaves; larvae produce blotch mines. Spray with carbaryl when feeding begins.

Sisal Weevil, *Scyphophorus acupunctatus* Gyllenhal. Breeds in agave or century plant in the Southwest and has been seen on grapevines.

Sitka Spruce Weevil*, *Pissodes sitchensis* Hopkins. Important in the Pacific Northwest, killing or injuring terminal shoots of young trees, causing a crook in the trunk and/or a forked, worthless tree. The weevil is so prevalent in much of Washington and Oregon that Sitka spruce is no longer planted. The weevil is light to dark brown with a prominent curved beak, $\frac{3}{10}$ inch long. There is no practical control.

Small Chestnut Weevil*, *Curculio sayi* Gyllenhal. More abundant than the large chestnut weevil, often destroying 90 per cent of nuts in Asiatic chestnut stands.

Southern Pine Root Weevil*, *Hylobius aliradicis* Warner.

Strawberry Root Weevil*, *Otiorhyncus ovatus* (Linnaeus). Present throughout northern United States, a special pest of strawberries and conifers—hemlock, arborvitae, Japanese yew, some spruce, junipers—also on raspberry, blackberry, cranberry, grasses, cucurbits, crucifers, deciduous trees and shrubs. It is recorded as severely injuring peppermint in Washington. This species is much like the black vine weevil in looks and habit. The beetles are mostly black, striated, ¼ inch long, with short, blunt snouts; the larvae are white, legless, curved. Strawberries are stunted, leaves bunched together, darkened, with fine roots and crown eaten. Root feeding by grubs often kills small hemlocks, but needle feeding by adults is negligible on this host. Arborvitae roots are not often seriously injured, but terminal twigs are girdled by adults and tender new foliage is eaten. The weevils start emerging from the soil in early June, feeding for 10 to 14 days before laying eggs through the summer. Eggs hatch in 7 to 10 days. Larvae feed on roots until cold weather, when they move down 6 to 14 inches, working up and feeding again in spring. Some winter as adults in trash.

Control. It is best to treat the soil before planting, working aldrin, dieldrin, or chlordane into the top 6 inches of soil, and spraying or dusting around the base of established plants with chlordane or malathion.

Another species, the **Rough Strawberry Root Weevil**, *Brachyrhinus rugostriatus,* works on about the same hosts as the strawberry root weevil. It is small, shining black with reddish brown antennae and legs. Adults feed on leaves and larvae on roots.

Strawberry Weevil*, *Anthonomus signatus* Say. An eastern pest of strawberry, raspberry, dewberry, also found on wild blackberry and cinquefoil. The dark, reddish brown, very small snout beetle winters under trash, is active early in spring when strawberries are coming into bloom. The female punctures buds with her long beak, inserts an egg, then crawls down and girdles the stem of the flower bud, causing it to wilt. The grubs feed in the buds for about 4 weeks, pupate, and adults emerge just before midsummer. Adults feed on pollen, sever stems of fruit buds, preventing formation of fruit. Spray with methoxychlor at the first sign of damage to flower buds; repeat in 2 weeks, if necessary.

Sweetclover Weevil*, *Sitona cylindricollis* Fåhraeus. On clover, alfalfa, soybean, and cowpea, burrowing in and girdling roots.

Sweetpotato Weevil*, *Cylas formicarius elegantulus* (Summers). Sweetpotato Root Borer. Formerly confined to the Gulf States, but now present also in Georgia, South Carolina, and New Jersey. The weevil feeds on sweetpotato, morning-glory, and other plants of the same family. The beetles are 1/4 inch long, slender, with blue head, wing covers, and abdomen, red thorax and legs, a long, straight black beak. The weevil attacks potatoes in the field, entering near the stems, and breeds in stored roots, which are honeycombed by fat, legless white grubs.

Control. Sort out infested potatoes at harvest and destroy; clean up all old vines; destroy volunteer sweetpotatoes and related weeds. Apply a 2 to 2½ per cent dieldrin dust along the row in a strip 6 to 8 inches wide, as soon as roots start to enlarge; repeat 2 weeks later. If dieldrin is banned, ask your Experiment Station for a substitute.

Thurberia Weevil*, *Anthonomius grandis thurberiae* Pierce. A variety of the boll weevil.

Vegetable Weevil*, *Listroderes costirostris obliquus* (Klug). A beetle from Brazil, first reported in Mississippi in 1922, now spread through the Gulf States and along the coast in California. The weevils are buff-colored with a lighter, V-shaped marking on the wing covers, ⅜ inch long. They have well-developed wings but seldom fly. They go into a summer resting period in late April or early May under trash or loose bark on trees, remaining inactive until early fall, when the parthenogenetic females crawl to vegetable crops to feed and lay eggs, continuing through the winter, except in coldest weather. They attack beet, cabbage, carrot, cauliflower, lettuce, mustard, onion, potato, radish, spinach, Swiss chard, tomato, turnip, feeding first in the crown, then defoliating whole plants, leaving only stem and midribs. This is also a pest of dichondra lawns in California.

Control. Spray or dust with rotenone. Rotate crops and cultivate thoroughly to destroy pupae in soil; keep down weeds.

Vetch Brucid*, *Bruchus brachialis* (Fåhraeus).

West Indian Cane Weevil*, *Metamasius hemipterus hemipterus* (Linnaeus).

West Indian Sweetpotato Weevil*, *Euscepes postfasciatus* (Fairmaire).

White Pine Weevil*, *Pissodes strobi* (Peck). The most serious pest of white pine in the East, a constant threat in home plantings, plantations, and forests, sometimes injuring Norway spruce, Scotch, pitch, and jack pines, other pines and spruces. You can tell the injury at a distance for the terminal leader is brown in sharp contrast to the rest of the tree. When the yellow, footless grubs, ⅓ inch long, mine in the bark and sapwood of the terminal shoot they girdle it. When this dies, a lateral branch grows up and tries to replace the leader. Sometimes 2 laterals grow up and the tree is forked. Sometimes the tree is killed back beyond the leader.

Adults are reddish to dark brown, somewhat mottled with brown-and-white scales, ¼ inch long. Adults hibernate under cover on ground, feed in May, lay 2 or 3 pearly eggs in cavities dug in bark of leaders. Egg laying continues through June. The grubs hatch in 6 to 10 days and feed on the inner bark as they girdle the shoot. They pupate in small, oval chambers in the wood and beetles emerge from late June to early September. There is only 1 generation. Wilting and drooping of terminal twigs in spring is the first sign of larval activity.

Control. Infested shoots must be cut off and burned as soon as noticed, making sure the cut is below all grubs. Tie a lateral to a stake to replace the leader and cut off the others. To protect shoots from infestation, spray in April with lindane.

Willow Flea Weevil*, *Rhynchaenus rufipes* (LeConte). A small, native snout beetle found from Maine to Iowa and in Oregon and California, Colorado, and New Mexico on willow, Lombardy poplar, aspen, sometimes red birch. The grubs—dirty-white, $\frac{1}{12}$ inch long, widest at the thorax—mine in leaves, mostly willow, sometimes poplar. The adult is a tiny, jet-black beetle, elliptical, covered with short gray hairs, with reddish-yellow antennae and legs. Weevils hibernate under loose bark or trash on ground, feed in May on opening buds and new leaves, eating circular holes, sometimes killing back twigs. They lay eggs in June, in pits on underside of leaves; larvae pupate in mined leaves, beetles emerge in August.

Woods Weevil, *Nemocestes incomptus* (Horn). Grayish brown with irregular gray spots on the back, found in the Northwest. Food plants include rhododendron, azalea, viburnum, camellia, rose, yew, and other shrubs. Guthion is recommended for treatment of established plantings.

Yosemite Bark Weevil*, *Pissodes yosemite* Hopkins. On ponderosa and other pines in California, Oregon, and Washington.

Yucca Weevil, *Scyphophorus yuccae* Horn. The adult, black with deeply grooved wing covers, feeds on sap of living yucca in southern California; the larvae breed in bases of green flower stalks and hearts of the same plants.

WHITEFLIES

Whiteflies are minute, sucking insects belonging to the family Aleyrodidae (meaning like flour) in the order Homoptera. The adults have 2 pairs of broadly rounded wings covered with snow-white waxy powder; they look like tiny white moths. Whiteflies are often present in great numbers on the underside of leaves but are rarely noticed unless the plant is disturbed, when they fly out in clouds. They are primarily tropical insects but are abundant in greenhouses and on house plants and are common on some garden plants in summer in the North, most of the year in the South.

The life history is much the same for all species of whiteflies. Oval eggs, $\frac{1}{100}$ inch long, are attached to underside of leaves by short stalks. They hatch in 4 to 12 days into active, pale-yellow, 6-legged crawlers. The crawlers, usually called larvae, sometimes nymphs, move about for a short time, avoiding strong light, then insert their beaks and start sucking sap. At the 1st molt they lose their legs and antennae and look like very small, very flat, oval scales, often with a marginal fringe of white waxy filaments, sometimes covered with rods or plates of wax. They secrete copious honeydew through a special opening on the upper surface of the body. After a 2nd molt, the insect becomes a pupa, larger and more distinctly segmented, and then the 4-winged adult leaves the pupal skin by a T-shaped opening in the back.

For many years summer oil sprays were used for the control of whiteflies; now more reliance is placed on dimethoate or malathion by home gardeners. Commercial growers sometimes use parathion, Guthion, or Vapona. Systemic insecticides applied to the soil may be helpful.

Acacia Whitefly, *Tetraleurodes acaciae* (Quaintance). On acacia, coffeeberry, and coraltree in California. The pupa case is shiny black with a short marginal fringe.

Avocado Whitefly*, *Trialeurodes floridensis* (Quaintance). A pest of avocado in Florida, also occurring on papaya, banana, guava, annona, citrus. The adult is very small, less than 1 mm, pale yellow with white wings; the larva has a white marginal fringe and remains affixed to foliage over winter. Adults appear in early March to lay white eggs in circles on leaves. There are 3 generations and a partial 4th. An oil spray is recommended in the fall when foliage begins to harden and in spring after fruit is set.

Azalea Whitefly*, *Pealius azaleae* (Baker & Moles). In eastern and southern United States and in California wherever the snow azalea, *Rhododendron mucronatum* (*R. ledifolia alba* and *R. indica alba*), and similar species are grown. This type has evergreen leaves covered with fine hairs and sticky bud scales. The eggs are pale yellow, pupae greenish white, oval, present in great numbers on underside of foliage. The leaves lose color from sucking of plant juices and are often covered with sooty mold growing in the honeydew. The mold interferes with photosynthetic function of leaves, the sapsucking reduces vigor and flowering. Spray with diluted summer oil emulsion before adults emerge in spring. Spray in summer with malathion or dimethoate, at weekly intervals if necessary.

Bandedwing Whitefly*, *Trialeurodes abutilonea* (Haldeman). On cotton, tobacco, etc. Vector of cottony leaf crumple and sweetpotato feathery mottle.

Barberry Whitefly, *Aleuroplatus berbericola* (Cockerell). Colorless pupal case; adult yellow with white wings. On barberry and Oregon grape (Mahonia).

Citrus Blackfly*, *Aleurocanthus woglumi* Ashby. Our federal government maintains biological and chemical control zones in Mexico to keep this serious Mexican pest from invading the United States. Many parasites are released in addition to eradicative treatments.

The insect has appeared and has been eradicated in Florida and Texas. The nymph has a black body with white fringe; the adult has a dark-brown body with dark-blue wings.

Citrus Whitefly*, *Dialeurodes citri* (Ashmead). The most important economic species of whitefly, a native of Asia introduced into Florida prior to 1885, when it was found on oranges. It appeared in California in 1907 and at later dates, but infestations have been fairly well eradicated so that it remains for the most part a pest in the Gulf States, where it is a most important citrus pest, ranking next to purple scale and rust mite. It injures through the consumption of sap and by the honeydew which encourages sooty mold all over fruit and foliage. It breeds in large numbers in chinaberry trees. Besides these, and citrus, preferred food plants are umbrella tree, cape-jasmine (gardenia), privets, Japanese and wild persimmons, lilac, coffee, prickly-ash. Occasionally infested shrubs or vines include allamanda, banana, cerasus, camellia, choisya, cherry-laurel, green ash, jessamine, pear, pomegranate, smilax, viburnum, wild olive, ailanthus, water oak, Osage-orange, palmetto.

Small yellow eggs, looking like dust, hatch in 10 to 12 days, those from unfertilized females turning into males. The larvae are thin, translucent, scalelike; they lose legs and antennae after the first molt, about 7 days after hatching. The 2nd molt is in 5 or 6 days, the 3rd after 10 to 12 days, after which the insect assumes the pupa or resting state, taking much less food, becoming thicker, the outline of the adult taking form, and finally the winged whitefly emerges through a T-shaped opening in the pupal skin. There are usually 3 generations in Florida, the spring brood of adults at its maximum in late March, the summer brood in June, and the fall (largest) brood in late August and early September.

Control. Oil or parathion sprays for scale insects control whiteflies fairly well. If special treatments are required, use malathion or dimethoate in summer. Cutting down chinaberry trees reduces infestations. There are a number of parasites and predators but they cannot be depended upon for control. Red-and-yellow fungi (species of Aschersonia) grow on whiteflies but are not considered as useful as formerly; they are dependent on proper weather conditions.

Cloudywinged Whitefly*, *Dialeurodes citrifolii* (Morgan). Similar to the citrus whitefly, chiefly a Florida pest, not found in California. Aside from citrus, special hosts are yam vines and a species of Ficus. The eggs are black, covered with a network of ridges, often laid on water sprouts; the adults have a dusky area in each wing. Maximum spring flight is early April; summer, early July; fall, late October. Remove and destroy water sprouts when most eggs are present—May, August, September, or January. Spray as for citrus whitefly or, if the cloudywinged is the only species, about 3 weeks later.

Crown Whitefly, *Aleuroplatus coronatus* (Quaintance). Abundant on live, valley, and tan oaks, Christmasberry, manzanita, wild coffeeberry throughout California. The pupa case is dark, surrounded by flat, waxy white plates that give the appearance of a crown. Adults have pale yellow-white wings.

Fern Whitefly, *Aleyrodes nephrolepidis* (Quaintance). Found on various ferns in homes and greenhouses. The pupa case is bright yellow, without covering.

Glacial Whitefly, *Trialeurodes glacialis* (Bemis). On bush fruits, blackberry, loganberry, boysenberry, raspberry, and on bean, columbine, wild clematis, coffeeberry, ninebark, sage, snowberry, tan oak in California. The young are yellow with a crystalline fringe; the adults are pure white.

Grape Whitefly*, *Trialeurodes vittata* (Quaintance). On leaves of European grape in California, but normally breeding on chaparral. The young appear in great numbers on underside of leaves, causing smutting of fruit and foliage with mold fungi. The pupa is dark brown with a marginal fringe.

Greenhouse Whitefly*, *Trialeurodes vaporariorum* (Westwood). The most common species in greenhouses and gardens. It does not overwinter outdoors in the North but it gets to the garden with greenhouse-grown seedlings of tomatoes and other plants. In my own garden practice I always expected to find whiteflies on ageratum, egg-

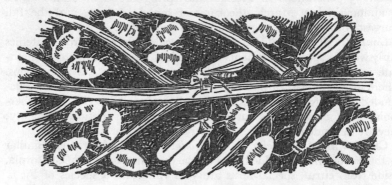

90. Nymph and adults of greenhouse whitefly, much enlarged, on underside of leaf.

plant, gourds, heliotrope, in dense quantities on underside of squash foliage, on tomatoes. In other sections they are also pests of aster, avocado, barberry, begonia, bignonia, blackberry, calceolaria, calendula, chysanthemum, cineraria, coleus, coffeeberry, cucumber, fern, fuchsia, geranium, grape, hibiscus, honeylocust, black locust, honeysuckle, Jerusalem-cherry, lantana, lettuce, loganberry, lupine, mallow, morning-glory, muskmelon, pea, pepper, potato, primrose, redbud, rose, sage, soybean, strawberry, watermelon. Infested plants lack vigor, turn yellow, sometimes wilt and die; leaves are sooted with black mold in the South, not so much outdoors in the North.

The eggs are elongated, pale yellowish green; the young are oval, thin, flat, pale green, semitransparent with white waxy threads radiating from their bodies. The larval stages last about a month; under greenhouse conditions there are several overlapping generations. Both male and female adults as well as larvae suck sap from underside of leaves.

Control. Spray or dust with malathion or dimethoate, being sure to cover undersurface of foliage. Greenhouse operators may use parathion or Vapona or Dithio (Bladafume, TEPP, very toxic).

Inconspicuous Whitefly, *Aleyrodes inconspicua* (Quaintance). Present along the West Coast on California laurel, Christmasberry, clematis, coffeeberry, maple, manzanita, live and tan oaks, Oregon grape (Mahonia), also reported from Florida. The pupa is pale or dark yellow with only a narrow fringe. The wings are dusky brown.

A **Jasmine Whitefly,** *Dialeurodes kirkaldyi* (Kotinsky). Known in Hawaii on citrus; reported in 1963 in Florida on several species of jasmine and on morinda. It is similar to the citrus whitefly.

Kellogg's Whitefly, *Pealius kelloggi* (Bemis). Often present in numbers on leaves of Catalina cherry, growing wild or used as an ornamental. The pupa is pale yellow, resting on dense white rods and covered with wide white wax ribbons so it looks like a minute flower.

Madroña Whitefly, *Trialeurodes madroni* (Bemis). Shiny black pupa case with wide white fringe. On madroña in California.

Manzanita Whitefly, *Trialeurodes merlini* (Bemis). Brown pupa case densely covered with white cottony wax. Often so numerous on manzanita, the bush appears covered with snow. Also infesting madroña.

Mulberry Whitefly*, *Tetraleurodes mori* (Quaintance). An eastern species that survives outdoors. Popular host plants include mulberry, dogwood, azalea, hackberry, holly, mountain-laurel, linden, maple, sycamore. The larvae are elliptical, very small, jet-black, edged with a white fringe of waxy filaments. Adults are around from June to Sep-

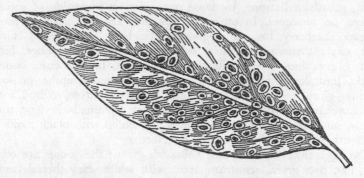

91. Nymphs of mulberry whitefly, black with white fringe.

tember, increasing in numbers late in the season. Apparently there is
no great injury to host plants.

Pruinose Whitefly, *Aleyrodes pruinosa* Bemis. Often present in enormous quantities on undersurface of Christmasberry (toyon) leaves,
causing serious smutting in central and southern California. The
pupa is yellow to dark brown with a frosty white covering. Adults
have yellow bodies with brown markings, 2 dusky spots on each fore
wing.

Rhododendron Whitefly*, *Dialeurodes chittendeni* Laing. Yellowish mottling on upper surface of leaves together with rolling of margins is caused by flat, greenish, almost transparent larvae. There is
much honeydew accompanied by sooty mold. Only rhododendrons
with smooth underleaf surfaces are infested. Spray with dimethoate
or diazinon. In the Pacific Northwest spraying with 2 per cent white
oil emulsion in autumn before frost has been effective.

Strawberry Whitefly*, *Trialeurodes packardi* (Morrill). The larva is
scalelike, covered with wax; overwintering is in the egg stage. Foliage
of infested plants loses vitality, may decay, is usually covered with
sooty mold growing in honeydew. This species is distributed throughout the United States. Spray with malathion.

Sweetpotato Whitefly*, *Bemisia tabaci* (Gennadius). Destructive
to sweetpotatoes in Florida, especially late-planted vines. Larvae are
$\frac{1}{12}$ inch long, flat, thin, nearly round, very inconspicuous on underside of leaves. Their honeydew encourages black mold. Spray with
malathion.

Woolly Whitefly*, *Aleurothrixus floccosus* (Maskell). Probably native to Florida on seagrape, later infesting citrus. It appeared in
California but prompt eradication measures were instituted. The pupa

is covered with white woolly filaments of wax, which gives the common name. Eggs are brown, curved, laid in circles as the female revolves around her inserted beak. The 1st larval stage is green, the others brown with a wide fringe of white wax. Adults are yellowish, do not fly much; there are 4 broods. Several parasites aid in control.

There are many other species of whiteflies found in gardens but they lack common names for easy reference and their habits and control are similar to those that have been treated.

WIREWORMS

Wireworms are the larvae of click beetles, order Coleoptera, family Elateridae. They occur throughout North America and over most of the world as destructive pests of corn, small grains, grasses, potatoes, beets, carrots, and other root crops. They may also injure other vegetables, beans, peas, lettuce, radish, and onions in particular, and flowers such as aster, dahlia, gladiolus, and phlox. Injury is usually most extensive in land recently taken over from sod, but in some sections wireworms are numerous in soil that has been continuously under cultivation. They eat seed, resulting in almost total loss of a planting of corn or peas; they feed on underground stems, causing death of seedlings; they eat the small roots of larger plants; they burrow into potatoes, carrots, beets, or bulbs. As larvae, they are entirely soil pests, working on underground plant parts.

The larvae are smooth, wiry worms, first white, with dark jaws, but after feeding and molting several times they are hard, jointed, and shiny, dark yellow to brown, with the last segment of the body pronged or forked, ¼ inch to ¾ inch long (Plate XXIII). Adults are hard-shelled, tapering beetles, gray-brown to black, with the joint in

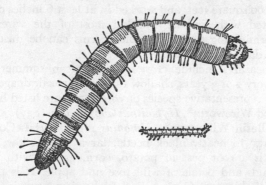

92. Wireworm, larva of a click beetle.

front of the wing covers loose and flexible. When they are placed or fall on their back, they right themselves with a sharp click.

The adults winter in soil cells, emerge in spring when soil temperature warms up, and crawl over the surface or make short flights to lay their eggs, in damp soil, 1 to 6 inches deep. The larvae feed little and do not cause much damage until their 2nd season. They sometimes change to white pupae in a year, but more often 2 or 3 years—sometimes 5 or 6 years—pass before they make a small cell 3 to 8 inches below the soil surface and pupate. The pupa changes to the adult in 3 weeks but the latter does not emerge until spring. Due to overlapping of generations, wireworms of all sizes and ages are present in the soil at the same time.

Control. The soil can be fumigated, treated with insecticides, or seeds and bulbs can be treated before planting, killing the wireworms present but with no long residual action. Treatment is for fallow soil only and planting should be delayed at least 2 weeks after treatment. Punch holes in the soil 1 foot apart and at least 6 inches deep and pour in ½ to 1 teaspoon of a 10 per cent solution of ethylene dibromide or 1 to 2 teaspoons D-D mixture and close the holes with soil. Special applicators are available for large plots. Both fumigants are poisonous to man; do not breathe the vapors; wash off immediately any liquid spilled on the skin. Ethylene dibromide is combustible.

Soil insecticides are easier to apply than fumigants and have a long-lasting effect, though the initial kill may be slow. Aldrin, dieldrin, and heptachlor have been effective but use of these chlorinated hydrocarbons is in disfavor. Diazinon may be used, broadcast at the rate of 6 pounds of dust per 1,000 square feet and worked into the top 8 inches of soil before planting. Chlordane is also recommended, 5 ounces of 40 per cent wettable powder in 2½ gallons of water applied to 1,000 square feet, and worked in at least 6 inches deep.

Seeds treated with lindane will kill most of the wireworms attracted to germinating seeds. Gladiolus corms can be dusted with 6 per cent chlordane before planting.

Cultural measures include crop rotation, clean summer fallowing of the land every 2 or 3 years, shallow tillage, proper drainage.

Only a few representative species of wireworms are listed here.

Abbreviated Wireworm*, *Hypolithus abbreviatus* (Say).

Columbia Basin Wireworm*, *Limonius subauratus* LeConte. A robust, slate gray to nearly black beetle, larva pale yellow, somewhat flattened. It is a root pest of potato, corn, grains, with the adults feeding on buds and petals of wild rose and apple. It is particularly injurious in Washington, Oregon, and Idaho, is present in California, Arizona, New Mexico and eastern states.

Dryland Wireworm*, *Ctenicera glauca* (Germar). Reported in the Northwest on wheat and potatoes.

Eastern Field Wireworm*, *Limonius agonus* (Say). Probably the most common eastern species, found even on land which has been under cultivation for many years. It is a serious pest in tobacco areas along the Connecticut River and in upstate New York, attacking potatoes, beets, carrots, radishes, onion; most injurious in early spring.

Great Basin Wireworm*, *Ctenicera pruinina* (Horn). Found in dry areas east of the Cascades in Washington, Oregon, Idaho. The beetle is black, slender; the larva is yellow.

Gulf Wireworm*, *Conoderus amplicollis* (Gyllenhal). A most important subterranean pest of sweetpotatoes in the Gulf States, its punctures followed by rots. It is also important on white potatoes.

Oregon Wireworm*, *Melanotus oregonensis* (LeConte). Common on the West Coast, Oregon, and California, on roots of grapes and figs.

Pacific Coast Wireworm*, *Limonius canus* LeConte. Infesting bulbs along with other root crops.

Plains False Wireworm*, *Eleodes opacus* (Say). Found between the Mississippi River and the Pacific Coast, preferring wheat but also attacking grasses, oats, corn, sugar beets, beans, and other garden crops. The beetle is black with a flat back sparsely clothed with white hairs. It cannot fly and when disturbed elevates the hind part of its body, keeping its head on the ground. The larvae are brown or yellow, prominently jointed.

Puget Sound Wireworm*, *Ctenicera aeripennis aeripennis* (Kirby).

Sand Wireworm*, *Horistonotus uhlerii* Horn. A southern pest, on cotton, corn, and peanuts.

Southern Potato Wireworm*, *Conoderus falli* Lane. The most abundant species in the commercial potato-producing areas in the Southeast, sometimes a pest of sweetpotatoes.

Sugarbeet Wireworm*, *Limonius californicus* (Mannerheim). Common in California and north to Washington. The adult is a small, elongate click beetle, 3/8 inch long, light or dark brown, with coarse punctures on the back. The larvae, typical shiny, yellow-brown hard worms, feed mostly on roots of young plants, aster, chrysanthemums, and other flowers as well as on sugar beets, beans, and corn.

Tobacco Wireworm*, *Conoderus vespertinus* (Fabricius). Spotted Click Beetle. Common in cornfields as well as a tobacco pest. The larva is hard, thick, 1/2 inch long, more destructive in dry than in wet soils.

Western Field Wireworm*, *Limonius infuscatus* Motschulsky. Associated with the sugarbeet wireworm on the West Coast, particularly injurious to potatoes in sandy river-bottom land.

Wheat Wireworm*, *Agriotes mancus* (Say). Pest of potato, corn, wheat, and a wide variety of plants across the country.

Chapter VI

HOST PLANTS AND THEIR PESTS

In this section there are sorted out under their different host plants (the plants they live or feed on) the nearly 2,000 garden pests included in Chapter V. Some have been dismissed in a line or two, some have been treated in detail. The list is by no means complete, but I hope it covers the major insect pests to be found in the various sections of continental United States. It has only a few references to Hawaii because I have had no personal experience with the exotic possibilities there.

Some of the pests are limited to one or two hosts, others may attack several hundred different kinds of plants. In the latter case, the more important food plants are given as I have observed them in my own practice or have found them in the literature. I have been greatly aided, in making up this Check List, by the *Cooperative Economic Insect Report* that comes weekly from the United States Department of Agriculture, as well as by the publications from various state institutions.

The pests are listed under each host alphabetically according to the groups under which they are described in the pest section, Chapter V, which is also in alphabetical order. The group name, **Aphid, Beetle, Borer, Bug, Caterpillar,** and so on, is given in boldface. For instance, under ABUTILON we have **Beetle,** Fuller Rose, which means that you find BEETLES in Chapter V and then run down **Fuller Rose Beetle** as if you were using a dictionary. So far as they are available, the common names are those presently approved by the Entomological Society of America. When an insect does not have a common name officially designated, I have supplied one that will aid in finger-tip reference. Approved names are marked with an asterisk. Other names frequently used as common names are given with the descriptions of the pests in Chapter V and also in the Index. See pages 486–612 for further help in finding the particular pest that is worrying you at the moment.

The list of insects under certain host plants is appallingly long, but don't let it be hopelessly discouraging. Many insects can be safely ignored; many will never appear in your particular region; and of those that may be a problem in your state, few will be disastrous in any one season. Some of the more important pests are singled out by a brief comment.

Having noted some of the possibilities, check back to Chapter V for a more complete description of the damage, the life history of the pest and suggested treatment. Always read the introduction to each group of pests as well as the text on a particular species. If typical life histories and control measures are given for the group as a whole, the details are not repeated under every species.

Remember also that control measures and particularly the chemicals recommended are constantly changing. They vary from state to state as well as year to year. For fruits, vegetables, and ornamentals be sure to ask for help from your local County Agent or State Experiment Station. They have free bulletins and spray schedules that are constantly being revised to keep up with our advancing knowledge. This book is definitely not the last word!

ABELIA
Scale, Florida Wax; Greedy; Latania; Lesser Snow; White Peach.

ABUTILON (Flowering Maple)
Beetle, Fuller Rose (feeds from leaf margins).
Bollworm, Pink. Mealybugs. Mites (red spiders).
Moth, Abutilon (looper caterpillar chews foliage).
Scale, Black Araucaria; Brown Soft; Cottony Taxus; Lesser Snow.
Weevil, Imported Longhorned (feeds from edge of leaf).
Whitefly, Greenhouse (minute white flies on underside of leaves).

ACACIA
Beetle, Fuller Rose. Borer, Branch and Twig. Butterfly, Sulfur.
Caterpillar, Omnivorous Looper; Orange Tortrix.
Mealybug, Citrus; Ground (white, powdery, on roots); Mexican.
Psyllid, Acacia.
Scale, Black Thread; California Red; Cottonycushion; Cyanophyllum; Dictyospermum; Fern; Florida Red; Florida Wax; Greedy; Lesser Snow; Long Soft; Mimosa; Mining; Oleander; Pustule; Quohogshaped; Rufous; San Jose; White Peach.
Spittlebugs. Whitefly, Acacia.

ACALYPHA (Copper-leaf; Chenille Plant)
Mealybug, Longtailed; Mexican; Striped.
Scale, Black; Brown Soft; Cottonycushion; Cottony Taxus; Cyanophyllum; Florida Red; Green Shield; Long Soft; Parlatorialike; Pyriform.

ACANTHOPANAX (Five-leaf Aralia)
Aphid, Foxglove; Spirea.
Bug, Fourlined Plant (dark, depressed circular spots in leaves).

ACONITE, Monkshood (*Aconitum*)
Bug, Fourlined Plant (dark, depressed spots in leaves).
Leafminer, Larkspur (tan blotches on foliage).
Mite, Cyclamen (leaves, buds deformed, blackened).

ACTINIDIA
Scale, Lesser Snow; San Jose.

AECHEMIA
Scale, Aechemia; Boisduval's; Latania; Pineapple.

AFRICAN-VIOLET (*Saintpaulia*)
Aphid, Foxglove; Potato.
Caterpillar, Soybean Looper.
Mealybug, Citrus (white cottony mass at leaf axils); Ground (several species at roots).
Mite, Broad (leaves glassy); Cyclamen (leaves deformed, stems twisted).
Scale, Fern.

AGAPANTHUS (African-Lily; Lily-of-the-Nile)
Mealybug. Scale, Latania. Thrips, Banded Greenhouse.

AGAVE (see Century Plant)

AGERATUM
Aphid, Bean. Beetle, Oriental. Budworm, Tobacco (feeds on buds).
Earworm, Corn (eats buds or foliage).
Leaftier, Celery (feeds inside rolled leaves).
Mite, Cyclamen (leaves, flowers deformed); Twospotted (leaves white).

Whitefly, Greenhouse (common in late summer; leaves stippled white).

AGRIMONY (*Agrimonia*)
Aphid, Potato.

AILANTHUS (Tree-of-Heaven)
Aphid, Melon. **Beetle.**
Borer, Brown Wood (brown beetle, yellow larva, winding galleries).
Moth, Cynthia (large green caterpillar); Whitemarked Tussock.
Scale, Oystershell.
Webworm, Ailanthus (brown caterpillars in fine webs); Fall.
Whitefly, Citrus.

AJUGA (Bugleweed)
Mealybug, Citrophilus. **Mite,** Bugle Bud.

AKEBIA
Scale, San Jose (small, round, grayish).

AKEE (*Blightia sapinda*)
Scale, Black; Green Shield; Pustule.

ALBIZZIA (see Mimosa)

ALDER (*Alnus*)
Aphid, Alder; Hop; Woolly Alder (common, goes over to maple).
Beetle, Alder Bark; Alder Flea (steel-blue, may defoliate); Elm Calligrapha.
Borer, Banded Alder; California Prionus; Pacific Flatheaded; Poplar-and-Willow.
Bug, Alder Lace. **Butterfly,** Western Swallowtail.
Casebearer, Birch.
Caterpillar, Chainspotted geometer; Omnivorous Looper; Western Tent.
Leafminer, European Alder. **Leaf Skeletonizer,** Birch.
Mite, Fruittree; Yellow Spider.
Moth, Gypsy; Smeared Dagger; Spotted Tussock.
Psyllid, Alder. **Sawfly,** Striped Alder.
Scale, Black; Brown Soft; Cottony Maple; European Fruit Lecanium; Green Shield; Oystershell; San Jose; Willow Scurfy.
Spittlebug, Alder.

ALFALFA (*Medicago*)

Aphid, Alfalfa; Pea; Spotted Alfalfa.
Armyworm, Western Yellowstriped.
Beetle, Alfalfa Snout; Palestriped Flea; Striped Blister.
Bug, Alfalfa Plant; Rapid Plant; Superb Plant.
Butterfly, Orange Sulfur.
Caterpillar, Alfalfa; Alfalfa Looper; Green Cloverworm.
Curculio, Clover Root.   **Leafroller,** Omnivorous.
Mite, Strawberry Mite.   **Moth,** Pine Tortrix.
Rootworm, Western Corn.   **Spittlebug,** Meadow.
Treehopper, Threecornered Alfalfa.   **Webworm,** Alfalfa; Garden.
Weevil, Alfalfa; Clover Head; Sweetclover.

ALLAMANDA

Mealybug, Longtailed.
Scale, Black; Cyanophyllum; Dictyospermum; Florida Red; Hemi-
    spherical; Mining; Purple; Pyriform; Tesselated; White Peach.
Whitefly, Citrus.

ALMOND (*Prunus communis*)

Aphid, Black Peach; Waterlily (winter host for).
Beetle, Western Striped Cucumber; Tobacco Flea.
Borer, American Plum; California Prionus; Peach Twig; Shothole;
    Western Peachtree.
Bug, Boxelder; Consperse Stink.   **Casebearer,** California.
Caterpillar, California Tent; Filbertworm; Navel Orangeworm; Om-
    nivorous Looper; Redhumped.
Leafhopper, Plum (transmits yellows).   **Leafroller,** Fruittree.
Mite, Clover; European Red; Pacific Spider; Peach Silver; Texas
    Citrus; Twospotted.
Scale, Black; Coconut; Cottonycushion; European Fruit Lecanium;
    Forbes; Greedy; Green Shield; Hemispherical; Howard; Olive;
    Oystershell; San Jose; Walnut.
Thrips, Citrus.

ALOE

Mites.
Scale, Brown Soft; California Red; Florida Red; Hemispherical; Ole-
    ander (pale yellow).

ALSTROEMERIA

Aphid, Green Peach.   **Thrips,** Banded Greenhouse.

ALTERNANTHERA
Scale, Parlatorialike.

ALYSSUM (Madwort, Basket-of-Gold)
and SWEET ALYSSUM (*Lobularia maritima*)
Beetle, Red Turnip.   Caterpillar, Imported Cabbageworm.
Leafhopper, Aster (transmits aster yellows).
Moth, Diamondback (green caterpillar).

AMARANTH (*Amaranthus*)
Aphid, Corn Root; Cowpea; Potato.   Beetle, Carrot.
Leafhopper, Southern Garden.   Scale, Cottonycushion; Green.
Webworm, Garden.

AMARYLLIS (*Hippeastrum*, other Genera)
Beetle, Black Blister.
Caterpillar, Convict (black with white bands).   Cutworm, Climbing.
Fly, Narcissus Bulb (one maggot inside); Lesser Bulb (several maggots).
Mealybug, Citrus.   Mite, Bulb (in rotting bulbs).
Scale, Brown Soft; Hemispherical.
Thrips, Banded Greenhouse; Gladiolus (foliage, flowers streaked);
   Greenhouse; Sugarbeet.

AMAZON-LILY (*Eucharis*)
Mealybug, Pineapple.   Scale, Dictyospermum.

AMPELOPSIS
Beetle, Rhabdopterus.   Scale, Barnacle; Hemispherical.
Weevil, Black Vine.

ANCHUSA (Alkanet; Bugloss)
Leafhopper, Aster.   Mites, Spider.

ANDIRA (Angelin-tree; Cabbage-tree)
Scale, Black Thread; Latania; Mining.

ANDROMEDA (*Pieris*, other genera)
Bug, Andromeda Lace (foliage of *Pieris japonica* stippled white).
Caterpillar, Azalea.   Mite, Twospotted (foliage yellow).
Scale, Azalea Bark; Florida Wax (waxy white tinged with pink);
   Cottony Maple; Latania; Nigra.
Whitefly, Azalea.

ANEMONE (Windflower)

Aphid, Crescentmarked Lily; other species.
Beetle, Black Blister (devours foliage, flowers of Japanese anemone).
Cutworms. Leaftier, Celery (webs foliage). Thrips, Pear.

ANISE-TREE (*Illicium floridanum*)

Scale, Brown Soft; Cottonycushion; Florida Red; Purple.

ANTHERICUM (St.-Bernards-Lily)

Scale, Cyanophyllum; Dictyospermum; Florida Red; Hemispherical.

ANTHURIUM

Mealybugs. Mites. Whiteflies.
Scale, Brown Soft; Boisduval's; Dictyospermum; Fern; Green Shield; Hemispherical; Proteus.

ANTIDESMA (Tropical Currant)

Scale, Black; Brown Soft; Cottonycushion; Green; Green Shield; Pyriform.

APPLE (*Pyrus malus*)

Aphid, Apple; Apple Grain; Clover; Hawthorn; Hop; Potato; Rosy Apple (curls leaves) ; Spirea; Woolly Apple.
Beetle, Apple Flea; Apple Twig; Bumbling Flower; Cherry Leaf; Fig; Fuller Rose; Grape Colaspis; Grape Flea; Green June; Imbricated Snout; Japanese; Potato Flea; Rose Chafer; Rose Leaf; Strawberry Leaf; Syneta Leaf; Western Striped Cucumber.
Borer, American Plum; Apple Twig; Broadnecked Root; Brown Wood; California Prionus; Flatheaded Appletree; Pacific Flatheaded; Pigeon Tremex; Roundheaded Appletree; Shothole; Western Peachtree.
Bud Moth, Eyespotted.
Bug, Apple Red; Boxelder; Dark Apple Red; Green Stink; Lygus; Pear Plant; Tarnished Plant.
Butterfly, Western Swallowtail. Cankerworm, Fall; Spring.
Casebearer, California; Cherry; Cigar; Pistol.
Caterpillar, Azalea; California Tent; Eastern Tent; Forest Tent; Linden Looper; Orange Tortrix; Palmerworm; Redhumped; Saddled Prominent; Schizura; Stinging Rose; Unicorn; Walnut; Western Tent; Western Tussock; Yellownecked.
Cicada, Periodical. Cricket, Blackhorned; Snowy Tree.
Curculio, Apple; Larger Apple; Plum.

Fruitworm, Green; Lesser Appleworm. Leaf Crumpler.

Leafhopper, Apple; Grape; Japanese; Mountain; Potato; Rose; Three-banded; Virginiacreeper; White Apple.

Leafminer, Apple Leaf Blotch; Apple Trumpet; Basswood; Spotted Tentiform; Unspotted Tentiform.

Leafroller, Fruittree; Obliquebanded; Redbanded.

Leaf Skeletonizer, Apple; Apple-and-Thorn.

Maggot, Apple (common cause of wormy apples).

Mealybug, Apple; Citrophilus; Comstock; Grape; Taxus.

Midge, Apple Leafcurling.

Mite, Clover; European Red (serious problem, foliage sickly); Four-spotted; Fruittree; McDaniel Spider; Pacific Spider; Pearleaf Blister; Pear Rust; Strawberry Spider; Twospotted; Willamette; Yellow Spider.

Moth, American Dagger; Apple Fruit; Browntail; Codling (most important apple pest; wormy, deformed fruit); Crinkled Flannel; Ermine; Gypsy; Hickory Tussock; Leopard; Oriental; Oriental Fruit; Resplendent Shield Bearer; Rusty Tussock; Spotted Tussock; Western Tussock; Whitelined Sphinx; Whitemarked Spinx; other species.

Psyllid, Apple Sucker. Rootworm, Strawberry.

Sawfly, Dock; European Apple.

Scale, Acuminate; Black; Brown Soft; California Red; Cottony-cushion; Cottony Maple; Cottony Peach; European Fruit Lecanium; Florida Red; Florida Wax; Forbes; Greedy; Green Shield; Howard; Italian Pear; Olive Parlatoria; Oystershell; Putnam; San Jose; Scurfy; Walnut.

Spanworm, Cleftheaded.

Termites, Subterranean. Thrips, Madroña; Pear.

Treehopper, Buffalo. Wasp, Apple Chalcid. Webworm, Fall.

Weevil, Apple Flea; Bronze Appletree; New York; Pea Leaf.

Wireworm, Columbia Basin.

Farmers have to apply a dozen or more combination sprays to obtain marketable fruit. Every state and county provides spray schedules for commercial growers and others for home gardeners, tailored to local pests and conditions. Combination fruittree sprays are available for home gardeners, and sometimes 5 properly timed applications will produce fruit fairly free from pests. The schedule usually calls for a dormant or delayed dormant spray for scale insects and aphids; a pink spray when buds show color, for caterpillars and other chewing insects as well as apple scab; a petal-fall or calyx spray when most of the petals have fallen (very important for controlling codling moth); and at least 2 cover sprays for codling moth. A summer spray may be needed for apple maggot.

APRICOT (*Prunus armeniaca*)

Aphid, Black Peach; Green Peach; Mealy Plum (slits and smudges fruit, stunts tree); Thistle; Waterlily.

Beetle, Fig; Fuller Rose; Green June; Plum Gouger; Western Spotted Cucumber (eats holes in fruits, spreads brown rot).

Borer, American Plum; Branch and Twig (small holes at base of buds, fruit spurs); Carpenterworm; Flatheaded Appletree; Pacific Flatheaded; Peachtree; Peach Twig; Shothole; Western Peachtree.

Bug, Largid. **Butterfly,** Western Swallowtail.

Cankerworm, Fall; Spring.

Caterpillar, California Tent; Orange Tortrix; Redhumped; Yellownecked.

Curculio, Plum. **Earwig,** European.

Fruitworm, Green. **Leafhopper,** Plum.

Leafroller, Fruittree; Oblique-banded.

Maggot, Apple. **Mealybug,** Grape.

Mite, Clover; Fruittree; Pacific Spider; Twospotted; Willamette.

Moth, Codling; Oriental Fruit; Western Tussock.

Sawfly, Cherry Fruit.

Scale, Black; Brown Soft; Cottonycushion; European Fruit Lecanium; Forbes; Italian Pear; Olive Parlatoria; Oystershell; San Jose; Walnut; White Peach.

Termites. Thrips, Citrus; Pear; Western Flower. **Weevil.**

ARABIS (Rockcress)

Aphid, Crescentmarked Lily; Lettuce Root.

ARALIA

Aphid, Ivy (Oleander); Spirea.

Caterpillar, Imported Cabbageworm; Omnivorous Looper.

Leafhopper, Japanese. **Leafminer,** Serpentine.

Mealybug, Citrus; Longtailed. **Mite,** Cyclamen; Tumid Spider.

Scale, Black; Brown Soft; Dictyospermum; Cottonycushion; Florida Red; Green; Green Shield; Hemispherical; Japanese Wax; Pyriform; Red Wax.

Thrips, Banded Greenhouse; Sugarbeet.

ARAUCARIA (Monkeypuzzle; Norfolk-Island-pine)

Aphid, Araucaria.
Mealybug, Citrus; Cypress; Golden (covered with yellow wax);
Ground.
Scale, Araucaria (white); Black Araucaria (very dark); Brown Soft;
Chaff; Dictyospermum; Florida Red; Proteus.

ARBORVITAE (*Thuja*)

Aphid, Arborvitae (brown with white bloom).
Bagworm (common, small bags on twigs).
Beetle, Northern Cedar Bark (twigs wilt, hang down); Western Cedar
Bark.
Borer, Cedar Tree (brown beetle; may girdle trees).
Caterpillar, Hemlock Looper.
Leafminer, Arborvitae (tips of twigs light-colored). Mealybug, Cypress.
Mite, False Spider; Spruce Spider (common, serious, foliage brown);
Tipdwarf; Twospotted. Moth.
Psyllid, Tomato. Sawfly, Arborvitae.
Scale, Dictyospermum; European Fruit Lecanium; Fletcher; Glover;
Juniper; Latania; Newstead's; San Jose.
Spittlebugs. Weevil, Arborvitae; Lilac; Strawberry Root.

ARBUTUS (see Madroña; Strawberry-tree)

ARDISIA

Orthezia, Greenhouse.
Scale, Brown Soft; Cottony Taxus; Cyanophyllum; Dictyospermum;
Fern; Florida Wax; Hemispherical; Latania; Lesser Snow; Yellow.

ARTEMISIA (Wormwood; Sagebrush)

Aphid, Artemisia; Pale Chrysanthemum.
Beetle, Goldenrod. Grasshoppers. Mealybug, Yucca.
Midge, Artemisia Gall. Mite, Artemisia Gall.
Psyllid, Artemisia; Knotweed.
Scale, Black Araucaria; Artemisia (large white sacs); Black.
Thrips, Artemisia.

ARTICHOKE, GLOBE (*Cynara scolymus*)

Aphid, Bean (black); Green Peach; Oleaster Thistle (pale yellow to
green).
Earworm, Corn. Leafminer, Chrysanthemum.

Moth, Artichoke Plume (yellow caterpillar in stems, heads).
Slug, Gray Garden; Greenhouse.
Termite, Western Subterranean.

ARTICHOKE, JERUSALEM (*Helianthus tuberosus*)
Aphid, Sunflower.

ARTILLERY PLANT (*Pilea*)
Scale, Lesser Snow.

ASCLEPIAS (see Butterfly Weed).

ASH (Fraxinus)
Aphid, Leafcurl Ash.   Beetle, Bark.
Borer, Apple Twig; Banded Alder; Brown Wood; California Prionus; Carpenterworm; Flatheaded Appletree; Lilac (common, in wood, scar tissue on trunk) ; Pacific Flatheaded; Redheaded Ash.
Bug, Ash Lace; Ash Plant; California Ash Mirid; Sycamore Lace.
Butterfly, Tiger Swallowtail.   Cankerworm, Fall.
Caterpillar, Forest Tent; Western Tent; Hickory Horned Devil.
Cricket, Snowy Tree (may injure bark in egg laying).
Fruitworm, Green.   Leafminer, Lilac (blotches in leaves).
Leafroller, Fruittree; Obliquebanded (caterpillars in rolled leaves).
Mite, Ash Flowergall; Privet.
Moth, Browntail; Great Ash Sphinx; Leopard; Polyphemus; Promethea (large green caterpillar) ; other species.
Sawfly, Blackheaded Ash; Brownheaded Ash (may defoliate).
Scale, Brown Soft; Cottony Maple; European Fruit Lecanium; Howard; Olive; Osborn's; Oystershell (often injurious) ; Putnam; San Jose; Scurfy; Terrapin; White Peach.
Webworm, Fall.   Whitefly, Citrus.

ASPARAGUS
Aphid, Asparagus; Bean; Crescentmarked Lily; Melon; Potato.
Beetle, Asparagus (feeds on shoots, foliage) ; Japanese (on foliage) ; Spotted Asparagus (larvae eat berries) ; Spotted Cucumber.
Bug, Garden Fleahopper; Say Stink; Harlequin.
Caterpillar, Orange Tortrix; Yellow Woollybear.
Centipede, Garden Symphylan (injures shoots, serious in California).
Cutworms.   Leafminer, Asparagus (maggots may girdle stems).
Mite, Bulb (may injure underground stems).
Scale, Black Thread; Dictyospermum; Latania; Lesser Snow.

ASPARAGUS FERN, "SMILAX," (*Asparagus plumosus*)
Aphid, Asparagus; Crescentmarked Lily; Green Peach.
Armyworm, Beet.   **Bug,** Garden Fleahopper; Rapid Plant.
Cutworm, Variegated (climbs plants, clips stems).
Mite, Twospotted (mealy webs, loss of color) ; Asparagus.
Scale, Black; Chaff; Coconut; Hemispherical; Lesser Snow; Olean-
der.
Thrips, Onion (silvering, curling of leaves; brown corky spots).

ASPEN (see Poplar)

ASPIDISTRA
Scale, California Red; Dictyospermum; Fern (white, conspicuous) ;
Florida Red; Lesser Snow; Proteus; Pyriform.

ASSONIA (Dombeya)
Scale, Black; Brown Soft; Chaff; Latania; Lesser Snow; Long Soft;
Pustule.

ASTER, CHINA (*Callistephus*)
Aphid, Brown Ambrosia; Corn Root; Crescentmarked Lily; Green
Peach; Leafcurl Plum; Lettuce Root; Melon; Potato; Solanum
Root; Sugarbeet Root; Western Aster Root; White Aster Root.
Beetle, Asiatic Garden; Black Blister (common on flowers); Clema-
tis Blister; June (grubs injure roots) ; Margined Blister; Potato Flea;
Spotted Cucumber; Striped Cucumber.
Borer, European Corn; Stalk.
Bug, Chrysanthemum Lace; Fourlined Plant; Tarnished Plant.
Caterpillar, Soybean Looper.   **Centipede,** Garden Symphylan.
Leafhopper, Aster (transmits aster yellows) ; Redbanded; Southern
Garden.   **Leafminer,** Wild Parsnip.
Leafroller, Obliquebanded.   **Leaftier,** Celery.
Mealybug, Solanum; Yucca.   **Mite,** Broad.
Scale, Black (not common); Green.
Thrips, Banded Greenhouse; Gladiolus.
Whitefly, Greenhouse.   **Wireworm,** Sugarbeet.

ASTER (Perennial)
Aphid, Aster (green, clustered thick on flower stems) ; Corn Root;
Grindelia; Little Blacklined Aster.

AUCUBA (Golddust Plant)

Aphid, Aucuba (greenish).

Scale, California Red (yellow strain, making wounds for leafspot fungi); Chaff; Cyanophyllum; Dictyospermum; Latania; White Peach.

Walkingstick, Twostriped.

ASTILBE

Beetle, Japanese (descends on flowers and foliage in hordes).

AUSTRALIAN-PINE (*Casuarina*)

Borer, Australian-pine.   Mealybug, Citrus; Longtailed.

Scale, Barnacle; Brown Soft; Cottonycushion; Dictyospermum; Latania; Long Soft; Mining (grayish, mines partly in bark).

AUSTRALIAN SILK-OAK (see Grevillea).

AVOCADO (*Persea americana*)

Ant, Argentine; Fire.   Aphid, Bean; Melon; Spirea.

Beetle, Ambrosia; Banded Flea; Bark; Blossom Anomala; Bronze Willow Flea; Darkling Ground; Fuller Rose; June (on young trees); Rhabdopterus.

Borer, Branch and Twig; Avocado Tree Girdler; Shothole.

Bug, Avocado Lace; False Chinch; Harlequin; Lygus.

Butterfly, Western Swallowtail.

Caterpillar, Avocado (skeletonizes leaves, scars fruit); Omnivorous Looper; Orange Tortrix.

Cricket, Snowy Tree.   Cutworm, Variegated (on young trees).

Mealybug, Citrophilus; Citrus; Coconut; Coleman's; Longtailed.

Leafroller, Avocado.

Mite, Avocado Brown; Avocado Bud; Avocado Red; Broad; Pallid; Platanus; Sixspotted.

Scale, Acuminate; Barnacle; Black; Brown Soft; Camphor; California Red; Cottony Maple; Cyanophyllum; Dictyospermum (important in Florida); European Fruit Lecanium; Florida Red; Florida Wax; Greedy; Green Shield; Hemispherical; Latania (gray to yellow, serious pest); Lesser Snow; Oleander; Oriental; Parlatorialike; Purple; Pyriform (serious in Florida); Red Bay; Rufous; Tea; Terrapin; Tesselated; Tuliptree.

Snail, Brown Garden.

Thrips, Avocado Blossom; Bean; Greenhouse (important, fruit scarred); Redbanded.

Weevil, Adaleres; Citrus Root.   Whitefly, Avocado; Greenhouse.

AZALEA (*Rhododendron*)

Aphid, Azalea; Mealy Plum; Rusty Plum.
Beetle, Asiatic Garden; Flea; Fuller Rose.
Borer, Azalea Stem (yellow grubs in twigs); Rhododendron (in wood near base); Raspberry Cane.
Bug, Andromeda Lace; Azalea Lace (most common and serious pest); Rhododendron Lace.
Caterpillar, Azalea; Saddleback. **Fruitworm,** Speckled Green. **Leafminer,** Azalea.
Mealybug, Citrophilus; Longtailed; Striped.
Mite, Azalea; Cyclamen; False Spider; Privet; Southern Red (causes defoliation); Twospotted.
Moth, Whitelined Sphinx. **Planthopper,** Citrus Flatid.
Scale, Acuminate, Azalea Bark (white cotton, black mold on twigs); Camellia Mining; Camphor; Cyanophyllum; Florida Red; Greedy; Latania; Oleander; Peony (serious in South; brown humps, white circles in branches); Pit; Pyriform; Red Bay; Soft Azalea (resembles Azalea Bark); Walnut.
Thrips, Greenhouse (leaves pale, covered with black dots); Madroña.
Walkingstick, Twostriped.
Weevil, Black Vine (grubs injure roots; beetles notch leaves at night, girdle stem); Japanese; Strawberry Root.
Whitefly, Azalea; Mulberry; Rhododendron.

Spraying to control azalea lace bug is almost always necessary. Bark and peony scales, thrips and mites are more of a problem in warm climates.

BALSAM-APPLE (*Momordica balsamina*)

Scale, Green; Hemispherical; Lesser Snow.

BALSAM, GARDEN (*Impatiens balsamina*)

Aphid, Impatiens; Spirea.
Beetle, Spotted Cucumber (eats holes in blossoms).
Bug, Tarnished Plant (blackens new shoots).
Mealybug, Citrus.

BALSAM FIR (see Fir)

BALSAM-ROOT (*Balsamorhiza*)

Bug, Lace. **Fly,** in flower head. **Mite,** Balsamroot.

BAMBOO (*Bambusa*)

Aphid, Bamboo (yellow with black markings).
Mite, Bamboo. **Mealybugs.**

Scale, Bamboo; Cottony Bamboo (white sacs at leaf axils) ; Cottony-cushion; Dictyospermum; Green; Hemispherical; Proteus.

BANANA (*Musa*)
Aphid, Banana; Green Peach. Borer, Banana Root.
Mealybug, Citrus; Longtailed; Pineapple; Yucca.
Scale, Acuminate; Black; Boisduval's; Brown Soft; California Red; Coconut; Cyanophyllum; Dictyospermum; Fern; Florida Red; Green; Hemispherical; Latania; Oleander; Oriental; Pyriform; Rufous; Tesselated.
Whitefly, Avocado; Citrus.

BANANA-SHRUB (*Michelis fuscata*)
Scale, Tuliptree. Whitefly, Citrus.

BANKSIA (Australian Honeysuckle)
Scale, Black Araucaria; Purple.

BANYAN (*Ficus benghalensis*)
Mealybug, Longtailed.
Scale, Black; Chinese Obscure; Green Shield; Mining.

BARBERRY (*Berberis*)
Aphid, Barberry (small, yellow-green, on new shoots).
Beetle, Asiatic Garden. Moth, Eightspotted Forester.
Scale, Barberry (convex, reddish brown, soft) ; Florida Wax.
Webworm, Barberry (webs over twigs).
Weevil, Japanese. Whitefly, Barberry; Greenhouse.

BASSWOOD (see Linden)

BAUHINIA (Mountain Ebony, Orchid Tree)
Beetle, Cuban May. Mealybug, Citrus; Longtailed. Mite, Yuma Spider.
Scale, Acuminate; Black; Black Thread; Brown Soft; Cottony-cushion; Cyanophyllum; Dictyospermum; Fern; Florida Red; Latania; Lesser Snow; Long Soft; Mining; Pustule; Proteus; Pyriform; Quahogshaped; Rufous; White Peach.

BAY, LOBLOLLY (*Gordonia lasianthus*)
Beetle, Rhabdopterus. Psyllid.

BAY, SWEET (*Laurus*—see Laurel)

BAY, SWEET (*Magnolia*—see Sweetbay)

BAYBERRY, WAX-MYRTLE (*Myrica cerifera*)
Beetle, Pine Colaspis.
Caterpillar, Chainspotted Geometer; Redhumped; Stinging Rose.
Moth, Crinkled Flannel. **Mealybug,** Longtailed; Striped.
Scale, Acuminate; Black; Barnacle; Dictyospermum; Florida Red; Florida Wax; Glover; Green Shield; Hemispherical; Long Soft; Latania; Nigra; Purple; Pustule; Pyriform; Tesselated.

BEAN, LIMA BEAN (*Phaseolus*)
Aphid, Bean (small, black); Cowpea; Green Peach; Melon; Pea; Potato; Solanum Root; Turnip.
Armyworm, Fall; Yellowstriped.
Beetle, Banded Cucumber; Bean Leaf; Fuller Rose; Grape Colaspis; June; Mexican Bean (yellow with black spots, the most serious bean pest); Oriental; Palestriped Flea; Potato Flea; Redheaded Flea; Red Turnip; Rose Chafer; Spotted Cucumber; Striped Blister; Striped Cucumber; Western Striped Cucumber; Whitefringed.
Borer, European Corn; Lesser Cornstalk; Lima-bean Pod; Lima-bean Vine.
Bug, Garden Fleahopper; Green Stink; Harlequin; Leaffooted; Lygus; Onespot Stink; Pumpkin; Rapid Plant; Say Stink; Tarnished Plant.
Caterpillar, Alfalfa; Green Cloverworm; Saltmarsh; Yellow Woollybear.
Cricket, Field. **Curculio,** Cowpea.
Cutworm, Black; Granulate; Western Bean. **Earworm,** Corn (feeds on pods).
Leafhopper, Beet; Potato. **Leafminer,** Serpentine.
Leafroller, Bean; Obliquebanded; Omnivorous.
Leaf Skeletonizer, Bean. **Leaftier,** Celery.
Maggot, Seedcorn (tunnels in sprouting seeds).
Mealybug, Grape. **Millipedes.**
Mite, Pacific Spider; Sixspotted; Strawberry Spider; Tumid Spider; Twospotted. **Moth,** Diamondback.
Springtail, Garden. **Termites.**
Thrips, Bean; Onion; Western Flower. Treehopper, Threecornered Alfalfa.
Webworm, Beet; Garden.
Weevil, Bean (grubs in stored beans); Bean Stalk; Citrus Root; Japanese (on lima bean).
Whitefly, Glacial; Greenhouse. **Wireworm,** Plains False; Sugarbeet.

Most gardeners have to spray or dust for Mexican bean beetles; often the other pests can be ignored.

BEARBERRY (*Arctostaphylos*)
Aphid, Manzanita Leafgall; Rose and Bearberry.
Whitefly, Bearberry.

BEAUTY-BUSH (*Kolkwitzia*)
Scale, Purple.

BEAUTY-LEAF (*Calophyllum*)
Mealybug, Coconut.
Scale, Coconut; Cottonycushion; Florida Red; Tesselated.

BEEBALM (*Monarda*)
Aphid, Green Peach; Melon; Mint.

BEECH (*Fagus*)
Aphid, Beech; Beech Blight (white, woolly) ; Giant Bark.
Beetle, Birch Bark; Grape Flea.
Borer, Brown Wood; Flatheaded Appletree; Oak Timberworm; Pacific
  Flatheaded; Pigeon Tremex; Twolined Chestnut.
Bug, Birch Lace.   Cankerworm, Fall; Spring.
Caterpillar, Eastern Tent; Hemlock Looper; Redhumped Oakworm;
  Saddled Prominent; Walnut; Yellownecked.
Leafcutter, Maple.   Leafhopper, Grape.   Leaftier, Beech.
Mite, Beech; Oak.
Moth, Gypsy; Imperial; Io; Leopard; Luna; Rusty Tussock.
Scale, Beech (circular, pale yellow with wax, associated with Nectria
  disease) ; Black; Cottonycushion; Cottony Maple; European Fruit
  Lecanium; Osborn's; Oystershell; Putnam; San Jose.
Spanworm, Elm.   Weevil, New York.

BEET (*Beta*)
Aphid, Bean; Corn Root; Green Peach; Melon; Solanum Root;
  Sugarbeet Root.
Armyworm, Beet.
Beetle, Asiatic Garden; Beet Leaf; Carrot (works on roots) ; Hop
  Flea; Oriental; Palestriped Flea; Potato Flea (minute, black, makes
  pinholes in leaves) ; Rose Chafer; Spinach Carrion; Spinach Flea;
  Spotted Cucumber; Striped Blister; Toothed Flea; Western Striped
  Cucumber.
Borer, Beet Petiole; European Corn.

Bug, Alfalfa Plant; False Chinch; Garden Fleahopper; Harlequin; Tarnished Plant.
Caterpillar, Cabbage Looper; Celery Looper; Yellow Woollybear.
Cutworm, Pale Western.
Leafhopper, Beet (important as vectory of curly-top disease).
Leafminer, Beet; Serpentine; Spinach (common).
Maggot, Cabbage; Seedcorn.   **Moth,** Whitelined Sphinx.
Springtail, Garden (occasional injury to seedlings).
Termites.   Thrips, Onion.
Webworm, Alfalfa; Cabbage; Garden; Southern Beet; Spotted Beet.
Weevil, Vegetable (injurious in the Gulf States).
Wireworm, Eastern Field.

BEGONIA

Aphid, Crescentmarked Lily; Melon.   **Beetle,** Fuller Rose.
Caterpillar, Orange Tortrix (rolls leaves).
Mealybug, Citrus (common; white cotton at leaf axils); Longtailed.
Mite, Broad (leaves glassy); Cyclamen (plants stunted); Twospotted.
Scale, Brown Soft; Cyanophyllum; Fern; Florida Red; Hemispherical; Latania.   **Termites.**
Thrips, Banded Greenhouse; Greenhouse; Sugarbeet.
Weevil, Black Vine (grubs destroy roots; serious on tuberous begonia).
Whitefly, Greenhouse (very common).

BERGAMOT (*Citrus bergamia*)
Scale, Hemispherical; Purple.

BIGNONIA (Cross Vine; Trumpet Flower)
Mealybug, Citrus.
Scale, Barnacle; Hemispherical; Lesser Snow.
Whitefly, Greenhouse.

BILLBERGIA
Scale, Boisduval's; Cyanophyllum; Dictyospermum; Flyspeck; Latania; Pineapple; Proteus.

BIRCH (*Betula*)
Aphid, Birch; European Birch; Foxglove; Giant Bark; Witchhazel Gall; Witchhazel Leafgall.
Beetle, Birch Bark; Japanese; June; Pitted Ambrosia.
Borer, Bronze Birch (kills from the top down); Sapwood Timberworm.
Bug, Alder Lace; Birch Lace.   **Butterfly,** Tiger Swallowtail.

Cankerworm, Fall, Spring. **Casebearer,** Birch; Birch Tubemaker.

Caterpillar, Chainspotted Geometer; Eastern Tent; Forest Tent; Hemlock Looper; Linden Looper; Redhumped; Saddled Prominent; Variable Oakleaf; Yellownecked.

Leafcutter, Maple.

Leafminer, Birch (serious, nearly half of each leaf blighted, brown).

Leafroller, Obliquebanded. **Leaf Skeletonizer,** Birch.

Mite, Oak.

Moth, American Dagger; Cecropia; Crinkled Flannel; Elm Sphinx; Gypsy; Io; Leopard; Imperial; Oriental; Polyphemus; Rusty Tussock; Spotted Tussock.

Sawfly, Birch; Dusky Birch.

Scale, European Fruit Lecanium; Greedy; Oystershell; San Jose; Terrapin; other species.

Spanworm, Bruce; Elm.

Wasp, Giant Hornet. **Webworm,** Fall. **Weevil,** Willow Flea.

BIRD-OF-PARADISE (See Strelitzia)

BISHOPWOOD (*Bischofia*)

Scale, Acuminate; Cockerell; Florida Red; Pyriform; Tesselated.

BITTERSWEET (*Celastrus*)

Aphid, Bean (black, common); Spirea (green).

Scale, Euonymus (almost always encrusting vines, covering leaves); Oystershell; San Jose.

Treehopper, Twomarked.

BLACKBERRY (*Rubus*)

Aphid, Blackberry.

Beetle, Fuller Rose; Green June; Imbricated Snout; Rose Chafer; Rose Leaf; Whitefringed.

Borer, Currant; Pacific Flatheaded; Raspberry Cane; Raspberry Crown; Rednecked Cane; San Jose.

Bud Moth, Eyespotted.

Bug, Consperse Stink; Negro (bad taste in berries).

Caterpillar, Redhumped; Saddled Prominent; Yellownecked; Yellow Woollybear.

Cricket, Blackhorned; Snowy Tree. **Horntail,** Raspberry.

Leafminer, Apple Trumpet; Blackberry.

Leafroller, Fruittree; Obliquebanded; Strawberry.

Maggot, Raspberry Cane (tips wilt).

Mealybug, Citrophilus; Coleman's.

Mite, Dryberry; Pacific Spider; Redberry; Twospotted.
Moth, Io; Strawberry Crown; Western Tussock.
Psyllid, Blackberry (occasional distortion, stunting).
Rootworm, Strawberry.
Sawfly, Blackberry (leaves eaten by blue-green larvae).
Scale, Cottony Maple; European Fruit Lecanium; Parlatorialike; Rose; San Jose. Wasp, Blackberry Knotgall.
Weevil, Apple Flea; Black Vine; Cribrate; Pea Leaf; Strawberry; Strawberry Root.
Whitefly, Glacial; Greenhouse.

BLACKBERRY-LILY (*Belamcanda*)
Aphid, Tulip Bulb.   Borer, Iris.
Scale, Florida Red.

BLEEDING-HEART (*Dicentra*)
Scale, Latania; Quohogshaped.

BLADDERNUT (*Staphylea*)
Scale, Putnam.

BLUEBERRY (*Vaccinium corymbosum*)
Beetle, Blueberry Flea; Green June; Pitted Ambrosia; Rhabdopterus.
Borer, Azalea Stem; Blueberry Crown Girdler; Blueberry Tip; Rhododendron.
Caterpillar, Azalea; Chainspotted Geometer; Forest Tent; Hemlock Looper; Yellownecked.
Curculio, Plum.   Cutworm, Black Army.
Fruitworm, Cherry; Cranberry (wormy berries).
Leafhopper, Sharpnosed (vector of stunt disease).
Leafminer, Blotch.   Leafroller, Redbanded.
Maggot, Blueberry (common cause of wormy berries).
Mite, Blueberry Bud; Yellow Spider.   Moths.
Scale, Azalea Bark; Barnacle; Cottony Maple; European Fruit Lecanium; Florida Wax; Japanese Wax; Oak Eriococcus; Oleander; Oystershell; Parlatorialike; Putnam; Red Bay; Terrapin.
Spanworm, Currant.   Spittlebug, Dogwood.
Thrips, Blueberry (curls, deforms buds and leaves).
Wasp, Blueberry Stem Gall. Webworm, Fall. Weevil, Blossom; Cranberry.

BOEHMERIA (Chinese Silk-plant)
Scale, Florida Red.

BOTTLE-BRUSH (*Callistemon*)
Caterpillar, Omnivorous Looper. Mealybug, Citrus.
Scale, Acuminate; Black; Black Thread; Brown Soft; Coconut; Cottonycushion; Cyanophyllum; Dictyospermum; Florida Red; European Fiorinia; Florida Wax; Green Shield; Long Soft; Latania; Proteus; Pyriform; Tea; Tesselated.

BOUGAINVILLEA (*Buginvillaea*)
Caterpillar, Bougainvillea. Mealybug, Longtailed.
Orthezia, Greenhouse.
Scale, Brown Soft; Cottonycushion; Cyanophyllum; Florida Red; Hemispherical; Latania; Mining; Pustule; Quohogshaped.

BOUVARDIA
Mealybug, Citrus.

BOYSENBERRY (*Rubus*)
Leafroller, Omnivorous. Sawfly.
Scale, Latania; Long Soft. Whitefly, Glacial.
See Blackberry, Raspberry for other possible pests.

BOXELDER (*Acer negundo*)
Aphid, Boxelder (green, hairy, with conspicuous honeydew).
Bagworm. Beetle, Sweetpotato Flea.
Borer, Boxelder Twig; Flatheaded Appletree; Pacific Flatheaded.
Bug, Boxelder (a common nuisance); Green Stink; Western Boxelder.
Caterpillar, Forest Tent; Greenstriped Mapleworm; Omnivorous Looper.
Leafroller, Boxelder; Fruittree; Obliquebanded.
Mite, Boxelder; Willamette. Mealybug.
Moth, American Dagger; Cecropia; Smeared Dagger; Spotted Tussock.
Psyllid, Boxelder.
Scale, Brown Soft; California Red; Cottony Maple; European Fruit Lecanium; Gloomy; Oystershell; Terrapin; Walnut.
Webworm, Fall.

BOXWOOD (*Buxus*)
Leafminer, Boxwood (common, injurious; blisters in leaves).
Mealybug, Comstock; Ground.
Mite, Boxwood (leaves grayish); Twospotted. Moth.
Planthopper. Psyllid, Boxwood (terminal leaves curled into cups).

Scale, California Red; Camellia Mining; Chaff; Coconut; Cottony-cushion; Florida Wax; Glover; Greedy; Holly; Japanese; Lesser Snow; Oleander; Oystershell; Proteus; Pyriform; Walnut; White Peach.
Wasp, Giant Hornet (tears bark). Webworm, Boxwood.

BRAZILIAN PEPPER-TREE (*Schinus terebinthifolius*)
Leafhopper.
Scale, Acuminate; Barnacle; Black; Black Thread; Brown Soft; Chaff; Cottonycushion; Florida Wax; Green Shield; Hemispherical; Mango Shield; Mining; Lesser Snow; Olive; Parlatorialike; Proteus; Purple; Pyriform; Quohogshaped; White Peach.

BREADFRUIT (*Artocarpus*)
Mealybug, Longtailed.
Scale, California Red; Latania; Red Wax.

BROADBEAN (*Vicia faba*)
Weevil, Broadbean.

BROCCOLI (*Brassica oleracea*)
Aphid, Cabbage (common, grayish lice on leaves, flower heads); Turnip.
Beetle, Potato Flea (shot holes in leaves).
Caterpillar, Cabbage Looper; Imported Cabbageworm.
Leafhopper, Flavescent. Maggot, Cabbage (common, seedlings wilt).
See Cabbage for other possible pests.

BROMELIADS (Air Plants)
Scale, Boisduval's; Brown Soft; Flyspeck; Latania; Pineapple; Proteus.

BROOM (*Genista*)
Aphid, Bean (black). Caterpillar, Genista.
Scale, Greedy (gray, convex); Oleander (round, flat, yellow).

BROOM, SCOTCH (*Cytisus*)
Bug, Plant; Lace. Leafhopper.
Scale, White Peach. Treehopper.

BROUSSONETIA (Paper Mulberry)
Scale, White Peach.

BROWALLIA
Aphid, Corn Root; Western Aster Root.
Leafhopper, Aster.

BRUNFELSIA (Raintree)
Scale, Barnacle; Mining; Oleander; Pryiform; Rufous.

BRUSSELS SPROUTS (*Brassica oleracea* var. *gemmifera*)
Aphid, Cabbage.
Beetle, Western Striped Flea.   Bug, Harlequin.
Caterpillar, Cabbage Looper; Imported Cabbageworm.
Maggot, Cabbage.
See also Cabbage.

BUCKEYE (*Aesculus*)
Beetle, Striped Cucumber.   Caterpillar, Omnivorous Looper.
Mealybug, Grape.   Moth, Whitemarked Tussock.
Scale, Cottonycushion; Cottony Maple.
See also Horsechestnut.

BUCKTHORN (*Rhamnus*)
Aphid, Buckthorn; Melon.   Moth, Oriental.
Scale, Barnacle; Florida Wax; Gloomy; Long Soft; San Jose; Terrapin.

BUDDLEIA (Butterfly Bush)
Beetle, Japanese.   Butterfly, Checker Spot.
Moth, Buddleia.   Scale, Latania; White Peach.
Thrips, Banded Greenhouse.

BUFFALOBERRY (*Shepherdia*)
Aphid, Oleaster-thistle; Russian-olive; Polygonum.

BUMELIA (False Buckthorn)
Fly, Bumelia Fruit.
Scale. Cottonycushion; Cottony Maple; Florida Wax; Proteus; Pyriform; Terrapin.

BUTTERCUP (*Ranunculus*)
Aphid, Corn Root; Poplar Foldedleaf.   Thrips.

BUTTERFLY-PEA (*Clitoria*)
Orthezia, Greenhouse.
Scale, Lesser Snow; Pustule.

BUTTERFLY WEED (*Asclepias*)

Aphid, Green Peach; Melon; Oleander.
Beetle, Argus Tortoise.   **Bug,** Small Milkweed.
Butterfly, Monarch (greenish caterpillar with dark bands).
Leafminer, Serpentine (winding tunnels in leaves).
Mealybug, Citrus.
Scale, Cyanophyllum; Pustule; San Jose.
Thrips, Western Flower.

BUTTERNUT (*Juglans cinerea*)

Beetle, Hickory Saperda; June.
Borer, Painted Hickory.   **Bug,** Walnut Lace.
Caterpillar, Hickory Horned Devil; Walnut; Yellow Woollybear.
Curculio, Butternut; Hickory Nut.
Moth, Hickory Tussock; Imperial; Luna; Walnut Sphinx.
Rootworm, Strawberry (beetle makes minute holes in foliage).
Sawfly, Butternut Woollyworm (leaves eaten by hairy larvae).
Scale, European Fruit Lecanium; Oystershell; Walnut (round, gray).
Treehopper, Twomarked.

BUTTONBUSH (*Cephalanthus*)

Aphid, Cephalanthus.
Scale, Green; Pyriform; San Jose; Tuliptree; White Peach.

CABBAGE (*Brassica oleracea*)

Aphid, Cabbage (gray lice, numerous on underside of leaves); Green Peach; Turnip.
Armyworm, Fall.
Beetle, Argus Tortoise; Black Blister; Cabbage Flea; Hop Flea; Imbricated Snout; Potato Flea; Red Turnip; Rose Chafer; Sinuate Flea; Spotted Cucumber; Striped Flea; Western Black Flea; Western Striped Flea; Whitefringed; Yellowmargined Leaf.
Bug, False Chinch; Green Stink; Harlequin (red and black, southern); Horned Squash; Tarnished Plant.
Caterpillar, Cabbage Looper; Crossstriped Cabbageworm; Gulf White Cabbageworm; Imported Cabbageworm; Purplebacked Cabbageworm; Southern Cabbageworm; Soybean Looper; Yellow Woollybear.
Cricket, Mole.   **Curculio,** Cabbage(ash-gray weevil); Cabbage Seedstalk.
Cutworms.   Earworm, Corn.
Leafminer, Serpentine.   **Leaftier,** Celery.
Maggot, Cabbage (wilts seedlings); Seedcorn.

Millipedes. Moth, Diamondback (green caterpillar).
Slugs (several species make holes in leaves, enter heads).
Termites. Thrips, Onion.
Webworm, Beet; Cabbage. Weevil, Vegetable.

CACTUS
Aphid, Tulip Bulb (on roots). Beetle, Fig; Longhorned.
Mealybug, Citrus; Ground (may kill plants); Longtailed; Striped;
other species.
Midge, Cactus Fruit Gall.
Mite, Desert Spider; Twospotted (plants gray, webby).
Orthezia, Greenhouse (dark with white wax).
Scale, Boisduval's; Cactus; Cottony Cochineal; Cyanophyllum; Dic-
tyospermum; Greedy; Latania; Lesser Snow; Oleander; Oriental;
Pineapple; Proteus; Pyriform; Tesselated; Walnut.
Thrips, Date Palm. Weevil.
Use sprays on cacti with some caution. A pointed stick or stiff
brush will help to remove scales and mealybugs. For ground mealy-
bugs on roots, wash off all soil and repot.

CAESALPINIA
Scale, Dictyospermum; Quohogshaped.

CAJEPUT (*Melaleuca leucadendra*)
Mealybug, Citrus.
Scale, Acuminate Black; Black Thread; Brown Soft; Chaff; Coco-
nut; Dictyospermum; Fern; Florida Red; Florida Wax; Green
Shield; Pyriform; Tea; Tesselated.

CALADIUM
Aphid. Beetle, Scarab. Mealybug, Pineapple.
Scale, Boisduval's; Brown Soft; Cottonycushion; Florida Red; Lesser
Snow.

CALABASH (*Crescentia cujete*)
Orthezia, Greenhouse. Scale, Black Thread.

CALATHEA
Scale, Cyanophyllum.

CALCEOLARIA
Aphid, Crescentmarked Lily; Geranium; Green Peach.
Whitefly, Greenhouse.

CALENDULA

Aphid, Bean (black, common); Crescentmarked Lily; Green Peach; Lettuce; Melon; Western Aster Root.
Beetle, Black Blister; Spotted Cucumber.
Borer, Stalk.   Bug, Tarnished Plant.   Butterfly, Painted Lady.
Caterpillar, Cabbage Looper; Soybean Looper; Yellow Woollybear.
Leafhopper, Aster (transmits aster yellows); Redbanded.   Mealybug, Mexican.
Scale, Ground Pearls.
Thrips, Composite (in flower head).   Whitefly, Greenhouse.

CALIFORNIA CHRISTMASBERRY,
TOYON (*Photinia arbutifolia*)

Aphid, Rose and Bearberry; Woolly Hawthorn.
Borer, California Buprestid; Pacific Flatheaded.
Bug, Toyon Lace (common, leaves lose color, have brown flecks).
Caterpillar, California Tent; Omnivorous Looper.
Mite, Blister; Platanus.   Moth, Western Tussock.
Scale, Black; European Fruit Lecanium; Italian Pear (shiny dark gray, sunken in bark; associated with lichens); Oystershell; San Jose.
Thrips, Greenhouse; Toyon.
Weevil, Black Fruittree.
Whitefly, Crown; Inconspicuous; Iridescent; Pruinose.

CALIFORNIA COFFEEBERRY (*Rhamnus california*)

Aphid, Buckthorn (?).
Borer, Flatheaded Cherrytree; Pacific Flatheaded.
Butterfly, Eurymedon.   Leafminer, Nepticula.
Moth, Ceanothus Silk; Western Tussock.   Thrips, Robust.
Whitefly, Acacia; Crown, Glacial; Greenhouse; Inconspicuous; Iridescent.

CALIFORNIA-LAUREL (*Umbellularia californica*)

Aphid, California-laurel; Crescentmarked Lily.
Borer, Banded Alder; Branch and Twig.
Caterpillar, Omnivorous Looper (yellow, green or pink, striped).
Leafminer, Cameraria Gall.   Scale, Brown Soft; Greedy.
Thrips, Onion; Pear.
Whitefly, Inconspicuous; Iridescent; Laurel.

CALIFORNIA-NUTMEG (*Torreya californica*)

Scale, Black; Parlatoria; Pineleaf; Proteus.

CALIFORNIA-POPPY (*Eschscholzia californica*)
Mealybug, Grape.

CALLA (*Zantedeschia*)
Aphid, Crescentmarked Lily; Geranium; Green Peach.
Beetle, Grapevine Hoplia.
Caterpillar, Yellow Woollybear.   Leaftier, Omnivorous.
Mealybug, Grape; Longtailed.   Mite, Narcissus Bulb; Twospotted.
Scale, Brown Soft.
Thrips, Banded Greenhouse; Greenhouse; Onion; Sugarbeet.

CALLIANDRA (Powder-Puff)
Scale, Parlatorialike; Pustule.   Treehopper, Thornbug.

CALLICARPA (Beauty-berry; French Mulberry)
Mealybug, Citrus.
Scale, Black; Brown Soft; Florida Wax; Green Shield; Latania;
   Pustule; White Peach.

CALYCANTHUS (Sweetshrub)
Scale, Dictyospermum; Florida Red; Latania.

CAMELLIA
Aphid, Black Citrus (curls new leaves); Melon; Green Peach; Or-
   nate.
Beetle, Fuller Rose; Rhabdopterus; Grape Colaspis.
Caterpillar, Omnivorous Looper; Orange Tortrix; Western Parsley.
Curculio, Cambium.   Cutworm, Spotted.
Leafroller, Fruittree.   Leaftier, Celery.
Mealybug, Citrus; Longtailed.
Mite, Camellia Bud; Camellia Rust (rusty foliage); Southern Red.
Planthopper, Citrus Flatid.   Rootworm, Cranberry.
Scale, Black; Black Thread; Brown Soft; Camellia (brown, leaves
   may drop, important in Southeast); Camellia Mining; Camellia
   Parlatoria (common on Pacific Coast); Camphor; Chaff; Cottony-
   cushion; Cottony Taxus; Cyanophyllum; Degenerate; Dictyosper-
   mum; European Fiorinia; Fern; Florida Red; Florida Wax;
   Greedy; Green Shield; Hemispherical; Japanese Wax; Latania;
   Mining; Oleander; Oystershell; Parlatorialike; Peony (white cir-
   cles on branches, sometimes serious); Proteus; Purple; Pyriform;
   Quohogshaped; Tea (the worst pest in Gulf States, white filaments
   on underside of leaves); San Jose.

Weevil, Black Vine; Cribrate; Japanese; Strawberry Root.
Whitefly, Citrus; Greenhouse.

An oil spray spring and fall has been standard for control of scales but phosphates are now popular, with dimethoate relatively safe and particularly effective for tea scale.

CAMPANULA (Bluebell, Canterbury Bells)

Aphid, Foxglove. Slugs. Thrips, Onion.

CAMPHOR-TREE (*Cinnamomum camphora*)

Mite, Avocado Red (leaves turn reddish) ; Platanus; Southern Red.
Scale, Brown Soft; Camphor (convex, dark brown, may cause death) ; Chaff; Cyanophyllum; Dictyospermum; Fern; Florida Red; Florida Wax; Greedy; Latania; Lesser Snow; Oystershell; Parlatoria-like; Pyriform; Red Bay; Tesselated.
Thrips, Camphor (most injurious; buds, branches die; bark cracks).

CANDLENUT, CANDLEBERRY-TREE (*Aleruites moluccana*)

Mealybug, Longtailed.
Scale, Florida Red; Latania; Lesser Snow.

CANDYTUFT (*Iberis*)

Moth, Diamondback.

CANNA

Aphid, Potato.
Beetle, Fuller Rose; Goldsmith; Japanese (common on flowers); Spotted Cucumber.
Caterpillar, Saddleback; Yellow Woollybear.
Barworm, Corn.
Leafroller, Larger Canna (green caterpillar rolls leaves); Lesser Canna.
Leaftier, Celery. Mealybug, Citrus, Pineapple.
Scale, Coconut; Dictyospermum; Florida Red; Green Shield; Latania (small, gray, convex) ; Oriental; Pineapple (white and gray).

CANTALOUPE (see Melon)

CAPE-HONEYSUCKLE (*Tecomaria*)

Scale, Black Thread; Barnacle; Brown Soft; Latania; Mining; Quohogshaped.

CAPE-JASMINE (see Gardenia)

CAPE-MARIGOLD (*Dimortheca*)
Leafhopper, Aster.

CARAGANA (Pea-Tree)
Aphids. Beetle, Caragana Blister. Bug, Caragana Plant.

CARAWAY (*Carum*)
Aphid, Willow.
Caterpillar, Celeryworm (green, black-banded).

CARDINAL-FLOWER (*Lobelia cardinalis*)
Aphid, Waterlily.
Bug, Negro (red to black, southern).
Leafroller, Redbanded. Wireworms.

CARISSA (Natal-plum)
Mite, Tuckerellid.
Scale, Black; Barnacle; Chaff; Cyanophyllum; Dictyospermum; Florida Red; Green Shield; Hemispherical; Latania; Lesser Snow; Oriental; Proteus; Purple; Pyriform; Quohogshaped; Tesselated; Yellow.
Thrips, Greenhouse.

CARNATION (*Dianthus caryophyllus*)
Aphid, Green Peach. Armyworm, Beet.
Beetle, Fuller Rose.
Caterpillar, Cabbage Looper; Salt-marsh; Soybean Looper.
Cutworm, Spotted (climbs stems).
Leafminer, Carnation.
Leafroller, Obliquebanded; Omnivorous. Leaftier, Celery.
Maggot, Carnation; Carnation Tip. Mealybug, Grape.
Mite, Carnation; Carnation Bud; Grass; Twospotted (leaves pale, dusty).
Scale, Brown Soft; Oriental; Parlatorialike.
Thrips, Gladiolus; Onion; Western Flower.

CAROB (*Ceratonia siliqua*)
Borer, Carpenterworm. Caterpillar, Navel Orangeworm.
Mealybug, Citrus; Longtailed; Mexican.
Scale, Brown Soft; California Red; Greedy; Latania; Long Soft; Lesser Snow; Oleander. Whiteflies.

CARROT (*Daucus carota*)

Ants, Pavement.
Aphid, Bean; Corn Root (white, powdery, at roots); Green Peach; Honeysuckle and Parsnip; Leafcurl Plum; Lettuce Root; Solanum Root; Tulip Bulb; Willow.
Beetle, Asiatic Garden, Black Blister; Carrot; Palestriped Flea; Potato Flea.
Bug, Rapid Plant.   Butterfly, Western Parsley.
Caterpillar, Celeryworm (green, black-banded); Yellow Woollybear.
Fly, Carrot Rust (rusty tunnels in roots); Onion Bulb.
Leafhopper, Aster; Mountain.
Millipedes.   Mite, Desert Spider.
Termites.   Thrips, Onion.   Webworm, Alfalfa; Beet.
Weevil, Carrot (tunnels in roots); Vegetable (eats foliage at night).
Wireworm, Eastern Field; Western Field; other species.

CASHEW (*Anacardium*)

Scale, Acuminate.

CASSAVA (*Manihot esculenta*)

Mealybug, Coconut.   Mite, Twospotted.
Scale, Black; Cassava; Lesser Snow.

CASSIA (Golden-shower)

Beetle, Cuban May.
Bug, Eggplant Lace (brown and yellow).   Caterpillar.
Mite, Texas Citrus.
Scale, Black; Brown Soft; Cottonycushion; Florida Red; Dictyospermum; Latania; Lesser Snow; Long Soft; Oleander; Oriental; Pustule; Pyriform; White Peach.

CASTOR-BEAN (*Ricinus*)

Armyworm, Southern (may defoliate and kill).
Bug, Alfalfa Plant.
Leafhopper, Potato.   Leafminer, Serpentine.
Mite, Lewis Spider; Texas Citrus; Twospotted.
Scale, Cottonycushion; Green; Lesser Snow; White Peach.
Webworm, Garden.

CATALINA CHERRY (*Prunus lyoni*)

Borer, Pacific Flatheaded.   Caterpillar, Filbertworm.
Leafminer, Apple.   Moth, Catalina Cherry (caterpillars in seeds).

Scale, European Fruit Lecanium.
Whitefly, Kellog's (looks like small white flower).

CATALPA
Aphid, Melon. Bug, Green Stink.
Mealybug, Comstock (white fluffs in bark crevices; serious).
Midge, Catalpa (small brown spots in leaves).
Moth, Catalpa Sphinx (large, dark caterpillar; defoliates).
Planthopper. Scale, San Jose; White Peach.

CATNIP (*Nepeta*)
Leafhopper, Grape. Webworm, Small Beet.

CATTAIL (*Typha*)
Aphid, Mealy Plum; Melon; Waterlily.
Borer, Potato Tuberworm. Grasshoppers. Mites.

CAULIFLOWER (*Brassica oleracea* var. *botrytis*)
Aphid, Cabbage; Turnip.
Beetle, Striped Flea; Western Black Flea; Western Striped Flea.
Bug, Harlequin; Tarnished Plant.
Caterpillar, Cabbage Looper; Imported Cabbageworm; Yellow
  Woollybear.
Curculio, Cabbage (weevil attacking seedlings).
Leaftier, celery.
Maggot, Cabbage (seedlings wilt). Moth, Diamondback.
Springtail, Garden (on seedlings). Thrips, Onion.
Webworm, Cabbage. Weevil, Vegetable.
  See Cabbage for other possible pests.

CEANOTHUS
Aphid, Ceanothus (red-brown to black); Cowpea; Crescentmarked
  Lily.
Borer, Flatheaded Cherrytree; Pacific Flatheaded.
Bug, Ceanothus Lace (black and brown; leaves whitened; common).
Butterfly, California Tortoiseshell.
Caterpillar, Western Tent.
Mealybug, Grape; Ground; Yucca. Mite, Lewis Spider; Ceanothus.
Moth, Douglas Fir Tussock; Ramosia.
Scale, Greedy; San Jose; Scurfy; Willow.
Spittlebug, Alder. Thrips, Madroña.

CEDAR (*Cedrus*)
>   DEODAR (*Cedrus deodara*) and Cedar of Lebanon
>   (*C. libanotica*)

Aphid, Bowlegged Fir.
Beetle, Cedar Bark; Northern Cedar Bark; Pine Colaspis; Western Cedar Bark.
Borer, Blackhorned Pine; Cedar Tree; Western Cedar.
Horntail, Western. **Mealybug,** Grape; Juniper; Taxus.
Sawfly, Cedar Cone; Redheaded Pine.
Scale, Black; Brown Soft; Cottonycushion; Florida Red; Florida Wax; Newstead's; Pine; Pine Needle.
Weevil, Deodar.

CEDAR, INCENSE (*Libocedrus*)
Beetle, Cypress Bark. **Mealybug,** Cypress.
Scale, Cypress; Juniper; Pine Needle; Putnam.

CELERIAC (*Apium graveolens* var. *rapaceum*)
Fly, Carrot Rust.

CELERY (*Apium graveolens* var. *dulce*)
Aphid, Crescentmarked Lily; Green Peach; Honeysuckle and Parsnip; Leafcurl Plum; Melon; Rhodes Grass; Willow.
Armyworm, Southern.
Beetle, Carrot; Potato Flea. **Borer,** European Corn.
Bug, Garden Fleahopper; Negro; Tarnished Plant.
Butterfly, Western Parsley.
Caterpillar, Cabbage Looper; Celery Looper; Parsleyworm (green with black bands); Yellow Woollybear.
Fly, Carrot Rust (plants wilt; outer leaves turn yellow).
Leafhopper, Aster; Beet. **Leafroller,** Obliquebanded; Omnivorous.
Leaftier, Celery (major pest, webbing foliage, mining in hearts).
Maggot, Cabbage. **Mite,** Desert Spider; Tumid Spider; Twospotted.
Thrips, Onion. **Webworm,** Parsnip. **Weevil,** Carrot.

CENTURY PLANT (*Agave*)
Borer, Stalk. **Mealybug,** Grape.
Scale, Black Thread; Brown Soft; California Red; Chaff; Dictyospermum; Fern; Florida Red; Lesser Snow; Oleander; Proteus; Pustule.
Thrips, Dracaena. **Weevil,** Sisal; Yucca (black billbug).

CEPHALOTAXUS (Plum-yew)
Scale, Dictyospermum.

CERIMAN (*Monstera deliciosa*)
Mealybug, Longtailed.
Scale, Acuminate; Black; Black Thread; Brown Soft; Chaff; Florida Red; Green Shield; Proteus; Pyriform.

CEROPEGIA
Mite, Privet.

CHALICE-VINE (*Solandra*)
Scale, Chaff; Green Shield; Pineapple.

CHAMAECYPARIS (see Retinospora)

CHASTE-TREE (*Vitex*)
Scale, Barnacle; Latania; White Peach.

CHAYOTE (*Sechium edule*)
Mealybug, Citrus.

CHERIMOYA (*Annona cherimola*)
Mealybug, Coconut.
Scale, Cyanophyllum; Coconut; Hemispherical; Oleander; Pyriform.
Thrips, Greenhouse.

CHERRY (*Prunus avium; P. cerasus*)
Aphid, Black Cherry (prevalent on young shoots, curls leaves); Green Peach; Malaheb Cherry; Oat Bird-cherry; Red and Black Cherry; Waterlily.
Beetle, Asiatic Garden; Cherry Leaf; Japanese; Imbricated Snout; Peach Bark; Plum Gouger; Rose Chafer; Syneta Leaf.
Borer, American Plum; Apple Twig; Brown Wood; California Prionus; Flatheaded Appletree; Flatheaded Cherrytree; Lesser Peachtree; Peachtree; Shothole.
Bud Moth, Eyespotted.
Bug, Boxelder; Green Stink; Harlequin.
Butterfly, Tiger Swallowtail; Western Swallowtail.
Cankerworm, Fall; Spring. **Casebearer,** California; Cherry; Cigar.
Caterpillar, Eastern Tent; Forest Tent; Omnivorous Looper; Orange Tortrix; Palmerworm; Phigalia Looper; Pruneworm; Redhumped; Saddleback; Saddled Prominent; Ugly Nest; Western Tent; Yellownecked; Yellow Woollybear.
Cricket, Snowy Tree.
Curculio, Apple; Cherry; Plum (wormy cherries).

Fly, Black Cherry Fruit; Cherry Fruit (maggots in fruit); Western Cherry Fruit.

Fruitworm, Green. **Leaf Crumpler.**

Leafhopper, Privet. **Leafminer,** Spotted Tentiform.

Leafroller, Fruittree; Obliquebanded; Redbanded.

Leaf Skeletonizer, Apple-and-Thorn.

Maggot, Apple. **Mealybug,** Citrophilus.

Mite, Clover; Fruittree; McDaniel Spider; Pacific Spieer; Pear Rust; Willamette.

Moth, Apple Fruit; Browntail; Codling; Crinkled Flannel; Ermine; Oriental; Oriental Fruit; Western Tussock; other species.

Sawfly, Cherry Fruit; Pearslug.

Scale, Barnacle; Calico; Cottony Maple; Dictyospermum; European Fruit Lecanium; Florida Red; Forbes; Glover; Greedy; Hemispherical; Latania; Pustule; Putnam; Pyriform; San Jose; Scurfy; Terrapin; Walnut; White Peach.

Termites, Subterranean. **Thrips,** Onion; Pear.

Treehopper, Buffalo (curved slits in bark).

Webworm, Fall. **Whitefly,** Citrus.

CHERRY, ORIENTAL FLOWERING, JAPANESE
(*Prunus* spp.)

Aphid, Waterlily (when tree is near ponds).

Beetle, Japanese.

Cankerworm, Fall; Spring. **Caterpillar,** Eastern Tent; other species.

Planthopper. **Scale,** White Peach.

See Cherry for other possible pests.

CHERRY, SAND (*Prunus pumila*)

Bug, Green Stink.

Sawfly, Plum Webspinning. **Scale,** San Jose.

Thrips, Greenhouse.

CHERRY-LAUREL, LAUREL-CHERRY (*Prunus laurocerasus*)

Aphid, Spirea.

Scale, Black Thread; Brown Soft; Cottonycushion; Chaff; Dictyospermum; Cyanophyllum; European Fruit Lecanium; Florida Red; Florida Wax; Glover; Latania; Mining; Pyriform; San Jose; Terrapin; Walnut; White Peach.

Whitefly, Citrus.

CHESTNUT (*Castanea*)

Although the American Chestnut was practically exterminated by blight, Asiatic chestnuts are being grown, hybrids are being produced, and there is still the native chinquapin in the South.

Aphid, Chestnut; Giant Bark (large, gray).
Bcetle, Japanese (very fond of chestnut foliage).
Borer, Broadnecked Root; Brown Wood; Chestnut Bark; Chestnut Timberworm; Dogwood; Flatheaded Appletree; Oak Sapling; Oak Timberworm; Filehorned Prionus; Twig Pruner; Twolined Chestnut.
Cankerworms.
Caterpillar, California Oakworm; Filbertworm; Omnivorous Looper; Stinging Rose.
Moth, Browntail; Gypsy; Hag; Imperial; Leopard; Luna; Whitemarked Tussock.
Scale, Dictyospermum; European Fruit Lecanium; Mining; Obscure; Oystershell; Putnam; San Jose; Terrapin.
Webworm, Fall.
Weevil, Asiatic Oak; Large Chestnut; Small Chestnut.

CHICKORY (*Chicorium*)

Aphids.

CHICK-PEA (*Cicer*)

Earworm, Corn.

CHINABERRY (*Melia azedarach*)

Mite, Pacific Spider (yellowing foliage).
Scale, Black; California Red; European Fruit Lecanium; Chaff; Greedy; Green Shield; Latania; Lesser Snow; Oleander; Pustule; Pyriform; White Peach.
Whitefly, Citrus (breeds profusely on this tree).

CHINESE EVERGREEN (*Aglaeonema simplex*)

Mealybug, Comstock; Pineapple. **Scale.**

CHINESE LANTERN (*Physalis*)

Beetle, Striped Cucumber (devours foliage; transmits mosaic).
Bug, Fourlined. **Weevil,** Imported Longhorned.

CHOISYA (Mexican Orange)

Mealybug, Citrophilus; Grape.
Whitefly, Citrus.

CHOKEBERRY (*Aronia*)
Beetle, Rhabdopterus. **Borer**, Roundheaded Appletree.
Scale, San Jose.

CHOKECHERRY (*Prunus virginiana*)
Aphid, Chokecherry. **Beetle**, Birch Bark.
Borer, Roundheaded Appletree.
Caterpillar, Chainspotted Geometer; Eastern Tent (almost inevitable); Hemlock Looper; Schizura; Stinging Rose; Ugly Nest.
Fly, Black Cherry Fruit; Cherry Fruit.
Leaf Crumpler. **Leafminer**, Apple Blotch; Unspotted Tentiform.
Moth, Cynthia; Io; Lappet; Polyphemus; Promethea; Resplendent Shield Bearer; Spotted Tussock.
Scale, Barnacle; Black; Cottonycushion; Florida Wax; Green Shield; Masked; Walnut.
Spittlebugs. **Walkingstick**. **Webworm**, Fall.

CHRYSANTHEMUM
Aphid, Chrysanthemum; Corn Root; Foxglove; Geranium; Goldenglow; Green Peach; Leafcurl Plum; Melon; Myrtle; Pale Chrysanthemum; Thistle.
Armyworm, Beet.
Beetle, Asiatic Garden; Black Blister; European Chafer; Fuller Rose; Goldsmith; Rose Chafer; Spotted Cucumber; Whitefringed.
Borer, European Corn; Stalk.
Bug, Alfalfa Plant; Chrysanthemum Lace; Fourlined Plant (round, depressed, tan spots in leaves); Garden Fleahopper; Harlequin; Tarnished Plant.
Caterpillar, Cabbage Looper; Soybean Looper; Yellow Woollybear; Zebra.
Leafhopper, Aster. **Leafminer**, Chrysanthemum.
Leafroller, Redbanded. **Leaftier**, Celery.
Mealybug, Citrus; Ground; Mexican (serious in greenhouses).
Midge, Chrysanthemum Gall (conical galls in stem, leaf, and bud).
Mite, Broad; Cyclamen; Eriophyid; Privet; Twospotted.
Orthezia, Greenhouse.
Scale, Black; Cottonycushion; Hemispherical; Latania.
Slugs. **Spittlebug**, Meadow (common). **Termites**.
Thrips, Banded Greenhouse; Chrysanthemum; Greenhouse.
Weevil, Cocklebur; Imported Longhorned; Japanese.
Whitefly, Greenhouse. **Wireworm**, Sugarbeet.

CHUFA (*Cyperus*)
Beetle, Whitefringed.

CINERARIA
Aphid, Geranium; Green Peach; Leafcurl Plum; Melon; Potato.
Caterpillar, Cabbage Looper; Orange Tortrix; Soybean Looper.
Cutworms. Leafhopper, Aster.
Leafminer, Chrysanthemum. Leaftier, Celery.
Mealybug, Citrus; Longtailed. Mite, Twospotted.
Slug, Spotted Garden; Greenhouse. Whitefly, Greenhouse.

CINNAMON-TREE (*Cinnamomum zeylandicum*)
Scale, Chaff; Dictyospermum; Fern; Florida Red; Florida Wax;
Lesser Snow; Pyriform; Tesselated.

CINNAMON VINE (*Dioscorea batatas*)
Scale, Pyriform; Tesselated.

CINQUEFOIL (*Potentilla*)
Aphid, Rose (small, green). Weevil, Strawberry.

CISSUS (Kangaroo Vine; Marine Ivy)
Aphid, Grapevine. Beetle, Fuller Rose.
Mealybug, Citrus. Scale, Greedy; Lesser Snow.

CITRON (*Citrus medica*)
Beetle, Fuller Rose. Scale, California Red; Cottonycushion.

CITRUS FRUITS
(Calamondin, Grapefruit, Kumquat, Lemon, Orange, Tangerine)
Ant, Argentine (disseminates scales, mealybugs, aphids); Fire; Little
Fire.
Aphid, Black Citrus; Cowpea; Green Peach; Melon; Potato; Spirea.
Armyworm, Beet. Bagworm.
Beetle, Citrus Root; Darkling Ground; Fuller Rose; Spotted Cu-
cumber; Tobacco Flea; Western Spotted Cucumber.
Borer, Branch and Twig; California Prionus; West Indian Sugarcane
Root.
Bug, Cotton Stainer; Green Stink; Harlequin; Leaffooted; Southern
Green Stink; Tarnished Plant; Western Leaffooted.
Butterfly, Western Parsley.
Caterpillar, Garden Tortrix; Navel Orangeworm; Omnivorous
Looper; Orangedog; Orange Tortrix (bores in rind of fruit);
Pink Scavenger; Puss.
Cutworms. Fly, Caribbean Fruit; Mediterranean Fruit.
Grasshoppers. Katydids.

Leafhopper, Potato.   **Leafroller,** Fruittree; Omnivorous.

Mealybug, Citrophilus; Citrus; Fruit; Grape; Japanese; Longtailed.

Mite, Broad; Citrus Bud; Citrus Flat; Citrus Red (purple mite in Florida, leaves grayish); Citrus Rust (fruit rusty, dry, rough); European Red; False Spider; Lewis Spider; Omnivorous; Pacific Spider; Sixspotted; Texas Citrus; Twospotted; Yuma Spider.

Moth, Raisin; Western Tussock; other species.

Planthopper, Citrus Flatid.

Scale, Barnacle; Black; Brown Soft; California Red; Camphor; Chaff; Citricola; Citrus Snow; Cottonycushion; Dictyospermum; Fern; Florida Red; Florida Wax; Lesser Snow; Mango Shield; Mining; Nigra; Oleander; Purple (major pest); Putnam; Rufous; San Jose; Tea; Yellow.

Slug, Banded; Gray Garden; Greenhouse. **Snail,** European Brown.
Termites.

Thrips, Bean; Citrus (scars fruit); Cotton; Florida Flower; Flower; Greenhouse; Orchid.

Weevil, Citrus Root.

Whitefly, Avocado; Citrus (trees devitalized, covered with sooty mold); Cloudywinged; Woolly.

It is impossible to suggest a spray schedule that would be generally applicable. The citrus whitefly so troublesome in Florida is not a problem in California. Conditions vary within a state; the citrus grower must have a program tailored for his own location. For the homeowner, using citrus trees as ornamentals, a cleanup spray in May or June with a summer oil is perhaps most important. Malathion aids in control of whiteflies and many scales.

CLARKIA

Leafhopper, Aster.

CLEMATIS

Aphid, Green Peach.

Beetle, Black Blister (devours flowers, foliage); Clematis Blister.

Borer, Clematis (works in roots).

Bug, Tarnished Plant.   **Caterpillar,** Omnivorous Looper.

Mite, Twospotted (webby, yellow foliage).

Scale, Brown Soft; Oystershell.

Weevil, Japanese.   **Whitefly,** Glacial; Inconspicuous.

CLEOME (Spider-flower)

Aphid, Green Peach.

CLERODENDRUM (Glorybower)
Mealybug, Citrus; Longtailed. **Orthezia,** Greenhouse.
Scale, Black; Brown Soft; Green Shield; Hemispherical; Latania; Pustule.

CLOVER (*Trifolium*)
Aphid, Clover; Corn Root; Cowpea; Hawthorn; Pea; Spotted Alfalfa; Sweetclover; Yellow Clover.
Armyworm, Fall.
Beetle, Beet Leaf; Grape Colaspis; Imbricated Snout; Palestriped Flea; Potato Flea.
Borer, Clover Root; Clover Stem; Sweetclover Root.
Bug, Alfalfa Plant. **Butterfly,** Clouded Sulfur.
Caterpillar, Clover Head; Clover Looper; Green Cloverworm.
Curculio, Clover Root. **Earworm,** Corn. **Leafhopper,** Corn.
Mite, Clover; Strawberry Spider. **Moth,** Pine Tortrix.
Wasp, Clover Seed Chalcid. **Webworm,** Garden.
Weevil, Alfalfa; Clover Head; Clover Leaf; Clover Seed; Lesser Clover Leaf; Sweetclover.

COCKSCOMB (*Celosia*)
Aphid, Green Peach.
Mite, Twospotted; other species (mealy webs; serious in hot weather).
Scale, Latania.

COCONUT (see Palms)

COFFEE (*Coffea*)
Aphid, Black Citrus.
Mealybug, Citrus; Longtailed. **Orthezia,** Greenhouse.
Scale, Black; Black Thread; Camellia; Cyanophyllum; Green; Green Shield; Hemispherical; Pyriform; Tesselated.
Whitefly, Citrus.

COFFEEBERRY (see California Coffeeberry)

COLEUS
Bug, Fourlined Plant.
Caterpillar, Soybean Looper; Yellow Woollybear.
Mealybug, Citrus; Grape; Longtailed (white fluffs at leaf axils).
Mite, Privet; Twospotted.
Orthezia, Greenhouse (dark scale with white wax).

Scale, Parlatorialike.   Slug, Greenhouse.
Weevil, Imported Longhorned (gray snout beetle).
Whitefly, Greenhouse (common problem).

COLLARDS (*Brassica oleracea* var. *acephala*)
Aphid, Cabbage; Turnip (grayish lice, common).
Beetle, Whitefringed; Yellowmargined Leaf.
Bug, Horned Squash; Harlequin; Southern Squash.
Caterpillar, Cabbage Looper; Imported Cabbageworm.
Moth, Diamondback; Whitelined Sphinx.
Webworm, Cabbage.
  See Cabbage for other pests.

COLUMBINE (*Aquilegia*)
Aphid, Blackbacked Columbine (pink and green); Columbine
  (cream-colored, abundant); Crescentmarked Lily; Foxglove;
  Melon; Potato; Spirea.
Beetle, Asiatic Garden.
Borer, Columbine (salmon caterpillar in crown); Stalk.
Budworm, Rose. Bug, Red-and-Black Stink. Butterfly, Columbine
  Skipper.
Curculio, Cambium.
Leafminer, Columbine (white winding tunnels); Wild Parsnip.
Mealybug, Citrophilus; Grape.   Mites.
Moth, Whitelined Sphinx.
Weevil, Imported Longhorned.   Whitefly, Glacial.

CONFEDERATE-JASMINE (*Trachelospermum*)
Scale, Black Thread; Acuminate; Camphor; Chaff; Dictyospermum;
  Florida Red; Florida Wax; Latania; Pustule; Pyriform; Quohog-
  shaped.
Whiteflies.

CONFEDERATE-ROSE (*Hibiscus mutabilis*)
Scale, Chaff; Pustule.

COOPERIA (Rainlily; Prairielily)
Fly, Narcissus Bulb.

CORAL BEAN, CORAL TREE (*Erythrina*)
Beetle, Cuban May.   Mealybug, Striped.
Scale, Lesser Snow.   Whitefly, Acacia.

CORALBELLS (*Heuchera*)
Mealybugs (occasional). Weevil, Strawberry Root (grubs at roots).

CORALBERRY (*Symphoricarpos*)
Scale, Barnacle; Black; Cottonycushion; Green Shield; Latania; Lesser Snow; Pustule; San Jose; Walnut.

CORAL-PLANT, BELLYACHE BUSH (*Jatropha*)
Mealybug, Longtailed; Mexican; Striped.
Scale, Brown Soft; Dictyospermum; Hemispherical; Latania; Lesser Snow; Oleander; Purple.

CORAL-VINE (*Antigonon*)
Scale, Black; Brown Soft; Black Thread; Cottonycushion; Hemispherical; Latania; Lesser Snow.

COREOPSIS (Tickseed)
Aphid, Coreopsis.
Beetle, Chrysomela Leaf; Spotted Cucumber.
Bug, Fourlined Plant. Leafhopper, Aster.

CORK TREE (*Phellodendron*)
Aphid, Potato.
Scale, Lesser Snow; Pustule.

CORN (*Zea mays*)
Ant, Cornfield.
Aphid, Bean; Corn Leaf; Corn Root (woolly white lice at roots; distributed by ants); English Grain; Greenbug; Potato; Rusty Plum.
Armyworm, Beet, Fall.
Beetle, Asiatic Garden; Argus Tortoise; Bean Leaf; Blister; Bumble Flower; Carrot; Cereal Leaf; Corn Flea; Corn Sap; Corn Silk; Desert Corn Flea; Dusky Sap; Green June; Imbricated Snout; Japanese; Palestriped Flea; Potato Flea; Redheaded Flea; Rose Chafer; Seedcorn; Slender Seedcorn; Spotted Cucumber (southern corn rootworm); Striped Blister; Striped Cucumber; Sweetpotato Flea; Toothed Flea; Western Black Flea; Western Spotted Cucumber; Western Striped Cucumber; Whitefringed.
Billbug, Maize; Southern Corn.
Borer, European Corn (cream-colored caterpillars at base of ears and on stalks); Elder; Lesser Cornstalk; Southern Cornstalk; Southwestern Corn; Stalk (dark, striped caterpillar); Sugarcane.

Bug, Chinch; Garden Fleahopper; Green Stink; Harlequin; Negro; Southern Green Stink.

Caterpillar, Range; Yellow Woollybear.

Cutworm, Bronzed; Claybacked; Palesided; Western Bean; Western W-marked.

Earworm, Corn (dark caterpillars at tip of ears; common).

Leafhoppers (vectors of corn stunt).

Leafminer, Corn Blotch. Maggot, Seedcorn.

Millipedes. Mite, Desert Spider.

Planthopper, Corn. Rootworm, Northern Corn; Western Corn.

Termites. Thrips, Grass.

Webworm, Corn Root. Weevil, Corn Stem.

Wireworm, Columbia Basin; Plains False; Sand; Sugarbeet; Tobacco; Wheat.

The two most important pests are the European corn borer, with control started when plants are young, and the corn earworm, treated just after silking.

CORNFLOWER, BACHELORS-BUTTON (*Centaurea*)

Aphid, Western Aster Root; other species.

Borer, Stalk. Leafhopper, Aster. Leaftier, Omnivorous.

Scale, Hemispherical.

COSMOS

Aphid, Bean (black); Coreopsis; Melon; Potato; Western Aster Root.

Beetle, Asiatic Garden; Japanese; Spotted Cucumber (on flowers).

Borer, European Corn (cream-colored); Stalk (dark, striped).

Bug, Fourlined Plant; Tarnished Plant.

Leafhopper, Aster (transmits aster yellows).

Mite, Twospotted (plant yellow or gray, mealy).

Termites, Subterranean.

COSTMARY (*Chrysanthemum balsamia*)

Aphid, Artemisia.

COTONEASTER

Aphid, Apple, Potato. Borer, Sinuate Pear.

Bug, Hawthorn Lace (leaves stippled gray, rusty flecks underneath).

Leafhopper, Privet. Leaf Crumpler. Mealybug, Hawthorn.

Mite, Pear Leaf Blister (small, reddish brown blisters); Platanus. Moths.

Scale, Acuminate; Dictyospermum; Florida Wax; Greedy; Latania; Olive; Oystershell; Pine Needle; Quohogshaped; San Jose; White Peach.

Webworm, Cotoneaster (webbing ends of branches).

COTTONWOOD (see Poplar)

COWPEA (*Vigna sinensis*)

Aphid, Bean (black, common); Cowpea.

Armyworm, Fall.

Beetle, Bean Leaf; Blister; Grape Colaspis; Mexican Bean; White-fringed.

Borer, Lesser Cornstalk.

Bug, Green Stink; Harlequin; Garden Fleahopper; Leaffooted; Pumpkin.

Caterpillar, Green Cloverworm; Velvetbean.

Cricket, Camel.   **Curculio,** Clover Root; Cowpea.

Cutworms.   Leafminer, Serpentine.

Treehopper, Threecornered Alfalfa.   **Webworm,** Garden.

Weevil, Cowpea; Sweetclover.   **Wireworms.**

CRABAPPLE, ORNAMENTAL (*Pyrus* spp.)

Aphid, Apple; Apple Grain.

Borer, Flatheaded Appletree; Roundheaded Appletree.

Bug, Alder Lace; Apple Red.   **Cankerworms.**

Caterpillar, Eastern Tent.   **Curculio,** Apple.

Leaf Crumpler.

Leafminer, Apple Blotch; Spotted Tentiform; Unspotted Tentiform.

Maggot, Apple.   **Moth,** Codling.

Rootworm, Strawberry.   **Sawfly,** European Apple.

Scale, San Jose.   **Weevil,** Apple Flea.

See Apple for other possible pests.

CRANBERRY (*Vaccinium macrocarpon*)

Beetle, Cranberry; Rhabdopterua.

Borer, Cranberry Girdler.

Budworm, Cranberry Blossomworm.

Caterpillar, Blackheaded Fireworm; Yellowheaded Fireworm (berries webbed); Chainspotted Geometer.

Fruitworm, Cranberry; Sparganothis (also leafroller).

Leafhopper, Bluntnosed (vector of false-blossom disease).

Midge, Cranberry Tipworm.
Moth, Gypsy; Crinkled Flannel; Tussock.
Rootworm, Cranberry.
Scale, Cranberry; Oystershell; Putnam.
Spanworm, Cranberry. Termites.
Weevil, Black Vine; Cranberry; Strawberry Root.

CRANBERRY, HIGH BUSH (*Viburnum opulus*)
Aphid, Bean.

CRAPEMYRTLE (*Lagerstroemia*)
Aphid, Crapemyrtle (profuse honeydew with sooty mold).
Beetle, Colaspis; Flea; Fuller Rose.
Mealybug, Citrus.
Scale, Black; Camellia Mining; Coconut; Cyanophyllum; Florida
Red; Florida Wax; Green Shield; Hemispherical; Latania; Pus-
tule; Pyriform.

CRASSULA
Mealybug, Citrus (white woolly bodies congested on stems).
Mite, Cyclamen (plants deformed).
Scale, Latania; Lesser Snow.

CRESS, GARDEN (*Lepidium*)
Aphid, Cabbage; Corn Root. Bug, Harlequin.
Beetle, Western Black Flea. Leafminer, Serpentine. Maggot, Cab-
bage.

CROCUS
Aphid, Crescentmarked Lily; Green Peach; Tulip Bulb.
Mite, Narcissus Bulb.

CROSSANDRA
Mealybug, Mexican. Orthezia, Greenhouse. Scale, Barnacle.

CROTON (*Codiaeum*)
Mealybug, Citrus; Longtailed; Striped.
Mite, Texas Citrus; Spider. Orthezia, Greenhouse.
Scale, Black; Brown Soft; Coconut; Cottonycushion; Croton; Dic-
tyospermum; Fern; Florida Red; Florida Wax; Glover; Green
Shield; Hemispherical; Latania; Lesser Snow; Long Soft; Orien-
tal; Parlatoria; Purple; Pyriform; Quohogshaped; Rufous.
Thrips, Greenhouse.

CROTALARIA
Mite, Twospotted; other species.
Scale, Black; Cyanophyllum; Dictyospermum; Florida Red; Lesser Snow; Pustule; White Peach.

CRYPTOMERIA
Scale, Maskell.

CUCUMBER (*Cucumis sativus*)
Aphid, Green Peach; Melon (carries bacteria causing wilt).
Armyworm, Fall; Beet.
Beetle, Banded Cucumber; Hop Flea; Imbricated Snout; Potato Flea; Spotted Cucumber (green with 12 black spots); Striped Cucumber (yellow-green with 3 black stripes); Western Spotted; Western Striped.
Borer, Squash Vine.
Bug, Garden Fleahopper; Horned Squash; Squash; Southern Green Stink; Tarnished Plant.
Caterpillar, Melonworm; Pickleworm (small, greenish, in blossom, fruit).
Centipede, Garden Symphylan. **Cricket,** Field. **Cutworms.**
Leafhopper, Beet (transmits curly top).
Leaftier, Celery. **Maggot,** Seedcorn.
Mite, Desert Spider; Twospotted.
Springtail, Garden. **Thrips,** Onion; Western Flower.
Whitefly, Greenhouse. **Weevil,** Strawberry Root.
Start plants under Hotkaps, later changing to cheesecloth or wire screening to protect young vines from aphids and cucumber beetles spreading disease. Start spraying or dusting as soon as plants are too large for covering.

CUNNINGHAMIA (China-fir)
Scale, Cottonycushion; Florida Wax.

CUPHEA (Cigarflower; Cigarette Plant)
Beetle, Pine Colaspis.
Scale, Black; Brown Soft; Cottonycushion; Florida Wax; Latania; Lesser Snow; Pustule.

CURRANT (*Ribes*)
(Including Flowering Currant)
Aphid, Currant (leaves crinkled, cupped down, green lice in pockets); Chrysanthemum; Dogberry; Ornamental Currant; Potato; Variable Currant.

Beetle, Fuller Rose.
Borer, Currant (canes die back); Currant Stem Girdler; Flatheaded
    Appletree; Pacific Flatheaded.
Bug, Fourlined Plant (circles in leaves).
Caterpillar, Western Tent; Yellow Woollybear.
Fly, Currant Fruit (maggots in fruit).
Fruitworm, Gooseberry.
Leafhopper, Grape; Privet; White Apple.
Leafroller, Fruittree; Obliquebanded. Mealybug, Ground.
Mite, Currant Bud; McDaniel Spider; Twospotted.
Moth, Io; Whitelined Sphinx.
Sawfly, Imported Currantworm (green with black spots).
Scale, Chaff; Cottony Maple; European Fruit Lecanium; Forbes;
    Green Shield; Oystershell; Putnam; San Jose; Scurfy; Walnut.
Spanworm, Currant (looper caterpillar).
Weevil, Currant Fruit.
    Cut out canes with borers. Spray for aphids and sawfly larvae.

CUSTARD-APPLE (*Annona reticulata*)
Mealybug, Coconut.
Scale, Florida Wax; Hemispherical; Latania; Long Soft; Quahog-
    shaped.

CYCAD, SAGO PALM (*Cycas*)
Mealybug, Citrus; Longtailed.
Scale, Araucaria; Black; Black Thread; Brown Soft; California
    Red; Chaff; Coconut; Cyanophyllum; Dictyospermum; European
    Fiorinia; Fern; Florida Red; Green Shield; Hemispherical (brown,
    convex, common); Latania; Oleander (yellow); Oriental; Proteus;
    Purple; Red Bay; Tesselated; White Peach.

CYCLAMEN
Aphid, Crescentmarked Lily; Melon.
Beetle, Oriental. Mealybug, Citrus.
Mite, Broad; Cyclamen (plants deformed, stunted, buds black).
Thrips, Greenhouse.
Weevil, Black Vine (grubs on roots may kill plants).
    Use insecticides cautiously on Cyclamen; some may be phytotoxic.

CYNOGLOSSUM
Aphid, Leafcurl Plum.

CYPRESS (*Cupressus*)
Aphid, Arborvitae (brown); Cypress (large green).

Beetle, Cedar Bark; Flea; June; Pine Colaspis.
Borer, Apple Twig; Western Cedar. **Horntail,** Western.
Mealybug, Citrus; Cypress; Longtailed; Redwood.
Midge, Monterey Pine.
Mite, Cypress; Date; Platanus; Southern Red.
Moth, Cypress Cone; Cypress Tip; Cypress Webber; Imperial; White-marked Tussock; other species.
Sawfly, Cypress.
Scale, Cottonycushion; Cypress Bark (serious on Monterey cypress); Dictyospermum; Juniper; Latania; Newstead's; Red Bay.
Thrips, Greenhouse.

CYPRESS, BALD (*Taxodium*)
Moth, Cypress. **Scale,** Taxodium.

CYPRESS-VINE (*Quamoclit*)
Scale, Black; Green Shield.

DAHLIA
Aphid, Bean (black, common); Green Peach; Leafcurl Plum; Melon; Potato.
Bee, Leafcutter.
Beetle, Asiatic Garden; Black Blister; Carrot; Grape Colaspis; Japanese; Rose Chafer; Spotted Cucumber (eats petals); Western Spotted Cucumber; Whitefringed.
Borer, Burdock; European Corn; Stalk.
Bug, Fourlined Plant; Tarnished Plant (new shoots blackened).
Caterpillar, Saddleback; Yellow Woollybear.
Earworm, Corn. **Leafcutter,** Morningglory.
Leafhopper, Potato (prevalent, serious; leaves curl, brown at margins; plants stunted); Southern Garden.
Leaftier, Celery. **Mealybug,** Citrus.
Mite, Cyclamen; Twospotted (mealy webs). **Planthopper.**
Scale, Black; Cottonycushion; Florida Wax.
Thrips, Flower; Greenhouse; Onion (transmits spotted-wilt virus).
Wasp, Giant Hornet (may tear stalks).
Weevil, Cocklebur. **Wireworms.**

DAISY, OXEYE (*Chrysanthemum leucanthemum*)
Aphid, Artemisia. **Beetle,** Whitefringed.
Bug, Daisy Plant (punctures leaves, flower buds).
Caterpillar, Omnivorous Looper.
Leafminer, Chrysanthemum. **Leaftier,** Celery.
Mealybug, Ground (works at roots).

DAISY, SHASTA (*Chrysanthemum maximum*)
Aphid, Myrtle.
Beetle, Spotted Cucumber (very common on flowers).
Bug, Daisy Plant; Fourlined Plant; Tarnished Plant.
Butterfly, Checker Spot.
Leafminer, Chrysanthemum (irregular light mines in leaves).

DAPHNE
Aphids, several species. **Mealybug,** Citrus.
Scale, Citricola; Cottonycushion; Dictyospermum; Greedy; Yellow.

DATE PALM (*Phoenix dactylifera*)
Beetle, Corn Sap; Dried Fruit; Fig.
Bug, Western Leaffooted (large, with leaflike legs).
Mealybug, Grape.
Mite, Date (webs leaves together; scars fruit).
Scale, Brown Soft; Oriental; Parlatoria Date (small, gray and white, presumably eradicated) ; Red Date.
Thrips, Banded Greenhouse.

DATURA (Angels Trumpet)
Aphid, Green Peach. **Bug,** Cotton Lace.
Leafhopper, Beet. **Mite,** Spider; Tomato Russet.
Psyllid, Tomato. **Scale,** Cottony Taxus; Latania.

DAYLILY (*Hemerocallis*)
Aphid, Daylily; Sand Lily. **Scale,** Coconut.
Thrips, Daylily; Flower; Tobacco; other species (blossoms streaked, foliage silvered).
Weevil, Imported Longhorned.

DELPHINIUM (Larkspur)
Aphid, Delphinium (red, on underside of cupped-down leaves); Green Peach; Crescentmarked Lily.
Beetle, Asiatic Garden; Black Blister; Japanese (rare on delphinium).
Borer, Burdock, Stalk. **Budworm,** Rose.
Bug, Fourlined Plant. **Cutworms.**
Leafminer, Larkspur (tan blotches in leaves). **Millipedes.**
Mite, Broad (leaves glassy); Cyclamen (the most important pest; plants stunted, leaves deformed; flower buds black) ; Twospotted.
Slugs. Sowbugs. Thrips, Gladiolus.

DEUTZIA
Aphid, Bean; Cowpea; Currant (leaves crinkled) ; Melon.
Beetle, Fuller Rose (leaves notched from margins).
Leafminer, Lilac (tan blotches in leaves). **Scale,** White Peach.

DEWBERRY (*Rubus flagellaris*)
Borer, Rednecked Cane.
Leafroller, Obliquebanded; Strawberry.
Maggot, Raspberry Cane. **Sawfly,** Dewberry; Raspberry.
Scale, Rose. **Weevil,** Strawberry.
  See Blackberry and Raspberry for other pests.

DIANTHUS (Garden Pink)
Aphid, Green Peach. **Beetle,** Black Blister.

DICHONDRA (Grass)
Beetle, Flea. **Cutworm,** Granulate. **Weevil,** Vegetable.

DIEFFENBACHIA
Aphid, Cotton; Waterlily.
Mealybug, Ground; Longtailed. **Scale,** Mango Shield.

DILL (*Anethum graveolens*)
Aphid, Honeysuckle and Parsnip; Willow.
Caterpillar, Celeryworm. **Weevil,** Carrot.

DOCK (Rumex)
Aphid, Dock. **Sawfly,** Dock. **Scale,** Green.

DOGWOOD (*Cornus*)
Aphid, Corn Root; Dogwood; Melon; Sunflower; Whitebanded Dogwood.
Beetle, Pitted Ambrosia.
Borer, Azalea Stem; Dogwood (kills branches) ; Dogwood Cambium; Dogwood Twig; Flatheaded Appletree (injures young trees) ; Pecan.
Bug, Green Stink.
Caterpillar, Phigalia Looper; Redhumped; Stinging Rose.
Cicada, Periodical (injures twigs by egg laying).
Leafhopper, Rose (foliage commonly stippled white) ; Eightlined.
Leafminer, Locust. **Leafroller,** Obliquebanded.
Midge, Dogwood Clubgall. **Sawfly,** Dogwood.
Scale, Cottony Maple; Cyanophyllum; Dogwood; False Cottony Ma-

ple; Florida Wax; Forbes; Obscure; Oystershell; Oleander; Purple; Putnam; San Jose; Tea; Tesselated; Tuliptree; Walnut; White Peach; Willow Scurfy.

Whitefly, Mulberry (round, black with white fringe). **Weevil.**

DORONICUM (Leopards-bane)

Aphid, Crescentmarked Lily; Spirea.

DOUGLAS-FIR (*Pseudotsuga*)

Aphid, Cooley Spruce Gall (alternate host for); Douglas Fir; Monterey Pine.

Beetle, Douglas Fir; Douglas Fir Engraver; Golden Buprestid; Obtuse Sawyer; Silver Fir.

Borer, California Prionus; Cedartree (may girdle and kill); Fir Flatheaded; Sculptured Pine; Western Larch Roundheaded; White Pine Shoot.

Bud Moth, Larch. **Budworm,** Spruce (serious).

Butterfly, Pine (green, whitestriped caterpillar; may defoliate).

Caterpillar, Phantom Hemlock Looper; Western Hemlock Looper; Douglas Fir Defoliator.

Horntails.

Midge, Balsam Gall; Douglas Fir Cone; other species.

Moth, Douglas Fir Cone; Douglas Fir Pitch; Douglas Fir Tussock; Pine Cone; Sequoia Pitch; Silverspotted Tiger; Zimmerman Pine.

Scale, Black Pineleaf; Hemlock; Pine Needle.

Weevil, Douglas Fir Twig; Strawberry Root.

DRACAENA

Beetle, Fuller Rose.

Mealybug, Citrus; Longtailed.

Scale, Boisduval's; Brown Soft; Cyanophyllum; Dictyospermum; Fern; Hemispherical; Long Soft; Pyriform; Tesselated.

Thrips, Banded Greenhouse; Dracaena.

DURANTA (Golden Dewdrop)

Orthezia, Greenhouse.

Scale, Acuminate; Black; Black Thread; Cottonycushion; Dictyospermum; Florida Red; Florida Wax; Hemispherical; Latania; Mining; Long Soft.

DUTCHMANS-PIPE (*Aristolochia*)

Butterfly, Pipevine Swallowtail (brown caterpillar).

Mealybug, Longtailed. **Scale,** Hemispherical.

ECHEVERIA
Scale, Lesser Snow. Weevil, Black Vine.

EGGFRUIT (*Lucuma nervosa*)
Scale, Green; Lesser Snow; Mining; Pyriform; Tesselated.

EGGPLANT (*Solanum melongena* var. *esculentum*)
Aphid, Green Peach; Melon; Potato.
Beetle, Asiatic Garden; Blister; Colorado Potato (yellow with black stripes) ; Eggplant Flea (tiny shotholes in leaves) ; Palestriped Flea; Potato Flea (injurious to seedlings) ; Spotted Cucumber; Tobacco Flea.
Borer, Potato Stalk; Potato Tuberworm.
Bug, Cotton Stainer; Eggplant Lace; Green Stink; Garden Fleahopper; Harlequin; Onespot Stink; Pumpkin; Southern Green Stink.
Caterpillar, Yellow Woollybear. Cutworms.
Hornworm, Tobacco; Tomato.
Leafhopper, Potato. Leafminer, Eggplant.
Maggot, Pepper (occasional; worms in fruit).
Mite, Strawberry Spider; Twospotted; other species.
Whitefly, Greenhouse (common on plants started in greenhouses).

ELAEAGNUS (Russian-olive)
Aphid, Oleaster-thistle (yellow and green) ; Russian-olive.
Mite, Citrus Red.
Scale, Brown Soft; Chaff; Cyanophyllum; Dictyospermum; Florida Red; Florida Wax; Hemispherical; Latania; Lesser Snow; Oleander; Olive; Olive Parlatoria; Oriental; Proteus; Purple; Pustule; San Jose; Walnut; White Peach.

ELDER (*Sambucus*)
Aphid, Elder; Bean.
Beetle, Potato Flea; Rose Chafer.
Borer, Currant; Elder; Elder Shoot. Bug, Green Stink.
Caterpillar, Omnivorous Looper. Cricket, Blackhorned Flea.
Mealybug, Citrus; Grape. Mite, Elderberry. Moth, American Dagger.
Scale, Black; Brown Soft; Green; Green Shield; Hemispherical; Walnut.
Thrips, Madroña. Weevil.

ELDER, YELLOW (*Stenolobium*)

Mealybug, Citrus. **Orthezia,** Greenhouse.

Scale, Acuminate; Black; Green Shield; Hemispherical; Lesser Snow; Mining; Proteus; Quohogshaped.

ELM (*Ulmus*)

Aphid, Elm Cockscombgall; Elm Leaf; Elm Sackgall; Giant Bark; Woolly Apple; Woolly Elm; Woolly Elm Bark; Woolly Hawthorn; Woolly Pear.

Beetle, Carrot; Elm Calligrapha; Elm Flea; Elm Leaf (serious; leaves skeletonized, may drop); Grape Flea; Japanese (chews leaves to lace); June; Larger Elm Leaf; Native Elm Bark; Red Elm Bark; Rose Chafer; Smaller European Bark (transmits Dutch elm disease); Striped Cucumber.

Borer, Azalea Stem; Brown Wood; Carpenterworm; Dogwood Twig; Elm; Flatheaded Appletree (injurious to new transplants); Flatheaded Cherrytree; Oak Timberworm; Pacific Flatheaded; Pigeon Tremex; Painted Hickory; Twig Girdler; Twig Pruner.

Bug, Alder Lace; Elm Lace.

Butterfly, Mourningcloak (spiny caterpillar).

Cankerworm, Fall; Spring (important, may defoliate).

Casebearer, Elm.

Caterpillar, Eastern Tent; Hemlock Looper; Omnivorous Looper; Redhumped Oakworm; Puss; Variable Oakleaf.

Cricket, Blackhorned Tree.

Leafhopper, Whitebanded Elm (transmits phloem necrosis); Virginiacreeper.

Leafminer, Elm; Locust. **Leafroller,** Fruittree.

Mite, Avocado Red; European Red; Fourspotted; Oak; Twospotted.

Moth, Browntail; American Dagger; Cecropia; Elm Sphinx; Gypsy; Leopard; Scurfy (important); European Elm; European Fruit Lecanium; Gloomy; Green Shield; Japanese Wax; Latania; Obscure; Oystershell; Putnam; Pyriform; San Jose; Scurfy; Walnut; White Peach.

Spanworm, Elm. **Treehopper,** Buffalo. **Webworm,** Fall.

Weevil, Apple Flea; Black Elm Bark; Japanese; Red Elm Bark.

The most serious problems are elm leaf beetles and the bark beetle vectors of Dutch elm disease.

ENDIVE (*Cichorium*)

Aphid, Bean (black); Brown Ambrosia; Green Peach; Pea (large, green).

EPILOBIUM
Aphid, Evening Primrose; Green Gooseberry; Malaheb Cherry.

ERIOPHYLLUM
Mealybug, Yucca.

ERYTHRINA
Mealybug, Mexican; Striped.   **Scale,** Lesser Snow.

ERYTHRONIUM
Aphid, Green Peach.

EUCALYPTUS
Aphid, Cowpea.
Borer, Californa Prionus; Nautical; Pacific Flatheaded.
Bug, Lygus.
Caterpillar, California Oakworm; Omnivorous Looper; Orange Tortrix.
Mealybug, Longtailed.
Mite, Avocado Red; Platanus; Southern Red.
Scale, Acuminate; Black; California Red; Cottonycushion; Dictyospermum; Florida Red; Greedy; Latania; Lesser Snow; Oleander; Oriental; Purple; Pyriform; San Jose.
Thrips, Greenhouse.

EUGENIA
Mealybug, Citrus; Longtailed; Mexican.
Scale, Black; Acuminate; Chaff; Coconut; Dictyospermum; Florida Red; Florida Wax; Mango Shield; Masked; Proteus; Purple; Pustule; Pyriform; Tesselated.
Thrips, Greenhouse.

EUONYMUS
Aphid, Bean; Ivy; Potato.   **Leafroller,** Omnivorous.
Scale, Araucaria; Barnacle; Black; Brown Soft; California Red; Chaff; Cottony Maple; Cyanophyllum; Dictyospermum; Euonymus (males thin, white, conspicuous; females brown; common and injurious); Florida Red; Florida Wax; Glover; Greedy; Latania; Proteus; Parlatorialike; Purple; Pyriform; San Jose; Tea; Yellow.
Euonymus scale is the chief problem.

EUPATORIUM (Mistflower)
Aphid, Brown Ambrosia; Coreopsis; Corn Root; Leafcurl Plum.
Fly, Eupatorium Gall.   Leafminer, Chrysanthemum.
Scale, Cassava; Cyanophyllum; Green; Latania; other species.

EUPHORBIA (Crown-of-Thorns)
Scale, Cyanophyllum; Dictyospermum; Florida Red; Latania; Long
Soft; Oriental; Proteus.   Thrips.

EUPHORBIA (Snow-on-the-Mountain)
Scale, Brown Soft.

EUPHORBIA (Spurge)
Aphid, Lettuce Root; Potato.
Scale, Cyanophyllum; Dictyospermum; Long Soft.

EURYA
Scale, Barnacle; Citrophilus; Cottonycushion; Camellia; Florida Red;
Florida Wax; Latania; Tea.

EVENING PRIMROSE (*Oenothera*)
Aphid, Evening Primrose; Melon; White Aster Root.
Beetle, Steelblue Flea.   Mealybug, Yucca.   Weevil, Cocklebur.

FATSHEDERA
Mealybug, Striped.   Mite, Privet.
Scale, Florida Red; Pyriform.

FATSIA
Psyllid.   Scale, Florida Red; Green Shield; Pyriform.

FEIJOA
Scale, Acuminate; Bamboo; Barnacle; Black; Brown Soft; Chaff;
Dictyospermum; Florida Red; Florida Wax; Green Shield; La-
tania; Pyriform; Red Bay; Tesselated.

FERNS
Aphid, Crescentmarked Lily; Fern (black) ; Latania.
Beetle, Japanese (feeds on some species).
Caterpillar, Florida Fern (feeds at night) ; Orange Tortrix (roll
leaves) ; Yellow Woollybear.
Mealybug, Citrus; Longtailed; Coconut.   Millipedes.   Moths.
Crickets.   Cutworms.   Grasshoppers.
Orthezia, Greenhouse.

Scale, Acuminate; Barnacle; Black; Black Thread; Brown Soft; Coconut; Cottonycushion; Chaff; Dictyospermum; European Fiorinia; Fern (white); Florida Red; Florida Wax; Green; Green Shield; Hemispherical (brown); Latania; Lesser Snow; Long Soft; Oleander (flat, yellow, common); Oriental; Parlatorialike; Proteus.
Slug, Gray Field. **Snail,** Fern (eats from lower leaf surface). **Thrips.**
Weevil, Black Vine (on maidenhair fern); Japanese.
Whitefly, Citrus; Fern; Greenhouse.
Use insecticides on ferns with caution; they are subject to chemical injury.

FETTERBUSH (*Lyonia lucida*)
Scale, Azalea Bark.

FIG, CREEPING (*Ficus pumila*)
Mealybug, Citrophilus.
Scale, Dictyospermum; Cottonycushion; Pyriform.
Whitefly, Citrus. **Thrips,** Cuban Laurel.

FIG, STRANGLER (*Ficus aurea*)
Orthezia, Greenhouse.
Scale, Black; Brown Soft; Chinese Obscure; Florida Red; Florida Wax; Green; Green Shield; Hemispherical; Pustule; Long Soft; Pyriform; Tesselated.

FIG, TREE (*Ficus carica*)
Beetle, Dried Fruit; Fig; Darkling Ground; Green June.
Borer, Branch and Twig (black and brown beetle bores in twigs).
Caterpillar, Navel Orangeworm.
Mealybug, Citrophilus; Fruit; Longtailed (prevalent); Mexican.
Mite, Dried Fruit; Fig Rust; Pacific Spider; Texas Citrus.
Psyllid, Fig.
Scale, Black; Cottonycushion; Dictyospermum; Fig (oystershaped, purple or brown); Florida Wax; Green Shield; Japanese Wax; Latania; Lesser Snow; Mining; Oriental; Oystershell; Pustule; San Jose; White Peach.
Thrips, Cuban Laurel. **Wireworm,** Oregon.

FILBERT (*Corylus*)
Aphid, Filbert.
Caterpillar, Filbertworm. **Mealybug,** Apple.
Mite, Filbert Bud. **Moth. Weevil,** Filbert.

FIR (*Abies*)

Aphid, Balsam Twig; Balsam Woolly; Bowlegged Fir; Flocculent Fir.
Bagworm.
Beetle, Fir Engraver; Lion; Mountain Pine; Obtuse Sawyer; Oregon
Fir Sawyer; Silver Fir; Western Balsam Bark.
Borer, California Prionus; Flatheaded Cone; Flatheaded Fir; Round-
headed Fir; SculpturedPine.
Budworm, Blackheaded; Spruce. **Bud Moth,** Larch.
Caterpillar, Chainspotted Geometer; Fir Cone Looper; False Hem-
lock Looper; Hemlock Looper.
Horntails. Leafminer, White Fir Needle.
Midge, Balsam Gall. **Mite,** Spruce Spider (needles cobwebby).
Moth, Douglas Fir Tussock; Fir Seed; Pine Tube; Silverspotted Ti-
ger; Spotted Tussock.
Sawfly, Balsam Fir. **Scale,** Oystershell; Pine Needle.

FLACOURTIA (Governors-plum)

Mite, Texas Citrus.
Scale, Acuminate; Brown Soft; Latania; Purple; Pustule; White
Peach.

FLAME VINE (*Pyrostegia*)

Mealybug, Citrus. **Orthezia,** Greenhouse.
Scale, Black Thread; Barnacle; Brown Soft; Cyanophyllum; Chaff;
Florida Wax; Green Shield; Lesser Snow; Mining; Proteus; Pus-
tule; Parlatorialike Pyriform.

FLEABANE (*Erigeron*)

Aphid, Corn Root Erigeron; Melon; Spirea.

FORGET-ME-NOT (*Myosotis*)

Aphid, Forget-me-not; Green Peach.
Beetle, Potato Flea (small, black; pinholes in leaves).
Butterfly, Painted Beauty (purple, yellow and green caterpillar).
Leaftier, Celery.

FORSYTHIA

Bug, Fourlined Plant (occasional; tan circles in leaves).
Scale, Latania; Purple; San Jose; Walnut.
Weevil, Japanese.

FOXGLOVE (*Digitalis*)

Aphid, Foxglove; Crescentmarked Lily; Melon.

Beetle, Asiatic Garden; Japanese; Rose Chafer.
Mealybug, Citrophilus. Scale, Cottonycushion. Thrips, Onion.

FRANGIPANI (*Plumeria*)
Mealybug, Longtailed.
Scale, Acuminate; Black; Brown Soft; Coconut; Cottonycushion; Cyanophyllum; Green; Green Shield; Hemispherical; Latania; Lesser Snow; Oriental; Pyriform.

FRANKLINIA (*Gordonia alatamaha*)
Scale, Red Bay; Walnut. Wasp, Giant Hornet.

FREESIA
Aphid, Crescentmarked Lily; Green Peach; Tulip Bulb.
Mite, Bulb (in rotting bulbs). Thrips, Gladiolus.

FREMONTIA
Psyllid, Fremontia.

FRINGE-TREE (*Chionanthus*)
Scale, White Peach; Rose.

FRITILLARIA
Scale, Latania.

FUCHSIA
Aphid, Crescentmarked Lily; Ornate; Green Peach; Potato.
Beetle, Fuller Rose; Strawberry Flea.
Caterpillar, Yellow Woollybear.
Mealybug, Citrus; Longtailed.
Mite, Broad; False Spider; Cyclamen; Privet (pits on underside of leaves); Twospotted.
Moth, Whitelined Sphinx.
Scale, Barnacle; Black; California Red; Greedy.
Thrips, Greenhouse (foliage with "pepper and salt" effect).
Whitefly, Greenhouse (prevalent; injurious); Iris.

FURCRAEA
Scale, Brown Soft; Hemispherical.

GAILLARDIA
Aphid, Potato; Goldenglow.
Beetle, Asiatic Garden; Japanese. Bug, Fourlined Plant.
Scale, Cottonycushion. Thrips, Flower; Onion. Wireworms.

GALLBERRY (*Ilex glabra*)
Scale, Acuminate; Florida Wax; Gloomy; Latania; Oak Eriococcus; Purple; Walnut.

GALTONIA
Fly, Narcissus Bulb.

GARDENIA (Cape-jasmine)
Aphid, Melon.   Beetle, Fuller Rose (notches leaves at night).
Mealybug, Citrus; Longtailed.   Mite, Gardenia.
Orthezia, Greenhouse.
Scale, Acuminate; Barnacle; Black; Brown Soft; Dictyospermum; Florida Red; Florida Wax; Green; Green Shield; Hemispherical; Long Soft; Mango Shield; Mining; Proteus; Pustule; Pyriform; Quohogshaped; Tesselated; Tea; Tuliptree.
Thrips, Banded Greenhouse; Flower.
Weevil, Black Vine.
Whitefly, Citrus (very common, accompanied by much sooty mold).

GAURA
Scale, Barnacle.

GEIGER-TREE (*Cordia*)
Beetle, Leaf.
Scale, Black; Brown Soft; Coconut; Green Shield; Hemispherical; Latania; Lesser Snow; Pyriform.

GERANIUM (Wild)
Aphid, Wild Geranium.

GERANIUM (*Pelargonium*)
Aphid, Foxglove; Geranium; Green Peach; Potato.
Beetle, Fuller Rose; Rose Chafer.
Budworm, Tobacco.   Bug, Fourlined Plant.   Cankerworm, Fall.
Caterpillar, Cabbage Looper; Omnivorous Looper; Orange Tortrix; Soybean Looper.
Earworm, Corn.
Leafroller, Beet; Obliquebanded; Redbanded.
Leaftier, Celery.   Mealybug, Citrus; Mexican.
Mite, Broad; Cyclamen (young leaves curl) ; Twospotted.
Moth, Geranium Plume.
Scale, Cottonycushion; Fern; Lesser Snow; Pustule; Rose; White Peach.

Weevil, Black Vine; Imported Longhorned; Japanese.
Whitefly, Greenhouse (almost inevitable on indoor geraniums).

GERBERA (African-daisy)
Aphid, Green Peach; Leafcurl Plum.
Caterpillar, Soybean Looper.
Mealybug, Citrus; Mexican. **Mite,** Broad; Cyclamen.
Scale, Black; Brown Soft; Coconut; Cottonycushion; Dictyospermum; Green Shield; Hemispherical; Latania; Mango Shield; Oriental; Pyriform.
Thrips, Banded Greenhouse.

GERMANDER (*Teucrium*)
Mite, Germander Leaf Crinkle.

GINGER-LILY (*Hedychium*)
Mealybug, Pineapple. **Scale,** Tesselated.

GINKGO
Caterpillar, Omnivorous Looper. **Leafroller,** Fruittree.
Mealybug, Grape. **Moth,** Whitemarked Tussock. **Scale,** Peach Lecanium.

GINSENG (*Panax*)
Mealybug, Longtailed. **Scale,** Hemispherical; Oystershell.

GLADIOLUS
Aphid, Crescentmarked Lily; Foxglove; Melon; Potato; Tulip Bulb.
Armyworm, Beet.
Beetle, Asiatic Garden; Black Blister; European Chafer; June; Whitefringed.
Borer, European Corn; Stalk.
Bug, Fourlined Plant; Garden Fleahopper; Tarnished Plant.
Caterpillar, Zebra. **Cutworms. Earworm,** Corn.
Leafhopper, Redbanded. **Leaftier,** Omnivorous.
Maggot, Seedcorn.
Mite, Bulb (in corms); Desert Spider; Twospotted.
Scale, Florida Red; Latania.
Thrips, Gladiolus (universal pest; leaves and flowers streaked); Banded Greenhouse; Greenhouse; Western Flower.
Weevil, Imported Longhorned. **Wireworms.**

GLOBE-AMARANTH (*Gomphrena globosa*)
Aphid, Crescentmarked Lily; Green Peach; Potato.

GLOBETHISTLE (*Echinops*)
Aphid, Bean; Green Peach (leaves curl down).
Bug, Fourlined Plant (small, circular tan spots in leaves).

GLORYBUSH (*Tibouchina*)
Scale, Florida Wax; Hemispherical; Parlatoria.

GLOXINIA
Aphid, Crescentmarked Lily; Green Peach.
Mite, Cyclamen.
Thrips, Greenhouse; Onion.   Weevil, Black Vine.

GOLDENCHAIN (*Laburnum*)
Aphid, Bean; Cowpea (infests ends of branches).
Mealybug, Grape.

GOLDENGLOW (*Rudbeckia*)
Aphid, Brown Ambrosia; Goldenglow (common; bright red on stems).
Beetle, Asiatic Garden; Fuller Rose.
Borer, Burdock; Stalk.
Bug, Fourlined Plant; Tarnished Plant.   Mite, Twospotted.
Sawfly, Goldenglow.   Slugs.

GOLDENRAIN-TREE (*Koelreuteria*)
Scale, Lesser Snow; Mining; White Peach.

GOLDENROD (*Solidago*)
Aphid, Corn Root; Goldenglow; Leafcurl Plum; Sugarbeet Root.
Beetle, Goldenrod; Black Blister.   Borer, Locust.
Bug, Chrysanthemum Lace; Leaffooted.
Caterpillar, Orange Tortrix.   Fly, Gall.
Leafhopper, Mountain.
Scale, Cottonycushion; Black; Florida Wax; Green; Goldenrod.
Thrips.   Treehopper, Buffalo.

GOOSEBERRY (*Ribes grossularia; R. hirtellum*)
Aphid, Currant (crinkled leaves); Dogberry; Gooseberry Witchbroom; Green Gooseberry.
Beetle, Imbricated Snout.   Borer, Currant; Pacific Flatheaded.
Bug, Fourlined Plant.   Caterpillar, Yellow Woollybear.   Fly, Currant.
Fruitworm, Gooseberry.   Leafhopper, White Apple.

Leafroller, Fruittree; Obliquebanded.
Mealybug, Grape, Ground. Moth, Whitelined Sphinx.
Sawfly, Imported Currantworm (green, blackspotted larvae).
Scale, Cottony Maple; European Fruit Lecanium; Oystershell; Peach Lecanium; Putnam; San Jose; Scurfy.
Spanworm, Currant.

GOURD (*Cucurbita*)
Aphid, Melon. Beetle, Spotted Cucumber; Striped Cucumber.
Borer, Squash Vine. Bug, Squash.
Whitefly, Cloudywinged; Greenhouse (very common pest).

GRAPE (*Vitis*)
Aphid, Cowpea; Grapevine; Grape Phylloxera.
Armyworm, Western Yellowstriped.
Beetle, Bumbling Flower; Darkling Ground; Fig; Grape Bud; Grape Colaspis; Grape Flea; Grapevine Hoplia; Japanese (serious on foliage); Green June; Rose Chafer; Rose Leaf; Small Darkling Ground; Spotted Grapevine; Steelblue Flea.
Borer, Apple Twig; Branch and Twig; Broadnecked Root; Grape Cane Gall Maker; Grape Root; Grape Trunk.
Bug, Boxelder; Consperse Stink; False Chinch; Harlequin.
Caterpillar, Badwinged Geometer; Omnivorous Looper; Yellow Woollybear.
Cricket, Blackhorned Tree. Curculio, Grape.
Cutworm, Brassy; Greasy; Variegated.
Earworm, Corn. Grasshoppers. Leaffolder, Grape.
Leafhopper, Grape; Southern Garden; Threebanded; Variegated; Virginiacreeper.
Leafminer, Grape. Leaf Skeletonizer, Grape; Western Grape.
Mealybug, Comstock; Fruit; Grape; Ground; Longtailed.
Midge, Grape Blossom; Grape Gall; Grapevine Tomato Gall.
Mite, Erineum; Grape Bud; Grape Rust; Pacific Spider; Willamette.
Moth, Abbott's Sphinx; Achemon Sphinx; Eightspotted Forester; Grape Berry (wormy berries, clusters webbed together); Grape Plume; Virginiacreeper; Whitelined Sphinx.
Planthopper (on wild grape).
Rootworm, Grape (chains of holes in leaves); Strawberry; Western Grape.
Sawfly, Grape.
Scale, Black; Brown Soft; California Red; Camphor; Cottonycushion; Cottony Maple; Cyanophyllum; European Fruit Lecanium; Florida Red; Grape (round, gray, on old canes); Greedy; Green; Lesser

Snow; Obscure; Olive; Osborn's; Oystershell; Peach; Pustule; Quohogshaped; White Peach; Ground Pearls.
Spittlebugs. Termites.
Treehopper, Twomarked (on wild grape).
Thrips, Bean; Citrus; Grape; Greenhouse; Pear; Western Flower.
Wasp, Grape Seed Chalcid.
Whitefly, Grape; Greenhouse; Woolly.   **Wireworms.**
Most spray schedules are planned primarily for control of the grape berry moth.

GRAPEFRUIT
Beetle, Fuller Rose.   **Mealybug,** Longtailed.
Mite, Citrus Red; Citrus Rust.
Scale, Black; California Red; Cottonycushion.
Thrips, Citrus.
See Citrus Fruits for many other pests.

GRASS (see Lawn Grasses)

GREVILLEA (Australian Silk-oak)
Budworm, Tobacco.   **Caterpillar,** Omnivorus Looper.
Mealybug, Citrophilus; Grape.   **Mite,** Avocado Red; Grevillea.
Scale, Black; Brown Soft; Chaff; Coconut; Cottonycushion; Cyanophyllum; Dictyospermum; Florida Red; Greedy; Green Shield; Latania; Lesser Snow; Long Soft; Mining; Oleander; Pustule; Pyriform; Quohogshaped.

GRINDELIA
Aphid, Grindelia.

GROUNDCHERRY (*Physalis*)
Aphid, Potato.
Beetle, Colorado Potato; Potato Flea; Tobacco Flea.
Borer, Potato Stalk.   **Budworm,** Tobacco.
Hornworm, Tobacco; Tomato.   **Maggot,** Pepper.
Mite, Tomato Russet.   **Mealybugs.**

GROUNDSEL (*Senecio*)
Aphid, Green Peach.   **Butterfly,** Painted Beauty.
Caterpillar, Omnivorous Looper.

GROUNDSELBUSH, SEAMYRTLE (*Baccharis*)
Scale, Acuminate; Black; Cyanophyllum; Florida Wax; Goldenrod; Green Shield; Green; Hemispherical; Latania; Pyriform.

GUAVA (*Psidium*)

Beetle, Rhabdopterus.
Fly, Caribbean Fruit; Mexican Fruit (only in part of Texas).
Mealybug, Citrus; Longtailed; Mexican; Striped.
Mite, Broad; False Spider. **Moth,** Ermine.
Scale, Barnacle; Black; Brown Soft; Chaff; Coconut; Cottonycushion; Cottony Taxus; Dictyospermum; Florida Red; Florida Wax; Greedy; Green; Green Shield; Hemispherical; Latania; Nigra; Oriental; Parlatorialike; Pyriform; Tesselated.
Termites. Thrips, Greenhouse; Redbanded.
Whitefly, Avocado; Woolly.

GUMBO-LIMBO (*Bursera simaruba*)

Scale, Black; Brown Soft; Coconut; Cottonycushion; Florida Wax; Japanese Wax; Pustule; Latania; Rufous.

GYPSOPHILA

Leafhopper, Aster.

HABRANTHIS

Fly, Narcissus Bulb.

HACKBERRY (*Celtis*)

Beetle, Hackberry Engraver.
Borer, Live Oak Root; Painted Hickory; Twig Pruner.
Bug, Hackberry Lace; Southern Green Stink.
Butterfly, Hackberry Empress. **Caterpillar,** Puss.
Leafhopper, Potato.
Mite, Hackberry Witches' Broom. **Moth,** Oriental.
Psyllid, Hackberry Nipplegall Maker.
Orthezia, Greenhouse.
Scale, Camphor; Citricola; Cottonycushion; Cottony Maple, Cyanophyllum; Elm Scurfy; European Fruit Lecanium; Gloomy; Green Shield; Lesser Snow; Obscure; Oystershell; Pustule; Putnam; San Jose; Walnut.
Spittlebug, Blueberry. **Whitefly,** Mulberry.

HAMELIA (Firebush; Scarletbush)

Mealybug, Citrus. **Orthezia,** Greenhouse.
Scale, Black; Green Shield; Hemispherical; Lesser Snow; Mining; Parlatorialike.

HAWTHORN (*Crataegus*)

Aphid, Apple; Apple Grain; Clover; Fourspotted Hawthorn; Grapevine; Hawthorn; Melon; Rosy Apple (curls young leaves) ; Spirea; Woolly Apple (white on branches) ; Woolly Hawthorn.

Beetle, Larger Elm Leaf; Striped Cucumber; Japanese.

Borer, Apple Bark; Flatheaded Appletree; Roundheaded Appletree; Shothole; Sinuate Peartree.

Bud Moth, Eyespotted.

Bug, Apple Red; Hawthorn Lace (stippled foliage).

Cankerworm, Fall; Spring.   **Casebearer,** Cigar.

Caterpillar, Eastern Tent (common); Forest Tent; Redhumped; Variable Oakleaf; Western Tent; Walnut.

Leaf Crumpler.   Leafhopper, Poplar.

Leafminer, Apple Blotch; Apple Trumpet; Spotted Tentiform; Unspotted Tentiform.

Leafroller, Obliquebanded.   **Leaf Skeletonizer,** Apple-and-Thorn.

Mealybug, Hawthorn.   **Mite,** Brown; Twospotted; Yellow Spider.

Moth, Browntail; Codling; Gypsy; Oriental Fruit; Western Tussock.

Planthopper.   Sawfly, Pearslug.

Scale, Barnacle; Brown Soft; Cottony Maple; European Fruit Lecanium; Florida Red; Florida Wax; Forbes; Latania; Putnam; San Jose; Scurfy; Terrapin; Walnut.

Weevil, Apple Flea.

HAZELNUT (*Corylus*)

Beetle, Larger Elm Leaf; Pitted Ambrosia.

Bug, Alder Lace.

Caterpillar, Filbertworm; Palmerworm; Western Tent; Yellownecked.

Leafhopper, Japanese.   **Leafroller,** Obliquebanded.

Scale, European Fruit Lecanium; Oystershell.

Weevil, Apple Flea; Hazelnut.   **Whitefly,** Hazel.

HEATH (*Erica*)

Scale, Greedy; Oleander; Oystershell.

HEATHER (*Calluna*)

Beetle, Japanese.   **Leaftier,** Greenhouse.

Mite, Twospotted.   **Scale,** Greedy; Mining; Oystershell.

HELENIUM (Sneezeweed)

Beetle, Helenium Snout.

HELIOPSIS

Bug, Fourlined Plant; Garden Fleahopper.

HELIOTROPE
Aphid, Crescentmarked Lily; Green Peach; Leafcurl Plum.
Bug, Fourlined Plant. **Leaftier,** Celery.
Mealybug, Citrophilus; Citrus. **Mite,** Twospotted.
Orthezia, Greenhouse. **Termites.**
Whitefly, Greenhouse (common, even outdoors).

HEMLOCK (*Tsuga*)
Aphid, Hemlock Woolly. **Bagworm.**
Beetle, Asiatic Garden (on seedlings) ; Fir Engraver; Lion; Mountain
Pine.
Borer, Blackhorned Pine; Flatheaded Cone; Flatheaded Fir; Hemlock
(destructive) ; Roundheaded Western Larch.
Caterpillar, False Hemlock Looper; Hemlock Looper (may defoliate) ;
Phantom Hemlock Looper; Western Hemlock Looper (serious).
Leafminer, Spruce Needle. **Leafroller,** Redbanded.
Mite, Hemlock; Spruce Spider (important, needles turn white) ; Two-
spotted.
Moth, Cypress; Gypsy. **Sawfly,** Hemlock.
Scale, Black Pine Leaf; Cottonycushion; Florida Wax; Grape; Hem-
lock (gray, circular) ; Latania; Lesser Snow; Pine Needle (white) ;
Red Bay; other species.
Webworm, Hemlock. **Weevil,** Strawberry Root.

HIBISCUS (Rose-mallow)
Aphid, Bean; Melon.
Beetle, Cuban May; Fuller Rose; Japanese.
Bollworm, Pink. **Bug,** Cotton Stainer. **Earworm,** Corn.
Katydids (large holes in foliage). **Moth,** Abutilon (green caterpil-
lar).
Sawfly.
Scale, Black; Brown Soft; California Red; Cottonycushion; Chaff;
Cyanophyllum; Fern; Florida Red; Florida Wax; Hemispherical;
Japanese Wax; Latania; Lesser Snow; Long Soft; Nigra; Olean-
der; Oriental; Parlatorialike; Pineapple; Pustule, Quohogshaped;
San Jose; Tesselated.
Weevil, Boll; Hibiscus. **Whitefly,** Greenhouse.

HICKORY (*Carya*)
Aphid, Blackmargined; Black Pecan; Blackspotted Hickory; Giant
Bark (large, gray and black) ; Hickory Phylloxera.
Beetle, Hickory Bark; Hickory Saperda; June.
Borer, Banded Hickory; Brown Wood: Flatheaded Appletree; Painted

Hickory; Pecan Carpenterworm; Redheaded Ash; Tiger Hickory; Twig Girdler; Twig Pruner.
Bug, Hickory Plant; Sycamore Lace.
Cankerworms. Casebearer, Cigar; Pecan.
Caterpillar, Hickory Horned Devil; Hickory Shuckworm; Linden Looper; Redhumped; Stinging Rose; Walnut; Yellownecked.
Cicada, Periodical. **Curculio,** Hickorynut.
Leafroller, Fruittree; Hickory. **Mealybug. Mite,** Oak.
Moth, Gypsy; Hickory Tussock; Imperial; Lappet; Luna; Oriental.
Sawfly, Butternut Woollyworm.
Scale, Cottony Maple; European Fruit Lecanium; Grape; Hickory; Latania; Osborn's; Obscure; Putnam; Scurfy; Tesselated.
Treehopper, Threecornered Alfalfa; Twomarked.
Walkingstick. Webworm, Fall. **Weevil,** New York; Pecan.

HOGPLUM (*Spondias*)
Mealybug, Striped.
Scale, Florida Wax; Mimosa; Obscure; Rufous; Walnut.

HOLLY (*Ilex*)
Aphid, Black Citrus; Foxglove; Melon; Potato; Rose.
Beetle, Black Blister; Ambrosia; Japanese; Potato Flea; Rhabdopterus.
Bud Moth, Holly. **Caterpillar,** Orange Tortrix; Saddleback.
Leafminer, Holly (blotch mines, very common); Native Holly (serpentine mines).
Leafroller, Obliquebanded. **Leaftier,** Holly.
Mealybug, Comstock. **Midge,** Holly Berry.
Mite, Southern Red (serious; leaves turn grayish); other species.
Moth, Gypsy; Lappet.
Scale, Acuminate; Barnacle; Black; Brown Soft; California Red; Camellia Mining; Chaff; Cottony Maple; Cyanophyllum; Dictyospermum; European Fruit Lecanium; Florida Web; Florida Wax; Forbes; Greedy; Green Shield; Hemispherical; Holly; Holly Pitmaking; Japanese; Japanese Wax; Latania; Oleander; Oystershell; Parlatorialike; Peach; Pustule; Pyriform; Red Bay; Rhododendron; Tea (common on Chinese Holly); Terrapin; Tesselated; Walnut; White Peach.
Spittlebugs. Webworm, Boxwood. **Weevil,** Black Vine; Japanese.
Whitefly, Citrus; Mulberry.
Spraying is usually necessary for holly leaf miners.

HOLLYHOCK (*Althaea rosea*)
Aphid, Bean; Green Peach; Hollyhock; Melon; Potato.

Beetle, Japanese (common on flowers); Oriental; Rose Chafer; Spotted Cucumber.
Borer, Burdock; European Corn; Stalk.
Bug, Hollyhock Plant; Lace; Tarnished Plant.
Butterfly, Painted Beauty; Painted Lady.
Caterpillar, Yellow Woollybear.
Leafminer. Leafroller, Redbanded. **Leaf Skeletonizer,** Cotton Leaf Perforator.
Mealybug, Mexican. **Mite,** Twospotted. **Moth,** Abutilon.
Scale, Brown Soft; Latania; Lesser Snow.
Slug, Spotted Garden (large holes in leaves).
Thrips, Gladiolus; Hollyhock. **Weevil,** Boll; Hollyhock.

HONEYLOCUST (*Gleditsia*)
Beetle, Ashgray Blister.
Borer, Honeylocust; Painted Hickory; Twig Girdler.
Bug, Plant; Lace. **Cankerworm,** Spring; Fall. **Caterpillar,** Walnut.
Leafhopper. Leafroller, Locust.
Midge, Honeylocust Podgall. **Mite,** Honeylocust Spider.
Moth, Oriental. **Scale,** Black; Cottony Maple; European Fruit Lecanium.
Webworm, Mimosa (very common and injurious). **Whitefly,** Greenhouse.

HONEYSUCKLE (*Lonicera*)
Aphid, Honeysuckle and Parsnip; Woolly Honeysuckle.
Beetle, Black Blister; Fuller Rose; Potato Flea.
Bug, Fourlined Plant. **Caterpillar,** Omnivorous Looper.
Leafroller, Obliquebanded; European Honeysuckle; Redbanded.
Mealybug, Comstock; Longtailed. **Midge.**
Moth, Snowberry Clearwing; Whitelined Sphinx.
Sawfly, Honeysuckle.
Scale, Camphor; Cottonycushion; Chaff; Coconut; Cyanophyllum; Dictyospermum; Greedy; Green Shield; Hemispherical; Latania; Lesser Snow; Mining; Oystershell; Parlatorialike; Pyriform; Quohogshaped; San Jose; Walnut; White Peach.
Webworm, Fall. **Weevil,** Japanese. **Whitefly,** Greenhouse; Iris.

HOP-HORNBEAM (*Ostrya*)
Aphid, Melon. **Beetle,** Pitted Ambrosia. **Borer,** Twolined Chestnut.
Bug, Birch Lace.
Scale, Cottonycushion; Latania.

HOP-TREE (*Ptelea*)
Scale, White Peach.   **Treehopper**, Twomarked.

HORNBEAM (*Carpinus*)
Scale, Maple Phenacoccus; Sourgum.

HORSECHESTNUT (*Aesculus*)
Aphid.   Bagworm.
Beetle, Japanese (very destructive) ; Potato Flea.
Borer, Flatheaded Appletree.
Caterpillar, Omnivorous Looper.
Leafroller, Fruittree; Obliquebanded.
Mealybug, Comstock; Grape.   **Mite,** Fourspotted; Rust.
Moth, Whitemarked Tussock.
Scale, Cottony Maple; Maple Phenacoccus; Oystershell; Putnam;
     Scurfy; Walnut.
Spanworm, Elm.
     See also Buckeye.

HORSERADISH (*Armoracia*)
Aphid, Western Aster Root.
Beetle, Horseradish Flea; Western Black Flea.
Bug, Harlequin.
Caterpillar, Cabbage Looper; Imported Cabbageworm.
Curculio, Cabbage.   **Moth,** Diamondback.   **Webworm,** Cabbage.

HOSTA (Plantain Lily)
Scale, Florida Wax.

HOYA (Wax-plant)
Aphid, Oleander.   **Mealybug,** Citrus.

HUCKLEBERRY (*Gaylussacia*)
Scale, Azalea Bark; False Cottony Maple; Latania; Oak Eriococcus;
     Putnam; Red Bay.

HUCKLEBERRY (*Vaccinium*) See Blueberry.

HYACINTH (*Hyacinthus*)
Caterpillar, Yellow Woollybear.
Fly, Lesser Bulb; Narcissus Bulb (large maggot in rotting bulb).
Mite, Bulb (minute, white, in rotting bulbs).

HYDRANGEA
Aphid, Crescentmarked Lily; Green Peach; Melon.
Beetle, Rose Chafer. **Bug,** Tarnished Plant. **Caterpillar,** Soybean Looper.
Leaftier, Hydrangea (leaves tied around flower bud).
Mite, Hydrangea; Twospotted.
Scale, Cottony Taxus; Hydrangea. **Thrips,** Banded Greenhouse.

HYMENOCALLIS (Spider Lily)
Caterpillar, Convict. **Fly,** Narcissus Bulb.
Scale, Boisduval's; Lesser Snow. **Thrips,** Banded Greenhouse.

HYPERICUM (St.-Johns-wort)
Scale, Hypericum; Latania; San Jose; White Peach.

HYSSOP
Scale, Black Araucaria.

IMPATIENS (*I. sultana*)
Aphid, Impatiens. **Mite,** Twospotted (serious pest on indoor plants).

INDIA-HAWTHORN (*Raphiolepis*)
Scale, Brown Soft; Cottonycushion; Camellia; Florida Red; Florida Wax; Dictyospermum.

INDIAN-LAUREL (*Ficus nitida*)
Scale, Black; Black Thread; Chinese Obscure; Cyanophyllum; Dictyospermum; Florida Red; Florida Wax; Green Shield; Proteus; Rufous.

INDIAN-PAINTBRUSH (*Castileja*)
Mealybug, Coleman's.

INKBERRY (see Gallberry)

IRESINE
Scale, Green.

IRIS
Aphid, Crescentmarked Lily; Brown Ambrosia; Potato; Tulip Bulb (white, cottony).
Beetle, Blister; Carrot; Oriental; Rose Chafer; Rose Leaf; White-fringed.

Borer, Burdock; Iris (chief pest, producing ragged leaves, hollow rhizomes); Stalk.
Bud Moth, Verbena (green caterpillars on seed pods).
Fly, Lesser Bulb. **Caterpillar**, Zebra.
Leaftier, Omnivorous. **Mites.**
Scale, Black Thread; Florida Red. **Slug**, Spotted Garden; other species.
Thrips, Gladiolus; Flower; Iris (prevalent on Japanese iris).
Weevil, Iris (in seed pods). **Whitefly**, Spirea. **Wireworm**, Pacific Coast.

IRONWOOD (*Ostrya virginiana*)

Aphid, Melon. **Beetle**, Pitted Ambrosia.
Borer, Twolined Chestnut. **Scale**, Cottonycushion; Latania.

IVY, BOSTON (*Parthenocissus tricuspidata*)

Beetle, Japanese (serious).
Leafhopper, Grape; Virginiacreeper (foliage white in summer).
Moth, Eightspotted Forester. **Scale**, Calico; Cottonycushion.
Weevil, Imported Longhorned.

IVY, ENGLISH (*Hedera helix*)

Aphid, Bean; Green Peach; Ivy.
Beetle, Black Blister. **Bug**, Fourlined Plant.
Caterpillar, Cabbage Looper; Omnivorous Looper; Puss.
Hornworms. **Leaftier**, Celery.
Mealybug, Citrus; Grape; Mexican.
Mite, Privet; Twospotted (very common, leaves gray, mealy).
Moth, Eightspotted Forester.
Scale, Brown Soft; Cottonycushion; Cottony Maple; Cottony Taxus; Dictyospermum; Florida Red (round, reddish brown); Green; Glover; Greedy; Florida Wax; Oleander (yellow, flat); Oak Eriococcus; Olive; Oriental; Parlatorialike; Peach Lecanium; Pineapple; Pit; Pustule; Proteus; Pyriform; Red Bay; Tesselated.

IXORA

Aphid, Black Citrus. **Beetle**, Colaspis.
Mealybug, Longtailed. **Moth**, Io.
Scale, Acuminate; Barnacle; Black; Black Thread; Brown Soft; Cottonycushion; Cyanophyllum; Florida Red; Florida Wax; Green; Green Shield; Hemispherical; Mango Shield; Mining; Oriental; Parlatorialike; Pustule; Pyriform; Tesselated.
Weevil.

JACARANDA
Aphid, Spirea. **Orthezia,** Greenhouse.
Scale, Black; Cottonycushion; Hemispherical; Lesser Snow; Long Soft; Purple; Pustule; Quohogshaped; Rufous.

JACOBINIA
Orthezia, Greenhouse.
Scale, Hemispherical; Mining; Parlatorialike; Proteus; Pustule.

JAMAICA-APPLE, CUSTARD-APPLE
(*Annona reticulata*)
Mealybug, Coconut.
Scale, Hemispherical; Latania; Long Soft; Quohogshaped.

JAPANESE PAGODA-TREE (*Sophora*)
Scale, Cottonycushion; Long Soft.

JAPANESE QUINCE (*Chaenomeles*)
Aphid, Hawthorn; Melon; Spirea. **Beetle,** Japanese.
Bug, Hawthorn Lace. **Mealybug,** Grape.
Scale, Black; Greedy; Florida Wax; Japanese Wax; Peach; San Jose; White Peach.

JASMINE (*Jasminum*)
Mealybug, Citrus; Longtailed. **Orthezia,** Greenhouse.
Scale, Acuminate; Barnacle; Black; Black Thread; Brown Soft; California Red; Camphor; Chaff; Camellia; Cyanophyllum; Dictyospermum; Florida Red; Florida Wax; Green; Green Shield; Hemispherical; Japanese Wax; Latania; Lesser Snow; Long Soft; Mimosa; Mining; Oleander; Olive; Oriental; Parlatorialike; Pineapple; Proteus; Purple; Pustule; Pyriform; Quohogshaped; Rufous; Terrapin; Tesselated.
Termites. Whitefly, Citrus; Jasmine.

JERUSALEM-CHERRY (*Solanum pseudocapsicum*)
Aphid, Green Peach; Potato. **Caterpillar,** Orange Tortrix (rolls leaves).
Scale, White Peach. **Thrips,** Flower; Onion. **Whitefly,** Greenhouse.

JESSAMINE (*Cestrum*)
Mealybug, Citrus; Longtailed. **Orthezia,** Greenhouse.
Scale, Acuminate; Black; Black Thread; Brown Soft; Cyanophyllum;

Chaff; Dictyospermum; Florida Red; Florida Wax; Green Shield; Hemispherical; Latania; Lesser Snow; Mining; Oleander; Oriental; Parlatorialike; Pineapple; Pustule; Pyriform; Quohogshaped; Rufous; Tesselated.

JESSAMINE, YELLOW (*Gelsemium*)
Mealybug, Longtailed.   Scale, Terrapin.

JOBS-TEARS (*Coix lacryma-jobi*)
Caterpillar, Orange Tortrix.

JUNEBERRY (see Shadbush)

JUNIPER, REDCEDAR (*Juniperinus*)
Aphid, Arborvitae; Redcedar; Rocky Mountain Juniper; American Juniper.
Bagworm (spindle-shaped bags on twigs; common).
Beetle, Cedar Bark; Golden Buprestid.
Borer, Blackhorned Pine; Flatheaded Cone.
Caterpillar, Redcedar Tortrix.
Mealybug, Juniper; other species.   Midge, Juniper.
Mite, Juniper Bud; Spruce Spider (foliage gray, webby); Twospotted.
Moth, Imperial; Juniper; other species.   Sawfly, Arborvitae.
Scale, Dictyospermum; Juniper (small, round, white, foliage yellow); Latania; Newstead's; Pine Needle; Red Bay; other species.
Spittlebugs.   Webworm, Juniper; Pale Juniper.
Weevil, Arborvitae; Deodar; Strawberry Root.

JUSTICIA
Mealybug, Citrus.   Scale, Black Thread.

KALANCHOE (*Bryophyllum*)
Aphids.   Mite, Cyclamen.   Scale, Lesser Snow.

KALE (*Brassica oleracea* var. *acephala*)
Aphid, Cabbage; Turnip.
Caterpillar, Cabbage Looper; Imported Cabbageworm.
Leaftier, Celery.   Moth, Diamondback.
Webworm, Cabbage.
See Cabbage for other pests.

KENTUCKY COFFEE-TREE (*Gymnocladus*)
Scale, Olive.

KERRIA
Beetle, Japanese (prevalent on this host).

KOHLRABI (*Brassica caulorapa*)
Aphid, Cabbage; Turnip.   Beetle, Asiatic Garden.
Bug, Harlequin.
Caterpillar, Cabbage Looper; Imported Cabbageworm.

KUDZU (*Pueraria*)
Beetle, Japanese.   Caterpillar, Velvetbean.
Scale, Brown Soft; Oleander; White Peach.

KUMQUAT
Thrips, Citrus.
   See Citrus for other pests.

LANCEWOOD (*Ocotea*)
Scale, Acuminate; Black Thread; Cottonycushion; Latania; Pyriform; Tesselated.

LANTANA
Beetle, Leaf.   Caterpillar, Orange Tortrix.
Fly, Lantana Gall.   Leaftier, Celery.
Mealybug, Citrus; Mexican; Yucca.   Mite, Broad; Cyclamen.
Moth, Lantana Plume; other species.   Orthezia, Greenhouse.
Scale, Brown Soft; Chaff; Cottonycushion; Green; Latania; Lesser Snow; Mango Shield; Mining; Pustule; Pyriform.   Whitefly, Greenhouse.

LARCH (*Larix*)
Aphid, Spruce Gall; Woolly Larch.
Bagworm (may defoliate).
Beetle, Douglas Fir; Eastern Larch; Douglas Fir Engraver; Japanese.
Borer, Flatheaded Fir; Western Larch Roundheaded.
Bud Moth, Eyespotted; Larch.   Budworm, Spruce.
Casebearer, Larch (leaves mined, used as cases).
Caterpillar, False Hemlock Looper.
Moth, Douglas Fir Pitch; Gypsy; Whitemarked Tussock.
Sawfly, Larch (green larvae may strip trees) ; Redheaded Pine.
Weevil, Pales.

LARKSPUR, ANNUAL (*Delphinium*)
Aphid, Delphinium (red, common on flower heads).

Borer, Stalk.   Leafhopper, Mountain.   Leafminer, Larkspur.
Mealybug, Ground.   Mite, Cyclamen.

LAUREL (*Laurus*)
Bud Moth, Eyespotted.   Mealybug, Ground.   Psyllid, Laurel.
Scale, Brown Soft; Chaff; Cottonycushion; Dictyospermum; Florida
Red; Florida Wax; Greedy; Green Shield; Glover; Latania; Purple; Pyriform; San Jose; Tesselated; Walnut; White Peach.

LAURESTINUS (*Viburnum tinus*)
Scale, Dictyospermum; Parlatorialike; White Peach.
Thrips, Greenhouse.

LAVATERA (Tree-mallow)
Psyllid, Lavatera.   Scale, Greedy.

LAVENDER
Butterfly, West Coast Lady.   Bug, Fourlined Plant.
Caterpillar, Orange Tortrix; Yellow Woollybear.

LAWN GRASSES
Ant, Argentine; Cornfield; Pavement; other species; (mounds in
lawns).
Aphid, Apple Grain; Chokeberry; Chokecherry; Corn Root; Elm
Cockscombgall; Elm Sackgall; English Grain; Lettuce Root;
Mealy Plum; Rose Grass; Rusty Plum; Solanum Root.
Armyworm, Fall; Lawn (on Bermuda grass).
Beetle, Asiatic Garden; Cuban May (on St. Augustine); European
Chafer; Japanese; June; Northern Masked Chafer; Oriental;
Southern Masked Chafer; Rose Chafer (all the preceding have
grubs working at grass roots) ; Palestriped Flea; Sweetpotato Flea.
Billbug, Bluegrass; other species.   Borer, Cranberry Girdler.
Bug, Chinch; False Chinch; Hairy Chinch (grass turns brown in
patches) ; Say Stink; Western Chinch.   Butterfly, Fiery Skipper.
Cricket, Changa; Mormon; Northern Mole; Southern Mole.
Cutworm, Bronzed; Glassy; Yellowheaded.   Earthworms.
Fly, Australian Sod; Frit.   Grasshoppers.
Leafhopper, Mountain; Painted; Yellowheaded.
Mealybug, Ground.   Millipedes.
Mite, Banks Grass; Bermudagrass; Clover.   Moths.
Scale, Bermudagrass; Ground Pearls; Rhodes Grass.   Slugs.   Snails.
Spittlebugs.   Termites.   Thrips, Flower; Grass.
Walkingstick, Prairie.   Wasp, Cicada killer (holes, mounds in lawn).

Webworm, Sod; Vagabond Crambus (silken nests).
Weevil, Annual Bluegrass; Cribrate; Strawberry Root.
Whitefly. Wireworm, Eastern Field; Plains False.
The usual treatments are for beetle grubs, chinch bugs, sod webworms, with spot treatment for ants.

LEMON (*Citrus limonia*)
Beetle, Fuller Rose. Mealybug, Grape; Longtailed; Yucca.
Mite, Citrus Bud; Citrus Rust; Lewis Spider; Strawberry Spider; Yuma Spider.
Scale, Black; California Red; Cottonycushion; Oleander.
Thrips, Citrus.
See Citrus Fruits for other pests.

LESPEDEZA
Webworm, Lespedeza. Weevil, Imported Longhorned.

LETTUCE (*Lactuca sativa*)
Aphid, Bean; Brown Ambrosia; Goldenglow; Green Peach; Lettuce Root; Potato; Turnip; White Aster Root.
Beetle, Palestriped Flea; Potato Flea.
Bug, Garden Fleahopper; Harlequin; Pitted Lygaeid; Tarnished Plant.
Caterpillar, Cabbage Looper; Celery Looper; Imported Cabbageworm.
Centipede, Garden Symphylan. Earworm, Corn.
Leafhopper, Aster; Potato.
Leafroller, Omnivorous. Leaftier, Celery.
Millipedes. Slugs. Thrips, Tubulifera.
Weevil, Vegetable. Whitefly, Vegetable.

LEUCOJUM (Snowflake)
Fly, Narcissus Bulb.

LIGNUM-VITAE (*Guaiacum*)
Scale, Barnacle; Florida Red.

LIGUSTRUM (see Privet)

LILAC (*Syringa*)
Aphid, Melon.
Beetle, Rhinoceros (occasionally feeds on roots, kills bushes).
Borer, Lilac (common; holes in trunk, protruding sawdust).

Butterfly, Tiger Swallowtail.   **Caterpillar,** Hickory Horned Devil.
Earwig, European.
Leafminer, Chrysanthemum; Lilac (tan or brown blotches).
Leafroller, Obliquebanded.   **Mite.**
Moth, Cynthia; Great Ash Sphinx; Leopard; Polyphemus; Promethea.
Scale, Cottony Maple; Euonymus; Florida Red; Latania; Olive; Oystershell (may completely encrust and kill branches); Pine Needle; Purple; San Jose; Scurfy; White Peach.
Wasp, Giant Hornet (tears off bark around branches).
Weevil, Cribrate; Japanese; Lilac.   **Whitefly, Citrus.**
A dormant spray is often advisable for scales.

LILY (*Lilium*)

Aphid, Crescentmarked Lily; Foxglove; Green Peach; Melon (dark green to brown, transmits mosaic); Purplespotted Lily; Tulip Bulb.
Beetle, Carrot; Fuller Rose; Whitefringed.   **Borer,** Stalk.
Caterpillar, Convict; Saddleback; Yellow Woollybear; Zebra.
Fly, Narcissus Bulb (large white maggot).
Mealybug, Citrus; Longtailed; other species.   **Mite,** Bulb.
Moth, Noctuid.   **Planthopper.**
Scale, Black Thread; Cyanophyllum; Dictyospermum; Florida Red; Hemispherical; Lesser Snow; Proteus.
Thrips, Lily Bulb.   **Weevil,** Lily.

LILY-OF-THE-VALLEY (*Convallaria*)

Weevil, Lily-of-the-valley.

LIME (*Citrus aurantifolia*)

Bug, Western Leaffooted.
Mealybug, Yucca.   **Mite,** Citrus Rust.
Scale, Cottonycushion; Dictyospermum; Terrapin.
Thrips, Citrus.
See also Citrus Fruits.

LINDEN, LIME, BASSWOOD (*Tilia*)

Aphid, Giant Bark; Linden (yellow and black, abundant).
Bagworm.
Beetle, Elm Calligrapha; Japanese (serious); Native Elm Bark.
Borer, American Plum; Brown Wood; Flatheaded Appletree; Linden.
Bug, Green Stink; Basswood Lace; Walnut Lace.
Cankerworm, Fall; Spring.

Caterpillar, Linden Looper; Redhumped; Variable Oakleaf; Yellow-necked.
Leafminer, Basswood. **Leafroller,** Basswood; Obliquebanded.
Mealybug, Taxus. **Mite,** Blister; Fourspotted; Gall.
Moth, American Dagger; Cynthia; Cecropia; Elm Sphinx; Gypsy; Whitemarked Tussock.
Sawfly, Elm.
Scale, Brown Soft; Cottony Maple; European Fruit Lecanium; Latania; Long Soft; Oystershell; Putnam; San Jose; Terrapin; Tesselated; Tuliptree; Walnut; White Peach.
Walkingstick. Whitefly, Mulberry (dark with white fringe).

LIPSTICK TREE (*Bixa*)
Scale, Mining; Quohogshaped.

LIRIOPE (Lily-turf)
Scale, Cyanophyllum; Dictyospermum; Florida Red; Lesser Snow; Proteus.

LIZARDS-TAIL (*Saururus*)
Mealybug, Coleman's.

LOBELIA
Aphid, Leafcurl Plum. **Bug,** Negro.
Leafhopper, Aster. **Leafroller,** Redbanded. **Leaftier,** Celery.

LOCUST (*Robinia*)
Aphid, Cowpea; Locust. **Bagworm.**
Beetle, Sweetpotato Leaf; Claycolored Leaf; Tenlined June.
Borer, Brown Wood; Carpenterworm; Lima Bean Pod; Locust (serious on black locust; young trees killed); Locust Twig; Painted Hickory; Twig Pruner.
Bug, Harlequin; Plant. **Butterfly,** Silverspotted Skipper.
Caterpillar, Redhumped; Velvetbean.
Leafminer, Locust (foliage looks "blighted"; very common).
Leafroller, Fruittree; Locust.
Mite, European Red. **Moth,** Crinkled Flannel; Io. **Sawfly.**
Scale, Black; Brown Soft; Cottonycushion; Cottony Maple; European Fruit Lecanium; Greedy; Oystershell; Putnam; San Jose; Walnut; White Peach.
Spanworm, Cleftheaded.
Treehopper, Buffalo; Threecornered Alfalfa; Twomarked.
Walkingstick, Twostriped.

LOGANBERRY (*Rubus loganobacchus*)

Aphid, European Raspberry. Beetle, Fuller Rose.
Bug, Consperse Stink. Cricket, Blackhorned Tree; Snowy Tree.
Fruitworm, Western Raspberry. Horntail, Raspberry.
Leafroller, Fruittree; Obliquebanded.
Maggot, Raspberry Cane. Sawfly, Raspberry. Scale, Rose.
Whitefly, Glacial; Greenhouse.
See Raspberry for other possible pests.

LOQUAT (*Eriobotrya japonica*)

Aphid, Apple; Melon.
Beetle, Flea; Western Spotted Cucumber; Western Striped Cucumber.
Borer, Pacific Flatheaded; Shothole.
Bug, Harlequin. Mealybug, Citrus.
Mite, Platanus; Southern Red. Moth, Codling.
Scale, Acuminate; Barnacle; Cyanophyllum; Florida Red; Florida
Wax; Mining; Latania; Olive; Pyriform; San Jose.

LOTUS (*Nelumbian*)

Aphid, Melon; Waterlily.

LUPINE (*Lupinus*)

Aphid, Essig's Lupine; Lupine (green with white wax; abundant).
Borer, Lima Bean Pod. Bug, Fourlined Plant.
Butterfly, Painted Lady. Fly, Lupine.
Weevil, Lupine (eats half moons out of leaves).
Whitefly, Greenhouse.

LYCHEE (*Litchi chinensis*)

Beetle, Rhabdopterus. Bug, Southern Green Stink.
Mite, Avocado Red; Litchi.
Scale, Black; Barnacle; Cottonycushion; Dictyospermum; Florida
Red; Florida Wax; Green Shield; Lesser Snow; Long Soft; Lata-
nia; Pyriform; Quohogshaped; Tesselated.
Thrips, Florida Flower; Greenhouse.

MACADAMIA

Beetle. Caterpillar, Navel Orangeworm. Mealybug, Grape.
Scale, Araucaria; Dictyospermum; Greedy; Latania; Mining; Olean-
der.
Thrips, Greenhouse.

MADRONA (*Arbutus menziesi*)
Aphid, Rose and Bearberry.
Borer, Branch and Twig; California Prionus; Flatheaded Cherrytree. Nautical. Butterfly.
Caterpillar, Western Tent. Leafminer, Blotch.
Moth, Madrona Shield Bearer; Polyphemus. Psyllid.
Scale, Brown Soft. Thrips, Madroña; Pear.
Whitefly, Kellogg's; Iridescent; Madroña; Manzanita.

MAGNOLIA
Aphid, Foxglove; Tuliptree.
Borer, Root Collar. Caterpillar, Omnivorous Looper; Saddleback.
Leafhopper, Japanese.
Mealybug, Comstock; Longtailed; Striped. Mite. Psyllid.
Scale, Acuminate; Black; Brown Soft; Camellia; Chaff; Coconut; Cottonycushion; Cyanophyllum; Dictyospermum; European Fruit Lecanium; Florida Red; Florida Wax; Glover; Greedy; Lesser Snow; Latania; Japanese Wax; Magnolia (soft, brown convex); Oleander; Parlatorialike; Purple; Red Bay; Tuliptree; White Peach.
Weevil, Sassafras. Whitefly, Citrus.

MAHOGANY (*Swietenia*)
Beetle, Cuban May. Caterpillars.
Scale, Black; Black Thread; Coconut; Latania; Lesser Snow.
Webworm. Weevils.
See also Mountain-mahogany.

MAHONIA (Oregon-grape; Oregon-holly)
Aphid, Barberry. Mealybug. Moth.
Scale, Greedy; Latania; Olive.
Whitefly, Barberry; Inconspicuous.

MALLOW (*Malva*)
Aphid, Potato. Beetle, Japanese. Bollworm, Hibiscus; Pink.
Butterfly, Painted Beauty; Painted Lady.
Mealybug, Citrophilus. Moth, Abutilon.
Whitefly, Greenhouse.

MALPIGHIA (Barbados-cherry)
Mealybug, Striped.
Scale, Barnacle; Black; Coconut; Florida Wax; Dictyospermum; Hemispherical; Masked; Pyriform.

MANDEVILLA
Thrips, Greenhouse.

MANGO (*Mangifera indica*)
Beetle, Bark; Rhabdopterus.
Fly, Mexican Fruit (in Texas); Papaya Fruit; West Indian Fruit.
Leafhopper, Potato; other species.
Mealybug, Citrus; Coconut; Longtailed; Striped.
Mite, Avocado Red; Broad; Tumid Spider.
Scale, Acuminate; Black; Black Thread; Brown Soft; California Red; Chaff; Coconut; Dictyospermum; Florida Red; Florida Wax; Glover; Green Shield; Hemispherical; Latania; Lesser Snow; Mango; Mining; Nigra; Oleander; Oriental; Purple; Pustule; Pyriform; Quohogshaped; Tea; Tesselated.
Thrips, Greenhouse; Redbanded. **Weevil.**

MANGROVE (*Rhizophera*)
Beetle, Australianpine. Scale, Green; Red Bay; other species.

MANZANITA
Aphid, Manzanita Leafgall. Borer, Pacific Flatheaded.
Butterfly, California Tortoiseshell. Moth, Western Tussock.
Scale, Brown Soft; Greedy; Manzanita.
Whitefly, Crown; Inconspicuous; Manzanita.

MAPLE (*Acer*)
Aphid, American Maple; Boxelder; European Birch; Giant Bark; Norway Maple; Painted Maple; Sycamore; Woolly Alder; other species.
Bagworm. Beetle, Columbian Timber; Green June; Japanese; Potato Flea.
Borer, American Plum; Boxelder Twig; Brown Wood; Carpenterworm; Flatheaded Appletree; Gallmaking Maple; Maple; Maple Callus; Maple Petiole; Pacific Flatheaded; Pigeon Tremex; Sugar Maple; Twig Pruner.
Bug, Birch Lace; Boxelder; Green Stink.
Cankerworm, Fall; Spring.
Caterpillar, Eastern Tent; Forest Tent; Greenstriped Mapleworm; Hemlock Looper; Linden Looper; Puss; Redhumped Oakworm; Saddled Prominent.
Cricket, Blackhorned Tree. Fruitworm, Green.
Leafcutter, Maple. Leafhopper, Grape; Japanese Maple; Norway Maple; Potato.

Leafroller. Obliquebanded; other species. **Leaf Skeletonizer,** Maple Trumpet.

Mealybug, Comstock; Taxus. **Midge,** Gouty Vein Gall; Spindle Gall.

Mite, Maple Bladder Gall; Oak.

Moth, American Dagger; Browntail; Cecropia; Gypsy; Io; Leopard; Oriental; Pale Tussock; Polyphemus; Spotted Tussock; White-marked Tussock.

Sawfly, Elm.

Scale, Black; Brown Soft; Calico, Chaff; Cottonycushion; Cottony Maple; Cyanophyllum; European Fruit Lecanium; False Cottony Maple; Florida Wax; Gloomy; Greedy; Japanese; Lesser Snow; Maple Phenacoccus; Obscure; Oystershell; Putnam; San Jose; Scurfy; Terrapin; Walnut.

Spanworm, Bruce; Elm. **Thrips,** Bean; Pear.

Whitefly, Inconspicuous; Mulberry; other species.

Maples seldom have as many pests as this list indicates but aphids are a common nuisance dropping honeydew. Use oil sprays with caution; avoid on sugar maple.

MARANTA (*Calathea*)

Mite, Tumid Spider. **Mealybug,** Citrus.

Scale, Boisduval's; Cyanophyllum; Florida Red; Latania; Long Soft; Proteus.

MARGUERITE (*Chrysanthemum frutescens*)

Aphid, Leafcurl Plum.

Leafminer, Chrysanthemum (Marguerite Fly). **Leaftier,** Omnivorous.

Mealybug, Ground. **Mite,** Broad; Cyclamen.

MARIGOLD (*Tagetes*)

Aphid, Green Peach; Melon.

Beetle, Japanese (prevalent on African, seldom on French marigolds).

Borer, Stalk. **Bug,** Garden Fleahopper; Tarnished Plant.

Caterpillar, Yellow Woollybear. **Cutworms.**

Leafhopper, Potato; Redbanded; Aster.

Mealybug, Citrus; Mexican. **Mite,** Broad; Cyclamen; Twospotted.

Slug, Greenhouse; Spotted Garden.

Thrips, Composite. **Weevil,** Imported Longhorned.

MARLBERRY (*Ardisia paniculata*)

Scale, Acuminate; Green; Green Shield; Florida Wax.

MATRIMONY VINE (*Lycium chinense*)
Aphid, Crescentmarked Lily.   **Borer,** Potato Tuberworm.
Scale, Latania.

MELON, CANTALOUPE (*Cucumis melo*)
Aphid, Melon (green to brown or black; curls leaves; transmits mosaic).
Armyworm, Western Yellowstriped.
Beetle, Fig; Grape Colaspis; Imbricated Snout; Palestriped Flea; Potato Flea; Squash; Spotted Cucumber; Striped Blister; Striped Cucumber; Western Striped Cucumber.
Borer, Squash Vine (vines wilt).
Bug, Squash (large, brown, shield-shaped) ; Horned Squash.
Caterpillar, Melonworm; Pickleworm; Cabbage Looper; Yellow Woollybear.
Leafhopper, Beet (transmits curly-top virus) ; Southern Garden.
Leafroller, Omnivorous.   **Maggot,** Seedcorn.   **Millipedes.**
Mite, Desert Spider; Carmine Spider; Strawberry Spider; Twospotted.
Termites.   Thrips, Onion; Western Flower.
Whitefly, Greenhouse.
Start melons under protective Hotkaps or screens. Most melons are sensitive to sulfur; some varieties can take it.

MESEMBRYANTHEMUM (Ice-plant)
Mealybug, Yucca.   **Orthezia,** Greenhouse.
Scale, Green Shield; Lesser Snow.   **Thrips,** Greenhouse.

MESQUITE (*Prosopis glandulosa*)
Borer, Huisache Girdler; Nautical; Pacific Flatheaded; Roundheaded Mesquite.
Bug, Green Stink.   **Grasshoppers.**
Leafhopper, Sugarbeet.   **Moth,** Gallmaking Clearwing.
Scale, Soft.   **Termites.   Treehopper,** Modest.

MIGNONETTE (*Reseda*)
Beetle, Potato Flea.
Caterpillar, Cabbage Looper; Imported Cabbageworm.
Earworm, Corn.   **Leafhopper,** Aster.
Mite, Twospotted.   **Thrips,** Onion.

MIGNONETTE-TREE (*Lawsonia inermis*)
Scale, Black; Coconut; Cyanophyllum; Green Shield; Latania; Pyriform; Quohogshaped; Rufous.

MIMOSA, SILK-TREE (*Albizzia julibrissin*)
Beetle, Blister; other species. **Mealybug, Citrus.**
Scale, Acuminate; Cottonycushion; Dictyospermum; Chaff; Latania; Long Soft.
Webworm, Mimosa (very common and injurious).

MINT (*Mentha*)
Aphid, Mint. **Beetle, Mint Flea; June.**
Bug, Fourlined Plant (common; dark spots in leaves).
Cutworm, Redbacked; Variegated.
Leafcutter, Morningglory. **Mealybug, Citrus.**
Mite, Twospotted. **Moth.**
Weevil, Strawberry Root.

MOCK-ORANGE (*Philadelphus*)
Aphid, Bean; Green Peach. **Scale, White Peach.**

MONKEYFLOWER (*Mimulus*)
Butterfly, Checker Spot. **Mealybug, Yucca.**
Mite, Desert Spider; Twospotted. **Thrips, Banded Greenhouse.**

MONKEYPUZZLE (See Araucaria)

MOONFLOWER (*Calonyction*)
Aphid, Green Peach.
Beetle, Argus Tortoise (holes in leaves); Blacklegged Tortoise.
Mealybug, Citrus; Longtailed.
Orthezia, Greenhouse. **Thrips, Banded Greenhouse.**

MORINDA (Indian Mulberry)
Scale, Cyanophyllum; Green. **Whitefly, Jasmine.**

MORNING-GLORY (*Ipomoea*)
Aphid, Melon; Myrtle.
Beetle, Argus Tortoise; Golden Tortoise; Mottled Tortoise; Spotted Cucumber; Striped Tortoise; Sweetpotato Flea; Whitefringed.
Bug, Fourlined Plant; Garden Fleahopper.
Leafcutter, Morningglory. **Leafminer, Morningglory.**
Mealybug, Citrus; Longtailed.
Scale, Black; Brown Soft; Green; Latania; Lesser Snow. **Thrips.**
Weevil, Sweetpotato. **Whitefly, Greenhouse; Inconspicuous.**

MOUNTAIN-ASH (*Sorbus*)

Aphid, Rosy Apple; Spirea; Woolly Apple. **Beetle,** Japanese.
Borer, American Plum; Apple Bark; Flatheaded Appletree; Lilac; Pacific Flatheaded; Roundheaded Appletree; Shothole; Sinuate Peartree.
Bug, Birch Lace.   **Mite,** European Red; Pear Leaf Blister.
Moth, Apple Fruit; Rusty Tussock. **Rootworm,** Strawberry.
Sawfly, Mountainash (eats all of leaf except veins) ; Pearslug.
Scale, Black; Cottony Maple; Oystershell; San Jose; Scurfy.

MOUNTAIN EBONY (see Bauhinia)

MOUNTAIN-HOLLY (*Nemopanthus*)

Scale, Greedy; Hemispherical; Oystershell.

MOUNTAIN-LAUREL (*Kalmia*)

Beetle, Strawberry Flea.
Borer, Azalea Stem; Rhododendron.
Bug, Rhododendron Lace (leaves stippled gray).
Scale, Azalea Bark; Chaff; Dictyospermum; Latania.
Weevil, Japanese. **Whitefly,** Mulberry (dark with white fringe).

MOUNTAIN-MAHOGANY (*Cercocarpus*)

Beetle, Pitted Ambrosia.
Borer, California Buprestid; Flatheaded Cherrytree; Pacific Flatheaded.
Caterpillar, Western Tent. **Psyllids.**

MUEHLENBECKIA

Scale, California Red; Dictyospermum; Florida Wax; Green Shield; Latania; Proteus; Tesselated.

MULBERRY (*Morus*)

Beetle.   Borer, Mulberry.
Bug, Southern Green Stink; Sycamore Lace.
Mealybug, Comstock; Longtailed. **Mite,** Carmine. **Planthopper.**
Scale, Black; Brown Soft; California Red; Cottony Maple; Cottony Taxus; Dictyospermum; European Fruit Lecanium; Florida Red; Florida Wax; Gloomy; Glover; Greedy; Green Shield; Japanese Wax; Olive; Latania; Lesser Snow; Peach; Pustule; Quohogshaped; San Jose; Terrapin; White Peach.
Whitefly, Mulberry (dark with white fringe).

MUSTARD (*Brassica*)

Aphid, Turnip.
Beetle, Horseradish Flea; Western Black Flea; Western Striped Flea; Yellowmargined Leaf.
Bug, Green Stink; Harlequin.
Caterpillar, Cabbage Looper; Imported Cabbageworm.
Curculio, Cabbage. **Maggot,** Cabbage.
Mealybug, Citrophilus. **Weevil,** Cabbage Seedpod; Cribrate; Vegetable.

MYRTLE (*Myrtus*)

Aphid, Clover; Crescentmarked Lily; Myrtle.
Leafhopper, Privet. **Mealybug,** Longtailed; Striped.
Scale, Acuminate; Barnacle; Black; Cottony Maple; Dictyospermum; Florida Red; Florida Wax; Glover; Greedy; Green Shield; Hemispherical; Latania; Long Soft; Nigra; Obscure; Purple; Pustule; Pyriform; Tesselated.
Thrips, Greenhouse.

MYRTLE, PERIWINKLE (see Vinca)

MYRTLE, WAX (see Bayberry)

NANDINA
Scale, Cottonycushion.

NARCISSUS (Daffodil)

Aphid, Tulip Bulb. **Caterpillar,** Convict.
Fly, Lesser Bulb (several maggots); Narcissus Bulb (1 large maggot).
Mealybug, Citrus; Solanum. **Millipedes.**
Mite, Bulb; Bulb Scale; Twospotted. **Moth,** Noctuid.
Slug, Introduced. **Thrips,** Flower; Gladiolus.

NASTURTIUM (*Tropaeolum*)

Aphid, Bean (black, inevitable); Buckthorn; Crescentmarked Lily; Green Peach.
Beetle, Flea. **Bug,** Tarnished Plant.
Caterpillar, Cabbage Looper; Imported Cabbageworm. **Earworm,** Corn.
Leafhopper, Beet. **Leafminer,** Serpentine (serious in the South).
Leaftier, Celery. **Mite,** Twospotted. **Thrips,** Greenhouse.

NECTARINE (see Peach)

NEMESIA
Aphid, Melon.

NEPHTHYTIS (see Syngonium)

NERINE
Thrips, Banded Greenhouse.

NEW JERSEY TEA (*Ceanothus americanus*)
Beetle, Rose Chafer.   Scale, Oystershell.

NICOTIANA (Flowering Tobacco)
Aphid, Green Peach.
Beetle, Colorado Potato; Potato Flea; Tobacco Flea; Whitefringed.
Cutworms.   Hornworms.   Whiteflies.

NINEBARK (*Physocarpus*)
Borer, Dogwood.   Whitefly, Glacial; Iris.

NOLINE (*Nolina*)
Scale, Black Thread; Chaff; Fern; Dictyospermum; Latania; Lesser
Snow; Proteus.

OAK (*Quercus*)
Aphid, Giant Bark; Oak; other species.
Beetle, Carrot; Goldsmith; Fuller Rose; Japanese; June; other spe-
cies.
Borer, Banded Hickory; Broadnecked Root; California Prionus; Car-
penterworm; Chestnut Bark; Chestnut Timberworm; Flatheaded
Appletree; Little Carpenterworm; Live Oak Root; Nautical; Oak
Sapling; Oak Timberworm; Pacific Flatheaded; Pecan Carpenter-
worm; Pigeon Tremex; Redheaded Ash; Sycamore; Tiger Hickory;
Tilehorned Prionus; Twig Girdler; Twig Pruner; Twolined Chest-
nut.
Bud Moth, Eyespotted.   Bug, Oak Lace (leaves whitened).
Cankerworm, Fall; Spring (may defoliate in peak years).
Caterpillar, Azalea; California Oakworm; Chainspotted Geometer;
Eastern Tent; Forest Tent; Greenstriped Mapleworm; Hemlock
Looper; Linden Looper; Orangestriped Oakworm; Orange Tor-
trix; Pacific Tent; Phigalia Looper; Pinkstriped Oakworm; Puss;
Redhumped Oakworm; Saddleback; Saddled Prominent; Spiny
Oakworm; Stinging Rose; Ugly Nest; Variable Oakleaf; Western
Oak Looper; Western Tent; Yellownecked.

Cicada, Periodical (twigs hang down, turn brown).
Leafminer, Basswood; Gregarious Oak; Solitary Oak.
Leafroller, Fruittree; Oak; Obliquebanded.
Leaf Skeletonizer, Oak. Leaftier, Oak.
Mite, Avocado Red; Oak; Platanus; Southern Red; Willamette.
Moth, American Dagger; Browntail; Buck; Cecropia; Crinkled Flannel; Gypsy (favors oak); Imperial; Io; Lappet; Leopard; Nevada Buck; Oriental; Polyphemus; Satin; Spotted Tussock; Western Tussock.
Sawfly, Pin Oak (leaves skeletonized); Red Oak.
Scale, California Red; Cottonycushion; Cottony Maple; Dictyospermum; European Fruit Lecanium; Florida Wax; Golden Oak; Greedy; Lesser Snow; Oak Eriococcus; Oak Kermes; Oak Lecanium; Obscure; Osborn's; Oystershell; Pit; Putnam; Pustule; Red Bay; Terrapin; Tesselated; Walnut; other species.
Treehopper, Oak; Threecornered Alfalfa.
Walkingstick, Twostriped. Wasp, Oak Gall (many species).
Webworm, Fall; Oak. Weevil, Asiatic Oak; Japanese; New York.
Whitefly, Citrus; Crown; Glacial; Inconspicuous.
Oaks often require a dormant spray for scale insects and a foliage spray for cankerworms, sometimes gypsy moths and other caterpillars.

OKRA (*Hibiscus esculentus*)
Aphid, Corn Root; Melon.
Beetle, Flea; Grape Colaspis; Japanese; Striped Cucumber; other species.
Bug, Green Stink; Harlequin; Pumpkin; Southern Green Stink.
Earworm, Corn. Leafhopper. Mite, Tumid Spider; Twospotted.
Moth, Abutilon (Okra Caterpillar).
Weevil, Boll. Whiteflies.

OLEANDER (*Nerium*)
Aphid, Bean; Green Peach; Oleander (yellow and black).
Caterpillar, Oleander. Leafroller, Omnivorous.
Mealybug, Citrus; Ground; Longtailed; Striped. Moth.
Scale, Araucaria; Black; Brown Soft; Chaff; Cottonycushion; Dictyospermum; Florida Red; Florida Wax; Green; Hemispherical; Latania; Lesser Snow; Oleander; Olive; Oriental; Parlatorialike; Peach; Pustule; Pyriform; Rufous; Tesselated.
Termites, Subterranean.

OLIVE (*Olea*)
Beetle, Olive Bark. Borer, American Plum; Branch and Twig.
Bug, Western Brown Stink.

Caterpillar, Omnivorous Looper.   Mealybug, Longtailed.
Mite, Lewis Spider; Olive Leaf; other species.
Scale, Araucaria; Black; California Red; Dictyospermum; Florida
Red; Florida Wax; Greedy; Hemispherical; Mining; Oleander;
Olive; Oriental; Pineapple; Purple; Red Bay; White Peach.
Thrips, Bean, Citrus.   Whitefly, Citrus.

ONION (*Allium*)

Aphid.   Armyworm, Fall.
Beetle, Blister; Imbricated Snout; Oriental.
Bug, Onion Plant.   Cutworms.
Fly, Lesser Bulb; Onion Bulb.   Leafminer, Pea.
Maggot, Onion (may kill seedlings); Seedcorn.   Mite, Bulb.
Thrips, Onion (leaves silvered, distorted).
Weevil, Vegetable.   Wireworm, Eastern Field.

OPHIOPOGON, WHITE LILYTURF (*Mondo*)

Scale, Brown Soft; Cyanophyllum; Dictyospermum; Fern; Florida
Red; Hemispherical; Lesser Snow; Proteus.

ORANGE (*Citrus*)

Beetle, Fuller Rose.
Bug, Cotton Stainer; Green Stink; Leaffooted; Western Leaffooted.
Caterpillar, Navel Orangeworm; Omnivorous Looper; Orange Tor-
trix.
Katydid, Angularwinged.
Mealybug, Grape; Ground; Japanese; Longtailed.
Mite, Citrus Red; Citrus Rust; Lewis Spider.
Scale, Black; Camphor; California Red; Cottonycushion; Greedy;
Oleander; San Jose; Tea.
Thrips, Bean; Citrus.
See also Citrus Fruits.

ORCHIDS

Ants, Florida Carpenter; Little Fire; other species.
Aphid, Crescentmarked Lily; Green Peach; Melon; Orchid; Palm.
Armyworm, Southern; Yellowstriped.
Beetle, Chinese Rose; Dendrobium.   Borer, Orchid Bulb.
Bug, Orchid Plant.
Caterpillar, Cabbage Looper; Parsleyworm; Pink Scavenger; Puss;
Saddleback.   Fly, Orchidfly (maggots in brown buds, small black
wasps).

Mealybug, Citrus; Longtailed; Orchid; Striped.
Mite, Omnivorous; Oncidium; Phaelenopsis; Tumid Spider; Two-spotted.
Moth, Morning Sphinx; Io; Great Southern White; other species.
Scale, Araucaria; Acuminate; Black; Black Thread; Brown Soft; Boisduval; Cactus; Chaff; Coconut; Cocos; Cockerell; Cyanophyllum; Cymbidium; Dictyospermum; False Brown Soft; False Parlatoria; Fern; Flyspeck; Florida Red; Florida Wax; Glover; Hemispherical; Ivy; Latania; Lesser Snow; Newstead's; Orchid; Oriental; Oystershell; Pineapple; Proteus; Pustule; Purple; Pyriform; Red Bay; Tea; Tesselated; Tesserate; Vanda Orchid; White Peach.
Slugs. Snails.
Thrips, Cuban Laurel; Banded Greenhouse; Florida Flower; Greenhouse; Lily Bulb; Orchid; Redbanded.
Weevil, Cattleya; Orchid.

ORCHID-TREE (see Bauhinia)

OSAGE-ORANGE (*Maclura*)
Borer, Mulberry. **Mealybug,** Citrus.
Scale, Cottonycushion; Cottony Maple; European Fruit Lecanium; Putnam; San Jose.
Whitefly, Citrus.

OSMANTHUS (Sweetolive; Tea Olive)
Scale, Acuminate; Brown Soft; Camellia; Black Thread; Chaff; Dictyospermum; Florida Red; Latania; Oleander; Parlatorialike; Red Bay; White Peach.

OXALIS
Aphid, Potato. **Mites.**

PACHYSANDRA (Spurge)
Mite, Twospotted (serious when plants are crowded).
Scale, Euonymus (thin, white, common); Florida Red; Oystershell; Purple; San Jose.

PALMETTO, CABBAGE PALM (*Sabal*)
Leaf Skeletonizer, Palm (major pest in Florida).
Moth, Fan Palm; other species. **Planthopper.**
Scale, Black Thread; Boisduval's; Coconut; Cocos; Dictyospermum;

Florida Red; Glover; Green; Oriental; Palmetto; Parlatorialike; Red Bay.
Whitefly, Citrus.

PALMS

Aphid, Green Peach; Latania; Palm.
Beetle, Fuller Rose.   **Borer,** Twig.   **Bug,** Royal Palm.
Caterpillar, Saddleback.
Leaf Skeletonizer, Palm (serious; leaves webbed).
Mealybug, Citrus; Coconut; Coleus; Grape; Longtailed; Palm.
Mite, Banks Grass; Privet; Tumid Spider.   **Moth,** Fan Palm.
Scale, Araucaria; Black; Black Thread; Boisduval's; Brown Soft; California Red; Chaff; Coconut; Cottonycushion; Cyanophyllum; Dictyospermum; Fern; Florida Red; Florida Wax; Glover; Greedy; Green Shield; Hemispherical; Latania; Oleander; Olive; Oriental; Palmetto; Parlatorialike; Pineapple; Purple; Pustule; Pyriform; Red Bay; Rufous; Tesselated; White Peach.
Thrips, Banded Greenhouse; Dracaena; Greenhouse.   **Weevil.**

PANDANUS (see Screwpine)

PANSY (*Viola*)

Aphid, Foxglove; other species.   **Beetle,** Flea.
Caterpillar, Yellow Woollybear.   **Cutworms.**
Leafhopper, Beet.   **Mealybug,** Solanum.   **Mite,** Twospotted.
Sawfly, Violet.   **Slugs.   Sowbugs.   Termites.   Wireworms.**

PAPAYA (*Carica papaya*)

Fly, Papaya Fruit.   **Leafhopper,** Papaya.
Scale, Coconut; Cottonycushion; Mining; Nigra; Parlatorialike; Pyriform.
Webworm, Papaya.   **Whitefly,** Avocado; Papaya.

PARKINSONIA (Jerusalem-thorn)

Mealybug, Citrus.
Scale, Barnacle; Brown Soft; Camphor; Chaff; Cottonycushion; Dictyospermum; Florida Wax; Latania; Lesser Snow; Long Soft; Quohogshaped.

PARSLEY (*Petroselinum*)

Aphid, Bean; Potato; Western Aster Root.   **Butterfly,** Western Parsley.

Caterpillar, Cabbage Looper; Parsleyworm.
Fly, Carrot Rust. **Leaftier,** Celery. **Mite,** Strawberry Spider.

PARSNIP (*Pastinaca*)
Aphid, Bean; Honeysuckle and Parsnip; Willow.
Beetle, Asiatic Garden; Carrot; Palestriped Flea.
Butterfly, Western Parsley.
Caterpillar, Parsleyworm; Yellow Woollybear.
Fly, Carrot Rust (tunnels in roots). **Leafhopper,** Aster.
Leafminer, Parsnip (blotch mines). **Millipedes.**
Webworm, Parsnip. **Weevil,** Carrot.

PASSION-FLOWER (*Passiflora*)
Butterfly, Brushfooted; Gulf Fritillary; Passion Vine; Zebra.
Caterpillar, Omnivorous Looper. **Leaftier,** Celery.
Mealybug, Citrus; Grape; Longtailed. **Orthezia,** Greenhouse.
Scale, Barnacle; California Red; Greedy; Green Shield; Latania;
  Lesser Snow; Purple; Proteus; Pustule.

PAWPAW (*Asimina triloba*)
Butterfly, Zebra Swallowtail. **Caterpillar,** Stinging Rose.

PEA (*Pisum*)
Aphid, Bean; Pea (large, green, important) ; Potato.
Armyworm, Beet.
Beetle, Bean Leaf; Imbricated Snout; Palestriped Flea; Spotted Cu-
  cumber; Striped Blister; Striped Cucumber; Western Striped Cu-
  cumber.
Borer, Clover Root; Lesser Cornstalk; Lima Bean Pod. **Budworm,**
  Tobacco.
Bug, Garden Fleahopper; Green Stink; Say Stink.
Caterpillar, Alfalfa; Cabbage Looper; Green Cloverworm; Velvet-
  bean; Yellow Woollybear.
Centipede, Garden Symphylan. **Curculio,** Cowpea. **Earworm,**
  Corn.
Leafminer, Pea. **Leaftier,** Celery; Omnivorous.
Maggot, Seedcorn. **Millipedes.**
Mite, Tumid Spider; Twospotted (serious in dry weather).
Moth, Pea (small caterpillars in pods).
Thrips, Onion; Western Flower. **Webworm,** Beet.
Weevil, Broad Bean; Pea; Pea Leaf. **Whitefly,** Greenhouse.

PEACH (*Prunus persica*)

(Including Nectarine, smooth-skinned peach)

Aphid, Black Cherry; Black Peach; Green Peach; Hop; Mealy Plum; Rusty Plum.

Beetle, Asiatic Garden; Bumbling Flower; Cherry Leaf; Fig; Fuller Rose; Green June; Japanese (prevalent, serious); Peach Bark; Plum Gouger; Redlegged Flea; Rose Chafer; Rose Leaf.

Borer, American Plum; Branch and Twig; California Prionus; Flatheaded Appletree; Lesser Peachtree; Nautical; Pacific Flatheaded; Peachtree (common, serious; gum at base of trunk); Peach Twig; Roundheaded Appletree; Shothole; Western Peachtree.

Bug, Boxelder; Dusky Stink; Green Stink (catfaces fruit); Leaffooted; Hickory Plant; Southern Green Stink; Tarnished Plant (new shoots black).

Cankerworm, Fall; Spring. **Casebearer,** California.

Caterpillar, Eastern Tent; Forest Tent; Walnut; Yellownecked.

Cicada, Periodical. **Cricket,** Blackhorned; Snowy Tree.

Curculio, Peach; Plum (common cause of wormy fruit).

Earworm, Corn. **Fly,** Mexican Fruit (in Texas) ; Walnut Husk.

Leafhopper, Mountain; Plum; Privet; Saddled.

Leafroller, Obliquebanded; Redbanded.

Mealybug, Citrophilus; Comstock; Ground.

Mite, Clover; Eriophyid (vector of peach mosaic); European Red; Fruittree; Peach Silver; Strawberry Spider; Twospotted.

Moth, Codling (wormy fruit) ; Oriental Fruit (blackens shoots).

Rootworm, Strawberry. **Sawfly,** Cherry Fruit; Peach.

Scale, Brown Soft; Cottonycushion; Cottony Maple; Cottony Peach; European Peach Lecanium; Florida Wax; Forbes; Grape; Howard; Latania; Italian Pear; Lesser Snow; Peach Lecanium; Pustule; Putnam; Pyriform; Rose; San Jose; Scurfy; Walnut; White Peach.

Thrips, Pear; Western Flower.

Treehopper, Buffalo. **Webworm,** Fall.

Peach spray schedules are timed primarily for control of brown rot and some other diseases with, usually, a dormant spray for scale insects, seasonal insecticides for plum curculio, Oriental fruit moth, and Japanese beetles, and late summer treatment for peachtree borers.

PEANUT (*Arachis hypogea*)

Armyworm, Fall.

Beetle, Elongate Flea; Palestriped Flea; Spotted Cucumber; Whitefringed.

Billbug, Southern Corn. **Borer,** Lesser Cornstalk. **Bug,** Burrowing Stink.

Caterpillar, Rednecked Peanutworm; Velvetbean (serious in Gulf States); Yellow Woollybear.

Cutworm, Granulate. **Earworm,** Corn.

Leafhopper, Potato (causes peanut "pouts"); Southern Garden.

Leafminer, Locust. **Mealybug,** Solanum. **Mite,** Twospotted. **Moth,** Bella.

Scale, Cottonycushion. **Termites.**

Thrips, Tobacco (terminal buds black). **Weevil. Wireworm,** Sand.

PEAR (*Pyrus communis*)

Aphid, Apple; Apple Grain; Clover; Cowpea; Hawthorn; Rosy Apple; Spirea; Woolly Apple; Woolly Pear.

Beetle, Fig; Fuller Rose; Green June; Palestriped Flea; Rose Chafer; Rose Leaf; Syneta Leaf.

Borer, American Plum; Apple Bark; Apple Twig; Brown Wood; Branch and Twig; Carpenterworm; Flatheaded Appletree; Pacific Flatheaded; Pear Fruit; Pigeon Tremex; Roundheaded Appletree; Shothole; Sinuate Peartree; Twig Girdler; Twig Pruner.

Bud Moth, Eyespotted; Pecan.

Bug, Apple Red; Consperse Stink; Pear Plant; Tarnished Plant.

Casebearer, California; Cigar.

Caterpillar, Eastern Tent; Forest Tent; Palmerworm; Redhumped; Stinging Rose; Yellownecked.

Cricket, Snowy Tree. **Curculio,** Apple; Plum; Quince (wormy fruit).

Earworm, Corn. **Fly,** Black Cherry Fruit; Cherry Fruit.

Fruitworm, Green. **Leaf Crumpler.**

Leafroller, Fruittree; Obliquebanded. **Leaf Skeletonizer,** Apple and Thorn.

Maggot, Apple.

Mealybug, Citrophilus; Comstock; Grape. **Midge,** Pear; Pear Leaf.

Mite, Clover; European Red; Fruittree; McDaniel; Pacific Spider; Pearleaf Blister (serious; dark blisters in leaves); Pear Rust; Strawberry Spider; Twospotted; Willamette.

Moth, Apple Fruit; Browntail; Codling; Hickory Tussock; Whitelined Sphinx.

Psyllid, Pear Psylla (leaves, fruit black; defoliation; tree decline).

Sawfly, California Pearslug; European Apple; Pearslug.

Scale, Barnacle; Black; Brown Soft; Calico; Cottony Maple; Cottonycushion; Dictyospermum; European Fruit Lecanium; Florida Wax; Forbes; Greedy; Howard; Italian Pear; Japanese Wax; Latania; Olive; Oystershell; Peach Lecanium; Pustule; Putnam; San Jose; Scurfy; Walnut; White Peach.

Thrips, Bean; Pear (blossoms appear burned).

Treehopper, Buffalo.   Webworm, Beet.
Weevil, New York.   Whitefly, Citrus.

The apple spray schedule often includes pears. Special treatment may be required for pearleaf blister mite and pear psylla.

PECAN (*Carya pecan*)

Aphid, Blackmargined; Black Pecan; Blackspotted Hickory; Giant Bark; Hickory; Pecan Leaf Phylloxera; Pecan Phylloxera.

Beetle, Cuban May; June.

Borer, American Plum; Apple Bark; Apple Twig; Dogwood; Flat-headed Appletree; Live Oak Root; Pecan; Pecan Carpenterworm; Shothole; Twig Girdler; Twig Pruner.

Bud Moth, Pecan.   Bug, Plant; Leaffooted; Southern Green Stink.

Casebearer, Pecan Cigar; Pecan Leaf; Pecan Nut.

Caterpillar, Hickory Horned Devil; Hickory Shuckworm (most serious pest) ; Omnivorous Looper; Walnut.

Curculio, Hickory Nut.   Mite, Avocado Red; Hickory; Pecan Leafroll; Twospotted.

Moths.   Sawfly.

Scale, Camphor; Cottonycushion; Cottony Maple; Dictyospermum; European Fruit Lecanium; Florida Red; Forbes; Greedy; Hickory; Latania; Obscure; Osborn's; Purple; Putnam; San Jose; Walnut; White Peach.

Spittlebug, Pecan.   Termites.

Webworm, Fall.   Weevil, Pecan (worms in nuts; serious).

PELARGONIUM (see Geranium)

PENSTEMON (Beard-tongue)

Aphid, Crescentmarked Lily; Foxglove; Potato.

Beetle, Fuller Rose.   Bug, Red-and-Black Stink.

Butterfly, Checker Spot.   Caterpillar, Orange Tortrix.

PENTAS

Caterpillar, Orange Tortrix.

Scale, Black; Cottonycushion; Pustule; Parlatorialike.

PEONY (*Paeonia*)

Ants (in buds, not injurious except for spreading Botrytis spores).

Beetle, Japanese (rare) ; Rose Chafer (common on flowers) ; Rose Leaf.

Bug, Fourlined Plant (tan circles in leaves) ; Tarnished Plant.

Curculio, Rose.

Scale, Oystershell; San Jose (present when old stalks not removed).
Thrips, Flower; Greenhouse (petals turn brown).

PEPPER (*Capsicum*)

Aphid, Green Peach; Melon; Mint; Potato. **Armyworm,** Beet.
Beetle, Asiatic Garden; Blister; Colorado Potato; Potato Flea; Rose
    Chafer; Spotted Cucumber; Tobacco Flea.
Borer, European Corn; Stalk.
Bug, Leaffooted; Pumpkin; Southern Green Stink; Garden Fleahop-
    per.
Cutworm, Granulate; Palesided.
Earworm, Corn. **Hornworm,** Tobacco; Tomato.
Leafhopper, Beet. **Leafminer,** Serpentine.
Maggot, Pepper. **Mealybug,** Ground.
Mite, Broad Cyclamen; Twospotted.
Orthezia, Greenhouse. **Psyllid,** Tomato.
Scale, Cottonycushion. **Weevil,** Pepper. **Whitefly,** Greenhouse.

PEPPER-TREE (*Schinus molle*)

Caterpillar, Omnivorous Looper. **Leafhopper. Mealybug,** Citroph-
    ilus.
Scale, Black (common); Barnacle; Chaff; Fern; Greedy; Green
    Shield; Hemispherical; Lesser Snow; Mining; Oleander; Parlatoria-
    like; Purple; Quohogshaped.
Thrips, Citrus.

PERSIMMON (*Diospyros*)

Beetle, Fuller Rose.
Borer, Flatheaded Appletree; Persimmon; Redheaded Ash; Twig
    Girdler (important in the East).
Caterpillar, Hickory Horned Devil; Redhumped; Variable Oakleaf.
Mealybug, Citrus; Mexican. **Moth,** Luna. **Psyllid,** Persimmon.
Scale, Acuminate; Bamboo; Barnacle; Black; Brown Soft; Cam-
    phor; Cottony Maple; European Fruit Lecanium; Florida Red;
    Florida Wax; Green Shield; Japanese Wax; Latania; Lesser
    Snow; Oleander; Osborn's; Oriental; Pustule; Putnam; San Jose;
    Tesselated; Walnut; White Peach.
Thrips, Greenhouse. **Whitefly,** Citrus. **Weevil.**

PETUNIA

Aphid, Green Peach; Potato.
Beetle, Asiatic Garden; Colorado Potato; Potato Flea (tiny shotholes
    in leaves); Spotted Cucumber.

Budworm, Tobacco. Bug, Garden Fleahopper; Tarnished Plant.
Caterpillar, Yellow Woollybear. Grasshoppers.
Hornworm, Tobacco; Tomato. Leafhopper, Aster. Leafminer, Pea.
Mealybug, Ground. Mite, Tomato Russet (transmits mosaic); Two-
  spotted.
Moth, Whitelined Sphinx. Orthezia, Greenhouse.

PHACELIA
Aphid, Leafcurl Plum.

PHILODENDRON
Mealybug, Citrus; Longtailed. Millipedes.
Mite, Carmine; Tumid Spider.
Scale, Black Thread; Brown Soft; Boisduval's; Dictyospermum; Fern;
  Latania; Orchid; Proteus; Red Wax.
Thrips, Banded Greenhouse.

PHLOX
Aphid, Melon; Spirea.
Beetle, Asiatic Garden; Black Blister; Golden Tortoise; June; Orien-
  tal; Potato Flea.
Borer, Stalk.
Bug, Fourlined Plant; Phlox Plant (reddish orange; deforms buds).
Earworm, Corn. Leafhopper, Aster.
Mite, Twospotted (very common; leaves yellow, webby).
Scale, Black; Brown Soft; Pyriform.

PHOTINIA
Beetle, Rhabdopterus.
Scale, Acuminate; Chaff; Dictyospermum; Florida Red; Florida Wax;
  Olive; San Jose; Walnut; White Peach. Thrips.
See also California Christmasberry.

PHYSOSTEGIA
Aphid, Foxglove. Budmoth, Verbena.

PIERIS
Bug, Andromeda Lace (on *Pieris japonica*).
See also Andromeda.

PINE (*Pinus*)
Aphid, Monterey Pine; Pine Bark (white fluffs on bark); Pine Leaf;
  Spruce Gall; Powdery Pine; White Pine; Woolly Pine Needle; other
  species.

Bagworm.

Beetle, Asiatic Garden (on seedlings) ; Black Hills; Black Turpentine; Coarsewriting; Claycolored Leaf; Englemann Spruce; Fivespined Ips; Golden Buprestid; Jeffrey Pine; June; Lion; Lodgepole Pine; Monterey Pine Cone; Monterey Pine Engraver; Mountain Pine; Northeastern Sawyer; Obtuse Sawyer; Oregon Fir Sawyer; Pine Chafer; Pine Colaspis; Pine Engraver; Pinyon Cone; Ponderosa Pine; Roundheaded Pine; Red Turpentine; Redwinged Pine; Southern Pine; Spotted Pine; Sugar Pine Cone; Western Pine Cone; other species.

Borer, Blackhorned Pine; Broadnecked Root; Brown Wood; Cedar Tree; California Prionus; Eastern Pineshoot; Flatheaded Cone; Flatheaded Fir; Pitch Mass; Ponderosa Pine Bark; Roundheaded Cone; Sculptured Pine; Turpentine; Western Larch Roundheaded.

Budworm, Spruce. **Butterfly,** Pine.

Caterpillar, Hemlock Looper; Monterey Pine Looper; Orange Tortrix; Pine Looper.

Horntail, California; Western.

Leafminer, Lodgepole Pine; Pine Needle; Pine Needlesheath.

Mealybug, Comstock; Cypress; Golden; Loblolly.

Midge, Gouty Pitch Gall; Monterey Pine; Monterey Pine Resin.

Mite, False Spider; Pine Bud; Spruce Spider; Pineneedle Sheath.

Moth, Cypress Tip; European Pine Shoot (common on ornamentals; tip yellow, crooked); Gypsy; Imperial; Monterey Pine Tip; Nantucket Pine Tip; Pandora; Pine Cone; Pine Tortrix; Pine Tube; Pine Tussock; Pitch Blister; Pitch Twig; Sequoia Pitch; Silverspotted Tiger; Zimmerman Pine; other species.

Sawfly, Balsam Fir; European Pine (serious, denudes branches) ; Introduced Pine; Jack Pine; Loblolly Pine; Lodgepole Pine; Monterey Pine; Redheaded Pine; Red Pine; Swaine Jack Pine; other species.

Scale, Barnacle; Black Pineleaf; Brown Soft; Cottonycushion; Cottony Pine; Florida Wax; Hemlock; Irregular Pine; Matsucoccus; Pine Needle (white, pearshaped, common) ; Newstead's; Pine Tortoise; Pinyon Needle; Prescott; Red Bay; Red Pine; Rufous; Walnut; other species.

Spittlebug, Pine; Saratoga.

Webworm, Pine; Pine False (needles webbed together).

Weevil, Deodar; Douglas Fir Twig; Lodgepole Terminal; Monterey Pine; Northern Pine; Pales; Pine Reproduction; Pine Root Collar; White Pine (leader dies back) ; Yosemite Bark.

A dormant spray of oil or lime sulfur for scales and later treatment for sawfly larvae takes care of many problems. Where allowed, use lindane for bark aphids; remove tips with shoot moths.

PINEAPPLE (*Ananas*)
Mealybug, Pineapple.   **Scale**, Boisduval's; Pineapple.

PISTACHIO (*Pistacia*)
Bug, Western Leaffooted.   **Scale**, California Red.   **Wasp**, See Chalcid.

PITHECELLOBIUM
Orthezia, Greenhouse.
Scale, Cottonycushion; Long Soft; Latania; Pustule.
Treehopper, Thornbug.

PITTOSPORUM
Aphid, Green Peach.   **Mealybug**, Citrophilus.
Mite, Tumid Spider; Twospotted.
Scale, Black; Brown Soft; Camellia; Cottonycushion (common);
    Chaff; Cyanophyllum; Florida Red; Florida Wax; Greedy; Green;
    Green Shield; Latania; Lesser Snow; Pit; Purple; Pustule; Pyriform.
Weevil, Cribrate.

PLUM, PRUNE (*Prunus domestica;* other species)
Aphid, Black Peach; Green Peach; Hop; Leafcurl Plum; Mealy
    Plum; Rusty Plum; Thistle; Waterlily.
Beetle, Cherry Leaf; Fuller Rose; Grape Flea; Green June; Japanese;
    Plum Gouger; Rose Leaf; Syneta Leaf.
Borer, American Plum; California Prionus; Flatheaded Appletree;
    Lesser Peachtree; Pacific Flatheaded; Peachtree; Peach Twig;
    Roundheaded Appletree; Shothole; Western Peachtree.
Bud Moth, Eyespotted.   **Bug**, Boxelder; Harlequin.
Cankerworm, Fall; Spring.   **Casebearer**, California; Cigar.
Caterpillar, Eastern Tent; Forest Tent; Orange Tortrix; Palmerworm;
    Pruneworm; Puss; Redhumped; Stinging Rose; Western Tent; Yel-
    lownecked.
Cricket, Snowy Tree.   **Curculio**, Plum (important).
Fly, Black Cherry Fruit; Cherry Fruit.
Leaf Crumpler.   **Leafhopper**, Grape; Plum; Privet; Prune.
Leafminer, Spotted Tentiform; Unspotted Tentiform.
Leafroller, Fruittree; Obliquebanded; Redbanded.
Leaf Skeletonizer, Apple.   **Maggot**, Apple.
Mealybug, Citrophilus; Ground; Longtailed.
Mite, Clover; European Red; Fourspotted; McDaniel Spider; Pacific
    Spider; Plum Rust.
Moth, Apple Fruit; Artichoke Plume; Browntail; Codling; Cynthia;

Leopard; Oriental; Oriental Fruit; Western Tussock; Whitelined Sphinx; Whitemarked Tussock.

Sawfly, Cherry Fruit; European Apple; Pearslug; Plum Webspinning.

Scale, Black; Brown Soft; Cottony Maple; Cottony Peach; European Fruit Lecanium; Florida Red; Florida Wax; Forbes; Green Shield; Howard; Italian Pear; Japanese Wax; Latania; Long Soft; Mimosa; Obscure; Olive; Oriental; Oystershell; Peach Lecanium; Purple; Pustule; Putnam; Quohogshaped; San Jose; Terrapin; Walnut; White Peach.

Thrips, Pear; Western Flower. **Weevil,** Cribrate.

For plums as for peaches the spray schedule is timed for the control of brown rot. Methoxychlor is safe to use in home gardens for the control of plum curculio.

PLUMBAGO (Leadwort)

Beetle, Fuller Rose.

Mealybug, Citrus. **Orthezia,** Greenhouse.

Scale, Cottonycushion; Florida Red; Pustule.

PODOCARPUS

Aphid, Podocarpus. **Mite,** Podocarpus.

Scale, Asiatic Red; California Red; Dictyospermum; Florida Red; Florida Wax; Glover; Japanese Wax; Latania; Long Soft; Proteus; Purple.

Treehopper, Thornbug.

POINCIANA

Beetle, Cuban May.

Scale, Coconut; Cottonycushion; Latania; Lesser Snow; Long Soft; Pustule; Quohogshaped.

POINCIANA, ROYAL (*Delonix regia*)

Moth, Noctuid (defoliates).

Scale, Black; Cottonycushion; Latania; Lesser Snow; Long Soft.

POKER-PLANT (*Kniphoffia*)

Thrips, Gladiolus.

POINSETTIA (*Euphorbia pulcherrinia*)

Aphid, Root. **Caterpillar,** Soybean Looper.

Mealybug, Citrus; Longtailed; Mexican; Striped.

Mite, Lewis Spider.

Scale, Barnacle; Black; Brown Soft; Coconut; Cottonycushion; Dictyospermum; Florida Red; Florida Wax; Lesser Snow; Long Soft; Nigra; Oleander; Pustule.
Termites.

POMEGRANATE (*Punica granatum*)
Aphid, Melon.   Beetle, Sap.   Bug, Western Leaffooted.
Caterpillar, Navel Orangeworm.   Mealybug, Citrus.
Mite, Pomegranate Leafroll.
Scale, Acuminate; Barnacle; Black; Citricola; Cottonycushion; Cyanophyllum; Florida Wax; Greedy; Latania; Mining; Olive; Rufous.
Thrips, Citrus; Greenhouse.   Weevil, Cribrate.   Whitefly, Citrus.

PONDAPPLE (*Annona glabra*)
Scale, Coconut; Oriental.

POPLAR, ASPEN, COTTONWOOD (*Populus*)
Aphid, Poplar Petiolegall; Poplar Twiggall; Poplar Vagabond; Sugarbeet Root; other species.
Beetle, Alder Flea; American Aspen; Aspen Leaf; Cottonwood Leaf; Goldsmith; Gray Willow Leaf; Imported Willow Leaf; June; other species.
Borer, Broadnecked Root; Bronze Birch; Bronze Poplar; California Prionus; Carpenterworm; Flatheaded Appletree; Linden; Pacific Flatheaded; Poplar; Poplar-and-Willow (small beetle may girdle trees); Sapwood Timberworm; Twig Girdler.
Bug, Ash Lace.
Butterfly, Mourningcloak (spiny elm caterpillar); Tiger Swallowtail; Viceroy.
Caterpillar, Chainspotted Geometer; Forest Tent; Poplar Tentmaker; Redhumped; Saddled Prominent; Western Tent; other species.
Cutworm, Western W-Marked.   Leafhopper, Poplar.
Leafminer, Aspen; Aspen Blotch; Cottonwood; Poplar.
Leafroller, Fruittree; Obliquebanded.
Mealybug, Comstock.   Mite, Fourspotted.
Moth, Cecropia; Hornet; Io; Leopard; Nevada Buck; Oriental; Polyphemus; Satin; Smeared Dagger; Rusty Tussock; Whitemarked Tussock; other species.
Sawfly, Willow; Willow Shoot.
Scale, Black; Brown Soft; Cottony Maple; European Fruit Lecanium; Greedy; Latania; Oystershell; Pine Needle; San Jose; Scurfy; Terrapin; Walnut; Willow Scurfy; White Peach.

Spanworm, Bruce; Cleftheaded. **Thrips, Pear. Treehopper,** Buffalo.
Wasp, Giant Hornet. **Webworm, Fall. Weevil,** Willow Flea.

POPPY (*Papaver*)

Aphid, Bean (black, common) ; Green Peach; Melon.
Beetle, Rose Chafer. **Bug,** Fourlined Plant; Tarnished Plant.
Leafhopper, Aster. **Mealybug,** Grape.

PORTULACA

Aphid, Bean; Corn Root; Potato.
Bug, Garden Fleahopper. **Moth,** Whitelined Sphinx.

POTATO (*Solanum tuberosum*)

Aphid, Buckthorn; Crescentmarked Lily; Foxglove; Green Peach; Potato; Solanum Root.
Armyworm, Fall; Southern; Yellowstriped.
Beetle, Ashgray Blister; Banded Flea; Black Blister; Carrot; Colorado Potato (convex, striped beetle devours foliage); Eggplant Flea; Eggplant Tortoise; False Potato; Fuller Rose; Hop Flea; Imbricated Snout; Margined Blister; Palestriped Flea; Potato Flea (tiny, black; minute holes in foliage) ; Spotted Cucumber; Strawberry Leaf; Striped Blister; Threelined Potato; Tobacco Flea; Tuber Flea; Western Potato Flea; Western Spotted Cucumber; Western Striped Cucumber; Whitefringed; Yellowmargined Leaf.
Borer, European Corn; Potato Stalk; Potato Tuberworm; Stalk; Tobacco Stalk.
Bug, Alfalfa Plant; Biglegged Plant; Eggplant Lace; False Chinch; Fourlined Plant; Garden Fleahopper; Harlequin; Leaffooted; Pumpkin; Rapid Plant; Say Stink; Southern Green Stink; Tarnished Plant; Western Plant.
Caterpillar, Cabbage Looper; Yellow Woollybear; Soybean Looper.
Cricket, Changa; Jerusalem; Northern Mole; Southern Mole.
Cutworm, Black; Dingy; Glassy; Pale Western; Spotted; Variegated.
Earwig, European. **Earworm, Corn. Fly,** Potato Scab Gnat.
Grasshopper, Clearwinged; Differential; Lesser Migratory; Redlegged; Twostriped.
Hornworm, Tobacco; Tomato.
Leafhopper, Arid; Aster; Beet; Clover; Potato (very injurious, rolls and burns leaves) ; Southern Garden; Western Potato.
Leafminer, Serpentine. **Maggot,** Seedcorn; Seedpotato.
Mealybug, Apple; Citrophilus; Grape; Solanum.
Millipedes. Mite, Tomato Russet.
Psyllid, Potato. **Scale,** Cottonycushion.

Slug, Gray Garden; Spotted Garden.   **Springtail,** Garden.
Termites.   Webworm, Beet; Garden.
Weevil, Vegetable.   **Whitefly,** Greenhouse; Iris.
Wireworm, Columbia Basin; Corn; Dryland; Eastern Field; Gulf; Pacific Coast; Prairie Grain; Southern Potato; Sugarbeet; Wheat.

POTENTILLA (Cinquefoil)

Aphid, Potato; Strawberry.   **Weevil,** Strawberry Root.

POTHOS

Mealybug, Longtailed.
Scale, Brown Soft; Florida Red; Latania; Proteus.

PRICKLY-ASH (*Zanthoxylum americanum*)

Scale, Barnacle; Black; Brown Soft; European Fruit Lecanium; Florida Wax; Howard; Lesser Snow; Pyriform; Scurfy; Walnut; White Peach.

PRIMROSE (*Primula*)

Aphid, Corn Root; Cowpea; Foxglove; Green Peach; White Aster Root.
Armyworm, Beet.
Beetle, Fuller Rose (leaves chewed in from margin); Potato Flea; Steelblue Flea; Strawberry Flea; Yellowmargined Leaf.
Mealybug, Longtailed; Yucca.
Mite, Twospotted (foliage always turns yellow in summer).
Slug, Spotted Garden (large holes in leaves).
Weevil, Black Vine (grubs work on roots) ; other species.
Whitefly, Greenhouse.

PRIVET (*Ligustrum*)

Aphid, Coreopsis; Privet.
Beetle, Sweetpotato Leaf; Tenlined June.
Borer, Mountain Ash.   **Caterpillar,** Omnivorous Looper.
Leafhopper, Privet; other species.   **Leafminer,** Lilac; Privet.
Mealybug, Citrophilus; Ground.
Mite, Citrus Flat; Privet (leaves dusty); Privet Bud; Privet Rust; Tuckerellid.
Planthopper.
Scale, Black; Black Thread; California Red; Camphor; Chaff; Coconut; Cyanophyllum; Dictyospermum; Forbes; Florida Red; Florida Wax; Forbes; Glover; Hemispherical; Japanese; Latania; Lesser Snow; Mining; Oleander; Green Shield; Olive; Pit; Privet;

Proteus; Purple; Pyriform; Quohogshaped; Red Bay; Rufous; San Jose; White Peach; Yellow.
Thrips, Privet (common, serious; leaves grayish).
Walkingstick, Twostriped.   **Weevil,** Cribrate; Japanese; Lilac.
Whitefly, Citrus (very common in southern gardens) ; Greenhouse.

PRUNE (see Plum)

PUMPKIN (*Cucurbita*)
Aphid, Melon; Potato.
Beetle, Blister; Palestriped Flea, Potato Flea; Spinach Carrion; Squash; Striped Cucumber; Western Striped Cucumber.
Borer, Squash Vine.   **Bug,** Garden Fleahopper; Squash.
Caterpillar, Melonworm; Yellow Woollybear.
Earworm, Corn.   **Maggot,** Seedcorn.   **Mealybug,** Citrus.
See Squash for other pests.

PYRACANTHA (Firethorn)
Aphid, Apple; Foxglove; Hawthorn; Rose; Spirea; Woolly Hawthorn.
Beetle, Rhabdopterus.
Bug, Hawthorn Lace (leaves stippled gray; more serious in South).
Mite, Platanus; Southern Red.   **Moth,** Phycitid.
Scale, Acuminate; Barnacle; Brown Soft; Cottonycushion; Dictyospermum; Florida Red; Florida Wax; European Fruit Lecanium; Greedy; Latania; Olive; San Jose; Walnut.
Webworm, Pyracantha (leaves, twigs webbed; prevalent in Southwest).
Weevil, Cribrate.

QUINCE (*Cydonia*)
Aphid, Apple; Apple Grain; Clover; Oat Birdcherry, Woolly Apple.
Beetle, Grape Flea; Japanese (serious).
Borer, Roundheaded Appletree.   **Casebearer,** Cigar.
Caterpillar, Eastern Tent; Forest Tent; Yellownecked.
Curculio, Apple; Quince (wormy fruit).
Leaf Crumpler.   Leafhopper, Privet.
Leafminer, Spotted Tentiform; Unspotted Tentiform.
Leafroller, Fruittree.   **Leaf Skeletonizer,** Apple.
Moth, Oriental Fruit; Codling; Rusty Tussock; Whitemarked Tussock.
Sawfly, Pearslug.
Scale, Barnacle; California Red; Cottonycushion; Cottony Maple; European Fruit Lecanium; Florida Wax; Greedy; Japanese Wax; Oystershell; Putnam; San Jose; Scurfy.

Treehopper, Buffalo; Quince.   Weevil, Apple Flea.

A spray schedule can be adapted from one for apples. Japanese beetles may be a problem in midsummer.

QUISQUALIS (Rangoon Creeper)
Scale, Brown Soft; Cyanophyllum; Latania; Mining; Proteus.

RADISH (*Rhaphanus sativus*)
Aphid, Cabbage; Green Peach; Potato; Turnip.
Beetle, Black Blister; Palestriped Flea; Potato Flea; Red Turnip; Sinuate Flea; Striped Blister; Western Black Flea; Western Striped Flea; Yellowmargined Leaf.
Bug, Harlequin.
Caterpillar, Cabbage Looper; Imported Cabbageworm; Yellow Woollybear.
Centipede, Garden Symphylan.   Curculio, Cabbage.
Leafminer, Serpentine.   Maggot, Cabbage (seedlings wilt); Seedcorn.
Moth, Diamondback.   Springtail, Garden.
Webworm, Cabbage.   Weevil, Cabbage Seedpod; Vegetable.
Wireworm, Eastern Field; other species.
See Cabbage for other possible pests.

RANDIA
Scale, Black Thread.

RASPBERRY (*Rubus*)
Aphid, Blackberry; European Raspberry; Potato; Spottedwinged; other species.
Beetle, Alfalfa Snout; Argus Tortoise; Fuller Rose; Green June; Imbricated Snout; Japanese (serious); Potato Flea; Rose Chafer; Rose Leaf; Sweetpotato Flea.
Borer, Flatheaded Appletree; Raspberry Cane; Raspberry Crown; Rednecked Cane; Rose Stem Girdler.
Bug, Negro (bad taste to berries); Consperse Stink.
Caterpillar, Green Cloverworm; Orange Tortrix; Yellow Woollybear.
Cricket, Blackhorned Tree.
Fruitworm, Raspberry; Western Raspberry (beetle may injure buds).
Horntail, Raspberry.
Leafhopper, Grape; White Apple.   Leafminer, Apple Trumpet.
Leafroller, Fruittree; Obliquebanded; Raspberry; Strawberry.
Maggot, Raspberry Cane (tips die back).

Mealybug, Citrophilus; Citrus.
Mite, Clover; McDaniel Spider; Willamette; Yellow.
Moth, Crinkled Flannel; Strawberry Crown.
Sawfly, Raspberry.
Scale, Brown Soft; Latania; Oystershell; Parlatorialike; Rose; Scurfy.
Spittlebug, Strawberry.
Weevil, Black Vine; Pea Leaf; Strawberry; Strawberry Root.
Whitefly, Glacial.

So far as possible, cut out infested canes. Use rotenone for Japanese beetles when berries are ripening.

RED BAY (*Persea borbona*)

Scale, Red Bay. **Whitefly**, Magnolia.

REDBUD, JUDAS TREE (*Cercis*)

Beetle, Rhabdopterus. **Caterpillar**, Western Tent.
Leaffolder, Grape. **Leafhopper. Leafroller**, Redbud.
Mite, Grevillea. **Moth**, Io; other species.
Scale, Brown Soft; Cottonycushion; European Fruit Lecanium; Gloomy; Greedy; Latania; Oleander; Parlatorialike; Pyriform; Terrapin; Walnut; White Peach.
Spittlebugs. **Treehopper**, Twomarked. **Whitefly**, Greenhouse.

REDWOOD (*Sequoia*)

Beetle, Redwood Bark.
Borer, Cedar Tree; California Prionus. **Horntail**, Western.
Mealybug, Cypress; Redwood; Yucca. **Moth**, Sequoia Pitch.
Scale, Black Araucaria; Brown Soft; Greedy; Oleander; Redwood.

RETINOSPORA (*Chamaecyparis*)

Aphid, Arborvitae. **Scale**, Newstead's; Red Bay.
Weevil, Arborvitae; Black Vine.

RHODODENDRON

Aphid, Rhododendron.
Beetle, Asiatic Garden; Pitted Ambrosia; Rhapdopterus.
Borer, Azalea Stem; Broadnecked Root; Rhododendron (common).
Bug, Rhododendron Lace (foliage yellow, stippled).
Fruitworm, Speckled Green. **Mealybug**, Taxus.
Midge, Rhododendron Tip. **Moths. Rootworm**, Cranberry.
Scale, Azalea Bark; Oleander; Pit; Rhododendron; Soft Azalea.
Thrips, Greenhouse; Madroña; Onion.
Wasp, Giant Hornet. **Weevil**, Black Vine; Japanese; other species.

Whitefly, Rhododendron.

Lace bugs and borers are most important.

RHUBARB (*Rheum*)

Aphid, Bean; Green Peach.   **Armyworm,** Western Yellowstriped.

Beetle, Alfalfa Snout; Hop Flea; Japanese; Oriental; Potato Flea.

Borer, European Corn; Stalk.

Caterpillar, Yellow Woollybear.   **Curculio,** Rhubarb (important).

Scale, Black.   **Termites.**

RIBBON-BUSH (*Homalocladium*)

Scale, Tesselated.

RICEPAPER-PLANT (*Tetrapanax*)

Mealybug, Citrus.

Scale, Green Shield; Latania; Purple; Pyriform; Tesselated.

ROCK-ROSE (*Cistus*)

Scale, Barnacle.

ROSARY-PEA (*Abrus precatorius*)

Scale, Brown Soft.

ROSE (*Rosa*)

Aphid, Black-and-red Rose; Crescentmarked Lily; Green Peach;
Hairy Rose; Melon; Potato (pink and green, common); Rose
(green); Rose and Bearberry; Rose Grass; Small Rose; Small
Green Rose; Strawberry; Woolly Apple; Yellow Rose.

Bee, Small Carpenter (borer in pith); Leafcutter (ovals and circles
cut from leaf margins).

Beetle, Asiatic Garden; Chinese Rose; Fuller Rose; Grape Colaspis;
Grapevine Hoplia; Green Rose Chafer; Japanese (major pest,
eats flowers, foliage); Oriental; Rhabdopterus; Rose Chafer (on
flowers); Rose Leaf; Sap; Spotted Cucumber (on flowers); Strawberry Leaf; other species.

Borer, Flatheaded Appletree; Pacific Flatheaded; Pigeon Tremex;
Raspberry Cane; Rose Stem Girdler; Rednecked Cane.

Budworm, Rose.

Bug, Fourlined Plant; Harlequin; Tarnished Plant; other species.

Cankerworms.   Casebearer.

Caterpillar, Eastern Tent; Forest Tent; Omnivorous Looper; Orange
Tortrix; Puss; Redhumped; Saddleback; Schizura; Stinging Rose;
Western Tent; Yellow Woollybear.

Curculio, Rose. Earwig, European (on flowers).

Earworm, Corn. Fruitworm, Speckled Green. Grasshoppers. Horntail.

Leafhopper, Apple (foliage white); Potato (brown tips, margins); Redbanded; Rose (coarse white stippling); Virginiacreeper; White Apple.

Leafroller, Fruittree; Obliquebanded; Omnivorous; Redbanded.

Leaftier, Celery. Maggot, Raspberry Cane. Mealybug, Citrophilus.

Midge, Rose (small buds turn black; occasional but very serious).

Mite, Citrus Red; European Red; Fourspotted; Southern Red; Two-spotted (leaves webby, yellow, may drop).

Moth, Browntail; Io; other species.

Sawfly, Bristly Roseslug; Curled Rose; Roseslug (leaves skeleton-ized); Rose Stem.

Scale, Black; Brown Soft; California Red; Camphor; Cottonycush-ion; Cottony Maple; Dictyospermum; European Fruit Lecanium; Florida Red; Greedy; Green Shield; Latania; Long Soft; Masked; Oleander; Olive; Oriental; Oystershell; Peach Lecanium; Pustule; Rose (round, white); Rose Palaeococcus; Rufous; San Jose; Wal-nut.

Thrips, Florida Flower; Flower (buds ball, petals turn brown); Greenhouse; Onion; Tobacco; Western Flower.

Treehopper, Buffalo (curved slits in bark).

Walkingstick, Northern. Webworm, Fall.

Weevil, Cribrate; Imported Longhorned; Japanese; Pea Leaf.

Whitefly, Greenhouse. Wireworm, Columbia Basin.

Most rose pests can be controlled with a single combination fungicide-insecticide-miticide spray, applied weekly from the time roses come into full leaf until hard frost. The more common prob-lems are aphids, leafhoppers, roseslugs, beetles, and spider mites but sprays are timed primarily to control rose blackspot.

ROSE-OF-SHARON, ROSE-ACACIA (*Robinia hispida*)

Aphid, Corn Root; Cowpea (dark, numerous at tips); Melon.

Beetle, Japanese (on flowers, foliage). Bug, Fourlined Plant.

Bollworm, Pink. Mealybug, Mexican.

Scale, Black; Brown Soft; Japanese; Latania; Lesser Snow; Mining; Quohogshaped; San Jose.

RUBBER PLANT (*Ficus elastica*)

Mealybug, Citrus; Longtailed.

Scale, Black; Black Thread; Brown Soft; Chinese Obscure; Chaff; Cyanophyllum; Dictyospermum; Florida Red; Florida Wax; Green

Shield; Japanese Wax; Latania; Lesser Snow; Nigra; Oleander;
Oriental; Proteus; Pustule; Pyriform; Rufous; Tesselated.
Thrips, Banded Greenhouse; Cuban Laurel; Dracaena; Greenhouse.

RUDBECKIA (Coneflower)
Aphid, Brown Ambrosia; Goldenglow; Crescentmarked Lily.
Bug, Garden Fleahopper.   **Leafhopper,** Aster.
Scale, Quohogshaped.

RUSSIAN-OLIVE (see Elaeagnus)

RUTABAGA (see Turnip)

SAGE, BLACK, WHITE (*Audibertia*)
Mealybug, Yucca.   **Scale,** Greedy; Olive.
Whitefly, Glacial; Greenhouse; Iridescent.

SAGE, SCARLET, BLUE (*Salvia*)
Aphid, Crescentmarked Lily; Foxglove.   **Beetle,** Asiatic Garden.
Borer, Stalk.   **Bug,** Tarnished Plant.
Leafhopper, Grape.   **Leaftier,** Celery.
Mealybug, Citrus.   **Mites.**
Orthezia, Greenhouse.   **Planthopper.**
Scale, Black; Brown Soft; Cottonycushion; Cassava; Greedy; Latania;
    Mining; Olive; Pit.
Whitefly, Glacial; Greenhouse.

SALAL (*Gaultheria*)
Caterpillar, Western Hemlock Looper.   **Leafminer,** Blotch.

SALSIFY (*Tragopogon*)
Aphid, Western Aster Root.   **Bug,** Tarnished Plant.
Caterpillar, Yellow Woollybear.

SANCHEZIA
Mealybug, Citrus; Longtailed.   **Scale,** Barnacle; Latania.

SANDALWOOD (*Santalum*)
Scale, Black.

SAND-LILY (*Leucocrinum*)
Aphid, Sand-Lily.

SANSEVIERIA
Scale, Lesser Snow.

SAPODILLA (*Achras sapota=Manilkara zapotilla*)
Beetle, Cuban May.
Mealybug, Citrus; Coconut. Mite, Texas Citrus.
Scale, Barnacle; Black; Acuminate; Cottonycushion; Coconut; Dictyospermum; Florida Wax; Greedy; Green Shield; Hemispherical; Japanese Wax; Latania; Lesser Snow; Mining; Masked; Proteus; Pustule; Pyriform; Rose Palaeococcus; Rufous.
Thrips, Greenhouse.

SAPOTE, WHITE (*Casimiroa*)
Mealybug, Longtailed.
Scale, Black; Brown Soft; Florida Red; Florida Wax; Green Shield; Japanese Wax; Latania; Lesser Snow; Mining; Oriental; Pyriform.

SASSAFRAS
Beetle, Japanese (important) ; Rose Chafer; Pitted Ambrosia.
Butterfly, Spicebush Swallowtail.
Caterpillar, Hickory Horned Devil; Phigalia Looper.
Leafroller, Fruittrcc.
Moth, Gypsy; Io; Polyphemus; Promethea.
Scale, European Fruit Lecanium; Florida Wax; Oystershell; Pyriform; San Jose.
Weevil, Sassafras.

SATINLEAF (*Chrysophyllum*)
Mealybug, Coconut.
Scale, Chaff; Coconut; Cottonycushion; Florida Red; Green; Latania; Mining; Tesselated.

SAUSAGE-TREE (*Kigelia pinnata*)
Scale, Black.

SAXIFRAGE (*Saxifraga*)
Rootworm, Grape. Slug, Spotted Garden.

SCABIOSA
Beetle, Fuller Rose. Bug, Chrysanthemum Lace; Garden Fleahopper.
Leafhopper, Aster.

SCHEFFLERA
Mite, Tumid Spider.
Scale, Acuminate; Black; Barnacle; Florida Red; Latania; Pustule; Pyriform.

SCHEMEA
Scale, Boisduval's.

SCHIZANTHUS (Butterfly-flower)
Leafhopper, Aster.

SCREWPINE (*Pandanus*)
Mealybug, Longtailed.
Scale, Black Thread; Boisduval's; Chaff; Coconut; Cyanophyllum; Dictyospermum; Fern; Florida Red; Latania; Lesser Snow; Nigra; Proteus; Rufous.

SEAGRAPE (*Coccolobis uvifera*)
Aphid, Black Citrus; Melon.   Borer, Seagrape.
Mealybug, Citrus; Comstock; Coconut; Striped.   Moth.
Scale, Black; Brown Soft; Chaff; Cyanophyllum; Florida Red; Florida Wax; Green; Green Shield; Hemispherical; Latania; Lesser Snow; Long Soft; Masked; Oleander; Pustule; Pyriform.
Weevil.   Whitefly, Woolly.

SEDUM
Aphid, Sedum; Green Peach; Melon.   Scale, Greedy; White Peach.

SEMPERVIVUM (Houseleek; Hen-and-chickens)
Mealybugs.

SERISSA
Scale, Cottonycushion; Cyanophyllum; Florida Wax; Latania; Pyriform; Quohogshaped.

SEVERINIA (Boxorange)
Mealybug, Citrus.
Scale, Black Thread; Chaff; Cottonycushion; Dictyospermum; Florida Red; Florida Wax; Hemispherical; Latania; Lesser Snow; Proteus; Purple.

SHADBUSH, SERVICEBERRY (*Amelanchier*)
Aphid, Woolly Elm; Woolly Hawthorn.

Borer, Apple Bark; Lesser Peach; Roundheaded Appletree; Shothole.
Butterfly, California Tortoiseshell. **Caterpillar,** Ugly Nest; Western Tent. **Curculio,** Apple.
Leafminer, Shadbush. **Mealybug,** Hawthorn.
Mite, Brown; European Red; Pearleaf Blister; Willamette; Yellow Spider.
Moth, Apple Fruit; Gypsy. **Sawfly,** Pearslug.
Scale, Oystershell; San Jose; Willow Scurfy.

SHALLOT (*Allium ascalonicum*)
Aphid, Shallot. **Fly,** Lesser Bulb.
See Onion for other pests.

SHAVING-BRUSH TREE (*Pachira fastuosa*)
Beetle, Cuban May.

SILVER LACE-VINE, FLEECE-VINE (*Polygonum aubertii*)
Aphid, Corn Root. **Beetle,** Flea; Japanese.

SHRIMP-PLANT (*Beloperone*)
Orthezia, Greenhouse.

SILVER-TREE (*Leucadendron argenteum*)
Scale, Greedy.

SILVER-VINE (*Actinidia polygama*)
Orthezia, Greenhouse. **Scale,** Lesser Snow; San Jose.

SMILAX (Greenbrier)
Scale, Chaff; Cyanophyllum; Green; Green Shield; Dictyospermum; Latania; Parlatorialike; Pustule; Red Bay; Smilax.
For the Smilax of florists see Asparagus Fern.

SMOKE-TREE (*Cotinus coggygria*)
Leafroller, Obliquebanded. **Scale,** San Jose.

SNAPDRAGON (*Antirrhinum*)
Aphid, Green Peach; Melon; Root. **Beetle,** Asiatic Garden.
Borer, Stalk. **Budworm,** Rose; Verbena.
Bug, Fourlined Plant; Red-and-black Stink; Snapdragon Lace; Tarnished Plant.

Caterpillar, Yellow Woollybear. Centipede, Garden Symphylan.
Leaftier, Celery. Mite, Broad; Cyclamen; Twospotted.
Moth, Snapdragon Plume. Slugs.

SNOWBALL (see Viburnum)

SNOWBERRY (*Symphoricarpos*)

Aphid, Crescentmarked Lily: Honeysuckle and Parsnip; Pulverulent
Snowberry; Snowberry. Beetle, Blister.
Borer, Flatheaded Cherrytree. Maggot, Apple.
Mealybug, Coleman's. Moth, Snowberry Clearwing. Sawfly.
Scale, Green; Green Shield; San Jose. Whitefly, Glacial.

SOAPBERRY (*Sapindus*)

Scale, Black; Gloomy; Green Shield; Obscure; Quohogshaped.

SOURGUM (see Tupelo)

SOURSOP (*Annona muricata*)

Mealybug, Coconut.
Scale, Black; Coconut; Flordia Red; Green; Green Shield; Hemispherical; Latania; Long Soft; Lesser Snow; Tesselated.

SOYBEAN (*Glycine max*)

Armyworm, Beet; Yellowstriped.
Beetle, Banded Cucumber; Bean Leaf; Japanese (makes lace of foli-
age) ; Mexican Bean; Spotted Cucumber; Striped Blister.
Bug, Brown Stink; Green Stink; Rapid Plant; Conchuela.
Borer, Beet Petiole; Lesser Cornstalk.
Caterpillar, Green Cloverworm; Soybean Looper; Velvetbean (may
defoliate).
Curculio, Clover Root. Cutworms. Earworm, corn. Grasshopper,
Redlegged.
Leafhopper, Potato. Leafminer, Locust.
Mite, Strawberry Spider; Twospotted.
Rootworm, Southern Corn; Western Corn.
Scale, White Peach. Thrips, Bean.
Webworm, Garden. Weevil, Alfalfa, Sweetclover. Whitefly, Banded-
wing.

SPANISH BAYONET (*Yucca aloifolia*)

Citrus, Mealybug. Orthezia, Greenhouse.
Scale, Black; Chaff; Cyanophyllum; Lesser Snow; Oleander; Purple.

SPANISH DAGGER (*Yucca gloriosa*)
Scale, Cyanophyllum; Lesser Snow; Purple.

SPANISH-LIME (*Melicocca bijuga*)
Beetle, Cuban May.
Scale, Barnacle; Black; Dictyospermum; Florida Wax; Green Shield; Latania; Lesser Snow; Mining; Rufous.

SPANISH NEEDLES (*Bidens*)
Caterpillar, Yellow Woollybear.
Mealybug, Citrus; Mexican. Orthezia, Greenhouse.
Scale, Black; Brown Soft; Cottonycushion; Chaff; Green; Green Shield; Mango Shield; Hemispherical.

SPARKLEBERRY (*Vaccinium arboreum*)
Mealybug, Longtailed.
Scale, Cyanophyllum; Dictyospermum; Florida Wax; Latania; Pyriform; Red Bay; Terrapin.

SPICEBUSH (*Benzoin aestivale*)
Butterfly, Spicebush Swallowtail.
Scale, Brown Soft; Cottonycushion; Dictyospermum; Florida Red; Lesser Snow; Pyriform.

SPINACH (*Spinacia*)
Aphid, Bean; Green Peach; Melon. Armyworm, Fall.
Beetle, Beet Leaf; Blister; Potato Flea; Spinach Carrion; Spinach Flea.
Caterpillar, Cabbage Looper. Cutworms. Grasshoppers.
Leafhopper, Beet. Leafminer, Serpentine; Spinach.
Leaftier, Celery. Maggot, Seedcorn. Mite.
Springtail, Garden.
Webworm, Beet; Southern Beet. Weevil, Vegetable.

SPIREA (*Spiraea*)
Aphid, Apple; Brown Spirea; Spirea (green; common).
Caterpillar, Saddled Prominent. Leafhopper, Privet.
Leafroller, Obliquebanded. Mite, Yellow Spider.
Scale, Black; Cottonycushion; Cottony Maple; Florida Red; Florida Wax; Latania; Oystershell; San Jose; Spirea; Walnut; White Peach.

SPREKELIA
Fly, Narcissus Bulb. Thrips, Banded Greenhouse.

SPRUCE (*Picea*)

Aphid, Balsam Twig; Black Polished Spruce; Bowlegged Fir; Cooley Spruce Gall (galls at tips of blue spruce twigs); Dark Brown Spruce; Eastern Spruce Gall (galls at base of Norway Spruce twigs); Green Spruce; Light Brown Spruce; Pine Leaf; Powdery Spruce; Spruce; Woolly Larch.

Bagworm.

Beetle, Alaska; Allegheny Spruce; Black Turpentine; Douglas Fir; Douglas Fir Engraver; Eastern Spruce; Engelmann Spruce; European Spruce; Fir Engraver; Golden Buprestid; Lodgepole Pine; Mountain Pine; Northeastern Sawyer; Pine Colaspis; Pine Engraver; Red Turpentine; Sitka Spruce; Southern Pine; White Pine Cone.

Borer, Blackhorned; Flatheaded Fir; Hemlock; Pitch Mass; Western Larch Roundheaded.

Budworm, Blackheaded; Spruce (very serious; needles webbed together, die). **Bud Moth,** Larch; Spruce.

Caterpillar, False Hemlock Looper; Hemlock Looper; Phantom Hemlock Looper; Western Hemlock Looper.

Leafminer, Spruce (needles webbed together). **Midge,** Spruce Gall.

Mite, Spruce Spider (common, injurious; needles gray, webby).

Moth, Douglas Fir, Pitch; Gypsy; Imperial; Pine Cone; Silverspotted Tiger; Spruce Epizeuxis; other species.

Sawfly, Balsam Fir; European Spruce; Greenheaded Spruce; Yellowheaded Spruce.

Scale, Balsam Fir; Pine Needle; Spruce Bud. **Spittlebug,** Pine.

Weevil, Engelmann Spruce; Pales; Sitka Spruce; Strawberry Root; White Pine.

Spruce budworm is very important in forests, spruce mite and gall aphids in home plantings.

SQUASH (*Cucurbita maxima*)

Aphid, Bean; Melon (common; curls leaves); Potato.

Beetle, Imbricated Snout; Spinach Carrion; Spotted Cucumber; Squash; Striped Cucumber; Tobacco Flea; Western Striped.

Borer, Squash Vine (common, serious; vines wilt).

Bug, Garden Fleahopper; Harlequin; Horned Squash; Squash.

Caterpillar, Melonworm; Pickleworm; Yellow Woollybear.

Earworm, Corn. **Leafhopper,** Beet.

Springtail, Garden. **Termites.**

Thrips, Onion; Western Flower.

Whitefly, Greenhouse (often abundant).

Many squash varieties are sensitive to sulfur.

SQUILL (*Scilla*)
Aphid, Tulip Bulb.

STAGGERBUSH (*Lyonia*)
Scale, Azalea Bark; Florida Wax; Oak Eriococcus; Red Bay.

STAR-APPLE (*Chrysophyllum cainito*)
Mealybug, Coconut; Longtailed.
Scale, Cottonycushion; Green Shield; Latania; Mining; Tesselated.

STEPHANOTIS
Mealybug, Citrus; Longtailed.
Scale, Black; Cottonycushion; Brown Soft; Cyanophyllum; Hemispherical; Pustule.

STOCK (*Mathiola*)
Beetle, Striped Flea; Western Black Flea; Western Striped Flea.
Caterpillar, Soybean Looper.
Mealybug, Mexican. Moth, Diamondback.
Spittlebug, Meadow. Springtail, Garden.
Weevil, Imported Longhorned.

STATICE (Sea-pink; Thrift)
Thrips, Greenhouse.

STRAWBERRY (*Fragaria*)
Ant, Cornfield.
Aphid, Bald Strawberry; Melon; Potato; Strawberry; Strawberry Root; Yellow Rose.
Beetle, Alfalfa Snout; Asiatic Garden; Darkling; European Chafer; Grape Colaspis; Hoplia; Oriental; Palestriped Flea; Rose Chafer; Rose Leaf; Strawberry Flea; Strawberry Leaf; Tenlined June; Whitefringed.
Borer, Strawberry Crown; Lesser Cornstalk.
Bug, Leaffooted; False Chinch; Lygus; Negro; Pameras (hard berries) ; Tarnished Plant.
Caterpillar, Green Cloverworm; Garden Tortrix; Salt Marsh; Woollybear.
Centipede, Garden Symphylan.
Cricket, Field; Northern Mole; Southern Mole.
Curculio, Cowpea. Cutworms. Earwig, European.
Leafhopper, Potato. Leafminer, Strawberry Crown.

Leafroller, Obliquebanded; Omnivorous; Strawberry; Western Strawberry.

Leaftier, Celery; Omnivorous.

Mealybug, Grape; Ground.   **Millipedes.**

Mite, Cyclamen (serious); Desert Spider; Strawberry Spider; Two-spotted.

Moth, Strawberry Crown.

Rootworm, Strawberry.   **Sawfly,** Strawberry.

Scale, Brown Soft; Rose; San Jose.   **Slugs. Snails. Sowbugs.**

Spittlebug, Meadow; Strawberry.

Thrips, Florida Flower; Western Flower.   **Webworm,** Garden.

Weevil, Black Vine (grubs on roots); Citrus Root; Imported Long-horned; Japanese; Pea Leaf; Strawberry; Strawberry Root.

Whitefly, Greenhouse; Iris; Strawberry.   **Wireworms.**

Buy certified strawberry plants and so start with clean stock. Cyclamen mite is a serious problem.

STRAWBERRY-TREE (*Arbutus unedo*)

Aphid, Rose and Bearberry.   **Caterpillar,** Western Tent.

Scale, Black; Brown Soft; Greedy.

STRAWFLOWER (*Helichrysum bracteatum*)

Beetle, Asiatic Garden.   **Leafhopper,** Aster.

Scale, Ground Pearls.

STRELITZIA (Bird-of-Paradise)

Mealybug, Citrus; Longtailed.

Scale, Boisduval's; Cockerell; Dictyospermum; Florida Red; Green; Greedy; Lesser Snow; Latania; Oriental; Pyriform.

STROBILANTHES (Lavenderbell)

Mealybug, Mexican.   **Orthezia,** Greenhouse.

Scale, Barnacle; Black; Cottonycushion; Black Thread; Florida Wax; Hemispherical; Latania; Mining; Nigra; Pustule; Tesselated.

SUGAR-APPLE (*Annona squamosa*)

Mealybug, Citrus; Coconut; Striped.

Scale, Barnacle; Brown Soft; Coconut; Cottonycushion; Dictyospermum; Florida Red; Florida Wax; Hemispherical; Latania; Lesser Snow; Long Soft; Oriental; Mining; Pustule; Rose Palaeococcus; Rufous.

SUGAR-BUSH (*Rhus ovata*)

Thrips, Toyon.

SUMAC (*Rhus*)
Aphid, Monell's Sumac; Sumac Gall.
Beetle, Potato Flea. **Borer,** Currant.
Caterpillar, Hickory Horned Devil; Omnivorous Looper; Walnut.
Leafroller, Obliquebanded. **Psyllid,** Sumac.
Scale, Black; Cottony Maple; Green; Lesser Snow; Pustule; Pyriform; Walnut; White Peach.

SUNFLOWER (*Helianthus*)
Aphid, Brown Ambrosia; Dogwood or Sunflower; Goldenglow; Green Peach; Hop; Leafcurl Plum; Melon; Potato; White Aster Root.
Beetle, Asiatic Garden; Carrot; Palestriped Flea; Potato Flea; Sunflower; Western Striped Cucumber; Whitefringed.
Bug, Biglegged; Fourlined Plant; Garden Fleahopper; Harlequin; Leaffooted; Say Stink; Tarnished Plant.
Butterfly, Painted Lady. **Caterpillar,** Yellow Woollybear.
Earworm, Corn. **Leafcutter,** Morningglory.
Leafroller, Obliquebanded. **Maggot,** Sunflower.
Mealybug, Citrophilus; Mexican. **Midge,** Sunflower Seed.
Mite, Desert Spider. **Moth,** Banded Sunflower; Sunflower.
Rootworm, Northern Corn.
Scale, Cottonycushion; Hemispherical; Lesser Snow; Latania.
Spittlebug, Sunflower. **Weevil,** Cocklebur; Seed.

SURINAM-CHERRY (*Eugenia uniflora*)
Mealybug, Citrus.
Scale, Black; Florida Red; Florida Wax; Dictyospermum.

SWEETBAY (*Magnolia virginiana*)
Scale, Brown Soft; Cyanophyllum; Dictyospermum; Florida Red; Florida Wax; European Fiorinia; Green Shield; Lesser Snow; Nigra; Oleander; Oriental; Parlatorialike; Red Bay; Terrapin; Tesselated; Tuliptree.

SWEETFERN (*Comptonia asplenifolia*)
Caterpillar, Chainspotted Geometer. **Moth,** Crinkled Flannel.
Spanworm, Cleftheaded. **Spittlebug,** Saratoga.

SWEETGUM (*Liquidambar*)
Aphid, Giant Bark. **Bagworm.** **Borer,** Twig Pruner.
Caterpillar, Forest Tent; Hickory Horned Devil; Redhumped.
Leafhopper. **Leaftier,** Sweetgum. **Mite.**
Moth, Azalea Sphinx; Luna; Polyphemus; Promethea.

Scale, Cottonycushion; Cyanophyllum; Gloomy; Latania; Sweetgum; Terrapin; Tuliptree; Walnut.
Webworm, Sweetgum.

SWEETPEA (*Lathyrus odoratus*)
Aphid, Corn Root; Pea; Potato; Solanum Root.
Beetle, Spotted Cucumber; Western Spotted Cucumber.
Bug, Fourlined Plant. Caterpillar, Zebra.
Centipede, Garden Symphylan.
Leafminer, Serpentine. Leaftier, Celery.
Mite, Desert Spider; Twospotted (common, leaves yellow, mealy).
Moth, Pea. Sowbugs.
Thrips, Banded Greenhouse; Onion; Western Flower.

SWEETPOTATO (*Ipomoea batatas*)
Aphid, Green Peach; Potato. Armyworm, Fall; Southern; Yellow-striped.
Beetle, Argus Tortoise; Blister; Golden Tortoise; Mottled Tortoise; Potato Flea; Striped Tortoise; Sweetpotato Flea; Sweetpotato Leaf; Whitefringed.
Caterpillar, Yellow Woollybear. Cutworm, Granulate.
Fly, Onion Bulb. Hornworm, Sweetpotato.
Leafhopper, Bean; Southern Garden.
Leafminer, Morningglory; Sweetpotato.
Maggot, Seedcorn. Mealybug, Citrus; Grape; Mexican.
Mite, Tumid Spider.
Scale, Lesser Snow. Termites. Thrips, Banded Greenhouse.
Weevil, Sweetpotato. Whitefly, Sweetpotato.
Wireworm, Gulf; Southern Potato.

SWEET-WILLIAM (*Dianthus barbatus*)
Leafhopper, Aster. Mites. Scale, Brown Soft.

SWISS CHARD (*Beta*)
Bug, Tarnished Plant. Leafminer, Spinach.
Weevil, Vegetable.
See also Beet for other possible pests.

SYCAMORE, PLANE (*Platanus*)
Aphid, Beech Blight; Giant Bark; Sycamore. Bagworm.
Borer, American Plum; Flatheaded Appletree; Flatheaded Cherry-tree; Pacific Flatheaded; Pigeon Tremex; Sycamore.
Bug, Sycamore Lace; Sycamore Plant.

Caterpillar, Hickory Horned Devil; Omnivorous Looper; Puss.
Leafhopper. Leafminer, Sycamore.
Mite, Platanus; Southern Red; Willamette.
Moth, Cynthia; Imperial; Io; Oriental; Sycamore Tussock; White-
marked Tussock.
Scale, Barnacle; Black; Brown Soft; Cottony Maple; Grape; La-
tania; Oystershell; Putnam; Sycamore (serious on oriental plane);
Terrapin.
Treehopper, Twomarked. **Webworm,** Fall. **Whitefly,** Mulberry.

SYNGONIUM (*Nephthytis*)
Mealybug, Longtailed; other species. **Mite.**
Scale, Hemispherical; Latania. **Thrips,** Greenhouse.

TABEBUIA
Aphid, Melon. **Scale,** Mining.

TABERNAEMONTANA
Scale, Acuminate; Barnacle; Brown Soft; Cyanophyllum; Florida Red;
Green Shield; Hemispherical; Latania; Mining; Oriental; Pustule;
Parlatorialike; Tesselated.

TAMARIND (*Tamarindus*)
Scale, Latania; Mining; Oriental; Quohogshaped; Rufous.

TAMARISK, SALT CEDAR (*Tamarix*)
Aphid, Green Peach. **Leafhopper. Mealybug,** Citrus.
Scale, Cottonycushion; Florida Wax; Oystershell.

TANGERINE (*Citrus nobilis*)
Beetle, Fuller Rose. **Bug,** Leaffooted.
Mite, Yuma Spider. **Scale,** California Red. **Thrips,** Citrus.
See also Citrus.

TANSY (*Tanacetum*)
Aphid, Green Peach.

TEA (*Thea sinensis*)
Scale, Acuminate; Chaff; Dictyospermum; Florida Red; Florida
Wax; Cyanophyllum; Latania; Oleander; Proteus; Tea.

TEASEL (*Dipsacus*)
Aphid, Goldenglow.

TECOMA
Caterpillar, Omnivorous Looper.   Mealybug, Longtailed.
Scale, Barnacle; Black; Florida Wax; Green Shield; Lesser Snow;
   Mining; Oleander.

TERNSTROEMIA
Scale, Camellia; Florida Red.

THEVETIA (Yellow Oleander)
Scale, Acuminate; Black; Brown Soft; Cyanophyllum; Florida Red;
   Florida Wax; Latania; Proteus; Pyriform; Tesselated.

THISTLE (Cirsium)
Aphid, Bean; Melon; Oleaster-thistle; Thistle.
Bug, Alfalfa Plant.   Butterfly, Painted Lady; Painted Beauty.
Leafroller, Obliquebanded.   Leaftier, Celery.
Moth, Artichoke Plum.   Scale, Green.

THORN, THORNAPPLE (see Hawthorn)

THUNBERGIA (Clockvine)
Mealybug, Citrus.   Orthezia, Greenhouse.
Scale, Acuminate; Black; Green Shield; Lesser Snow; Purple; Pro-
   teus; Pyriform; Tesselated; White Peach.

THYME (Thymus)
Mealybug, Ground.

TOMATILLO (Physalis ixocarpa)
Mite, Tomato Russet.

TOMATO (Lycopersicon esculentum)
Aphid, Green Peach; Potato (both common).
Armyworm, Beet; Fall; Western Yellowstriped.
Beetle, Black Blister; Colorado Potato; Darkling; Fig; Hop Flea;
   Palestriped Flea; Margined Blister; Potato Flea (minute holes in
   foliage); Spotted Cucumber; Striped Blister; Tobacco Flea; West-
   ern Potato Flea.
Borer, Potato Stalk; Potato Tuberworm; Stalk.
Bug, Eggplant Lace; Garden Fleahopper; Green Stink; Leaffooted;
   Onespot Stink; Pumpkin.
Caterpillar, Cabbage Looper; Soybean Looper; Tomato Pinworm.

Centipede, Garden Symphylan. Cricket, Camel; Field.

Cutworm, Granulate; Palesided. Earworm, Corn (tomato fruitworm).

Hornworm, Tobacco; Tomato (large green caterpillars).

Leafhopper, Beet. Leafminer. Maggot, Pepper. Mealybug, Solanum.

Mite, Cyclamen; Tomato Russet; Twospotted. Moth, Whitelined Sphinx.

Psyllid, Potato or tomato (plants deformed, appear diseased).

Scale, Lesser Snow. Slugs. Springtail, Garden.

Thrips, Banded Greenhouse; Flower; Onion; Western Flower.

Treehopper, Threecornered Alfalfa. Weevil, Vegetable.

Whitefly, Greenhouse (tiny white "moths" on underside of leaves).

Tomato pests vary in different sections. Fleabeetles and cutworms are rather general.

TRAVELERS-TREE (*Ravenala madagascariensis*)

Mealybug, Coconut; Longtailed.

Scale, Boisduval's; Brown Soft; Black Thread; Coconut; Dictyospermum; Florida Red; Green Shield; Latania; Lesser Snow; Nigra; Proteus; Tesselated.

TRUMPET VINE (*Campsis radicans*)

Planthopper.

Scale, Olive; Oriental; Pyriform; Quohogshaped; Tesselated.

Whitefly, Citrus.

TUBEROSE (*Polianthes tuberosa*)

Caterpillar, Convict.

TULIP (*Tulipa*)

Aphid, Green Peach; Potato; Tulip Bulb; Tulip Leaf.

Fly, Lesser Bulb; Narcissus Bulb. Millipedes.

Mite, Bulb; Twospotted. Scale, Black.

TULIPTREE (*Liriodendron*)

Aphid, Tuliptree (green, secreting much honeydew, with sooty mold).

Beetle, June. Borer, Sapwood Timberworm. Moth, Promethea.

Scale, Oystershell; Putnam; Tuliptree (serious); Walnut; Willow Scurfy.

Weevil, Sassafras.

TUNGOIL-TREE (*Aleutites fordii*)

Scale, Chaff; Cyanophyllum; Latania; Lesser Snow; Cottonycushion; Oleander; Olive; White Peach.

TUPELO, SOURGUM, BLACKGUM (*Nyssa sylvatica*)

Aphid, Coreopsis.　Borer, Twig Girdler.
Leafminer, Tupelo (cuts pieces from leaves).
Moth, Azalea Sphinx.　Scale, San Jose; Sourgum; other species.

TURKS-CAP, SLEEPING HIBISCUS (*Malvaviscus arboreus*)

Katydids, (large holes in foliage).　Moth, Abutilon.
Mealybug, Citrus; Longtailed; Mexican.
Scale, Black; Brown Soft; Hemispherical; Japanese Wax; Latania; Nigra.

TURNIP (*Brassica rapa*)

Aphid, Cabbage; Potato; Turnip.　Armyworm, Fall.
Beetle, Asiatic Garden; Palestriped Flea; Red Turnip; Sinuate Flea; Striped Blister; Western Black Flea; Western Striped Flea; Whitefringed; Yellowmargined Leaf.
Borer, Lesser Cornstalk.
Bug, Green Stink; Harlequin; Tarnished Plant.
Caterpillar, Cabbage Looper; Imported Cabbageworm; Yellow Woollybear.
Curculio, Cabbage.　Leafminer, Serpentine.
Maggot, Cabbage; Seedcorn.　Millipedes.
Moth, Diamondback; Whitelined Sphinx.
Termites.　Thrips, Onion.
Weevil, Cabbage Seedpod; Vegetable.

TURQUOISE VINE (*Ampelopsis brevipedunculata*)

Beetle, Japanese (very fond of this vine).

UMBRELLA PLANT (*Cyperus*)

Mealybug, Citrus; Longtailed.　Scale, Oleander.
Thrips, Citrus.　Whitefly, Citrus.

UMBRELLA-TREE (*Magnolia tripetala*)

Mite, Fourspotted.　Scale, Greedy; Lesser Snow; Oleander.
Thrips, Citrus.　Whitefly, Citrus.

VALLOTA (Scarboro-lily)
Fly, Narcissus Bulb.

VELVETBEAN (*Stizolobium*)
Beetle, Whitefringed. Caterpillar, Velvetbean. Mite, Texas Citrus.

VERBASCUM (Mullein)
Bug, Red-and-black Stink.

VERBENA
Aphid, Foxglove; Geranium; Green Peach; Melon.
Beetle, Clematis Blister. Bud Moth, Verbena.
Bug, Snapdragon Lace; Tarnished Plant; Garden Fleahopper.
Caterpillar, Omnivorous Looper; Yellow Woollybear.
Leafminer, Verbena (light blotches in leaves; common).
Leafroller, Obliquebanded. Mite, Broad; Cyclamen; Twospotted.
Orthezia, Greenhouse.
Scale, Brown Soft; Cottonycushion; Latania; Oleander.
Thrips, Flower; Greenhouse. Webworm, Garden. Whitefly, Greenhouse.

VERBESINA (Crownbeard)
Mealybug, Citrus.

VERONICA
Aphid, Foxglove.

VETCH (*Vicia*)
Aphids. Borer, Lima Bean Pod. Earworm, Corn.
Moth, Pea. Weevil, Broadbean; Vetch Bruchid.

VIBURNUM (Snowball)
Aphid, Bean; Crescentmarked Lily; Currant; Foxglove; Grapevine; Ivy; Snowball; Spirea; Viburnum.
Beetle, Asiatic Garden; Potato Flea. Borer, Dogwood Twig.
Bug, Tarnished Plant; Fourlined. Caterpillar, Schizura.
Hornworm, Tobacco; Tomato. Mealybug, Citrus; Longtailed. Moths.
Planthopper, Citrus Flatid.
Scale, Barnacle; Brown Soft; Camellia Mining; Chaff; Cottonycushion; Cottony Maple; Cyanophyllum; Dictyospermum; Florida Red; Florida Wax; Hemispherical; Japanese Wax; Latania; Obscure; Olive; Oystershell; Parlatorialike; Pyriform; Putnam; San Jose; Tesselated; Walnut.

Thrips, Flower; Greenhouse.
Treehopper, Threecornered Alfalfa; Twomarked.
Whitefly, Citrus; Greenhouse.
 The foliage of common snowball is usually curled up with aphids.
Viburnum carlesii is sensitive to sulfur.

VINCA (Myrtle; Periwinkle)

Aphid, Green Peach; Melon; Potato; Solanum Root.
Beetle, Fuller Rose.   Leafhopper, Aster.
Mealybug, Citrus; Longtailed.   Orthezia, Greenhouse.
Scale, Brown Soft; Dictyospermum; Florida Red; Florida Wax;
 Hemispherical; Latania; Olive; Oleander; Proteus.

VIOLET (*Viola*)

Aphid, Crescentmarked Lily; Foxglove; Green Peach; Red Violet;
 Shallot; Violet.
Beetle, Asiatic Garden; Potato Flea; Whitefringed.
Caterpillar, Omnivorous Looper; Yellow Woollybear.
Leafcutter, Morningglory.   Leafroller, Redbanded.
Leaftier, Celery.   Midge, Violet Gall.
Mite, Cyclamen; Twospotted (prevalent; leaves yellow).
Sawfly, Violet (blue-black larvae feed at night).
Scale, Fern.   Slug, Spotted Garden (large holes in leaves).
 Avoid nicotine on violets.

VIPERS-BUGLOSS (*Echium*)

Bug, Echium Lace.

VIRGINIA-CREEPER (*Parthenocissus quinquefolia*)

Aphid, Rusty Plum; other species.
Beetle, Grape Flea; Japanese (serious) ; Rose Chafer.
Caterpillar, Grapevine Looper.   Hornworm, Tobacco; Tomato.
Leaffolder, Grape.
Leafhopper, Grape; Threebanded; Virginiacreeper (foliage gray).
Moth, Abbott's Sphinx; Achemon Sphinx; Eightspotted Forester;
 Virginiacreeper.
Scale, Brown Soft; Calico; Cottonycushion; Cottony Maple; Cyano-
 phyllum; Florida Red; Green; Latania; Olive; Oystershell; Peach
 Lecanium; San Jose.
Weevil, Imported Longhorned.

WALLFLOWER (*Cheiranthus*)

Aphid, Crescentmarked Lily.

Beetle, Red Turnip; Western Black Flea; Western Striped Flea.
Moth, Diamondback.

WALNUT (*Juglans*)

Aphid, Blackmargined; Duskyveined Walnut; European Walnut; Giant Bark; Walnut; other species.
Borer, Brown Wood; California Prionus; Nautical; Pacific Flatheaded; Painted Hickory; Tiger Hickory; Twig Pruner.
Bug, False Chinch; Walnut Lace. **Casebearer,** Pecan Cigar.
Caterpillar, Filbertworm; Hickory Horned Devil; Navel Orangeworm; Omnivorous Looper; Orange Tortrix; Redhumped; Variable Oakleaf; Walnut (black with white hairs); Yellownecked.
Curculio, Black Walnut; Butternut. **Fly,** Walnut Husk.
Leafroller, Fruittree. **Mealybug,** Citrophilus; Grape.
Mite, European Red; Pacific Spider; Platanus; Southern Red; Strawberry Spider; Twospotted; Walnut Blister.
Moth, Codling; Hickory Tussock; Leopard; Luna; Walnut Sphinx; Western Tussock.
Rootworm, Strawberry. **Sawfly,** Butternut Woollyworm.
Scale, Black; Calico; California Red; Citricola; Cottonycushion; Dictyospermum; European Fruit Lecanium; Frosted; Greedy; Italian Pear; Obscure; Oystershell; Purple; Putnam; San Jose; Tuliptree; Walnut; White Peach.
Spanworm, Elm; Walnut. **Termites. Webworm,** Fall.
The walnut aphid and the codling moth are serious problems of commercial growers.

WANDERING-JEW (*Tradescantia*)

Caterpillar, Orange Tortrix. **Leafcutter,** Morningglory.
Leaftier, Celery. **Mealybug,** Citrus; Longtailed. **Scale,** Chaff.

WATERCRESS (*Nasturtium officinale*)

Aphid, Bean; Green Peach; Spinach.
Beetle, Watercress Leaf; Western Black Flea; Western Striped Flea.
Moth, Diamondback. **Sowbugs.**

WATERLILY (*Nymphaea*)

Aphid, Corn Leaf; Waterlily. **Beetle,** Waterlily Leaf.
Leafcutter, Waterlily. **Midge,** False Leafmining.

WATERMELON (*Citrullus vulgaris*)

Aphid, Melon (common; serious).
Beetle, Hop Flea; Imbricated Snout; Potato Flea; Squash; Spotted Cucumber; Striped Cucumber.

Bug, Horned Squash; Western Leaffooted.
Caterpillar, Melonworm; Pickleworm.　Cricket, Camel.
Leafminer, Serpentine.　Millipedes.　Mite, Spider.
Scale, Black; California Red.
Treehopper, Threecornered Alfalfa.
Whitefly, Greenhouse.　Wireworms.
See Melon for other pest.

WATERPRIMROSE (*Jussiaea peruviana*)

Mealybug, Citrus.　Scale, Black Thread.

WEIGELA

Aphid, Melon.　Borer, Shothole.
Bug, Fourlined Plant.　Mealybug, Comstock.
Scale, Barnacle; Cottonycushion; Latania.
Weevil, Japanese.

WILLOW (*Salix*)

Aphid, Black Willow; Giant Bark; Giant Willow; Green-and-pink Willow; Little Black-and-Green Willow; Willow; other species.
Beetle, Alder Flea; Cottonwood Flea; Elm Calligrapha; Goldsmith; Gray Willow Leaf; Imported Willow Leaf (skeletonizes leaves, especially weeping willow; small, metallic-blue beetle); Pacific Willow Leaf; Rose Leaf; Striped Cucumber; Willow Flea; other species.
Borer, Banded Alder; Bronze Birch; Brown Wood; Carpenterworm; Cottonwood; Flatheaded Appletree; Pacific Flatheaded; Poplar-and-Willow (may be serious).
Bug, Mountain Ash; Willow Lace.
Butterfly, Mourningcloak; Viceroy; Western Swallowtail.
Casebearer, California.
Caterpillar, Chainspotted Geometer; Eastern Tent; Forest Tent; Hemlock Looper; Omnivorous Looper; Orange Tortrix; Poplar Tent Maker; Redhumped; Schizura; Unicorn; Walnut; Western Tent.
Leafhopper, Poplar; Southern Garden; other species.　Mealybug, Grape.
Midge, Willow Beakedgall.　Mite, Platanus; Yellow.
Moth, American Dagger; Browntail; Buck; Cecropia; Cottonwood Dagger; Gypsy; Douglas Fir Tussock; Hornet; Io; Leopard (borer); Luna; Nevada Buck; Oriental; Rusty Tussock; Satin; Smeared Dagger; Spotted Tussock; Whitemarked Tussock.
Psyllid.　Sawfly, Willow; Willow Redgall; Willow Shoot.
Scale, Black; Brown Soft; California Red; Cottonycushion; Cottony

Maple; Dictyospermum; European Fruit Lecanium; Greedy; Green;
Nigra; Obscure; Oleander; Putnam; San Jose; Scurfy; Terrapin;
Willow Scurfy.
Spanworm, Cleftheaded. **Spittlebug,** Saratoga.
Thrips, Citrus; Pear. **Treehopper,** Twomarked.
Wasp, Giant Hornet. **Webworm,** Fall. **Weevil,** Cribrate; Willow
Flea.

WISTERIA (*Wistaria*)
Aphid, Melon.
Beetle, Rose Chafer; Sweetpotato Leaf; Tenlined June.
Butterfly, Silverspotted Skipper. **Leafroller,** Honeylocust.
Mealybug, Longtailed; Citrus; Mexican. **Planthopper.**
Scale, Brown Soft; Cottonycushion; European Fruit Lecanium; Flor-
ida Red; Lesser Snow; Mining; Peach Lecanium.
Weevil, Black Vine. **Webworm,** Fall.

WITCH-HAZEL (*Hamamelis*)
Aphid, Elm Cockscombgall; Witchhazel Leafgall; Spiny Witchhazel
Gall.
Caterpillar, Saddled Prominent.

WYETHIA
Lace Bug.

YAM (*Dioscorea*)
Whitefly, Cloudywinged.

YARROW (*Achillea*)
Aphid, Artemisia; Lettuce Root; Leafcurl Plum; Sugarbeet Root.
Thrips.

YAUPON (*Ilex vomitoria*)
Beetle, Rhabdopterus. **Psyllid.**
Scale, Acuminate; Cottony Maple; False Cottony Maple; Florida
Wax; Japanese Wax; Latania; Parlatorialike; Red Bay; Tea; Tes-
selated.

YEW (*Taxus*)
Beetle, Asiatic Garden. **Mealybug,** Taxus. **Mite,** Taxus Bud, False
Spider.
Scale, Cottonycushion; Cottony Taxus; California Red; Dictyosper-
mum; Fletcher; Hemlock; Oleander; Purple.

Termites.
Weevil, Black Vine (grubs at roots; plants die) ; Strawberry Root.

YUCCA
Bug, Yucca Plant.   **Borer,** Stalk.
Mealybug, Citrus; Yucca.   **Moth,** Yucca (effects pollination).
Scale, Black; Boisduval's; Brown Soft; California Red; Cassava; Chaff; Cyanophyllum; Dictyospermum; Florida Wax; Latania; Mining; Lesser Snow; Oleander; Oystershell; Purple; Red Bay; Yucca.
Thrips, Flower; Yucca.   **Weevil,** Yucca.

ZAMIA
Mealybug, Striped.
Scale, Brown Soft; Boisduval's; Cyanophyllum; Chaff; Dictyospermum; Fern; Florida Red; Hemispherical; Latania; Lesser Snow; Oleander; Oriental; Parlatorialike; Proteus; Purple; Red Bay; Zamia.

ZEPHYRANTHES (Zephyr-lily; Rain-lily)
Fly, Narcissus Bulb.   **Scale,** Brown Soft.

ZINNIA
Aphid, Bean; Corn Root.
Beetle, Asiatic Garden; Black Blister; Japanese (serious) ; Spotted Cucumber; Western Spotted Cucumber; Whitefringed.
Borer, European Corn; Stalk.
Bug, Fourlined Plant; Garden Fleahopper; Tarnished Plant.
Leafcutter, Morningglory.   **Leafhopper,** Beet; Redbanded.   **Leafminer.**
Leafroller, Redbanded.   **Mealybug,** Longtailed.
Mite, Broad; Cyclamen; Desert Spider; Twospotted.

ZIZYPHUS (Jujube)
Mealybug, Citrus.   **Mite,** Texas Citrus.
Scale, Lesser Snow; Cottonycushion; Mining; Oriental; Pustule.

LIST OF LAND-GRANT INSTITUTIONS AND AGRICULTURAL EXPERIMENT STATIONS IN THE UNITED STATES

For help in diagnosing and controlling plant pests write to the Extension Entomologist at the College of Agriculture of your State University or to your State Experiment Station. Bulletins, circulars, and spray schedules are available free from the Bulletin Room or Mailing Clerk.

ALABAMA: Auburn University, Auburn 36830.

ALASKA: University of Alaska, College 99735; Experiment Station, Palmer 99645.

ARIZONA: University of Arizona, Tucson 85721.

ARKANSAS: University of Arkansas, Fayetteville 72701; Cooperative Extension Service, P. O. Box 391, Little Rock 72203.

CALIFORNIA: University of California, Berkeley 94720; Riverside 92502; Davis 95616.

COLORADO: Colorado State University, Fort Collins 80521.

CONNECTICUT: University of Connecticut, Storrs 06268; Connecticut Agricultural Experiment Station, New Haven 06504.

DELAWARE: University of Delaware, Newark 19711.

FLORIDA: University of Florida, Gainesville 32603.

GEORGIA: University of Georgia, Athens 30601; Agricultural Experiment Station, Experiment 30212; Coastal Plain Station, Tifton 31794.

HAWAII: University of Hawaii, Honolulu 96822.

IDAHO: University of Idaho, Extension Service, Boise 83702; Agricultural Experiment Station, Moscow 83843.

ILLINOIS: University of Illinois, Urbana 61801.

INDIANA: Purdue University, West Lafayette 47907.

IOWA: Iowa State University, Ames 50010.

KANSAS: Kansas State University, Manhattan 66502.

KENTUCKY: University of Kentucky, Lexington 40506.

LOUISIANA: Louisiana State University, University Station, Baton Rouge 70803.

MAINE: University of Maine, Orono 04473.

MARYLAND: University of Maryland, College Park 20742.

MASSACHUSETTS: University of Massachusetts, Amherst 01002.

MICHIGAN: Michigan State University, East Lansing 48823.

MINNESOTA: University of Minnesota, St. Paul 55101.

MISSISSIPPI: Mississippi State University, State College 39762.

MISSOURI: University of Missouri, Columbia 65202.

MONTANA: Montana State University, Bozeman 59715.

NEBRASKA: University of Nebraska, Lincoln 68503.

NEVADA: University of Nevada, Reno 89507.

NEW HAMPSHIRE: University of New Hampshire, Durham 03824.

NEW JERSEY: Rutgers, The State University, New Brunswick 08903.

NEW MEXICO: New Mexico State University, University Park 88070.

NEW YORK: Cornell University, Ithaca 14850; Agricultural Experiment Station, Geneva 14456.

NORTH CAROLINA: North Carolina State University, Raleigh 27607.

NORTH DAKOTA: North Dakota State University, Fargo 58103.

OHIO: Ohio State University, Columbus 43210; Ohio Agricultural Research & Development Center, Wooster 44691.

OKLAHOMA: Oklahoma State University, Stillwater 74075.

OREGON: Oregon State University, Corvallis 97331.

PENNSYLVANIA: Pennsylvania State University, University Park 16902.

PUERTO RICO: University of Puerto Rico, Rio Piedras 00927.

RHODE ISLAND: University of Rhode Island, Kingston 02881.

SOUTH CAROLINA: Clemson University, Clemson 29631.

SOUTH DAKOTA: South Dakota State University, Brookings 57007.

TENNESSEE: University of Tennessee, Knoxville 37901.

TEXAS: Texas A & M University, College Station 77841; Agricultural Experiment Station, Lubbock 79414.

UTAH: Utah State University, Logan 84321.

VERMONT: University of Vermont, Burlington 05401.

VIRGINIA: Virginia Polytechnic Institute, Blacksburg 24061.

VIRGIN ISLANDS: Virgin Islands Extension Service, Kingshill, St. Croix 00850.

WASHINGTON: Washington State University, Pullman 99163: Western Washington Experiment Station, Puyallup 98371.

WEST VIRGINIA: West Virginia University, Morgantown 26506.

WISCONSIN: University of Wisconsin, Madison 53706.

WYOMING: University of Wyoming, Laramie 82070.

GLOSSARY

Abdomen. The third, posterior, division of the insect's body.

Aerosol. An atomized fluid with very small particles, usually appearing as a fog or smoke.

Alternate Host. A second type of plant required for the completion of the life cycle of an insect.

Antenna (pl. *antennae*). Paired segmented appendages, one on each side of the head, sometimes called "feelers."

Anus. The posterior opening of the alimentary tract.

Apterous. Wingless.

Asymmetrical. Not alike on the two sides.

Beak. The protruding mouth part structure of a sucking insect; proboscis.

Bilateral Symmetry. With parts arranged more or less symmetrically on either side of a medium vertical plane.

Brood. Individuals which hatch from the eggs laid by one mother, or individuals which hatch and normally mature at about the same time.

Caterpillar. Immature form—larva—of a moth, butterfly, or sawfly, having cylindrical body, well-developed head, thoracic legs, and abdominal prolegs.

Caudal. Near the tail.

Cephalothorax. United head and thorax, found in the Arachnida and Crustacea.

Cercus (pl. *cerci*). One of a pair of appendages at the end of the abdomen.

Chitin. A colorless, nitrogenous substance occurring in the outer layer of the body wall of arthropods.

Chrysalis (pl. *chrysalids*). The pupa of a butterfly.

Class. A subdivision of a phylum, containing a group of related orders.

Clypeus. A hardened plate on the lower part of the face, just above the labrum or upper lip.

Cocoon. A silken case inside which the pupa is formed.

Compatible. A material that can be used with another without counteracting or changing its effect.

Compound Eye. An eye composed of many individual elements, each represented externally by a facet.

Contact Poison. One that is effective on contact, as contrasted with a poison that must be swallowed.

Constricted. Narrowed.

Corium. The elongate, usually thickened, basal portion of the front wing, found in the Hemiptera.

Cornicle. One of a pair of dorsal tubes on the posterior part of the abdomen of aphids, secreting a waxy liquid.

Coxa (pl. *coxae*). The basal segment of the leg, by which it is joined to the body.

Crawler. The first active instar of a scale insect.

Crotchets. Hooked spines at tip of prolegs of caterpillars.

Cuneus. A more or less triangular piece of the corium.

Cuticle. The noncellular outer layer of the body wall.

Deciduous. Having a part or parts that may fall off or be shed.

Diapause. A period of arrested development or suspended animation.

Diluent. Inert material used in the preparation of a spray or dust.

Dormant. Inactive, usually in winter. The term is applied to the host plant, the insect, or the spray applied during the inactive period.

Dorsal. Pertaining to the back or upper side.

Dust. A finely divided or pulverized powder, applied dry.

Ectoparasite. A parasite that lives on the outside of its host.

Elytra (pl.). The thickened, leathery, or horny front wings of beetles, occasionally other insects.

Emergence. The act of an adult insect leaving the pupal case or last nymphal skin.

Endoparasite. A parasite that lives inside its host.

Esophagus. The narrow portion of the alimentary canal posterior to the mouth cavity.

Exoskeleton. A skeleton or supporting structure on the outside of the body.

Exuviae (always used in plural). The cast skins of an arthropod.

Family. Subdivision of an order containing a group of related genera. Family names end in *idae*.

Femur (pl. *femora*). The third leg segment, between the trochanter and the tibia.

Filiform. Hairlike or threadlike.

Frass. Sawdust or wood fragments, made by a wood-boring insect, mixed with excrement.

Furcula. The forked springing apparatus of the Collembola, springtails.

Fusiform. Spindle-shaped; tapering at each end.

Gall. Abnormal growth of plant tissue caused by stimulus of an animal or another plant.

Gaster. Rounded part of the abdomen of an ant.

Generation. From any given stage in the life cycle to the same stage in the offspring.

Genus (pl. *genera*). A group of closely related species; the first capitalized name in a scientific binomial.

Glabrous. Smooth, without hairs.

Globose. Spherical or nearly so.

Gregarious. Living in groups.

Grub. Immature form—larva—of a beetle; thick-bodied with well-developed head, thoracic legs but no prolegs.

Halter (pl. *halteres*). A small, knobbed structure in place of the hind wings in the order Diptera, flies.

Head. The anterior body region, bearing eyes, antennae, and mouth parts.

Hermaphroditic. Possessing both male and female sex organs.

Hibernation. A period of suspended animation in animals during seasonal low temperatures.

Honeydew. A sweet substance discharged from the anus of aphids, mealybugs, scales, and whiteflies.

Host Plant. Plant attacked by, or supporting, insects or diseases.

Hyperparasite. A parasite whose host is another parasite.

Inactivated. Made inactive or inefficient.

Instar. The form of an insect between successive molts. The first instar is the stage between hatching and the first molt.

Integument. The outer covering of the body.

Labium. The lower lip.

Lanceolate. Spear-shaped, tapering at each end.

Larva (pl. *larvae*). Immature form of an insect having complete metamorphosis. The name is also applied to the six-legged first instar of mites (Acarina).

Lateral. On or pertaining to the side.

Maggot. A legless wormlike larva, without a well-developed head; immature state of Diptera, flies.

Mandibles. The first or anterior pair of jaws.

Maxillae (sing. *maxilla*). The second pair of jaws, immediately posterior to the mandibles.

Mesothorax. The middle or second segment of the thorax.

Metamorphosis. Change in form during development.

Millimeter. 0.001 meter, about $\frac{1}{25}$ inch.

Molt. A process of shedding the skin.

Nocturnal. Active at night, flying or feeding.

Nymph. The immature stage of an insect with incomplete metamorphosis, one that does not have a pupal stage; also the eight-legged immature stage of Acarina.

Ocellus (pl. *ocelli*). The simple eye of an insect or other arthropod.

Order. Subdivision of a class, containing a group of related families.

Oviparous. Reproducing by laying eggs.

Ovipositor. Specialized organ in the female for depositing eggs.

Ovisac. An egg sac, conspicuous in mealybugs and some scale insects.

Palpus (pl. *palpi*). A segmented process borne by the maxillae or labium.

Parasite. An animal that lives in or on the body of another living animal, at least during part of its life cycle. Also, a plant living on or in another plant.

Parthenogenesis. Reproduction by development of unfertilized eggs.

Pedicel. The "waist" or stem of the abdomen (between thorax and gaster) in ants; also the second segment of the antenna.

Pheromone. A substance secreted to the outside of the body where it causes specific reactions by another individual of the same species. Sex attractants are pheromones.

Phylum (pl. *phyla*). One of the major divisions of the animal kingdom.

Plumose. Feather-like.

Posterior. Rear.

Predator. An animal which attacks and feeds on another animal.

Proboscis. Extended beaklike mouth parts.

Proleg. One of the fleshy "false" abdominal legs of a caterpillar.

Prothorax. First segment of the thorax.

Protonymph. Second instar of a mite.

Pubescent. Downy, covered with short fine hairs.

Pulvillus (pl. *pulvilli*). A soft pad or lobe beneath each tarsal claw.

Punctate. Pitted, with punctures.

Pupa (pl. *pupae*). Stage between the larva and adult in insects with complete metamorphosis; nonfeeding, usually inactive.

Puparium (pl. *puparia*). The thickened, hardened last larval skin in which the pupa is formed in the Diptera, flies.

Pupate. Transform to a pupa.

Scavenger. An animal that feeds on dead plants or animals or decaying material.

Segment. A subdivision of the body or an appendage between joints.

Seta (pl. *setae*). A bristle.

Sessile. Incapable of moving from place to place.

Species. A group of individuals similar in structure and physiology, capable of interbreeding and producing fertile offspring, and differing in structure and physiology from other such groups.

Spinneret. Organ used by certain insects in making silk or spinning webs.

Spiracle. A breathing pore, external opening of the tracheal system.

Spray. A liquid dispersed in fine drops.

Stem Mother. Female aphid giving birth to living young without fertilization.

Striate. With grooves or depressed lines.

Stylet. A needle-like structure, used for piercing by insects with sucking mouth parts.

Systemic Insecticides. Compounds which, applied to soil or foliage, are absorbed by the plant or translocated within it, rendering the sap toxic to certain insects.

Tarsus (pl. *tarsi*). The part of the leg beyond the tibia, consisting of one or more segments, bearing at the apex claws and pulvilli of the insect "foot."

Tegmina. Hard fore wings of grasshoppers.

Thorax. The body region behind the head, bearing claws and wings.

Tibia (pl. *tibiae*). The fourth segment of the leg, between the femur and the tarsus.

Tolerance. The amount of a spray or dust that can be left as residue on harvested fruits or vegetables without danger when they are used as food.

Trachea (pl. *tracheae*). A spirally ringed internal elastic air tube in insects, part of the respiratory system.

Trap Crop. A crop, usually planted in advance, to lure insects so they can be destroyed before attacking the desired crop.

Triungulin. The first instar larva of a blister beetle.

Trochanter. The second segment of the leg, between the coxa and femur.

Tubercle. A small rounded or knoblike protuberance.

Tympanum. A vibrating auditory membrane or eardrum; in grasshoppers.

Vector. A carrier of disease-producing fungi, bacteria, or viruses.

Vein. A thickened line in the wing.

Ventral. Pertaining to the lower side of the body.

Viviparous. Giving birth to living young, not egg-laying.

SELECTED BIBLIOGRAPHY

Anderson, Roger F. *Forest and Shade Tree Entomology*. 428 pp. John Wiley & Sons, Inc., New York, 1960.

Arnett, Ross H. *An Introduction to the Study of Beetles*. 40 pp. The Catholic University of America Press, Washington, D.C., 1963.

Billings, Samuel C., Chairman. *Consolidated List of Approved Common Names of Insecticides and Certain Other Pesticides*. Entomological Society of America, College Park, Md., 1970.

Blickenstaff, C. C., Chairman. *Common Names of Insects*. 36 pp. Entomological Society of America, College Park, Md., 1970.

Borror, Donald J., and Dwight M. DeLong. *An Introduction to the Study of Insects*. 3rd ed., 812 pp. Holt, Rinehart & Winston, New York, 1971.
A fine textbook, not too complicated for the serious gardener.

Borror, Donald J., and Richard E. White. *A Field Guide to the Insects of America North of Mexico*. 404 pp. Houghton Mifflin Company, Boston, 1970.
Very useful.

Brues, Charles T., A. T. Lelander, and Frank M. Carpenter. *Classification of Insects*. 917 pp. Bulletin of the Museum of Comparative Zoology at Harvard College, Vol. 108. Cambridge, Mass., 1954.

Carson, Rachel. *Silent Spring*. 368 pp. Houghton Mifflin Company, Boston, 1961.

Clausen, C. P. *Biological Control of Insect Pests in the Continental United States*. 151 pp. U. S. Department of Agriculture Tech. Bull. 1139. U. S. Government Printing Office, Washington, D.C., 1956.

Connecticut Agricultural Experiment Station. *Plant Pest Handbook*. 194 pp. Bull. 600. New Haven, Conn., 1956.

Craighead, E. C., et al. *Insect Enemies of Eastern Forests*. 679 pp. U. S. Department of Agriculture Misc. Publ. 657. U. S. Government Printing Office, Washington, D.C., 1950.

Davidson, Ralph H., and Leonard M. Pears. *Insect Pests of Farm, Garden and Orchard*. 6th ed., 675 pp. John Wiley & Sons, Inc., New York, 1966.

DeBach, Paul, editor. *Biological Control of Insect Pests and Weeds*. 844 pp. Reinhold Publishing Corporation, New York, 1964.

Dekle, G. W., and L. C. Kuitert. *Orchid Insects, Related Pests and Control.* 28 pp. Florida Department of Agriculture Bull. 8. Gainesville, 1968.

Dowden, Philip B. *Parasites and Predators of Forest Insects Liberated in the United States Through 1960.* 70 pp. U. S. Department of Agriculture Agricultural Handbook 226. U. S. Government Printing Office, Washington, D.C., 1962.

Eberling, Walter. *Subtropical Fruit Pests.* 436 pp. University of California, Berkeley, 1959.

Essig, E. O. *Insects of Western North America.* 1,035 pp. The Macmillan Company, New York, 1926.
My copy of this remarkable compilation has been in constant use. There is a 1958 edition, *Insects and Mites of Western North America,* but it is not in my personal library.

Felt, Ephraim Porter. *Plant Galls and Gall Makers.* 364 pp. Comstock Publishing Company, Inc., Ithaca, N.Y., 1940.

Frear, D. E. H., editor. *Pesticide Handbook—Entoma.* 24th ed., 280 pp. College Science Publishers, State College, Pa., 1972.
This edition lists 7,765 pesticides.

Goetsch, Wilhelm. *The Ants.* 173 pp. University of Michigan Press, Ann Arbor, Mich., 1957.

Graham, Kenneth. *Concepts of Forest Entomology.* 388 pp. Reinhold Publishing Corporation, New York, 1963.

Keen, E. P. *Insect Enemies of Western Forests.* 280 pp. U. S. Department of Agriculture Misc. Publ. 273. U. S. Government Printing Office, Washington, D.C., 1952.

Klots, Alexander B. *A Field Guide to the Butterflies of North America, East of the Great Plains.* 349 pp. Houghton Mifflin Company, Boston, 1951.

———. *The World of Butterflies and Moths.* 207 pp. McGraw-Hill Book Company, Inc., 1958.

Klots, Alexander B., and Elsie B. Klots. *Living Insects of the World.* 304 pp. Doubleday & Company, Inc., Garden City, N.Y., 1959.
Marvelous color photographs, fascinating text.

Klots, Alexander, and Elsie Klots. *Insects of North America.* 250 pp. Doubleday & Company, Inc., Garden City, N.Y., 1971.

Irons, Frank. *Hand Sprayers and Dusters.* 12 pp. U. S. Department of Agriculture Home and Garden Bulletin No. 63. U. S. Government Printing Office, Washington, D.C., 1967.

Leonard, Mortimer Demarest. *A List of Aphids of New York.* Proceedings of Rochester Academy of Science, Vol. 10, No. 6, pp. 289–432. Rochester, N.Y., 1963.

Leonard, Mortimer D., and Theodore L. Bissell. *A List of Aphids of District of Columbia, Maryland and Virginia.* 129 pp. Maryland Agricultural Experiment Station Cont. 4390. College Park, Md., 1970.

Lutz, Frank E. *Field Book of Insects.* 510 pp. G. P. Putnam's Sons, New York, 1935.

Mason, Hamilton. *Your Garden in the South.* 358 pp. D. Van Nostrand Company, Inc., Princeton, N.J., 1961.

Maxwell, Lewis S. *Handbook of Florida Insects and Their Control.* 106 pp. Great Outdoors Publishing Co., Inc. St. Petersburg, Fla., 1959.

McMillan, Wheeler. *Bugs or People?* 228 pp. Appleton-Century-Crofts, New York, 1965.

Meister, R. T., editor. *1972 Farm Chemicals Handbook.* 424 pp. Meister Publishing Co., Willoughby, Ohio, 1972.

Merrill, G. B. A. *A Revision of the Scale-Insects of Florida.* 143 pp. State Plant Board of Florida Bull. 1. Gainesville, Fla., 1953.

Metcalf, C. L., and W. F. Flint, rev. by R. L. Metcalf. *Destructive and Useful Insects.* 4th ed., 1,087 pp. McGraw-Hill Book Company, Inc., New York, 1962.
Even more useful, if possible, than previous editions.

National Academy of Sciences. *Principles of Plant and Animal Pest Control.* Vol. 3. *Insect-Pest Management and Control.* 508 pp. Publ. 1695. Washington, D.C., 1969.

———. *Scientific Aspects of Pest Control.* 470 pp. Publ. 1402. Washington, D.C., 1966.

New England Section, Society of American Foresters. *Important Tree Pests of the Northeast.* 2nd ed., 191 pp. Evans Printing Company, Concord, N.H., 1952.

New York State College of Agriculture. *A Guide to Safe Pest Control Around the Home.* 41 pp. Cornell Misc. Bull. 74. Cornell University, Ithaca, N.Y., 1971.

Palmer, Miriam A. *Aphids of the Rocky Mountain Region.* Vol. V, 452 pp. Thomas Say Foundation, 1952.

Pimentel, David. *Ecological Effects of Pesticides on Non-Target Species.* 220 pp. Executive Office of the President, Office of Science and Technology. U. S. Government Printing Office, Washington, D.C., 1971.

Pennsylvania State University. *1972 Approved Pesticides for Pennsylvania.* 80 pp. College of Agriculture Extension Service, University Park, Pa., 1972.

Pirone, Pascal P. *Diseases and Pests of Ornamental Plants.* 4th ed., 546 pp. The Ronald Press Company, New York, 1970.

———. *Tree Maintenance.* 576 pp. Oxford University Press, New York, 1972.

Pratt, Robert M. *Florida Guide to Citrus Insects, Diseases, and Nutritional Disorders in Color.* 191 pp. Agricultural Experiment Station, Gainesville, Fla., 1958.

Pritchard, A. Earl, and Edward W. Baker. *Revision of the Spider Mite Family Tetranychidae.* 472 pp. Pacific Coast Entomological Society, San Francisco, 1955.

Reed, L. B., and Raymond E. Webb. *Insects and Diseases of Vegetables in the Home Garden.* 50 pp. U. S. Department of Agriculture Home and Garden Bull. 46, revised 1971. U. S. Government Printing Office, Washington, D.C., 1971.

Riddick, Eloise. *A List of Florida Plants and the Scale-Insects Which Infest Them.* 78 pp. State Plant Board of Florida Bull. 7. Gainesville, Fla., 1955.

Rutgers, the State University. *1972 Pesticides for New Jersey.* Extension Service College of Agricultural and Environmental Science, New Brunswick, N.J., 1971.

Schread, John C. *Control of Mites and Aphids on and in Bulbs.* 11 pp. Connecticut Agricultural Experiment Station Bull. 699. New Haven, 1969.

——. *Control of Scale Insects and Mealybugs on Ornamentals.* 27 pp. Connecticut Agricultural Experiment Station Bull. 710. 1970.

——. *Leaf Miners and Their Control.* 19 pp. Connecticut Agricultural Experiment Station Bull. 693. 1971.

Schuder, Donald L. *Insect Pests of Shade Trees and Shrubs.* 36 pp. Purdue University Mimeo E-41. Lafayette, Ind., 1962.

Smith, Floyd F. *Controlling Insects on Flowers.* 81 pp. U. S. Department of Agriculture Agriculture Information Bull. 237. U. S. Government Printing Office, Washington, D.C., 1967.

Swain, Ralph B. *The Insect Guide.* 261 pp. Doubleday & Company, Inc., Garden City, N.Y., 1952.

U. S. Department of Agriculture. *Insects.* The Yearbook of Agriculture, 1952. 780 pp. U. S. Government Printing Office, Washington, D.C., 1952.

——. *Suggested Guide for the Use of Insecticides to Control Insects Affecting Crops, Livestock, Households, Stored Products, Forests and Forest Products—1968.* Agriculture Handbook No. 331. U. S. Government Printing Office, Washington, D.C., 1968.

U. S. Department of Health, Education and Welfare. *Report of the Secretary's Commission on Pesticides and Their Relationship to Environmental Health.* Parts I and II. 677 pp. U. S. Government Printing Office, Washington, D.C., 1969.

Washington State University. *Control of Insect and Mite Pests of Ornamental Trees, Shrubs, and Lawns for Home Owners.* 31 pp. E.M. 3310. College of Agriculture, Pullman, 1971.

——. *Control of Insect and Mite Pests of Home and Garden.* 34 pp. E.M. 3318. College of Agriculture, Pullman, 1971.

Watkins, John V., and Herbert S. Wolfe. *Your Florida Garden.* 319 pp. University of Florida Press, Gainesville, 1954.

Weigel, C. A., and L. G. Baumhofer. *Handbook on Insect Enemies of Flowers and Shrubs.* 115 pp. U. S. Department of Agriculture Misc. Publ. 626. U. S. Government Printing Office, Washington, D.C., 1948.

Westcott, Cynthia. *Plant Disease Handbook.* 3rd ed., 843 pp. Van Nostrand Reinhold Company, New York, 1972.

Consult pp. 253 to 276 for the material on Nematodes that has been omitted from this edition of the *Bug Book.*

——, editor. *Handbook on Biological Control of Plant Pests.* 97 pp. Brooklyn Botanic Garden, Brooklyn, N.Y., 1960.

Whitten, Jamie L. *That We May Live.* 251 pp. D. Van Nostrand Company, Princeton, N.J., 1966.

This very selective Bibliography is limited to some of the well-thumbed material in my personal library. It includes a mere sampling of the many helpful bulletins from the U. S. Department of Agriculture and state universities and experiment stations. Of the professional publications that come to my desk the most useful are the *Journal of Economic Entomology* and the *Bulletin*, both published by the Entomological Society of America, and the weekly *Cooperative Economic Insect Report* from the U. S. Department of Agriculture. The latter has been of great assistance in deciding which pests are important enough to be included in this *Bug Book*, in keeping me up-to-date on new insects, and on the frequent changes in insect names. In preparing the third edition more help on names came from Louise M. Russell, W. H. Anderson, and E. W. Baker of the U.S.D.A. For this fourth edition, Theodore L. Bissell, of the University of Maryland, checked the names in some of the insect groups.

Other publications regularly scanned for entomological information include: *Agricultural Chemicals; American Forests; American Fruit Grower; American Rose; Arborist's News; Audubon; Florist & Nursery Exchange; Flower & Garden; Frontiers of Plant Science* (Connecticut Agricultural Experiment Station); *The Garden Journal* (New York Botanical Garden); *Home Garden* (now *Natural Gardening*); *Horticulture; International Shade Tree Conference Proceedings;* New Jersey *Insect-Disease Newsletter;* New York *Insect & Disease Report; Plant Disease Reporter* (from U. S. Department of Agriculture); *Plants & Gardens* (Brooklyn Botanic Garden); *Science; Trees Magazine; Westchester Agricultural News*.

INDEX

(Boldface numerals indicate line drawings; plate numbers in roman numerals refer to color illustrations following pages 308, 356)

Calico scale, 391
California ash mirid, 194
California casebearer, 218
California Christmas-
berry, 510
California coffeeberry,
510
California fivespined ips,
113
California flatheaded
borer, 162
California green lacewing,
280
California harvester ant,
56
California horntail, 276
California-laurel, 510
aphid, 69
borer, 160
California-nutmeg, 510
California oakworm, 223
California pear sawfly,
375
California peppertree
chalcid, 453
California-poppy, 511
California prionus, 162
California red scale, 392
California tent caterpillar,
223, 239
California tortoiseshell,
211
California tussock moth,
363
Caliothrips fasciatus, 440
Caliroa cerasi, 381
lineata, 381
Calla, 511
Calliandra, 511
Callicarpa, 511
*Callidium antennatum
hesperum,* 160
Calligrapha scalaris, 118
Callipus lactarius, 326
Callistemon, 505
Callistephus, 496
Callisto geminatella, 299
Callopistria floridensis,
226
Callosamia promethea,
360
Callosbruchus maculatus,
466

Calluna, 548
Calomicrus brunneus, 115
Calomycterus setarius,
468
Calonyction, 567
Calophya californica, 371
flavida, 371
nigripennis, 371
triozomima, 371
Calophyllum, 501
Calopitrimerus thujae,
340
vitis, 334
Calosoma calidum, 120
frigidum, 125
scrutator, 125
sycophanta, 120
Calpodes ethlius, 301
Calycanthus, 511
Cambala annulata, 326
Cambium curculio, 249
Camel cricket, 245
Camellia, 511
bud mite, 330
mining scale, 392
parlatoria, 392
scale, 393
Cameraria cincinnatiella,
294
hamadryadella, 297
Camnula pellucida, 273
Campanula, 512
Camphor scale, 393
Camphor-tree, 512
Camphor thrips, 440
*Camponotus abdominalis
floridanus,* 56
carolinensis, 274
ferrugineus, 58
pennsylvanicus, 56
Campsis radicans, 605
Campylenchia latipes, 449
Campylomma verbasci,
203
Canadian fleabane aphid,
69
Candleberry-tree, 512
Candlenut, 512
Candytuft, 512
Cankerworm(s), 215
fall, 215, Plate XVIII
spring, 215, 216
Canna, 512

Cantaloupe, 512, 566
Canterbury bells, 512
Cantharidae, 105
Cantharidin, 111
Cape-honeysuckle, 512
Cape-jasmine, 513, 542
Cape-marigold, 513
Capitophorus elaegni, 83,
89
hippophaes, 85
Capsicum, 579
Capsus bugs, 197
Capsus simulans, 197
Carabidae, 104, 124
Caragana, 513
aphid, 69
blister beetle, 113
plant bug, 197
Caraway, 513
Carbamult, 23
Carbaryl, 14
Carbofuran, 14
Carbon bisulfide, 14
Carbon disulfide, 14
Carbon tetrachloride, 14
Carbophenothion, 14
Cardinal-flower, 513
Caribbean fruit fly, 261
Caribbean pod borer, 162
Carica papaya, 574
Carissa, 513
Carmine spider mite, 330
Carnation, 513
maggot, 310
mite, 330
tip maggot, 310
tortrix moth, 347
Carnocephala flaviceps,
288
Carob, 513
Carolina grasshopper, 273
Carolina mantid, 312
Carpenter ant, 56
black, 56
Florida, 56
red, 58
Carpenter bee, 101
Carpenterworm, 162, 163
moths, 343
Carpinus, 552
Carpocapsa pomonella,
347
Carpoglyphidae, 327

western hemlock looper,
239
western oak looper, 239
western tent, 239
yellowheaded fireworm,
240
yellownecked, 240
yellow woollybear, 240
zebra, 240
Catnip, 515
Cattail, 515
Cattleya fly, 267
Cattleya midge, 321
Cattleya weevil, 465
Cauliflower, 515
Caulocampus acericaulis,
174
Cavariella aegopodii, 95
essigi, 95
Ceanothus, 515
aphid, 69
clearwing, 347
lace bug, 197
silk moth, 347
spittlebug, 434
Ceanothus americanus,
570
Cecidomyia catalpae, 321
citrulli, 322
ocellaris, 323
piniinopsis, 322
resinicoloides, 323
viticola, 322
Cecidomyiidae, 260, 320
Cecidophyopsis psilaspis,
340
Cedar, 516
bark beetle, 113
cone sawfly, 375
tree borer, 163
Cedar, incense, 516
Cedar of Lebanon, 516
Cedrus deodara, 516
libanotica, 516
Celama sorghiella, 460
Celastrus, 503
Celeriac, 516
Celery, 516
leaftier, 306
looper, 223
Celeryworm, 224, 232,
Plate XIX
Celosia, 523

Celtis, 547
Centaurea, 526
Centipede(s), 45, 241,
242
garden, 241
Century plant, 516
Cepaea nemoralis, 427
Cephalanthus, 508
Cephalosporium lecanii,
387, 425
Cephalotaxus, 516
Cephidae, 165, 275, 373
Cerambycidae, 105, 160,
161, 162, 163, 166,
172, 174, 181, 186
Ceramica picta, 240
Cerasphorus cinctus, 160
Cerataphis lataniae, 80
orchidearum, 80, 83
variabilis, 80, 84
Ceratina spp., 102
Ceratitis capitata, 264
Ceratocystis ulmi, 144
Ceratomia amyntor, 350
siliqua, 513
Cercis, 589
Cercocarpus, 568
Cercopidae, 433
Cereal leaf beetle, 113
Ceriman, 517
Cerococcus deklei, 416
kalmiae, 416
quericus, 411
Cerodontha dorsalis, 294
Ceropegia, 517
Ceroplastes ceriferus, 408
cirripediformis, 388
floridensis, 403
rubens, 419
Cerotoma trifurcata, 110
Cestrum, 555
Ceutorhynchus assimilis,
465
quadridens, 249
rapae, 249
*Chaetanaphothrips orchi-
dii,* 445
Chaetocnema confinis,
150
denticulata, 151
ectypa, 117
pulicara, 115
Chaetosiphon fragaefolii,
91

minor, 65
Chaff scale, 393
Chainspotted geometer,
224
Chaitophorus populellus,
86
populifoliae, 86
viminalis, 95
Chalcididae, 451
Chalcidoidea, 450
Chalcids, 451, 452, 453,
454, 455
Chalcodermus aeneus,
249
Chalcophora angulicollis,
181
Chalice-vine, 517
Chamaecyparis, 589
Chamaemyiidae, 260
Changa, 245
Charcoal beetle, 114
Chaste-tree, 517
Chayote, 517
Checkered beetles, 105
Checkerspot butterfly, 211
Cheiranthus, 608
Chelymorpha cassidea,
108
Chemicals, garden, 1, 3–4
8, 9–29
alphabetical listing, 12–
29
care in use of, v, 28–29
in combination, 27–28
and control of insect
pests, 4, 8, 9–29
microbial, 5–6
new, introduction of,
10–12
spraying and dusting,
30–43
sterilants, control by, 6,
12
Chenille plant, 487
Cherimoya, 517
Chermidae, 60
Cherry, 517
casebearer, 218
curculio, 249
fruit fly, 262
fruit sawfly, 375
fruitworm, 269
leaf beetle, 114